Multicultural Counseling and Psychotherapy

Multicultural Counseling and Psychotherapy: A Lifespan Approach, Sixth Edition, offers counseling students and professionals a distinctive lifespan approach that emphasizes the importance of social justice and diversity in mental health practice. Chapters include case studies, reflection questions, and examinations of current issues in the field. Each chapter also discusses the ways in which a broad range of factors—including sexuality, race, gender identity, and socioeconomic conditions—affect clients' mental health and gives students the information they need to best serve clients from diverse backgrounds.

Leroy G. Baruth is professor and chair of the department of human development and psychological counseling in the Reich College of Education at Appalachian State University in Boone, North Carolina. He received his doctorate from the University of Arizona in Tucson.

M. Lee Manning is professor and eminent scholar in the department of teaching and learning in the Darden College of Education at Old Dominion University in Norfolk, Virginia. He specializes in diversity and development. He received his doctorate from the University of South Carolina in Columbia and has published more than 175 journal articles and 35 books.

Multicultural Counseling and Psychotherapy

A Lifespan Approach

Sixth Edition

Leroy G. Baruth and M. Lee Manning

Routledge
Taylor & Francis Group

NEW YORK AND LONDON

Sixth edition published 2016
by Routledge
711 Third Avenue, New York, NY 10017

and by Routledge
2 Park Square, Milton Park, Abingdon, Oxon, OX14 4RN

Routledge is an imprint of the Taylor & Francis Group, an informa business

© 2016 Leroy G. Baruth and M. Lee Manning

The right of Leroy G. Baruth and M. Lee Manning to be identified as authors of
this work has been asserted by them in accordance with sections 77 and 78 of the
Copyright, Designs and Patents Act 1988.

This book was previously published by: Pearson Education, Inc.

First Edition published by Pearson 1991

Fifth Edition published by Pearson 2012

Library of Congress Cataloging in Publication Data
Baruth, Leroy G.
   Multicultural counseling and psychotherapy : a lifespan approach / Leroy G.
Baruth, M. Lee Manning. — Sixth edition.
      pages cm
   Includes bibliographical references and index.
 1. Cross-cultural counseling—United States.   2. Psychotherapy—United States—
Cross-cultural studies.   3. Developmental psychology—United States—Cross-cultural
studies.   I. Manning, M. Lee.   II. Title.
   BF637.C6B283 2016
   158.3—dc23
   2015029447

ISBN: 978-1-138-95353-6 (hbk)
ISBN: 978-1-138-95354-3 (pbk)
ISBN: 978-1-315-65996-1 (ebk)

Typeset in Galliard
by Apex CoVantage, LLC

To all my students who have taught me so much during my 40 years in the counseling field.

LGB

To Marianne, Jennifer, Michael, Richard, Jada, Abigail, and Luke.

MLM

Contents

2   Identity Development and Models   25

13 Understanding Hispanic American Clients

Preface

The United States, which historically has been a haven for various cultural and ethnic groups, continues to benefit from the rich diversity of its people. The increasing cultural diversity of the U.S. population has given rise to a more intense need for effective multicultural counseling. Clients of various cultural backgrounds may bring to counseling sessions problems related to a particular lifespan stage or to the frustrations and challenges that often face cultural groups struggling to cope in U.S. society. Although few basic counseling strategies are designed for multicultural situations in particular, an understanding of client differences—cultural, ethnic, racial, gender, sexual orientation, disability, socioeconomic, individual, and the need for rehabilitation counseling—is important in using existing strategies to their best advantage. Integrating multicultural and lifespan considerations is crucial to counseling effectiveness. Problems associated with multicultural intervention arise not only when majority-culture professionals counsel minority clients but also when minority counselors intervene with majority-culture clients.

NEW TO THIS EDITION

Multicultural Counseling and Psychotherapy: A Lifespan Approach was written to address the aforementioned concerns. It provides majority- and minority-culture elementary and secondary school counselors, marriage and family therapists, rehabilitation agency counselors, mental health counselors, counselors in higher education, and social workers with an exploration of the lives and potential counseling challenges of African American, American Indian, Asian American, European American, and Hispanic American clients at the various stages along the lifespan continuum. We also focus on understanding and counseling clients who identify as lesbian, gay, bisexual, or transgender (LGBT). In addition, we address new topics such as the Jewish Identity Model, rehabilitation counseling, social class and socioeconomic conditions, and the complex interrelationships between development and counseling. To clarify and enliven the text and to provoke the reader's thoughts, several new features are included:

- Case studies describing individuals representing a multitude of cultures and age groups. Various members of the fictional families are introduced, as are LGBT individuals in the four lifespan stages, providing a portrait of the child, the adolescent, the adult, and the elder within the family and/or the culture and within the society at large (Chapters 4–16).
- All new suggested readings, providing readers with additional opportunities for learning (Chapters 1–17).
- Expanded sections on social class and socioeconomic conditions, including (but not limited to) poverty rates, poverty definitions, and health insurance coverage (Chapter 1 and other appropriate chapters).

- An expanded section on cultural identities, including new coverage of the Jewish Identity Model (Chapter 2).
- Four counseling and development pedagogical aids in each counseling chapter—a feature that looks at development and offers specific counseling suggestions (Chapters 6, 8, 10, 12, 14, and 16).
- Reflection questions after each Case Study in all counseling chapters (Chapters 6, 8, 10, 12, 14, and 16).
- Updates to approximately one-half of the Case Studies (Chapters 5–16).
- Focus on the 2014 *ACA Code of Ethics*, with appropriate Internet sites for additional information (Chapters 3 and 17).
- Alignment with the CACREP Standards, published inside the front cover.
- Sections on spirituality and religious communities (Chapter 1 and appropriate chapters).

THE LIFESPAN PERSPECTIVE AND SELECTION OF CULTURES

The lifespan perspective that provides a framework for this text reflects the current emphasis on lifespan development and stresses that mental health issues and counseling problems differ for children, adolescents, adults, and elders. Effective multicultural counseling requires that counselors understand the problems unique to each client's culture, as well as the problems unique to the client's developmental period. It takes only a few examples to illustrate the need to consider culture as well as development in counseling intervention: Mental health issues of the American Indian child differ from those of the Asian American elder; similarly, African American children have unique problems that differ from those of Asian American children or even from those of African American adults.

Our emphasis on five cultural groups—African American, American Indian, Asian American, European American, and Hispanic American—was determined by two main factors. First, these five groups currently represent the most populous cultures in the United States. Second, these five cultural groups all have significant challenges that will increasingly require counseling intervention. Moreover, acculturation of younger generations threatens the continuance of the cherished values, traditions, and customs associated with each of these five cultures.

ORGANIZATION OF THE TEXT

Multicultural Counseling and Psychotherapy: A Lifespan Approach is organized into three parts and 17 chapters. Part I (Chapters 1–3) provides background knowledge for intervening with clients of differing backgrounds. Part II (Chapters 4–16) centers on understanding and counseling African American, American Indian, Asian American, European American, and Hispanic American clients as well as LGBT clients in the various lifespan stages. Part III (Chapter 17 and the Epilogue) discusses professional issues in multicultural counseling and explores future directions in the field.

The organization of the text is consistent with our goal of enhancing understanding of seven broad concepts:

1. The United States is a nation of many cultural groups and will continue to be enriched by increasing cultural diversity (Chapter 1).
2. A prerequisite to effective multicultural counseling is for minority- and majority-culture counselors to understand their own cultural identities and how their identities affect counseling intervention (Chapter 2).
3. Majority-culture counselors can be trained to intervene effectively with minority clients and minority counselors with majority-culture clients; minority counselors can be also trained to intervene effectively with minority clients of differing cultural backgrounds (Chapter 3).

4. Knowledge of a client's developmental period and the problems and challenges of each lifespan period contributes to the counselor's expertise (Chapter 4).
5. Knowledge of a client's cultural background provides the counselor, regardless of cultural background, with a sound basis for multicultural counseling intervention (Chapters 5, 7, 9, 11, 13, and 15).
6. Counselors and their clients benefit from the selection and implementation of counseling strategies and techniques that are appropriate for specific cultural groups (Chapters 6, 8, 10, 12, 14, and 16).
7. In the coming years, counselors intervening in multicultural settings will be challenged by issues that deserve to be understood and addressed as multicultural counseling continues to gain recognition and respect (Chapter 17).

SPECIAL FEATURES AND PEDAGOGICAL AIDS

To help readers develop a sense of professionalism and further their learning, we have included:

* *Suggested Readings*, which list journal articles that may be of special interest to readers who wish to improve their multicultural counseling effectiveness
* *Appendix*, which lists experiential activities that can be used as a part of the multicultural counseling course

At various points in the text, the reader is cautioned to keep in mind that each client is unique; that is, individual differences related to gender, sexual orientation, disability, generation, geographic location, and socioeconomic class must be accounted for in planning appropriate counseling intervention. Intracultural differences, as evidenced in the many Asian American, European American, and Hispanic American subgroups, also must be considered. To avoid stereotyping of cultures, we refer to specific populations whenever possible. It is crucial for counselors to recognize that the line between cultural descriptions and cultural stereotypes is very narrow and that the consequences of stereotypical thinking are potentially damaging to clients of all cultures and at all lifespan stages.

Part I
Overview

1 Introduction to Multicultural Counseling and Psychotherapy

QUESTIONS TO BE EXPLORED

- What is multicultural counseling and psychotherapy, why should counselors understand clients' many differences, and why should counselors plan culturally appropriate counseling intervention?
- What clients comprise the U.S. populations? How can counselors define culture in its "broadest" terms, especially since clients have several different cultures?
- What diversities challenge mental health counselors in a pluralistic society, e.g., culture in all its forms, race, ethnicity, worldview, social class, spirituality, generational differences, gender, sexual orientation, disabilities, and lifespan developmental differences? How does White privilege result in the lack of privilege for many others? What is social justice and how can this specific action toward social justice contribute to the welfare of all people?
- What are the important tenets of multicultural counseling?
- What counseling considerations deserve consideration when planning individual, group, family, and rehabilitation counseling?

OVERVIEW

America's doors have been open to people of diverse cultural, ethnic, and racial origins for many years. Some people entered the country with hopes of realizing the American dream. Others came to escape oppressive conditions in their home countries. Still others were brought against their will and were expected to conform culturally. Then there were those who already inhabited the land that is now the United States. Through experiences commonly associated with daily living and working together, it was thought that this diverse range of people would acculturate or adopt "American" customs and values and, as in a "melting pot," assimilate into mainstream society. For any number of reasons, however, many people opted to hold on to their cultural heritages, traditions, and customs; they wanted their cultural characteristics and values recognized as different, rather than as inferior or wrong.

Considerable evidence suggests that the melting pot metaphor does not provide an accurate description of the many cultural groups living in the United States. For example, some groups have failed (or have elected not to try) to forsake cherished cultural characteristics in order to become "Americanized." Asians and Hispanics,[1] regardless of their generation, often reluctantly give up ethnic customs and traditions in favor of "middle-class American habits" that appear to them to be in direct contradiction to beliefs they acquired early in life. African Americans have fought to overcome cultural dominance and discrimination and, through efforts such as the civil rights movement, have sought to understand and maintain their cultural heritage. In essence, the United States is a nation of diverse peoples, and although cultural groups can be described with some accuracy, cultures are not monolithic in nature. This need to recognize

3

and respect individual differences and similarities within cultures becomes clearer when one considers the generational differences and social class differences among the African American, American Indian, Asian American, European American, and Hispanic American cultures. The knowledgeable counselor can use these differences in working with a multicultural clientele.

CLIENTS: TODAY AND IN THE FUTURE

The range of the U.S. multicultural society and the role it plays in shaping people's lives will continue to become apparent to counseling professionals as increasing numbers of clients from diverse cultures seek mental health services. Undoubtedly, counselors and psychotherapists will increasingly counsel clients with differing customs, traditions, values, and perspectives toward life events and the counseling process. Will counselors, regardless of their cultural background, be able to provide effective counseling services for clients of differing backgrounds? The attitudes and skills that counselors bring to the multicultural counseling situation will depend significantly on their knowledge of cultures, their counseling effectiveness with clients, and their willingness to perceive cultural characteristics as differences rather than deficits.

For purposes of this text, we have chosen to concentrate on five cultures: African American, American Indian, Asian American, European American, and Hispanic American. The first determining factor was population numbers, particularly the estimated growth increases associated with them. To date, these cultures have shown significant increases and are expected to continue to do so, either by increased birth rate or by immigration. The numbers are currently sufficiently large that counselors—in schools, private practices, mental health institutions, or other settings of service delivery—will likely encounter clients from these cultures. Second, most available research data were drawn from these five groups. Third, these cultural groups have needs that warrant counseling, but individuals often are reluctant to seek counseling. Fourth, few counselors have sufficient knowledge of clients' cultural and other differences (especially the African, Asian, Hispanic, and American Indian cultures) and how these differences affect the process of providing effective, culturally responsive counseling intervention.

African Americans

Whether termed African Americans, Black Americans, or Afro-Americans, the majority of this group can trace its origin to regions of Africa. The term *African American* appears most popular as a replacement for *Black* or *Black American* because it recognizes cultural ties with Africa. It also includes groups who indicate their race as "Black," "African Am.," or "Negro" or provide written entries such as African American, Afro-American, Kenyan, Nigerian, or Haitian.

The term *African American* continues to be debated. The term is being questioned by some Blacks who have long lived in the United States, just as their ancestors did. Also, it is being questioned by some people with roots in sub-Saharan Africa. Others simply prefer the term *Black*. It will take a number of years to determine which term will actually be selected to designate Black people and their culture. While correct names or labels are important, it is more important to understand the African American culture and its diversity.

American Indians

Ancestors of the people who are now known as Indians, Native Americans, or Native American Indians have continuously occupied North America for at least 30,000 years. Rather than emigrating from other lands and facing cultural assimilation into the majority culture, American Indians faced an influx of outsiders to their land who expected them to relinquish cherished cultural traditions. Again, the U.S. Census Bureau categorizes American Indians or Alaska Natives as any of the original peoples of North and South America (including Central America) who maintain tribal affiliation or community attachment. The American Indian people have been categorized into one group (see Chapter 7).

Asian Americans

Risking violation of sacred family traditions, many young Asians headed for the promised land of America around the turn of the twentieth century. Asian Americans were often forced to accept the lowest-paid menial jobs and were denied the rights of citizenship and ownership of land. As discussed in Chapter 9, Asian Americans and Pacific Islanders in the United States include the following Asian cultures: Chinese, Filipino, Japanese, Korean, Asian Indian, and Vietnamese. Hawaiians, Samoans, and Guamanians are known as Pacific Islanders. The recent influx of another group of Asian Americans from Southeast Asia has further contributed to the diversity of the Asian cultures. Many Indochinese started their journey from rural and poor areas to refugee camps and finally to American towns and cities. Originating from such countries as Vietnam, Cambodia, Laos, and Thailand, these people differ from the most populous Asian groups (Japanese and Chinese). Southeast Asians are a diverse group. For example, refugees from Southeast Asia can include Blue, White, and Striped Hmong; Chinese, Krom, and Mi Khmer Cambodians; Chinese Mien, Thai Dam, and Khmer Laotians; and Lowlander and Highlander Vietnamese. Each group has its own distinct history and culture. However, a discussion of all the many Asian groups currently living in the United States is beyond the scope of this text.

European Americans

As discussed in Chapter 11, 53 categories of European Americans live in the United States. Although ambiguous, the term *White ethnic* originally referred to Southern and Eastern European immigrants, rather than to Americans of British or German ancestry. In later years, the term has referred to a broader range of people. European Americans have not received notable attention in the discussions of multiculturalism and diversity. It is also important to mention that European Americans are a diverse people in terms of thought, emotions, and group loyalty. European Americans emigrated from widely diverse places, such as Western and Southern Europe as well as Eastern Europe and the former Soviet Union. People of Greek, Italian, Lebanese, Near Eastern, Arab, Polish, Irish, French, and German descent are well known in the United States, whereas those from the Netherlands, Portugal, Spain, and Switzerland are less well known.

Hispanic Americans

The Hispanic American culture includes Mexican Americans, Chicanos, Spanish Americans, Latinos, Mexicans, Puerto Ricans, Cubans, Guatemalans, and Salvadorans. All are recognized as Hispanics and share many values and goals. The soaring Hispanic population in the United States has been driven largely by waves of new immigrants—legal and illegal—as well as by more accurate counts by census takers. Hispanics are a large, young, rapidly increasing, highly diverse group of people. *Hispanic* is widely used to cover a disparate array of people from various nationalities. In fact, Hispanics should be considered an aggregate of distinct subcultures, rather than a homogeneous cultural group. For example, although Hispanics have cultural similarities, each Hispanic subgroup has its own distinct social and cultural practices. This increasing population is currently influencing mainstream American culture in such areas as communication, employment, education, and the arts. Chapter 13 describes the Hispanic population in more detail.

UNDERSTANDING DIVERSITY AMONG CLIENTS IN A PLURALISTIC SOCIETY

Culture, Subculture, and Intraculture

Culture can be defined as institutions, communication, values, religions, genders, sexual orientations, disabilities, thinking, artistic expressions, and social and interpersonal relationships.

It should not be thought of as an abstract or relatively fixed set of attributions, shared traditions, country of origin, or even shared agreement about norms for living, common beliefs, and the like. Culture is fluid and emergent as people constantly recreate themselves, their narratives, and their contexts and, in turn, are themselves changed. Culture is always a matter of intersections—of class, race, ethnicity, gender, age, and experiences—which themselves are diverse and changing (Gallardo & McNeill, 2009; Robinson-Wood, 2009). Although counselors need to have an understanding of culture and its effects on counseling, an inclusive perspective of culture recognizes that client differences exist. Acquiring an objective picture of others' cultural backgrounds requires an understanding of the many differences that make up an individual. One cannot group all Asian Americans into one cultural group or assume that all European or Hispanic American women are alike.

Subculture can be defined as a racial, ethnic, regional, economic, or social community (e.g., gang, drug, gay, elderly) that exhibits characteristic patterns of behavior sufficient to distinguish it from others in the dominant society or culture. A subculture provides its members with a history, social values, and expectations that may not be found elsewhere in the dominant culture. Therefore, meaningful communication between people who appear similar may be hampered because of differing subcultures.

Intraculture can be defined as a client's educational background, socioeconomic status, acculturation, and urban and rural background. A client may be a member of several subcultures and intracultures, each influencing the process and outcome of counseling intervention. For example, a client may be disabled, gay or lesbian, first generational, and socioeconomically poor.

Race

Race refers to the way a group of people defines itself or is defined by others as being different from other groups because of assumed innate physical characteristics. It is based on characteristics such as skin and eye color and shape of the head, eyes, ears, lips, and nose. Despite large numbers of people moving from one geographic region to another and increasing numbers of interracial marriages, the concept of race continues to play a role in distinguishing people. However, race contributes little to understanding clients' culture, ethnicity, sexual orientation, and lifespan differences. Considered as a single entity, racial identity does not reveal an individual's nationality, communication, or religion. Cultural groups that are defined by nationality, geography, communication, and religion seldom correspond with racial categories, at least not to the extent necessary to provide culturally relevant information. Therefore, although counselors should be cognizant of their clients' race, they will learn more about their clients' strengths, weaknesses, and challenges when other, more individual, aspects are identified.

Ethnicity

Ethnicity is the most distinguishing characteristic of Americans because we are categorized primarily based on our cultural identity or nationality. Robinson-Wood (2009) maintains that ethnicity refers to a connectedness based on commonalities (e.g., religion, nationality, region) in which specific aspects of cultural patterns are shared and transmission over time creates a common history and ancestry. Ethnicity refers to commonality in which unique cultural aspects refer to a nationality and country of origin. For others, religion describes either ethnicity or values and lifestyles. Characteristics associated with ethnicity include (1) a shared group image and sense of identity derived from values, behaviors, beliefs, communication, and historical perspectives; (2) shared political, social, and economic interests; and (3) shared involuntary membership with a specific ethnic group. Because of interracial marriage, many Americans have multiple ethnic and racial identities. Some persons of mixed lineage prefer to assume identities; for example, they label themselves as "White," "Black," "Indian," "Latino," "Asian," or merely "American." Still, the effects of ethnicity and race are pervasive and influence people's opinions and actions.

Worldview

This section defines *worldview* and discusses overall aspects of the term. Worldview may be defined as one's individual experiences and social, moral, religious, educational, economic, or political inputs shared with other members of one's reference group, such as culture group, racial or ethnic group, family, state, or country. Increasing attention has focused on the notion that different counseling and psychotherapy approaches reflect different worldviews. It is important that counselors understand worldviews when planning professional intervention. Western counseling theories and research often depend heavily on abstractions, abstract words, cause-and-effect relationships, linear analytic thinking, and inductive and deductive reasoning—a thinking style that reflects Western worldviews.

Understanding one's own worldview and those of other cultures, as well as perceiving their similarities and differences, facilitates interculturally sensitive relationships and communication. For example, if a school counselor wishes to facilitate the educational process of immigrant Chinese in the United States, he or she may be more successful if there is a clear understanding of the Chinese view of the structure, roles, functions, and purpose of hierarchical relationships compared with the American view of egalitarian relationships. In other words, understanding worldviews is important because a client's worldview is an overriding cognitive frame of reference that influences most of his or her perceptions and values. To understand an individual's response to a situation and to avoid a breakdown in communication, the counselor needs to understand the client's worldview.

Social Class and Socioeconomic Status

Social class and socioeconomic status continue to be significant aspects of people's lives. Still, in the twenty-first century, many professionals might misunderstand the effects of social class and socioeconomic status. Although social class is potentially associated with many human experiences, the topic has not received much attention in counseling intervention. Counselors intervening with clients of culturally diverse backgrounds benefit from knowing the client's social class. Looking only at cultural backgrounds might produce limited results. Clients' socioeconomic status affects nearly all aspects of their lives. Factors such as household income, health insurance, and overall wealth can affect physical and psychological health as well as one's outlook on life. The sad reality is that significant numbers of people in the United States live in poverty, with barely adequate incomes, or without health insurance. Effective counselors also avoid assuming that whether a person has succeeded or failed socioeconomically is a result of his or her motivation and determination. Failing socioeconomically can result from any number of reasons, from poor life decisions to our societal ills, such as prejudice and discrimination. Counselors and clients might see life events from different perspectives and neither might be able to understand the other's perspectives on events. Readers can think of a multitude of examples:

- a middle-class African American might have far more in common with a middle-class Asian American than she or he would with a lower-class African American;
- the middle- to upper-class counselor may experience difficulty understanding the challenges (e.g., low wages, unemployment, feelings of helplessness) that a client from a lower socioeconomic level may experience on a daily basis. The U.S. Census Bureau offers a wealth of current and reliable data on people's poverty levels and access to health insurance. For example, the official poverty rate in 2013 was 15.4%, up a point or two from

previous years. Instead of listing economic data here, we suggest interested readers refer to the U.S. Census Bureau (https://www.census.gov/population/projections/data/national/2014.html). The site also provides individual data on the various ethnic groups that will be valuable when planning mental health interventions.

While the majority of the data presented earlier provide a general and cursory look at people and their poverty levels, the poverty definitions list that follows provides several key definitions that describe poverty and challenges faced by some people in the United States.

Another indication of social class and socioeconomic conditions is people's ability to get health insurance. One cannot purchase or acquire health insurance if her or his main concern is providing housing and nutrition. People's socioeconomic level is often reflected in their health insurance coverage. Several interesting (and somewhat disturbing) numbers describe health insurance coverage during 2008. The percentage of people without health insurance in 2008 was not statistically different from 2007 at 15.4%. The number of uninsured increased to 46.3 million in 2008, from 45.7 million in 2007. The good news here is the Affordable Care Act, which insured millions of people who had previously been uninsured. On the other hand, the United States still has many Americans without health-care insurance.

Poverty: Definitions

Annual poverty rate–Percent of people in poverty in a calendar year.

Chronic or long-term poverty–Percent of people in poverty every month for the duration of time (typically three to four years).

Poverty definition–Money income levels that vary by family size and composition to determine poverty levels. If a family's total income is less than the family's threshold, all family members are considered in poverty. The official poverty thresholds do not vary geographically, but they are updated for inflation. The official poverty definition uses money income before taxes and does not include capital gains or noncash benefits (such as public housing, Medicaid, and food stamps).

Poverty rate–The percentage of people (or families) below poverty levels.

Poverty thresholds–Dollar amounts used to determine a family's or person's poverty status.

Ratio of income to poverty–People and families are in poverty if their income is less than their poverty threshold. If their income is less than half their poverty threshold, they are below 50% of poverty; less than the threshold itself, they are in poverty (below 100% of poverty); less than 1.25 times the threshold, below 125% of poverty, and so on. The greater the ratio of income to poverty, the more people fall under the category, because higher ratios include more people with higher incomes.

Working poor–The Census Bureau does not use the term "working poor." The "working poor" may mean different things to different data users, such as:

–People who worked, but who, nevertheless, fell under the official definition of poverty.

–People who were in poverty and had at least one working family member.

–People who may not necessarily be "in poverty" according to the official measure of poverty, but who fall below some percentage of the poverty level (for instance, 200% of poverty).

–"Below 100% of poverty" is the same as "in poverty."

–"Below 200% of poverty" includes all those described as "in poverty" under the official definition, plus some people who have income above poverty but less than two times their poverty threshold.

Adapted from: U.S. Bureau of the Census, Current Population Survey, Annual Social and Economic Supplements. Poverty and Health Statistics Branch/HHES Division.

Spirituality

Spirituality and religion are important to people across cultures (Blanks & Smith, 2009). Although the terms *religion* and *spirituality* are sometimes used synonymously, they are actually separate concepts. The foremost distinction between religion and spirituality is made by Phillips (2003), who stated that religion is "an extrinsic organized faith system grounded in institutional standards, practices, and core beliefs while spirituality is intrinsic personal beliefs and practices that can be experienced within or without formal religion" (p. 249) (as cited in Glover-Graf, Marini, Baker, & Buck, 2007, p. 21).

While some counselors have been reluctant to address religious and spiritual issues, spiritual aspects of mental health efforts can be dated back to the Middle Ages, when physicians were clergy members and the church granted medical licenses. Acceptance of spirituality is part of a movement that includes acupuncture, meditation, herbal medicine, prayer, therapeutic touch, and transactional psychology. Spiritual values may include intuition and vision, being in harmony, living in the moment, self-responsibility, peace-wellness-balance, and viewing illness as a lesson and a path as alternative healthy responses. Ethical concerns sometimes arise when spirituality and religion are intertwined. Prior to professional intervention, counselors should become familiar with the religious values and beliefs of clients. Untrained counselors may be in a quandary whether to broach client religious beliefs, knowing the importance of religion in people's lives (Glover-Graf et al., 2007).

Religious and spiritual beliefs have long been influential in the healing process. For example, many older-generation Hispanics believe in the healing powers of *curanderos*, or folk healers, whereas many Asians believe physical and mental health are determined by the balance of nature encompassed in the principles of yin and yang. Also important is that counselor disinterest, discomfort, or lack of awareness regarding religious–spiritual practices may be perceived by the client and the client's family as indicating judgmental or negative responses, which might lead to early termination of counseling (Glover-Graf et al., 2007).

Spiritual approaches to mental health interventions can be identified. Several questions deserve answering prior to initiating intervention (Gold, 2010).

1. How open is the spiritual stance that I will be modeling with my clients?
2. Which themes and practices of spiritual traditions resonate with me? Which do not?
3. How able am I to express my benevolent connectedness with each client?
4. How do I understand the presence or absence of transcendence in my own spiritual practices?
5. How do my spiritual beliefs contribute to my sense of meaning and purpose?

After considering these and other questions, eight descriptions will guide counselors in determining a client's religiosity or spirituality (Gold, 2010).

1. Religiously committed clients see the world and their issues through their religious convictions.
2. Religiously loyal clients integrate religious norms into culture in order to create guiding principles.
3. Spiritually committed clients are oriented toward spiritual themes rather than organized religions.
4. Religiously and spiritually committed clients present without orientation toward any specific religion or spiritual tradition, but they may come to welcome the opportunity to integrate such practices.
5. Superficially religious clients claim a religious affiliation, but their prime motive may be social rather than spiritual.
6. Religiously tolerant and indifferent clients can accept the need for others to hold such belief systems but dismiss the relevance of such beliefs in their own lives.
7. Nonreligious clients reject the value of religion overtly.
8. Religiously hostile clients are not accepting of those who see any merit in adherence to such belief systems (Gold, 2010).

A look at spiritualism should not neglect the Jewish faith. Almost like an invisible minority, the Jewish people have been virtually ignored in multicultural literature. Because Jews are classified as White and are seen as highly assimilated, their histories have placed them in a difficult situation where they have been basically overlooked. There are three denominations of Judaism: Orthodox, Conservative, and Reform. Orthodox refers to a form of Judaism that follows all of the commandments and regulations of the traditional Jewish scripture, including the rules of Sabbath observances and dietary laws. Conservatism accepts traditional Judaism, while absorbing aspects of the predominant culture and accepting modernization through their belief in gender equality and driving to synagogues on the Sabbath. Reform Judaism emphasizes the importance of individual decisions about the commandments and observances and the need for continuing change and revision of practices and belief over time (Altman, Inman, Fine, Ritter, & Howard, 2010). A more in-depth examination of the Jewish ethnic identity will be explored in Chapter 2.

Generational Differences

Generational differences within a particular culture result in varying beliefs and values and represent another obstacle to achieving homogeneity within a culture. Older generations may be more prone to retain Old World values and traditions because of the tendency to live in close proximity to people of similar language, traditions, and customs. Because of public schooling and a tendency (or a requirement) to adopt the values of the majority culture in school, younger generations are more likely to accept values different from those of their elders. Older generations may have lived in cultural enclaves with others speaking their native languages, but younger generations who can communicate effectively in English cope better in a predominantly English-speaking society. Although acculturation plays a role in generational differences, one's place on the lifespan continuum also plays a significant role. Whether because of wisdom, experience, or the way events are perceived during each lifespan stage, opinions and beliefs change as one matures. Generational differences often lead to interpersonal conflicts that have the potential to create psychological and emotional problems that warrant counseling intervention.

Gender

The influence of a client's gender in the counseling process and outcome has been vigorously debated. Counselors should recognize and understand gender-based differences or those characteristics and traits that are unique to males and females and that affect their unique orientations toward problems and solutions. There are numerous possibilities for exploring gender-based differences in counseling. It is clear that gender plays a significant role during counseling, but research focusing specifically on females of different cultural backgrounds does not consistently allow for generalizations across cultures.

In her excellent research study of gender, Deutsch (2007) argued that gender is not something we are but something we do. Gender must be continually socially reconstructed in light of "normative conceptions" (Deutsch, 2007, p. 106) of men and women. People act with awareness that they judge according to what is deemed appropriate feminine or masculine behavior. These normative conceptions of men and women vary across time, ethnic group, and social situation, but the opportunity to behave as manly men or womanly women is ubiquitous. Thus, gender is an ongoing emergent aspect of social interaction. Rather than internalize a set of behaviors and practices or identities that were rewarded and modeled by parents, teachers, and other authority figures, men and women create gender within social relationships throughout their lives. Theories about gender differ. Some theorists suggest that the difference is not gender per se; the problem is power. Men have more say; they get more money, more attention, more interesting jobs, more status, and more leisure (Deutsch, 2007).

Yakushko and Chronister (2005) maintain that global changes have resulted in an increase in the number of immigrant women in the United States. They believe that serving the mental health needs of immigrant women is a new frontier for American counselors and research scholars. They used Urie Bronfenbrenner's ecological theory as a guide for counselors working with immigrant women, because it highlights the significance of individual factors and larger social contexts on immigrant women's lives. Essentially, Yakushko and Chronister proposed the following contexts for consideration:

Individual–factors such as age, sex, physical and cognitive abilities, and language proficiency

Microsystem–factors such as family composition, urban or rural environment, occupational status, and racial and ethnic composition

Mesosystem–factors such as relations among immigrants' social support networks in the microsystem

Exosystem–factors such as political and economic climate of home and environment, relations between home and host countries, and legal immigration status

Macrosystem–factors such as cultural values of the home and host environment, gender and sexual identity, and political and economic values of the home and host countries.

These factors are only representative examples of the kind of information that might be helpful in working with immigrant women clients.

Sexual Orientation

Decades ago, many counselors did not address the clients' sexual orientation either, because clients did not share their sexual preferences or the counselor felt uncomfortable or unprepared for dealing with the challenge. Hebard and Hebard (2015) call for counselors to make a conscious shift in their understanding of gender as it relates to the human body. Their article actually calls for moving from LGB to LGBT to include transgender clients. They provide a long glossary of terms. It is important that counselors have familiarity with privilege and oppression as social constructs that create power dynamics. More on this important topic will be addressed in Chapters 15 and 16.

We believe that the multicultural counseling movement should include people of differing sexual orientations. Lesbians, gays, bisexuals, and transgender (LGBT) clients have a unique culture of their own, and they experience many of the same problems seen in other minorities. Sexual orientation should be perceived as a unique characteristic, just as gender, culture, ethnicity, and social class are considered unique. Counselors working with gay and lesbian clients must understand the special challenges (e.g., job discrimination, loneliness, isolation, ridicule) that gays and lesbians experience. Also, as discussed in Chapter 15, models that show the different stages of identity development have been proposed for gays and lesbians. Effective counselors working with gay or lesbian clients should base professional intervention on the clients' worldviews and overall perspectives of life. Understanding and counseling of LGBT clients are the topics of Chapters 15 and 16.

It is important to know at this point that sexual orientation might lead to several additional challenges: HIV risk behavior and internalized homophobia among Black men who have sex with men (Amola & Grimmett, 2015). Other problems mentioned by Amola and Grimmett (2015) include depression and low self-esteem. In this introductory section, it is important to note that the challenge might be far more complex than a client admitting her or his sexual orientation—clients have a professional and ethical responsibility to understand the accompanying problems as discussed by Amola and Grimmett (2015).

Ethical standards and accreditation standards as well as professional guidelines challenge counselors to provide sensitive and competent services for lesbian, gay, and bisexual clients. Effective counselors understand that people with differing sexual orientations have a culture of their own, perhaps several cultures, just as other people do. We are convinced that multicultural counselors can develop competence in working with clients with differing sexual orientations. Such competence can be developed through supervision, consultation, and additional training. Ideally, this effort should provide guidance for professionals familiar with multicultural counseling to extend their work to counselor competence with LGBT clients and will provide a framework for professionals in LGBT psychology to build on the foundations established by multicultural counseling. The authors maintain that conceptualizing counselor competence includes knowledge, attitudes, and skills. Training in these three areas involves the content, the means of conveying the content, and the training environment (one that accepts and promotes an affirming environment).

DePaul, Walsh, and Dam (2009) focused their research on issues of sexual orientation among middle and secondary school students. All students benefit from a greater awareness of sexual orientation. Heterosexual students develop an awareness of the process of discovery experienced by their LGBT peers. Such awareness can enhance their appreciation of the various dimensions of sexual identity. For some students, a heightened awareness of sexual orientation may result in their beginning to acknowledge their identity as lesbian, gay, or bisexual. Recent trends show the age of first awareness typically ranges from 8 to 11 years, and the age of identifying as LGBT typically ranges from 15 to 17 years. DePaul et al. (2009) report that LGBT students are at high risk for dropping out of school, suicidal ideation, self-harm, substance abuse, loneliness, social dissatisfaction, and risky sexual behavior.

DePaul et al. (2009) proposed a three-tier action plan. First, *whole-school prevention* includes such practices as enhancing the school climate by teaching acceptance of LGBT students, having a safe place for LGBT students, and offering a supportive dialogue for LGBT issues. Second, *targeted prevention* is aimed at specific groups of people who face established risks (e.g., classism, racism, and heterosexualism). Such practices seek to thwart chronic and predictable risks, focusing on specific issues such as system inequities. Third, *intensive intervention* provides a comprehensive approach to addressing mental health in schools, for example, working individually with students who have already experienced negative outcomes.

Disabilities

We think people with disabilities also have a culture of their own—the way they perceive themselves and think they are perceived by others; the mind-sets and worldviews they share;

and, unfortunately, the prejudice and discrimination they often experience. Smith, Foley, and Chaney (2008) defined *ableism* as a form of discrimination or prejudice against individuals with physical, mental, or developmental disabilities. Approximately 20% of Americans have some type of disability. Because disabilities have been viewed as defects rather than differences, they have not been widely recognized as a multicultural concern.

The most common psychological theories about clients with disabilities are based on the assumption that psychological adjustment accompanies the disability. Some counselors assume that all people with disabilities need counseling to help them deal with their losses. Such an opinion often comes from the belief that disabled people are bitter and self-pitying because of their disability. Because people with disabilities are individuals and thus respond differently, some need counseling, whereas others do not. Those who do seek counseling deserve counselors with knowledge, attitudes, and skills for intervening with clients with disabilities. Some people with disabilities experience problems similar to those without disabilities. However, people with disabilities may experience additional difficulties that they may seek to resolve through counseling services. Special problems may include coping with pain, frustration, and discrimination. Counselors should help clients with disabilities (just as with all clients) understand what counseling can and cannot do.

Hart (2009) looked specifically at the prevailing assessment and instructional issues related to culturally and linguistically diverse students with special needs. A dilemma facing educators and counselors is the need for effective instruction for all children, including those who come from diverse backgrounds and who experience problems with learning difficulties and disabilities. It is clear that students with disabilities require specialized professional intervention and strategies.

Graf, Blankenship, Sanchez, and Carlson (2007) conducted an interesting study involving people with disabilities among Mexicans and Mexican Americans at the U.S.–Mexico border. They began with data that reported the percentage of Hispanics with disabilities as being 10.4%, far lower than assumed. This number could be artificially low, since many immigrants actively avoid contact with government institutions out of fear of deportation and general apprehension.

Graf et al. (2007) concluded that, overall, participants tended to hold positive attitudes toward family members with disabilities and being with persons with disabilities. Of particular note is the attitude toward family members with disabilities and the general belief that family members with disabilities need others to take care of them. Participants in the study did not believe that spending time with a person with a disability reflected poorly on the person, nor did they believe that it was embarrassing to have a family member with a disability. The researchers found significant differences among Mexicans and Mexican Americans. Mexicans indicated much less discomfort around, and less avoidance of, persons with disabilities. They were less embarrassed by having a family member with a disability, and they believed that people with disabilities should automatically be treated kindly. They also believed that people with disabilities should be excused more often for bad behaviors, bad temper, and hurting others. However, they also believed that people with disabilities were less likely to succeed and have a "real future" (Graf et al., 2007, p. 163). Thus it appears the Mexicans have less hope in terms of success for people with disabilities but are kinder and more forgiving toward them (Graf et al., 2007).

Withrow (2008) maintained that culture influences the way a family views disability as well as how a family views intervention. For example, some Mexican Americans view disability as an act of God, a punishment for something done by the family, or the work of evil spirits. Also, the U.S. emphasis on fixing the disability is countered by some Mexicans' emphasis on acceptance of one's destiny and living in harmony with the disabling condition.

Lifespan Development

A major premise underlying this text is that clients differ with respect to their lifespan stages. Each lifespan stage (childhood, adolescence, adulthood, old age) has its own unique developmental characteristics and counseling problems. The dilemma is compounded, however, when counselors consider that their clients' lifespan differences and cultural characteristics are often closely intertwined. Examples include elderly Asian Americans, who may exhibit considerable anxiety over the younger generation's acculturation, or the health concerns of elderly African Americans, or the machismo that is so important to Hispanic American adolescents. An adolescent client and an elderly client of the same culture, race, and ethnic group will probably perceive an issue from different perspectives. Problems, values, and beliefs vary so greatly with development that people functioning within the same lifespan stage may actually constitute a subgroup.

Human development is an ongoing process that starts at birth and continues until death, with cultural and individual variations existing within each lifespan period. The problems of children obviously differ from those of adults. Culturally perceptive counselors recognize that although African American and American Indian children may share similar developmental characteristics, they may be vastly different in many other respects. Likewise, although the elderly in all cultures often have common characteristics, elderly Asian Americans experience problems that differ from those of elderly American Indians or Hispanic Americans. It is important that counselors understand each client's cultural background and lifespan period as well as the intricate relationships between the two. Although studies in multicultural psychology and human development have become more sophisticated during the past decade or so, counselors are urged to draw conclusions and generalizations cautiously; the existing literature often does not allow for definitive conclusions. Sufficient evidence does indicate, however, that cultural differences undoubtedly exist across and within cultures, between generations, and throughout the lifespan. In this text, we examine cultural differences in terms of a lifespan approach and discuss their implications for counselors and psychotherapists in multicultural settings.

Research on human development relative to cultural diversity is limited. The paucity of literature in this area, however, does not excuse the counselor from making every effort to gain the maximum knowledge of the client's place on the lifespan continuum. Increased recognition of cultural differences (and their implications for the counseling profession) has led to more and better research on multicultural populations and multicultural counseling processes. Nonetheless, much of the available literature must be considered as beginning points. Journals that publish research and scholarly opinion are too many to name here; however, a few representative journals that provide information for counselors include *Counseling Psychologist, Counseling and Human Development, Journal of Counseling and Development, American Psychologist, Journal of Cross-Cultural Psychology*, and *Journal of Multicultural Counseling and Development*. Readers interested in information pertaining to children and adolescents should consider *Child Development* and *Professional School Counseling*; those interested in adult development should consult *Human Development*; those counseling the elderly will benefit from reading selected issues of *Gerontologist* or *Journal of Gerontology*. In summary, client differences such as culture, race, ethnicity, worldview, social class, lifespan, generation, gender, sexual orientation, and disability deserve counselors' attention and should be reflected in all aspects of multicultural counseling.

COUNSELING AND PSYCHOTHERAPY IN A MULTICULTURAL SOCIETY

Multicultural counseling (sometimes called cross-cultural counseling) and psychotherapy have become major forces in counselor training and are recognized and endorsed by leading counselor education accrediting agencies. The National Council for Accreditation of Teacher Education (NCATE) and the Council for Accreditation of Counseling and Related Educational Programs (CACREP) have adopted the position that multicultural education should be a part of the educational program for counselors. Considering our increasingly diverse society, it seems clear that culture will become an important construct for assessing, interpreting, and changing psychological processes in the future. However, the process of making culture central to the counseling process will require reconceptualizing our theories, tests, methods, strategies, and outcomes.

A Brief Historical Overview of Multicultural Counseling

Multicultural counseling as a specialization started with a small group of counselors and psychologists who were interested in cross-cultural differences. The civil rights movement of the 1960s provided tremendous impetus to the development of multicultural counseling. In addition, the growing recognition of racism and other forms of discrimination in American society resulted in ethnicity and minority status becoming a focus of interest within the field of counseling.

Until the mid-1960s, counseling and psychotherapy in America tended to overlook clients of differing cultural backgrounds, who were at a disadvantage in a predominantly majority culture and a middle-class society. Likewise, psychotherapy limited its practice primarily to clients of the middle and upper classes and neglected people from lower classes and differing cultural backgrounds. However, by the mid-1970s, the number of studies focusing on the effects of race on counseling and psychotherapy had increased.

The movement gained momentum as people began to realize that certain minority-group clients were receiving unequal and poor mental health services. Questions were posed such as: Can middle-class, European American counselors work successfully with African American clients of any social class? Did existing counselors have the knowledge, skills, and attitudes to work with clients of a different gender, culture, or ethnicity? Obviously, more culturally relevant counseling services were needed, which mandated counselor education programs taking a more comprehensive approach to diversity. Counselors needed to feel confident that they had the knowledge, skills, and attitudes to provide effective and professional counseling intervention. The number of publications on counseling minority groups in the United States began to increase. While initial efforts focused on Asian Americans, African Americans, and American Indians, the term *multiculturalism* was expanded to include other groups: various subcultures, racial groups, developmental periods, sexual orientation groups, gender groups, age groups, and social classes.

Although the history of multicultural counseling and psychotherapy has been brief, current research and writing provide a basis for the prediction that the enthusiasm for counseling across cultures will continue.

Definitions

Although many scholars have offered definitions, we prefer our definition of multicultural counseling, one that reflects our beliefs about clients and their various diversities:

> Professional intervention and counseling relationships in which the counselor and the client belong to different cultural groups, subscribe to different worldviews, and have distinguishing differences such as gender, sexual orientation, disabilities, social class, spirituality, and lifespan period.

Although counseling professionals often differ on their definition of multicultural counseling, most agree on several key aspects:

- Professional intervention techniques should reflect culturally different clients' cultural and ethnic backgrounds, lifespan period, socioeconomic status, gender perspectives, disabilities, and sexual orientation.
- Counseling professionals plan accordingly for differences during counseling intervention as the dissonance between the cultural backgrounds of the counselor and the client increases.

- Counseling is perceived as culturally based, meaning that both the counselor and the client bring their worldviews and cultural perspectives to the counseling process.
- Clients differ in the concerns they bring to counseling due to their cultural and ethnic backgrounds, lifespan period, gender perspectives, and sexual orientation.
- Counselors and their clients might vary in their perceptions of the counseling process as well as expected outcomes of the professional intervention.

Counseling and Culture

To understand the close relationship between counseling and culture, counseling must be considered in its cultural context. Counselors in multicultural settings carefully avoid three situations that can influence professional intervention and limit its effectiveness. First, they avoid overemphasizing similarities (e.g., culture, gender, sexual orientation, and lifespan period), which can lead to a mind-set that fails to recognize the differences that actually exist and thereby affect counseling outcomes. The second situation is overgeneralizing differences, which lead to stereotyping. The third is assuming that one must emphasize either similarities or dissimilarities. These three situations can be avoided by focusing on the uniqueness of the client without dwelling on the client's similarities or differences.

Counseling and Counselor's Identity

A counselor's identity is influenced by several factors: culture, lifespan period, gender, sexual orientation, developmental period, and prejudicial beliefs. Likewise, the counselor's perspectives toward individualism or collectivism affect counseling effectiveness. Why does all this matter, and does counselor identity have the potential to affect the outcome of professional counseling intervention? Without doubt, the counselor's identity (and perspectives toward others) affects his or her ability to counsel effectively.

Effective counselors see the need to prepare and accept the responsibility to prepare for professional intervention in multicultural settings. Such responsibility and commitment require the close examination of one's own identity. Counselors cannot understand others' cultural beliefs and worldviews until they understand their own; therefore, they should recognize their distinguishing cultural characteristics, beliefs, attitudes, and worldviews. In other words, they must learn "who they are" and "what they are becoming." This is especially true when counseling in multicultural situations, because clients will undoubtedly perceive events and situations through different lenses. Counselors need to understand the bases of their identities—their culture, ethnicity, social class, and gender—and how these orientations affect their response to clients.

A counselor's identity will influence how he or she intervenes. The European American counselor might emphasize rugged individualism; the Asian American and Hispanic American might feel obligated to show more concern for others. The African American counselor might expect European Americans to show more regard for family. Readers can likely name numerous other examples. The point is that counselors need to understand how their identities affect their feelings about clients' events and situations and, ultimately, counseling effectiveness. Perceptive counselors realize the necessity of working toward a neutral position regarding the value of these feelings and that clients' attributes affect how they perceive the forces affecting their lives.

Most counselor education programs provide training and firsthand experiences in individual and group counseling. Such training helps prospective counselors learn personal issues that might later interfere with their counseling effectiveness. This experience should also help prospective counselors become aware of their own ethnic and racial identities and how these views have shaped their personal identities, including their attitudes toward other ethnic and racial groups, the other gender, and people with differing sexual orientations. Counselors who completed counselor education programs prior to the emphasis on intervening with clients in multicultural settings and, more specifically, on understanding how counselor identity affects counseling intervention have the professional responsibility to become aware of their own racial and ethnic identities, their perspectives toward differing cultural groups, and how their identities and perspectives affect the outcome of the counseling relationship.

Mental health counseling extends far beyond perceiving the client's problems through a cultural lens. Many factors should be considered, such as race, ethnicity, spirituality, social class, and disabilities. Also, as we will address later in this chapter, White privilege and social injustices occur all too often, which limits a client's success during the counseling process. Mental health counseling efforts might be limited when the counselor only considers one or two aspects of the client's life conditions.

Resources and Guidelines

Counselors have several *resources* at their disposal when planning professional interventions in multicultural situations, including:

- research-based findings on the cross-cultural counseling process;
- published accounts of personal experiences by other counselors;
- personally transmitted accounts;
- the counselor's own experiences with clients of differing backgrounds; and
- the counselor's professional, cultural, and personal sensitivity.

The following *guidelines* can potentially improve the overall effectiveness of multicultural counseling. Counselors should:

- be aware of their clients' and their own cultural group history and experiences;
- develop sensitivity toward their own personal beliefs and values;
- develop awareness and comprehension of their clients' histories and experiences within the cultural group;
- develop an awareness and comprehension of their clients' experiences in mainstream culture;
- develop perceptual sensitivity toward their clients' personal beliefs and values;
- demonstrate active listening and a broad repertoire of genuine verbal and nonverbal responses; and
- demonstrate genuine concern for their clients' individual situations.

Ethics

Ethics, without doubt, plays a significant role in multicultural counseling and influences its professional status, as well as its growth and progress. Because the topic of ethics is examined in Chapter 3 (mainly the American Counseling Association's 2014 *Code of Ethics*) as a counselor responsibility, here we only briefly discuss the special ethical responsibilities of counselors who intervene with clients of culturally different backgrounds. Counseling clients of various cultural backgrounds requires more than just knowledge of a particular client's cultural background. The client's perceptions, expectations, and expression of symptoms also warrant understanding from a cultural context. In fact, these should be understood both from the client's perspective and from that of the majority culture. Ethics comes into play when counselors try to understand (and subsequently plan interventions) that all people function from a culturally determined worldview, which includes values, belief systems, lifestyles, and modes of problem-solving and decision making. Ethical standards need to focus on professional training, assessment, and intervention practices, especially as these aspects relate to counseling with clients of diverse cultural backgrounds.

When a mental health professional joins a professional association and agrees to abide by the code of ethics, it is assumed that the individual acts in accordance with its publicly acknowledged set of standards. Having a common document addressing multicultural competence helps the mental health professions achieve greater sophistication, preparation, and practice.

Challenges and Barriers

Several challenges have the potential to limit the effectiveness of multicultural counseling. Although counselors can address challenges such as their own abilities to understand and counsel others who are different from themselves, they have less control over other challenges, such as society's racism and discrimination.

Possible Disparities in Health Access

Unfortunately, health-care disparities exist in the United States. Children and the elderly might be the most disadvantaged. Children in the child welfare system have been shown to have disproportionately high rates of health problems. The elderly are often ignored or lack the knowledge to access health care. The Affordable Care Act will provide improved health care to people of all ages. Still, as we have mentioned, some people are not covered under this landmark act. Counselors need to understand the act and be able to offer recommendations for health care or be able to suggest other professionals who are more acquainted with the health-care mandates.

Counselors' Mind-Sets and Efforts

Challenges counselors may encounter when intervening with clients of differing cultural backgrounds include:

- lack of communication resulting from communication difficulties;
- counselor misunderstandings of a client's culture, racial group, ethnicity, worldviews, gender, or sexual orientation, as well as how and to what extent these characteristics affect counseling intervention;
- erroneous assumptions about cultural assimilation;
- differing social class values and orientations;
- stereotypical generalizations about clients of other cultures;
- assumptions of racism or cultural bias on the part of either the counselor or the client; and
- lack of understanding of the client's worldview.

The existence of barriers does not imply that the counselor's challenge is too overwhelming to be tackled. Perceptive counselors can learn about clients' cultures, interact with people from different backgrounds, learn appropriate techniques for dealing with different clients, and, perhaps most important, examine their own beliefs and opinions concerning people of different cultures.

Lifespan Differences

The increasingly pluralistic nature of the United States signifies a vast array of cultural, ethnic, gender, and racial differences deserving of counselors' respect and appreciation. It is important for counselors to understand, however, that lifespan differences contribute to human diversity and, in many cases, are as important as a group's unique physical and cultural characteristics. A major premise of this text is that counselors should consider not only a client's cultural differences but also the client's lifespan period and the characteristics associated with each developmental stage, including potential psychological and emotional problems associated with each stage.

Stereotyping

Stereotyping prohibits the effectiveness of multicultural counseling. Stereotypes produce a generalized mental picture of a person or an entire culture. Although a stereotype may hold some validity in a particular case, effective counselors have a professional responsibility to consider all stereotypes with skepticism and to acknowledge that prejudice and approval or disapproval accompany these images. Because stereotypes all too often contribute to racism and ageism, effective counselors should seek to understand and respond appropriately to their own and others' cultural and age-level beliefs.

Stereotypes about lifespan stage also affect one's perceptions of clients. Do children lack the power to change their lives? Are adolescents rebellious troublemakers obsessed with sex? Are adults always preoccupied with progress and material gains? Are the elderly "over the hill" without power or purpose? A counselor who holds such beliefs could place clients in a difficult situation. Likewise, if a client subscribes to these beliefs, then the therapeutic relationship may be undermined.

Racism

According to Malott and Schaefle (2015), racism has been defined as a system of oppression, whereby persons of a dominant racial group (Whites, in the United States) exercise power or privilege over those in nondominant groups. Such actions may be made out of bias or in an effort to maintain advantaged access to social, economic, and educational resources. Forms of racism vary by context and exist at both micro (individual) and macro (structural/societal) levels. As laws and social standards in the United States have changed, expressions of racism have become less obvious (Malott & Schaefle, 2015). Because of racism's varied and often covert formations, scholars have described the phenomenon as insidious, systematic, and pervasive, capable of affecting people of color in all areas of their lives.

Acts of racism still occur, and with the rapidly expanding technological innovations, racism might be more covert than overt. Racism and its effects continue to affect society with great force. The impact can be seen within various societal institutions, including education, government, business, housing, and criminal justice. The disturbing reality is that racism remains deeply embedded in many of our value systems and in economic, political, and social institutions.

Racism appears in various forms and dimensions. For example, people (a) harbor negative feelings about another group because they consider that group to be a threat to their cultural beliefs; (b) harbor negative feelings about another cultural group, yet will not openly admit their racial feelings; (c) demonstrate friendly attitudes to other cultural groups only in some situations; and (d) fail to understand others' cultural beliefs and traditions and therefore harbor negative feelings because of ignorance and misunderstanding. Unfortunately, racism or general dislike of those who are "different" often results in crimes committed against people based on their culture, social class, sexual orientation, or other differences. Racism sometimes results in new forms of extremism manifesting itself in actions that hurt others, both physically and psychologically.

Institutional racism is defined as different access to the goods, services, and opportunities of society and impedes social acceptance and economic progress. While the more obvious forms of racism can be identified and addressed, institutional racism may be more covert, including policies and practices of decision making. Because this type of racism can be legal and often has been codified in institutions of law and custom, there may be no identifiable perpetrator. Institutionalized racism may involve limited access to quality education, housing, employment, medical facilities, and a safe environment.

Personally mediated racism is defined as prejudice and discrimination, where prejudice means different assumptions about the abilities, motives, and intentions of others based on their race, and discrimination means different actions toward others based on their race. This type of racism can take many forms, including lack of respect, such as poor or no service; suspicion, such as shopkeepers' vigilance, avoidance of others, street crossing, purse clutching, and standing when empty seats are available; and devaluation, such as surprise at competence and the discouraging of aspirations.

Internalized racism is defined as acceptance of negative messages by members of stigmatized races about their own abilities and intrinsic worth. It is characterized by their not believing in others who look like them and not believing in themselves. It involves accepting limitations to one's full humanity, including one's spectrum of dreams, one's right to self-determination, and one's range of allowable self-expression.

The effects of racism are often denied and considered a taboo subject in racially mixed settings. Also, many people, regardless of their racial group membership, have been socialized to think of the United States as a just society and fail to recognize the impact of racism on their own and others' lives.

White Privilege

White privilege has been described as benefits simply because of the color of one's skin. These benefits may result in better treatment at banks, department stores, and restaurants. White people are treated better and with more respect only because they are White. White privilege can also be defined as the belief that only one's own standards and opinions are accurate. Or as some might say, "White means I am right!" White privilege brings several advantages. Whites can feel confident when they look at the newspaper or television that they will see other Whites. Having white skin usually allows people to assimilate into the dominant culture in a way that most people of color cannot. Generally speaking, Whites do not have to spend the psychological effort or economic resources recovering from others' prejudices. Privilege can also be considered in terms of power, access, advantage, and a majority status. *Power* is having control, choice, autonomy, and authority or influence over others. *Access* is having money, opportunities, and/or material possessions. *Advantage* is having connections, favorable treatment, entitlement, social support, or lack of concern for others. *Majority* is simply being part of the majority in number, social standing, and/or social norms. The opposite of privilege, *oppression*, is the lack of privilege, power, access, and majority status (Hays, Chang, & Dean, 2004).

White guilt describes a feeling or emotion felt by European Americans who see their group as responsible for advantages held over other racial groups. White guilt can include White people feeling good about their favored social position. Some evidence suggests that the advantaged can experience something akin to pride when they see themselves as superior to members of other groups. Still, even feeling a sense of pride, these people might also feel bad when systemic inequality illegitimately favors their group and disadvantages others. For example, European Americans can feel guilty about the ways in which racial inequality advantages them and disadvantages other groups.

What does all this have to do with counselors? White counselors respond to White privilege and oppression with varying levels of awareness. Depending on their level of awareness, White counselors report anger, guilt, confusion, defensiveness, sadness, and a sense of responsibility and need for advocacy when discussing these topics. Other counselors might not have such a sense of awareness. Because Whiteness remains invisible to Whites, they might look at racial discrimination with detachment and feel little responsibility for changing the status quo. Although discussing these realities may create strong emotions, it is helpful in increasing counselors' awareness of advocacy, oppression, and cultural identity (Hays et al., 2004).

Social and Economic Justice

The Center for Economic and Social Justice (http://www.cesj.org/learn/definitions/defining-economic-justice-and-social-justice/) defines social justice as a set of universal principles that guide people in judging what is right and what is wrong, no matter what culture and society they live in. Justice is one of the four "cardinal virtues" of classical moral philosophy, along with courage, temperance (self-control), and prudence (efficiency). (Faith, hope, and charity are considered to be the three "religious" virtues.) Virtues or "good habits" help individuals to develop fully their human potentials, thus enabling them to serve their own self-interests as well as work in harmony with others for their common good.

Social justice encompasses economic justice. Social justice is the virtue which guides us in creating those organized human interactions we call institutions. In turn, social institutions, when justly organized, provide us with access to what is good for the person, both individually and in our associations with others. Social justice also imposes on each of us a personal responsibility to work with others to design and continually perfect our institutions as tools for personal and social development (http://www.cesj.org/learn/definitions/defining-economic-justice-and-social-justice/).

McCabe and Rubinson (2008) focused on committing to social justice by advocating school psychology programs to teach advocacy for LGBT youth. Their study explored how graduate students in school psychology programs can be prepared to ensure an equal and safe environment for youth identifying as LGBT. They found that although graduate students had strong positive attitudes toward social justice (e.g., race, class, and language), they revealed inadequate attitudes and knowledge of issues faced by LGBT youth. They were unlikely to become change agents for LGBT youth due to institutional barriers, ambivalent attitudes, and insufficient knowledge. The results did not imply that graduate students were unwilling or resistant to social justice. Rather, it showed that many did not understand the issues and difficulties faced by LGBT youth or the complexity of social justice issues.

Value of Understanding a Client's Developmental Stage

The number of research studies on lifespan development has resulted in a broad spectrum of publications, textbooks, and conference proceedings. Counselors who understand the developmental characteristics and unique cultural characteristics of their clients and the complex relationship between these two dimensions bring an enhanced perspective to counseling and psychotherapy.

As we have already mentioned, a major premise of this text is the importance of recognizing and understanding a client's developmental stage when planning and implementing counseling intervention. Rather than assuming a developmental homogeneity that may not actually exist, counselors benefit from knowing the problems, tasks, and challenges of each developmental period. The decision to use a specific technique should always be based on a sound rationale, rather than simply on a counselor's style, training, or preference. The relevance of human development theories becomes clear as counselors select techniques and counseling strategies based on the client's developmental level and the goals being worked toward. Counselors need to know counseling strategies that reflect cultural (and other) differences and developmental levels as well as short-term and long-term counseling goals.

COUNSELING INTERVENTION: CULTURAL CONSIDERATIONS

Regardless of culture and social class, professionals must often reach difficult decisions concerning whether to use individual, group, or family therapy for their clients. In multicultural situations, such decisions can be particularly difficult as cultural, intracultural, and generational differences are brought into play.

Individual and Group Therapy

Selecting individual or group counseling techniques becomes intricately complex, considering that some cultures may not react favorably to traditional counseling situations. For example, because of the commitment of Asian Americans to protecting the family name and honor at all costs, an Asian American client may be reluctant to reveal significant personal or family information; a Hispanic male client may be reluctant to disclose events or situations that may reflect negatively on his family or his manhood; the Western society's tendency to encourage the sharing of one's personal feelings runs counter to American Indians' reluctance to allow "outsiders" to intervene in their personal affairs. Where a client may be reluctant to disclose significant information during individual therapy, this reluctance might grow more acute during group therapy. Clients, both minority and majority culture, may distrust the counselor, again both minority and majority culture, because they believe that the counselor does not understand a cultural perspective other than his or her own.

The terms *multicultural group counseling* and *multicultural counseling groups* are used interchangeably to refer to group counseling situations in which counselors and clients differ in their cultural, ethnic, or racial characteristics. Many counselors agree that group counseling services can be used in both a preventive and a remedial manner with people from diverse ethnoracial backgrounds. Although intervening with group counseling may foster positive psychological outcomes, the effective and ethical practice of multicultural group counseling depends largely on the practitioner's understanding and competence in this area.

Marriage and Family

The Western world's tradition of encouraging males and females to share feelings and to communicate openly, freely, and on an equal footing may not be accepted by many Asian Americans, who have long accepted the superiority of the male and his valued role as the family spokesperson. In fact, it is unlikely that certain minority women will assume a significant speaking role during marriage and family counseling sessions. Although younger generations may have acculturated somewhat, the dominance of the male and his control over the family in some cultures should be understood by mental health professionals who may have intervened predominantly with clients of other cultural backgrounds.

When planning intervention strategies, the counselor should consider the extent to which the client's cultural traditions affect therapy sessions and their outcome. Specifically, how will the client in a multicultural setting respond to the presence of a spouse or children during a session? Will the wife respond during family therapy or will she let the husband speak for the family? Such questions can be answered only by considering individual clients; their cultural characteristics, generation, and degree of acculturation; and the nature and severity of the problem.

Rehabilitation Counseling

Rehabilitation counselors are concerned with assisting individuals who have disabilities to maximize their potential and their independence. Rehabilitation counselors work with individuals who have a variety of physical, mental, and emotional disabilities, as defined in the Rehabilitation Act of 1973 and the 1998 Amendments to the Rehabilitation Act as well as in the Americans with Disabilities Act (ADA). They assist individuals who have disabilities in vocational, independent living, and educational pursuits.

The current trend for people working in the rehabilitation counseling field is to obtain a master's degree in rehabilitation counseling or a closely related field and to obtain national certification as a Certified Rehabilitation Counselor (CRC). The CRC is administered through the Commission on Rehabilitation Counselor Certification (CRCC). The MA degree has recently been affirmed in the 1998 Amendments to the Rehabilitation Act. Individuals who receive the MA degree in rehabilitation counseling are also eligible for most counseling licensure exams after taking an additional three classes. It is important to check with the state in which you would like to practice for licensing requirements. Individuals who want to become rehabilitation counselor educators, researchers, or administrators need to go beyond the master's degree and obtain a doctoral degree.

Rehabilitation counselors work in a variety of settings, the typical categories of settings being public, private nonprofit, and private for-profit rehabilitation settings. Typical settings in which rehabilitation counselors may be employed include:

- State vocational rehabilitation agencies
- Community-based rehabilitation agencies (often specializing with populations such as individuals who have developmental disabilities, chronic mental health issues, or specific medical disabilities such as HIV/AIDS)
- Private rehabilitation agencies
- Insurance companies
- Public school systems
- Hospitals
- Colleges/universities
- Independent living centers
- Employee assistance programs within a corporation
- Job training centers

Rehabilitation counselors may also be employed in nontraditional settings, such as in community counseling agencies, substance abuse agencies, and human resource departments.

SUMMARY

Multicultural counselor education and mental health centers indicate that the growth of this field will continue. Clients will benefit even more with the increasing recognition of lifespan differences. Predicted population trends indicate that the nation's increasing diversity suggests counselors will increasingly be called on to provide professional intervention to people of differing cultural backgrounds and lifespan periods. Understanding concepts of culture, race, and ethnicity as well as lifespan differences will be prerequisite to effective multicultural counseling.

The appendix provides counselors with "Suggested Multicultural Experiential Activities" as they learn more about multicultural counseling.

NOTE

1 Some scholars (e.g., Comas-Diaz, 2001) prefer other terms such as Latino/a for this cultural group. Although we respect Comas-Diaz's opinion and the right of individuals to select a name for their culture, we have chosen to use the term Hispanic throughout this book, mainly because that is the term used by the U.S. Census Bureau. Still, whenever possible, we will refer specifically to persons from specific cultural backgrounds, such as Mexican Americans.

SUGGESTED READINGS

Appiah, K.A. (2015). Race in the modern world: The problem of the color line. *Foreign Policy*, *94*(2), 3–8. Biological traits such as skin color, facial shape, and hair color and texture defined racial boundaries—still, there was no scientific reason for doing so.

Clauss-Ehlers, C.S., & Parham, D. (2014). Landscape of diversity in higher Education: Linking demographic shifts to contemporary university and college counseling center practices. *Journal of Multicultural Counseling & Development*, *42*(2), 69–76. American institutions of higher education are increasingly called upon to respond to demographic changes—current and future shifts in the environmental, academic, social, and emotional climate of campuses are likely to spawn both concerns and opportunities for academic and student services personnel and students.

Dykes, F., & Thomas, S. (2015). Meeting needs of the hidden minority: Transition planning tips for LGBT youth. *Preventing School Failure, 59*(3), 179–185. Although this reading focuses on instruction, related services, employment, and post-school living arrangements, it continues to be appropriate for counselors seeking to meet the needs of lesbian, gay, bisexual, transgender, and questioning students.

MacLeod, B. P. (2014). Addressing clients' prejudices in counseling. *Counseling Today, 56*(8), 50–55. The article focuses on how counselors address the prejudices of their clients during counseling, e. g., the shift of counseling profession to a multicultural and social justice paradigm, making it difficult for the counselors to treat prejudiced clients, the need of the counselors to address the racist statements and beliefs of their clients, and the need to know clients' experiences with racism, social history with prejudice, and parents' reaction to race during counseling.

Pica-Smith, C., & Poynton, T. A. (2014). Supporting interethnic and interracial friendships among youth to reduce prejudice and racism in schools: The role of the school counselor. *Professional School Counseling, 18*(1), 82–89. Supporting interethnic and interracial friendships in schools among children and adolescents is an important part of a progressive educational agenda informed in equity, social justice frameworks, and critical multicultural education that leads to a reduction in racial prejudice.

West-Olatunji, C. (2014). Multicultural counseling: The next frontier. *Counseling Today, 56*(9), 5–7. The article discusses the accomplishments of multicultural counseling scholars. It highlights six frontiers for multicultural counselors including transnationalism, the impact of oppression and marginalization on cultural identity and understanding multiple identities.

2   Identity Development and Models

QUESTIONS TO BE EXPLORED

- How do factors such as culture, gender, sexual orientation, and development affect counselor identity?
- How do prejudice, social justice, and White privilege affect counselor identity, and how should the counselor respond to it?
- How does the American belief in individualism and self-sufficiency affect counselor identity as well as counselor perception of clients who may feel more regard and concern for the welfare of others?
- What is meant by Helms's (1984, 1990, 1994) White racial identity attitude theory (WRIAT) model and Rowe, Bennett, and Atkinson's (1994) White racial consciousness (WRC) model, and what are their similarities?
- Why should counselors develop an awareness of the perspective of their own culture, gender, sexual orientation, and development stage as well as those of their clients?
- What difficulties and hurdles are associated with counselors understanding their own identity in an effort to achieve more effective intervention with clients in multicultural settings?

OVERVIEW

Counselor identity plays a major role in shaping how counselors perceive themselves and how they perceive others and their cultural backgrounds. Counselors in multicultural settings often face seemingly confusing situations, customs, and worldviews that differ from their own and have the potential to affect the efficacy of counseling intervention. Their clients, regardless of the lifespan stage, can have attitudes and beliefs that contradict counselors' long-held and valued beliefs. For example, the African American counselor may fail to understand the American Indian perspective toward sharing and love of the earth, or males may not understand females' perspectives and vice versa. Misunderstandings that result from differences between the counselor and the client, such as differing cultural backgrounds, social class, or gender perspectives, can cloud judgments and inhibit decision-making processes. Plus, factors such as social justice and White privilege must be factored into identity development. This chapter focuses on counselor identity, how identity can affect the counseling relationship, and the need for counselors, regardless of cultural background, to understand their own and others' cultural identities.

UNDERSTANDING IDENTITY

Scholars of social psychology, personality theory, feminist thought, and psychoanalytic theory have developed detailed theories of the self and identity that have implications for the counseling profession, especially counselors in multicultural situations.

Identity has been defined as a phenomenological experience of coming to understand oneself; identity is lived discourse. Individuals need to infuse values, beliefs, behaviors, and lifestyle into their identities. *Social identity* is the part of an individual's self-concept that derives from knowledge of membership in a group along the attached emotional significance (Thomas, Hacker, & Hoxha, 2011). *Cultural identity* can be defined as one's cultural identification—the distinguishing character or personality of an individual and her or his self-perception as a cultural being as well as beliefs, attitudes, and worldviews. The definition can also be viewed in terms of personal identity or who one is. Identity is the partly conscious, largely unconscious sense of who one is, both as a person and as a contributor to society. Undoubtedly, counselors can offer other definitions; however, regardless of the selected definition, a well-grounded, mature psychosocial identity is necessary. Identity, a complex and multifaceted entity, can be perceived in terms of culture, development, and gender and directly influences how counselors perceive situations as well as their counseling effectiveness.

Racial identity development is important for at least two reasons. First, it helps shape individuals' attitudes about themselves, their attitudes about other individuals in their racial-ethnic minority group, and their attitudes about individuals from the majority. Second, it emphasizes that individuals from a particular cultural group differ, with widely varying attitudes and preferences.

Culture and Identity

Identity is inseparable from the specific culture that shapes it. One's culture—communication, social structures, rituals, and taboos—shapes one's identity in terms of what one thinks about situations and events. In other words, identity is influenced by how people perceive their communication, both as their native communication and in comparison with the majority communication. For example, an Asian American woman may look favorably on her native language within her enclave yet perceive her native language as inferior when forced to participate in the broader English-speaking society. Similar conclusions can hold true for mannerisms, beliefs, and values. For example, a Hispanic American counselor might have difficulty understanding a European American's motivation to achieve and to excel at the expense of others. Before counselors can understand the cultural orientation of others, it will be necessary for them to understand their own culture and its effects on their counseling intervention.

Identity is firmly based on culture, cultural backgrounds, and opinions of how others perceive their culture. Although all people need to be aware of the relationship between culture and identity, counselors have an even greater responsibility to examine perceptions of their own and others' cultures and identities. The counselor needs an identity that contributes to the acceptance of culturally different people. Counseling effectiveness will be diminished when the counselor places value judgments on clients' cultures and judges events and situations through his or her identity expectations.

Identity is well grounded in the developmental changes that occur from childhood to old age. Identity formation begins early in life, but it continues to develop throughout the lifespan. Other factors that affect identity include the passage of time, social change, role requirements, and one's perceptions of others' opinions.

Pope (2000) examined the relationship between psychosocial development and racial identity of Black American (Pope used the term *Black American* because some participants were Caribbean American), Asian American, and Hispanic American traditionally aged undergraduate college students to learn the developmental needs and issues of college students of color and the impact of race and racial identity on their development. Implications of Pope's study included (1) ensuring that programs targeted at assisting students in the development of these areas (psychosocial development and racial identity) reflect consideration for differences in Asian American students; (2) focusing on individual interactions, such as advisement and career counseling sessions, to pass on important information and skills for psychosocial development and racial identity; (3) avoiding making assumptions about the students' levels of psychosocial development without first considering their racial identity and how they perceive themselves as racial beings; (4) addressing students' unique histories, cultural values, and perspectives of the various racial groups by targeting different types of workshops, personal approaches, mentoring, and advising and counseling efforts; and (5) considering both race and racial identity as important factors in understanding the development of students of color.

As we have said, identity formation actually begins in young children (as they learn the identifying characteristics of their culture), and significant development occurs during adolescence, when maturational ability allows self-determination, abstract future-oriented thought, expanding social roles, and more astute recognitions of one's culture and those of others. Thus counselors working in multicultural settings need to understand both culture and development. Understanding one entity and not the other limits the counselor's ability to intervene, especially with clients of differing cultural backgrounds.

It is often difficult for people to understand the perspectives of others in differing lifespan stages. Although many people remember certain events of their childhood, they may forget what it is like to be a child. Likewise, it is difficult for an adolescent to imagine life as a middle-aged or an elderly person. The lifespan period of the client has serious implications for counselors. First, counselors need to understand the various tasks and challenges of each developmental stage. Second, they need to understand the value placed on the elderly in some cultures. Third, and probably most important, counselors need to understand their own developmental period in itself and in relation to other developmental stages.

Gender and Identity

Gender can be defined as the differences in masculinity and femininity—the thoughts, feelings, and behaviors that suggest masculine or feminine orientations. Effective counselors accept and understand that individual and societal expectations of acceptable behavior for men and women vary across cultures. As with culture, gender has a direct influence on identity and vice versa. All people's identities, regardless of cultural background, are influenced by gender and gender expectations.

Research by Moore (2005) explored how women with severe disabilities attributed meaning to their lives, experiences, and decisions. Unquestionably, women with severe work disabilities face substantial barriers to participation in social, educational, and work roles.

Moore provided several implications for working with and counseling women with severe disabilities:

1. Connection with others–counselors should assess the loss of relationships and relational opportunities in clients' lives.
2. Unpaid and paid work counselors can explore the meaning of work in clients' lives because they need to feel their abilities are being utilized, their needs are being met, and their lives are being valued.
3. Religion/spirituality–counselors should realize that church involvement and spirituality can be significant avenues that help to clarify meaning in life. Moore also thinks that the traditional medical model of counseling and rehabilitation disregards the inherent tendency in human beings toward wellness, self-actualization, and growth.

Thomas et al. (2011) studied 17 African American young women between the ages of 15–21. Participants were asked about meaning and salience of gendered racial identity. The participants identified with negative stereotypes and images of African American women, issues of colorism, and standards of beauty. Furthermore, when asked directly about the meaning of race and gender in their lives, the participants indicated that race and gender simultaneously influenced their perceptions. After looking at gendered racial identity, early awareness of racism, beauty standards, and self-determination, Thomas et al. (2011) concluded that promoting resilience and strength is an important developmental outcome for African American students. Needing to be tough and living with stereotypes may be an additional burden for African American girls and young women to bear alone. Therefore, programs that vocalize their experiences and provide support to one another regarding the societal pressures they face will be crucial in the development of resilience. Programs that focus on self-concept and identity development need to address issues of gendered racial identity. African Americans girls and young women need to develop the ability to critically deconstruct images and stereotypes and the ability to engage in self-determination. This would include being able to develop standards of beauty that reflect a variety of norms for hair and combats the issue of colorism (Thomas et al., 2011).

Several issues surface when counselors consider gender and its effects. Counselors need to understand their own gender—their maleness or femaleness—and how these orientations affect their counseling orientations and effectiveness. Likewise, counselors need to understand others' cultural orientations toward gender, such as cultures that place females in less-valued positions. Also, changing gender orientations deserve consideration; that is, some people in Western cultures have been more accepting of males adopting traditionally female expectations and vice versa. Counselors should use considerable caution, however, not to transfer Western perspectives to people of other cultural backgrounds. Similarly, counselors from cultures that traditionally have adhered to strict gender roles, such as some Asian cultures, should be conscious of their own gender perspectives when intervening with Western-culture clients.

Prejudice, Social Injustice, White Privilege, Racism, and Identity

Identity can lead to prejudice and racism when people consider their culture or values to be better than those of another person. Prejudice and racism result when people believe their identities to be superior to others' and others' beliefs, attitudes, and worldviews to be wrong or inferior. Rather than perceive differences as enriching and worthy, people harboring prejudicial thoughts attempt to convince, subtly or blatantly, that others' cultural characteristics are wrong. Prejudice has harmful effects on both the harborer and the recipient. Racism can exist in many forms (e.g., aversive racism can refer to only ethnic discrimination). Other forms of racism and discrimination can be disablism, sexism, or homophobia (Rodenborg & Boisen, 2013), all of which can lead to social injustices. The identity of the prejudiced person is based on a belief of superiority that clouds her or his perspective of others and limits her or his ability to provide psychological intervention. The person to whom prejudice is directed does not have a fair chance of being understood and accepted.

Focusing solely on race and health consequences, Smedley (2012) reported that people of color might experience racism and discrimination in their health diagnosis and treatment. Smedley reported an overwhelming body of literature demonstrates that minority patients receive a lower quality of health care than Whites. Disparities include poorer health outcomes, including policies and practices of health-care systems and the legal and regulatory climate in which they operate. Smedley's research also indicated strong evidence of racial bias, discrimination, stereotyping, and clinical uncertainty. White privilege in health care also plays a role. The implications for mental health counselors are clear: Understanding multicultural counselors might not suffice. Counselors also need to evaluate their racism toward others, how their counseling decisions might be based on cultural and ethnic stereotypes, and how a client's sexual orientation might affect their opinions of others.

Case (2012) maintained that there is an "invisibility of Whiteness and White Privilege" (p. 79). Often, White or Whiteness defines the norm, which results in race-neutral charades and myths that perpetuate racial oppression. These unrecognized White norms result in racism focusing on people of color. Speaking only of White women, Case (2012) maintained that women who engage in self-reflection of racism have a better understanding of White privilege and the acceptance of White norms, and they may have a head start in developing an antiracist identity.

White women can begin to view the world through a filter of race that no longer hides Whiteness but rather highlights White privilege and the centrality of Whiteness.

It is imperative that counselors of all cultures determine whether they harbor traces of prejudice before they intervene with clients of differing cultural backgrounds. Counselors need to erase all personal prejudices before intervening with clients who are different in some way. For example, Hispanic American counselors should eliminate (or reduce as much as possible) all prejudices when intervening with European Americans and vice versa. Addressing one's prejudices requires understanding one's cultural identity and the perceptions of others.

Some counselors adhere to Western identity norms of individualism that can lead to a lack of acceptance of others or even outright prejudice. This constitutes a serious but not insurmountable challenge; counselors, regardless of cultural background, need to perceive situational events from their clients' cultural perspectives. Rather than use their own cultural perspectives when intervening with Eastern clients, Western counselors should intervene from the clients' perspectives. The reverse also holds true; counselors with Eastern cultural backgrounds should consider Westerners' cultural perspectives.

Denevi (2004) researched White racial identity and racism. Although Denevi focuses on schools and educators, many of her thoughts on White racial identity, privilege, and racism apply to counselors. She maintains that professionals committed to the development of a multicultural community need to confront the question of White racial identity and privilege. Rather than using guilt, Denevi's work has focused on the research on identity development and social justice initiatives. Many White people have been taught that their way of living is the American way and often feel a need to defend their culture, thus creating animosity and fear of interaction with others and equating Whiteness as rightness. One way of looking at White identity development is through the establishment of White affinity groups. These groups refer to a gathering of people who all share a similar experience—in this case, being White. This does not mean that everyone shares the same experiences, but rather that participants recognize that racial identity has an effect on the way they move through the world.

Denevi suggests that White professionals:

- explore their Whiteness and recognize their ethnic identity—in other words, think about what it means to be White;
- consider themselves as diverse and recognize that multicultural does not mean "other than White";
- distinguish between group and individual identity;
- understand the social, political, and historical roles of teaching (or in this case, providing counseling intervention); and
- learn the distinction between speaking for someone and speaking with someone.

Individualism and Identity

Our nation's emphasis on individualism has resulted in a preoccupation with fulfilling the needs of self rather than emphasizing equality for all. In the United States, the trend toward individualism and self-centrality reflects the American idea of the person, yet these concepts do not contribute to an understanding and acceptance of identity in other cultures. Autonomy, a traditional American value, places priority on self and personal achievement. Although "self" and "identity" differ for different cultures, it is possible for people to share common ground with others in a manner that extends beyond individualism. Professional intervention needs to be done with caution, because some clients—for example, American Indians or Hispanic Americans, who often feel responsible for others' welfare—may perceive individualism as antithetical to their sense of collectivism. Counselors who understand their own and others' identities can match the interviewing style to the level of client awareness. For example, many non-African

American therapists may be ineffective when intervening with African Americans because of an inability to relate to the client's cultural identity. Likewise, African American therapists might experience some difficulties with African American clients who have differing worldviews from their own. Social class differences might also influence counseling intervention as middle- or higher-class counselors intervene with people of differing social class backgrounds. Counselors who have achieved considerable materialistic accomplishments might have difficulty working with clients who are more concerned about rent, food, and medical insurance.

Several models of identity development have appeared (sexual orientation, female, and biracial) in recent years. Although an examination of all identity models is beyond the scope of this text, selected models are examined briefly in terms of how counseling intervention will be influenced.

THE COUNSELOR'S IDENTITY: DEVELOPING SELF-AWARENESS

Healey and Hays (2012) maintained that a counselor's professional identity development is a process by which an individual reaches an understanding of her or his profession in conjunction with her or his own self-concept, enabling the articulation of occupational role, philosophy, and professional approach to people within and outside the individual chosen field. One's professional identity includes the values and beliefs ascribed by a profession as a whole as well as the way one engages in the chosen profession. To build a relationship with one's field of work, an individual must establish a clear foundation and construct a professional relationship that distinguishes and clarifies the profession from other similar vocations. Healey and Hays (2012) also maintained that the counselor's professional identity resulted from the philosophical beliefs and values that might be influenced by factors such as socially defined gender role expectations, personal values, and engagement in professional activities.

Some researchers (Moss, Gibson, & Dollarhide, 2014) believe counselors experience specific transformational tasks during their professional identity development. However, Moss et al. (2014) maintain only limited research exists that examines the various points in the career lifespan. Transformational tasks describe the work counselors must accomplish at each stage of their professional development. They concluded six themes are influential to counselors' professional identity development: (a) adjustment to expectations, (b) confidence and freedom, (c) separation versus integration, (d) experienced guide, (e) continuous learning, and (f) work with clients. The actual professional tasks are idealism toward realism, burnout toward rejuvenation, and compartmentalization toward congruency (e.g., developing a congruency toward work and life). We have seen these professional tasks evolve with many counselors we know.

Self-awareness includes

1. a person's consciousness of factors and events that influence his or her psychological, social, emotional, and cultural attributes;
2. one's sense of identity as influenced by the perception of self and others;
3. a broad array of factors such as culture, race, ethnicity, gender, social class, and sexual orientation.

Ideally, counselors should develop an awareness of their cultural heritage and how it has shaped their beliefs, attitudes, and values, especially those involving other people. To provide effective counseling intervention, counselors have a professional responsibility to acquire specific knowledge about differing groups of clients. Counselors also need a general understanding of the sociopolitical systems operative in the United States with respect to minorities and the institutional barriers that prevent minorities from using mental health services.

Counselors can develop or promote self-awareness by examining personal attitudes and beliefs. This process of increasing understanding of oneself and one's identity should begin with exploration of one's culture and how it affects personal psychosocial development. Of particular importance is a careful examination of factors that have contributed to the formation of the counselor's ethnic identity during childhood and adolescence. Such self-exploration leads to self-awareness, which is crucial in developing a set of personal attitudes and beliefs to guide intervention with differing cultures.

For cross-cultural awareness and subsequent effective counseling to occur, counselors need to develop several "awarenesses" in addition to just self-awareness (however, these additional awarenesses do not negate the importance of self-awareness). In addition to self-awareness and awareness of one's own culture, other awarenesses include an understanding of racism, sexism, culture, social class, and sexual orientation, as well as individual differences.

Conducting research specifically on school counselors, Akos and Ellis (2008) maintained that school counselors who engage in understanding their own racial identity increase their ability to understand the impact of thoughts, attitudes, feelings, and beliefs regarding racial issues. Such an understanding allows the counselor to be more effective by increasing her or his own awareness and recognize barriers that may impede the counseling process. Counselors' goals should be to identify strategies that reduce stress and enhance bicultural and multicultural abilities, so students can function equally well with their own groups and with others.

Awareness of One's Culture and Sensitivity to One's Cultural Heritage

Counselors in multicultural situations should be able to:

identify the culture(s) to which they belong;

identify specific cultural groups from which they derived fundamental cultural heritage and significant beliefs and attitudes;

recognize the impact of their beliefs on their ability to respect others;

identify specific attitudes, beliefs, and values from their own cultural heritage that support behaviors demonstrating respect; and

recognize the influence of other personal dimensions of identity and their role in self-awareness.

The next section looks at how these self-awarenesses affect psychological processes and counseling intervention.

Awareness and Attitudes, Values, and Biases About Psychological Processes

To gain understanding of personal identity and development of self-awareness, effective counselors develop an awareness of how their own cultural backgrounds and experiences that influence their attitudes, values, and biases about psychological processes. For example, counselors need to be able to:

- identify the history of their culture in relation to educational opportunities and current worldview;
- identify relevant personal cultural traits and explain their influences on cultural values;
- identify social and cultural influences on cognitive development;
- identify social and cultural influences in their history that have influenced their views, which may affect counseling; and
- articulate the beliefs of their own cultural and religious groups as they relate to sexual orientation, able-bodiedness, and the impact of these beliefs on counseling relationships.

Several factors suggest a need for a section in this text concerning the White counselor. First, realistically speaking, the United States has more White counselors than non-White counselors.

As members of the majority culture, White counselors might have a greater need to understand minority cultures and the racism, prejudice, and discrimination that minority cultures often face. Second, substantial research has not focused on the identity development of counselors of other cultural backgrounds. Perhaps researchers do not see a need for studying minority counselors' identities, but the fact remains that research has focused primarily on White counselor trainees and practicing counselors.

THE PONTEROTTO MODEL–THE WHITE COUNSELOR'S IDENTITY

Ponterotto, Utsey, and Pedersen (2006, cited in Ivey, D'Andrea, Ivey, & Simek-Morgan, 2012) proposed a model of identity development for White counselor trainees; according to this model, the White counselor often works through the following stages when confronted with multicultural concerns.

Step 1. *Pre-exposure:* The White counselor trainee has not thought about counseling and therapy as a multicultural phenomena. The trainee may believe that people are just people and in counseling practice may engage in unconscious racism or sexism or try to treat all clients the same.

Step 2. *Exposure:* The counselor trainee recognizes multicultural issues, learns about cultural differences and discrimination and oppression, and realizes that previous educational experiences have been incomplete. In this stage, the trainee may become perturbed and confused by the many apparent incongruities.

Step 3. *Zealotry and Defensiveness:* Counselor trainees are faced with the challenge of multicultural issues and may move in one of two directions: Some may become angry and active proponents of multiculturalism, whereas others may retreat into quiet defensiveness and continue to use Eurocentric perceptions and worldviews. These individuals become passive recipients of information and return to the safer perspectives of the White culture.

Step 4. *Integration:* The counselor trainee acquires respect for and awareness of cultural differences, understanding how personal and family history can affect the counseling intervention plan. An acceptance evolves that one cannot know all the dimensions of multicultural counseling and therapy at once and that developing multicultural counseling expertise takes time and practice.

Although Ponterotto and colleagues (2006, cited in Ivey et al., 2012) developed their model for White counselors, the model also has implications for counselor trainees of other cultural backgrounds. For example, an Asian American counselor may have developed an awareness of her or his own culture and be aware of some cultures but may not have had contact with Hispanic Americans, African Americans, or clients with social class differences or differing sexual orientations. Therefore, it is likely that all counselors will have to face issues in multicultural counseling that Ponterotto and colleagues suggested.

IDENTITY DEVELOPMENT MODELS

Minority Racial/Cultural Identity Model

The Racial/Cultural Identity (R/CID) development model (Sue & Sue, 2013) is a conceptual framework to aid therapists in understanding their culturally different clients' attitudes and behaviors. The model describes five stages of development that people experience as they struggle to understand themselves in terms of their own culture, the dominant culture, and the relationships between cultures: conformity, dissonance, resistance and immersion, introspection, and integrative awareness.

In the *conformity stage*, minority individuals prefer dominant cultural values over their own. Physical and cultural characteristics toward the self (or one's own racial/cultural group) are perceived negatively, as something to be avoided or denied. Basically, in this stage, minority individuals identify with and appreciate White Americans and their lifestyles, value systems, and cultural/physical characteristics. The attitudes and beliefs toward members of the same minority group might be similar to those they perceive as held by the majority culture, yet they see themselves as different or an exception to the rule. Little thought or validity is given to other cultural viewpoints. To be more like the majority culture, some minority individuals in this stage might attempt to mimic what is perceived as White mannerisms, speech patterns, dress, and goals (Sue & Sue, 2013).

In the *dissonance stage*, no matter how much one attempts to deny his or her own racial/cultural heritage, an individual will encounter information or experiences that are inconsistent with culturally held beliefs, attitudes, and values. For example, an Asian American who believes that Asians are inhibited, passive, inarticulate, and poor in people relationships may encounter an Asian leader who seems to break all these stereotypes. In all probability, movement into the dissonance stage is a gradual process. The individual is in conflict between different information and experiences that challenge his or her current self-concept. People generally move into this stage slowly, but a traumatic event may propel some individuals to move into dissonance at a much more rapid pace. Attitudes and beliefs about the self include a growing sense of personal awareness that racism does exist, that not all aspects of the minority or majority culture are good or bad, and that one cannot escape one's cultural heritage. The person begins to accept the possibility of positive attributes in the minority cultures and an accompanying sense of pride in self. Attitudes toward members of the same minority change (Sue & Sue, 2013).

During the third stage, the *resistance and immersion stage*, the person tends to endorse minority-held views completely and to reject the dominant value of society and culture. The person seems dedicated to reacting against White society and rejects White social, cultural, and institutional standards. Desire to eliminate oppression of the individual's minority group becomes an important motivation of the individual's behavior. Three feelings—guilt, shame, and anger—surface. Feelings of guilt and shame result from thinking that, in the past, minority individuals have rejected or downplayed their own cultural and racial groups. These feelings are associated with a sense of anger at the oppression and feelings of being brainwashed by forces in the White society.

This stage includes a sense of rediscovery of one's own history and culture. People seek information that enhances a person's sense of identity and worth. Cultural and racial characteristics that once elicited feelings of shame and disgust become symbols of pride and honor. Negative self-esteem resulting from prejudice and racism is now actively challenged in order to raise self-esteem. A growing sense of comradeship develops with persons from his or her own minority group, and a strong sense of cultural pride develops. There are fewer attempts to reach out and understand other racial/cultural minority groups and their values and customs. Characterized by both withdrawal from the dominant culture and immersion in one's cultural heritage, there is also considerable anger and hostility directed at White society (Sue & Sue, 2013).

The *introspection stage* is the fourth level; it includes the individual beginning to discover that this level of anger directed at White people is psychologically draining and does not permit one to devote more critical energies to understanding him or herself or his or her own racial/cultural group. The person now feels that he or she has too rigidly held on to minority group views and notions in order to submerge personal autonomy. This conflict now becomes significant in terms of responsibility and allegiance to one's own minority group versus notions of personal independence and autonomy. Thus the individual begins to spend more and more time and energy trying to sort out these aspects of self-identity and begins to demand individual autonomy. The person might also see his or her own group taking positions that might be considered extreme. There is a greater uneasiness with culturocentrism, and an attempt is made to reach out to other groups and to learning what types of oppression they experienced and how they handled oppressive experiences. Finally, the person experiences distrust for the dominant society and culture. Conflict occurs because the person begins to recognize that there are many elements in U.S. culture that are highly functional and desirable, yet there is confusion as to how to incorporate these elements into the minority culture (Sue & Sue, 2013).

In the fifth and last stage, the *integrative awareness stage*, minority persons have developed a sense of security and now can own and appreciate unique aspects of their culture as well as others' cultures. Minority culture is not necessarily in conflict with White dominant cultural ways. Many conflicts and discomforts are resolved, allowing greater individual control and flexibility. There is now the belief that there are acceptable and unacceptable aspects in all cultures and that it is very important for the person to be able to examine and accept or reject those aspects of a culture that are not seen as desirable.

The person develops a positive self-image and experiences a strong sense of self-worth and confidence. Racial pride in identity and culture develops, as well as a sense of autonomy. In essence, the individual becomes bicultural or multicultural. There is no longer a conflict over disagreeing with group goals and values. He or she reaches out to other minority groups to understand their cultural values and ways of life. In the end, the individual experiences a sense of trust and liking from members of the dominant group who seek to eliminate oppressive activities. The individual becomes open to constructive elements of the dominant culture (Sue & Sue, 2013).

The R/CID development model has several implications for counseling intervention. First, an understanding of cultural identity development should sensitize counselors to the role that oppression plays in a minority individual's development. Second, the model will aid counselors in recognizing differences between members of the same minority group with respect to their cultural identity. Third, the model allows counselors to realize the potentially changing and developing nature of cultural identity among clients (Sue & Sue, 2013).

Biracial Identity Development Model

Although having parents of different racial and ethnic backgrounds has a long history in the United States, the 2000 census was the first official opportunity for mixed-race to identify as biracial or multiracial. Two factors contributed to the emergence of the biracial identity option in the United States. First, the demographic reality changed. Decriminalization of interracial marriage in 1967, the number of interracial unions, and the number of mixed-race individuals grew substantially. Second, the biracial and multiracial identity movement also contributed to the emergence of the biracial identity option in the United States (Townsend, Fryberg, Wilkins, & Markus, 2012).

Poston (1990) proposed a five-stage, progressive, developmental model for biracial identity development. (Although the article is nearly 25 years old, it continues to be one of the best in describing identity development for biracial identity development.) Poston's model includes:

Step 1. *Personal Identity:* People in this stage are commonly very young, and membership in any particular ethnic group is just becoming salient. Children will tend to have a sense of self that is somewhat independent of their ethnic background. However, they develop an awareness of their race and ethnicity. Opinions vary as to how much racial awareness actually occurs. Young children often demonstrate idiosyncratic and inconsistent feelings about such matters, sometimes showing no awareness of race and identity. Older children have a greater sense of ethnic identity.

Step 2. *Choice of Group Categorization:* Individuals in this stage feel a need to choose an identity, usually of one ethnic group. Although individuals differ, this stage can be a time of crisis and alienation. Many biracial people feel forced to make a specific racial choice in order to participate in or belong to peer, family, and social groups. Biracial people think they have two choices: (1) They can choose a multicultural existence that emphasizes the racial heritage of both parents, or (2) they can choose one parent's culture or racial heritage as dominant over the other. Factors influencing this decision include the status of the parents' ethnic backgrounds; neighborhood demographics; ethnicity of peers; acceptance and participation in cultures of various groups; and parental and familial acceptance, physical appearance, knowledge of languages other than English, cultural knowledge, age, political involvement, and individual personality differences. It would be unusual for an individual to choose a multiethnic identity, because this requires some level of knowledge of multiple cultures and a level of cognitive development beyond that which is characteristic of this age group.

Step 3. *Enmeshment/Denial:* This stage is characterized by confusion and guilt at having to choose an identity that is not fully expressive of one's background. Individuals in this stage often experience feelings of guilt, self-hatred, and lack of acceptance of one or more groups. A multiethnic child, unable to identify with both parents, may experience feelings of being disloyal and of guilt over rejection of one parent. During this stage, the biracial adolescent might be ashamed of and might fear having friends meet the parent whose racial background differs from the norm in the neighborhood. Eventually, these feelings must be resolved and the individual must learn to appreciate both parental cultures.

Step 4. *Appreciation:* Individuals begin to appreciate their multiple identities and to broaden their reference group orientation. They may not only begin to learn about their racial/ethnic heritages and cultures but also continue to identify with only one group. The choice of which group to identify with continues to be influenced by the factors described in Stage 2.

Step 5. *Integration:* Individuals in this stage experience a wholeness and tend to recognize and value all their ethnic identities. At this stage, they have developed secure, integrated identities (Poston, 1990).

Poston's (1990) model of biracial identity introduces several important issues and assumptions. First, biracial individuals may tend to have identity problems when they internalize outside prejudice and values. Second, numerous factors, such as family and peer influences, affect individuals' identity choices. Third, biracial individuals may experience alienation at the choice phase and may make a choice even though they are uncomfortable with it. Fourth, the choice of one identity over another at the choice phase and the resultant denial can be associated with feelings of guilt and disloyalty. Fifth, integration is important and is associated with positive indicators of mental health. Finally, the most difficult adjustment and identity confusion occur during the enmeshment/denial stage.

White Racial Identity Attitude Theory (WRIAT) Model

Although we value the most current research, some classics in the field continue to be worth mentioning. Helms's (1984, 1990, 1994) work on the White counselor's racial identity is one of these classics. Helms's research focused on the White counselor's racial identity and how it affects counseling intervention. Racial identity development can be defined as the process or series of stages through which a person passes as the person's attitudes toward his or her own racial/ethnic group and the White population develops, ultimately achieving a healthy identity. Although the number of stages and the specifics of each stage vary among models, the first stage typically involves acceptance of the stereotypes that the dominant society has attributed to the group. The second stage is typically one of conflict or dissonance, in which the individual begins to question previously held stereotypes. The third stage involves an immersion in the culture of the racial/ethnic group and a militant rejection of individuals and values outside the group. In the final stage, the individual retains a positive racial/ethnic identity while coming to accept the positive attributes of individuals and cultures outside the reference group.

Several White racial identity development models (e.g., Helms's White racial identity attitude theory (WRIAT) model and Rowe et al.'s White racial consciousness model (WRC)) have
been proposed in the last decade or so. The model selected for discussion is Helms's WRIAT
model (Helms, 1984, 1990, 1994).

Helms (1984, 1990, 1994) proposed that White racial identity develops through six stages:
contact, disintegration, reintegration, pseudoindependence, immersion/emersion, and autonomy. Each stage involves conceptions of self as a racial being as well as conceptions of others
and of oneself relative to other racial groups. Helms's model includes two phases: the abandon-
ment of racism and the development of a positive White identity.

The six stages of WRIAT are as follows:

Step 1. *Contact:* This stage involves a lack of consciousness of one's own race and a naïve curiosity or timidity with respect to other groups. People usually pretend that racial differences
do not matter, perhaps because they lack meaningful contact with members of other cultural groups or were raised in a familial atmosphere that did not discuss racial differences.

Step 2. *Disintegration:* This stage involves guilt and confusion. This stage represents Whites'
first acknowledgment of social implications that often force them to face moral dilemmas that arise from being considered superior to other groups. These feelings can
lead to guilt and anxiety when discussions and life experiences focus on racial issues.
During this stage, people may embrace immoral racial values and beliefs because these
are the norms for the White group to which they have been exposed. The identity
may become exclusively White as people attempt to escape from the painful feelings
by denying that racism exists.

Step 3. *Reintegration:* Because of the intrapersonal conflict experienced in the previous
stage, the reintegration stage involves people adopting an orientation in which all
aspects of being White are considered superior. People have a tendency to stereotype other groups negatively and to exaggerate the differences between one's own
group and others. Common reactions include rigidity in beliefs, reclusiveness, and
out-group aggression and hostility in mixed racial environments. Feelings include
views of cultural superiority and denigration and hostility toward other groups.

Step 4. *Pseudoindependence:* This stage represents the initial step toward a positive, nonracist
identity. People in this stage attempt to control tumultuous feelings aroused during
earlier stages by thoughtfully considering other people's racial problems and by trying to acculturate them to the White culture. These people continue to believe in
the superiority of the White race; that is, they believe that other racial issues can be
resolved by learning the White culture and by associating with Whites.

Step 5. *Immersion/emersion:* This stage involves White people beginning to seek a personally meaningful definition of Whiteness and to reeducate other White people about
race and racism. People are consciously aware of being White and may have feelings
of anger and confusion and an insensitivity to other Whites. They sometimes believe
that they should relate to, and identify with, other Whites in their environment but
that the other Whites perhaps have not resolved their own racial issues.

Step 6. *Autonomy:* This stage might best be thought of as an ongoing process of refinement
of one's racial identity. Primary themes include internalizing, nurturing, and applying
the new personal definition of Whiteness that has evolved in earlier stages. Individuals in this stage are nonracist Whites and are able to conceive of being White without
being racist; they recognize that core values and beliefs are absorbed from the White
culture. Because these people can actively question the tenets of the White culture,
they now have the capacity to choose those aspects of White culture that feel right to
them. People in this stage are actually multiracial; that is, they increasingly become
aware of the commonalities inherent in various forms of oppression and try to eliminate all forms of oppression from society.

Asian Identity Model

Sue and Sue (2013) maintain that Asian American identity models have not been advanced as far as some other identity models. They explain that while some models have been proposed, the early models had several shortcomings. First, the early models failed to provide a clear rationale as to why an individual develops one ethnic type over another. Second, the early proposals seemed too simplistic to account for the complexity of racial identity development. Third, these models were too population specific in that they described only one Asian American cultural group. In response to these criticisms, theorists have begun moving toward the development of stage/process models of Asian American identity development. Sue and Sue (2013) describe John Kim's model involving third-generation Japanese American women to posit a progressive and sequential stage model of Asian American identity development. His model integrates the influence of acculturation, exposure to cultural differences, environmental negativism to racial differences, personal methods of handling race-related conflicts, and the effects of group or social movements on the Asian American individual.

The *ethnic awareness stage* begins around the age of three or four, when the child's family members serve as the significant ethnic group model. Positive or neutral attitudes toward one's own ethnic origin are formed, depending on the amount of ethnic exposure conveyed by caretakers.

The *White identification stage* begins when children enter school, where peers and the surroundings become powerful forces in conveying racial prejudice that negatively impacts their self-esteem and identity. The realization of "differentness" (quotes in Sue & Sue, 2013) from such interactions leads to self-blame and desire to escape racial heritage by identifying with White society.

The awakening to the *social political consciousness stage* means the adoption of a new perspective, often correlated with political awareness. The civil rights movement and the women's movement, as well as other significant political events, often precipitate this new awakening. The primary result is an abandoning of identification with White society and a consequent understanding of oppression and oppressed groups.

The *redirection stage* involves recommendation or renewed connection with one's Asian American heritage and culture. This is often followed by the realization that White oppression is the culprit in the negative experiences of youth. Anger against White racism may become a defining theme, with concomitant increases of Asian American self-pride and group pride.

The *incorporation stage* represents the highest form of identity evolution. It encompasses the development of a positive and comfortable identity as Asian American and consequent respect for other cultural/racial heritages. Identification for or against White culture is no longer an important issue (Sue & Sue, 2013).

Pilipino American Identity Development Model

Nadal (2004) explains *F/Pilipino*, the term he uses to describe Americans of Philippine backgrounds from different geographic regions and different stages of identity development who use both Filipino and Pilipino as ethnic identities. Some F/Pilipinos will use Pilipino as a political statement because there is no "F" in the Tagalog/Pilipino language. However, some F/Pilipinos will identify with Filipino because it is the term that has been used most commonly for centuries.

Nadal (2004) maintains that the sociocultural experience of F/Pilipino Americans is distinct from that of their Asian American counterparts due to a variety of factors, including a lower socioeconomic status, F/Pilipino American-specific health concerns, educational barriers, and marginalization within the Asian American community. All these factors have the potential to influence cultural identity development.

Nadal (2004) examines identity development in F/Pilipino Americans. In his article, he proposes a six-stage identity development model. The model describes the process of ethnic identity formation for native-born, second-generation F/Pilipino Americans in the United

States. This nonlinear model will not be completed by all F/Pilipino Americans. Plus, the stages should not be viewed as positive or negative but should be used to understand the acculturation levels of F/Pilipino Americans for more accurate and appropriate therapeutic or psychological practice. While Nadal provides a detailed description and discussion of the six stages, space allows us only to list the stages:

Step 1. Ethnic Awareness
Step 2. Assimilation to Dominant Culture
Step 3. Social Political Awakening
Step 4. Panethnic Asian American Consciousness
Step 5. Ethnocentric Realization
Step 6. Incorporation

Nadal also provides several excellent implications for counseling F/Pilipino Americans. First, the model is nonlinear, meaning that participants may advance through the stages in a progressive manner but may occasionally move back and forth between stages. Second, it is important to understand that some people may not progress through all the stages. Depending on their environments, surroundings, and influences, clients may remain in certain stages for their entire lives. Third, it is important to realize that it is not the duty of the counselor to help a client progress through these stages. The counselor may challenge the client to think in different perspectives yet should not and could not force the client to advance to any other stage.

Hispanic Identity Model

Robinson (2005) cites the work of Ferdman and Gallegos (2001) in her discussion of Hispanic identity development. It is worth noting that Robinson chooses to use the term *Latino* rather than *Hispanic*. Still, her synopsis of Ferdman and Gallegos's (2001) work is valid and helpful to counselors intervening with Hispanic clients. According to Robinson (2005) and Ferdman and Gallegos (2001), there are key dimensions involved in defining a nonlinear Hispanic orientation. The first dimension is the *lens* (italics Robinson's) toward identity, how a person chooses to identify herself or himself, how Latinos as a group are seen, how Whites are seen, and how race fits into the equation. The various orientations are described in what follows.

Hispanic (or Latino) Integrated

Persons who have reached this orientation are able to embrace the fullness of the Latino identity and integrate this into other identities, such as class, profession, and gender. These persons feel comfortable with all types of Latinos, because they use a broad lens to see themselves, White people, and others.

Hispanic Identified

This group has more of a pan-Hispanic identity, with a view of race as uniquely Hispanic or Latin. A deep and abiding understanding exists of the political struggle and a desire to be united with other Hispanics in racial unity. Despite the awareness of and vigilant stand against institutional racism, Hispanic-identified persons may see Whites, Blacks, and others in a rigid way.

Subgroup Identified

Persons in this group see themselves as distinct from White people but do not necessarily identify with other Hispanics or with people of color. These people do not reflect broad pan-Hispanic orientations. Other Latino subgroups may be viewed as inferior. People's allegiance to a particular subgroup is nearly exclusive. Race is not a central or clear organizing concept but nationality, ethnicity, and culture are primary.

Hispanic as "Other"

Persons with this orientation see themselves as people of color. This may be a function of biracial or multiracial status, ambiguous phenotype, or dominant construction of race. In certain contexts, the person sees herself or himself as a minority person and not as White. There is no identification with Latino cultural norms or with White culture, and an understanding of Latino history and culture is missing.

Undifferentiated

Persons with this orientation regard themselves as simply "people" (quotes Robinson's) with a color-blind eye. The emphasis on racial classification is not a part of their framework. The desire to associate with other Latinos is not prominent because contact with others is distinct from a person's race or ethnic identity.

White Identified

White-identified persons perceive themselves as White and sometimes feel superior to people of color. Assimilation into White culture is a possibility, as is connection to other subgroups. There is an acceptance of the status quo and a valuing of Whiteness to the extent that marrying White is preferred over marrying dark.

Although not a linear model, the strength of this model is that it helps counselors and clients ascertain identity development for Hispanics who differ greatly across acculturation level, skin color, national origin, and political ideology (Robinson, 2005).

Feminist Identity Model

Examining feminist identity development for White women is important due to women's experience of both White privilege and marginalization. Exploring the relationships between these aspects of identity and attitude development provides a means of understanding how both a dominant identity (Whiteness) and historically marginalized identity (women) develop and function (Wolff & Munley, 2012).

Downing and Roush (1985), another classic study, offer a model of feminist identity development. They base their theory on the premise that women who live in contemporary society must first acknowledge, then struggle with, and repeatedly work through their feelings about the prejudice and discrimination they experience in order to achieve an authentic and positive feminist identity. The authors assert that feminist and nonsexist counseling and psychotherapies are needed to reflect a developmental model of feminist identity.

The Downing and Roush (1985) model of feminist identity development has five stages:

Step 1. *Passive Acceptance:* The woman is unaware of or denies the individual, institutional, and cultural prejudice and discrimination against her. She considers traditional sex roles to be advantageous; that is, when asked to use such terms as woman or man, she prefers to use girl or boy because she thinks the terms have some type of advantage. Likewise, she accepts the White male social system and the perspective of the dominant, majority culture.

Step 2. *Revelation:* This stage evolves from a series of crises that result in open questioning of self and roles and feelings of anger and guilt. Although events leading to such revelations vary with individuals, typical events include attending consciousness-raising groups, realizing discrimination against female children, ending a relationship, getting a divorce, being denied credit or employment, or becoming involved in a women's empowerment movement.

Traditional female socialization includes a distrust of one's perceptions, a mechanism that helps perpetuate women's subordinate status. An increased sense of trust in one's perceptions is necessary in order to begin the process of questioning oneself and one's role and to eventually make the transition to the revelation stage. During revelation, women primarily experience feelings of anger and secondary feelings of guilt because they believe that they have participated in their own past oppression. They see men as negative and women as positive. They perceive other women in this stage as having mature, positive identities, when in reality they have developed "pseudo-identities" (Downing & Roush, 1985, p. 700) based on negation of traditional femininity and the dominant culture.

Step 3. *Embeddedness-Emanation:* Women attaining this stage encounter several barriers. These barriers are subtle in nature, are chronic in duration, and may be posed by significant others as well as by society. Most women are so integrally involved in the dominant culture through marriage, work, and children that it is difficult for them to embed themselves in a female subculture. Because they often are considered only as wives, mothers, lovers, sisters, and daughters of men, women in this stage commonly feel the need to end their marriages or significant relationships as they immerse themselves in female subcultures. Women's centers, women's studies classes, and women's support groups serve as havens for women experiencing embeddedness.

During the latter part of this stage, women experience emanation—the beginnings of an openness to alternative viewpoints and to a more relativistic rather than dualistic perspective. Although the need to reduce dissonance between the newly emerging identity and the repeated experience of being treated as subordinate may cause some women to revert to earlier stages, others tolerate these discrepancies and emerge from this uncomfortable state with a healthier, multidimensional, and adaptive perspective. Interaction with men during the latter part of embeddedness-emanation is usually cautious.

Step 4. *Synthesis:* In this stage, women increasingly value the positive aspects of being female, and they are able to integrate these qualities with their unique personal attributes into a positive and realistic self-concept. They are able to transcend traditional gender roles, make choices for themselves based on well-defined personal values, and evaluate men on an individual, rather than a stereotypical, basis. They have reached a balance with others and are able to channel their energies productively but also to respond appropriately to experiences of oppression and discrimination.

Step 5. *Active Commitment:* This stage involves the transition of the newly developed, consolidated identity into meaningful and effective action. Women carefully select an issue based on their unique talents and the possibility of both personal gratification and effecting social change. A consolidation of the feminist identity occurs and actions are personalized and rational. Women consider men as equal yet not the same as women. Few women truly evolve to the active commitment stage. Most women dedicated to working for women's equal rights may actually be functioning out of needs from earlier stages, such as revelation and embeddedness-emanation.

Jewish Identity Model

Jewish identity development models have been basically ignored in the study of multiculturalism. Who is a Jew? The question is becoming ever more pressing for Jews around the world. It looks like a religious issue, but it is bound up with history, Israeli politics, and the rhythms of the diaspora. Addressing it means deciding whether assimilation is a moral threat, as many Jews think, or a phenomenon to be accommodated. The struggle over the answer will shape Israel's society, its relations with Jews elsewhere, and the size and complexion of the global Jewish community ("Who is a Jew?," 2014).

In the diaspora, too, history has reframed the question of who counts as a Jew. In much of Eastern Europe, communist strictures made worship perilous and observance lapsed. Even circumcision was discouraged. By the time the system imploded, lots of Jews had forgotten much of their heritage. Yet they still consider themselves as Jews ("Who is a Jew?," 2014).

Little consensus exists on what factors align Jews as an ethnic group. Altman, Inman, Fine, Ritter, and Howard (2010) studied Jewish identity models, drew several conclusions, and designed a model of Jewish ethnic identity (see Figure 2.1). These writers maintained that the Jewish identity included connection and commonality, Jewish lifestyle and values, religious behaviors and traditions, cultural celebrations, and remembrance and awareness of the Holocaust. The Jewish identity has several reinforcers: family, Jewish community and friends, acceptance by and attraction to other Jews, experiences with those who are tolerant and respectful, and Jewish dating and marriage. In their excellent article, they summarized the essential aspects (family influences and support, community influences and support, and personal identification) of the Jewish identity. These aspects are summarized in Figure 2.1.

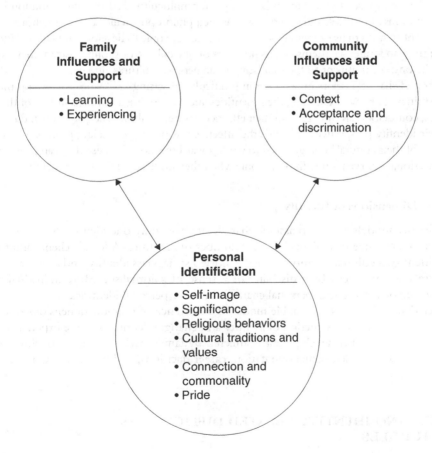

Figure 2.1 The Jewish Identity

Source: Altman, A. N., Inman, A. G., Fine, S. G., Ritter, H. A., & Howard, E. (2010). Exploration of Jewish identity. *Journal of Counseling and Development, 88*, 163–173. Reprinted with permission by John Wiley and Sons.

It is also important to state that the Jewish people in the study associated themselves with multiple cultures, for example, American, Jewish, and minority status. We think it is also safe to say other factors are involved, including social class, economic status, geographic location, and sexual orientation.

Implications for counseling practices involving the Jewish identity play a salient role for many American Jews. Counselors have a professional responsibility to consider the client's identity in a therapeutic session. They should also consider stereotypes (e.g., all Jews are wealthy; feelings of lack of consideration by the majority society; Altman et al., 2010).

Lesbian/Gay Identity Model

Several models of lesbian and gay identity development have been proposed. Proposing various numbers of stages and times of acceptance of lesbian and gay identity development, each model can help counselors better understand their own sexual orientations and identities as well as identity development in gay and lesbian clients. It is not feasible to explore in detail all the models of gay and lesbian identity development here; however, several models are examined in Chapter 15.

Multicultural Identity Model

People who are exposed to diversity and challenges for multicultural adaptation continuously modify their opinions of both self and others as well as their philosophy of life. These modifications and a commitment to growth by examining self and others lead people to develop multicultural identities wherein they no longer see themselves as products of one culture or group. Instead, they express a strong, lifelong commitment to the well-being of all peoples, cultures, and groups.

It is hoped that counselors intervening in multicultural settings will work to develop multicultural identities. Through examining their identities and developing an understanding of their own identities, counselors can emerge from their ethnocentrism or cultural encapsulation and recognize how their identity perspectives influence the effectiveness of the counseling process. Counselors, regardless of their cultural heritage, need to work toward this goal, because they can provide effective professional intervention with others only when they understand their own identities.

Multiple Dimensions of Identity

Most identity models appear to assume that clients have only one identity. Such an assumption fails to recognize that clients have any number of identities. A female client might have a lesbian identity, a cultural identity, a racial identity, a social class identity, and a gender identity. These are also influenced by a disability or a sense of spiritualism. More individual factors might be personal attributes, personal characteristics, or personal identities.

Rather than being a fixed or stable model, the existence of multiple dimensions of identity suggests a continuing construction of identity and changing contexts in the experience of the identity. Overall identity development is affected by family background, sociocultural conditions, social class, gender, sexual orientation, career decisions, and life planning, to name just a few factors.

ADDRESSING IDENTITY-RELATED DIFFICULTIES AND HURDLES

Achieving an understanding of the many dimensions of identity and how identity affects counseling intervention and effectiveness will not be an overnight task; it might take years for the counselor to come to terms with his or her identities and how they have been shaped by such factors as culture, race, development, gender, disability, and sexual orientation. Several difficulties and hurdles can be highlighted.

Achieving Objectivity

A direct relationship exists between one's conscious and unconscious biases and the ability to help others who do not share one's culturally derived views. Counselors, like most people, sometimes have difficulty developing objective perspectives of others. Opinions, perspectives, and worldviews forged by cultural heritage, gender expectations, and sexual orientation (to name a few influencing factors) often lead people to think that their perspectives, views, and ways of thinking are right, whereas all others are wrong. For example, a European American male counselor must not condemn an American Indian woman for wanting to share material wealth nor condemn an African American or Hispanic American for placing family welfare over individual desires. Such objectivity requires counselors of both genders and all cultural backgrounds to perceive clients' differences as worthy and enriching rather than as wrong or in need of change or remediation.

Avoiding Western Identity Perspectives of Individualism

As previously mentioned, counselors should avoid using perspectives based on Western notions of individualism during intervention. European American counselors, perhaps men more than women, might have a tendency to intervene by using perspectives that suggest individualism. Counseling from Western perspectives can create conflict between counselor and client worldviews; that is, the counselor's perspectives on such issues as individualism, family welfare, and concern for others do not coincide with the client's.

SUMMARY

Counselors in multicultural situations (and in fact, all situations) can take several paths, all with potential for developing respect for the identities of both counselor and clients. Counselors can:

• develop an understanding and respect for clients' different worldviews and the effects of those differences;
• consider and accept perspectives that vary from their own identity perspectives;
• accept and respect their cultural identity, values, and perspectives, yet be open to those of others; and
• listen carefully; ask sensitive questions; and read and study about clients' cultural, social class, racial, and ethnic backgrounds as well as sexual orientation.

Counselors need to understand their own identities and the factors that contribute to their development. Counselor identity shapes how counselors perceive themselves and how they perceive others and their cultural backgrounds. Counselors in multicultural settings may face different situations, customs, and worldviews that could affect counseling effectiveness. Clients in multicultural situations may have attitudes and beliefs that threaten or disturb a counselor of another cultural background. It is important for counselors to understand their identities and how these are affected by culture, gender, parental expectations and teachings, and sexual preference. Undoubtedly, counselor identity affects counseling intervention and therefore should be understood in relation to both self and others.

The appendix in this volume provides counselors with "Suggested Multicultural Experiential Activities" as they learn more about counselor identity.

SUGGESTED READINGS

Degges-White, S. & Stoltz, K. (2015). Archetypal identity development, meaning in life, and life satisfaction: Differences among clinical mental health counselors, school counselors, and counselor educators. *Adultspan Journal, 14*(1), 49–61. Adults pursuing careers in counselor education and clinical mental health counseling participated in a study that examined relationships among archetypal identity development, meaning in life, and life satisfaction. Significant differences between groups existed for five archetypal identities, and meaning in life was significantly related to life satisfaction.

Kerr, B. A., & Multon, K. D. (2015). The development of gender identity, gender roles, and gender relations in gifted students. *Journal of Counseling & Development, 93*(2), 183–191. This article describes the interaction of giftedness with gender identity, gender role, and gender relations, and explores ways in which many gifted educational practices are gendered.

Malott, K. M., Paone, T. R., Schaefle, S., Cates, J., & Haizlip, B. (2015). Expanding White racial identity theory: A qualitative investigation of Whites engaged in antiracist action. *Journal of Counseling & Development, 93*(3), 333–343. This article presents outcomes of a qualitative exploration of White racial identity and offers suggestions intended to enhance White racial identity theory and provide empirical support for characteristics of Whites who are engaged in antiracist activities.

Prosek, E. A., & Hurt, K. M. (2014). Measuring professional identity development among counselor trainees. *Counselor Education & Supervision, 53*(4), 284–293. This study examined the differences in professional identity development between novice and advanced counselor trainees.

Schnall, E., Kalkstein, S., Gottesman, A., Feinberg, K., Schaeffer, C. B., & Feinberg, S. S. (2014). Barriers to mental health care: A 25 year follow-up study of the Orthodox Jewish community. *Journal of Multicultural Counseling and Development, 42,* 161–172. The Orthodox Jewish people are often overlooked—there seems to be an increased acceptance of mental health illness and its treatment and satisfaction with quality of health, along with decreased mistrust of the mental health field.

3 The Culturally Effective Counselor

QUESTIONS TO BE EXPLORED

- How does cultural diversity affect counseling intervention? Why should counselors seek special preparation for counseling clients of differing cultures?
- How can counselors develop a new identity that promotes social justice?
- What barriers, myths, assumptions, and stereotypes interfere with effective multicultural counseling?
- What characteristics describe effective counselors?
- What specific beliefs and attitudes, understandings, skills, and ethical concerns should be addressed during professional preparation for multicultural counseling?
- What is a worldview, and does it affect counseling intervention?
- What ethical standards pertain to multicultural counseling?
- How can experiential learning enhance ethical decision making?
- How do competent counselors provide a positive and supportive counseling environment for clients of differing sexual orientations? What ethical and legal consequences might counselors face who decline to counsel an LGBT client?
- How do competent counselors provide a positive and supportive counseling environment for clients with disabilities?

OVERVIEW

American society undoubtedly benefits from the richness of cultural diversity. Counselors who are trained in traditional counseling approaches, however, often experience difficulty when working with clients of differing cultural backgrounds. Formal preparation and firsthand experiences with people of differing cultural backgrounds are essential for multicultural counseling to be effective.

Effective counselors in multicultural situations also understand and address social justice issues. In fact, Kottler (2013) suggests reenvisioning a new counselor identity, one that includes an emphasis on social justice. He believes that counselors entered the profession because of a strong belief in advocacy, working on the behalf of the marginalized and oppressed. Counselors need to become actively involved in altruism beyond their professional responsibilities. Similarly, social justice is part of counselors' ethical codes and moral obligations (Kottler, 2013).

The concept of social justice was defined in Chapter 1. In this chapter, we look at why counselors need multicultural counseling competence (e.g., attitudes, knowledge, and skills) as well as an understanding of social justice and appropriate intervention techniques.

CULTURAL DIVERSITY AND THE COUNSELING PROFESSION

As the population of the United States grows more pluralistic and all forms of diversity are increasingly recognized, counselors will be called on to provide professional intervention with clients of differing backgrounds and worldviews. Counselors will be challenged to provide culturally appropriate counseling intervention. Such contact can initially lead to questioning, confusion, guilt, and anxiety about topics of diversity. Regardless of the counselors' diverse background, counselors will be expected to intervene with clients of differing cultural backgrounds. Mental health professionals need multicultural counseling training programs because mental health services should differ depending on the culture and lifespan period of the individual client.

The already complex nature of the counseling process is further complicated when client and counselor come from different cultures and different social classes. Problems and issues may arise during counseling sessions when, for example, the counselor is a middle-class European American and the client is a lower-class African American or vice versa. Generational, intracultural, lifespan, social class, and sexual orientation differences complicate the counseling process to an even greater degree.

Increased attention is also being given to multiculturalism and marriage and family counseling or, more specifically, to how cultural and other forms of diversity affect families and marriage and family counseling. The traditional family unit (a married man and woman parenting two children) of the 1950s and 1960s is no longer the norm. Counselors cannot assume that the practices that are effective with traditional family structures are effective with diverse family systems. Counselors will increasingly work with diverse family systems, such as single-parent families, stepfamilies, families of mixed cultural heritages, and families of different sexual orientations. Effective marriage and family counselors consider the various family arrangements, the need for different approaches and ways of thinking about families, and how differences need to be reflected in counseling.

Minority Counseling Professionals

The question may be raised as to whether problems resulting from differing cultural backgrounds can be reduced by carefully matching clients with counselors of similar cultural and socioeconomic backgrounds. Realistically, however, the relatively small number of minority counselors reduces the possibility of such counselor-client matchups. There may be several reasons for the relatively small number of minorities entering the counseling profession. First, minority students considering the profession may be dissuaded by the small number of minorities in the profession. Where would these students find mentors? Who could guide them appropriately or offer needed support? Second, institutional racism may discourage students wanting to become counselors.

It is essential that counselor education programs employ faculty members of diverse backgrounds because they can serve as role models for minority students. Similarly, having diverse faculty members in tenure-track positions serves as a highly visible statement that cultural diversity is respected and valued in the counseling program.

Barriers to Effective Multicultural Counseling

Barriers have impeded counselors' efforts with clients in multicultural settings. Counselors intervening in multicultural settings should recognize and then formulate a plan for addressing the barriers.

Differing Class and Cultural Values

Counselors' class values, which are partly determined by their own socioeconomic class, influence the effectiveness of multicultural counseling. We believe that professional mental health services are class-bound and that a dangerous situation develops when the counselor (especially the counselor with a middle- or upper-class background) attributes mental health disorders to a client's culture or social structure. The importance of being aware of class- and culture-bound values should be recognized, especially when counselors consider the consequences that could result from misunderstanding those values.

Cultural differences that affect counseling relationships include the varying amounts of time needed to establish deep personal relationships, some clients' tendencies not to disclose personal information to an unfamiliar person, and differing definitions of psychological well-being. In fact, some cultures (e.g., American Indians) may consider traditional counseling to be in violation of their basic philosophy of life.

Differing Languages Between Counselor and Client

Language, dialect, or overall communication differences between counselor and client may present formidable barriers to effective counseling relationships. The monolingual nature of Western society may unfairly discriminate against clients from bilingual and lower-class backgrounds. Regardless of the client's native communication and cultural background, building rapport during counseling sessions depends significantly on communication between counselor and client. For example, a middle- or upper-class African American professional may experience difficulty and frustration in trying to understand the street talk of a lower-class African American client. A Spanish-speaking person of Puerto Rican descent may not understand the dialect of a Mexican American migrant worker from California. These examples illustrate the importance of counselors exercising caution in communication to avoid assumptions that may affect diagnosis and counseling intervention.

Fuertes's (2004) research provides a framework for the delivery of bilingual services. With respect to linguistically diverse clients, the guidelines are clear that the client be offered services in the language that she or he prefers and, if this is not possible, that the counselor refer the client to a professional who speaks the client's language. The guidelines also instruct counselors, as an option, to offer their services to the client with the use of a properly trained translator who shares the client's cultural background. Supervisors have definite roles as they work with their supervisees: (1) Supervisors should educate their supervisees about the American Psychological Association (APA) guidelines and model them as part of the supervision process; (2) they should assess any disparities in language ability or cultural knowledge between themselves and their interns or students; (3) they may communicate their comfort with either language and allow, or even encourage, variations in English use in supervision; and (4) they should monitor when and why language mixing and switching occur.

Stereotyping Clients

Counseling professionals, regardless of whether they are from a minority or majority culture, need to consider their stereotypical beliefs toward clients of differing cultures. It is often easier to rely on stereotypical beliefs about others than to learn about cultures and to get to know people on a firsthand basis. Stereotyping can result from a counselor's personal prejudices and biases as well as from a lack of factual information about cultures and individuals.

Stereotyping crosses cultural lines and deserves the attention of counseling professionals of all cultural backgrounds. Just as European American counselors might hold stereotypical perceptions about African American, Asian American, Hispanic American, and American Indian clients, counselors from these cultural groups might also hold stereotypical perceptions about European American clients. Significant problems can accrue from counselors using stereotypical generalizations to describe their clients: It is ethically wrong, the resultant counseling is based on erroneous information, and the counselor is guilty either of not having sufficient knowledge of cultural backgrounds or of failing to take the initiative to learn factual and accurate information.

Counselor Encapsulation

Counselor encapsulation can be described as substituting stereotypes for the real world, disregarding client differences, and emphasizing a technique-oriented definition of the counseling process. Based on personal opinion and personal worldviews, the counselor may value assumptions that he or she believes are best for clients and society as a whole. Counselors need to become culturally sensitive individuals with new knowledge and skills and to reorganize old knowledge that no longer applies to current situations. Such a change also requires counselors to use counseling interventions that reflect clients' differences and worldviews rather than counseling techniques thought to be effective for all people.

Counselors Understanding Their Own Cultures

Counselors need to understand their own diversities in order to successfully understand others' diversities. Such a task is a prerequisite to effective counseling intervention in multicultural situations. These diversities include far more than just culture, although culture plays a major role. Counselors should consider all forms of differences mentioned in this book, for example, social class, ethnicity, gender, and sexual orientation. Also important is the counselor's sense of spiritualism and its role in mental well-being. Such an examination includes looking at one's (as well as others') differences in an objective, nonprejudicial fashion. A counselor must understand her or his differences, but she or he has a professional responsibility to avoid thinking, "My uniqueness (whether culture, social class, ethnicity, gender, or sexual orientation) is better than the client's." An understanding of oneself does not always come easily—it may take years to develop a sound understanding of oneself and one's worldview.

Client Reluctance and Resistance

Some cultural groups prefer to discuss personal, emotional, and other problems with parents, friends, and relatives rather than with professional counselors. The lack of minority counselors in many counseling agencies may contribute to the underuse of professional services by minorities. American Indians may believe that counseling services are not responsive to their cultural and individual needs. Other clients, such as Chinese Americans (and many other Asian American people), traditionally seek family assistance with personal problems rather than disclose problems to outsiders. In the Asian American culture, it is a social taboo to ask detailed questions about physical and mental illnesses. Recognizing these cultural beliefs, the culturally effective counselor will want to avoid explicit questions that clients might consider an invasion of their privacy.

Differing Worldviews and Lack of Cultural Relativity

An understanding of counselor and client worldviews is key in multicultural counseling situations. *Worldview* can be defined as a person's values, beliefs, and assumptions about life aspects, such as relationships with others and with the broader world, as well as perspectives of past and present events and outlook about the future. Although definitions of worldview vary, effective counselors in multicultural settings understand their own and their clients' worldviews, how these worldviews affect the outcomes of counseling intervention, and how to provide culturally sensitive intervention that reflects their clients' worldviews.

Why should counselors consider worldviews, especially in multicultural settings? One's worldview is a culturally based variable that influences the essence of the counseling relationship. Additionally, the counselor's and client's lack of cultural relativity can result in disparate perceptions of problems. An effective counselor in a multicultural situation must perceive the client's problems from a cultural perspective. What a client perceives as a problem may not be so perceived by the counselor and vice versa; it is the counselor's responsibility to attempt to perceive situations from the client's worldview.

Labeling Women, Multicultural Populations, Sexual Preferences and the Poor

Cultural groups, as well as women and the poor, often have been labeled as mentally ill when they have varied from so-called normal patterns of behaving. Likewise, counselors sometimes label women's physiological illnesses as psychogenic and label mental health disorders in African American clients as psychoses.

Expecting All Clients to Conform to Counselors' Standards and Expectations

Another common barrier in multicultural counseling is presented when counselors expect (perhaps unconsciously) clients to conform to the counselors' cultural standards and expectations. For example, expecting African American women to emulate European American standards of beauty (or vice versa) has a demoralizing effect. Putting pressure on adolescent African American mothers to undergo sterilization denies them an important source of self-worth and fails to consider the extended kinship network that figures so prominently in child rearing and mothering among African American women.

Clients of various cultural backgrounds may also be treated differently from European clients. Certain approaches may reflect paternalistic behavior or the counselor's belief that he or she is doing what is best for the client. In some cases, the counselor may even distort information if she or he thinks such a practice benefits the client.

Another equally serious issue that may threaten the counselor-client relationship involves the cultural dictates surrounding gender roles. Traditional and stereotypical gender roles prohibit strong disagreement between authority figures and clients. Thus communication and individual decision making by women may be discouraged.

Counselors who strive to be culturally effective will respond to a variety of issues: the different ways cultural backgrounds influence counseling relationships; the need to evaluate their own cultural biases and stereotypes; the ways problems and solutions vary among cultures; and the extent to which cultural encapsulation affects counseling intervention and outcomes. Will counselors understand, for example, the strong sense of family and community shared by many African Americans? Will they understand American Indians' love of nature or commitment to sharing or the loyalty of Hispanic American men to machismo? Such understanding, together with the knowledge of development factors during each stage of the lifespan, significantly determines the effectiveness of counseling efforts. Likewise, African American, Asian American, Hispanic American, and American Indian counselors need to understand the European American perspectives of individualism, family, and other cultural characteristics.

CULTURALLY EFFECTIVE COUNSELORS

This section examines the characteristics of culturally effective counselors, such as being aware of self, developing multicultural counseling competencies (in terms of attitudes and beliefs, understandings, and skills), and recognizing and addressing their values and biases, as well as understanding clients' worldviews, learning culturally appropriate intervention strategies, and understanding and adhering to ethics associated with multicultural counseling.

Awareness of Self

Ideally, counselors should develop an awareness of their own cultural heritage and how it has shaped their cultural beliefs, attitudes, and values, especially those involving other people.

To provide effective counseling intervention, the counselor working with clients of a particular racial or ethnic minority has to acquire specific knowledge about the particular groups.

Developing self-awareness also includes developing an awareness of how one's own cultural background and experiences influence one's attitudes, values, and biases about psychological processes. For example, counselors should be able to do the following (Arredondo et al., 1996 prepared this list in 1996, but it continues to be an excellent guide for counselors in multicultural situations as well as counselors in training):

- Identify the history of their culture in relation to educational opportunities and current worldview.
- Identify relevant personal cultural traits and explain their influences on cultural values.
- Identify social and cultural influences on cognitive development.
- Identify social and cultural influences in their history that have influenced their views (which would affect counseling).
- Articulate the beliefs of their own cultural and religious groups as they relate to sexual orientation, able-bodiedness, and so forth, and the impact of these beliefs on the counseling relationship.

Counselors should also be able to do the following (Arredondo et al., 1996):

- Identify the culture(s) to which they belong.
- Identify specific cultural groups from which they derived fundamental cultural heritage and significant beliefs and attitudes.
- Recognize the impact of their beliefs on their ability to respect others.
- Identify specific attitudes, beliefs, and values from their own cultural heritage that support behaviors demonstrating respect and valuing.
- Engage in an ongoing process of challenging their own beliefs and attitudes that do not support respecting and valuing of differences.
- Appreciate and articulate positive aspects of their own heritage that provide them with strengths in understanding differences.
- Recognize the influence of other personal dimensions of identity and their role in self-awareness.

Multicultural Counseling Competencies

While all counselors need an array of professional competencies, those who provide multicultural counseling need specific competencies related to culture and its effects on counseling. Culturally competent counselors need an understanding of their own cultural characteristics and of how their cultural values and biases may affect clients, an ability to resolve differences of race and beliefs between counselor and client, and an ability to know when a client should be referred to a counselor of the client's own race or culture. They also need a wide range of verbal and nonverbal response skills, acknowledge of the client's developmental stage, and the skill to send and receive accurate and appropriate verbal and nonverbal messages.

Arredondo and coworkers (1996) also published an extensive article focusing on multicultural counseling competencies. One key reference tool in the process of developing these competencies was the dimensions of the personal identity model. Premises of this model are as follows:

- We are all multicultural individuals.
- We all possess a personal, political, and historical culture.
- We are all affected by sociocultural, political, environmental, and historical events.
- Multiculturalism also intersects with multiple factors of individual diversity.

Dimensions of the personal identity model are as follows:

- *A Dimensions:* Age, culture, ethnicity, gender, language, physical disability, race, sexual orientation, social class.
- *B Dimensions:* Educational background, geographic location, income, marital status, religion, work experience, citizenship status, military experience, hobbies/recreational interests.
- *C Dimensions:* Historical moments/eras.

Although the work of Arredondo and colleagues (1996) may appear too old for a book today, it continues to be a comprehensive list of multicultural counseling competencies.

I. Counselor Awareness of Own Cultural Values and Biases

   A. Attitudes and Beliefs

      1. Culturally skilled counselors believe that cultural self-awareness and sensitivity to one's own cultural heritage is essential.

      2. Culturally skilled counselors are aware of how their own cultural background and experiences have influenced attitudes, values, and biases about psychological processes.

      3. Culturally skilled counselors are able to recognize the limits of their multicultural competency and expertise.

      4. Culturally skilled counselors recognize their sources of discomfort with differences that exist between themselves and clients in terms of race, ethnicity, and culture.

   B. Knowledge

      1. Culturally skilled counselors have specific knowledge about their own racial and cultural heritage and how it personally and professionally affects their definitions of and biases about normality/abnormality and the process of counseling.

      2. Culturally skilled counselors possess knowledge and understanding about how oppression, racism, discrimination, and stereotyping affect them personally and in their work. This allows individuals to acknowledge their own racist attitudes, beliefs, and feelings. Although this standard applies to all groups, for White counselors it may mean that they understand how they may have directly or indirectly benefited from individual, institutional, and cultural racism as outlined in White identity development models.

      3. Culturally skilled counselors possess knowledge about their social impact on others. They are knowledgeable about communication style differences; how their style may clash with or foster the counseling process with persons of color or others different from themselves based on the A, B, and C Dimensions; and how to anticipate the impact it may have on others.

   C. Skills

      1. Culturally skilled counselors seek out educational, consultative, and training experiences to improve their understandings and effectiveness in working with culturally different populations. Being able to recognize the limits of their competencies, they (a) seek consultation, (b) seek further training or education, (c) refer to more qualified individuals or resources, or (d) engage in a combination of these.

      2. Culturally skilled counselors are constantly seeking to understand themselves as racial and cultural beings and are actively seeking a nonracist identity.

II. Counselor Awareness of Clients' Worldview

    A. Attitudes and Beliefs

        1. Culturally skilled counselors are aware of their negative and positive emotional reactions toward other racial and ethnic groups that may prove detrimental to the counseling relationship. They are willing to contrast their own beliefs and attitudes with those of their culturally different clients in a nonjudgmental fashion.

        2. Culturally skilled counselors are aware of stereotypes and preconceived notions that they may hold toward other racial and ethnic minority groups.

    B. Knowledge

        1. Culturally skilled counselors possess specific knowledge and information about the particular group with which they working and are aware of the life experiences, cultural heritage, and historical background of their culturally different clients. This particular competency is strongly linked to the minority identity development models available in the literature.

        2. Culturally skilled counselors understand how race, culture, ethnicity, and so forth, may affect personality formation, vocational choices, manifestation of psychological disorders, help-seeking behavior, and the appropriateness or inappropriateness of counseling approaches.

        3. Culturally skilled counselors understand and have knowledge about sociopolitical influences that impinge on the life of racial and ethnic minorities. Immigration issues, poverty, racism, stereotyping, and powerlessness may affect self-esteem and self-concept in the counseling process.

    C. Skills

        1. Culturally skilled counselors should familiarize themselves with relevant research and the latest findings regarding mental health and mental disorders that affect various ethnic and racial groups. They should actively seek out educational experiences that enrich their knowledge, understanding, and cross-cultural counseling behavior.

        2. Culturally skilled counselors become actively involved with minority individuals outside the counseling setting (e.g., community events, social and political functions, celebrations, friendships, neighborhood groups) so that their perspective of minorities is more than an academic or helping exercise.

III. Culturally Appropriate Intervention Strategies

    A. Attitudes and Beliefs

        1. Culturally skilled counselors respect clients' religious and spiritual beliefs and values, including attributions and taboos, because these affect worldview, psychosocial healing, and expressions of distress.

        2. Culturally skilled counselors respect indigenous helping practices and respect help-giving networks among communities of color.

        3. Culturally skilled counselors value bilingualism and do not view another language as an impediment to counseling ("monolingualism" may be the culprit).

    B. Knowledge

        1. Culturally skilled counselors have a clear and explicit knowledge and understanding of the generic characteristics of counseling and therapy (culture-bound, class-bound, and monolingual) and how they may clash with the cultural values of various cultural groups.

2. Culturally skilled counselors are aware of institutional barriers that prevent minorities from using mental health services.
3. Culturally skilled counselors have knowledge of the potential bias in assessment instruments and use procedures and interpret findings in a way that recognizes the cultural and linguistic characteristics of the clients.
4. Culturally skilled counselors have knowledge of family structures, hierarchies, values, and beliefs from various cultural perspectives. They are knowledgeable about the community where a particular cultural group may reside and the resources in the community.
5. Culturally skilled counselors should be aware of relevant discriminatory practices at the social and the community level that may be affecting the psychological welfare of the population being served.

C. Skills

1. Culturally skilled counselors are able to engage in a variety of verbal and nonverbal helping responses. They are able to send and receive both verbal and nonverbal messages accurately and appropriately. They are not tied down to only one method or approach to helping but recognize that helping styles and approaches may be culture-bound. When they sense that their helping style is limited and potentially inappropriate, they can anticipate and modify it.
2. Culturally skilled counselors are able to exercise institutional intervention on behalf of their clients. They can help clients determine whether a problem stems from racism or bias in others (the concept of healthy paranoia) so that clients do not inappropriately personalize problems.
3. Culturally skilled counselors are not averse to seeking consultation with traditional healers or religious and spiritual leaders and practitioners in the treatment of culturally different clients when appropriate.
4. Culturally skilled counselors take responsibility for interacting in the language requested by the client and, if not feasible, make appropriate referrals. A serious problem arises when the linguistic skills of the counselor do not match the language of the client. This being the case, counselors should (a) seek a translator with cultural knowledge and appropriate professional background or (b) refer the client to a knowledgeable and competent bilingual counselor.
5. Culturally skilled counselors have training and expertise in the use of traditional assessment and testing instruments. They not only understand the technical aspects of the instruments but are also aware of the cultural limitations. This allows them to use test instruments for the welfare of culturally different clients.
6. Culturally skilled counselors should attend to, as well as work to eliminate, biases, prejudices, and discriminatory contexts in conducting evaluations and providing interventions and should develop sensitivity to issues of oppression, sexism, heterosexism, elitism, and racism.
7. Culturally skilled counselors take responsibility for educating their clients as to the processes of psychological intervention, such as their goals, expectations, legal rights, and the counselor's orientation.

Providing a Supportive Environment for Lesbian, Gay, Bisexual, and Transgender Clients' Therapy

Effective and competent counselors in multicultural settings provide supportive environments for lesbian, gay, bisexual, and transgender (LGBT) clients and also provide appropriate professional intervention (see Chapter 16). As with all aspects of this text, readers should remember

LGBT clients pass through all four lifespan stages; therefore, it is important to clarify misconceptions (e.g., children and the elderly do not face LGBT issues). Some counselors might harbor negative attitudes that are harmful to a humane and supportive counseling environment. LGBT clients may be perceived as weaker, more powerless, and less active than heterosexual clients are. Others might hold stereotypical beliefs about LGBT clients or consider LGBT clients as pathological, disordered, and deviant.

Other obstacles limit supportive counseling environments for these clients. Because LGBT clients fall outside the heterosexual norm, they must create their own identities, relationships, and communities. Therapists who work with LGBT clients must understand challenges associated with these tasks. Because some therapists lack exposure to information and to LGBT clients, they do not have the resources or firsthand contact to counter the prejudices faced by these clients. Competent counselors for LGBT clients seek accurate and objective information as well as firsthand contact with them. Therapists must also confront problems resulting from religious biases, societal norms, gender restrictions, and fears surrounding sexuality resulting in homophobia, heterosexism, prejudice, and discrimination against LGBT clients. Similarly, lesbian or gay counselors should seek to understand heterosexism and the challenges these clients bring to counseling.

In their research on how to instill social justice, McCabe and Rubinson (2008) maintained that some counselor trainees had strong positive attitudes toward social justice, such as race, class, or language. Still, McCabe and Rubinson (2008) reported that some counselor trainees felt indifferent or unsympathetic regarding knowledge of issues faced by LGBT clients. These trainees did not see themselves as change agents in schools and were unlikely to correct an LGBT social justice issue. Reasons cited included institutional barriers, lack of positive feelings about affirming LGBTs, and lack of sufficient knowledge about sexual orientation.

What about counselors who refuse to intervene with LGBT clients? Hermann and Herlihy (2006) research the legalities in just such a legal case. In 2001, a federal appeals court upheld the job termination of a counselor who requested to be excused from counseling a lesbian client on the grounds that homosexuality conflicted with the counselor's religious beliefs. Legal consequences include: (1) An employer's legal obligation to make reasonable accommodations for a counselor's religious beliefs does not include accommodating a counselor's request to refer homosexual clients who ask for assistance with relationship issues; and (2) counselors who engage in such behavior (and discrimination) may face significant legal liability. Furthermore, this case clearly showed that a counselor refusing to intervene with a homosexual client could be considered as a violation of the *ACA Code of Ethics*, which is discussed later in this chapter. Finally, the counselor likely would be considered liable should the client file a malpractice lawsuit.

Therapists who demonstrate competence with LGBT clients take responsibility for professional development and for confronting biases. They want to project positive feelings toward LGBT clients and, in doing so, contribute to client growth and healing. Likewise, they avoid attributing all the LGBT clients' problems to sexual orientation. Similarly, competent therapists encourage the development of a positive LGBT identity. Finally, therapists whose gender role orientations are particularly rigid must avoid making incorrect assessments of LGBT clients (and vice versa) who do not fit the societal gender roles. To promote a positive and supportive environment for LGBT clients, the therapist should:

- avoid overemphasizing similarities and differences, regardless of the therapist's sexual orientation;
- be comfortable with his or her sexuality, others' sexual orientation, as well as same-sex marriage;
- provide therapy to LGBT clients only when the counselor is comfortable with his or her own sexual orientation;

- avoid assuming that lesbian, gay, and bisexual couples are similar to or very different from his or her own sexual orientation; and
- refuse to believe that simply changing a sexual orientation will solve many of one's problems.

Other strategies that contribute to a positive and supportive counseling environment include the counselor respecting client confidentiality, being supportive and accepting, allowing clients to consider their sexual orientation, making a genuine offer of help, providing accurate and objective information, and being informed when making referrals to community and social organizations.

As emphasized in Chapters 15 and 16, clients' sexual orientation should be considered a part of their culture. Therefore, culturally effective counselors will understand and respect a client's sexual orientation in addition to practicing appropriate counseling techniques.

Providing Counseling for People With Disabilities

Chapters 1 and 17 advance the idea that people with disabilities have a culture of their own. Based on that idea, counselors should provide a supportive environment and effective professional intervention with clients with disabilities—perhaps a counseling approach called *disability counseling*.

In their recent research, Smart and Smart (2006) maintained that because of the increasing number of people with disabilities, counselors of all specialties will be called on to provide services to people with disabilities. Disability is a natural part of the human existence and is growing more common as a larger proportion of the U.S. population experiences some type of disability. Due to medical advances and technology, wider availability of health insurance, and a higher standard of living generally, people who would have died in the past now survive with a disability.

In the past, clients with disabilities were served primarily by rehabilitation counselors, probably because of concern that the disability was the important concern. However, because disability is a common and natural part of life and because all individuals, including people with disabilities, have multiple identities, roles, and functions, clients with disabilities require the services of counselors in all specialty areas: aging and adult development; gay and lesbian issues; multicultural concerns; community mental health; school counseling; group counseling; marriage and family counseling; and spiritual, ethical, and values (Smart & Smart, 2006).

Smart and Smart (2006) offered several implications that we consider helpful to counselors working with disabled clients.

- Counselors should engage in ongoing examination of clients' feelings about the experience of disability and the resulting interaction of the counselor's own identity with that of the client.
- Counselors should recognize that the disability is simply one part of the individual's identity.
- Counselors should guard against imposing their own values on the client with the disabilities.

ETHICS OF MULTICULTURAL COUNSELING

Ethics are rules of conduct or moral principles that guide the practices of professional counselors. Multicultural principles have been included in the APA's *Ethical Principles* and the American Counseling Association's (ACA's) *Ethical Standards*. Ethically conscientious counselors want to provide the best possible services to their clients and practice in a manner that reflects the profession's highest standards. The nature of the counseling process—that is, the close involvement between counselor and client—makes ethical standards a crucial aspect of the counseling process.

2014 ACA Code of Ethics

The *2014 ACA Code of Ethics* offers helpful suggestions for counselors.

1. *The Counseling Relationship addresses important issues that arise in forming, maintaining, and ending the counseling relationship.*
2. *Confidentiality, Privileged Communication, and Privacy emphasizes the client's right to privacy of records and information shared during sessions.*
3. *Professional Responsibility contains standards related to maintaining competence.*
4. *Relationships with Other Professionals highlights the importance of respecting professionals in related mental health professions.*
5. *Evaluation, Assessment, and Interpretation contains standards that govern the use of tests in counseling.*
6. *Teaching, Training, and Supervision includes ethical guidelines for counselor educators and trainers, for counselor preparation programs, and for students and supervisees.*
7. *Research and Publication addresses a range of issues, including protection of human subjects, informed consent for research participants, honesty and accuracy in reporting research results, and ethical problems in seeking publication.*
8. *Resolving Ethical Issues emphasizes the responsibility of counselors to know their ethical standards and explains procedures for resolving and reporting suspected ethical violations.*

(We strongly suggest counselors and counselors in training read *ACA Code of Ethics* at http://www.counseling.org/Resources/CodeOfEthics/TP/Home/CT2.aspx.)

Lonborg and Bowen (2004) discuss the ethical implications of spiritual diversity for school counseling in rural communities, an area they think should be in the multicultural counseling realm. Their opinions and suggestions, however, apply to nearly all counselors who at least sometimes deal with spiritual issues. By design, members of the counseling profession assist students and clients in the important process of identity development, of which spiritual identity is one important aspect. School counselors should work with their colleagues to create a school environment in which people of differing spiritual traditions feel welcome. Counselors as individuals may be on their own spiritual journeys; however, as school professionals, their challenge is to find ways to live out their own spiritual traditions and beliefs while carrying out their important responsibilities to a school community that likely enjoys tremendous spiritual and religious diversity.

Lonborg and Bowen (2004) provide practical suggestions for school counselors working with spiritual issues. First, school counselors should anticipate the ethical challenges associated with their highly visible lives. Second, counselors should identify and be prepared to use an ethical decision-making model when confronted with questions about multiple relationships, confidentiality, and boundaries of competence. Third, counselors must become familiar with community norms and values so that they may thoughtfully consider the impact of their personal and professional behavior on the school community as well as on the lives of their current and future clients. Fourth, ethical school counseling requires an understanding of one's own worldview, including spirituality as well as an awareness of diverse worldviews that exist in the community. Fifth, in light of their important role in promoting school climate, school counselors should advocate for multicultural competence in all members of the school community.

Counselors in multicultural settings have a responsibility to provide a diversity-sensitive counseling practice. Counselors may work toward this professional responsibility in several ways:

•   Understand one's own prejudices and assumptions.
•   Understand one's overt and covert attitudes toward sexual orientation, regardless of whether the counselor is homosexual or heterosexual (or questioning).

- Enhance intervention strategies to include nontraditional roles and system-oriented approaches that might be appropriate for diverse clients.
- Read some of the excellent articles and new books available on multicultural counseling.
- Attend workshops and seminars to broaden your knowledge and understandings of different cultures in the United States.
- Seek consultation or work under supervision while stretching boundaries of competence in working with diverse client populations.

Professional Training and Preparation

The vast cultural and ethnic differences that characterize the U.S. population provide a sound rationale for including culturally appropriate professional experiences in training for counselors. Rather than counselors merely using slightly modified techniques that were originally designed for European, middle-class clients, current thought calls for culturally effective counselors to have special professional preparation in counseling clients of various cultural backgrounds.

Kim and Lyons (2003) describe the use of experiential learning activities as a method of instilling multicultural competence in counselor trainees. Experiential learning can be a powerful means to stimulate multicultural awareness and can be used to help individuals confront and overcome racial/ethnic biases. When used with didactic methods, experiential learning can provide trainees with opportunities to observe and practice skills that they have read and have been taught. The appendix of this book offers examples of experiential learning activities.

Arthur and Achenbach (2002) maintain that students can experience cultural similarities and differences through experiential learning. Students can be encouraged to process their experience in both cognitive and affective domains. First, cognitive learning challenges students to examine their worldviews and beliefs about self and others. Cognitive behavior can be examined by including topics such as social and cultural bases of behavior, attitudes, and beliefs to be reflective about the impact of the professional role. Second, curriculum designed to increase counselors' self-awareness needs to go beyond cognitive learning and to encourage students to engage in affective learning. To challenge ethnocentrism, students require experiences that help them to bring feelings, attitudes, and values to the surface. Experiential learning can promote self-awareness through demonstrating the important influences of thoughts and feelings in the counseling role. Third, experiential learning facilitates students' experience of cultural similarities and differences in a structured environment with relatively low risk. Thus students may be able both to process and to resolve new information prior to working directly with culturally diverse clients.

Playing the role of counselor or client may not necessarily challenge students to process cultural information in new ways. Assuming a specific role during experiential learning may lead to externalizing the behavior, thoughts, and feelings that emerge without personalizing learning. Therefore, special efforts must be made to explore hidden messages of clients and counselors (Arthur & Achenbach, 2002).

Counseling faculty members have a responsibility to address several ethical considerations. First, to protect students, educators should make it clear that participation in the experiential learning is voluntary and not a condition of the course or evaluation. Second, educators should seek informed consent from participants prior to engaging in experiential learning. Third, a safe context must be fostered during experiential learning to prevent levels of stress that could be counterproductive for learning goals or harmful to students. Fourth, counselor educators should limit the amount of student self-disclosure in reaction to experiential learning. Fifth, faculty must be knowledgeable about the content in multicultural counseling, and they must be skillful facilitators at orchestrating learning environments, skillful supporters of individual learners' reactions, and able to help students link their personal experiences to the development of multicultural competencies.

Several suggestions for using experiential learning to foster multicultural counseling experiences include the following:

- Select experiential learning exercises to match specific learning goals in the domains of self-awareness, knowledge, and skills.
- Review experiential learning exercises to consider which values are reinforced and which values may be excluded or devalued.
- Review ethical considerations, including the competence of faculty, safety in the learning environment, student consent for voluntary participation, and sufficient time for debriefing.
- Be aware that experiential learning based on the simulation of oppression may lead to defensiveness and pose a barrier to student learning.
- Personalize experiential learning and encourage students to pay attention to feelings, thoughts, and behaviors in exploring their worldviews.
- Encourage discussion in which contrasting points of view, values, and beliefs can help students experience cultural diversity with their peers.
- Structure learning so that students can be reflective about self-awareness, knowledge, and skills.
- Help students identify strategies beyond the experiential learning exercise to review and incorporate their learning into professional practice.
- Encourage students to continue the process of reflective practice beyond course work and in their professional work as multicultural counselors.
- Incorporate both process and outcome measures to evaluate the ways that students' multicultural competencies are affected through experiential learning (Arthur & Achenbach, 2002).

They emphasize that one cannot speak of one feminist therapy—counselors need to realize there are many feminist therapies, but they all share a valuing of gender as a central organizing aspect in an individual's life and the tenet that people cannot be separated from their culture.

Feminism and feminist therapy has impacted family therapy, which has existed since the 1940s, but only in the past decade has it become a driving force in counseling and psychotherapy. The authors also explore career counseling and state that one of the most significant advantages of the feminist movement is to emphasize that women should have the same opportunities as men.

TRAINING AND PREPARATION ISSUES

Counselor educators often face the reality that counseling professionals are not adequately trained to meet the mental health needs of clients of various cultures. They also question counseling methods and techniques that are most effective with clients of differing cultural backgrounds.

Should counselor educators provide training in multicultural counseling for undergraduate students, or should such training be reserved only for the graduate level? Estrada, Durlak, and Juarez (2002) believe that it is possible to promote multicultural counseling competencies in undergraduate students. Their goal was to train students who have little knowledge of multicultural counseling and to provide a highly structured and supportive academic environment for undergraduate students to explore diversity. Although multicultural counseling competency cannot be achieved completely in a single course, exposing undergraduate students to multicultural concepts can enhance some competencies and motivate students to develop additional expertise.

Training in multicultural counseling previously occurred in a one-semester course that was designed to introduce undergraduate students to current multicultural concepts and principles in counseling and psychotherapy, to increase students' awareness of multicultural concepts and knowledge about the clinical needs of clients from culturally diverse backgrounds, and to increase students' ability to conceptualize counseling cases from multicultural perspectives. Instead of teaching actual counseling skills, the counseling course adopted a broad definition of multiculturalism to include racial and ethnic issues, sex, socioeconomic status, sexual orientation, and national origin. The beginning of the course focused on providing a rationale for and a definition of multicultural counseling, including a review of sociopolitical, historical, and developmental factors that may account for the existence of clinically underserved populations. Assigned readings focused on racism, sexism, and other forms of oppression; ethical issues in multicultural counseling; the notion of within group differences or variance; and the etic or universal approaches as contrasted to emic or culturally specific approaches to understanding human behavior. The second part of the course was a review and critique of traditional theories of psychotherapy from multicultural perspectives. The last part of the course was a review of the psychotherapy literature on sex, gays, and lesbians as well as the most visible racial and cultural minority groups in the United States, including African Americans, Asian Americans, Hispanic Americans, and Native Americans.

Counselor education and counseling psychology programs are increasingly devoting attention to how to train counselors to work with people of differing backgrounds most effectively. Counselor supervision is an important topic in counselor education literature. Recommendations included that supervisors (1) acquaint themselves with recent counselor education models designed to promote the effectiveness of multicultural counseling, (2) recognize the complex nature of cultural factors and mental health variables, and (3) learn about prospective counselors' cultural backgrounds as well as their other diversities.

Counselor self-development is an important element in counselor education. Current programs use a variety of models to provide training in multicultural counseling. However, the question remains: How can counselors who were trained prior to the emphasis on cultural diversity most effectively plan a program of self-development? Although any efforts of these counselors to improve their multicultural competence are commendable, clients deserve (and the ethics of the counseling profession require) counselors who are qualified and competent to intervene in multicultural situations. Counselors who are planning a program of self-development may take several approaches:

- Make a commitment to recognize the value of a client's cultural, ethnic, racial, socioeconomic, lifespan, sexual orientation, and all other differences.
- Strive to participate in firsthand social interactions with people from various cultures, individually and in groups.
- Become familiar with the literature on multicultural counseling, including professional publications that focus on cultural diversity and lifespan issues; attend seminars offered by counseling organizations; and participate in additional formal course work.
- Use exercises of this type to provide opportunities to gain a better understanding of one's own personal values and attitudes and those of others from different backgrounds.
- Engage in critical reflection to identify possible racist attitudes and to examine personal behaviors, perceptions, and feelings that might compromise effective and competent multicultural counseling.

Effective counselors also benefit from an understanding of the "concept or culture of *Whiteness*." Whiteness can be defined as a socially constructed phenomenon that reflects historical cultural practices and beliefs that give an advantage to people with lighter skin color. Because "Whiteness" is embedded in the social, economic, and legal structure of the United States, it has become a normative phenomenon that affects people of all cultures, races, and ethnicities (Rothman, Malott, and Paone, 2012).

Last, and certainly not least, is the counselor's commitment to social justice. Chung and Bemak (2013) emphasize broadening the discussion of multiculturalism to include social justice in graduate counselor training. Although some counselor education programs have integrated social justice into course work, very few have a stand-alone class or have infused social justice throughout the curriculum. Even so, social justice remains an important concern in in the counseling profession.

As with other professional tasks to be mastered, the success a counselor achieves toward improving multicultural counseling effectiveness depends significantly on the level of enthusiasm and commitment brought to the effort.

SUMMARY

There are three essential aspects to becoming an effective counselor. First, the counselor needs to have an appreciation for cultural diversity, an understanding of the individual culture, and a sense of empathy for clients. Second, the counselor needs appropriate beliefs and attitudes, understandings, and skills to intervene effectively in multicultural situations. Third, professional preparation, firsthand experiences with people of various cultures, and an adherence to ethical standards established by the counseling profession can reduce the barriers to effective multicultural counseling.

The appendix provides counselors with "Suggested Multicultural Experiential Activities" as they learn more about the qualifications and characteristics of effective counselors.

SUGGESTED READINGS

American Counseling Association (2014). *2014 ACA Code of Ethics*. Author: American Counseling Association, ct@counseling.org. We highly recommend counselors read and digest the *2014 ACA Code of Ethics*. It provides a preamble, purpose, and detailed information on the counseling relationship and is a must read document for all counselors.

Carrola, P., & Corbin-Burdick, M.F. (2015). Counseling military veterans: Advocating for culturally competent and holistic interventions. *Journal of Mental Health Counseling 37*(1), 1–14. The large number of military personnel returning from combat operations in Iraq and Afghanistan with symptoms of mental illness has led to increased focus on specialized veteran mental health treatment and post-traumatic stress disorder.

Hooper, L.M. (2014). Mental health services in primary care: Implications for clinical mental health counselors and other mental health providers. *Journal of Mental Health Counseling, 36*(2), 95–98. Though the idea of incorporating mental health services into primary care is not new, there is a clear need to promote the transportability of counseling theories and culturally sensitive counseling practices to primary care settings.

Kim, B.S.K., & Park, Y.S.J. (2015). Communication styles, cultural values, and counseling effectiveness with Asian Americans. *Journal of Counseling & Development, 93*(3), 269–279. This study examined counseling intervention designed for Asian Americans. Participants rated session effectiveness after viewing a videotape of a counselor using a culturally congruent or incongruent communication style.

Loos, J, Manirankunda, L., Hendrickx, K., Remmen, R., & Nöstlinger, C. (2014). HIV testing in primary care: Feasibility and acceptability of provider initiated HIV testing and counseling for Sub-Saharan African migrants. *AIDS Education & Prevention, 26*(1), 81–93. Provider-initiated HIV testing and counseling is recommended to reduce late HIV diagnoses, common among Sub-Saharan African migrants (SAM) residing in Europe.

Part II

Understanding and Counseling Clients in Multicultural Settings and Throughout the Lifespan

4 Multicultural Human Growth and Development

QUESTIONS TO BE EXPLORED

- Why are the prenatal and infancy stages important in a lifespan approach?
- How do historical and contemporary perspectives of infancy, childhood, adolescence, adulthood, and old age differ?
- Does each lifespan stage have a "culture?" What makes each stage unique? What role do cultural differences play during each lifespan stage?
- What are some issues and questions that pertain to multicultural lifespan development?
- What are the physical, psychosocial, and intellectual characteristics of clients at each lifespan stage?
- What special problems and concerns face African American, American Indian, Asian American, European American, and Hispanic American clients at each lifespan stage?
- What are some research findings in the multicultural development area? What implications do they have for mental health professionals?
- What challenges confront counselors working with clients at the various lifespan stages, and what resources can be suggested?

OVERVIEW

Although most counseling professionals have recognized for some time that understanding cultural differences enhances intervention, the need to take the client's lifespan stage into account has been emphasized only recently. Understanding developmental characteristics and the unique crises, tasks, and problems associated with a particular lifespan period provides counselors with insights into the counseling needs of children, adolescents, adults, and the elderly. To underscore the importance of recognizing and understanding lifespan differences, this chapter begins with a discussion of cross-cultural research and an overview of lifespan development, followed by a description of developmental characteristics of the four lifespan stages and relevant issues occurring during each.

Human development and the various types of diversity are complexly related, a fact that has implications for counselors working with the various developmental periods and with various cultures and socioeconomic groups. The list below presents several questions that need to be addressed for more enhanced understanding of the effects of culture on development.

Cross-Cultural Child Development: Crucial Questions

- How do the various types of diversity (e.g., culture, ethnicity, social class, sexual orientation, and gender) affect children's development?
- What developmental similarities do children share across cultures and other diversities?

- How do children differ developmentally across cultures and other diversities?
- How do cultural beliefs about maternal and paternal parenting affect child development?
- How should professional intervention reflect both culture and the childhood stage of development?
- Do the research findings of Piaget, Vygotsky, and Erikson have relevance for development in minority children?
- How can mental health professionals most effectively intervene with children of differing cultures?

Wainryb (2004) maintains that the emphasis on the study of diversity, a growing area of research in developmental psychology, reflects an increasing awareness of the need to recognize the value of the differences among people. Wainryb reviews scholarly writing that maintains that the field of developmental psychology is an ethnocentric one dominated by European American perspectives. When one group, the majority, has the exclusive power to define the nature of itself and all other groups in a society, all minority groups are disenfranchised. Such an ethnocentric approach does not yield an accurate account of human development. The call to address these biases has been taken seriously. Minority groups are now routinely included in developmental research. In this context, psychologists have championed culture as the main source of development—the origin and organizer of the self, emotion, cognition, and values.

In Table 4.1, Papalia, Feldman, and Martorell (2014) divided the lifespan into eight periods rather than the four stages chosen for this volume; for example, they have three childhood stages and three adulthood stages.

Although Papalia, Feldman, and Martorell (2014) provided a detailed look at development, the counseling chapters will discuss only the four main lifespan stages. Also, readers are encouraged to remember that all clients differ according to socioeconomic class, sexual orientation, disability, and cultural factors.

PRENATAL AND INFANCY STAGES

Crucial Periods

The nine months preceding birth are so obviously significant in lifelong development that their inclusion here requires no explanation. An infant's overall size, health, and weight are all affected by the mother's nutritional intake during pregnancy. Smoking and drug and alcohol use can harm the fetus. Improper nutrition may be a result of lack of financial resources, lack of knowledge, the tendency to rely on relatives rather than to consult physicians, and/or communication barriers that cause misunderstanding. Also, the ingestion of certain medications and toxins during early pregnancy can harm the fetus (Vander Zanden, Crandell, & Crandell, 2006). For these and other reasons, minority children or those from lower socioeconomic backgrounds may begin life at a disadvantage.

A closely related issue is infant mortality in the United States. Despite leading the world in remarkable advances in newborn care, the United States has the highest infant mortality rate of all affluent industrialized nations. In fact, a growing number of not-so-affluent nations also outperform the United States in infant survival. African American infants currently experience more than twice the risk of dying in their first year of life compared with white infants.

Table 4.1 Developmental Characteristics Throughout the Lifespan Continuum

Age Period	Physical Developments	Cognitive Developments	Psychosocial Developments
Prenatal (conception to birth)	Conception occurs. The genetic endowment interacts with environmental influences from the start. Basic body structures and organs form. Brain growth spurt begins. Physical growth is the most rapid in the lifespan. Fetus hears and responds to sensory stimuli. Vulnerability to environmental influences is great.	Abilities to learn and remember are present during fetal stage.	Fetus responds to mother's voice and develops a preference for it.
Infancy and Toddlerhood (birth to age 3)	All senses operate at birth to varying degrees. The brain grows in complexity and is highly sensitive to environmental influence. Physical growth and development of motor skills are rapid.	Abilities to learn and remember are present, even in early weeks. Use of symbols and ability to solve problems develop by the end of second year. Comprehension and use of language develop rapidly.	Attachments to parents and others form. Self-awareness develops. Shift from dependence to autonomy occurs. Interest in other children increases.
Early Childhood (3 to 6 years)	Growth is steady; appearance becomes more slender and proportions more adultlike. Appetite diminishes, and sleep problems are common. Handedness appears; fine and gross motor skills and strength improve.	Thinking is somewhat egocentric, but understanding of other people's perspective grows. Cognitive immaturity leads to some illogical ideas about the world. Memory and language improve. Intelligence becomes more predictable.	Self-concept and understanding of emotions become more complex; self-esteem is global. Independence, initiative, self-control, and self-care increase. Gender identity develops. Play becomes more imaginative, more elaborate, and more social. Altruism, aggression, and fearfulness are common. Family is still focus of social life, but other children become more important. Attending preschool is common.
Middle Childhood (6 to 11 years)	Growth slows. Strength and athletic skills improve. Respiratory illnesses are common, but health is generally better than at any other time in lifespan.	Egocentrism diminishes. Children begin to think logically but concretely. Memory and language skills increase. Cognitive gains permit children to benefit from formal schooling. Some children show special educational needs and strengths.	Self-concept becomes more complex, affecting self-esteem. Coregulation reflects gradual shift in control from parents to child. Peers assume central importance.

(Continued)

Table 4.1 (Continued)

Age Period	Physical Developments	Cognitive Developments	Psychosocial Developments
Adolescence (11 to about 20 years)	Physical growth and other changes are rapid and profound. Reproductive maturity occurs. Major health risks arise from behavioral issues, such as eating disorders and drug abuse.	Ability to think abstractly and use scientific reasoning develops. Immature thinking persists in some attitudes and behaviors. Education focuses on preparation for college or vocation.	Search for identity, including sexual identity, becomes central. Relationships with parents are generally good. Peer groups help develop and test self-concept but also may exert an antisocial influence.
Young Adulthood (20 to 40 Years)	Physical condition peaks; then declines slightly. Lifestyle choices influence health.	Cognitive abilities and moral judgments assume more complexity. Educational and career choices are made.	Personality traits and styles become relatively stable, but changes in personality may be influenced by life stages and events. Decisions are made about intimate relationships and personal lifestyles. Most people marry, and most become parents.
Middle Adulthood (40 to 65 years)	Some deterioration of sensory abilities, health, stamina, and prowess may take place. Women experience menopause.	Most basic mental abilities peak; expertise and practical problem-solving skills are high. Creative output may decline but improve in quality. For some, career success and earning powers peak; for others, burnout or career change may occur.	Sense of identity continues to develop; stressful midlife transition may occur. Double responsibilities of caring for children and elderly parents may cause stress. Launching of children leaves empty nest.
Late Adulthood (65 years and over)	Most people are healthy and active, although health and physical abilities decline somewhat. Slowing of reaction time affects some aspects of functioning.	Most people are mentally alert. Although intelligence and memory may deteriorate in some areas, most people find ways to compensate.	Retirement from workforce may offer new options for use of time. People need to cope with personal losses and impending death. Relationships with family and close friends can provide important support. Search for meaning in life assumes central importance.

Adapted from: Experience Human Development, 13th Edition by Diane Papalia, Ruth Feldman, and Gabriela Martorell. 2014. New York: McGraw Hill. Used with permission by McGraw Hill Education.

Unfortunately, this mortality gap has widened over several decades. Some might blame the high mortality rate of African Americans for raising the national average, but that is assuming the white rate is low, which it is not. Understanding the high rates of African American infant mortality in the United States requires analysis of the effects of race as a social construct, thus addressing discrimination and racism in its various forms (David & Collins, 2014).

Although smoking and use of alcohol or drugs is a conscious choice made by the pregnant woman, maternal malnutrition is more difficult to control and particularly affects minority groups. Malnutrition-related problems, such as low birth weight, rickets, physical and neural defects, and failure to thrive, occur most frequently in African American, American Indian, and Hispanic American children whose mothers are more likely to be undernourished than are mothers of European American children (Vander Zanden et al., 2006).

Single mothers can face increased stress due to housing and financial problems as well as the challenges of raising children alone. Some unmarried women may also lack adequate health care during pregnancy. They may be unable to afford proper health care, be too embarrassed to seek help, or be unaware or uninformed of available health services due to inadequate English-speaking skills. The stress, frustration, and anxiety that sometimes accompany single motherhood can result in problems that require counseling intervention. Still, it must be acknowledged that not all unmarried women experience such problems—some women have the financial means and English-language skills to seek assistance and the emotional support of extended family members.

Multicultural Differences

Is infant behavior universal or does even infant behavior vary according to culture? Surprisingly to some observers, research suggests that infants demonstrate culture-specific behaviors. A typical behavior of Western newborns is the Moro reflex. To test this reflex, the baby's body is lifted, with the head supported. The head is then released and allowed to drop. Typical European American newborns extend both arms and legs, cry persistently, and move about in an agitated manner. In contrast, Navajo newborns typically respond in a more reduced reflex extension of the limbs; crying is rare, and agitated motion ceases almost immediately. African American infants appear to be more precocious in gross motor skills, as are Asian American infants to a lesser degree, than infants of European origin. Asian American infants are typically more docile and may tend to stay closer to their parents (Papalia et al., 2014).

Learning about cross-cultural developmental studies helps mental health professionals avoid inappropriate generalizations about aspects of children and their social world. A knowledge of cultural differences and an understanding of child growth and development are essential for counselors working with children of differing cultural backgrounds. In one sense, counselors should be able to think from a child's perspective and to see situations from a child's point of view. This will often include recognizing and understanding how a child of a particular age thinks—the child's self-perception of physical growth and changes, the child's psychosocial self-concept, and the child's level of intellectual development.

CHILDREN

Understanding the unique position of children in the lifespan continuum and the historical and contemporary perspectives surrounding the concept of the childhood years presents professionals with challenging tasks. Because their physical, psychological, and intellectual characteristics differ from those of their older counterparts on the lifespan, children have unique developmental characteristics that professionals should understand and consider when planning counseling intervention. Although all children progress in the same developmental sequence, it is imperative to recognize the effects of diverse cultural and ethnic backgrounds on young clients.

Childhood Years: Historical and Contemporary Perspectives

Interest in the unique growth and developmental aspects of children and recognition of the need for special counseling for children have been demonstrated only fairly recently. Because they lacked social standing and legal rights, children were considered by many to be possessions and were treated as the adults pleased. There was no concept of childhood—children were seen as miniature adults. The prevailing opinion of the adult culture was that "children should be seen and not heard." It proved difficult for society to accept that children also differed culturally.

Contemporary perceptions of the childhood years hold that childhood has its own unique culture that differs significantly from other lifespan cultures. Although children differ across cultures, they have their own characteristics that differ substantially from those of adults. Children, by virtue of their developmental characteristics, have their own communication patterns, senses of humor, likes and dislikes, and types of social activity and play. Their unique ways of speaking, acting, and perceiving events in their lives indicate that professionals should duly consider the distinct culture of the childhood years.

Counseling professionals who consider children to be unique and developing individuals rather than miniature adults tend to counsel children more effectively. In essence, counselors and psychotherapists who intervene with children from varying cultures should understand (a) the culture of childhood; (b) the physical, psychosocial, and intellectual characteristics of developing children; and (c) the cultural differences among children.

Multicultural Differences

A discussion of cultural differences in children should consider differences from a cultural perspective. Some cultures differ sharply in dimensions of individualism versus collectivism. Some European Americans harbor a sense of individualism, while Hispanics and American Indians value a sense of collectivism, meaning they feel responsible for the group, whether it be close family or neighbors. Likewise, African Americans value the immediate family as well as the extended family. Individualism and collectivism are not matters of right and wrong; it is simply the worldview of individual cultures regarding how they consider others.

Actual physical differences also exist between cultures. In the United States, African American children tend to have longer legs and be taller than European American children, who, in turn, are taller than Asian American children. In Canada, English-speaking children tend to be taller than French-speaking children. Similarly, African American boys and girls tend to grow faster than European American children, and thus be a bit taller and heavier at the same age. By about six years of age, African American girls have more muscle and bone mass than European American or Hispanic American girls. Hispanic American girls have a higher percentage of body fat than European American girls of the same age (Papalia et al., 2014).

Child Development

The present-day emphasis on child growth and development illustrates the recognition and value currently being placed on the childhood years. Developmentally, an array of physical, psychosocial, and intellectual changes occur simultaneously: Muscles and body proportions grow, social interests increasingly move outside the immediate family to a broader community and society, and intellectual problem-solving and reasoning skills increase.

Three physical changes are (1) the rapid growth of legs and arms, resulting in a slimmer appearance; (2) a lengthening of the jaw and an increase in face size as permanent teeth replace baby teeth; and (3) an increase in muscle tissue in boys and adipose tissue (fat) in girls.

Children emerge from the socially secure confines of a parent-centered home into a socially expanding world of extended family, with closer and more meaningful friendships and a recognition of peers. As children build their complex social networks of friends and significant peers, they also change their self-concept, their opinions of others, and their perceptions of the world in relation to themselves. Closely related to physical and psychosocial-emotional development is intellectual development, which opens vast new worlds of increased thinking ability. No longer confined to the physical or concrete worlds, a child now experiences increased flexibility of thought, ability to reverse operations, enhanced memory, and ability to share another's point of view. As always, culturally perceptive counselors need to remember that physical, psychosocial, and intellectual development differs across cultures and that each client should be considered unique (Papalia et al., 2014).

Development, family relationships, and culture are complexly intertwined. In her cross-cultural research with Asian and Australian children, Keats (2000) reported that far-reaching changes challenge traditional cultural values in family relationships and child-rearing practices. The author examines aspects such as the role of communication, development of values, and culturally related differences. Western ideas of desirable practices in the development of children often conflict with an Asian culture's traditional views and more recent ideologies. Examples of conflicts include Islamic views of child development and the attitudes of many Westerners toward China's one-child policy. Also, Asian countries have all been undergoing massive lifestyle changes, including economic, social, and psychological, which threaten many traditional child-rearing practices and values.

One problem facing children is obesity. Pan, May, Wethington, Dalenius, and Grummer-Strawn (2013) examined obesity in low-income non-Hispanic whites, American Indian, and Alaska Native families. These researchers found that, compared to non-Hispanic whites, the risk of obesity was 35% higher among American Indians and Alaskan Natives but 8% lower among non-Hispanic African Americans. The high incidence underscores the importance of early-life obesity prevention in multiple settings for low-income children and their families.

Gender Differences

Although physical gender differences are fairly easy to recognize, other differences between girls and boys are more subtle. Counselors and other professionals should carefully avoid stereotyping girls and boys. For too many years, people have considered girls and boys in gender-specific terms, to the detriment of both genders. The list below looks at selected gender differences.

Selected Gender Differences in Children

- In infancy, girls are slightly shorter and lighter and have a higher ratio of fat to muscle than boys; girls in some Asian cultures are below growth norms for North American children of the same age; and African American girls are slightly ahead of European American children of all ages.
- Attention-deficit hyperactivity disorder (ADHD) is diagnosed five to ten times more often in boys than in girls; however, many girls with ADHD may be overlooked because their symptoms usually are not as obvious.
- Boys are more likely to have asthma, although heredity contributes to this condition in both boys and girls.
- Temperamental differences may result from gender-differentiated maternal child-raising attitudes as well as inherited genetic differences.

- Boys sometimes exhibit a tendency to be active and daring, whereas girls may be more anxious and timid, perhaps because parents often teach boys to be physically active and teach girls to seek help and physical closeness.
- During the early childhood years, boys are slightly ahead of girls in skills that emphasize force and power, perhaps because boys and girls are encouraged to engage in different activities.

Source: Developed from *Experience Human Development* (13th ed.), by Diane Papalia, Ruth Feldman, and Gabriela Martorell, 2014, New York: McGraw Hill.

Self-Concept

Two closely related aspects surface as the social status of children changes: self-concept and locus of control. Children around six or seven years of age begin to think of themselves in external terms—what they look like, where they live, and what they are doing. This developing self-concept takes two forms: the real self and the ideal self. The former refers to the child's concept of what she or he is actually like; the latter refers to what the child would like to be like (Papalia et al., 2014). Thus children continually evaluate themselves to determine their degree of self-worth and their sense of adequacy. Positive self-concept comes from development of the sense of industry, when children feel successful in learning the knowledge, tasks, and technology of their society. The negative side of this sense of industry—feelings of inferiority and inadequacy—results in anxiety and poor self-concept (Erikson, 1963).

Self-concept varies among children of differing cultural backgrounds. Kenny and McEachern (2009) look at multicultural differences in children's self-concepts. Children's self-perceptions will significantly influence academic achievement, social achievement, and actual behavior. In fact, low self-esteem can lead to depression, eating disorders, suicide, and adjustment problems. Understanding multicultural differences will allow counselors to improve students' thoughts and feelings about themselves and thus perhaps prevent occurrences of behavioral and emotional difficulties. It is also important to note that certain cultural or ethnic factors may pose ongoing stressors related to acculturation, racial discrimination, academic difficulties due to language barriers, and other challenges associated with adjusting to the mainstream culture. Unfortunately, language differences among speakers of African American English have often been considered language deficits, based on a lack of understanding of the language (Pearson, Conner, & Jackson, 2013). Being told one's language is a deficit and in need of improvement can lead to lower self-concepts.

Specific findings included the fact that Blacks score significantly lower than Hispanics on total self-concept but were not significantly different from White students. White students scored significantly higher on the behavior scales, which means that Whites considered themselves better behaved than Black and Hispanic students, for example, complying with school and home rules and expectations. School counselors need to evaluate the self-concept of children from diverse ethnic backgrounds—feeling good about oneself is important for constructive life choices, helps prevent destructive behaviors, and may lead to improvement in academic achievement (Kenny & McEachern, 2009).

Locus of control refers to the degree to which a person perceives control over his or her life. Briefly put, children who have an internal locus of control believe that they can determine what happens to them; on the other hand, children who have an external locus of control believe that outside forces control their lives. Locus of control has implications for counselors intervening in multicultural settings; children (as well as adults and the elderly) may think that racism and discrimination prohibit them from taking control of their lives.

ADOLESCENTS

The adolescent years have traditionally gone unrecognized as a genuine developmental period on the lifespan. As a result, adolescence has been plagued with misconceptions, general misunderstandings, and damaging stereotypes. No longer children but not yet adults, adolescents very often experience feelings that tend to lower their self-esteem. Psychosocial and intellectual changes that parallel the more visible physical changes cause adolescents to adopt childlike behaviors at times and to conform to adult standards at other times. Adolescents often experience identity confusion. Professionals working with adolescent clients need a sound understanding of this lifespan period; they also need to recognize cultural differences that influence adolescent behavior.

Adolescent Years: Historical and Contemporary Perspectives

Some observers define adolescence in terms of a specific age range, whereas others equate the beginning of adolescence with the onset of puberty and its ending with certain cultural factors.

Contrary to popular belief, the term *adolescence* has not been in use very long; in fact, it was hardly accepted before the nineteenth century. Moreover, proposing the term to suggest a continuation of childhood beyond puberty was considered even more ludicrous than not recognizing it at all.

Multicultural Differences

Adolescents vary from culture to culture, just as children do. What is considered normal behavior in one culture may be considered inappropriate in another. For example, many European American adolescents feel a strong need to act in accordance with peer pressure, whereas Asian American adolescents may believe that loyalty to parents takes precedence over any peer pressure that may be experienced. Similarly, the sense of "machismo" that so strongly influences the behavior of many Hispanic Americans is less important to their European American and Asian American counterparts. Other differences include allegiance to family, self-esteem, collectivism versus individualism, and overall worldviews. Without knowing the individual client, it is difficult to generalize about multicultural differences. Counselors also need to consider that clients in some cultures have been adversely affected by discrimination and social injustice.

Adolescent Identity

Adolescents ask themselves: Who am I? What am I to become? One main task of adolescence is to build a reasonably stable identity. Identity refers to a person's sense of placement within the world; in other words, it is the meaning that one attaches to oneself in the broader context of life (Vander Zanden et al., 2006).

Adolescents often develop individual and cultural identities under difficult circumstances involving racism, discrimination, and injustice. The "culture of poverty" image may influence American Indian identities; similarly, African Americans who hear repeatedly that their culture is inferior may develop negative identities. In fact, African American youths have historically been confronted with many challenges to their cultural identity that have negatively affected their physical and psychological development. They have encountered problems with education, unemployment, delinquency, substance abuse, adolescent pregnancy, and suicide. Evidence in schools includes declines in grade point averages and attendance and in rates of participation in extracurricular activities as well as increases in psychosocial stress and problem behaviors. One must carefully avoid blaming the victim in this case—African Americans, just as adolescents in other cultures, have faced serious racism and discrimination.

Gender Differences

Perceptive counselors understand the importance of gender differences and their effect on adolescent girls and boys. Considerable caution is needed when considering gender. People often make statements such as "Boys like to compete; girls like to collaborate" or "Boys like a large social network; girls like a few close friends." Although such statements can be true, counselors should avoid basing professional intervention on these and similar assumptions. With that said, the list below looks at several selected gender differences among adolescent girls and boys.

Selected Gender Differences in Adolescents

- Typically girls satisfy communal needs through friendships, whereas boys satisfy status and mastery needs.
- Girls normally seek more emotional closeness in friendships, whereas boys look for more physical activity—for example, sports and competitive games.
- Girls experience greater decreases in self-esteem, perhaps because they are concerned about physical abilities and feel more insecure about these abilities.
- Girls often develop a sense of infant-caregiver, which carries over for future intimate ties; boys often form a masculine gender identity, stressing individuation and independence.
- Girls are more prone to depression (but this is limited to industrialized nations); however, suicide rates are higher for boys (probably four- or five-fold greater).

Source: Developed from *Development Through the Lifespan* (6th ed.) by L. E. Berk, 2008, Boston: Allyn and Bacon; *Experience Human Development* (13th ed.) by Diane Papalia, Ruth Feldman, and Gabriela Martorell, 2014, New York: McGraw Hill.

Yager and Rotheram-Borus (2000) investigated ethnic, gender, and developmental differences in the social expectations of African American, Hispanic American, and European American high school students. The four domains included group orientation, expressiveness, assertiveness, and aggressiveness. Yager and Rotheram-Borus reached several conclusions, but only their findings on gender will be briefly mentioned here. Males' social expectations were less group-oriented and assertive and more expressive and aggressive. Females' expectations for assertiveness increased with grade level. Ethnic and gender differences were similar across youths of different ages.

Self-Concept

The significance of self-concept during all periods of the lifespan cannot be overstated. An adolescent's degree of self-worth can have long-lasting effects on identity formation, social development, and academic achievement. Self-perception is vital in determining whether the adolescent will become alienated from parents, peers, and society or whether he or she will become a sociable person who is capable of sustaining satisfactory relationships.

Although self-concept begins to develop at birth and continues to develop until death, the real crisis in identity occurs during adolescence. Emerging from this crisis with a strong, healthy, and independent self-concept allows the adolescent to progress further and to face the challenges of the adult world. Adolescents who are unable to develop positive self-concepts may withdraw from others or develop negative identities. Successful mastery of the developmental tasks that lead to a healthy self-concept is even more difficult for minority group members. Failure can result in academic problems, loneliness, and isolation.

We think and hope the self-concept among African Americans has improved over the years due to the civil rights movement and the Black consciousness movement. Still, understandably, some African American adolescents have high self-esteem and others have lower self-esteem. As readers recall, self-esteem can differ from area to area; for example, an adolescent might have excellent athletic self-esteem but may differ significantly in academic areas.

The self-concept of adolescents of all cultures may be enhanced by (a) learning about their respective cultural histories, (b) identifying the effects of past and contemporary relationships (both intracultural and intercultural), (c) learning historical and contemporary accomplishments and contributions of respective cultural groups, and (d) working to reduce acculturative stress, especially for immigrants and first-generation adolescents.

Adolescents Who Are at Risk

Although suicide, accidents, and homicides account for most adolescent deaths, many adolescents are at risk due to eating disorders, drug abuse, and sexually transmitted diseases (STDs). Common eating disorders include anorexia nervosa and bulimia, which are characterized by a distorted body perception and a preoccupation with food. Substance abuse may involve alcohol, tobacco, and marijuana or other illicit drugs, which may lead to the use of still more powerful drugs. AIDS and STDs are becoming increasingly serious problems, with particular implications for adolescents. Three out of four cases of STDs involve young people from 15 to 24 years of age. Chlamydia, gonorrhea, syphilis, and herpes simplex are a few STDs that take a considerable toll on adolescents (Papalia et al, 2014)

It takes special commitment and expertise to intervene with adolescents of various cultures. Adolescents may experience frustrations not only from being at an age between childhood and adulthood but also from being a minority in a predominantly European American society. At a time when development of positive self-concept and identity is crucial, adolescents often find themselves caught between their parents' admonitions and their peers' pressure to experiment with risky behavior. In fact, being culturally different has the potential for making the already difficult adolescent years even more so. The American Indian adolescent who values noninterference with others and the Asian American adolescent who believes that errant behavior brings shame and disgrace on the family can encounter problems with identity formation. Understanding the complex relationship between development and cultural diversity provides counselors with clearer insights into counseling adolescents from differing cultures.

Speaking only of African American students, Cokley et al. (2014/2015) maintained African American students are overidentified for behavior issues at schools and underidentified for mental health services. Often related to these issues are socioeconomic status and race. Experiences common to low SES populations include single-parent households, overcrowded homes, multigenerational experiences of financial stress, exposure to neighborhood violence, and substance abuse. All of these bring their own share of challenges and can be difficult for low-income black adolescents already dealing with developmental stressors related to puberty, peer-related stress, academic motivation, and identity formation to cope with.

Cokley et al. (2014/2015) examined cultural considerations and depression. Depression is one of the most prevalent and debilitating mental illnesses in the United States. Depression should not be mistaken for the typical bouts of sadness and/or irritability that usually subside within a few hours or days. In addition to the sadness and/or irritability, common symptoms of depression include loss of interest in pleasurable activities, changes in appetite and sleep, decreased energy, difficulty concentrating, and feelings of guilt, worthlessness, and/or helplessness. However, understanding depressive symptoms is culturally oriented around White Americans. Black students are often diagnosed with schizophrenia rather than an accurate diagnosis of a depressive disorder.

ADULTS

Although adults are often thought to be "grown and not developing," they do, in fact, continue to experience physical, psychosocial, and intellectual developmental changes. Tasks that face counselors of adult clients include a commitment (a) to consider adulthood a unique developmental period between adolescence and the elderly years and (b) to take into account multicultural differences among adults.

Adulthood Years: Historical and Contemporary Perspectives

The term *adulthood* has only recently begun to receive attention and respect as a valid period on the lifespan. Because it lacks the specific developmental characteristics of childhood or adolescence, adulthood was used as an all-encompassing term to describe all developmental changes in adults, beginning at age 18, 21, or some other age. Researchers consider the adult stage a largely unexplored phase of the lifespan. Once thought to be homogeneous, fully developed "products," adults are currently recognized by researchers and scholars as diverse and continually changing and developing.

Adult Development

As previously mentioned, to assume that adults do not continue to experience both visible and invisible developmental changes demonstrates a lack of knowledge of human development. From the time of conception, humans experience many developmental changes, both desirable and undesirable, that continue until death. Considerable individuality is associated with these developmental changes: Some adults experience them without psychological turmoil, whereas others require counseling interventions.

While Erikson's classic works (1963, 1968) are nearly 50 years old, we believe his theories have potential for counseling intervention with clients of differing cultural backgrounds, especially when counselors consider *individuals'* worldviews. Admittedly, Erikson's theories have received considerable criticism from feminist groups who believe that females need their own developmental theory and feminist-based counseling models. The theory is dominated by a male, Eurocentric perspective, with emphasis on the emergence of the individual. Feminists claim that, in Erikson's theory, the male is seen as the model of normal development. His theory emphasizes individualism, whereas females need to be connected and to be able to develop and maintain relationships.

Adult developmental stages basically can be divided into three arbitrary age ranges: early, middle, and late. The early adult age range is 20 to 40 years. During these years, early adults make decisions regarding marriage and careers that will affect the rest of their lives. The middle age range is approximately 40 to 65 years. (The late age range arbitrarily begins at age 65; it is discussed in the next section.) Middle age brings with it an aging physical appearance, development of a distinct adult intelligence, and changes in personality. Although the transition from early adult to middle age may go virtually unnoticed, counselors can still benefit from determining the stage at which clients think they are. Transitions are culture based, which means that middle age in one culture may not coincide with the previously suggested age range of 40 to 65 that is often considered appropriate for the Western world (Papalia et al., 2014).

Saucier (2004) looks at issues confronted by aging women, particularly those related to ageism and body image, emphasizing society's role in influencing women's perceptions of their bodies. Issues include unattainable beauty (e.g., the ideal female body represents the thinnest 5% of women), the influence of the media, and declining self-concept about one's body. Saucier offered several implications for counseling professionals. First, the impact of ageism should be explored, and issues that could be affected by this cultural bias should

be discussed: Saucier suggests assertiveness training and creating a more positive attitude toward aging. Second, women need help in acknowledging changes in their physical
appearance and in dealing with emotions associated with these changes: Saucier suggests
cognitive-behavioral approaches and also help for women to understand that there is nothing
inherently pathological and irrational about wanting to achieve a culturally valued appearance. Third, the influence of the media takes a toll on women: Saucier suggests encouraging
women to view the media with a more critical eye and to view the marketing schemes emphasizing youth and beauty as hype. Also, she suggests that feminist therapy can be beneficial in
dealing with the media, because it encourages the expression of anger toward injustices and
teaches assertiveness.

It is essential that readers realize that developmental tasks may differ among cultures, genders, disabilities, and sexual orientations. A developmental task in one culture might appear
earlier or later, or possibly not at all, in another culture.

Gender Differences

The list below looks at several selected gender differences among adult women and men. As
mentioned in the other sections of this chapter, readers should avoid gender stereotyping. The
only accurate and reliable way to determine specific gender characteristics is to gain firsthand
knowledge about individual clients.

Selected Gender Differences in Adults

- About 13% of men and 3% of women are heavy drinkers. About one-third of heavy
  drinkers are alcoholics.
- The number of single adults (individuals not living with an intimate partner) has
  risen six-fold since 1970 to 29% in never-married males and 21% in similar females.
- Disability due to arthritis affects 45% of men over age 65; in women, the number is
  higher—50% of those ages 65 to 75 and 60% of those over age 75.
- Men and women experience reproductive health problems; in other health areas,
  men experience more lung cancer (although this cancer is increasing in women), and
  women experience more eating disorders, rheumatoid arthritis, and osteoporosis.
- Women tend to have higher life expectancies than men and lower death rates
  throughout life.

Source: Developed from *Development Through the Lifespan* (6th ed.) by L. E. Berk, 2008,
Boston: Allyn and Bacon; *Experience Human Development* (13th ed.) by Diane Papalia, Ruth
Feldman, and Gabriela Martorell, 2014, New York: McGraw Hill.

Concerns and Tasks of Adulthood

Adults, perhaps unknowingly, experience several concerns and tasks during the adult years.
Challenges may include growing older, developing adult identities, forming positive self-esteem,
and progressing through the stages of moral development. These are all affected by adults' cultural backgrounds, their opinions of their cultural heritages, and their acculturative stress. People of all cultures may experience problems associated with poverty, alcoholism, drug use, and
violence. Concerns and tasks undoubtedly reflect the stage of adulthood (between early adult

and middle-aged adult). Other differences in developmental concerns and tasks occur among clients of differing sexual orientations. The counselor's challenge is to understand problems from the adult's perspective and to plan intervention that reflects both the client's lifespan stage and the culture.

Havighurst (1972) compiled a list of developmental tasks that he maintained were age-level appropriate for both early and middle adulthood. Success or failure in these tasks determined future happiness or unhappiness. Tasks during early adulthood include selecting a mate, learning to live with a partner, starting a family, rearing children, managing a home, and getting started in an occupation. Tasks during middle adulthood include assisting teenage children to become responsible adults, assuming social and civic responsibility, performing satisfactorily in one's chosen occupation, developing leisure activities, relating to one's spouse as an individual, accepting the physiological changes of middle age, and adjusting to aging parents.

In recognizing the role of cultural and socioeconomic factors in mastering these developmental tasks, Havighurst (1972) acknowledges that they are extremely important. A person in one culture might be encouraged to seek financial independence; in another culture, financial dependence might be the norm. Whereas a successful middle-aged European American might be established and performing satisfactorily in an occupation, the unemployed middle-aged African American, American Indian, or Hispanic American with few marketable skills might still be seeking gainful employment. Similarly, socioeconomic differences affect one's leisure activities, degree of social and civic responsibility, and ability to manage a home. Although Havighurst's work is 40 years old, it is still applicable as counselors consider diversity and its effects on developmental tasks. Although Havighurst's developmental theories undoubtedly contribute to our knowledge of adults, many questions still remain as to the complex interaction of development, culture, and socioeconomic class in a nation of increasing diversity.

Developmental changes during the substages of the adult period are as distinctive as the previously discussed child and adolescent developmental changes; hence, the need for specific counseling strategies planned for early, middle, and late adulthood. Intervening with adults of various cultures requires an understanding of the physical and psychosocial effects of aging, the different tasks and crises among cultures, and the complex relationship between an individual's development and culture.

Stress and Stress-Related Illnesses

The more stressful the changes that occur in a person's life, the greater the likelihood that illness will occur within the next year or two. Change, even positive change, can be stressful, and some people react to stress by becoming ill. In addition, there are different types of stressors or stressful experiences. Hassles of everyday living are associated with minor physical ills such as colds and may have a stronger effect on mental health than major life events or transitions. Stress is currently being examined as a factor in such diseases as hypertension, heart disease, stroke, peptic ulcers, and cancer. The most frequently reported symptoms of stress include headache, stomachache, muscle pain or tension, and fatigue. The most common psychological symptoms include nervousness, anxiety, tension, anger, irritability, and depression (Papalia et al., 2014).

Lovejoy (2001) compares body image disturbance and eating disorders among African American and White women to determine major ethnic differences in these areas. In her feminist sociological analysis, Lovejoy offers three arguments for the differences among African American and White women: (1) African American women may develop a strong positive self-valuation and an alternative beauty aesthetic to resist societal stigmatization, (2) African American women may be less likely to acquire eating disorders due to differences in the cultural construction of femininity in Black communities, and (3) positive body image among African American women may sometimes reflect a defensive need to deny health problems such as compulsive eating and obesity.

Several societal factors have the potential for contributing to stress and stress-related illnesses. Racism, prejudice, discrimination, and the threat of hate crimes can all act as stressors. Minorities, regardless of their cultural and ethnic backgrounds, can experience stress in housing or work situations where the majority culture (whatever it might be) fails to treat them fairly and equitably. Also, the lack of English-language proficiency and the accompanying problems can result in stress.

Counselors who identify a client's problem as stress or stress-related should look for the actual stressor and, whenever possible, assist the client in reducing the stressful experiences. Still, counselors should not automatically assume that a client's stress is a result of racism, prejudice, and discrimination.

Early Adulthood and Middle Adulthood

Adult concerns differ with each substage (early, middle, late) and with culture and socio-economic status. Concerns associated with specific cultures might include (being careful to avoid basing counseling on stereotypes) high unemployment rates among African Americans, Hispanic Americans, and American Indians; alcoholism among American Indians; acculturation (and attendant rejection of old-world values) of Asian Americans; the portrayal of African American males as violent and prone to drug use; and the emerging role of African American women as family heads.

Racial Identity and Self-Esteem

How adults develop and perceive their racial identity will affect their mental health and overall outlook on life. Developing a positive racial identity can be difficult in U.S. society because of racism, sexism, classism, and heterosexism. The identity development process, initiated during the childhood years, requires each individual to build a sense of self: personal and cultural beliefs, feelings about the self and culture, and perceptions about one's "place" in the overall U.S. society. A close relationship exists between racial identity and self-esteem: Both are intertwined and affect each other. How one feels about one's culture undoubtedly affects feelings about oneself and vice versa.

THE ELDERLY

America's population is undeniably growing older. People are increasingly living longer. Since 1900, the percentage of people over age 65 has grown from 4% to 13%; by the year 2030, 20% of the U.S. population will likely be in that group. The elderly population itself is also aging. Its fastest-growing segment consists of people 85 and older, and by 2030 their number could more than double.

Ethnic diversity is also increasing among the elderly, as in other age groups. By 2030, 25% of older Americans will be members of a minority group. The proportion of older Hispanic Americans is likely to more than triple from 5.1% to 17.4% by 2030, exceeding the older African American population (Papalia et al., 2014).

The graying of the population can be attributed to several factors, primarily high birthrates, high immigration rates during the early to mid-twentieth century, better medical care, and healthier lifestyles. At the same time, the trend toward smaller families has reduced the relative size of younger age groups (Papalia et al., 2014).

Elderly Years: Historical and Contemporary Perspectives

What does it mean to be elderly in a culture that emphasizes youth? What does it mean to be an elderly minority person in such a culture? Chronological age alone is a poor measure of physical condition or aging, especially because elderly people are so diverse in terms of physical, psychosocial, and cognitive abilities. An improved awareness of nutrition, better health care, and improved knowledge of the benefits of exercise have all contributed to healthier lifestyles during the later years. Still, we live in a nation that places emphasis on youth and beauty (although one's perception of beauty depends on one's culture and overall worldviews).

Although views of aging differ within cultures and with individual people, indications are that the European culture favors youthfulness. The elderly are often perceived as incapable of thinking clearly, of learning new things, of enjoying sex, of contributing to the community, and of holding responsible jobs. The elderly in many other cultures, however, do not suffer such negative attitudes. For example, in the Chinese and Japanese cultures, the elderly are accorded a higher status than their American counterparts. Papalia and colleagues (2009) reported that although it is considered rude in most Western countries to ask a person's age, people are often asked their age in other countries (e.g., Japan), so that they can be accorded greater respect and proper deference.

In the United States, aging is generally seen as undesirable. Even today, older people often are categorized in derogatory terms such as "fading fast," "over the hill," "out to pasture," "geezer," and "biddy." Other terms are kinder (e.g., "older Americans," "golden-agers," "senior citizens"), but we seem to be somewhat baffled as to how to describe the elderly, especially those from various cultures.

Stereotypes about elderly people reflect widespread misconceptions: Older people are usually tired, poorly coordinated, and prone to infections and accidents; most of them live in institutions; they can neither remember nor learn; they have no interest in sexual activity; they are isolated from others; they do not use their time productively; that they are grouchy and self-pitying (Papalia, Feldman, & Martorell, 2014).

Myths and stereotypes surrounding the elderly have long cast them in an undesirable light. They are often misunderstood, neglected, and abused. Undoubtedly, the elderly client may present difficult problems for the counselor: Planning appropriate intervention requires an understanding of the declining capacity of the body to function properly and the health problems and concerns that often plague the elderly of differing cultural backgrounds.

Orel (2004) maintains that the gay, lesbian, and bisexual (GLB) senior population is growing, yet there has been little attention given to identifying and understanding the needs of this population. She reports on the results of a series of focus groups and in-depth interviews with GLB elders. The beliefs, attitudes, and opinions of the participants revealed seven major areas of concern: physical health, legal rights, housing, spirituality, family, mental health, and social networks. While the numbers of GLB elders will likely increase during the next few decades, obtaining accurate population numbers is difficult, since sexual orientation as a research variable has been absent in almost all gerontological research. Although attitudes toward people with differing sexual orientations have improved, some GLB elders have been reluctant to come out.

Elderly Development

Changes in physical appearance, such as graying hair, balding, and wrinkling skin, usually indicate advancing age; however, many other less visible changes occur as people age. Understanding the elderly requires conscientious effort, because various cultures perceive and treat the elderly differently.

Desselle and Proctor (2000) reported that one in four adults aged 65 through 74 years is hearing impaired, and almost two in five adults aged 75 and older experience disabling hearing loss. Hearing impairment is an "invisible disability," and these authors want social workers to be aware that sounds amplified by hearing aids may be fuzzy, unclear, and confusing. In addition, hearing aids amplify background noises and jumble sounds the user is trying to hear. Although Desselle and Proctor (2000) wrote their article primarily for social workers, their conclusions and recommendations are also relevant for counselors with hearing-impaired clients:

- Face the person, maintain eye contact, speak slowly, pause between words, and enunciate each word clearly.
- Speak in a louder tone, but do not shout or yell (which can embarrass these clients).
- Never speak directly into the person's ear, to do so will eliminate visual cues.
- After finishing a thought, check with the person to determine whether he or she understands what was said.
- If the client is having trouble understanding a phrase, try rephrasing it.
- Be an advocate. If someone is ignoring the hearing-impaired person, explain that the hearing-impaired person is interested in what is being said.
- Be patient and treat the client with respect.
- Help these clients accept the natural consequences of hearing impairment by teaching them to be assertive and to cultivate a sense of humor about inevitable conversation errors.
- Get the client's attention before beginning to speak.

Gender Differences

Gender differences exist among the elderly, just as they do among individuals in the other three lifespan stages (see the list that follows entitled "Selected Gender Differences in the Elderly"). Some characteristics are gender specific (such as reproductive system problems), whereas others such as sleeping difficulties, sexual relations, and suicide vary among individuals. Therefore, when counseling elderly women and men, awareness of selected gender characteristics can be worthwhile, but it does not eliminate the need to assess women and men as individuals.

Health Problems and Concerns of the Elderly

There are common misperceptions about the health status of the elderly. Most people over age 65 do not have to limit any significant activities for health reasons, and not until age 85 do more than half of the elderly population report such limitations. Even those aged 85 and older are usually able to take care of their own basic needs. Thus the stereotype of the elderly as helpless is not based on reality Papalia, Feldman, and Martorell (2014). This is not meant to imply, however, that the health problems of the elderly do not warrant special attention.

Selected Gender Differences in the Elderly

- Men and women have varying sleeping difficulties, a trend that starts earlier for men than women; until age 70 or 80, men experience more sleep disturbances than women, probably due to enlargement of the prostate gland (causing more frequent urination) and sleep apnea, a condition where breathing stops for 10 seconds or longer.
- Nearly 50% of women aged 65 and older are widowed, compared with only 15% of men.
- Among unmarried people over 65, about 70% of men and 50% of women have sex occasionally.

- Women experience a greater dissatisfaction when marital dissatisfaction exists—they usually try to confront marital problems in an attempt to solve them, which can be taxing to physical and mental health.
- Suicide rates peak during late life, climbing to their highest levels in people aged 75 years and older.

Source: Developed from *Experience Human Development* (13th ed.) by Papalia, Feldman, and Martorell (2014).

Krause (2004) examines the relationships among lifetime exposure to traumatic events, emotional support, and life satisfaction in older adults. He divided his subjects into three groups: the old-old (65–74 years old), the older-old (75–84 years old), and the oldest-old (85 years and older). Examples of traumatic events include a spouse or child dying, a child given up shortly after birth, life-threatening illness or accident, or a near-fatal accident. Life satisfaction includes statements of one's opinion of her or his life. Emotional support includes the support one has been given within the past year. Krause (2004) suggests older adults who have been exposed to lifetime trauma are at risk; elderly who do not have sufficient emotional support should be included in the intervention group, especially the oldest-old group; and third, when working with members of the oldest-old group, the results indicate that elders who encountered traumatic events between the ages of 18 and 64 appear to be the most vulnerable.

The need to consider the cultural aspects of health is becoming increasingly clear. Keeping in mind individual differences, as well as differing environmental conditions, we can now summarize the health problems facing the elderly in several cultures.

African Americans

African Americans have a number of risk factors (Papalia et al., 2014).

- Almost one-third of the excessive mortality of middle-aged African Americans can be traced to six risk factors: high blood pressure, high cholesterol levels, obesity, diabetes, smoking, and alcohol intake.
- The death rate for middle-aged African Americans is nearly twice that for European Americans.
- Almost twice as many African Americans as European Americans ages 45 to 64 die of heart disease, close to one and a half times as many die of cancer, and more than three times as many die from stroke.
- About one in three African American adults has hypertension, compared with one in four European Americans; hypertension accounts for one in five deaths of African Americans, twice the number occurring in European Americans.
- African American women are at higher risk of hypertension and are more likely to be overweight than European American Women.

Elder abuse also occurs among elderly African Americans, just as in all cultures. Elder abuse is a difficult term to define and depends on how physicians, social workers, lawyers, or other professionals choose to define it. It is often a catchall term used to describe physical maltreatment, financial exploitation, neglect (by self or others), misuse of medication, violation of rights, and psychological abuse. Regardless of the definition and type, elderly African

Americans are increasingly susceptible to abuse and deserve the attention of mental health professionals.

American Indians

The average life expectancy for American Indians is only 65 years, eight years less than that of European Americans. The major health problems of elderly American Indians are tuberculosis, diabetes, liver and kidney disease, high blood pressure, pneumonia, and malnutrition. The majority of elderly American Indians rarely visit a physician, primarily because they often live in isolated areas and lack transportation. Other reasons relate to a long-standing reliance on ritual folk healing and a different cultural understanding of disease.

Asian Americans

Hypertension, tuberculosis, and certain types of cancers are major health concerns of elderly Asians and Pacific Islanders. This population is less likely to use formal health-care services, such as those reimbursed under Medicare, primarily because of cultural and language differences, a reliance on folk medicine, and a distrust of Western medicine.

European Americans

The concerns of elderly European Americans include health problems and long-term illnesses and hospital care, fear of living alone, lack of financial means, inability to deal with medical professionals and social service workers, and increased medical bills. They also experience lack of physical mobility and terminal diseases and often worry a great deal about health concerns and about paying for needed medical care.

Hispanic Americans

Twenty-four percent of Hispanic Americans aged 65 and over live in poverty, which contributes to their health problems and overall poor living conditions. Also, Hispanics between the ages of 65 and 84 experience health problems at a greater rate than the general population. Primary health problems in this population include cardiovascular disease and diabetes (Berk, 2008).

Educational, occupational, and income advantages of Cuban Americans in early adulthood may translate into better overall health for them, compared with other Hispanics. The greater impoverishment of Puerto Ricans points to higher morbidity rates among this population compared with Cuban Americans and Mexican Americans. A larger proportion of older Cuban Americans and Puerto Ricans reported more illnesses than Mexican Americans. A significantly smaller proportion of Mexican Americans than Cubans and Puerto Ricans reported being hospitalized during the past 12 months (Berk, 2008).

Some other statistics include:

* Central/South American men and Puerto Rican women are most likely to live alone.
* Central/South American women and Cuban men are most likely to live with family.
* Cuban women prefer living alone relative to living with family members.
* Older Central/South American men may have migrated as individual workers rather than as household heads and consequently have few kin available for coresidence.

SUMMARY

Counselors need to understand the insights that can be gained from understanding multicultural differences from a lifespan perspective. Counselors who work with clients at the four lifespan stages face several challenges that have potential for improving the counseling intervention and enhancing the client-counselor relationship, including

- understanding the historical and contemporary perspectives of each lifespan stage;
- understanding the importance of human growth and development in the counseling process;
- understanding that clients differ both within and across cultures; and
- understanding the complex relationship among counseling, culture, and human growth and development.

SUGGESTED READINGS

Goldsmith, J.S., & Kurpius, S.E. Robinson. (2015). Older adults and integrated health settings: Opportunities and challenges for mental health counselors. *Journal of Mental Health Counseling, 37*(2), 124–137. The growing number of older adults and the increasing recognition and growth of integrated health teams are creating expanded career opportunities for mental health counselors (MHCs).

Hayden, L., Cook, A., Scherer, A., Greenspan, S. Silva, M.R., Cadet, M., & Maki, E. (2014). Integrating physical activity, coach collaboration, and life skill development in youth: School counselors' perceptions. *Journal of School Counseling, 12*(3), 1–38. Given the social, emotional, and academic benefits of physical activity related to youth development coupled with the minimal research regarding how school counselors can use physical activity for life skill development, this article focuses on school counselors' beliefs about collaborating with coaches and using physical activity to develop life skills.

Konstam, V., Cook, A.L., Tomek, S., Mahdavi, E., Gracia, R., & Bayne, A.H. (2015). What factors sustain professional growth among school counselors? *Journal of School Counseling, 13*(3), 1–40. This study examined relationships among self-reported professional expertise, organizational support of evidence-based practices (EBP), and professional growth—school counselors with higher self-reported expertise reported that they were more likely to improve their school counseling skills.

Qasqas, M.J., & Jerry, P. (2014). Counselling Muslims: A culture-infused antidiscriminatory approach. *Canadian Journal of Counselling & Psychotherapy, 48*(1), 57–76. There are approximately 1.57 billion Muslims in the world, with approximately 940,000 living in Canada—despite the high numbers and anticipated growth of this population, there still exists a dearth of research on the worldviews and intracultural differences of Muslims.

Smith, A., & Koltz, R.L. (2015). Supervision of school counseling students: A focus on personal growth, wellness, and development. *Journal of School Counseling, 13*(2), 1–34. The researchers used focus groups over a two-year period to better comprehend students' experiences of growth, e.g., defining personal growth, wellness, and clinical growth, as a professional school counselor.

5 Understanding African American Clients

QUESTIONS TO BE EXPLORED

• What are the childhood, adolescent, adult, and elderly years like in the African American culture?
• What social and cultural, familial, religious, and communication characteristics describe African Americans along the lifespan continuum?
• What unique challenges (e.g., social injustices, discrimination, and prejudices) face African Americans during the various lifespan stages?
• What unique challenges face counselors providing mental health services to African Americans in the four lifespan stages?
• What sources of information are available for counselors intervening with African American children, adolescents, adults, and elders?

OVERVIEW

Counselors who work effectively with African American children, adolescents, adults, and elderly recognize the challenges associated with each lifespan stage as well as the rich diversity of African American culture. Providing appropriate counseling intervention for African American clients requires an understanding of each individual's culture, family, and communication, all of which interact in a complex fashion to create clients with unique needs. Effective counselors also recognize and gain an understanding of the decades of racism and discrimination that the African American people have experienced. This chapter examines African Americans in all stages of the lifespan continuum and explores counseling issues germane to these clients.

AFRICAN AMERICANS: DEMOGRAPHICS

Black or African Americans include persons of any origin in any of the Black racial groups of Africa. The term includes people who indicate their race as "Black," "African American," or "Negro," or who report entities such as African American, Kenyan, Nigeria, or Haitian (U.S. Census Bureau, 2015d).

African Americans comprise one of the nation's largest ethnic minority groups. In fact, projected population numbers suggest that African Americans will increase from 41.2 million in 2012 to 61.8 million in 2060, from 13.1% to 14.7% (U.S. Census Bureau, 2015a). In addition, the African American population is young, and one can project significant birth rates in the next several decades. Although significant numbers of African Americans live in metropolitan areas such as New York; Detroit; Washington, D.C.; New Orleans; Baltimore; Chicago; and Memphis, the majority of African Americans live in the South (55%), 18% live in the Northeast and Midwest, and 9% live in the West. Selected states with significant numbers of

African Americans include New York, Florida, Texas, Georgia, California, Illinois, and North Carolina. Mental health professionals practicing in metropolitan areas will increasingly work with significant numbers of African Americans; however, many African Americans continue to live in rural areas in the South and will need professional intervention for problems throughout their lifespan continuum.

While this section looks only at population numbers and regions of residences, other figures in this chapter focus on the age of children, educational attainment, socioeconomic factors (e.g., poverty rates), marital status, and family characteristics.

AFRICAN AMERICAN CHILDREN

Social and Cultural Description

Describing African American children requires an understanding of the differences within their culture. Lower, middle, and higher socioeconomic groups live differently; likewise, significant differences characterize urban and rural African Americans. Table 5.1 shows population numbers for African American children. Numbers appear to be increasing, especially during the first decade of the twenty-first century.

The number of African American students enrolled in U.S. schools has fluctuated widely, and in some cases, actually decreased. Still, counselors will be called upon to intervene with African American children and adolescents. One reason is that African American children interact with two cultures on a daily basis: the African American culture of their home/neighborhood and other cultures in schools and other social institutions. It is important for counselors to remember that the actions of other children and sometimes adults may cause feelings of inferiority in African American children. Such thinking results from the culturally deficient model in which people consider cultural differences to be inferior. African American children should be afforded the opportunity to grow up in a society in which unique characteristics are considered different rather than deficient.

Governmental social programs such as Head Start and Follow-Through have undoubtedly improved the lives of many African American children. Still, many African American children under the age of 18 (number 4,008,000 or 39%) continue to live below the federal poverty level (Annie E. Casey Foundation, 2014).

These numbers provide a bleak picture of the future of many Black children. Unfortunately, the self-concept may be the most influential factor in a child's development. African American children's self-concepts (i.e., what children think of themselves, their abilities, and their culture) influence not only academic achievement but also many other social and psychological aspects of their development. For example, African American children may tend to accept others' views, either negative or positive, of themselves and their culture. Racism and discrimination undoubtedly have affected the African American community; however, increased pride in the African American experience has resulted in considerable gains relative to African American self-concept. Other gains may be attributed to African American parents fostering positive self-concept development in their children. Self-concept is also affected by children's perceptions of their socioeconomic status and the problems associated with being poor and disadvantaged.

Table 5.1 Population: African American Children

Age	Number
Under 5 years	2,840,429
5 to 14 years	5,846,346

Source: Adapted from U.S. Census Bureau. (2015b). *Sex by age (Black or African American alone, 2009–2013 American Community Survey 5 year estimates).* Washington, DC: Author.

Counselors and educators should also objectively consider the African American child's achievement (which is closely related to self-concept), rather than rely on traditional stereotypes of achievement expectations. Although some African American students lag behind other students on standardized tests, there is considerable controversy about where the responsibility for lower academic performance lies. School officials often blame the child's "disadvantaged" or "culturally deprived" home. Although we believe children may be "disadvantaged," we do not agree with the term "culturally deprived." Black children have cultures of their own (e.g., culture, race, lifespan period, and socioeconomic status); however, some of their cultural experiences might not be conducive to school success. One has to be very careful about stereotyping all Black children as being underachievers. Some educators now call for effective schools where teachers have an objective understanding of African American children and similar expectations for these children as well as for children from other cultural backgrounds.

Communication

The degree to which African American children experience communication problems varies considerably with socioeconomic class, geographic location, and language of the parents. Children of educated and socially mobile urban African American parents may speak a different dialect than children of rural parents of a lower socioeconomic status.

African American children are likely to face several problems:

- Their dialect, albeit an excellent means of communication in the African American culture, might result in communication difficulties and other problems generally associated with not being understood by the majority culture.
- Their self-esteem might be lowered as they hear negative statements about their dialect and are urged to change to a more standard form of English.
- Children might not experience communication difficulties at home or in the neighborhood; however, problems may result when speech patterns vary considerably between home/neighborhood and school settings. Children's communication skills often determine their scores on intelligence and achievement tests or, perhaps more accurately, linguistic intelligence.

What directions should counselors take when working with African American children? Rather than imply that Black dialect is wrong, inferior, or substandard, they should attempt to understand the role that dialect plays for people who have experienced a history of injustice and struggle for survival. Counselors should not expect African American children to change their dialect during counseling sessions or to abandon it in all situations in favor of Standard English; however, African American children and their educators should understand the frustrations and problems that might result from speaking differently among people who speak predominantly Standard English.

Families

African American children grow up in homes that may be very different from other cultures. Two examples follow.

1. African Americans rely extensively on family kinship networks, which include blood relatives and close friends called *kin*. Young African American children are often taken into the households of their grandparents. These arrangements reflect a sense of family responsibility; that is, children belong to an extended family, not merely to the parents. Consequently, uncles, aunts, cousins, and grandparents all exert considerable authority in the family and are responsible for the care and rearing of children and for teaching them appropriate skills and values. These strong kinship bonds probably originated from the African ethos of survival of the tribe

and the oneness of being. Kinship care can be an important factor in an examination of African American families.

Kinship care is the full-time nurturing and protection of children by relatives subsequent to a legal parent-child separation. In most cases, these children have been removed from parents' homes because of neglect or abuse. African Americans represent the largest percentage of children in kinship care. These children encounter numerous challenges—they frequently contend with economic hardship and the stress associated with the estrangement from their birth parents. One problem or challenge is that 50% of African American children live in a familial situation without a father present (U.S. Census Bureau, 2015h).

Such challenges suggest the most critical family dynamic is adaptability or the ability to adjust to family roles in response to change—kinship caregivers with resilient children demonstrated a clear awareness of new family issues. Virtually all kinship caregivers believed that the immediate family was close—they emphasized themes such as loyalty and interdependence and also felt open communication promoted their sense of family cohesion.

Brandon (2007) maintains that weak connections still exist between African Americans and schools, despite the advantages of parental involvement. Several reasons might explain this disconnect. First, cultural and language differences might result in conflicts between parents and schools. Second, some parents might assume it is the schools' responsibility to educate their children. Third, cultural and school expectations for achievement and behavior might exist. Other reasons might include the high proportion of parents living in poverty or single parents who simply do not have the time to become involved in school activities. Brandon (2007) also calls for educators and counselors to collect information from parents about their perceptions of the racial climate in the school.

Religion is another important aspect of African American life; however, there has been little research focused on the role of religion in the development of the African American child. More attention has been focused on religion with respect to the civil rights movement, economic leadership, and the quest for equal opportunities. It is clear, though, that children perceive the church as a hub of social life, friendship, the provider of a peer group, advice and comfort, and a source of leadership in the community.

Islam and African American Families

Raising children in an Islamic family in a non-Islamic society is a difficult task. Some African American Muslims enroll their children in public or private secular schools; others may home-school or educate their children in private Islamic schools.

Children in these families are sometimes subject to all the pressures of the lifespan period as well as challenges associated with defining their identity and the place that Islam has in their lives. Because of the restriction on dress, girls will often struggle with wearing a hijab in their adolescence unless they are in a supportive community. Some Muslim girls who go to secular high schools wear a hijab, but others choose not to because of negative stereotypes about covering their hair. Parents must work very hard to ensure that their children have a large enough peer group with whom to relate. Muslim women are not supposed to marry non-Muslim men, but Muslim men may marry outside their religion as long as their intended wife believes in the oneness of God (e.g., Christian, Jewish). Because the man is expected to be the spiritual leader in the home, a woman is thought to be vulnerable to oppression for her beliefs if she marries a non-Muslim.

Maslim and Bjorck (2009) conducted some interesting research on reasons for conversion to Islam in the United States. It is important to say that only 38% of their participants were African American, but the authors still offer some excellent information about reasons some women convert to Islam. Reasons included Islamic views against secular values, dissatisfaction with former faiths, the need to solidify one's identity, the appeal of Islamic views regarding gender and ethnicity, and an appreciation for the Islamic tenets. The researchers concluded that the decision to become a Muslim was a thought-out decision based on sound beliefs and reasoning.

Religion has always played an important role in many African Americans' lives. A complex relationship exists between African Americans' family and religious beliefs, regardless of the specific religion. Counselors can neither ignore nor condemn the family's religious background. Successful counseling intervention will depend on an acceptance of the family's and the child's religious beliefs—and this acceptance will include a knowledge of and appreciation for the client's religious beliefs.

Unique Challenges Confronting African American Children

African American children growing up in an increasingly multicultural society face difficult problems that can impede their overall development into adulthood. These problems result from their culture being different from mainstream American culture and from years of discrimination and misunderstanding with respect to their culture and their developmental period. Communication barriers, lower academic achievement, and poor self-esteem are a few problems that confront these children. Thus it is imperative that counselors and other professionals consider individual differences rather than perpetuate stereotypical images of the African American child—not all African American children are struggling and problem-laden. Counselors need to take into account individuality among African American children and recognize that motivation and determination are powerful determinants of success, even in the face of hardship.

Case Study 5.1 describes Carl, an African American child.

Case Study 5.1: Carl, an African American Child

Five-year-old Carl lives with his mother, father, grandmother, one older brother, and two older sisters in a lower-middle-class neighborhood in a large city. Several aunts and uncles and six cousins live in the immediate neighborhood. William, his father, has completed 11 years of schooling and works in a local manufacturing plant. His mother, Cynthia, has had a similar formal education. She works as a hospital aide.

Carl spends a considerable amount of time with his grandmother. He considers his aunts and uncles to be "parents away from home." He visits them often and plays with his cousins and other children in the neighborhood. The closeness of the family has its advantages. When Carl is ill and unable to attend kindergarten, he stays home with his grandmother or at the homes of other relatives; hence, his parents do not have to miss work.

Carl's neighborhood is predominantly African American, although several Puerto Rican and Cuban families have recently rented houses in the area. Carl already realizes that people of different ethnic groups have different customs and lifestyles. He attends the neighborhood integrated school with a racial composition that is approximately 50% African American, 30% European American, and 20% Hispanic American. The teachers are predominantly middle-class African Americans. Although Carl tries in school, his readiness scores and performance on kindergarten objectives place him below average. His teacher assumes that his problems stem from a poor home environment and blames Carl and his parents for the difficulties. Carl's self-esteem is low; sometimes he blames himself for not doing as well as the other children. Although his dialect works well with his parents and in the neighborhood, it is not viewed favorably at school. Sometimes he does not understand his teacher or class materials. The teacher frequently corrects Carl's speech because, she says, students will need to use "correct English" when they enter the real world.

Reflection Questions:

1. Is Carl beginning to think one culture (or socioeconomic class) is wrong and one right? Will he conclude from his middle-class teachers that his life experiences are socioeconomically different or inferior?
2. What are the positive or negative effects of his teacher correcting his speech? (Remember, his dialect works well with his parents and in his neighborhood.)
3. What will an effective counselor perceive Carl's future challenges might be at present?

AFRICAN AMERICAN ADOLESCENTS

Social and Cultural Description

Census reports indicate that 3,315,656 African Americans aged 15 to 19 currently reside in the United States, and these numbers are expected to increase significantly by 2025 and 2050 due to the high birth rates of African Americans (U.S. Census Bureau, 2015b).

Counselors should expect to see increasing numbers of African American clients in this developmental period. Undoubtedly, some adolescents will seek counseling at school, while others will have court-ordered counseling. Seeking counseling, of course, is not limited to African American adolescents—adolescence can be a challenging period for all cultures.

Counselors with an understanding of the African American culture will appreciate the predicament of many African American adolescents. These adolescents want to retain the cultural heritage with which they feel comfortable; however, they may also believe that some acculturation must take place for their economic and psychological survival. A balance must be struck whereby African American adolescents can retain their cultural heritage and at the same time achieve success in a pluralistic society. African American youth face several challenges that effective counselors will at least consider: identity development, stereotypes of the culture and developmental period, delinquent and criminal behavior, and high school graduation rates.

Identity development is a major task for all adolescents but more so for racial and ethnic minorities given their often oppressive environments. Unfortunately, many African American youth have numerous obstacles to overcome, such as poverty, substandard housing, and inferior schools. In addition, their socialization and identity development occur in the context of racial discrimination and oppression, an environment that is not conducive to mental health.

African American adolescents face overcoming the stigma of negative social stereotypes; too often they are portrayed as school dropouts, drug abusers, and lawbreakers. Negative stereotypes used to describe the African American culture and the adolescent lifespan period lower the self-esteem of these adolescents. It is imperative that counselors recognize the considerable individual differences among African American adolescents rather than automatically stereotyping them.

While all cultures have adolescents with delinquent and criminal behavior, Bell (2007), in her research, looked at gender and gangs. Bell used the National Longitudinal Study of

Adolescent Health to address whether males and females differ in risk factors associated with gang memberships (e.g., community characteristics, parent-child relationships, and association with deviant friends). Integrating theory and research from social disorganization, social control, and feminist perspectives on crime/delinquency, few differences were found between boys and girls in terms of risk factors associated with gang membership and outcomes associated with gang involvement. Instead, the results indicate that parental control, attachment, and involvement; school safety; peer fighting; age; sex; and race similarly influence boys' and girls' gang preferences.

Although African American youth accounted for only 17% of the youth population ages 10–17, African American juveniles were involved in 51% of juvenile Violent Crime Index and 32% of juvenile Property Crime Index arrests (Dinkes, Kemp, Baum, & Snyder, 2009). Such an occurrence can be attributed to many factors, such as self-fulfilling prophecies (often prejudicial and stereotypical) that African American youth will misbehave, outright discrimination, and racism.

Caire (2009) claims that hundreds of thousands of African American students do not graduate from high school. Some specific numbers for African Americans' graduation rates include Indianapolis, Indiana (19%); Detroit, Michigan (20%); Norfolk, Virginia (27%); and Rochester, New York (47%). He also questions the economic losses of children, families, and our economy as well as the vast amounts of money spent on prisons (Caire, 2009). More attention to individuals' worldviews, cultural perceptions, and improved educational opportunities for diverse learners has the potential for improving graduation rates.

Communication

Appreciation of one's own language and communication styles, along with the development of communication skills sufficient for understanding others and for being understood, significantly influences an adolescent's ability to adjust to societal expectations. Emphasis should be placed on understanding and accepting adolescents' valuing of their language and communication styles rather than on subscribing to a language-deficit belief in which some languages are judged to be unworthy and destined for extinction.

The dialect of African Americans, sometimes called Black English (or African American Language (AAL) or Ebonics), is used in varying degrees, depending on the individual person and the situation. Its widespread use among African Americans continues to arouse concern among people who do not understand the language, its background, and the African American culture. Some educators question whether language differences may result in severe consequences for African American students, both during school and later in the workplace. The importance of one's language and communication style cannot be underestimated.

Some people have sought to change the African American dialect—some, no doubt with good intentions. The African American dialect, however, persists as an integral aspect of the culture for several reasons. First, it provides a vehicle for expressing the uniqueness of the African American culture. Second, it binds African Americans together and traverses the barriers of education and social position.

Rather than perceive the Black dialect as wrong or substandard, the counselor should help these adolescents understand that Black English is a unique and valuable aspect of their culture. As they develop into adulthood and into an ever-widening social world, they must also be made to realize the implications of using a language that is not wholeheartedly accepted by the majority culture. During the crucial time of moving away from the safe confines of family and home, adolescents will benefit from speaking a language that is accepted and understood outside the predominantly African American community. Feeling and being understood in their own community but being rejected by the prevailing culture has the potential for damaging self-concept and retarding development.

Families

Counselors intervening with African American adolescents need to understand the African American family from a historical perspective rather than allow misconceptions and stereotypes to cloud their perceptions. Throughout centuries of cultural oppression and repression, the African American family has developed an appreciation for extended family networks. The family plays a crucial role in determining an adolescent's capacity and readiness to develop a sense of self and an identity.

Understanding African American family customs contributes to effective counseling intervention. Also, European American counselors and counselors from other cultures will benefit from an objective understanding of the adolescent developmental period. It should be recognized that not all African American adolescents experience role confusion. They are not all impoverished or uneducated. Nor do they all come from single-parent households. African American adolescents must be perceived in a more objective light.

Considerable concern has been expressed for adolescent identity formation, especially in African American households and in single-parent homes from which the father is absent. A disturbing number of African American families live in poverty, and there is a growing trend of female-headed families and households. The number of children living with their mothers without a father present varied widely among racial groups in 2009, from 8% for Asian American children and adolescents to 50% for African Americans (U.S. Census Bureau, 2015a). Two points should be noted: First, it is important for counselors to avoid blaming the victim for her or his poverty status, and second, it is important to understand the dire long-term consequences of poverty. High unemployment, mass incarceration rates, prejudice, and discrimination all contributed to African American poverty.

Unique Challenges Confronting African American Adolescents

African American adolescents face several challenges that will significantly influence their identity development and transition into adulthood. First, they must accept the challenge of combating the racism and discrimination that have plagued their culture for decades. Second, they must reject stereotypes of their culture and developmental period. Acceptance of misperceptions and stereotypes precludes an objective examination of one's personal abilities and, without doubt, may retard the development of a cultural identity and a strong self-concept. Third, they must develop identities that embody the African American culture; adolescence; and their own individual abilities, skills, and characteristics. Doing otherwise results in role confusion and a loss of potential. The shift from two-parent to one-parent families influenced African American children and adolescents, just as they have the offspring of all people. A larger proportion of births occurred to unmarried women in 2015, thus increasing the proportion of never-married parents. A partial explanation is that the delay of marriage increased the likelihood of nonmarital birth. Another factor was the growth of divorce among couples with children. These trends may have important implications for the well-being of children and for the programs and policies that relate to welfare, family leave, child care, and other areas of work and family. We are not saying that one-parent homes are bad for children and adolescents, but we do think that single parents, whether female or male, experience more economic, social, and parenting hardships.

African American adolescents are also challenged to understand the importance and necessity of education in their lives. Adolescents living in poor neighborhoods often perceive little reward from working for academic achievement and may underestimate their opportunities. Counselors can make significant contributions when they help these adolescents understand the benefits of education.

Case Study 5.2 focuses on Tyrone, an African American adolescent.

Case Study 5.2: Tyrone, an African American Adolescent

Tyrone, a 16-year-old African American, is in the ninth grade and lives with his parents, grandmother, younger brother, and two younger sisters. Because most of Tyrone's relatives also live in his lower-middle-class neighborhood, he enjoys the extended family network. Tyrone feels free to visit his relatives in their homes, and they often spend time at his home. When Tyrone cannot attend school because of illness, he usually goes to the home of his adolescent cousins.

Tyrone has experienced several "identity crises." He has questioned his success in developing from childhood to adulthood, and he has also questioned the significance of being African American in an increasingly diverse society. Although he has learned much about his cultural heritage and is proud to be African American, he also realizes he might have limited opportunities. Also, being an adolescent has not been easy. Even though his parents and siblings view him as "not yet grown," his peers think he is ready for adult activities. Should he listen to his family, or should he go along with his friends?

Another problem confronting Tyrone is his education. Quite frankly, he is not sure he will graduate from high school. His grades in elementary school were below average, but his grades are even lower now, and this is his second year in the ninth grade. He thinks he could do the work, but his recent academic record discourages him, and he admits to a changing world of many interests. He does not have many behavior problems in school (except perhaps talking with his friends too much at times), but he thinks his teachers are not too interested in him. Also, although he has both African American and European American teachers, he doubts whether any of them really understand what it is like being an African American adolescent in a large school. His parents talk with him often about the importance of education and encourage him to do his best work, but neither parent is able to help him much with homework.

Tyrone continues to speak his dialect. He communicates well with his parents, extended family, and friends. In fact, he is proud of his Black English, even though his teachers do not like it. Language puzzles Tyrone. His teachers "don't sound right," he says. It appears, however, that he will have to be the one to change.

Reflection Questions:

1. What is the relationship between Tyrone's language and culture? Does culture affect language or vice versa? Or both?
2. What professional interventions might contribute to his African American identity, his questioning of his school and teachers, and his "identity crises," for example, his developmental period, cultural background, and socioeconomic status?

AFRICAN AMERICAN ADULTS

Social and Cultural Description

Describing the African American population is difficult because of its tremendous diversity. Differences resulting from social class, intracultural aspects, sexual orientations, geographic location, educational attainment, and individuality contribute to the tremendous diversity of the African American people.

Familial structure can have a significant influence on child rearing, economic status, and psychological satisfaction. In 2011, there were 8,726,419 African American households in the United States. Of these, 3,804,021were married. Other family structures included 836,460 male householders and 4,085,938 female householders (U.S. Census Bureau, 2015c).

African Americans are disproportionately affected by poverty, food insecurity, and unemployment. They are also more likely to receive emergency food assistance than their Latino and White, non-Hispanic peers. According to the 2012 U.S. Census Bureau American Community Survey, the poverty rate for all African Americans in 2012 was 28.1%, which is an increase from 25.5% in 2005. Actually, the poverty rate increased between 2005 and 2012 for every demographic of African Americans except those ages 65 and over who experienced a decrease from 21.2% to 19%. Black families with children under 18 headed by a single mother have the highest rate of poverty (U.S. Census Bureau, 2015c) at 47.5 compared to only 8.4% of married-couple Black families.

In 2010, the poverty threshold was $22,314 for a family of four. Among racial and ethnic groups, African Americans had the highest poverty rate, 27.4%, followed by Hispanics at 26.6% and Whites at 9.9%. Nearly 46% of young Black children (under age six) live in poverty, compared with 14.5% of White children. Workers earning poverty-level wages are disproportionately female, Black, Hispanic, or between the ages of 18 and 25.

In 2013, African Americans were nearly twice as likely to be unemployed (13%) as their White non-Hispanic counterparts were (7%). African Americans are three times as likely to receive assistance through the Feeding America network compared with their White non-Hispanic peers. Median income for African American households ($34,600) is significantly lower than their non-Hispanic White counterparts ($58,300). Poverty rates for African Americans (27%) in 2013 were nearly triple that of non-Hispanic Whites (10%). Twelve percent of African Americans live in deep poverty (less than 50% of the federal poverty threshold), compared with 6% of all people in the United States. Counselors and other professionals must avoid the temptation to "blame the victim." Poverty is caused by a number of factors (many of which African Americans cannot control), including decades of discrimination, social injustices, prejudice, and lack of educational opportunities.

The high incidence of health problems in African American males is so serious that their life expectancy is declining. African Americans experience disturbingly high rates of HIV. In fact, African Americans are the racial/ethnic group most affected by HIV. The rate of new HIV infection in African Americans is eight times that of Whites based on population size. Gay and bisexual men account for most new infections among African Americans; young gay and bisexual men aged 13 to 24 are the most affected of this group.

African Americans accounted for an estimated 44% of all new HIV infections among adults and adolescents (aged 13 years or older) in 2010, despite representing only 12% of the U.S. population; considering the smaller size of the African American population in the United States, this represents a population rate that is eight times that of Whites overall. In 2010, men accounted for 70% (14,700) of the estimated 20,900 new HIV infections among all adult and adolescent African Americans. The estimated rate of new HIV infections for African American men (103.6/100,000 population) was seven times that of White men, twice that of Latino men, and nearly three times that of African American women. In 2010, African American gay, bisexual, and other men who have sex with men represented an estimated 72% (10,600) of new infections among all African American men and 36% of an estimated 29,800 new HIV infections among all gay and bisexual men. More new HIV infections (4,800) occurred among young African American gay and bisexual men (aged 13–24) than any other subgroup of gay and bisexual men. In 2010, African American women accounted for 6,100 (29%) of the estimated new HIV infections among all adult and adolescent African Americans. This number represents a decrease of 21% since 2008. Most new HIV infections among African American women (87% or 5,300) are attributed to heterosexual contact. The estimated rate of new HIV infections for African American women (38.1/100,000 population) was 20 times that of White women and almost 5 times that of Hispanic/Latino women (Centers for Disease Control, 2013).

A problem related to poverty and AIDS is African Americans' health insurance coverage, but this should be changing and improving with the Affordable Care Act. The cumulative effects of health disadvantages and the tendency to avoid medical visits until conditions are serious predispose African American adults to higher incidences of chronic disability and illness.

The African American culture is diverse in many ways: social class—urban, suburban, or rural—as well as geographical regions of the United States. Another area of diversity is their religious beliefs. While the United States is generally considered a highly religious nation, African Americans are markedly more religious on a variety of measures than the U.S. population as a whole, including level of affiliation with a religion, attendance at religious services, frequency of prayer, and religion's importance in life. Compared with other racial and ethnic groups, African Americans are among the most likely to report a formal religious affiliation, with fully 87% of African Americans describing themselves as belonging to one religious group or another, according to the U.S. Religious Landscape Survey conducted in 2007 by the Pew Research Center's Forum on Religion & Public Life. Latinos also report affiliating with a religion at a similarly high rate of 85%; among the public overall, 83% are affiliated with a religion. As with all cultures, African Americans choose a number of individual religions: Evangelical Protestant (15%), historically Black Protestant (59%), Catholic (5%), unaffiliated (12%), and other (5%). (Note: Due to rounding, the total does not equal 100%).

The Landscape Survey also finds that nearly eight in ten African Americans (79%) say religion is very important in their lives, compared with 56% among all U.S. adults. In fact, even a large majority (72%) of African Americans who are unaffiliated with any particular faith say religion plays at least a somewhat important role in their lives; nearly half (45%) of unaffiliated African Americans say religion is very important in their lives, roughly three times the percentage who says this among the religiously unaffiliated population overall (16%). Indeed, on this measure, unaffiliated African Americans more closely resemble the overall population of Catholics (56% say religion is very important) and mainline Protestants (52%).

Additionally, several measures illustrate the distinctiveness of the Black community when it comes to religious practices and beliefs. More than half of African Americans (53%) report attending religious services at least once a week, more than three in four (76%) say they pray on at least a daily basis and nearly nine in ten (88%) indicate they are absolutely certain that God exists. On each of these measures, African Americans stand out as the most religiously committed racial or ethnic group in the nation. Even those African Americans who are unaffiliated with any religious group pray nearly as often as the overall mainline population (Pew Research Center, 2009).

Undoubtedly, the Black church, as an institution, has been a vital social, economic, and political resource for the African American community. Churches have had a long-standing tradition of actively addressing social needs, organizing educational initiatives, mobilizing economic support for Black businesses, promoting civil rights awareness, and providing a safe haven for the expression of the Black experience. As a social institution, the Black church serves as a significant support network for its congregation. Members experience fellowship, develop friendships, and assist each other in times of need. Churches are also an important support system for families, providing a sense of tradition; moral guidance; and services for parents, children, and the elderly. As a religious institution, the Black church provides spiritual and moral guidance. The church has also been shown to have a positive effect on the health and well-being of its members. Counselors need to understand that the Black church provides a source of strength. They need to be trained to understand the role and function of Black churches in the lives of their members. Counselors also need to understand the importance of religion and spirituality to many African Americans; in fact, the communalism of the Black church environment provides a sense of shared identity, values, and mutual support.

Some African Americans, either by choice or by necessity, have somewhat adopted the social and cultural patterns of the larger society in which they live. Significant cultural adaptation among middle- and upper-class African Americans often makes these groups barely distinguishable culturally from Americans of comparable socioeconomic levels. Some evidence points to an overconforming to middle-class standards in religious observances, dress, sexual behavior, and child-rearing practices.

On the other hand, many African Americans have been influenced by Islam and Islamic values in their search for identity and self-determination. Much of what African Americans learn about Islam comes through organizations or individuals that have attempted to blend the culture of African Americans with the practice of Islam. This reconciliation of culture and religion is not an unusual occurrence in the Islamic world. Although the tenets of the religion do not change from culture to culture, usually each culture puts its distinct cultural stamp on the everyday habits and practices of the religion.

Communication

Considerable differences are found in the speech patterns of African Americans and those of other cultural groups. First, African Americans are more likely to interject such comments as "all right," "make it plain," and "that all right" into conversations, whereas European Americans are more likely to sit quietly or perhaps smile or nod. To the speaker, the oral comments are perceived as signs of encouragement; African Americans do not consider them rude or annoying.

Although the subject is controversial, Black English has been considered a full-fledged linguistic system with the range of inherent variation of all languages. As a language, Black English is systematic and rule-governed in its syntax, phonology, and semantics. The major pronunciation differences between Black English and Standard English include word variability, sound variability, contrast variability, and final consonants. Although some studies have shown that African Americans hold Black English in high regard, other studies indicate that African Americans prefer Standard English. Black English has traditionally been viewed by the dominant culture as an inferior system of communication and its speakers as ignorant or lazy. However, some African Americans engage in code switching (using two or more linguistic varieties)—they speak one dialect or the other, depending on the communicational situation. Although code switching has been espoused as a goal for African Americans, it has not been universally accepted and has been subject to objections; some people consider it racist for African Americans to have to shoulder the entire burden for language and communication.

Still, people's communication styles and their culture often are inseparable. Although not all African Americans speak Black English, the linguistic elements of the language are believed to represent important markers of group identity and group solidarity. This idea holds that African Americans should feel positive about themselves, because it is an important way to distinguish themselves from other groups. Still, negative stereotypes of Black English are often inconsistent with upwardly mobile individuals. To maintain cultural ties and at the same time advance in mainstream society, code switching or switching communication styles becomes the necessary and preferred mode of interaction. In their struggle for equality and self-esteem, African Americans often feel they should balance the need to identify with their own culture with the need to function effectively within the context of the larger dominant culture.

African Americans' nonverbal communication may play an important role in the counseling relationship. Effective counselors understand such communication and work toward correct interpretations. The directness of some African Americans during counseling may be considered offensive or hostile. For example, African Americans, especially males, may act overly confident and unconcerned, which may be a means of defense that limits disclosure, involvement, and revealing embarrassing or difficult issues.

Families

The previously discussed effects of unemployment and underemployment on African American men and their families present a clear problem. One result of unemployment is family disruption, which increases homicide and robbery rates. The high crime rates in urban African American communities appear to stem from the combination of unemployment, economic deprivation, and family disruption. Changes in the family include higher divorce rates, decreased marriage rates, increasing numbers of female-headed households, and increasing percentages of children living in single-parent households. A female householder heads many African American households during difficult economic times. Being a single parent and holding a job can take a tremendous toll. Also, women who have never married represent the large number of females heading households. Another challenge to economic security: the large number of births to unmarried mothers. Consequences of these situations become clear when one considers that most African American children in single-parent households also live in lower socioeconomic circumstances.

Unique Challenges Confronting African American Adults

African Americans face several problems. First, as previously mentioned, dialect differences will present a continuous challenge. Although their distinctive dialect is a unique cultural characteristic, some African Americans are beginning to view it as a handicap to academic and financial success. Second, African Americans must address the problem of their negative image. Third, their low socioeconomic status must also be addressed. Complicating these problems is the fact that many African Americans live in an environment in which social conditions are often detrimental to self-improvement.

Historically, suicide rates for European Americans have exceeded those of African American by a ratio of 2:1. These low rates for African Americans are attributable to misclassification of suicides for African Americans, underreporting due to the heightened stigma associated with suicidal behavior in this population, and the presence of a number of protective factors. Actually, the number of suicides among African Americans may be higher if the number of deaths misclassified as homicides or accidents was included. The rates of suicide in the African American community, particularly among younger men, are on the rise. Also, across racial and ethnic lines, men are four times more likely than women to commit suicide (Kaslow et al., 2004).

In their article, Kaslow et al. (2004) maintain that only recently have investigators examined psychological factors associated with suicidal behavior in African Americans. Their discussion contends that several factors affect suicidal behaviors: psychological, aggression and impulsivity, substance abuse, spirituality and religiosity, and ethnic diversity. The findings have several implications for clinical practice. First, when assessing African Americans, one should query those with elevated levels of psychological distress, aggression, and substance use; maladaptive cognitive processes; and low levels of religiosity, spirituality, and ethnic identity regarding suicidal tendencies and history of suicidal behavior. Second, preventive interventions for suicidal African Americans and those at risk for suicidal behavior should target reducing psychological symptoms, increasing feelings of helpfulness, and reducing substance use via the teaching of effective strategies for the management of aggression.

Case Study 5.3 focuses on Cynthia, an African American adult.

Case Study 5.3: Cynthia, an African American Woman

Cynthia, age 33, considers herself fairly fortunate. Her family consists of her husband, William; two sons, Tyrone and Carl; two daughters, Karen and Jennifer; and the children's grandmother. William has not been laid off recently at the manufacturing plant, and she works as a hospital aide. Although Cynthia knows that William is worried about being laid off, she feels fairly secure about her job. Having William's mother in the home is another plus; she looks after the family when Cynthia is at work.

Cynthia's life is not problem-free, however. Providing for four children is often difficult, especially when William is without work. Furthermore, her own lack of formal education and marketable skills is holding her down. She is also concerned about her lower-middle-class neighborhood, which appears to be deteriorating in several areas. Drugs are becoming increasingly visible, the police are being called more frequently, delinquency and vandalism are more rampant, and it is rumored that there are three cases of AIDS. Just the other day, she thought she overheard Carl ask Tyrone whether he had smoked pot. Cynthia questions whether her children should be growing up in such an environment. She understands the temptations that 5-year-old Carl and 16-year-old Tyrone may experience. Also, she wonders about the safety of her family. She tends to be nonaggressive and has always been opposed to guns in the home. Recent neighborhood events, however, are making her more receptive to William's suggestion of buying a gun for protection. Also, although her two young daughters are not currently on the streets much, they are developing rapidly and will soon be leaving the safe confines of their home.

Cynthia sometimes thinks of herself, too—her frustrations and accomplishments.

Reflection Questions:

1. How would effective counselors intervene with Cynthia? Shouldn't life be more than just work and survival?
2. Considering Cynthia's lifespan period, her being a working mother, and her marketable skills, she has challenges. How can a counselor intervene? Cynthia is not overly concerned at this time, but she has concerns that will likely call for counseling intervention.

AFRICAN AMERICAN ELDERLY

Social and Cultural Description

African American elderly are the fastest growing segment of the African American population. Approximately 20% of African American elderly live in nonmetropolitan areas, and most are concentrated in the Southeast. Table 5.2 shows the population of African Americans 65 and older.

Three closely related factors influence the quality of life of the African American elderly: education, employment, and income.

First, some African American elderly who seek counseling have little formal education. The income levels tend to be lower for elderly African Americans. Lack of income is probably the

Table 5.2 African American Population 65 and Older (in thousands)

Age	Numbers
65–74	1,214,748
75–84	695,585
80–84	291,437
85 and older	250

Source: Adapted from U.S. Census Bureau. (2015b). *Sex by age (Black or African American alone, 2009–2013 American Community Survey 5 year estimates)*. Washington, DC: Author.

most serious problem faced by aging African Americans. Perhaps due to a double jeopardy, elderly African American women are usually worse off financially than African American men and people of other cultural backgrounds.

Second, although housing costs consume a substantial portion of African Americans' incomes, the money spent does not contribute to their general life satisfaction. In addition, increasing rents and maintenance costs cause additional financial hardships for those with fixed incomes. Urban-dwelling elderly African Americans tend to be clustered in low-income areas in the central districts of cities, often in crowded apartments.

Third, elderly African Americans, especially those living in rural areas, experience serious health and social problems. Common health problems include high blood pressure, musculoskeletal disorders, and cancer. (In fact, cancer is a leading cause of mortality among elderly African Americans.) Yet elderly African Americans, especially rural residents, often have limited access to health care. Many elderly African Americans view themselves as sick and disabled and as being in poor health. There is a higher incidence of chronic disease, functional impairments, and risk factors, such as high blood pressure. African American men have the highest incidence of prostate cancer, and they tend to be hospitalized more frequently and for longer periods of time.

On the positive side, religion plays a major role in the lives of many elderly African Americans. Their family-oriented belief system enables them to cope with the stress of their daily lives. Participation in church-related activities is valued early in life and continues to be important later in life. Historically, the church served as a frame of reference for African Americans coping with racial discrimination, and it continues to play a key role in their survival and advancement. The church has been one of the few institutions to remain under African American control and relatively free from the influence of the majority culture. The church often embraces many religions, including the traditional African American Protestant denominations, such as Baptist and Methodist, as well as other, more fundamentalist groups. African American religious services tend to be celebrations; worshipers are inclined to be more demonstrative than worshipers in other cultures are.

Effective counselors should prepare to intervene with African American elders, a quickly growing segment of the geriatric population. Population numbers of African American elders are expected to continue to increase, and, in fact, by the year 2030, they could possibly constitute the highest number of minority elders in the United States, depending on Hispanic influxes and birthrates.

Communication

The aging process takes its toll on the vocal mechanisms, just as it does on the rest of the body. Elderly African Americans' health problems extend to their language mechanisms. Age-related losses can be seen in at least two aspects of language production. The first is retrieving words from long-term memory. When conversing with others, elderly clients may have difficulty thinking of the correct words to convey their thoughts. Consequently, their speech contains a greater number of pronouns and other unclear references than it did at younger ages. They may also speak more slowly and pause more often, in part because they need time to search their memory for certain words. Second, the elderly need time to plan what to say and how to convey their thoughts. Consequently, their speech may contain more hesitations, false starts, word repetitions, and sentence fragments as they age.

The language used in church has relevance for elderly African Americans and for the congregation as a whole. The congregation responds to the minister with frequent "amens" or "right-ons" to offer encouragement and to indicate agreement. Dialectal differences in language on the part of minister and congregation have genuine meaning for African American elderly.

Families

Accurate perceptions of the role of elderly African Americans and their contributions to immediate and extended kinship networks contribute to counseling effectiveness. The African American family has long existed within a well-defined, close-knit system of relationships. Several underlying themes, such as respect for the elderly, strong kinship bonds, and pulling together in efforts to achieve common family goals, characterize African American family relationships. For example, family responsibility involves combining resources so that all family members will feel economically and emotionally secure.

African American elderly occupy a unique position in the family that differs considerably from the position of European American elderly. In the African American family structure, the elderly are often regarded as immediate family members; hence, they are expected to care for the young. Elderly African American women in particular play an important role in this extended family network. African Americans often value elderly family members because they are important role models. For example, they are valued for their accumulation of wisdom, knowledge, and common sense about life; their ability to accomplish much with little; their ability to accept the reality of aging; and their sense of hope and optimism for a better future.

Living arrangements of elderly African Americans are important for counselors, especially marriage and family counselors, to comprehend. The majority of African American and European American men aged 65 and older are married, whereas the majority of women are widowed.

Unique Challenges Confronting the African American Elderly

Problems that pose challenges for elderly African Americans include the following:

- They are reluctant to participate in health-related activities because only a few health-care providers and researchers are African Americans.
- Low annual income affects housing, nutrition, health care, and nearly all other aspects of their living standards.
- Widowed, separated, or divorced elderly African Americans who are not accepted into the extended kinship network must live alone and face potentially serious problems; not being a part of a traditional family unit is likely to be especially difficult for African Americans, because they place such a high value on the kinship network.
- They experience more frequent and longer hospitalization stays than the elderly of other cultures; health problems, or the fear of health problems, may require counseling intervention.
- They may experience discrimination and unequal treatment on two counts: age and minority status.

Case Study 5.4 looks at Eloise, an elderly African American woman.

Case Study 5.4: Eloise, an Elderly African American Woman

Eloise, better known as Miss Eloise to her younger friends and as Aunt Ellie to her grandchildren, is 74 years old. She moved in with her son William and his family after her husband died. Eloise has worked hard all her life, usually at low-paying jobs with no retirement plans. She lives primarily off her Social Security payments, which allow for necessities. Although she cannot contribute financially to William's household, Eloise does take care of the children and helps his wife, Cynthia, with light housecleaning. She also makes a few extra dollars caring for several children for a neighbor who works. She often cares for nieces and nephews, too, but free of charge because they are family. Eloise enjoys living with her son and his family. It has proved to be a mutually satisfying relationship, and it means a lot to her.

Eloise's problems are common to many elderly African Americans. If she did not have a home with William and Cynthia, she would barely be able to afford a place of her own. Although her health is still fairly good, she worries about falling ill, especially because so many of her friends are in poor health or have died. Another worry, the increasing incidence of crime in the neighborhood, is one she shares with William. When she grew up, times were difficult for African Americans, but the problems that her grandchildren must face—drugs and AIDS—were not a concern back then.

Eloise has always gone to church and she continues to attend. Her religion has seen her through some difficult times and is still a source of strength for her. William and the family also give her strength. Because of them, she has avoided serious financial woes, loneliness, and the fear of growing old alone. In fact, Eloise may be luckier than most other elderly people; she enjoys good health, she has her family by her, and she feels needed.

Reflection Questions:

1. How must Eloise feel about medical care as she ages?
2. Does she think about the past, for example equal opportunities in education and employment?
3. Some people in the elderly lifespan experience depression and hopelessness. If Eloise feels this way, what intervention strategies should counselors use?

SUMMARY

Counselors who intervene with African American children, adolescents, adults, and elderly will have several difficult, but not insurmountable, challenges, for example:

- understanding both historical and contemporary perspectives of the African American culture and its people;
- understanding the challenges that African Americans commonly experience during each lifespan stage;
- understanding changing African American family structures and how these changes can affect marriage, child rearing, and gender perceptions;
- recognizing and responding appropriately to the dilemma surrounding use of Black English; and
- understanding intracultural, geographic, socioeconomic, and other differences that contribute to individuality.

Understanding African American people and the challenges commonly associated with respective lifespan periods is prerequisite to acquiring the knowledge, attitudes, and skills necessary for counseling African American children, adolescents, adults, and elderly.

SUGGESTED READINGS

Adkison-Johnson, C. (2015). Child discipline and African American parents with adolescent children: A psychoeducational approach to clinical mental health counseling. *Journal of Mental Health Counseling, 37*(3), 221–233. Parents from all backgrounds often grapple with child-rearing issues when their children reach adolescent age, and for African American families, the task of addressing problematic adolescent behaviors is complicated by their interaction with external systems (e.g., agencies, schools, legal systems) whose workers often struggle to meet the mental health and social service needs of an increasingly diverse society.

Baskin, T.W., Russell, J.L., Sorenson, C.L., & Ward, E.C. (2015). A model for school counselors supporting African American youth with forgiveness. *Journal of School Counseling, 13*(7), 1–17. The authors describe how practicing school counselors can appropriately and effectively work with African American youth regarding forgiveness.

Roscoe, J.L. (2015). Advising African American and Latino students. *Research & Teaching in Developmental Education, 31*(2), 48–60. Students entering colleges and universities will increase significantly over the next 35 years. Many of these students are statistically underprepared both academically and socially for the higher education environment.

St. Lawrence, J.S., Kelly, J.A., Dickson-Gomez, J., Owczarzak, J., Amirkhanian, Y.A., & Sitzler, C. (2015). Attitudes toward HIV voluntary counseling and testing (VCT) among African American men who have sex with men: Concerns underlying reluctance to test. *AIDS Education & Prevention, 27*(3), 195–211. In the United States, African American men who have sex with men (MSM) bear a disproportionate burden of HIV and have high rates of undetected and untreated HIV infection. Contemporary antiretroviral therapy (ART) can produce viral suppression of HIV, maintain health, and prevent onward HIV transmission from infected persons to their sexual partners, giving rise to the concept of treatment as prevention.

Trahan, D.P. & Lemberger, M.E. (2014). Critical race theory as a decisional framework for the ethical counseling of African American clients. *Counseling & Values, 59*(1), 112–124. The authors introduce critical race theory as a decisional framework for ethical counseling, with a focus on racial disparities when working particularly with African American clients.

6   Counseling African
       American Clients

QUESTIONS TO BE EXPLORED

- What unique challenges and differences can counselors expect when intervening with African American children, adolescents, adults, and elderly?
- How can counselors, especially those from differing cultural backgrounds, effectively plan counseling intervention for African American clients, considering African Americans' many geographic, socioeconomic, and individual differences?
- How can counselors assist in lessening the effects of racism, prejudice, social injustices, and discrimination that have long affected African Americans?
- How can counselors accommodate for African Americans' differences when selecting individual, group, or family therapy?
- What concerns and problems related to development might African American clients at different lifespan stages present to counselors?
- How can counselors of differing cultural backgrounds and lifespan stages intervene with African Americans of other lifespan stages?
- What additional resources are available for professionals intervening with African American clients?

OVERVIEW

As a cultural group, African Americans have been victims of discrimination and racism for many years. In general, African Americans have higher unemployment rates; lower economic status and, in some cases, poverty; more drug abuse problems; overall poorer health; lower life expectancy; and higher infant mortality rates than other U.S. groups. Also, as with other cultural groups, African American clients will have problems that are unique to specific developmental stages. For example, this chapter looks at biracial children, counselor-parent collaboration, empowerment groups, and challenges facing the elderly. At the outset, it is important to note that considerable geographic, socioeconomic, religious, and individual differences exist among African Americans, and therefore all clients should be considered individually.

Regardless of the developmental period of African American clients, counselors should always remember that religion is deeply rooted in the African American culture. Religious observances may involve scared ceremonies, symbols, expressions, or behaviors related to God or some supreme being. The African American church is perhaps the most recognizable symbol of African American religion and spirituality and maintains a rich history within the culture. Moreover, the church holds considerable moral sway because of the sense of connection, purpose, and empowerment it instills in African Americans, even those who do not maintain regular church attendance or membership. Again, regardless of the client's developmental period, counselors should consider African Americans' spirituality, and religious beliefs. Counselors should avoid stereotypical assumptions about the African American church, as differences may result on the basis of denomination, socioeconomic status of the congregation, or geographic location.

AFRICAN AMERICAN CHILDREN

Potential Problems Warranting Counseling Intervention

Problems that African American children may experience include

- failure to develop a strong African American identity and self-esteem;
- adverse effects of stereotypes, prejudices, social injustices, White privilege, and injustices against African American children and the childhood years in general;
- adverse effects of inappropriate value judgments based on differences;
- academic problems because of either the children's lack of educational experiences or the school's inability to build on such experiences;
- inability to overcome society's perception of African American children as "behavior problems";
- language problems and different nonverbal communication styles;
- different home life and cultural concepts of "family";
- physical, psychosocial, and intellectual differences;
- health and nutritional problems associated with low-income families;
- increasing desire to move from a parent-centered world to a peer-centered world; and
- failure to attain competence in developmental tasks, such as getting along with peers (from the same culture and other cultures) and in learning appropriate masculine or feminine social roles.

Counseling Considerations

Counselors intervening with African American children are often at a loss in choosing appropriate strategies. Before making counseling decisions involving these children, professionals should assess their abilities and personal biases objectively. Often African American children are assessed by instruments designed primarily for European Americans, which could result in a culturally biased picture. If the counseling professional views a child in an unfavorable light, the child's self-perception may be affected.

Examples of tests that are designed specifically for African American children or are appropriate for them include:

- *The Black Intelligence Test of Cultural Homogeneity*–a test to identify early indicators of intelligence in Black children. Included are items on Black American folklore, history, life experiences, and dialect.
- *Themes of Black Awareness (TOBA)*–a 40-item, sentence-completion instrument that elicits thematic material relative to an individual's level of Black awareness.
- *Themes Concerning Black (TCB)*–an instrument to measure various aspects of a Black person's personality.
- *Multicultural Pluralistic Assessment (MPA)*–a test to be used with culturally diverse children ages 5 to 11 years. Based on the assumption that American society is pluralistic, both culturally and structurally, this assessment tool includes an interview with parents, a medical examination, and a Wechsler Intelligence Scale for Children (WISC).

Bradley, Johnson, Rawls, and Dodson-Sims (2005) maintained the changing demographics of public schools have been a catalyst for examining the role of school counselors, especially their multicultural competence to deal with students of color and to work with parents for the benefit of students' academic and developmental success. Nine strategies for counselors collaborating with African American parents follow:

1. Explore your own attitudes about African American families and their children.
2. Obtain an accurate and well-balanced perspective of African American family life.
3. Establish respectful and positive rapport.
4. Make flexible meeting times.
5. Establish community relationships.
6. Perceive African American students as at promise.
7. Establish parent groups.
8. Advocate on behalf of African American parents and children.
9. Appreciate the strengths of African American families.

Elementary school counselors working with African American children should respect and appreciate cultural differences, actively participate in the African American community, ask questions about the African American culture, and hold high academic and social expectations for African American children.

Milan and Keiley (2000) believe that biracial youth are a particularly vulnerable group in terms of self-reported delinquency, difficulty in school, internalizing problems, and self-regard. As a group, they are more likely to receive some form of psychological intervention than their counterparts from other cultures are. They report more misbehaviors, school problems, and general self-worth. When counseling biracial clients, counselors should be careful to avoid assuming that clients' problems result from their biracial cultural backgrounds. Since this article is 16 years old, we hope circumstances have improved. Still, we think the counseling strategies below continue to be important.

Counseling strategies suggested by Milan and Keiley (2000) include the following:

- Have both parents construct a cultural genogram that focuses on their ancestors' identities, coping strategies, childbearing practices, strengths, and adversities.
- Use reflecting teams that consist of a group of therapists and therapists-in-training who watch a therapy session and then discuss their reactions with each other and with family members.
- Use externalizing language whereby the therapist attempts to separate the problem from the client by talking about the problem as an adversarial entity (e.g., bulimia) that is trying to gain control of the family.

Individual and Group Therapy

Groups often provide a more natural setting than individual counseling for working with children. Children function as members of groups in their daily activities (e.g., in the family, in the classroom, in the peer group). Group counseling has been advocated as an effective method of counseling several children simultaneously. An even more important advantage is that children can learn appropriate behaviors and new ways of relating more easily through interaction and feedback in a safe situation with their peers.

Steen, Bauman, and Smith (2007) summarized suggestions for small-group counseling in schools: prevention groups (e.g., dealing with peer pressure), problem-focused support groups (e.g., dealing with parental divorce), and information-focused psychoeducational groups (e.g., study skills). Working with students in the small-group modality is a viable way to assist students who are not achieving to their potential and who may be experiencing emotional and behavioral problems.

Family Therapy

Counseling African American children in family therapy settings can be particularly useful. First, all family members are part of a counseling process in which each member works to achieve unity and working order. Second, family relationships can be redefined during the session as each family member adds input. The close-knit nature of the African American family (both immediate and extended) may also contribute to the effectiveness of family therapy.

What status and what role will the African American child be accorded during family therapy? In essence, how will the child be perceived by the family and the counselor? Three factors are particularly relevant in answering these questions. First, African American families generally accord equal status to sons and daughters. Second, clear responsibilities are assigned to siblings on the basis of age. Third, the firstborn, regardless of gender, receives special preparation for the leadership role in the child group. Also, because of the reality of racism and discrimination, some African American parents feel determined to create a more favorable environment for their children.

Several strategies will contribute to counselors' success with African American children and their families in group sessions. First, as a matter of procedure, the counselor should meet with the child, the family, and school officials to clarify issues and to facilitate change. Second, successful counselors communicate respect and openly acknowledge the family's strengths. Third, the counselor should avoid using jargon and relate to the family in a direct but supportive manner. Fourth, counselors should avoid assuming familiarity with adult family members; for example, the counselor who uses first names prematurely and without permission may offend adult family members, who may view this as showing disrespect in front of their children. Case Study 6.1 looks at Carl, a five-year-old African American child.

Case Study 6.1: Carl, a Five-Year-Old African American Child

What concerns and needs will five-year-old Carl bring to the counseling session? Carl's kindergarten teacher referred him to the counselor because she thought Carl was not achieving at the appropriate level for a five-year-old. After talking with Carl, the Hispanic American counselor thought that, although his readiness scores and kindergarten objectives were below average, he indeed had been putting forth considerable effort. The counselor concluded that Carl's poor self-concept was adversely affecting his schoolwork: Carl believed that he could not do the work the teacher expected. The counselor also thought that Carl's dialect was another factor contributing to his problems. The dialect worked well at home but did not seem to be acceptable at school. Although his teacher was a middle-class African American, she encouraged Carl to give up the neighborhood language for a "school language." Although Carl did not want to change, he did recognize that his dialect was quite different from the language he heard at school.

Also apparent to the counselor was Carl's confusion regarding his cultural identity. Carl wondered why so many people encouraged him to change his "ways," especially because his family spoke and acted the same way at home and in the community. The counselor summed up the assessment: If Carl could improve his self-concept and establish a strong cultural identity, his overall school achievement might improve and he might show an increased interest in school.

Reflection Questions:

1. How should the counselor address possible self-concept issues?
2. What should be the counselor's response, if any, to the teacher trying to impose two languages (e.g., his neighborhood/home language and school language) on Carl?
3. How could the counselor implement a partnership approach among Carl, the teacher, parents, and herself?

Compared to other cultural groups, urban African American male adolescents experience disproportionately higher rates of discipline referrals, suspension, and expulsion, which have been related to ecological factors, including misunderstandings between a student's culture of origin and school. Counseling and Development 6.1 examines Jocelyn, a 12-year-old African American girl.

Counseling and Development 6.1: The Childhood Years

Jocelyn, a 12-year-old African American girl, was falling behind in her schoolwork and appeared concerned about "something in her life." She seemed to be more concerned with her friends than with her schoolwork. The teacher could see a trend toward fewer "girlfriends" and more (and older) "boyfriends." Concerned that Jocelyn might be considering some form of sexual experimentation in her life, her teacher referred her to the school counselor.

The counselor considered several childhood developmental characteristics, for example, forming cultural and sexual identities, declining self-esteem, increasing friendship networks, and increasing independence.

Counseling Strategies:

1. Ask Jocelyn about her immediate and extended family relationships to determine family strengths and weaknesses as well as other sources of support.
2. Understanding that a developmental characteristic of this age group is moving toward "cross-sex" friendships, ask Jocelyn about her friendships, especially her sudden interest in older boys.
3. Evaluate Jocelyn's self-esteem to determine whether she is feeling less secure with her girlfriends, thus causing her to seek the attention of older boys.

AFRICAN AMERICAN ADOLESCENTS

Potential Problems Warranting Counseling Intervention

Problems that African American adolescents may experience include:

*   failure to develop a positive self-esteem and a strong African American identity;
*   poor academic achievement;
*   communication problems, both verbal and nonverbal, in part because Black English is accepted in the home and community but is deemed inappropriate at school;
*   absence of the father from the home;
*   adverse effects of the culture being perceived as inferior or in need of change;
*   cultural and social-class differences;
*   developmental differences (e.g., height, weight, coordination);
*   problems associated with increasing socialization of the adolescent outside the African American community;
*   adverse effects of racism, prejudice, social injustices, and discrimination;
*   role confusion because of stereotypes and prejudices involving both the adolescent developmental period and the African American culture; and
*   achievement of developmental tasks, such as getting along with peers and progressing toward personal independence. This may be difficult for adolescents who differ racially and culturally from the mainstream and for those with disabilities or different sexual orientation.

One of the most important mental health issues to understand relative to Black students is depression. Depression is one of the most prevalent and debilitating mental illnesses in the United States. Depression should not be mistaken for the typical bouts of sadness and/or irritability that subside within a few hours to a few days. In addition to sadness/irritability, common symptoms of depression include loss of interest in pleasurable activities; changes in appetite and sleep; decreased energy; difficulty concentrating; and feelings of guilt, worthlessness, and/or helplessness. However, understanding depressive symptoms is culturally oriented around White Americans. Black adolescents are often diagnosed with schizophrenia more than the more accurate diagnosis of a depressive disorder, in part due to differential symptoms and clinician bias. Instead of the standard feelings of sadness and hopelessness, Black adolescents often exhibit increased irritability, anger, and aggression. In addition, although not included in the criteria for depressive disorders, somatic symptoms—headaches, stomachaches, back pain, and limb pain—are among the prominent signs of depression among racial and ethnic minority adolescents (Cokley et al., 2014/2015).

Cokley et al. (2014/2015) explained that experiences common to low SES populations include single-parent households, overcrowded homes, multigenerational experiences of financial stress, exposure to neighborhood violence, and substance abuse. All of these bring their own share of challenges and can be overwhelming to cope with for low-income Black adolescents already dealing with common development stressors related to puberty, peer-related stress, academic motivation, and identity formation. The interaction of race, low socioeconomic status, and culture interact in ways that make the detection of mental health issues among Black students more challenging.

Exploring how counselors perceive and respond to Black students' behavior affects mental health outcomes. Educators are gatekeepers for the interventions students can receive when problems are identified. If educators fail to critically interrogate their responses to diverse students, they risk criminalizing what are essentially symptoms of psychological distress. Furthermore, the pervasive negative stereotyping of Blacks can bias teachers toward addressing externalizing symptoms (e.g., delinquent and aggressive behavior) rather than being sensitive to their underlying internalizing causes (e.g., depression and anxiety). This limited focus on underlying mental health concerns can, in turn, lead to punitive responses from educators. For more than three decades, Black students have been disproportionately affected by exclusionary discipline practices, such as special education placements, suspensions, alternative learning center placement, and expulsions. These practices are often based on interpreting culture and behavior within a universal perspective rather than seeking to understand culture and behavior within a Black context. Exclusionary discipline practices start early (Cokley et. al, 2014/2015).

Day-Vines and Day-Hairston (2005) suggest intervention strategies for African American male adolescents. Some of the problems of urban, African American male adolescents result from cultural perspectives, male subcultures, and communication styles. First, cultural perspectives include a mainstream American cultural orientation that endorses competition, individualism, a nuclear family, and religion as separate from other aspects of life. The African American cultural orientation endorses collective orientation, extended family networks, and religion as integral to family life. The authors maintain that these characteristics apply to many people, but certainly not all. Second, the urban African American male often endorses values that reflect the direct antithesis of healthy psychosocial functioning, for example, academic underachievement, aggression, substance abuse, sexual promiscuity, and illegal activity. Third, communication styles sometimes exhibit characteristics that do not conform to norms and expectations in mainstream educational settings.

Day-Vines and Day-Hairston (2005) recommend culturally congruent strategies for urban males:

1. Use individual and small-group counseling and mentoring programs.
2. Overcome the counselor's own inhibitions.

3. Use bibliotherapy.
4. Provide instruction in social skills.
5. Teach students that behavior in some situation (e.g., home) may not be acceptable at school. Day-Vines and Day-Hairston (2005) called this "code switching" (p. 241).
6. Promote democratic values, such as civic responsibility, service learning, and collaboration.

Counseling intervention should also include a consideration of religious commitments and beliefs. Molock and Barksdale (2013) concluded African American adolescents (aged 13–19) were more likely to attend church and describe themselves as very religious. They also concluded African American females took more active involvement in church activities than African American males.

Counseling Considerations

Moore-Thomas and Day-Vines (2008) maintained that counselors should provide culturally competent strategies for religious and spiritual African American adolescents. Religiosity and spirituality should be considered especially important in the determination of culturally relevant counseling strategies.

Moore-Thomas and Day-Vines (2008) offer several counseling implications: First, professional school counselors should increase their awareness of personal spiritual and religious development. For example, counselors can read articles and books on religiosity and spirituality and engage in conversations and experiential activities that facilitate reflection and personal growth. Second, professional school counselors should work to understand students' personal narratives, including religious and ethnic histories and the implications of related phenomena, such as racism and discrimination. Third, in order to address spiritual and religious needs of African American adolescents, school counselors need to become familiar with basic principles of faith development and racial identity development.

Bailey and Paisley (2004) describe the challenging situations facing African American males as follows. African American males often give up on schools and education because they do not see schools and social systems as places for them to succeed. The poor academic and social performance of African American males has been linked to the lack of role models, low self-esteem, hopelessness, and low expectations of schools and communities.

Henfield (2013) maintained the counseling profession should recognize gifted Black male students' needs and identify ways to meet their needs, especially opportunity gaps that disproportionately place gifted Black male students at an academic disadvantage. Without such recognition and understanding, school counselors are left with an inadequate or less than comprehensive understanding of the potential issues associated with being Black, male, and identified as a gifted student.

Given the strong connection between opportunity gaps and achievement gaps and denying Black male students opportunities afforded to other students, many schools are guilty of systematically placing Black males in positions to fail and otherwise not reach their potential. School counselors are as responsible for closing opportunity gaps as any other educator in school settings—teachers, support staff, and administrators. It is clear that Black male students have much to process and consider such as the attempt to successfully navigate their schools and, in particular, the gifted classrooms where they receive instruction. While the design and implementation of services specifically for gifted Black males are important, school counselors can provide other services for educators, administrators, families, and community to support development of gifted Black male learners. A significant component of school counselors' responsibilities is the alleviation of barriers that interfere with students' ability to thrive and flourish. For gifted Black male students, these barriers exist in the form of lowered teacher expectations, teachers' disinclination to nominate Black male students to gifted programs, and socio-emotionally unwelcoming gifted classrooms.

Davis, Davis, and Mobley (2013) wrote about the school counselor's role in addressing advanced placement equity for African American students. School counselors who wish to address gaps in Advanced Placement participation and success for African American students may consider adopting a policy of recruitment that identifies African American students with untapped academic potential as well as encourage students to enroll in AP programs. This approach challenges the traditional policies of application and recommendations; instead of asking students who may not fully grasp their academic potential to make application to AP programs, schools can identify students who have shown potential in the past and can encourage these students to enroll in AP courses. Gifted African American students benefit from a sense of community and family that values academic achievement, emphasizes open discussion, and acknowledges culture. Students involved in the study began to develop a concept of themselves as scholars, formed tight relationships with peers that were supportive in nature, and thought of each other and the adult leaders as family. Davis et al. (2013) also suggest that collaboration of school counselors with other educators can be a key component of success. School counselors can build collaborative teams by working with teachers who are open to new approaches and who recognize the importance of the whole child in the learning process. Although these authors focused on closing the AP excellence and equity gaps, school counselors could be encouraged to actively seek to close achievement gaps at every level. School counselors can pursue the practitioner.

Suggestions for European American counselors working with African American females include that counselors should be honest, open, relaxed, respectful, and good listeners. They should not be afraid to make mistakes, refrain from taking things personally, ask for help or for clarification from the group when needed, communicate honestly even when discussing sensitive topics, and avoid being overly sensitive to issues related to racism, prejudice, and stereotyping. As with all cross-cultural counseling, professional counselors must be aware of the limitations of their own beliefs and assumptions about others. European American professionals need to consider their own prejudices (as should counselors of all cultures) and be open to and genuinely respectful of culturally different attitudes and behaviors (Muller, 2000).

As previously mentioned, language differences and communication barriers can be factors in determining the success of counseling intervention. In fact, the ability to communicate effectively is considered more important than similarity to the client's racial membership group. What, then, must counselors of African American adolescents recognize to ensure effective communication? First, some African Americans resent counselors' attempts to use slang to show understanding. Second, counselors who are unfamiliar with the directness of some African Americans may find their style of communication offensive and may interpret directness as hostility. Some clients may be hesitant to speak altogether for fear that their speech will be evaluated negatively; thus therapists sometimes label African Americans as nonverbal and incapable of dealing with feelings. In fact, African Americans often deal with anxiety by becoming either passive or aggressive: Either they say nothing or they become loud, threatening, and abusive. Passive or aggressive behavior during therapy may be a manifestation of frustration and displaced anger toward the therapist, particularly the European American therapist. Consider the following dialogue between Jessie and her counselor:

JESSIE: Well, you're the one who wanted to talk, so talk.
COUNSELOR: Yes, the absence list showed you weren't in school for three days. Didn't we have an agreement that when things weren't going right for you, we'd talk, rather than you cutting out?
JESSIE: All this same White counselor talk. You Whites always coming down on us and jiving us.
COUNSELOR: Jessie, I thought we were going to talk about what happened during the three days of absence.

JESSIE:	This whole damn system of yours—it's hooked us all into money.
COUNSELOR:	Would you cut out all that crap about the system and talk about what's been going on with you the last three days? You know we can talk about what you can do for you, but that other thing is out there and not in here.
JESSIE:	Uh? Tell me more, ha!
COUNSELOR:	Jessie, I know you believe unfair things happen to you, but I want you to talk about what's been happening to you the last few days and try to forget that other for now.
JESSIE:	Uh? Well, uh, see. Our check didn't come in, and we had the bills, and I had to get us some quick bread and.[1]

Competent skills and techniques needed for counseling African Americans include the consideration of family and community life from an African American perspective. African American counselors should be available in areas that have large African populations. When an African American high school student goes to a counselor, particularly a European American counselor, and is reluctant to reveal information, the student may be experiencing inner conflicts with racial identity and may choose not to participate in the counseling relationship. Because having access to only European American counselors may have a detrimental impact on African American adolescents, it is important for these adolescents to experience feelings of acceptance in counselor-client relationships.

Advocacy, proactive services, and outreach should figure prominently in school guidance programs designed to effectively address the career development needs of African American adolescents. Advocacy activities include in-school action to address policies and procedures that may affect educational opportunities negatively.

Concerns that African American adolescents bring to counseling sessions include establishing a meaningful personal identity, academic performance, interpersonal relations, autonomy, sexual and aggressive feelings, and long-term career plans.

Individual and Group Therapy

A primary task for counselors during initial counseling intervention is to determine the appropriateness of individual and group therapy. Deciding which technique to use requires a basic understanding of intervention strategies and a careful consideration of the client's culture and developmental period.

Counselors of African American adolescents (and in fact, all cultures and ethnicities) should consider whether the adolescent is more likely to disclose personal information during individual or group interventions. In individual and group therapy, how effective is counseling if the family is not involved? Although adolescents tend to prefer group therapy sessions because their age-level peers may have similar problems, will African American adolescents speak of personal matters in the presence of adolescents from other cultures? Answering these questions requires getting to know the individual adolescent and the nature of the problem.

Johnson and Johnson (2005) recommend effective counseling of African American youths:

- Encourage African American students to talk about themselves, their families, and their experiences to determine strengths.
- Ask students to describe their social-class status rather than make assumptions based on their behaviors.
- Ask students to describe their social kin networks.
- Ask students to describe concerns about whether the counselor will be able to help them.
- When possible, visit the homes of African American youths.

Johnson and Johnson (2005) suggest that counseling strategies should include using a group leader, establishing a set number of meetings, setting individual objectives, and building group cohesion and support. However, the model goes beyond the traditional approach by including a multicultural approach that is sensitive to students living in urban settings. The approach also uses the strengths of an unstructured process group, with clearly defined goals to develop individual student success.

Factors affecting the outcome of individual/group counseling include developmental levels and gender roles. Possible interventions include group assertiveness training, which has been found to reduce classroom displays of aggression; expressive group therapy, which has positive effects on male youths; and self-instructional techniques, which modify African American adolescent males' behavioral risks.

Bemak, Chung, and Siroskey-Sabdo (2005) maintain that urban schools face unique challenges as they provide culturally responsive experiences for diverse populations. The many problems facing at-risk urban African American girls include academic achievement, high drop-out rates, negative stereotyping, and fewer educational resources—many of which result from social problems, poverty, violence, and discrimination. Case Study 6.2 looks at a counselor's efforts with Tyrone, a 16-year-old African American adolescent.

Case Study 6.2: Tyrone, an African American Adolescent

Tyrone, age 16, was recommended by his teacher for a districtwide school dropout prevention program. A requirement for enrolling in the at-risk program was at least one session (one part of an overall assessment) with a community agency counselor. After the initial visit, the counselor used established guidelines in deciding whether additional sessions were warranted. Tyrone was brought from his school to the 35-year-old European American counselor, who met with students individually at the agency. Tyrone's greatest in-class behavior problem was talking too much with his friends; he was adamantly opposed to being placed in the at-risk drop-out program and being sent to the counselor.

The counselor introduced herself and explained to Tyrone the reason for the referral. Tyrone stated, "Nothin's wrong with me. The problem's the teacher, who don't like me 'cause I'm Black. I'll be glad to get out of that honky school. I'd quit now if my parents wouldn't find out about it." Tyrone mostly looked down at the floor or at the picture on the office wall. His failure to look her in the eye concerned the counselor, but she realized it was a common habit among her African American clients.

The counselor assessed Tyrone's case. His academic problems qualified him for the dropout program, and he appeared to harbor strong feelings that he was a victim of racism in his school. Still, she had to note that not all of Tyrone's teachers were European American. Could it be that his African American teachers, who had been academically successful, had lost perspective about what it meant to be poor and African American? Although the counselor did not want to imply that racism was not a factor, she hoped to help Tyrone get the situation in perspective.

During Tyrone's first session, the counselor tried to make him feel comfortable talking to her. She was of European cultural background and might not understand what it was like to be poor and African American, but she sought to learn more about him, his friends, and his culture. She realized that establishing rapport was all-important.

She informed Tyrone that she wanted him to return for additional counseling. She carefully explained that this was not punishment. She wanted to help him and would not "put him and his race down," as he thought his teachers did. Another decision was to continue individual therapy until she could determine whether there were enough students in Tyrone's situation to form a small group. Also, she considered future family counseling because the referral slip mentioned that Tyrone's parents were interested in his academic work. Yes, she thought, maybe Tyrone's parents could help with this situation.

Reflection Questions:

1. Tyrone's perception of racism (whether valid or not) in the school was undoubtedly a major factor in the possibility of him dropping out of school; how should the counselor address this perception without denying the possibility of racism being a major factor?
2. The European American counselor admitted (at least to herself) that her worldviews were different from Tyrone's; how might she gain a better perception of Tyrone's worldviews as her own worldviews?
3. What do you think of her decision to begin with individual therapy and then perhaps switch to small-group therapy?

Family Therapy

As with individual and group therapy, a fundamental step is to consider whether the adolescent will disclose personal information during family counseling sessions. Another point to consider is the extent to which the family can assist during and after the counseling session. The likelihood of family members helping to facilitate change may be greater when they are involved in therapy sessions.

The family therapist sees a client's problems as a result of family interactions, as affecting other family members, or as being amenable to family members providing assistance and insights. Although African American families differ in many aspects and deserve individual consideration, two cultural characteristics that might contribute to family counseling include their concern for group welfare and their extended family networks. Grandparents, aunts and uncles, and cousins might also play active roles in family counseling. They might be able to offer insights that the parents do not realize.

Unless there is a court-ordered mandate for family counseling, an individual interview is probably the most effective means of deciding whether the client will benefit from family members being included. Counseling and Development 6.2 looks at James.

Counseling and Development 6.2: The Adolescent Years

James, 17-year-old African American young man, is engaging in illegal behaviors (e.g., vandalism, shoplifting, and smoking marijuana) in his community. He and some friends were arrested for vandalism, which meant his mother (the father does not live with them) had to miss work so she could accompany James to juvenile court. The judge ruled 40 hours of community service and that James attend 12 counseling sessions.

The counselor considered James's self-esteem, developing cultural identity, and his choice of friends. She realized that perhaps James's friends were getting him in trouble, but she also realized the situation could be the other way around—he could be getting his friends into trouble.

Counseling Strategies:

1. Ask James about his friends and overall friendship networks, and raise the possibility of more constructive activities with his friends.
2. Discuss James's short- and long-term orientations in an attempt to get James to think about his education and behavior.
3. Ask James about whether he has spoken with his school counselor about his educational achievement and possibilities for his future.

AFRICAN AMERICAN ADULTS

Potential Problems Warranting Counseling Intervention

Problems African American adults may experience include

- suicide rates that have been escalating for 20 years;
- communication problems caused by misunderstood communication patterns and dialects;
- African American women often being more religiously active than their mates;
- adverse effects of myths and stereotypes regarding the African American culture;
- historical and contemporary ill treatment from other cultures;
- low self-esteem, confused cultural identity, and feelings of rejection;
- lack of education;
- differing cultural characteristics and customs;
- unequal employment and housing opportunities;
- underemployment, unemployment, and low socioeconomic status;
- increasing number of single-parent and/or female-headed households;
- inability to cope with problems associated with adulthood (e.g., appearance and personality changes, psychosocial crises, marital discord);
- depression and depressive symptoms resulting from living in high-stress environments (e.g., low income, high crime rate, high unemployment);
- coping with signs of aging (e.g., strength and stamina decrease, gray hair and wrinkles increase, the body frame begins to stoop) Papalia, Feldman, and Martorell (2014).
- taking stock of one's life during the adult period, including past accomplishments and the possibilities of attaining future goals (financial, personal, and societal); and
- perception of how age has affected sexuality.

Counseling Considerations

Counseling services for adults are based on the premise that all individuals have the capacity for controlled growth and development in psychosocial, vocational, emotional, and other areas. Furthermore, life transitions in adulthood often give rise to conflict; such conflict may cause individuals to be less effective in coping with aspects of daily living. Counselors of adults seek to provide services that maximize the growth and coping abilities of clients and that help them explore these areas of their lives.

Effective intervention with African American clients includes a mutual understanding on the part of client and counselor about their racial identities and how racial identity influences counseling dynamics. Counselors who are knowledgeable about the African American identity development process and assess the interactive nature of racial identities have a better understanding of these clients and can provide more effective intervention.

Depression is a mental condition, typically with lack of energy and difficulty maintaining concentration and interest in life. Typical changes include agitation (emotional disturbance, unsettlement, or lack of calm); procrastination (delaying an action to a later time); hibernation (avoiding invitations and avoiding social activities); diet (either lower or higher appetites); and sleeping (have trouble sleeping or sleeping more than usual) (Ryan, 2013). Ryan (2013) offered several suggestions: Learn about depression (what it is and is not), view one's self as part of a support team, understand how depression affects a person's life, encourage the client to exercise and engage in physical activities, and encourage the depressed person to avoid being alone. Also, very important, it is important that counselors avoid judging or criticizing the depressed client.

Racial discrimination has negatively affected African Americans in the United States for centuries and produced one of the most publicly recognized histories of social oppression. The deleterious effects of racism on African American people clearly demonstrate that perceived racism and discrimination may negatively affect the lives of the oppressed. Perceived racism refers to the subjective experience of prejudice and/or discrimination and has been pervasive among African Americans. It can be a threat to encouragement. It is difficult for an African American individual to maintain a healthy self-concept or feel competent when he or she is consistently confronted with unjust prejudice and negative discrimination.

It is important to recognize that not all African Americans have fallen victim to the deleterious effects of racism but instead have risen above it by active coping. Spirituality, ethnic pride, and racial socialization experiences are important aspects of African American adults' experiences and may play important roles in their lives. Finally, promoting spirituality and ethnic pride may be an effective preventive and intervention strategy for helping African American adults counteract the negative effects of perceived racism. In counseling, a strength-based perspective on the part of the counselor could potentially help African American clients actively use resources, such as spirituality and ethnic pride, in dealing with perceived racism (Rowles & Duan, 2012).

African American Muslims might feel distrustful of European American counseling professionals, and in fact, counselors of other cultures. Distrust of the therapist and beliefs about counselors' attitudes toward Muslims may hinder therapeutic relationships with African American Muslims. These feelings of distrust might also extend to African Americans of other religious beliefs. African Americans often underuse counseling services because they perceive counselors as insensitive to their needs and as not accepting, understanding, or respecting their cultural differences. Other reasons for underuse include attitudes of mental health professionals as well as clients and the limited number of African American counselors. African Americans also often rely heavily on their church (and other forms of spiritualism) rather than on counseling intervention. Mental health professionals increasingly recognize the mental health benefits of religious involvement and the extent to which a strong spiritual base is central to the client's improved mental health.

Because of segregation and lack of African American counselors and psychotherapists, African Americans who seek counseling have very little chance of seeing an African American regardless of their preference (Townes, Chavez-Korell, & Cunningham, 2009). Ferguson, Leach, Levy, Nicholson, and Johnson (2009) maintained that some African American clients have a preference for racially similar counselors, whereas other clients do not have significant preferences. Attitudes and feelings of African American individuals toward White people (and possibly counselors of other cultures as well) may play a role in a person's willingness to attend counseling with a culturally different counselor. African American clients who have negative attitudes toward the cultural background of the counselor at the outset of therapy may benefit from being assigned or referred to a counselor with a similar cultural background. Such preferences might be problematic because the majority of counselors are White and middle class, making it difficult to meet the needs of minority populations.

Mental health help seeking among African American women is influenced by factors such as age, socioeconomic status, education, cultural beliefs, religion, and unique life experience. A large number of middle-class, working-class, and low-income African American women seek help from sources (e.g., churches and extended family members) other than traditional mental health institutions. If and when African American women seek help from traditional mental health service providers, the problem is often serious.

If there had been a taboo related to speaking about menopause in the African American culture, it did not appear to affect this population of women. Relatively few had any problem discussing the topic. It appears that this taboo has not only weakened in the larger U.S. culture but also in the African American community.

Implications for counselors include the following:

1. Realize that both commonalities and differences regarding menopause exist within ethnic/cultural groups.
2. Remember that although most women reported an overall positive attitude toward menopause and similar symptoms, individual experiences may vary greatly from the norm.
3. Understand that women considering menopause for the first time might also be considering for the first time what it means to grow older in a society that supports ageism.
4. Understand that African American women might have to deal with ageism, sexism, and racism—all hurdles that threaten their well-being.
5. Network with other health-care professionals through initiatives such as community coalitions whose agendas support both psychological and medical care needs.

The question remains whether a non–African American therapist can intervene effectively with African American clients. Perhaps it would be preferable to match counselors and clients whenever possible with respect to race. Some African Americans may not want to see an Asian American therapist, just as some women may not want to see a male therapist. A client's choice of therapist usually is indicative of self-perceptions and certain expectations of the counseling relationship.

Some problems may result from African Americans' racial, historical, cultural, and structural position in American society. A major task for the counselor continues to be engaging reluctant African American men to participate in counseling. Men often feel they should work out their own difficulties; consequently, they do not want to disclose personal feelings, which further complicates the counseling process.

Individual and Group Therapy

When planning intervention for African American clients, the counselor must decide whether to use individual or group counseling. While some counselors might prefer individual counseling, group counseling often has advantages and deserves consideration. Some advantages are that group counseling can be more cost-effective in terms of the counselor's time, and clients often feel support from other participants who have similar problems and challenges. Still, the welfare of the client is always the final determinant. The decision about whether to use individual or group approaches should depend on several factors.

First, is the group developmentally compatible with a particular client? For example, an African American adolescent will likely face different problems than an African American elderly person. Although they both might experience discrimination, the younger client may be experiencing job discrimination or identity concerns, whereas the older one may be facing health problems and financial concerns. As always, individual differences and challenges deserve consideration. While the counselor might be able to plan counseling intervention that addresses some diversity in age and level of development, participants might benefit from having all group members in a similar developmental period.

Second, how will the African American adult respond in group counseling? Some clients who are quite vocal in individual counseling are reluctant to speak in front of groups, especially when they feel their situations reflect negatively on their ability to provide for the family, maintain a job and the household, and serve as suitable role models for children and adolescents. Do they have the social skills, communication skills, and emotional stability to benefit from group interaction? Are they receptive to sharing feelings as well as accepting others' feelings? These decisions can be made only through consideration of individual clients.

Whether individual or group interventions, Marbley, Bonner, McKisick, Henfield, and Watts, (2007) offered several recommendations for multicultural counseling and therapy:

1. Have a wealth of counseling theories, tools, and techniques that are culturally appropriate for the African American culture.
2. Be prepared to disclose your cultural self—the individual or group needs to understand your worldviews, privileges, and feelings of oppression. (It is wise to avoid thinking the individual or group perceives challenges result from oppression and the ills of racism.)
3. Recognize your culturally different paradigms and epistemologies and how worldviews determine the direction of counseling.
4. Take advantage of African Americans' indigenous systems, such as the church, community, and extended family.

Gender differences also deserve consideration when deciding between individual or group therapy. Although African American women are more likely than their spouse/significant other to be receptive to discussing problems in groups, women in mixed gender groups may not be as willing to discuss their push for equality and the problems associated with female-headed households. Counselors providing group therapy with African American women should assume the role of an active facilitator; understand nonverbal communication, such as the meanings of gestures, postures, and movements; enlist group members' feedback; and experiment with exercises that help group members gain greater awareness.

Family Therapy

To work effectively with African American families, therapists must be willing to explore the impact of the social, political, socioeconomic, and broader environmental conditions of families. Therapists must also be willing to expand the definition of family to a more extended kinship system. Relatives often live in proximity to and expect to rely on one another in times of need. They may interchange functions, and they frequently share responsibilities for child rearing. This is an important point to understand, because counseling sessions may be attended by family members who counselors usually would not expect to do so.

Counseling interventions that emphasize social functioning over inner feelings are most appropriate for African Americans. Counselors need to attend to the specifics of African Americans' historical and cultural experiences as well as their socioeconomic conditions. Family therapists should also be aware of the important roles that extended family members, social institutions, and churches play in the lives of African American families.

A therapist working with an African American Muslim family needs to know to which community the family belongs and how its members feel about their particular religious community.

Essentials for successfully counseling African American families include discussing their goals for the intervention; understanding and respecting the African American culture, especially family traditions; assisting the family to adopt the counseling plan; and assisting the family to evaluate the plan and its effectiveness.

Counselors should avoid assuming too many generalizations about African Americans. They differ in many ways, such as socioeconomic status and place of origin, to name a few areas. For example, African Americans do not always experience similar problems: Lower-class families may experience economic problems, high crime and mortality rates, and employment and social discrimination. Although counseling intervention always has potential, some social problems facing African Americans are beyond their control. A helpful approach is for the therapist to point out areas of life where they do have control and empower them to make changes where they can.

Suggestions for providing family therapy for African Americans include understanding the worldview of these families as being different from that of the larger society; considering family strengths, such as religious/spiritual orientations, adaptability of family roles, acknowledging differences between counselor and client, and exploring how these differences can influence the counseling process; and learning to acknowledge and to feel comfortable with the family's cultural differences.

Recommendations or principles for counselors working with African American families experiencing divorce, separation, or other problems include encouraging couples to (a) maintain an open, honest, and direct communication with children about divorce or separation; (b) maintain a strong coalition despite marital discord; (c) provide understanding, availability, and support to the children; (d) build a new life, establish a new identity, and redefine the relationship with the ex-spouse or estranged spouse; and (e) maintain an image of competence and self-confidence.

Respect is key to successfully engaging the family during a family counseling session. The therapist should openly acknowledge the family's strengths, avoid professional jargon, and relate to the family in a direct but supportive manner.

The literature has focused primarily on urban African American families whose lives differ from those of non–African American, middle-class therapists. Family therapy may not always be the treatment of choice in such situations. Again, individual consideration of African American clients is essential. In essence, until definitive research suggests appropriate treatment strategies, the wisest policy continues to be the consideration of individual clients and their particular circumstances. Case Study 6.3 looks at Cynthia, an African American adult.

Case Study 6.3: Cynthia, an African American Adult

Cynthia, age 33, referred herself for counseling through a counseling program operated for the hospital staff. In this program, counselors, who are in private practice or are employed by community mental health organizations, conduct counseling sessions at the hospital on a regular basis.

During Cynthia's first session, the 38-year-old Asian American female counselor discussed Cynthia's reasons for the self-referral. Speaking in Black dialect interspersed with Standard English, Cynthia explained that she felt trapped. Her husband tried hard to make a living: His work record was good, he never did time in jail, and he did not have a drinking problem. Still, Cynthia wanted more; she was already over 30, and nothing much was changing in her life. Although she had not spoken with her husband about her plans, Cynthia was thinking about attending school at night. She had a desire to improve her life. The counselor listened intently, took notes, and encouraged Cynthia to examine her goals carefully and to consider the impact of her decision on her family. The counselor accepted Cynthia as a client. First, she would meet with her several times individually; then move to a group session (other women working in the hospital likely had similar concerns); and finally, depending on Cynthia's progress and her husband's reaction, she might schedule family sessions during which other family members could see the reasons for Cynthia's concerns and understand her goals.

Reflection Questions:

1. What counseling approach should be taken to address Cynthia's feelings of being "trapped"?
2. Would it be appropriate at some time to invite the husband to a counseling session so he could better understand his wife's feelings? Why or why not?
3. "Still, Cynthia wanted more; she was already over 30, and nothing much was changing in her life." Considering the adult developmental stage, what intervention techniques might be used to help Cynthia decide whether additional education was the best approach?

Counseling and Development 6.3 looks at Catherine, a 40-year-old female.

Counseling and Development 6.3: The Adult Years

Catherine is a 40-year-old female with three teenage children. In addition to taking care of her elderly mother who lives in the neighborhood, she works part-time in a job without much potential for the future. Catherine is becoming increasingly depressed, stressed, and worried about the future. Her primary care physician recommended her for psychological counseling. Her husband has a job with insurance that partially funds counseling.

Catherine's counselor reflected on Catherine's developmental characteristics and related circumstances: 40 and in a job without much future, hormonal changes, and taking care of both her children and her mother.

Counseling Strategies:

1. Ask Catherine about her feelings about her depression, stresses, and worries in an attempt to learn what factors trigger these feelings.
2. Discuss with Catherine why she thinks her primary care physician encouraged her to attend counseling, for example, sexual concerns, developmental concerns, or suicidal thoughts.
3. Ask Catherine about the possibility of attending small-group counseling sessions with women with similar problems (only after a client-counselor relationship has been established).

AFRICAN AMERICAN ELDERLY

Potential Problems Warranting Counseling Intervention

Problems that elderly African Americans may experience include

- adverse effects of stereotypes about the culture and elderly status;
- the possibility of multiple jeopardy (i.e., combination of being culturally different, aged, and/or disabled);
- lack of education, lack of employment, and low socioeconomic status;
- cultural differences, traditions, and customs;

- high divorce/separation rates;
- problems with generational differences because of the acculturation of younger African Americans; and
- health problems; longer and more frequent hospital stays; chronic diseases, functional impairments, prostate cancer, and risk indicators such as high blood pressure (U.S. Census Bureau, 2009).

Cohen, Goh, and Yaffee (2009) explained the importance of understanding depression among biracial depressed urban elders. Many factors affect the prevalence and extent of depression among biracial elders: age, external locus of control, somatic illness, dysfunctional personality, inadequate coping strategies, previous psychopathology, social networks, stressful life events, lower income, and female gender. Counselors working with the elderly, whether monoracial or biracial, will be challenged to understand depression among the elderly. Although an understanding of the culture is essential, counselors must understand the worldviews of the elderly client. The aging process is difficult for some clients, and counselors need to understand the complex relationship between growing older and depression.

Pinguart and Sorensen (2005) investigated ethnic differences in caregiving backgrounds, stressors, beliefs about filial obligations, psychological and social resources, coping processes, and psychological and physical health. Ethnic minority caregivers had a lower socioeconomic status, were younger, were less likely to be a spouse, and were more likely to receive informal support. They also provided more care than White caregivers and had stronger beliefs about filial obligations than White caregivers. Asian caregivers, but not African and Hispanic caregivers, used less formal support than non-Hispanic White caregivers. Whereas African American caregivers had lower levels of caregiver burden and depression than White caregivers, Hispanic and Asian caregivers were more depressed than their White non-Hispanic peers. All non-White groups of caregivers reported worse physical health than Whites.

Counseling Considerations

Counselors should first try to gain an understanding of what it means to be elderly and African American and to be aging in a society that glorifies youth. As with other stages of human development, counselors working with elderly African Americans should be aware of the body of knowledge pertaining to the elderly developmental period in this culture. Specific research and scholarly opinion on counseling African American elderly, however, is scarce. Counselors must synthesize their understanding of the culture with their knowledge of the lifespan period to form a basis for counseling decisions.

Most techniques used in counseling adults also apply to the elderly. What steps, then, can counselors take to improve the likelihood of a positive counselor-client relationship? First, rapport should be established by convincing the client that the counselor empathizes with the concerns of the elderly, such as health problems, financial problems, loneliness, and expectations of family and church. The elderly client may think, "You're too young and too White to know my problems and to know how I feel," but the counselor can still try to gain the client's confidence by demonstrating a "feel" for the various aspects of aging. Several characteristics of African American family life may result in the need for counseling intervention for the elderly. One example is the orientation toward kinship bonds, wherein a wide array of uncles, aunts, "big mamas," boyfriends, older brothers and sisters, deacons, preachers, and others frequent the African American home. The increasing number of three-generation families may result in boundary or responsibility problems involving the elderly. Another example is African Americans' strong religious orientation. Consider the following family dialogue that illustrates the powerful influence of the church:

COUNSELOR: (*To Ms. K.*) Do you understand why your children worry about you?
MS. K: No.

COUNSELOR:	Find out from them now.
Ms. K:	Why? Do you think I'm gonna die?
CYNTHIA:	The way daddy be hitting on you.
Ms. K:	Ray don't hit on me.
KAREN:	What he fought you that time.
Ms. K:	John, you think I'm gonna die?
JOHN:	The way you two get in serious arguments sometimes (*pause*)—someone might get injured.
Ms. K:	Nobody gets serious injuries. You know the Bible says everybody is gonna die but they come back, John.
JOHN:	I know.
Ms. K:	Then you all don't have anything to worry about. Jehovah tells you that you're not supposed to worry about anything like that 'cause he'll take care of his people, and we'll live right back here on this earth. If you be good. Dying is something to get out of all this agony now. (Hines & Boyd-Franklin, 2005, p. 97)

Clearly, the children's valid concerns for Ms. K's safety are being blocked by her religious beliefs. Counselors who are confronted with such situations are in a better position to intervene successfully if they understand the traditional role of the church and the influence that it exerts.

Individual and Group Therapy

The first several sessions should focus mainly on individual therapy directed toward building rapport and letting the elderly client know what to expect from a counseling relationship; however, if other clients with similar problems participate (and, in all likelihood, there will be such clients), group therapy may be feasible. Group therapy for elderly African Americans is most beneficial when several clients have problems in common with their culture, their age, or racism and discrimination.

Case Study 6.4 looks at a counselor's efforts with Eloise, a 74-year-old African American woman.

Case Study 6.4: Eloise, an Elderly African American

Eloise, age 74, visited her community medical doctor for stomach pains and was referred to a community mental health counselor. She decided to keep her appointment, mainly because the agency was near her son's home. The 34-year-old European American female counselor recognized that Eloise had a few problems, but generally she was in much better shape than most other elderly African American clients were. Although Eloise was poor, she was better off financially than many African American women; her health was relatively good; and she felt needed by her grandchildren, nieces, and nephews. The counselor decided that the best strategy for this first session was to gain Eloise's confidence and to learn more about her. Conversation focused on Eloise's life, her age, and her family and church. At the end of the session, Eloise concluded that the counselor was, indeed, interested and that she knew a little about what being an elderly African American woman was like.

The counselor reached several conclusions during this first session. Although Eloise did not have any serious problems, she did feel that she lacked control over her life. Financial problems were a possibility, and her neighborhood was becoming more dangerous. The counselor decided to meet with Eloise again one-on-one and then maybe a group session could be arranged. Also, the supportiveness of Eloise's family suggested to the counselor that a family session might be beneficial.

Reflection Questions:

1. How could the counselor use Eloise's spirituality to lessen her challenges?
2. How could the young European American counselor learn more about being African American and the elderly years? Did a degree of double jeopardy exist?
3. What intervention techniques might the counselor use to better understand Eloise as well as herself?

Family Therapy

Family therapy may be particularly appropriate for elderly African American clients in certain situations. Consider the following example of a boundary problem in which the therapist worked with three generations:

> A ten-year-old boy was brought in for treatment because of stealing. The first session was attended by the parents and their two children. Both parents appeared bewildered and unsure of their parenting skills. Upon learning the grandmother had the primary child-care responsibility, the counselor asked her to join the family sessions. It became apparent that the grandmother ran the household. She had her way of handling the children, and the parents had theirs.

The therapist's goal was to form a working alliance between the parents and the grandmother so that the children were no longer given conflicting messages. This was accomplished by having a number of joint meetings with the parents and the grandmother to discuss family rules, division of labor, and child-care policies. Disputes and differences of opinions were discussed. Later, the children were included in sessions in order to clarify the boundaries of the family (Hines & Boyd-Franklin, 2005, p. 92).

What other problems might African American elderly bring to counseling sessions? Possibilities include problems with adult children, interracial marriages, and divorces or remarriages. Of course, some problems are specific to aging—for example, grief and growing old in a society that favors youth. In summary, counselors need to understand the elderly period in the lifespan, the problems experienced by elderly African Americans, and the strategies employed in family therapy. Counseling and Development 6.4 looks at Rob, a 72-year-old African American man.

Counseling and Development 6.4: The Elderly Years

Rob, a 72-year-old African American man, was recommended for counseling at a health services center. He is fearful of what his future might bring. He is married and has two grown children—one lives nearby and one lives in another state. Rob had a heart attack seven years previously. He has had biopsies for an enlarged prostate (benign). Rob remembers when he was more sexually active and, generally speaking, could do more physical activities.

The counselor looked at Rob's developmental period: heart problems, enlarged prostate, reduced sex life, and thought processes a little slower.

Counseling Strategies:

1. Ask Rob how he sees his life—past accomplishments, future goals, familial concerns, and other areas of concern.
2. Try to ascertain whether Rob feels a certain degree of double jeopardy—being African American and elderly.
3. Ask Rob about his opinions of his health conditions, for example, the heart problem, enlarged prostate, less energy, and sleep habits.

SUMMARY

Counseling African American clients can be a rewarding experience when counselors understand these clients' cultural backgrounds and developmental periods. Knowing when to use individual, group, and family therapy and where to seek additional knowledge about cultural differences are prerequisites to planning and implementing effective counseling for these clients. Simply having knowledge, however, is insufficient; it is necessary to appreciate the life circumstances of African American clients. To determine appropriate counseling interventions, such factors as racial and ethnic differences, language and communication barriers, and concerns associated with lifespan differences must be understood. Particularly challenging to counselors are class and generational differences and other cultural group differences that sometimes may not be so obvious. Because few professionals have been trained to work with African American clients from all four lifespan stages, it is imperative that counselors seek such training, either through accredited training programs or through other professional development avenues, or refer clients to colleagues with the appropriate expertise.

NOTE

1 Dialogue from *Counseling and Development in a Multicultural Society* (p. 432), J.A. Axelson, 1999, Monterey, CA: Brooks/Cole.

SUGGESTED READINGS

Bowman, N.A., & Park, J.J. (2014). Interracial contact on college campuses: Comparing and contrasting predictors of cross-racial interaction and interracial friendship. *Journal of Higher Education*, 85(5), 660–690. Research on diversity in higher education has evolved to consider the nature of interracial contact and campus climate as well as the factors that may foster meaningful interactions.

Cokley, K., Cody, B., Smith, L., Beasley, S., Miller, I. S. K., Hurst, A., Awosogba, O., Stone, S., & Jackson, S. (2014/2015). Bridge over troubled waters: Meeting the mental health needs of black students. *Kappan*, 96(4), 40–45. These authors maintained Black children are overidentified for behavior issues at schools and underidentified for mental health concerns.

Roscoe, J.L. (2015). Advising African American and Latino students. *Research & Teaching in Developmental Education*, 31(2), 48–60. 13. The volume of minority students entering colleges and universities will increase significantly over the next 35 years—many of these students (particularly those from African American and Hispanic cultures) are statistically underprepared both academically and socially for the higher education environment.

Trahan, D.P., & Lemberger, M.E. (2014). Critical race theory as a decisional framework for the ethical counseling of African American clients, *Counseling & Values*, 59(1), 112–124. The authors introduce critical race theory as a decisional framework for ethical counseling, with a focus on racial disparities when working particularly with African American clients.

Williams, J.M., Greenleaf, A.T., Albert, T., & Barnes, E.F. (2014). Promoting educational resilience among African American students at risk of school failure: The role of school counselors. *Journal of School Counseling*, 12(9), 1–34. While the educational difficulties of African American students from low-income households are well documented and widely discussed in the literature, far less attention has been paid to students who succeed in school despite significant challenges, such as poverty, housing instability, and food insecurity.

7 Understanding American Indian Clients

QUESTIONS TO BE EXPLORED

- What are the childhood, adolescent, adult, and elderly years like in the American Indian culture?
- What social and cultural, familial, and communication characteristics describe American Indians along the lifespan continuum?
- What unique challenges (e.g., low educational attainment, poverty, health) face American Indians during the various lifespan stages?
- What cultural discontinuities do American Indian children and adolescents experience as they deal with issues in their homes and communities and in majority-culture or reservation schools?
- What do psychologists and researchers mean by two-spirit people, especially concerning American Indians?
- What unique challenges face counselors providing mental health services to American Indians in the four lifespan stages?
- What sources of information are available for counselors intervening with American Indian children, adolescents, adults, and elders?

OVERVIEW

Professional intervention with American Indian children, adolescents, adults, and elders requires an understanding of the challenges associated with each lifespan stage, the tremendous diversity within the American Indian culture, and the many challenges this culture faces. Providing appropriate counseling intervention for the American Indian client requires an understanding of the individual's culture, family, communication, spirituality, and many problems, all of which interact in a complex fashion. To be effective, counselors need to recognize and gain an understanding of racism and injustices forced, and still being forced, on American Indians. This chapter examines American Indian children, adolescents, adults, and elders; their characteristics; and their daily challenges.

AMERICAN INDIANS: DEMOGRAPHICS

Early American colonists treated American Indians with contempt and hostility and engaged in wars against them that bordered on genocide. Later, the native peoples were driven from the coastal plains to make way for a massive movement by White settlers pushing west. History is filled with examples of racism and discrimination against American Indians, and they continue to face such realities and the accompanying effects of poverty, unemployment, and low educational attainment. Research suggests a dismal picture for many American Indians.

American Indian and Alaskan Native includes a person having origins in any of the original peoples of North and South America (including Central America) and who maintains tribal affiliation or community attachment. This category includes people who indicate their race as "American Indian or Alaskan Native" or report entries such as Navajo, Blackfeet, Inupiat, Yup'ik, or Central American Indian groups or South American Indian groups (U.S. Census Bureau, 2015d).

"American Indians by the Numbers" (U.S. Census Bureau, 2015e) reports the following data: population (5.2 million, about 2% of the United States population), fourteen states with a population over 100,000, 432,343 age 65 or over, median age of 30.8 in 2013, 325 federally recognized reservations, 566 tribes, 1,698,815 families, 82.2% of American Indians 25 and over had a at least a high school education, median single-race household income was 36,252 in 2013 compared with 52,176 for the nation as a whole, and 26.9% lacked health care. The Alaska population identifies as American Indian and Alaskan Native, alone or in combination, in 2012, the highest rate for this race group of any state. Alaska was followed by Oklahoma (13.4%), New Mexico (10.4%), South Dakota (10.0%), and Montana (8.1%) (https://www.census.gov/population/estimates/state/rank/aiea.txt). Table 7.1 shows the cities in which significant numbers of American Indians live.

The U.S. Census Bureau offers other facts about American Indians and their demographics; however, caution is urged as counselors and social workers intervene with American Indians. This culture is very diverse: American Indians constitute a significant cultural group with very different values, problems, and resources compared with the general population. Therefore, to avoid basing professional decisions on stereotypes and misinformation, counselors need to consider tribal, language, educational, and other differences.

First, American Indians are a young and growing population. The median age of the American Indian population is considerably younger than the U.S. median. Also, the relatively young age of the population results in higher fertility rates overall.

Second, educational attainments of American Indians, Eskimos, and Aleuts are dismal but improving: 82.2% of American Indians and Alaskan Natives age 25 and older have at least a high school diploma, and 17.6% have at least a bachelor's degree. In comparison, 86.3% of the overall population had a high school education and 29.1% had a bachelor's degree or higher (U.S. Census Bureau, 2015e).

Third, significant numbers (29.2%) of American Indians live below the poverty line. The proportion of American Indian, Eskimo, and Aleut persons and families living below the poverty level is considerably higher than for the total population (U.S. Census Bureau, 2015e). For example, Standing Rock Reservation (which straddles North Dakota and South Dakota, with a population of 8,956) has a poverty rate of 43% compared with all the United States at 15%. About one in four American Indians and Alaskan Natives lived in poverty in 2012 (U.S. Census Bureau, 2015i).

Table 7.1 American Indian Population for Selected Cities

City	
New York	111,749
Los Angeles	54,236
Phoenix	43,724
Oklahoma City	36,572
Anchorage	36,062

Source: "Top 5 Cities with the Most Native Americans." U.S. Census Bureau. (2015e). American Indians by the numbers. Washington, DC: Author. Retrieved 3 June 2015 from http://www.infoplease.com/spot/aihmcensus1.html.

AMERICAN INDIAN CHILDREN

Social and Cultural Description

It is crucial that professionals intervening with American Indian children understand the history of the United States from the American Indian point of view and from the child's perspective. The assumption that American Indians belong to one homogeneous tribe is far from the truth. They are a culture of many peoples, with diverse educational attainments, economic levels, and tribal differences.

Although physical and cultural diversity has long characterized American Indians, certain similarities with respect to values and beliefs allow for a broad-based description of the American Indian child. As mentioned previously, caution must be exercised when developing such a portrait, because considerable intracultural variation is to be expected. Particularly relevant is the location of a child's residence (on or off the reservation), the child's school (predominantly American Indian or European American), and the parents' socioeconomic class.

The values and beliefs of American Indians often differ from those of other Americans. Whereas European American children are taught that they have considerable freedom as long as their actions remain within the law, American Indian children are taught that their actions must be in harmony with nature. American Indians also prize self-sufficiency and learning gained from the natural world. Children are taught to respect and protect the aged, who provide wisdom and acquaint the younger generations with traditions, customs, and legends. Elderly American Indians teach younger family members traditional crafts and handiwork as well as cultural morals. Other distinct cultural values are reflected in interpersonal relationships. For example, children receive the same degree of respect as adults, group cooperation and harmony are encouraged, and individuals are judged by their contribution to the group. American Indians have an unhurried lifestyle that is present time-oriented. A deep respect for tradition is evident.

For more than a century, tens of thousands of American Indians were sent to Indian boarding schools. The federal Bureau of Indian Affairs began opening boarding schools in the late 1870s, similar to religious boarding schools operated by Christian missionaries. The stories of misery and abuse told by native children in these schools are disturbing, especially since the goal was to obliterate all that was Indian. Some schools banned parents from visiting, because they might influence children with tribal cultures. Today, about 93% of American Indian and Alaskan Native students attend regular public schools, and 7% attend schools administered by the U.S. government's Bureau of Indian Affairs, a system of 184 schools for educating American Indian students spread over 23 states. American Indian and Alaskan Native students were more likely than students of other racial and ethnic groups to receive services under the Individuals with Disabilities Education Act (IDEA) (National Education Association, 2008).

The Indian Child Welfare Act (ICWA) was passed in 1978 to reaffirm tribal authority to protect children. ICWA aimed at stopping the inappropriate removal of pictures of American Indian leaders. In the 1970s, studies documented the horrifying experiences of thousands of American Indians: One out of every four children was being removed from their homes. Often such placement meant that many children were cut off forever from loving extended families, their culture, community, and entire tribes (Cross, 2014).

The ICWA has been hampered by lack of funding, jurisdictional barriers, lack of trained personnel, lack of information about the extent of abuse and neglect, lack of culturally appropriate service models, and community denial of these problems. Programs designed to serve tribal communities should have sufficient funds, tribal funds should be distributed so as to emphasize need and equity, regulations that provide tribes with the ability to design and operate a program that meets the unique circumstances and values of their communities, and understandable application procedures and more realistic reporting requirements.

Unfortunately, some American Indians, just like all cultures, have disabilities. Interestingly, disability is an idea familiar to Western culture but with no direct parallel in American Indian culture. The American Indian culture considers disability as disharmony of spirit. The main cause of preventable intellectual disabilities in the United States is prenatal alcohol use. Fetal Alcohol Spectrum Disorders (FASD) prevalence rates for Native Americans range from 1.0 to 8.97 per 1000 births. Native Americans have higher rates of alcohol use, frequency of use, and increased rates of fetal alcohol syndrome compared with other ethnic groups. American Indians and Alaskan Natives (AI/AN) have the second highest rates of intellectual and learning disabilities, only surpassed by African Americans. Other disabilities include hydrocephalus, atrial septal defect, valve stenosis, and atresia, cleft palate without cleft lip, cleft lip without cleft palate, rectal atresia and stenosis, fetal alcohol syndrome, and autosomal abnormalities.

Communication

American Indian languages can be divided into about a dozen stocks, with each stock divided into distinct languages. Most classifications of American Indians into nations, tribes, or peoples have been linguistic rather than political. This broad and diversified communication background, albeit personal and sacred to the American Indian, has not contributed to the European American definition of school success. Moreover, widespread differences exist in American Indians' ability to speak English.

Nonverbal communication of American Indian children adds another dimension to counseling intervention. It is essential for professionals to understand American Indian gestures, body movements, and general social behavior. Although considerable diversity exists, American Indian children speak more softly than European children and at a slower rate. They also tend to avoid direct interaction between speaker and listener as expressed by signs such as head nods and similar gestures.

Twenty-nine percent of American Indians and Alaskan Natives five years and older speak a language other than English in the home. While we understand and appreciate that language and communication is central to American Indian cultures, these children might experience a conflict between home language and community language. American Indians, of course, are not the only cultural group that speaks another language in the home. Still, school success (which can be defined in many ways) depends heavily on language and communication skills. We are not suggesting American Indians should forsake their native languages, but we are saying effective counselors with the American Indian culture are aware of challenges resulting from dual languages.

Families

American Indian immediate and extended families contribute to their children's cultural identities and play a significant role in overall child development. Extended family members offer both symbolic and actual leadership in family communities. They monitor children's behavior and offer advice and support with child-rearing practices.

American Indian children are respected, and they are also taught to respect others. American Indian child-rearing methods are marked by extraordinary patience and tolerance; that is, Indian children usually are brought up without restraint or severe physical punishment. Obedience is achieved through moral or psychological persuasion, building on tribal beliefs in supernatural beings. Many tribes have stories of supernatural beings who watch children. Through the telling of myths and legends, children are given a clear picture of expectations for desired behavior and the consequences of deviant behavior. The American Indian family thinks of children as gifts worthy of sharing with others, with fewer rules to obey in the American Indian culture. Also, the American Indian family places more emphasis on group welfare.

In the American Indian culture, family extends beyond the immediate relatives to extended family relatives through second cousins, members of one's clan, members of the community, all other living creatures in this world, nature as a whole, and the universe itself. The entire universe is thought of as a family, with everyone serving a useful and necessary function. American Indian children develop a heightened sensitivity for everything of which they are a part, for the cyclical motion of life, and for customs and traditions.

American Indian child-rearing practices and differing cultural family expectations for behavior sometimes result in confusion for American Indian children growing up with other cultures. They may demonstrate feelings of isolation, rejection, and anxiety that can result in alienation, poor self-image, and withdrawal. Such feelings undoubtedly affect achievement aspirations of American Indian children and can cause them to question the worth of their family life.

Unique Challenges Confronting American Indian Children

Several obstacles may hinder counseling interventions for American Indian children. First, American Indian children might harbor feelings of suspicion and distrust of professionals, whether European American or some other culture. Second, communication problems, such as nonverbal or body language, may result in misunderstanding, mistrust, and inability to develop rapport, which may hinder counseling efforts. The American Indian child who may appear to be unemotional or detached may only be overly sensitive to strangers. Third, as with Bill (see Case Study 7.1), counselors need to provide intervention to emphasize that cultural expectations are not a matter of right and wrong—they are simply different and deserve understanding and appreciation. Fourth, children with disabilities deserve attention, as do their parents and families. Counselors can play vital roles as they work with teachers and parents (and extended families) to assist American Indian children with their psychological challenges. Four, the National Education Association (NEA) publication, *American Indians/Alaska Natives: Education Issues*, reports a somewhat dismal picture of education issues American Indians and Alaskan Natives face:

- The AI/AN community faces educational issues similar to other minority groups, including the need for adequate funding for schools serving minority and disadvantaged students, as well as other issues with a special impact on the community.
- Student achievement gaps need to be aggressively addressed. For example, while 71% of AI/ANs age 25 or older had a high school diploma or more in the 2000 census, only 11% had a bachelor's degree or more, compared to 27% of Whites.
- There is an increasing need for quality teachers in Indian schools. Due to rural isolation, low teacher salaries, high poverty, and differences in languages and cultures, it is difficult to recruit and retain quality teachers in Indian schools. Further, the need for special education teachers is growing since representation of AI/AN students in special education is at 18%, almost double the rest of the student population at 10%.
- Native schools continue to be plagued by safety concerns, with high suspension and expulsion rates, and the highest percentage of all groups to report injury with weapons and fights on school grounds.

Case Study 7.1: Bill Lonetree, an American Indian Child

Eight-year-old Bill Lonetree lives with his parents, 10-year-old sister, 15-year-old brother, and elderly grandmother. The Lonetree family home is in a small community several miles from a reservation. Although the family's financial status is above the poverty level, money often poses a problem. For many years, Bill's ancestors lived on the reservation, but his grandparents moved off the reservation to better their deteriorating financial status. After Bill's grandfather died, his grandmother moved in with Bill's parents.

Bill, a quiet and often reflective child, is a third grader at the local European American school. Although he generally likes his school and has several American Indian friends, he experiences difficulty making friends of other cultures.

Bill's schoolwork is below average. In home and neighborhood situations, he appears to be relatively bright and thoughtful. His European American teacher, who recently began teaching at the school, encourages Bill to try harder, to listen attentively, and to be more proactive in his learning. In her attempts to motivate Bill, she sometimes tells him of her learning experiences in high school and college and encourages him to prepare for similar experiences that he can someday enjoy. She hopes that Bill will speak up and give her some indications that he is at least listening to her. Bill's parents think he is trying hard in school, although he is not performing at the level they would like. They hope that his grades will not decline further at about sixth grade, as was the case with Bill's older brother.

When Bill is asked about his academic problems, he responds that he is trying but admits that he does not always understand what the teacher is saying. He admits that reading the textbooks and other materials is difficult for him. Understanding (and speaking) two languages is often confusing for him.

In Bill's family, there is a sense of mutual respect and appreciation for one another. His grandmother, although elderly and unable to contribute financially, is close to Bill. He has tremendous respect for her and listens attentively when she tells him of the rich heritage of the American Indian culture. Also, he feels a sense of loyalty to her. On the days when she is ill, Bill stays home from school to watch over her and to assist her with her needs.

Bill is looking for a sense of self-worth (although perhaps not the same "self-worth" his teacher considers important) and he desires friendships. His poor self-concept, however, makes it difficult for him to find new friends and to develop self-worth. He sometimes feels "caught in the middle" between his American Indian home and peers of other cultures.

Reflection Questions:

1. How will you explain to Bill's teacher that his perception of "trying" and "success" differs from hers?
2. How will you intervene with Bill to improve his self-worth? How will you explain to Bill that his culture and cultural expectations are different rather than right or wrong?
3. What advice will you offer Bill's parents (and elderly grandmother) to improve his grades and social skills?

AMERICAN INDIAN ADOLESCENTS

Social and Cultural Description

Although the words *Indian* and *adolescent* combined tend to evoke stereotypical images, this developmental period in the American Indian culture varies greatly. Significant physical and cultural variance is found within the American Indian population, but individual differences during the adolescent years are even more marked. Some common characteristics emerge when studying American Indian adolescents, but one must be careful not to oversimplify or ignore intracultural and individual differences.

Each day, American Indian youths face the dilemma of constant change in our dynamic multicultural society. Conflicts include being expected to adapt to new and changing values and traditions. American Indian youths are an extremely high-risk population, with higher rates (compared with national averages) of dropping out of high school, alcohol and drug abuse, teenage pregnancy, learning disabilities, out-of-home placement, and suicide. Many American Indian youths also experience racism from other cultural groups as well.

Cultural beliefs and traditions of the American Indian people particularly influence developing adolescents and their evolving identity. Adolescents who live in American Indian families and attend schools with differing cultures may experience cultural confusion and often question allegiance to their cultural identity. This can be particularly serious for adolescents who want to retain their rich cultural heritage and at the same time be accepted in European American mainstream society.

Cooperation, Competition, and Sharing

Many Americans place value and emphasis on competition. American society values individuality and achievement; for many people, being successful means having the most cars, wealth, and material possessions. Many American Indians, however, view success communally, by contributing toward the group identity and by promoting harmony. They value sharing and seeking to acquire only what is necessary to satisfy current needs. In games requiring talent and skills, players may choose to play in such a way as to place group cooperation over individual winning. A similar situation may occur in the classroom, where competitive academic achievement may be shunned to avoid causing some students to be perceived as underachievers.

Patience and Passivity

American Indian adolescents learn to be patient, to control emotions, and to avoid passionate outbursts over small matters. Such attributes as poise under duress, self-containment, and aloofness often conflict with European American tendencies toward impatience and competitiveness. Therefore, people of other cultures sometimes perceive American Indians as lazy or uncaring. American Indians show patience and poise as they lower their voices when angry, unlike adolescents of some other cultures, who tend to be strident in expressing their anger. Other differences exist; for example, some American Indian groups indicate respect by looking downward to avoid eye contact.

Noninterference

Generally speaking, American Indians strive to attain a harmonious relationship with nature and all living things. Noninterference with others and a deep respect for the rights and dignity of individuals constitute a basic premise of the American Indian culture. Adolescents are taught early on to respect the rights and privileges of others and to work together toward common goals in harmony with nature. American Indians place high regard on building relationships and on an all-encompassing sense of belonging with one's people and the practice of noninterference. Although many individual differences must be considered, American Indians do not interfere with another person's ability to choose. Noninterference means caring in a respectful way.

The school dropout rate of American Indian adolescents is high. Factors that undoubtedly contribute to the high dropout rate include growing feelings of isolation, cultural conflicts between American Indian adolescents and teachers of other cultures, cultural and individual rejection, and anxiety resulting from differences in cultural values. Many American Indian adolescents often experience school curricula and program development that result in difficult challenges. Counselors working with American Indian adolescents need to move beyond stereotypical generalizations and rely on accurate knowledge and firsthand contact.

Communication

American Indian adolescents, like adolescents of other cultures, need the security and psychological safety provided by a common language. However, this may be complicated by the fact that some American Indian adolescents speak only their American Indian language, some speak only English, and others are bilingual. As previously noted, some speak English in school and another language at home. Self-concept and individual and cultural identities are being formed during the adolescent's transition from the family-centered world to a wider social world. No longer is communication limited to that with elders, parents, and siblings. An American Indian adolescent's ability to reach out to a wider world depends greatly on his or her ability to speak and understand the language of the majority and other cultures.

Attending a school staffed by teachers of other cultures and facing problems associated with not being understood may affect the adolescent's perceived ability to cope successfully in a culturally diverse world. Communication problems also may contribute to the adolescent's tendency to decline in academic achievement and self-esteem. They can also contribute to lower cultural and adolescent identities. Adolescents often have to decide which language to speak. American Indians respect their language as a part of their culture. This regard for their native language, however, conflicts with the opinion that English is the means to success, depending on one's definition of success.

Aguilera and LeCompte (2007) conducted research on the language experiences of three indigenous communities with language immersion models in preschool through twelfth grades. Specifically, they summarized the history and implementation of language instruction for American Indian, Alaskan Native, and Native Hawaiian children in three different language communities. Each community chose a different way to provide instruction, and each faced considerable difficulties. Aguilera and LeCompte (2007) explained that indigenous languages have been difficult to implement because of the overwhelming pressure to teach English and the recent emphasis on high-stakes testing. Still, revitalization is important to maintain the American Indian heritage, including knowledge of medicine, religion, cultural practices and traditions, music, art, human relations, and child-rearing practices. Their research evidence did not reveal the superiority of one immersion model over another; however, their research did show that total immersion is a more effective approach to achieving proficiency in native languages.

Families

Although an adolescent's developing social consciousness results in a gradual transition from a family-centered to a more peer-centered environment, the traditional American Indian respect for and commitment to the family continue. Adolescents seek social acceptance and approval from older members of the family as well as from younger ones. American Indian culture places family before self and fosters a great respect for elders and their wisdom. Wisdom is gained through interaction with older people, whose task is to acquaint the young with the traditions, customs, legends, and myths of their culture. All family members care for the aged and accept death as a natural fact of life.

Unique Challenges Confronting American Indian Adolescents

Three specific issues have particular relevance for American Indian adolescents: (1) Should American Indian or European American values (or some "cultural combination") provide the basis for the adolescent's developing identity? (2) Should proficiency in both the American Indian language and English be encouraged? And (3) Can harmony with family and nature be maintained while the adolescent is surviving in the European American world? Survival in the majority culture often requires American Indians to question the priorities of their own culture.

American Indian adolescents are in a unique and often difficult situation. Not only must they reconcile the values of American Indian and European American cultures, they must also deal with the usual problems of adolescence as a developmental period on the lifespan continuum. Educational and societal dilemmas, as well as cultural conflicts, during these crucial developmental years often cause feelings of frustration, hopelessness, alienation, and loss of confidence. The steady decline often seen in adolescents' academic achievement may further contribute to feelings of hopelessness.

Some researchers advocated a strengths approach rather than a weakness approach. McMahon, Kenyon, and Carter (2013) maintained that historically, the majority of research with American Indian youth and communities has focused on vulnerabilities, problems, and needs rather than resilience, strengths, and assets. These researchers concluded Alaskan Indian youth have a positive orientation toward themselves and their communities, which was evidenced by the fact that the youth identified more strengths than challenges in their lives. Somewhat unexpectedly, when asked what aspects of their lives and communities they would most like to change, a significant number of the youth identified they wanted to change "nothing" about their personal lives. Furthermore, a significant number of youth indicated they would not change anything about their communities as well. At first glance, this finding was somewhat surprising given that poverty, substance abuse, homicide, and suicide among residents have been continuous and serious problems on the reservations. To build upon youth resilience, programs should be directed toward not only the individual but also the families and communities. The people in their lives, especially their families, were repeatedly cited as sources of strength by Alaskan Indian youth. Therefore, families may be an important, yet previously neglected source of strength as an integral component of community-based interventions (McMahon et al., 2013).

Compared to other races and ethnicities, American Indians and Alaskan Natives (AI/AN) experience considerable health disparities. A better understanding of AI/AN adolescents' risk behaviors may help to improve future interventions and programs to prevent substance abuse, teen pregnancy, STIs (sexually transmitted infections), and sexual violence. Alcohol and substance abuse are contributing factors to sexual risk-taking among adolescents and can result in STI transmission, unintentional pregnancy, and sexual violence. In one study (grades 9–12) of AI/AN students, 14.2% had been hit, slapped, or physically hurt on purpose by their boyfriend or girlfriend; 11.6% had been forced to have sexual intercourse when they did not want to; 76.7% had indulged in alcohol; 29.3% drank alcohol before 13 years of age; 42.5% were current alcohol users; 22.8% engaged in binge drinking; and 6.6% had consumed alcohol on school property. The study concluded AI/AN engaged in health risk factors such as disproportionately high rates of STIs, teen pregnancy, and alcohol and drug abuse. Interventions should include targeted, adolescent-specific interventions aimed at reducing behaviors that put AI/AN adolescents at risk for teen pregnancy, STIs and other health conditions (de Ravello, Jones, Tulloch, Taylor & Doshi, 2014). Case Study 7.2 introduces Ed Lonetree.

Case Study 7.2: Ed Lonetree, an American Indian Adolescent

Ed, age 15, lives with his parents, sister, elderly grandmother, and his eight-year-old brother, Bill. The family still lives several miles from the reservation and continues to have some financial difficulty.

Ed, who is midway through his adolescent years, has problems that Bill has yet to experience. Although Ed was a relatively small child, his growth spurt began at about age 12, accompanied by considerable physical and psychosocial changes. He thinks about these changes and does not always understand what is happening. He wonders whether all the changes are normal. Sometimes he admits to feelings of confusion. "How can I be a child, an adolescent, and an adult?" Ed asks himself.

Ed is in the eighth grade for the second time. Although he thought he was trying last year, the schoolwork was difficult and he experienced language problems. In fact, language may be his greatest problem. He thinks his "choice of language" will depend on where he lives when he grows up. He will speak the American Indian language if he returns to the reservation; he will speak English if he lives in the local community. Meanwhile, he speaks the American Indian language with his grandmother (and sometimes with his father) and English at school.

Ed is thinking of joining the Indian League when he turns 16. The organization is concerned with the civil rights of American Indians and generally promotes their interests. Ed's dad thinks he will be too young and that finishing school and speaking English would be best for Ed. Secretly, Ed knows that he will not join if his grandmother opposes the idea. Disappointing his grandmother would not be worth joining the group. And, after all, she has always given him good advice in the past.

Ed has experienced a few problems at school. His teachers continue to write notes on his report cards referring to his lack of interest. Ed thinks he is interested and motivated, but the issue is not worth confronting the teachers. Also, he has tried to make friends with some European American adolescents but has not had a great deal of success.

Reflection Questions:

1. How can counselors intervene when Ed wonders, "How can I be a child, an adolescent, and an adult?" or when Ed questions whether he is a child or adolescent?
2. How can counselors address Ed's seeming "lack of interest"? Or is this a problem that should be addressed with both Ed and his teacher? In other words, perhaps Ed *is* interested, yet his teacher perceives otherwise.

AMERICAN INDIAN ADULTS

Social and Cultural Description

The U.S. Census Bureau provides some interesting data on the American Indian and Alaskan Native population. American Indians and Alaskan Natives have a population of about 5.2 million (about 2% of the United States population). Projected populations for these groups vary with the sources, but it is clear the population is growing, albeit slowly.

Several problems (although no fault of their own) plague the American Indian population. First, poverty affects about 22% of the American Indian population (Krogstad, 2014). In addition, they are more likely to have a family member with a disability (38% for American Indian and Alaskan Native families). Second, and related, American Indians continue to experience higher rates of chronic diseases, mortality, suicide, and alcoholism. American Indians are 770% more likely to die from alcoholism, 650% more likely to die from tuberculosis, 420% more likely to die from diabetes, and 280% more likely to die from accidents.

Historically, in American Indian communities, adults were universally responsible for child rearing. Every adult played a role in teaching and caring for younger members of the tribe. Grandparents often raised firstborn children and taught them about social mores and values, including sexuality and appropriate behaviors that ensured the tribe's survival. Children learned creation stories, naming ceremonies, spiritual teachings, puberty ceremonies, spiritual and social songs, and dances.

An estimated one in three Native American women are assaulted or raped in their lifetime and three out of five experience domestic violence. For decades, when a Native American woman was assaulted or raped by a man who was non-Indian, she had little or no recourse. Under long-standing law in Indian country, reservations are sovereign nations with their own police departments and courts in charge of prosecuting crimes on tribal land. But Indian police have lacked the legal authority to arrest non-Indian men who commit acts of domestic violence against native women on reservations, and tribal courts have lacked the authority to prosecute the men.

Congress approved a law that for the first time allowed Indian tribes to prosecute certain crimes of domestic violence committed by non-Indians in Indian country. While the law was praised by tribal leaders, native women, and the administration as a significant first step, it still falls short of protecting all Indian women from the epidemic of violence they face on tribal lands. The new authority went into effect for most of the country's 566 federally recognized Indian tribes in 2015. It covers domestic violence committed by non-Indian husbands and boyfriends, but it does not cover sexual assault or rape committed by non-Indians who are "strangers" to their victims. It also does not extend to native women in Alaska.

More than 75% of residents on Indian reservations in the United States are non-Indians. In at least 86% of the reported cases of rape or sexual assault of American Indian and Alaskan Native women, both on and off reservations, the victims say their attackers were non-native men.

On the modern-day reservation, Indians and non-Indians often live side by side. One home belongs to a White family and the next one belongs to an Indian family. It is a recipe for conflict over who is in charge and who has legal jurisdiction over certain crimes (Horwitz, 2014).

Spirituality plays a major role in the lives of many American Indians and thus should be recognized by counselors during intervention. Basic American Indian spiritual and traditional beliefs include the following:

1. A single higher power is known as Creator, Great Creator, Great Spirit, or Great One; plants and animals, like humans, are part of the spirit world. The spirit world exists conjointly with and intermingles with the physical world.
2. Human beings are made up of a spirit, mind, and body, all of which are interconnected; therefore, illness affects the mind and spirit as well as the body.
3. Wellness is harmony in body, mind, and spirit; unwellness is disharmony in mind, body, and spirit.
4. Natural unwellness is caused by a violation of a sacred social and natural law of creation (e.g., participating in a sacred ceremony while under the influence of alcohol, drugs, or having had sex within four days of a ceremony).
5. Unnatural unwellness is caused by conjuring (witchcraft) from those with destructive intentions.
6. Each individual is responsible for his or her own wellness by being attuned to self, relations, environment, and universe (Garrett & Wilbur, 1999).

Moghaddam, Momper, and Fong (2013) examined discrimination and participation in traditional healing in American Indians and Alaskan Natives (AI/AN). In light of the aversive experiences they face, AI/AN people have followed the tenets of ritual and traditional healing to address imbalances in the body, mind, and spirit. For providers working with AI/AN clients, it is important to understand who is using traditional healing and why they are using alternative services. Nearly a quarter of the sample reported discrimination in a health-care setting. Roughly half of the sample had used traditional healing, and the majority of those who had used traditional healing were women ages 35–44 (27%). Conclusions included roughly half (48%) of the study sample had participated in some form of traditional healing. The majority of those who used traditional services were women. The largest proportion of those who used traditional services were married (36%). Thirty-seven percent of traditional service users had dependent children.

Most professionals agree that the American Indian population has a proportionately greater percentage of problems than other minority populations. Compared with African and Asian Americans, American Indians have significant income, education, and medical needs. In addition, arrest, alcoholism, and unemployment rates are higher among American Indians than among other ethnic groups.

Although American Indians' diversity should always be considered, several cultural practices and lifestyles characterize American Indians. Common traits include (a) relative passivity and shyness in dealing with professionals, (b) sensitivity to strangers (resulting in soft-spokenness), (c) a tendency to focus on the present, (d) a fatalistic view of life, (e) strong family obligations, (f) noninterference with others, and (g) avoidance of assertive or aggressive situations.

Communication

At one time or another, American Indians have spoken over two thousand different languages. The difficulty of categorizing these languages into major families attests to the fact that understanding the communication patterns of this culture requires considerable effort.

The U.S. government has attempted to accommodate, assimilate, and terminate the Indian for centuries. This impact is felt today as traditional Native American languages are becoming extinct, and the future tribal leaders are struggling to perform on comparable levels with mainstream American students. Tribal sovereignty at its core is threatened by the upcoming generation of future leaders not knowing their traditional culture or language. Preserving Native American culture and language will not only improve the individual Native American student's success, but culture and language preservation will also preserve tribal sovereignty (Meza, 2015).

Littlebear (2003) claims that the United States is a graveyard for hundreds of native languages. Some are only a generation away from extinction. The loss of American Indian languages has been well chronicled by ethnologists, linguists, anthropologists, missionaries, and even some government-run schools. Although there is nothing wrong with American Indian languages, systematic attempts have been made to eradicate these languages and have the potential for damaging American Indian identities.

Families

American Indian families, just as individuals of the culture, have widely differing personality traits, cultural practices, and lifestyles. Several common characteristics of families, however, appear to pertain to large segments of the culture.

In the American Indian culture, because survival of the individual is synonymous with that of the community, the family holds a prominent place in the lives of American Indians, who view the concept of family much more broadly than mainstream America. Structural characteristics of the extended family network and the tribal network function as facilitators of social responsibility, reciprocity, and values transmission. Family relationships extend far beyond the biological connections of the nuclear family.

Several characteristics of American Indian families are worth mentioning. Each has implications for counselors planning professional intervention.

First, the culture expects adults to demonstrate strong allegiance to, respect for, and protection of the elderly.

Second, American Indian child-rearing practices include an emphasis on self-sufficiency, with physical development and psychological learning being in harmony with knowledge gained from the natural world.

Third, with respect to women, American Indian society differs from other ethnic minority groups. Historically, African, Latin, and Asian cultures have exhibited a patriarchal structure. Some American Indian subcultures, however, have perceived the roles of women differently. In the past, American Indian women held great political and economic power.

Fourth, indigenous residents of Alaska (Alaskan Natives) die by suicide at a rate nearly four times the U.S. average. An astonishing 7% of Alaskan Natives indicated that they had seriously contemplated suicide within the past year. Studies have shown that alcohol is directly or indirectly involved in most of these deaths. Although Alaskan Natives have encountered alcohol for well over a century, the high suicide risk is an entrenched but comparatively recent phenomenon affecting only the past two generations. The results for community risk factors suggested that both opportunities in the modem economy (higher median incomes) and a strong traditional presence (linguistically isolated households) offer some protection against young male suicide. A strong economy and presence of traditional elders provided opportunities and role models for identification and integration with the majority and minority cultures, respectively (Berman, 2014).

Unique Challenges Confronting American Indian Adults

Several challenges facing American Indian adults deserve counselors' attention.

First, the lack of acceptance of American Indian culture has contributed to the difficulties faced by American Indians. Currently, American Indians continue to struggle to overcome others' negative images of them; even worse, they may have to overcome their own negative self-images.

Second, the previously mentioned overall health-care concerns continue to be an ongoing concern. Chronic diseases, mortality rates, suicide, and alcoholism are all problems deserving counselors' attention. Still, in order to maintain objectivity and avoid stereotypes, counselors realize the dire need to base professional decisions on careful and objective evaluations.

Third, education has always been a controversial issue that basically revolves around value conflict and self-determination. Regardless of these factors, however, commitments to education and academic achievement of American Indians have been major drawbacks to their progress.

Both clients and their counselors must seek solutions to the challenges confronting American Indian adults in a cooperative spirit. Although the reasons for American Indians' personal and social conditions should be recognized and understood, counseling interventions should focus on solutions to the obstacles hampering personal and social progress.

Case Study 7.3 looks at John Lonetree, an American Indian adult.

Case Study 7.3: John Lonetree, an American Indian Adult

John, age 38, shares traits common to fathers of all cultural backgrounds. His main goals are to provide financial support and a home for his 8-year-old and 15-year-old sons, his 10-year-old daughter, his wife of 17 years, and his elderly mother. John works at a manufacturing plant and wonders where he could find another job if he was laid off. He realizes the difficulty that job hunting would entail, especially with his limited education, lack of marketable skills, and poor English.

Through hard work at the same job for nine years, John's condition is not that of the stereotypical American Indian. John has a job, does not have a drinking problem, has never been in jail, and is not overly self-critical, as many American Indians are thought to be. The fact that he does not have extensive material possessions is of little concern to him; he thinks people should appreciate him as a person rather than for what he owns. He is aware that he has experienced fewer problems than many of his friends.

John has several family concerns that adults of other cultures often share. He sometimes worries about his children's education. They will need a better education than he has had in order to compete in the predominantly European American society. He is concerned about his mother, who is showing signs of advancing age. Although she doesn't make a direct financial contribution to the family, she is an important source of advice and counsel. Also, she takes care of the children when they are too ill to attend school. Because of her age, she deserves to be protected and respected. John often seeks her advice on how to raise the children.

Although John is fairly content and happy compared with many of his friends, he does have problems. As previously mentioned, he wants his children to finish high school. Then he wants to do something to help those friends who have not been as fortunate as he has been. He would also like to rid himself, his family, and his people of the stereotypical image of the drunken, lazy, uneducated American Indian that continues to be so demoralizing. Finally, because he is accustomed to speaking a combination of two languages with his friends, he sometimes experiences communication difficulties when he travels outside his American Indian community.

Reflection Questions:

1. How should effective counselors provide intervention to address John's doubts about his future, his current employment skills, and his changing family?
2. How should John deal with family change when his mother dies, as well as with the psychological aspects of a close relative dying?

AMERICAN INDIAN ELDERLY

Social and Cultural Description

Counselors need to have an objective understanding of the population, education, employment, income, and health of elderly American Indians.

Knowledge of several interesting facts will help mental health professionals understand elderly American Indian clients:

- About one-fourth of Native American elderly live on American Indian reservations or in Alaskan Native villages. Almost half are concentrated in the southwestern states of Oklahoma, Arizona, New Mexico, and Texas. Most of the remainder live in states along the Canadian border.
- Educationally, elderly American Indians lag significantly. In fact, nearly 10% of all American Indian elderly do not have any formal education, and only about one-third have a high school diploma. Those who did receive an education almost exclusively attended school systems that—either on or off the reservation—often have been considered poor quality.

- Twenty-two percent of American Indians live in poverty; 26% of American Indian elderly live in poverty (*EP Magazine*, 2008).
- The health status of elderly American Indians also poses problems. American Indians' life expectancy is about eight years shorter than other cultures. American Indians and Alaskan Natives are ten times more likely than European Americans to develop diabetes. In addition, alcohol abuse is a leading cause of health problems in American Indians. Other health problems of elderly American Indians include injuries from accidents, suicide, homicide, tuberculosis, liver and kidney diseases, high blood pressure, pneumonia, and malnutrition.

Counseling professionals should focus their efforts on the prevention and management of chronic illnesses and conditions in this population. Disease patterns in American Indians have followed several trends, including a shift from acute, infectious diseases to those of a more degenerative type. Chronic illnesses and conditions seen in significant numbers of American Indians include diabetes, heart disease, substance use, and fetal alcohol syndrome.

As a result of increased morbidity and mortality rates, the life expectancy for American Indians is 71 years, less than the rest of U.S. population. Stark realities for elderly American Indians include, social and cultural barriers, racial and ethnic biases and discrimination; cultural understanding and language, socioeconomic status, health behaviors and lifestyles, financial issues, remoteness of facilities, aging and outdated facilities, ability to recruit and maintain health providers; and limits in funding and entitlement (*EP Magazine*, 2008).

It is imperative that counselors be aware of the often disturbing living conditions of American Indian elderly. Social programs cannot immunize American Indian elderly from a lifetime of deprivation, including inadequate nutrition, housing, and health services. Significant changes will be needed for future generations of elderly American Indians to witness improvement in their standard of living. Professional intervention must take into consideration all the conditions affecting the American Indian elderly.

Communication

American Indian elderly seem to experience communication problems similar to those of American Indian adults; however, there is no evidence that they encounter special problems as a result of their age. American Indian elderly experience frustration in seeking attention to their health and retirement benefits. Also, as with other minority adults, differing cultures may misunderstand or misinterpret the elderly American Indian's nonverbal communication style.

Families

As previously mentioned, the elderly receive considerable respect in the American Indian culture. This may be because of their advanced age or cultural tradition. Regardless of the reason, younger generations seek the opinions of elders and consider their advice with reverence.

Understanding the actual role the elderly play in American Indian families provides counselors with insights about their problems and the questions that might be raised during counseling sessions. The extended family continues to play a significant role in family life. Elderly family members provide significant services, such as assisting with traditional child-rearing practices. In turn, younger family members respect the symbolic leadership of the elderly and expect them to have an official voice in child rearing. Parents defer to the authority of their elders and rarely overrule the latter's decisions regarding the children. Relationships with all family members are an important source of strength for the elderly.

It is important for counselors to understand the living arrangements of American Indian elderly. Among Native American and European Americans age 65 and older, the majority of men are married and the majority of women are widowed.

Unique Challenges Confronting the American Indian Elderly

First, American Indians' poverty results in serious health problems: mortality, suicide, alcoholism, a host of diseases, and medical conditions, just to name a few. Second, the relatively small size of the elderly American Indian population has not been sufficient to attract attention to their problems. Dealing successfully with government agencies, such as the Bureau of Indian Affairs and the Public Health Service, continues to be frustrating, especially for American Indians who lack English proficiency and knowledge of their legal rights.

Case Study 7.4: Wenonah Lonetree, an American Indian Elder

At age 72, Wenonah Lonetree does not doubt that she is growing old. She senses it in the way she feels and in the way she is treated by her family and others. Growing old has both rewards and drawbacks. She realizes that attaining the age of 72 is unusual for a person in her American Indian culture; she has already outlived many of her friends. Although Wenonah is financially poor, not having money is nothing new to her. She lives with her son John, his wife, and their family and contributes to the family by helping with the children. In fact, she has assumed virtually all responsibility for child rearing. The children have learned that Wenonah's word represents authority; their parents never question her decisions. The family equates Wenonah's years with great wisdom.

Wenonah has the typical problems of elderly members of the American Indian culture. Her only schooling was a few years in a reservation school, and she suffers the usual ailments of the aged. Although her community does not lack medical facilities, Wenonah seldom visits the physician. She has no means of transportation when John and his wife are at work; besides, she places her trust in healing rituals. Finances are also a problem, because living with John and his family off the reservation has lowered her government benefits.

Living with John's family can be both rewarding and frustrating. She likes being close to the children, and her son conscientiously works to provide a good home. Also, telling the children stories and teaching them about customs and traditions allows her to relive old memories. However, she is troubled by the growing problems of her grandchildren. The school apparently has little regard for American Indian youths, and her grandson Ed is talking about joining the Indian League. "That's just not the way to make progress," Wenonah says quietly, yet adamantly.

Reflection Questions:

1. What counseling issues might Wenonah bring to the counselor? What will the next few years bring? Once the counselor has reached objective conclusions, what approaches do you suggest?
2. How can Wenonah reconcile the differences between her and the younger generations? How might the counselor help?

SUMMARY

American Indians during all four lifespan stages have problems that might be brought to counseling sessions. Professionals who counsel American Indian children, adolescents, adults, and elders have a responsibility to understand the American Indian culture as well as the specific challenges commonly associated with each lifespan period. American Indian women are perceived differently from women in most other cultures, and they have traditionally played significant family and tribal roles. Providing effective mental health intervention to such a diverse and challenged cultural group requires training and experience. Counselors will need to develop appropriate counseling skills and to make the commitment to provide culturally effective counseling intervention.

SUGGESTED READINGS

Ballard, E. D., Musci, R. J., Tingey, L., Goklish, N., Larzelere-Hinton, F., Barlow, A., & Cwik, M. (2015). Latent class analysis of substance use behavior in reservation-based American Indian youth who attempted suicide. *American Indian & Alaska Native Mental Health Research: The Journal of the National Center, 22*(1), 77–94. American Indian (AI) adolescents who attempt suicide engage in substance abuse and aggressive behaviors; and clinical correlates of subgroup membership included risky sexual behavior and recent exposure to suicidal behavior.

Henderson, D., Carjuzaa, J., & Ruff, W. G. (2015). Reconciling leadership paradigms: Authenticity as practiced by American Indian school leaders. *International Journal of Multicultural Education, 17*(1), 211–231. The study described how these leaders have to reconcile their Westernized educational leadership training with their traditional ways of knowing, living, and leading.

Meza, N. (2015). Indian education: Maintaining tribal sovereignty through culture and language preservation. *Brigham Young University Education & Law Journal,* Issue 1, 353–366. The article focuses on the role of culture and language preservation in promoting the sovereignty of tribes of Native Americans in the United States.

The Washington Post. (2014, November 29). From broken home to broken system. http://www .washingtonpost.com/sf/national/2014/11/28/from-broken-homes-to-a-broken-system/, accessed 29 November 2014. This excellent piece looks at an Oglala Lakota teenager with a long braid and tattoos—she had a broken home and then experienced a broken legal system.

Wexler, L., Chandler, M.; Gone, J. P., Cwik, M., Kirmayer, L. J., LaFromboise, T., Brockie, T., O'Keefe, V., Walkup, J., & Allen, J. Framing health matters: Advancing suicide prevention research with rural American Indian and Alaskan Native populations. *American Journal of Public Health,* 105 (5), 891–899. As part of the National Action Alliance for Suicide Prevention's American Indian and Alaskan Native (AI/AN) Task Force, a multidisciplinary group of AI/AN suicide research experts convened to outline pressing issues related to this subfield of suicidology.

8 Counseling American Indian Clients

QUESTIONS TO BE EXPLORED

- What unique challenges and differences can counselors expect when intervening with American Indian children, adolescents, adults, and elders?
- How can non-American Indian counselors effectively plan counseling intervention for American Indian clients, considering the latter's diverse cultural, tribal, and individual differences?
- How has a history of ill treatment (e.g., taking land, building America Indian schools, and harboring prejudice) affected American Indians and their worldviews?
- How can counselors address American Indians' tendency toward early withdrawal from counseling services?
- How can counselors conduct individual, group, and family therapy for American Indians?
- What developmental concerns and problems might American Indian child, adolescent, adult, and elderly clients present to counselors?
- How can counselors address American Indians' many problems, such as low educational attainment, high unemployment levels, and low socioeconomic conditions?
- What additional sources provide information for professionals intervening with American Indian children, adolescents, adults, and elders?

OVERVIEW

Counselors intervening with American Indian children, adolescents, adults, and elders need both an understanding of and an appreciation for the American Indian culture and worldview. Such a task will not be easy, considering the differing languages, lifestyles, religions, kinship systems, tribes, and reservations. Counseling therapy that may be appropriate for an American Indian adult living on the East Coast may be inappropriate for such an adult living in the western plains region. Each tribe's customs and values affect both individual identity and family dynamics. Counselors will find that American Indians withdraw from counseling at alarmingly high rates. The initial consultation should be substantive in nature; and the nature and process of counseling intervention should be explained to the client. Also, counselors need to understand that mainstream individual and group counseling processes often conflict with American Indians' values and perspectives—for example, cooperation, harmony, generosity, sharing, living in the present, ancient legends and cultural traditions, peace, and politeness. Finally, lifespan differences will also determine American Indians' worldviews as well as their perceived problems.

AMERICAN INDIAN CHILDREN

Potential Problems Warranting Counseling Intervention

Problems American Indian children may experience include

- failure to develop a strong cultural identity and a positive self-concept;
- adverse effects of misperceptions about American Indians and the childhood years;
- adverse effects of discrimination;
- distrust of European American professionals;
- poor English proficiency and confusion in communication;
- nonverbal communication style, which may result in misunderstandings;
- inability to reconcile American Indian cultural values with other cultural values;
- lower academic achievement after the fourth grade;
- increasing socialization from a parent-centered to a peer-centered world;
- physical, psychosocial, and intellectual differences;
- differences in size and growth rate resulting from cultural factors, genetics, environment, and socioeconomic status;
- hair texture, facial features, and skin colors of American Indian children, which may be considered by other cultures as inferior or wrong rather than different; and
- academic difficulties, which may cause American Indian children to conclude that they simply are not smart enough to achieve success in school.

Many American Indian children have problems in traditional American schools. Still, one should not blame the victim—American Indian children did nothing to create their problems. One indication is the high drop-out rates among American Indian students. Reasons might include schools' failing to recognize differing learning styles, failing to avoid the dangers of stereotyping American Indians as being too much alike, and failing to understand the many different American Indian cultures. Educators and counselors can learn more about American Indians' learning styles, values toward humility and harmony, tendencies to learn by demonstration and observation, and the need for more reflection time when asked questions (Morgan, 2010). Selected student characteristics, such as language ability, traditional knowledge, motivation, positive life experiences, early goal setting, basic skills, and the ability to balance conflicts between home and school, all contribute to the child's ability to succeed in school. Perceptive counselors will recognize these characteristics as they plan professional intervention with American Indian children.

American Indian youth often face social and cultural challenges during identity development. Newman (2005) maintains that the identity development process for ethnic minority adolescents provides an added dimension highlighting the importance of ethnicity in developing a sense of self. Her conclusions include: (1) Impulsive adolescents had the least developed ethnic identities and highest levels of interpersonal vulnerability; (2) conformist adolescents expressed positive feelings about ethnic group affiliation and described relationships as harmonious but demonstrated social anxiety; and (3) post-conformist adolescents had the highest levels of social competence and identity achievement but also had high levels of psychological distress and family conflict.

American Indians also face a number of challenges to their ego development and ethnic identity formation. For example, they are influenced by the mainstream media: the imagery of American Indians, omission of their history in social and political history, references to American Indians as being savages, and the various cultural stereotypes.

Counseling Considerations

Counselors who work with American Indian children should first learn as much as possible about the American Indian culture. Well-informed, objective, and appropriate counseling requires an unbiased perception of American Indian children and their many cultural and individual variations.

Behavior that may appear bizarre to the counselor might be the cultural norm for American Indian children. For example, American Indian children may pilfer objects from teachers, peers, or the counselor. When confronted, they will usually admit taking the objects; however, they are likely to be both surprised and hurt if the act is referred to as "stealing." These children have been taught that people of rank and importance share. The counselor could tell the children that sharing with one's family is acceptable but that one should ask before "borrowing" objects outside the home. In addition, freedom in the American Indian culture extends to the childhood years: Children are allowed considerable involvement in decision making and are usually given choices. Counselors working with American Indian children may want to provide them with opportunities to make decisions during counseling sessions.

Although mental health clinics have programs that address the needs of children, elementary school counselors probably represent the largest group of counselors working with American Indian children. These counselors should consider the stereotypical perceptions of the American Indian people and culture, the contributions of the culture, the special needs of young American Indians, and the barriers that hamper communication between American Indians and their counselors. To promote counseling effectiveness, these counselors may want to improve their understanding of the American Indian child's perceptions, language (both verbal and nonverbal), values, and cultural heritage.

Individual and Group Therapy

Current counseling orientations require American Indian children to adopt unfamiliar ways of acting and thinking and to reject their traditional ways of storytelling and participation in healing rituals and ceremonies. Counselors working with American Indian children should remember several key points. First, eye contact, which is valued in European American society, may be considered rude or discourteous by some American Indian children (depending on the tribe), who may be taught to listen without looking directly at the speaker. Second, counselors should exercise caution in placing children in situations requiring self-praise, because speaking of one's accomplishments may be considered in poor taste. Particularly in group sessions, considerable strain is placed on children who are asked to talk about their strengths. They may resort to telling unbelievable stories or may refuse to speak altogether; praise must always come from someone else. Third, it is important that clients receive positive reinforcement during group therapy; however, it may be more appropriate to provide reinforcement in individual situations. Receiving praise in front of one's peers in the initial stages of group therapy may be embarrassing and culturally inappropriate when working with American Indians. Once group cohesion is developed, group members may provide positive support to one another.

Group therapy appears to be a worthwhile intervention for American Indian children, because their culture places more value on group contributions than on individual successes and accomplishments. As with other cultures, many topics are appropriate for group counseling with children: discussing developmental concerns, dealing with death and divorce, developing friendships, or improving study skills.

Counselors working with American Indian children should

- provide individualized counseling intervention that addresses the specific needs of the American Indian child;
- provide assessment that has minimal socioeconomic or cultural bias;
- recognize that "life purposes" of American Indians differ from most other cultures; and
- intervene with strategies that value the child's culture as well as place high value on self-worth.

American Indian children learn early that nonverbal communication plays an important role in their lives. A significant factor in counseling effectiveness will be the counselor's own nonverbal communication style and personality. For example, communication will break down and the client may wish to leave if the counselor gives the impression of being busy or preoccupied.

Family Therapy

Because the extended family is a major source of support for American Indian people, counselors should plan intervention strategies that involve the entire family. Although individual situations exist, generally speaking, the American Indian people prefer counseling intervention that involves the entire family.

Prior to counseling American Indian children in family situations, the counselor needs to understand American Indian children and families. Counselors should understand the reason for participants seeking counseling, establish relationships that American Indians will deem positive, respond appropriately to children's and family's distrust, and explain how counseling procedures work. The counselor should also explain clearly to the family who he or she is, his or her role in counseling intervention, and the reason for the session. Case Study 8.1 looks at a counselor's efforts with Bill, an American Indian child.

Case Study 8.1: Counseling Bill Lonetree, an American Indian Child

Eight-year-old Bill's African American teacher referred him to counseling. She reported that Bill does not listen, shows little emotion, and appears anxious or stressed at times. The counselor, a European American, has met with Bill weekly for about four weeks, and Bill is just beginning to open up to him. Bill was suspicious at first, but slowly and reluctantly he has begun to confide that the teacher urges him to try harder, to listen attentively, and to take a more active role in the learning process. Bill does not understand the teacher's suggestions: He is listening and he does try; however, he admits to a lack of interest in the future. The counselor has noticed that Bill tends to look away as he speaks, although he appears to listen attentively. The counselor has also observed that Bill seems nervous when he talks about his schoolwork. Bill has admitted that he wants to do well in school, but school is not like home. Things are different in school—the communication, for example. Besides, he has no European American friends. The counselor has reached several conclusions: (a) Bill's comments indicate that some of his problems might stem from the teacher, who neither understands the American Indian culture nor recognizes the differences between Bill's home life and school life; (b) Bill is experiencing stress because of his lack of school progress; and (c) Bill should be counseled in individual sessions several times and then participate in a group session with other American Indian children.

Reflection Questions:

1. Comment on the teacher's opinion that "Bill does not listen, shows little emotion, and appears anxious or stressed at times." What could cause such an opinion? Could it be the teacher does not understand American Indian cultural characteristics?
2. What factors might cause Bill to conclude, "He wants to do well in school, but school is not like home?"
3. Do you agree with the counselor about having individual counseling first, and then switching to small group counseling? Remembering the American Indian culture and the developmental period, what is your rationale for such a counseling decision?

Group sessions with American Indian families may involve participation of extended family members, members of the clan or tribe, or significant others. These sessions may need to be informal and may require long periods of time to develop relationships and to achieve desired goals.

Counseling and Development 8.1: The Childhood Years

Ashutosh is a 12-year-old American Indian boy who was recommended for counseling by his teacher. His teacher felt he was not doing his best work and in fact was showing little interest in school. Although he was attending the school off the reservation, there were other American Indian children in his class. He seemed to be in an "in-between" period—not altogether a child, yet not functioning as an adolescent.

The counselor considered Ashutosh's attitudes toward learning and school, his developing cultural identity in the off-the-reservation school, and his lack of school achievement. The counselor concluded Ashutosh's problem might be both cultural and developmental.

Counseling Strategies:

1. Talk with Ashutosh about his developmental period—does he perceive himself as a child or an adolescent?
2. Try to learn Ashutosh's perceptions of his school life, his teacher, his seeming lack of motivation, and his "interest" in school.
3. Meet with Ashutosh's teacher to determine whether she is misinterpreting his lack of school interest and motivation—perhaps the teacher is looking at Ashutosh through a European American worldview.

AMERICAN INDIAN ADOLESCENTS

Potential Problems Warranting Counseling Intervention

Problems American Indian adolescents may experience include

- suicide, alcohol abuse and other substance abuse (e.g., tobacco and inhalants), and high school and college drop-out rates;
- failure to develop positive individual and American Indian identities;
- misperceptions and stereotypical images of American Indian adolescents that may result in poor self-image;
- communication problems (e.g., English as a second language, nonverbal communication being misunderstood, and differences between "reservation" or "tribal" languages and "school" languages);
- conflict between loyalty to family and elders and a desire to conform to peer standards;
- adverse effects of being misunderstood by other-culture teachers;
- poor academic achievement;
- poor self-concept;
- drug or alcohol addiction;
- adverse effects of racism and discrimination;
- generational conflict caused by parents' allegiance to American Indian values and the adolescent's acculturation into mainstream culture; and
- disagreements between adolescents and families about appropriate ages for certain activities—for example, one culture allowing or encouraging activities that another culture frowns upon.

Counseling Considerations

As previously stated, because there are relatively few American Indian counselors, most American Indian adolescents will probably be counseled by European American counselors or perhaps by other minority counselors. The non-American Indian counselor planning intervention with American Indian adolescents should consider the following questions: What unique American Indian cultural and developmental characteristics are important to know? In what stage is the American Indian adolescent's identity? How can the counselor develop trust, rapport, and genuine respect for American Indian adolescents? Will individual, family, or group therapy be most effective?

Although diversity among the various tribes does not allow for the establishment of clear rules for counseling American Indians, the counselor's understanding of the culture's unique characteristics is prerequisite to effective counseling. The following are several aspects of the culture that are important for counselors to remember:

- Adolescents are respected to the same degree as adults.
- Cooperation and harmony are valued.
- Generosity and sharing are important, and individuals are judged on their contributions.
- Competition may be encouraged as long as it does not hurt anyone.
- Life is lived in the present, with little concern for planning for the future.
- Some behaviors may be considered strange or rude (e.g., loud talking, reprimands).
- Ancient legends and cultural traditions are important.
- Peace and politeness are essential; confrontation is considered rude.

The American Indian adolescent's attitude toward silence differs significantly from that of adolescents in other cultures. The American Indian does not feel a need to fill time with meaningless speech just to avoid silence. Also, it is culturally appropriate to avoid eye contact with the speaker during conversation. The non-American Indian counselor might treat silence, embellished metaphors, and indirectness as signs of resistance, when they actually represent forms of communication. Professionals working with these adolescents need to monitor their feelings about these communication differences. They must resist the urge to interrupt and must be willing to admit to confusion and misunderstanding. Therapists should be especially aware of nonverbal communication, particularly when "nothing is taking place." How one enters the room, what is in it, and how one responds to silence are all forms of communication (Sutton & Broken Nose, 2005).

Perceived trust is the most important variable in how an American Indian adolescent decides whether a counselor should be viewed as a helper. The American Indian may harbor a general distrust of counselors of another cultural background. Once trust in the counselor and the counseling process is established, rapport and mutual respect likely will follow.

The first meeting with the American Indian adolescent should be designed to build trust. Effective listening and empathic responding are helpful in this regard. Counselors who are able to show genuine appreciation for the American Indian culture and its values and traditions likely will reduce their clients' distrust. During the first session, it is important that counselors work diligently to accommodate the American Indian time orientation and fatalistic view of life.

Individual and Group Therapy

In counseling American Indian adolescents, as in counseling other adolescents, cultural perceptions (the counselor's as well as the client's) play a large part in shaping counseling goals and intervention techniques. Once an adolescent has been referred or has initiated a self-referral, the counselor can decide whether individual or group therapy will be the most effective approach.

Counselors often prefer group sessions because most adolescents find it easier to speak freely in a group setting. They believe that their peers will understand and accept their deficiencies more readily than will adults.

As previously mentioned, group therapy may be the most valuable counseling approach for working with American Indian students. Group therapy relieves individual students of some of the pressures to talk and self-disclose and allows them to learn from the experiences of other adolescents. Groups should be kept small and should include some students who have successfully handled problems. Leaders must be respected and trusted by group members. Group counseling should take a general approach in which the students are asked to suggest topics to consider.

Counseling adolescents in individual or group situations has drawbacks. Clients may change their behavior, but on returning to the family, they might return to old behaviors. It is also important to remember that in some cases group therapy may cause American Indian adolescents to be somewhat reserved because of their lack of trust or their tendency toward noninterference with others. Their soft-spokenness and suspicion of strangers might also impede the counseling process in a group situation.

Family Therapy

Practical and immediate solutions to problems during family therapy may be more relevant than future-oriented philosophical goals. As a reflection of American Indian values, group decisions will take precedence over individual decisions during family counseling sessions. Whenever possible, the therapist should involve all family members, even extended family members, in selecting therapy goals. This process of involving all family members is often so therapeutic in itself that further counseling intervention may be unnecessary.

Ho (1987) related the cases of Phillip and Debbie. In Phillip's case, the misunderstanding regarded the extended family:

> Phillip, a 15-year-old probationer, was brought to the attention of a court-related worker when she received a complaint that Phillip was running around from house to house visiting female friends without parental supervision. When the worker inquired about Phillip's family background, she discovered that he had several aunts and cousins. When the worker called all Phillip's aunts and cousins together for a family conference, she discovered that all his cousins were young girls. The worker later learned that Phillip's behavior was very natural in the extended family system.
>
> (p. 97)

In the case of adolescent Debbie, it was necessary to mobilize a social support network to assist her:

> Although she had been a "good" student in the past, Debbie, the teenage daughter of the Tiger family, has recently been missing school. When her parents were informed of this, they displayed no surprise, but expressed willingness to cooperate with the school official in getting Debbie back to school regularly. The school social worker, who served as a family therapist, happened to live in the same neighborhood as the Tigers, and she volunteered to transport Debbie back and forth to school. Through this consistent relationship, the therapist became a trusted friend of the Tiger family. To express the family's gratitude and friendship, Mrs. Tiger provided the therapist with a regular supply of home-grown vegetables. Through this informal exchange, the therapist learned that the Tigers were totally shut off from the community, with Mr. Tiger labeled as "crazy" and "not to be trusted." Mr. Tiger did not have a regular job. On his days off, "he managed to get drunk," according to Mrs. Tiger. Although Mrs. Tiger was willing to get some therapy for their family problems, Mr. Tiger insisted that he would not have any of "that stuff"

(therapy). After learning that the Tigers were religious individuals who attended church regularly, the therapist referred the Tigers to a minister for consultation. The minister, although a non-Indian, was highly respected by the Indians who also attended the same church but belonged to different tribes. Through such extended interaction with other Indians, Mrs. Tiger became more relaxed and paid attention to Debbie, who managed to attend school regularly without the family therapist's assistance.

(pp. 100–101)

Case Study 8.2 looks at a counselor's efforts with Ed, an American Indian adolescent.

Case Study 8.2: Counseling Ed Lonetree, an American Indian Adolescent

Ed, age 15, was referred to the school guidance counselor by his teacher for poor academic achievement. On the referral slip, the teacher's notation read "poor grades, lack of interest, and unmotivated." During Ed's first session, he demonstrated some apprehensiveness and distrust of the European American counselor. The counselor and Ed discussed Ed's development and his American Indian culture. Ed was somewhat hesitant to share information ("You can't trust people in this school."), and he made vague references to the counselor "doing something to him."

During the first session, the counselor sought to lessen Ed's anxiety and to develop rapport. Ed's poor communication skills made conversation a bit difficult, but the counselor worked to overcome this barrier. The counselor noticed that Ed paused a lot in his speech—it seemed as if he could not find anything to say. Yet silent periods didn't seem to bother him.

After talking at length with Ed, the counselor came to two conclusions. First, Ed's academic problems resulted from poor language skills; second, Ed's teacher did not understand American Indian mannerisms. The teacher failed to recognize that Ed was indeed interested in school and motivated to learn.

The counselor decided to do three things: First, he would offer to assist Ed's teacher in understanding Ed's behavior. Then, because many of Ed's academic problems stemmed from his communication problem, the counselor would recommend Ed for special language classes. Finally, he would follow up on Ed's progress in individual sessions. The prospect of Ed speaking up in group therapy sessions seemed unlikely unless all other members of the group had similar academic and communication problems. After Ed's communication problem improved, however, the counselor thought that he could be considered for group therapy.

Reflection Questions:

1. What would come to a perceptive counselor's mind if she or he read a teacher's referral saying "poor grades, lack of interest, and unmotivated"?
2. How could the counselor work to build the client's trust in people in the school as well as the client-counselor relationship?

Counseling and Development 8.2: The Adolescent Years

Robert is the 16-year-old son of an American Indian father and a European American mother. Robert has been in two fistfights at school and has the reputation of being belligerent.

His school has American Indians, Hispanic Americans, and a few European Americans. His principal asked the counselor to speak with Robert in an effort to understand the problem and eventually help him change his behavior. The counselor met with Robert in an individual counseling session to determine whether she needs to intervene with family therapy.

The counselor knew she had to consider Robert's mixed parentage as well as the struggles often associated with the developmental period. Could the problem result from self-esteem or identity confusion?

Counseling Strategies:

1. Try to talk with Robert to determine whether he is being assertive or actually aggressive.
2. Talk with Robert about his adolescent years, his mixed family, and his friends to determine whether cross-cultural friendships exist.
3. From what you know now, what makes you think family therapy might or might not be needed?

AMERICAN INDIAN ADULTS

Potential Problems Warranting Counseling Intervention

Problems American Indian adults may experience include

- difficulties in overcoming myths that their culture is lazy, savage, and inferior;
- adverse effects of injustice, discrimination, hardship, and degradation;
- adverse effects of a "culture of poverty," such as high unemployment and low socioeconomic status;
- differing cultural characteristics;
- high suicide rate and low life expectancy;
- communication problems, including "on reservation" and "off reservation" languages and the majority culture's misunderstanding of nonverbal mannerisms;
- midlife difficulties such as coping with the effects of aging, marriage crises, psychosocial crises, and developmental tasks;
- problems with alcohol or other drugs;
- poor self-concept and feelings of rejection; and
- low educational level.

On a more positive note, Skogrand et al. (2008) reported on their study of strong Navajo marriages. The researchers concluded many Navajos had strong marriages due to several marital strengths: maintaining communication, nurturing their relationships, learning about marriage, preparing for marriage, and having a strong foundation.

Garrett and Carroll (2000) report that clear answers about alcohol use and abuse do not exist. According to these authors, American Indians may actually have an abstinence rate higher than that of the general U.S. population; 70% of Americans say they drink compared to 63% of those in American Indian tribes/nations. This may suggest that those American Indians who do drink experience more adverse consequences than others, contrary to the perception that alcoholism among American Indians is innate. Still, Garrett and Carroll (2000) think alcoholism in this culture is a problem that counselors need to address. For example, alcohol-related deaths among American Indians are 4.8 times greater than in the general U.S. population, and the mortality rate from chronic liver disease and cirrhosis is 4.5 times greater than in other racial or ethnic groups. Garrett and Carroll also report that 75% to 80% of American Indian suicides involve the use of alcohol or other mind-altering drugs.

Counseling Considerations

From an American Indian perspective, the entire ordeal of substance dependence is a matter of mental, physical, spiritual, and environmental dimensions. Factors that seem to be related to alcohol abuse in American Indians include cultural disassociation (not feeling a part of the traditional American Indian culture or the general U.S. culture), the lack of clear sanctions or punishments for alcohol abuse, and strong peer pressure and support for alcohol abuse. Other factors related to alcohol abuse include poverty, school failure, unemployment, poor health, feelings of hopelessness, and the breakdown of American Indian family life. Compared with the majority population, the alcohol-related mortality rate in American Indians is fourfold greater, and the rates of alcohol-related accidental death, suicide, and homicide are threefold greater (Thomason, 2000).

American Indians may be more successful in stopping or controlling their alcohol use if the treatment approach includes a family, group, or community component. However, this may be true only for traditionally oriented American Indians who are not highly acculturated into the general U.S. culture. Although acculturative stress, poverty, and racism may influence drinking behavior, there is no evidence to suggest that these are causative factors.

Thomason (2000) offers several conclusions:

- There is no evidence that a single treatment modality works especially well with American Indians.
- Counseling interventions should include assessment of the client's identity and acculturation level and modalities, such as brief interventions, social skills training, motivational enhancement, and community reinforcement.
- Clients who have a strong American Indian identity and are involved in their traditional culture may respond better to a treatment program that considers their culture; for example, it has been reported that treatment programs that incorporate the use of sweat lodges, talking circles or medicine wheels, and other American Indian rituals and traditional ceremonies are helpful.
- Group therapy with an American Indian counselor and American Indian clients may be difficult to initiate because of the shortage of American Indian treatment providers and the lack of standardized American Indian treatments. The shortage of American Indian counselors also presents difficulties because traditional American Indian healing strategies are meant to be practiced only by trained American Indian healers.

Working with American Indian clients presents counselors with numerous challenges: tribal and individual diversity, lifestyle preferences that can vary considerably from one client to another, verbal and nonverbal language differences, and the reluctance of clients to disclose personal or embarrassing thoughts. Still, counselors should learn about and plan sessions for American Indian clients as individuals and be cautious about making assumptions. The goals of counseling will largely depend on the tribal values and traditions of the American Indian client.

Lokken and Twohey (2004) maintain that the history of oppression of American Indians has resulted in American Indians being distrustful and reluctant to become involved with mental health professionals.

Garrett and Carroll (2000) explain the American Indian concept of the circle as a symbol of power, relation, peace, and unity. The circle reminds people of the sacred relationship humans share with all living things and of humanity's responsibility as a helper and contributor to the flow of the Circle of Life by living in harmony and balance with all living things. They explain the importance of the following concepts in a Native context: life energy, harmony and balance, spiritual practices, and substance dependence.

Six practical recommendations for counseling American Indians with substance abuse problems include the following:

- *Greeting.* Offer a gentle handshake if any handshake at all. A firm handshake is considered an aggressive show of power and can be construed as an insult.
- *Hospitality.* Offer a beverage or snack because American Indians have a traditional emphasis on generosity and kindness.
- *Silence.* Maintain a time of quietness at the beginning of the session to give both the counselor and the client a chance to orient themselves to the situation, get in touch with themselves, and experience the presence of the other person.
- *Acculturation.* Get a sense of the client's acculturation by formally assessing his or her values, geographic origin/residence, and tribal affiliation.
- *Eye contact.* Respect American Indians' practice of avoiding eye contact—the eyes are considered a pathway to the spirit. It may be acceptable to glance occasionally at the client, but generally it should be remembered that listening is "something that happens with the ears and heart." (Garrett & Carroll, 2000, p. 386)
- *Direction.* Offer suggestions rather than directions due to clients' respect for personal choice. (Garrett & Carroll, 2000)

Although American Indians often distrust European American mental health professionals, ethnically similar counselors are not always available, and when they are, their communication styles sometimes remain a salient factor in American Indians' perceptions of helpfulness. Some American Indian clients perceive negative consequences for participating in counseling: having children taken away, being treated in a condescending manner, and having medications prescribed without getting to the cause of the problem. In one example, when parents sought help to stop abusing, they were reported for abusing their children, a process that is very shameful for parents. Reported barriers to counseling include inaccessible locations, lack of availability of counselors, lack of knowledge about counseling, and lack of money for mental health counseling.

Factors associated with perceptions of counselor trustworthiness include authenticity, respectfulness, signs of listening behavior, self-disclosure, and slow pace. American Indian clients who seek counseling are usually hoping for concrete, practical advice about problems that is sensitive to their cultural beliefs and differences. Historically, American Indians have had negative experiences with professionals who were supposedly there to "help" them. Missionaries, teachers, and social workers have tried to address American Indians' needs by changing American Indians' value systems, thereby alienating them from the strength and support of their own people and traditions (Sutton & Broken Nose, 2005).

It is the counselor's task to help these clients accept and value their culture and to help them resolve difficult conflicts that can impede personal and social growth. Consider the following example (Axelson, 1999) in which a European American counselor helps an American Indian client consider his cultural beliefs about religion.

CLIENT: Where can I start? Take religion, for instance. Okay? I have a strong traditional Indian background . . . and I try to cope with whatever is good in the non-Indian society. But, coming from the Indian way of life, I feel that how I can relate myself to the way of praying to nature is not the same as saying I got to be good and go to church on Sunday and pray to a certain god. How can I relate myself to that way?

COUNSELOR: You're saying that you are religious, that you don't find that the White religion is in harmony with what you are; you find conflict in some practices of the White religion.

CLIENT: I'm not sure that you understood.
COUNSELOR: Would you try to explain to me again?
CLIENT: I know that I feel there is something around me that is good. I can take a piece of rock and say that it was formed from something that I believe in. I can take a tree branch and say that I pray to this tree and feel good. I feel the obligation that is imposing on me to make me go to church; and I don't want to do that.
COUNSELOR: You feel an obligation to go to church and somehow you want to resist the obligation. You're caught in the middle in giving in to it and fighting against it. You'd rather fight against it than do it; somehow you're not quite free to do that.
              (*Pause*)
CLIENT: Do you think I should? . . . go to church?
              (*Pause*)
COUNSELOR: I'm wondering if going to church would help you, like anybody else, since you feel so reluctant. It just doesn't seem to be you.
CLIENT: Eh . . . they tell me I should go to church.
COUNSELOR: Who are "they"?
CLIENT: The people who taught me about their religion. The Catholic Church.
COUNSELOR: You don't want to do this. Somehow I'm puzzled because you don't want to do it; in other words, you feel an obligation to go to church because they told you to. And yet you don't feel a real need inside yourself to go.
              (*Pause*)
CLIENT: I think . . . (*Pause*) . . . I think the need is there.
COUNSELOR: The need to go to church on Sunday?
CLIENT: Eh . . . I think the need is there because . . . I don't know . . . I don't know what to say. It's kind of confusing now.
COUNSELOR: You sound like you don't understand yourself. It's almost like someone sneaked up and put this need in you.
CLIENT: I think I know what is good, and I know that there is something there that is good. You know, why should I go to church on Sunday when I know that there is the same thing outside the church?
COUNSELOR: One thing. You see yourself as a good man. Is that right? And, as a good man, you recognize good within this Catholic religion and that gives a . . .
CLIENT: I don't know what's good within the Catholic religion.
COUNSELOR: You feel some kind of obligation or attraction to the good that you see there, but not enough obligation to make you feel that you want to go to church, or go to that church. That you can be good by praying before the stone or tree branch. Or by doing whatever you do on Sunday besides going to church.
CLIENT: What do you think I should do?
COUNSELOR: (*Sighs*) . . . What do you want to do?
              (*Pause*) What do you think a good man would do in your situation?
              (*Pause*)
CLIENT: I'm confused. I don't want to talk about it.[1]

American Indians often judge people by who they are rather than by what they are. On entering a therapist's office, they will probably look for indications of who the therapist is rather than for a particular diploma on the wall. Thus personal authenticity, genuine respect, and concern for the client are essential for initiating a relationship between counselor and client (Sutton & Broken Nose, 2005).

Traditionally, many counselors have not received training in counseling the American Indian population; therefore, they often do not feel the need to discuss the family's American Indian background and culture, to ask questions in a manner that does not cause discomfort, and to use cultural information in assessment decisions.

Also, traditionally, the contributions and roles of American Indian women have not been considered. Historical and counseling literature has generally failed to provide explanations of their contributions to the American Indian culture. Awe, Portman, and Garrett (2005) maintain that historically women have wielded a remarkable amount of sociopolitical power with tribal nations, yet as a rule, counseling professionals rely heavily on theories and interventions that reflect a Western, masculinized worldview. Awe and colleagues (2005) provide a look at the historical leadership of American Indian women and the cultural teachings they modeled and valued.

Examples of questions and statements that can open lines of communication and reveal culturally relevant information include the following:

- Where do you come from?
- Tell me about your family.
- What tribe or nation are you? Tell me a little about that.
- Tell me about yourself as a person, culturally and spiritually.
- Tell me how you identify yourself culturally.
- Tell me how your culture and spirituality plays into how you live your life.
- Tell me about your life as you see it—past, present, and future. (Garrett & Wilbur, 1999)

Awe and colleagues (2005) provide an alternative view of American Indian leadership and attempt to build a bridge between American Indian perspectives of nurturing leadership. Rather than Indian governance being filled with the notion of wise, supreme, and all-knowing chiefs, decisions were made by tribal councils or communities made up of multiple male and female leaders holding leadership positions.

Selected implications for the counseling profession include the idea that institutions of higher education, as well as other organizations, should move to a more collectivistic organization mentoring style; that mentoring of women should occur in a collectivistic relationship that fosters interdependence among colleagues and group success as relational norms; and that women require relationships to develop their own sense of identity and purpose—nurturing and mentoring women require an examination of a women's sense of place and being in the world (Awe et al., 2005).

Counseling American Indian adults requires techniques that are carefully planned to accommodate these clients' cultural characteristics. Using counseling techniques developed for clients of other cultural backgrounds with only slight modifications is not sufficient. Counseling and psychotherapy often are based on Western values that may be antagonistic to American Indian value systems. Not only should culturally appropriate counseling be planned, but counselors should also be aware of personal characteristics that may offend or confuse the client.

It is essential that counselors working with American Indian clients be adaptive and flexible in their professional intervention and understand that a counselor's personal identification with the culture of the client does not guarantee sufficient understanding of the client. Counselors should recognize their own personal biases and stereotypes and should use counseling approaches that involve empathy, caring, and a sense of the importance of the human potential.

Although some counseling strategies are effective for all cultures, the following strategies have the potential to enhance the effectiveness of counseling sessions with American Indians:

- Counselors may admit to not fully understanding the American Indian culture and request to be corrected if a cultural error is made.
- Counselors who empathize with others appreciate the greatness of the American Indian culture and its many accomplishments.
- Counselors should take the attitude that they can help best by listening.

- Counselors should have a small, homey, lived-in office. Pictures in the office of American Indians may help put clients at ease. Rather than sit side by side, some clients may prefer that the counselor sit behind a desk (to provide a form of separation).
- Counselors should not lean toward clients to study them. They also should not be upset with long pauses in the conversation. Counselors may want to take short notes and summarize at the end to let clients know they have been listening.

Counselors should give special attention to their manner of speaking. It is wise to summarize or confirm the client's thoughts after he or she has been talking for a while. In particular, counselors should not talk for too long and should not "talk down" to the client. Instead, the counselor's sentences should be short and lucid and should make clear that the counselor's views are only general opinions rather than absolute truths or facts.

Garrett and Wilbur (1999) offer several implications for counseling:

1. Counselors should recognize culturally specific meanings and practices that may play a critical role in understanding the client's issues (and appropriate ways of dealing with the issues) and also understanding the world in which the client lives.
2. Counselors should seek to understand the client's level of acculturation.
3. Counselors should pose questions in a respectful and unobtrusive manner.
4. Counselors should not assume that a client who "looks Indian" (p. 202) is traditional; similarly, it should not be assumed that a client who "does not look Indian" (p. 202) is not traditional.

The counselor might also explore such practical resources as a communication class, participation in ceremonies at a local powwow, or involvement with American Indian organizations or centers (Sutton & Broken Nose, 2005).

Individual and Group Therapy

Counselors working with American Indians need to remember several points. First, they should understand that counseling interventions do not always effectively address the problems of American Indians. Second, counselors need to understand American Indians' emphasis on nonverbal communication. American Indians express many thoughts in natural-world metaphors. Third, counselors need to understand the special needs of American Indians—that is, understand their familial structures and their values. Fourth, counselors need to show sincere interest in American Indians, carefully considering family theories, individual counseling styles, and assessment instruments.

The decision whether to use individual or group therapy should be based on the individual client's needs and culture. One advantage of group therapy is that clients may share similar problems and frustrations. Disadvantages of group therapy include American Indian clients' possible reluctance to share personal concerns and their cultural tendency toward noninterference with others.

It is worth reiterating the following important points with regard to counseling American Indians. First, the client is apt to be silent for what may seem like a long time. Second, restating or summarizing the client's comments at the end of the session may enhance understanding.

Family Therapy

Family therapy often has more successful outcomes for American Indians than individual counseling sessions. The American Indian family structure allows for the growth of bonding between generations. Counselors should incorporate as many family members as possible in family sessions, particularly during the first two or three sessions.

The American Indian culture emphasizes harmony with nature, noninterference with others, and a strong belief that people are inherently good and deserving of respect. Such traits, however, make it difficult for families experiencing problems to seek counseling or other professional help. Their fear and mistrust of European Americans make it difficult for them to allow a European American family therapist entry into their family system. Also, American Indians' lack of knowledge as to what a family therapist actually does often contributes to their reluctance to initiate or participate in counseling.

In American Indian culture, families work together to solve problems. Fortunately, family therapy, with its systemic approach and emphasis on relationships, is particularly effective in working with American Indians, whose life-cycle orientation blends well with this therapy approach (Sutton & Broken Nose, 2005).

As previously mentioned, the American Indian attitude toward silence can be extremely frustrating to counselors providing family therapy. This silence may sometimes be used as a safe response to defend against outsiders who are perceived as intruders; still, counselors sometimes experience frustration when several sessions are needed to get effective counseling under way.

The close-knit family structure of American Indians and their cultural tradition of keeping family matters private may result in few opportunities for family therapy. After engaging the family, the counselor should proceed cautiously to allow family members to deal with problems at their own pace. An overbearing or manipulative counselor will almost certainly alienate American Indian clients.

Case Study 8.3 looks at a counselor's efforts with John, an American Indian adult.

Case Study 8.3: Counseling John Lonetree, an American Indian Adult

John Lonetree, age 38, was referred by his physician to a community mental health clinic that provides free counseling to qualified American Indians. John had complained of headaches for several months, and the physician had been unable to pinpoint the cause.

The 45-year-old European American counselor greeted John at the office door and tried to make him feel as comfortable as possible. The counselor sat behind a small desk and requested that John sit across from him. The counselor took special care to let John know that he was fairly unaccustomed to counseling American Indians. He also encouraged John to make him aware of any misconceptions he might have about the culture. The counselor avoided looking John in the eye for long intervals while speaking. Being off the reservation, John experienced problems with English, which made communication somewhat difficult.

The counselor concluded that John had several problems related to his age and to the financial and emotional demands placed on him. First, John was nearly 40; relative to his life expectancy, 40 was "older" for him than for his age peers in other cultures. Second, with John's advancing age, his responsibilities seemed to be growing heavier and harder to bear. He was concerned about his children and their schoolwork. In addition, he was concerned about what he would do if he lost his job. So many people depended on him for financial support. The counselor suggested additional sessions, to which John agreed, somewhat to the surprise of the counselor, who was aware that American Indians often place a high premium on noninterference. Also, because John considered his problems to be family-oriented, the counselor decided that group counseling was inappropriate at this stage. The decision whether to include John's family would have to wait until the counselor knew more about the family situation.

Reflection Questions:

1. What intervention techniques do you think the counselor should employ?
2. Consider how the counselor should intervene with John being "older" than 40; how would you broach this topic?
3. How will the counselor equate "counseling intervention" and some American Indians' placing emphasis on "noninterference"?

Counseling and Development 8.3: The Adult Years

Chenoa (meaning "Pure Dove" or "Bird of Peace") is a 40-year-old female American Indian married to a 44-year-old of the same cultural heritage. Her problem is her 17-year-old daughter, who talks of moving off the reservation when she becomes self-sufficient. Chenoa worries that once the daughter moves, she will change her American Indian ways. To make the situation worse, her husband is concerned yet feels that such change is inevitable.

The counselor met with Chenoa and listened intently.

Counseling Strategies:

1. Ask Chenoa about "life tasks" or her progressing into her 40s and beyond.
2. Talk with Chenoa about why she thinks her husband is not joining her in the effort to keep the daughter on the reservation.
3. Would you support counseling between Chenoa and her husband? Should it be extended to family counseling (and include the daughter)?

AMERICAN INDIAN ELDERLY

Potential Problems Warranting Counseling Intervention

Problems that elderly American Indians may experience include

- difficulties overcoming culture- and age-related stereotypical images;
- double or multiple jeopardy as a result of being elderly, minority, and perhaps disabled;
- low socioeconomic status;
- inadequate nutrition and housing;
- low life expectancy;
- health problems, such as tuberculosis, diabetes, pneumonia, liver and kidney disease, and high blood pressure;
- inadequate health services, either because of lack of communication skills or overdependence on folk rituals;
- low self-esteem and poor self-concept;
- lack of education;
- generational differences because of the acculturation of younger American Indians;

- physical changes, such as visible signs of aging or a deteriorating skeletomuscular system or psychosocial-emotional changes, such as adjusting to poor health, the death of a spouse, or relocation to a reservation for economic reasons;
- lack of health-care opportunities that contribute to physical and mental well-being; and
- lack of transportation to acquire mental health counseling and other health services.

Counseling Considerations

Counselors working with older American Indians have a special task in understanding the trials and joys of the elderly period from the standpoint of American Indians. Many problems require an understanding of the complex relationship between age and cultural background.

Although the literature on counseling American Indian elderly as a specific population is sketchy at best, counselors can use their existing knowledge of the elderly and their knowledge of the American Indian culture as a basis for formulating appropriate counseling strategies. It is also important for counselors to acknowledge the centuries of deprivation and discrimination that American Indians have endured, the current status of uneducated American Indian elderly trying to live and cope with the stress common in contemporary society, and the elderly client's hesitation to seek professional counseling from a non-American Indian professional.

In addition to understanding the culture and the lifespan period, there are other prerequisites for effective counseling of the American Indian elderly. For example, counselors must build rapport with their elderly clients. American Indian history is full of broken treaties and promises. American Indian clients often must be convinced that professionals can be trusted to think in terms of American Indian welfare and well-being. Also, counselors must use their knowledge about the aging process in the counseling relationship. Finally, they should make sure that clients understand the counselor's role and know what to expect in the counseling relationship.

What specifically can counselors do to promote an effective counseling relationship? The following strategies may be considered:

- Allow adequate time to get acquainted. The atmosphere should be relaxed. Counseling professionals will not want to give the impression that they are uninterested or in a hurry.
- Allow for pauses and be patient when the client avoids eye contact or appears to just sit and think.
- Let elderly clients know that their age is accepted. Although counselors may not be aware of the realities of being elderly, it is imperative that they communicate a willingness to listen to and learn from their elderly clients.
- Allow a paraprofessional from the client's ethnic background to assist with communication barriers.
- Understand the client's cultural background and elderly status and the complex relationship between the two.

Individual and Group Therapy

The decision regarding what type of therapy to use should be based on the individual American Indian client. One intervention approach is to use individual therapy at first and then to move to a group therapy session. Of course, the individual client's willingness to speak in group sessions should be considered. How willing are elderly American Indians to disclose feelings of grief in group settings? What about concerns over decreasing strength or sexual abilities? Counselors should first explore the elderly American Indian's problems in individual sessions and then decide on the feasibility of group therapy.

Family Therapy

Counselors intervening with American Indian families first need to be relaxed. Elderly American Indians, who are accustomed to noninterference with others and unaccustomed to counseling procedures, tend to be silent for prolonged periods. Conversational exchanges may be relatively short. This pattern might last throughout the session or perhaps stretch into two sessions.

During the initial session with an elderly American Indian client, it may be useful to ask open-ended questions designed to elicit a family history. Showing genuine interest without being judgmental helps to establish rapport. It allows the client and the family members to get to know the therapist and vice versa.

Effective counseling sessions might emphasize the elder's "place" in the family structure and the counselor's awareness of the respect traditionally given to American Indian elderly. The counselor should keep in mind that elderly clients may not want to disclose personal information with their families present and that family members may look to the elderly client to act as spokesperson for the family,

---

Case Study 8.4: Counseling Wenonah Lonetree, an Elderly American Indian

Wenonah, age 72, was referred to a free counseling clinic when she went to a government office to try to increase her monthly benefit check. Wenonah's poverty, lack of education, and communication problems indicated that she could qualify for counseling assistance. Although Wenonah at first refused to go, her son John convinced her to visit the clinic, especially because he was off work that day and could take her there. However, she was not at all sure that she was doing the right thing.

The 38-year-old female European American counselor immediately recognized Wenonah's many problems. It was clear that she rarely visited a physician and saw her only role in life as taking care of her grandchildren. The counselor spoke to Wenonah alone while John waited outside. She began very slowly with Wenonah—she did not urge her on nor confront her when she paused or looked the other way during conversations. The counselor made Wenonah feel that her age was respected and that her problems were important and deserving of attention.

The counselor decided that Wenonah's problems were related primarily to communication difficulties and poverty. She suggested that Wenonah meet with the agency's language specialist, but Wenonah immediately responded that she did not have regular transportation to the clinic. In the meantime, the counselor told Wenonah that she would speak to the government agency to see whether Wenonah's benefits could be raised sooner. What about another session? What could be addressed? The counselor pointed to several issues, including Wenonah's feelings about growing old and about how society was changing. The counselor asked Wenonah to return, and she managed to schedule an appointment when John was off work and could bring her. In future sessions, the counselor would try to convince Wenonah to see a physician for a medical checkup.

Reflection Questions:

1. How might the 38-year-old female counselor better understand Wenonah's worldviews of being American Indian, somewhat elderly, and poor?
2. Did the counselor act prematurely in deciding Wenonah's problems were primarily communication and poverty? What other conclusions could she have drawn?
3. What other counseling techniques should she have used?

Counseling and Development 8.4: The Elderly Years

Alaqua is a 90-year-old American Indian woman. She is quite old for her cultural group, and she realizes her youthful days are over. She has numerous health problems: cancer that is in remission, diabetes, and heart problems. Her husband died about 15 years earlier; one of her sons died and one is in prison. She gets very depressed when she thinks about her life situation. Her medical doctor prescribed antidepressants, but Alaqua was at the maximum dosage, so he had to recommend a counseling session.

The counselor considered several concerns: Alaqua's age, her medical conditions, isolation after her husband's death, her dead son, and her son in prison. The counselor knew she needed to equate Alaqua's development and culture.

Counseling Strategies:

1. Talk with Alaqua about her culture and her cultural expectations of growing older.
2. Impress upon her the need to rely on the spirituality that was always a pillar of her culture and her family.
3. Family counseling was not a possibility, but the counselor did think about small group therapy since she had several American Indian females in similar circumstances.

SUMMARY

Counselors, psychotherapists, and social workers working with American Indian children, adolescents, adults, and elders need a comprehensive understanding of the American Indian culture, the four lifespan stages, and American Indians' specific challenges. Effective counselors understand American Indians' diversity: individual, tribal, communication, geographic, and so forth. Counselors will also be challenged to understand American Indians' proud heritage, appreciation of land and nature, and love of peace and harmony. Any of the following problems may be brought to counseling sessions: children's challenges in school, adolescents forming self-esteem and cultural identities while torn between two worlds, adults' financial and educational problems, and the elders' health problems. Effective counselors provide counseling intervention that reflects American Indian values and perspectives rather than using professional intervention techniques that reflect the perspectives of other cultures.

NOTE

1   *Source: Dialogue from Counseling and Development in a Multicultural Society* (pp. 428–430) by J.A. Axelson, 1999, Monterey, CA: Brooks/Cole. Reprinted with permission.

SUGGESTED READINGS

Agoratus, L. (2014). Alternatives to out-of-home placement for families. *Exceptional Parent, 44*(12), 48–49. Agoratus focuses on alternatives to out-of-home placement in the United States for families of individuals with disabilities.

Ballard, E.D., Musci, R.J., Tingey, L., Goklish, N., Larzelere-Hinton, F., Barlow, A., & Cwik, M. (2015). Latent class analysis of substance use behavior in reservation-based American Indian youth who attempted suicide. *American Indian & Alaska Native Mental Health Research: The Journal of the National Center, 22*(1), 77–94. American Indian (AI) adolescents who attempt suicide engage in substance abuse and aggressive behaviors; and clinical correlates of subgroup membership included risky sexual behavior and recent exposure to suicidal behavior.

Henderson, D., Carjuzaa, J., & Ruff, W. G. (2015). Reconciling leadership paradigms: Authenticity as practiced by American Indian school leaders. *International Journal of Multicultural Education*, *17*(1), 211–231. The study described how these leaders have to reconcile their Westernized educational leadership training with their traditional ways of knowing, living, and leading.

Limb, G. E., White, C., & Holgate, M. (2014). American Indian couples' relationship quality to improve parenting. *Journal of Human Behavior in the Social Environment*, *24*(2), 92–104. This study examined the impact that relationship quality has on American Indian parenting and its consequences on children, e.g., the more support American Indian parents received from one another, the more positive interactions they had with their child.

Meza, N. (2015). Indian education: Maintaining tribal sovereignty through culture and language preservation. *Brigham Young University Education & Law Journal*, Issue 1, 353–366. The article focuses on the role of culture and language preservation in promoting the sovereignty of tribes of Native Americans in the United States.

9 Understanding Asian American Clients

QUESTIONS TO BE EXPLORED

- What are the childhood, adolescent, adult, and elderly years like in the Asian American culture?
- What social and cultural, familial, and communication characteristics describe Asian Americans along the lifespan continuum?
- What unique challenges face Asian Americans during the various lifespan stages?
- What communication problems affect Asian Americans, and how do these problems affect educational attainment, employment, and the seeking of health-care services?
- What unique challenges face counselors providing mental health services to Asian Americans in the four lifespan stages?
- What sources of information are available for counselors intervening with Asian American children, adolescents, adults, and elders?

OVERVIEW

Planning counseling intervention for Asian American clients requires an understanding of their cultural characteristics, communication style and languages, families, and individual challenges. The diversity among Asian American clients also requires a consideration of their geographic, generational, and socioeconomic differences, as well as their intracultural and individual characteristics. Although clients from all cultures have been labeled with stereotypical beliefs, the notable successes of Asian American people have resulted in a "model minority" stereotype that sometimes leads mental health professionals to expect exemplary achievement and behavior as well as few mental health problems. This chapter examines the social and cultural, communicational, and familial characteristics of Asian Americans so that counselors working with children, adolescents, adults, and elders in the Asian American culture will have a valid and objective basis for counseling decisions and strategies.

ASIAN AMERICANS: DEMOGRAPHICS

"Asian" refers to people with origins in any of the original peoples of the Far East, Southeast Asia, or the Indian subcontinent, including people from Cambodia, China, India, Japan, Korea, Malaysia, Pakistan, the Philippine Islands, Thailand, and Vietnam. "Pacific Islander" refers to people with origins in any of the original peoples of Hawaii, Guam, Samoa, or other Pacific Islands. The Asian and Pacific Islander population is not a homogeneous group; rather, it comprises many groups who differ in language, culture, and length of residence in the United States. Some of the Asian groups, such as the Chinese and Japanese, have been in the United States for several generations. Others, such as the Hmong, Vietnamese, Laotians, and Cambodians, are comparatively recent immigrants. For simplicity, we often "lump" all Asian Americans together, but it is a serious mistake to think they all share the same characteristics and traits.

The amount of available information on Asian groups varies. Although considerable demographic information can be found on Asian groups from China, Korea, and Japan, less information is available about groups from India, Pakistan, and Bangladesh. Still, counselors should realize that the latter are Asian groups and that the diversity of all Asian groups calls for individual consideration during counseling.

Nearly three-fourths of all Asians lived in ten states. The ten states with the largest Asian alone-or-in-combination populations in 2010 were California (5.6 million), New York (1.6 million), Texas (1.1 million), New Jersey (0.8 million), Hawaii (0.8 million), Illinois (0.7 million), Washington (0.6 million), Florida (0.6 million), Virginia (0.5 million), and Pennsylvania (0.4 million). Together, these ten states represented nearly three-fourths of the entire Asian population in the United States. Although the Asian American population is small compared to other minority groups (such as African Americans and Hispanic Americans), they represent a rapidly growing, diverse culture in America (U.S. Census, 2015f).

Immigrants to the United States sometimes experience psychological problems. In addition, some immigrants enter the United States without adequate English-speaking skills, which can contribute to or create psychological problems, which call for help-seeking behaviors. Some Asian cultures may continue to use some form of spiritualism to address psychological issues. They tend to rely on their spouses or ministers (or their choice of spiritual advisor). Others may perceive seeking psychological help as a weakness and a negative reflection on their family. Again, one should consider acculturation levels, because while older people might be reluctant to seek counseling intervention, younger people might be acculturated to a point where professional intervention might be considered the norm.

While we often hear that Asian Americans are the "model minority," a closer look at their economic situation shows that not all people of Asian cultural backgrounds fit this stereotype. Poverty and its accompanying circumstances affect Asian Americans as well, just as they do people of all cultures. The following list looks at Asian Americans and their income, poverty and health insurance.

Asian Americans–Income, Poverty, and Health Insurance

$74,272 The median income of households headed by single-race Native Hawaiians and Other Pacific Islanders.

12.7% The poverty rate for those who classified themselves as single-race Native Hawaiian and Other Pacific Islander.

14.6% The percentage without health insurance for single-race Native Hawaiians and Other Pacific Islanders.

Source: U.S. Census Bureau. (2015j). Facts-for-features. Washington, DC: Author. Retrieved 2 December 2015 from http://www.census.gov/newsroom/facts-for-features/2015/cb15-ff 07.html.

ASIAN AMERICAN CHILDREN

Social and Cultural Description

Table 9.1 shows the population of Asian American children by age group. Because of their achievements and behavior in schools, Asian American children are often considered to be a

Table 9.1 Asian American Children by Age Group–Predictions

Age (years)	2010	2015
Under 5	943,000	1,004,000
5–9	927,000	1,018,000
10–14	894,000	1,034,000

Source: U.S. Census Bureau (2009). *Statistical Abstracts of the United States 2009* (128th ed.). Washington, DC: Author.

model minority. Teachers often consider Asian children ideal students—studious, high achieving, and well-behaved, Asian American students spend more time doing homework, attend more lessons out of school (e.g., tutoring sessions), and participate in more educational activities (e.g., library trips) than non-Asian American students.

It may be that Asian American parents who have high expectations of their children are unwilling to negotiate these terms. Children understand their parents' message and are obligated to their parents to do well in school. Perhaps Asian American students think their parents will feel displeasure with low school performance. Just perceiving how their parents might feel about their achievement may be a motivating factor.

The diverse nationalities comprising the Asian American culture make a general description difficult. Wide variation is found in physical characteristics as well as in attitudes, values, and ethnic institutions. For example, Japanese Americans have been described as quiet, reticent, or aloof. Compared with European American children, Asian American children may be more dependent, conforming, obedient to authority, and willing to place family welfare above individual wishes (Sue & Sue, 2013).

Some Asian American students, like students of all cultures, experience academic problems. Some have learning problems, some lack motivation or proficiency in English, and some have parents who do not understand the American school system because of cultural differences and language barriers.

Communication

The considerable emphasis that Asian cultures place on education has contributed to the academic success of many Asian American children. Sometimes this success overshadows the fact that some communication difficulties do exist and must be overcome. Communication difficulties may be traced to the fact that Asian Americans often come from bilingual backgrounds. Furthermore, cultural traditions and customs often restrict or impede verbal communication. For example, some Asian American children learn to value one-way communication in which parents are the primary speakers in the family.

Counselors should remember several factors relative to Asian American children's languages to avoid stereotypical thinking. First, it should be remembered that many Asian American students communicate in a second language. Although English may be their predominant language, these children may still continue to speak and hear their parents' native language at home and in their neighborhoods. Second, the Asian American child should not be viewed as good with numbers and poor with words. Third, although many Asian American children have proved to be quite successful academically, all children deserve individual consideration of their unique strengths and weaknesses. Fourth, generational differences and socioeconomic factors warrant consideration; second- and third-generation children with educated and successful parents will probably have fewer communication problems than first-generation children of lower socioeconomic status do.

Lo (2008) conducted research on expectations toward American schools among Chinese families with disabilities and special needs. The research suggested more training in cultural sensitivity for professionals working with Chinese families. Some Chinese families considered teachers disrespectful when schools sent home documents that were written only in English. Others felt the school did not want to be equal partners. One parent reported the teacher did not teach her child pronunciation because she would not look her in the eye. Several aspects need to be considered. The child might be learning languages both at home and at school as well as being challenged by a disability. Plus, there might be self-esteem issues associated with communication difficulties.

Families

Family allegiance and respect for parents and family significantly affect the achievement and behavior of Asian American children. In traditional Asian American families, children

- *View elders with great reverence and respect.* Children are taught that the father is the head of the family, with absolute authority.
- *Learn specific family roles.* The primary duty of the boys and men is to be good sons; the obligation to be a good husband or father is second to duty as a son. Females are primarily the child bearers and nurturing caretakers and are responsible for domestic chores. Children obey their parents and elders, and parents and elders are responsible for the support, upbringing, and education of the children. Both parents and children demonstrate respect for elders of the household; in return, ancestral spirits are believed to protect the family. The interdependency of family members works as a mechanism to keep the family together (Sue & Sue, 2013).
- *Feel their families have high expectations for their achievement and behavior.* Children are expected to excel in American society yet retain the values and traditions of their Asian American culture.
- *Sense a powerful message not to bring embarrassment and shame to the family.* The inculcation of guilt and shame is the principal technique used to control the behavior of family members. Parents emphasize the children's obligation to the family and their responsibility to meet family expectations. If a child acts contrary to the family's wishes, the child is considered selfish, inconsiderate, and ungrateful. Aberrant behavior is usually hidden from outsiders and is handled within the family. Outstanding achievement, in contrast, is a source of great pride; it, too, reflects not only on the child but also on the entire family (Sue & Sue, 2013).

The Asian and Pacific Islander family structure has the potential for creating conflicts and the need for counseling intervention. American-born children sometimes defy and reject their ancestors' ways of living. They may feel torn between the demands of becoming Americanized and the desires of parents to adhere to traditional values. If they believe that their parents have unreasonable expectations and are at odds with American expectations of life, children may openly voice their opposing opinions—for example, disdain for their cultural background. They may even make rude remarks about their parents' national origin.

Second-generation children often differ dramatically from their parents who immigrated to the United States. Many values, such as bringing honor and praise to the family by practicing filial piety, expressing deference to elders, and making personal sacrifices for family members, may become less meaningful to Asian American children.

Case Study 9.1 introduces Mina, an Asian American child.

Case Study 9.1: Mina, an Asian American Child

Mina, a ten-year-old Japanese American, lives with her parents, older sister, younger brother, and elderly grandfather. Although her community is predominantly Asian American, the immediate area in which she lives is as diverse as the broader culture; she has many opportunities to meet both Asian American as well as children of other cultures.

Mina lives in a close-knit family. Her father works two jobs, and her mother works one; together, they provide a comfortable standard of living. Mina's grandfather does not work outside the home, but he does take an active part in child rearing and has other household responsibilities. The whole family looks to him for advice in making everyday decisions. In essence, the family is an interdependent unit working toward common goals and toward solving its own problems. Each member accepts his or her own specific role and is committed to not disappointing other family members. Mina does not question the dominance of her father's authority, but she does notice her younger brother seems to have more important roles and privileges than she has.

Mina has demonstrated above-average academic achievement. She plays the piano, works part-time at the school library, and is a member of the school's Honor Society. Her family views education as an avenue to success and has always insisted that Mina excel in whatever she does. Although her teacher is concerned that Mina is a bit quiet and aloof, she also appreciates Mina's obedience and fine academic work. Mina does not think she is too quiet, but she does realize that her commitment to fulfill family expectations influences her interpersonal conduct and social standing. She feels pressured to excel in both personal conduct and academics. To do otherwise would bring shame and disappointment to her family.

Although Mina wants very much to please the members of her family, their high expectations have given rise to several problems. English does not come easily for her; it requires a considerable amount of work. Also, her friends think she is somewhat aloof—a bit of a goody-goody, in fact. Mina thinks her academic success has caused some of her fellow students to reject her. Of course, she wants to have friends and to be accepted by her peers, but family expectations must come first. Meanwhile, Mina continues to work diligently to fulfill her family obligations and to maintain her excellent academic standing. At the same time, she is trying to develop her own identity.

Reflection Questions:

1. How should effective counselors of Asian American children respond to Mina's perception that "she does notice her younger brother seems to have more important roles and privileges than she has." If that is her worldview, should counselors even broach the subject? Or should they wait for to mention her perception?
2. Suppose Mina mentions that she feels torn between her family's expectation and her peers' expectations—what approaches might be effective?

Unique Challenges Confronting Asian American Children

Asian American children face several challenges. One challenge is their ability to speak English. Speaking English and being understood can be a source of difficulty for Asian American children. A second challenge for Asian American children are the previously mentioned terms, acculturation and enculturation, whereby the child must decide whether to remain with Asian cultural tradition or adopt the dominant cultural perspectives (Omizo et al., 2008). Third, the model minority stereotype presents a significant dilemma for these children. Not all of them fit the mold, and even those who do may have trouble meeting unrealistic expectations. Fourth, some Asian Americans experience low socioeconomic status, with its inherent problems and risk factors.

ASIAN AMERICAN ADOLESCENTS

Social and Cultural Description

Asian Americans and Pacific Islanders' diversity creates an often overlooked disparate educational need. When one thinks of Asian Americans, for most people what comes to mind are well-educated, high-income earners; overachievers; and hard workers whose children are destined for spots at elite Ivy League schools. But this model minority perception is just that: a perception. It also overlooks one big issue: Asian Americans are far from homogenous. Some Asian Americans feel a sense of frustration in higher education. One of the challenges faced by many Asian American students at predominantly White institutions is a feeling of a lack of inclusiveness. This can be particularly true for students of Southeast Asian extraction (Oguntoyinbo, 2015). Also, adolescents differ according to maturity, geographical region, and socioeconomic class.

Brydolf (2009) maintains that Asian Americans are challenged by the "model minority" (p. 37) stereotype when it comes to academic achievement and other crucial measures of prosperity, health, and overall success. The stereotype of Asians as quiet, "model minorities" (Ly, 2008, p. 24) helps hide serious problems. Ly (2008) looks at the need for mental health services for Asian Americans and maintains that European American students may wrestle with the same problems but tend to seek help or be helped sooner. When problems such as social anxiety and depression arise, cultural barriers prevent many from seeking help. Talking about problems to outsiders is considered taboo and shameful. Getting help from family often is not an option. Many Asians attach a strong stigma to mental health problems or simply deny their existence. In addition, even the Asian Americans who do seek mental health services have higher rates of dropping out of therapy (Ly, 2008). Finally, focusing on health risk behaviors, Lee and Rotherham-Borus (2009) also studied the model minority stereotype and concluded that protected sexual relations are lower in Asian Americans and Pacific Islanders and that there are increasing trends in lifetime drinking and marijuana use.

The importance of identity formation and personality development during the adolescent years must be considered from a cultural perspective. Family beliefs and values play an important role in shaping the emerging adult. Asian Americans often adopt a more practical approach to life and problems than do European Americans. Although some acculturation has occurred, cultural emphasis continues to be placed on diligence, harmony, taking responsibility, respect for authority, emphasis on education, respect for elders, and family loyalty.

A client's self-concept can be instrumental in the need for counseling intervention. Omizo, Kim, and Abel (2008) examined the differences among Asian American adolescents living in Hawaii. The researchers first defined the terms acculturation and enculturation. Acculturation was defined as adaptation to the norms and expectations of the dominant group. Enculturation was defined as the retention of the norms of the indigenous group. They concluded that the more Asian American adolescents adhere to both Asian and European American values, the better they feel about the unique ethnic groups to which they belong. They also concluded that the adolescents who adhered to Asian cultural values also judged themselves to be "good" (Omizo et al., 2008, p. 24) members of their ethnic group. Counseling implications of this study will be explored in Chapter 10.

One study (Rivas-Drake et al., 2014) suggests that diverse aspects of ethnic and racial identity (ERI) were generally associated with positive psychosocial functioning and mental health outcomes among adolescents. The outcomes most often examined—and for which more consistently positive associations with ERI were found—pertain to psychosocial functioning and mental health. One key finding of their work is that several aspects of ERI, particularly positive feelings about their ethnic or racial group (e.g., affirmation, private regard), are consistently associated with positive psychosocial adjustment among African American and Latino youth, and with academic outcomes among African American, Latino, and Asian American and Pacific Islander youth to some extent. Findings regarding psychosocial functioning and academic outcomes were more inconsistent among Native American youth. The least consistent findings were in the area of health risk outcomes. Discrepancies in findings preclude making definitive statements about the relation of ERI with health risk outcomes, particularly substance use, among Latino and Native American youth. Similar caution is warranted for Asian American and Pacific Islander youth due to a dearth of studies among this group. The extent to which affective-cognitive dimensions of ERI can and need to be parsed from cultural participation and engagement remains an important conceptual and empirical question. Recent research on ethnic exploration has suggested that the process of exploration can be either positively or negatively associated with psychosocial adjustment, depending on whether it involves searching for an ethnic identity or participating in ethnically related activities. Thus for those studies that include exploration and adjust for the influences of cultural practices, ERI likely refers to a cognitive-affective searching process, which may be predictive of risk taking.

Many Asian American adolescents spend more time on homework, take more advanced high school courses, and graduate with more credits. In addition, a higher percentage of these young people complete high school and college than do their European American peers. However, the high expectations for Asian American adolescents often work to their disadvantage, for example, expectations based on stereotypes mask individuality. Not all Asian American adolescents excel; indeed, many have academic problems that are serious enough to warrant their dropping out of school.

Yeh et al. (2008) conducted research on Chinese immigrant students' cultural interactions. They studied the relationship of English fluency, help seeking, acculturation, and family responsibilities to intercultural competence concerns. Intercultural competence was defined as challenges relating to others, such as European Americans, one's own ethnic group, and one's family. Results that have relevance for counselors include:

- Participants with low English proficiency had higher intercultural competency concerns.
- A greater number of family responsibilities significantly predicted higher intercultural competency concerns.
- A greater openness to other Asian American groups is significantly associated with fewer intercultural competence concerns.
- Higher levels of comfort in seeking help for career, college, and academic concerns are significantly associated with fewer intercultural competence concerns.
- Participants who reported more social support from a special friend had significantly fewer concerns about their intercultural competence.

(Yeh et al., 2008)

Communication

For effective multicultural counseling, it is crucial that the counselor recognize the problems some Asian Americans have with English and understand their unique forms of nonverbal communication. Without doubt, communication barriers and problems confronting Asian American adolescents make educational attainment even more significant. Although many Asian American parents encourage the use of English, large numbers of adolescents live in homes where the primary language spoken continues to be the native language.

In many cases, additional course work is recommended to remedy the language and communication deficiencies of Asian American students. Some of these students have such difficulty understanding English and making themselves understood that considerably more study is required to achieve even minimal competency. Moreover, the direct teaching of English communication skills to correct language and communication deficiencies indicates a failure to understand Asian Americans' difficulty with English and has caused remedial programs to become generally ineffective (Sue & Sue, 2013).

Some nonverbal behavior patterns demonstrated by Asian Americans differ distinctly from those of other cultures. For example, the forward and backward leaning of the body indicates feelings: A backward lean indicates a degree of discomfort with the conversation and a withdrawal from it, whereas a forward lean lets the speaker know the listener is interested, concerned, and flexible. Also, counselors should be aware that Japanese American females express anxiety through increased vocalization, whereas Japanese American males express anxiety through silence. Also, Japanese Americans often communicate nonverbally through gestures. Rubbing or scratching the back of the head or neck, for example, indicates shame or discomfort.

Families

Children learn early on that the father is the head of the household in the traditional Asian American family. Each family member recognizes and respects rigidly defined roles. The father-son relationship is held in the highest esteem. A son is a prized and valued family member who receives greater privileges and responsibilities than does a daughter. A son is obligated to respect and obey his father; in turn, the father assists his son with his education and marriage and provides him with an inheritance. Also, sons have a greater voice in family decisions and enjoy freedoms that daughters do not. Understandably, in this culture, adolescent boys are given more freedom than adolescent girls are. Perceptive counselors realize that acculturation has resulted in changes in some family structures. Asian cultural traditions may also vary according to generational status, socioeconomic level, and a host of other factors.

Respect for family values and expectations influence the behavior of adolescents. If adolescents demonstrate disrespect or any form of undesirable behavior, it reflects poorly on the entire family. The Chinese American family serves as a source of emotional security and personal identity and as a reference point for individual members. In turn, the family exerts control over interpersonal conduct and social relations, even over the choice of a career or marriage partner. Although acculturation has contributed to increasing individualism, such cultural characteristics as avoidance of shame, indirect communication, self-effacement, and modesty appear to be maintained in recent generations. Adolescent behavior will continue to be strongly influenced by old-world family expectations.

Unique Challenges Confronting Asian American Adolescents

Because they live in a predominantly European American culture and yet must continue to meet the expectations of their respective cultures, Asian American adolescents will probably experience problems that may warrant counseling intervention. Loyalty to Asian American family expectations may result in conflicts, especially during this period of pressure to conform to European American standards and to make the transition into a wider social world.

One of the authors taught a Japanese American student whose achievement record outpaced all others in the class. Her language problems often exacted a burdensome toll: She studied far longer and more conscientiously, sought more assistance, relied heavily on her Japanese American dictionary, and usually requested additional time for in-class assignments. With all her language difficulties, however, her persistence and determination overcame her deficiencies in English.

Yeh (2003) maintains that her research has particularly helpful implications for research, training, and counseling Asian immigrant youth. Yeh concludes that Korean immigrant students

- experience higher levels of mental health symptoms in comparison with Chinese and Japanese students;
- experience shame and humiliation in seeking help for their cultural conflicts;
- face particular challenges as they approach adulthood, such as child care, working for money, and increased housework; and
- experience increasing parent-adolescent conflict due to contrasting ideas about youth authority and autonomy.

Understanding the factors contributing to mental health symptoms in Chinese, Korean, and Japanese immigrant youth will help educators, administrators, and counselors better serve these groups through direct services, program development, and counselor training.

The European American emphasis on individualism presents challenges for Asian American adolescents seeking to satisfy the demands of contemporary society and still remain loyal to family traditions. Asian American girls, in particular, may experience the cultural conflict between traditional values and the more contemporary European American values and thus question their role in life: Will females continue to be relegated to second-class status in the Asian American family? Should they seek more equitable standing, such as exists in European American families? Female Asian Americans are often forced to make additional cultural compromises to achieve success in the majority culture.

Case Study 9.2 introduces Rieko, an Asian American adolescent.

Case Study 9.2: Rieko, an Asian American Adolescent

Rieko, a 16-year-old Japanese American, lives with her parents, younger sister, Mina, her younger brother, and her elderly grandfather. Rieko enjoys the closeness of her family and in particular seeks the advice of her grandfather, who is always available to listen to her concerns.

Rieko is in the tenth grade and does above-average work, but her studies take up most of her time. She is not sure why her studies take so much more time than for other students, but she suspects that her language problem is the reason. She has not discussed this with her family, however, because they continually emphasize the value of education. Also, she does not want them to know that her English is not as good as that of other students. Rieko does pride herself, however, on being able to speak Japanese. In fact, she and her grandfather sometimes speak his native tongue. She enjoys the fact that speaking Japanese makes her grandfather proud of her.

Besides excelling in schoolwork, Rieko has also learned the responsibilities of running a household. She can cook, clean, sew, and shop for groceries. Because her mother is responsible for these tasks, Rieko was encouraged to learn them, too. She is aware, though, that her younger brother is not being taught how to care for the household. She accepts the fact that girls must assume more responsibility despite having fewer privileges, but she sometimes envies her European American girlfriends, who have considerably more freedom. What will it be like after she finishes high school and college (if her family can afford to send her) and enters a predominately European American world? Secretly, she wonders whether she will be drawn away from her Asian American culture.

Sometimes, but not often, Rieko worries about her situation. Will she be more accepted by her fellow students next semester? Are they a bit standoffish because of her culture, because of her good grades, or because she tries to satisfy her teachers? If it is her grades and behavior, there isn't much she can do. She would never disappoint her family. Will her English improve? She has been working very hard on it lately, but there is only so much time between schoolwork and household chores. She also wants to spend some time with her grandfather. Right now, these problems do not seem overwhelming to Rieko. She has always persisted, and besides, she knows her family is there to support her.

Reflection Questions:

1. Assume Rieko suggests that she has a problem with English, and she is trying to hide the problem from her parents and family. What would be an effective approach to helping her resolve the concern?
2. As Rieko realizes that freedom and independence accompany adolescence (at least in some cultures), how can a counselor help her to resolve differences in cultural expectations?

ASIAN AMERICAN ADULTS

Social and Cultural Description

Historically, Asians and Pacific Islanders were often forced to accept the lowest paid menial jobs and were denied the rights of citizenship and of land ownership. Without the opportunity to live and work in European American communities, Asian Americans often formed their own cultural enclaves, such as Chinatowns. In these isolated enclaves, they continued to speak their native language and maintain their old-world traditions (Sue & Sue, 2013).

Phan, Rivera, and Roberts-Wilbur (2005) believe that there is a lack of knowledge about the identity development of Vietnamese women. Although statistics indicate that many Asian Americans have experienced considerable economic and academic success, a comprehensive picture deserves consideration before reaching conclusions. In an effort to understand Vietnamese refugee women, Phan and colleagues (2005) provide a brief history of Vietnamese populations and their problems (e.g., culture shock, depression, homesickness, and stresses). Next, they maintain that traditional models of identity development do not assist counselors in understanding ethnic minorities in the United States. One cannot assume that all women have the same issues—there is not a universal women's experience. Likewise, similarities between racial and ethnic identity exist, but gender is not always included.

Implications for practice include that counselors should

- understand issues of identity such as gender stereotypes, racial stereotypes, family, marriage, gender role conflict, and interracial marriage;
- recognize the multiple dimensions of Vietnamese refugee women, such as the influence of sociopolitical, sociohistorical, and inherited traditional aspects of the Vietnamese culture;
- understand that Vietnamese women have become better educated over the years, which has led them to freedom and progressive thinking; and
- realize that traditional ways of thinking about the Vietnamese culture may no longer be valid.

First, the stereotype of economic success does not take into account that the culture has a high percentage of more than one wage earner per household. It is true that some Asian Americans work in high-paying occupations, in part, because of high educational attainments. Second, taking care to avoid stereotyping, Asian Americans as a whole have impressive academic achievements. Eighty-two percent of the 25-and-older Asian population have at least a high school diploma. This compares with 86.6% of the total population. Fifty-one percent of the Asian population 25 and older have a bachelor's degree or higher level of education. This compared with 29.6% for all Americans 25 and older. Nearly 22% of 25-and-older Asian population have a graduate or professional degree. This compared with 11.2% for all Americans 25 and older (U.S. Census Bureau, 2015f).

Some Asian Americans believe that discussing unpleasant events will actually cause them to happen. In fact, discussing sickness, mental illness, or death with members of the Chinese culture often constitutes a social taboo. In some situations, an entire family might be ostracized if it is learned that one family member has a mental illness; however, that is also true in some other cultures.

Religious rites and ceremonies play a significant role in the lives of many Asian Americans. Formal religions include Buddhism, Protestantism, and Catholicism. Protestant and Buddhist churches serve specific Asian groups, such as the Japanese, Chinese, Filipino, Korean, and Vietnamese, whereas members of the Catholic Church are generally integrated with other ethnic groups in a geographic parish. Religious values of Asian Americans tend to be closely intertwined with family obligations and expectations.

Communication

Asian Americans speak many primary languages. Within each cultural subgroup, various dialects are spoken. Proficiency in English varies greatly among the different groups. English is generally the first and often the only language of American-born Asians. In contrast, most foreign-born Asian Americans speak a language other than English. Many are fluently bilingual and even multilingual or speak more than one dialect of their native Asian language. Those with limited English proficiency generally live in households where a language other than English predominates.

Many Asian Americans feel uncomfortable with direct forms of communication, especially those involving challenges, confrontation, interruption, and assertiveness. Asians often use subtle, indirect means of communication to allow all those involved to save face. Many Asian American people convey information nonverbally, such as through silence and eye contact. Maintaining silence during a conversation often indicates an expression of respect. Direct eye contact is usually avoided, especially with an elder, because it might indicate disrespect. Again, we must emphasize that acculturation has changed some Asians' communication styles. Factors such as generational status, country of origin, educational attainment, and socioeconomic status all affect communication styles.

Understanding that an Asian American's communication structure changes with differing situations provides counselors with additional cultural insights. Communication forms change with regard to syntax, word endings, and terminology, depending on the individuals involved and the nature of relationships.

Effective communication, regardless of the counselor's cultural background, is essential when working with Asian and Pacific Islander clients. Infusing cultural sensitivity into professional intervention requires counselors to be aware of communication that is reflective of cultural styles and mannerisms

Families

The Asian American family is characterized by unique familial roles and expectations that warrant the counselor's attention. Of great importance is the fact that this culture consists of many different populations shaped by environmental, historical, and social pressures. These groups differ not only among themselves but also in important aspects from the broader European American culture.

Most Asian American families are headed by married couples. Table 9.2 shows the family types among Asian Americans.

The family-first concept of Asian and Pacific Islander families plays a significant role in promoting and maintaining cohesiveness and stability in the family. The cultural obligation to

Table 9.2 Family Types Among Asian Americans (percentages)

Family Types	Total
Total	100
Married	59.6
Widowed	4.6
Divorced	5.0
Separated	1.3
Never Married	29.4

Source: U.S. Census Bureau. (2010). Marital status. *American fact finder*, S1201. Washington, DC: Author. Retrieved 3 January, 2010, from http://factfinder.census.gov.

place the family's needs above one's personal needs can result in problems that need counseling intervention.

Despite some changes in values and the shifting trend toward increasing individualism, such concepts as family loyalty, respect and obligation, and harmony and group cooperation all continue to play significant roles in determining family and individual behavior. Many Asians continue to hold on to a cultural value of humility and an orientation toward collectivism. These beliefs, which emphasize the connections among self, family, and community, stand in stark contrast with Western individualistic values. Counselors with cultural backgrounds that value individualism and independence may want to examine how these values affect their personal attitudes toward Asian American families who value harmony and interdependence.

Family honor is often maintained through highly developed feelings of obligation. The family provides a reference point, a source of personal identity and emotional security. The concept of loss of face involves not only the exposure of an individual's actions for all to see but also the possible withdrawal of the confidence and support of the family, community, or society.

In an effort to understand psychosocial post-migration adjustment, Chung, Bemak, and Wong (2000) studied variables such as acculturation, social support, and psychological distress in Vietnamese refugees. Chung and colleagues offer several recommendations for counselors:

1. Provide therapeutic interventions for existing dysfunctional families and social networks.
2. Support and reinforce already-established health social networks that go beyond the counseling interventions for troubled families and groups.
3. Re-create social networks where there is an absence of family or friends in order to facilitate interpersonal awareness and experiences.

Unique Challenges Confronting Asian American Adults

Communication problems, dismal employment opportunities for unskilled minorities, the model minority stereotype, and conflicting familial roles and expectations all create unique challenges for Asian American adults. First, communication problems will continue to challenge selected Asian groups. Second, the commonly held stereotype of Asian Americans achieving academic and financial success poses a problem. Third, problems may arise when family roles and expectations conflict with those of the European American culture. With acculturation, Asian Americans place increasing emphasis on the European ideals of individuality and personal achievement. Fourth, Hwang, Chun, Takeuchi, Myers, and Siddarth (2005) investigated depression in Chinese Americans and concluded that although most people experience depression during the late teens and early adulthood, Chinese Americans differ in the onset of depression. In fact, Chinese Americans in their study evidenced low risk during late teens and early adulthood. They also concluded that depression onset with Chinese Americans varies as a function of age at immigration and length of residence in the United States.

Sharma (2004) maintained that approximately one-fourth of Americans over the age of 15 have a physiological dependence on at least one substance. Still, while there is not any particular predilection for or prevalence of substance abuse, there is a glaring omission of data from groups with culturally diverse backgrounds.

Another challenge is life satisfaction after immigration to the United States. Chinese American immigrants who experience problems with communication and social isolation expressed less satisfaction. Counselors intervening with Chinese Americans, especially immigrants, need to realize the factors (e.g., language, discrimination, social isolation) that affect life satisfaction and thus plan counseling strategies to address these life stressors.

Despite serious gaps in the research and conclusions, Sharma (2004) concludes that Asian Americans bear a disproportionate burden of substance abuse. One-third of Asian American youth are smokers, which is much greater than among other ethnic groups. Recent reviews of the tobacco industry have revealed aggressive marketing directed toward Asian Americans. Several reasons exist for these marketing efforts: Asian Americans' rapidly increasing population growth, higher purchasing power of some Asian Americans, higher rates of tobacco use in countries of origin, higher proportions of retail businesses under Asian American ownership, and Asian Americans' difficulties adapting to mainstream American society. In Asian societies, youth are taught to be more dependent on others (e.g., parents, elders, and peers) in making decisions. As a result, Asians often get confused while making decisions that focus on everyday living and problems.

Educational interventions aimed at preventing the initiation of substance abuse, such as developing refusal skills, developing media interpretation skills, restoring people's sense of purpose and meaning, training in relaxation, and meditation methods, are available.

Case Study 9.3 introduces Han, an Asian American adult.

Case Study 9.3: Han, an Asian American Adult

Han, a 36-year-old Japanese American, lives in a predominantly Asian American neighborhood with his elderly father, his wife, 10-year-old daughter Mina, 16-year-old daughter Reiko, and his son. Han really appreciates the grandfather's presence in his household, especially when his two jobs leave him weary and in need of encouragement. Han's full-time job is with a European American company; his part-time job is with an Asian American friend who owns a small, struggling construction company. Although he likes his friend, Han would prefer to have only one job. The extra money is handy, but he has little time to spend with his family.

Han views his role as crucial to the welfare of the family. He makes most financial and household decisions. Some of his European American friends question his strong, authoritarian hand, but he feels that's the way it was with his father and that's the way it should be. Han is not sure he could change even if he wanted to. What would his wife and children think? What would the grandfather think? Everyone in his family expects him to make all the important decisions.

Han is proud of his daughter Mina. Her part-time library job, her musical gifts, and her recent initiation into the school's Honor Society please him. In fact, all his family members are worthy. Only once did Mina's younger brother appear to be a bit lax in his behavior at school. Before taking action, Han went to the grandfather to seek his advice. The solution was to approach the problem indirectly and with great tact. The boy did not suffer great shame or embarrassment, but he knew what his father expected him to do.

Han acknowledges that he has problems: working two jobs, uncertainty about his wife working to supplement his salaries, and his aging father. He is fairly content and is proud of his close-knit family, but today's changing society is likely to change the family, too. Han is uncertain about what the future will bring.

Reflection Questions:

1. How would you respond to Han feeling so much responsibility—for his children, wife, and father?
2. Developmentally speaking, what concerns do you think Han might have about his health and seeing his older parent growing elderly? What counseling strategies might be appropriate?

ASIAN AMERICAN ELDERLY

Social and Cultural Description

Counselors should remember that many elderly Asian Americans who seek counseling experienced considerable hardships decades ago (and, in many cases, still do). After arriving in the United States, Asians (especially the Japanese) experienced racism, injustice, and discrimination, such as legal acts forbidding them to own land. They also had limited educational and political opportunities. During World War II, many Japanese Americans were moved to internment camps in the western United States, where they remained until the end of the war. Counselors working with elderly Asian Americans who have suffered the effects of racism and discrimination need to understand how injustices affect these clients' current outlooks and worldviews.

It is a popular misconception that Asian American elderly have no need for assistance because they do not have significant problems and their adjustments to mainstream society have been relatively simple. Although many Asian Americans have demonstrated an amazing ability to achieve success in the predominantly European American society, Asian Americans, especially the elderly, should not be saddled with such an "all is well" image.

Compared with other minorities, the Asian American culture ranks closest to the European American in education and income, but professionals must still remember that most studies have focused on Asian Americans in general rather than on the elderly in particular. An appropriate perception of the elderly requires knowledge of the culture, the elderly years, and the elderly as individuals. Compared with elderly European Americans, elderly Asian Americans fall short in several areas crucial to individual well-being. For example, although the more recent Asian American immigrants include well-educated professionals, the percentage of Asian American elderly who lack formal education continues to be disturbingly high.

Pennachio (2004) offers information on the special needs of Chinese, Japanese, and Korean patients. Her article outlines some cultural clues to help professionals working with these cultures. Although we like Pennachio's (2004) suggestions, we remind readers of the vast diversity among Chinese, Japanese, and Korean patients. Examples of Pennachio's suggestions include:

Filipinos

Filipinos sometimes think

- rapid shifts from hot to cold lead to illness, and a warm environment is essential to maintaining optimal health;
- illnesses result from ancestors because of unfulfilled obligations, which can be countered by healers or priests with massage, herbal treatments, incantations, and offerings;
- they should resist screening programs such as mammograms, Pap smears, and blood tests for cholesterol and glucose.

Southeast Asians

Southeast Asians sometimes think

- elders should be involved in medical decision making;
- actions of the past affect the circumstances in which one is born and lives his life, as well as reincarnation of ancestral spirits;
- the head is sacred—if the head must be touched, touch both sides of the head so the person will think balance is being respected and maintained.

Indians

People from India sometimes think

- ayurvedic medicine, an ancient, intricate system of healing, is effective and worthy of respect;
- professionals should take charge and have answers to their problems;
- maintaining spiritual peace is an essential part of health.

While Pennachio's beneficial article focuses primary emphasis on medical practice, counseling professions will gain significant information about working with these cultural groups.

Although acculturation undoubtedly continues to occur, most elderly in the Asian American culture continue to receive considerable respect. For example, many Japanese Americans equate old age with prestige and honor. Respect for elders is evident in the language used when addressing the elderly and in behavior such as bowing to them and observing strict rules of etiquette. Each Japanese American generation has a unique title, which emphasizes the importance of the role that generations play:

Generation	Name
First	Issei
Second	Nisei
Third	Sansei
Fourth	Yonsei

The values brought to America by first-generation Chinese Americans are often quite different from the prevailing views of American society. For example, Chinese society discourages financial independence from parents and instead encourages interdependence. The American values of achievement, upward mobility, and competition are contrary to Chinese beliefs. In the Chinese culture, the elderly maintain control over income, property, and jobs, whereas European American culture does not recognize such control or power of the elderly.

First-generation Asian American elders have come to expect a reverence and respect that second and third generations (who have adopted many European American customs) may no longer support. Thus these Chinese Americans have difficulty maintaining the old-world traditions, lifestyle, and status they were taught to cherish in their homeland.

Watari and Gatz (2004) investigated Alzheimer's disease among Korean Americans. Barriers to seeking help for mental health symptoms include both structural and cultural barriers. Structural barriers include lack of health insurance, low income, and limited knowledge of the English language. Cultural barriers include how patients and families view illness and whether the illness was conceptualized in religious terms. For example, if the person considered the illness to be related to religious aspects, he or she was less likely to seek mental health counseling. Watari and Gatz (2004) conclude that Korean Americans underutilize community health services for dementia-related problems, delay visits to seek mental health service, and depend on family to buffer symptoms that sometimes result in more cognitive declines.

As do all older Americans, elderly Asian Americans experience various changes related to advancing age: declining physical strength, increased leisure time, and the imminence of death. In addition, elderly Asian Americans must adjust to challenges to their established traditions. In short, the difficulties faced by Asian Americans are also faced by other cultural groups.

Communication

Communication barriers cause considerable problems and frustrations for Asian American elderly. Communication problems have undoubtedly played a major role in preventing Asian Americans from seeking community services as well as public social and health services. Communication difficulties have also hampered their adjustment to a predominantly European American culture. Because elderly Chinese Americans have lived most of their lives in predominantly Chinese-speaking communities, communication poses a major barrier for them. They may not have the option to improve their living conditions by moving outside their ethnic neighborhoods. They may also not seek medical attention unless their illnesses are extremely severe, and then they visit only Chinese-speaking doctors in their neighborhood.

For Asian American elderly, communication problems are compounded by attitudes and limitations associated with advanced years. Because of the lack of motivation, the difficulty of learning a second language, or the lack of proper professional assistance, it is unlikely that the elderly will undertake any serious effort to improve their communication skills. The feeling that "it's too late in life to begin such an enormous task" or the lack of motivation to improve language skills continues to be a contributing factor to such hardships as substandard housing and inadequate medical attention and nutrition experienced by many elderly Asian Americans.

Families

Families, both immediate and extended, have traditionally played a significant role in the Asian American culture and are characterized by specific roles, relationships, and respect for elders. Although historically the responsibility for the elderly rested with the oldest son, more contemporary expectations do not include the oldest son accepting such responsibility. Elderly family members do, however, expect their children to assist them. In the traditional Japanese and Chinese cultures, the extended family unit functions as a supportive institution, and all family members share individual incomes. Although these values carried over to some degree in the United States and continue to be appreciated by first-generation Asian Americans, cultural changes in younger generations indicate that practices toward the elderly might be changing. It is ironic that, at the very time the elderly need stability and adherence to cultural traditions, many younger-generation Asian Americans are beginning to emphasize the values of the traditional European American society, such as financial independence from parents and extended family. Without doubt, the "Americanization" of Asian American youths is forcing many older Asian Americans to compromise their old-world values.

Unique Challenges Confronting Asian American Elderly

Asian American elderly have been erroneously portrayed as a cultural group without need of assistance and as an age group that has all of its financial and emotional needs met by younger generations. Professionals with a knowledge and understanding of Asian American elderly clearly recognize the fallacy of such thinking. Elderly Asian Americans experience challenges unique to their age on the lifespan and to their culture:

- Certain types of cancers, high blood pressure, and tuberculosis are major health concerns of elderly Asian/Pacific Islander Americans (U.S. Census Bureau, 2009).
- Elderly Asian Americans are less likely to use formal health-care services, such as those reimbursed under Medicare. Reasons include communication differences and a distrust of Western medicine.
- Language continues to be a serious problem for elderly Asian Americans. Because of lack of proficiency in English, they may be forced to live in low-income neighborhoods, where they often receive inappropriate medical care and cannot take advantage of social services.

- Because of low wages, lack of education, and limited skills, significant numbers of elderly Asian Americans live in poverty.
- An alarmingly high rate of drug use and suicide exists among older Asian Americans, especially in older men without family or ideological ties to the larger community.
- Increasing generational differences put additional stress on the elderly at a time when they especially need stability.

It is ironic that an age group and a culture with so many problems and challenges can be stereotyped as a cultural group without significant problems. Elderly Asian Americans are not likely to seek assistance for a variety of reasons: pride, communication barriers, fear of discrimination outside Asian American communities, and a mistrust of Western medicine. Furthermore, Asian American elderly may be forced to accept rejection of their traditional values as their children and grandchildren assimilate into the majority culture.

Case Study 9.4 introduces Grandfather Sukuzi, an elderly Asian American.

Case Study 9.4: Grandfather Sukuzi, an Asian American Elder

Eighty-five-year-old Grandfather Sukuzi lives with Han and his wife, their daughters, Mina and Rieko, and their youngest child, a son. He feels very fortunate to live in the same house with his family; some of his elderly friends are not as fortunate and must live either alone or with other elderly people in small apartments. He no longer works outside the home and does very little housework. "Keeping the house is women's work," Grandfather says. Besides, Han's wife and daughters do a very good job taking care of the house. Grandfather does feel needed, however; he helps the family by giving advice and instructing the children in traditional Japanese customs.

Grandfather's health is generally good, but he does have the usual problems associated with growing old, such as dizziness, aches and pains, and a slight loss of hearing. He is somewhat frail and moves slowly. His forgetfulness worries him. Could it be Alzheimer's disease? He has heard of it, but he does not know much about it. Grandfather seldom sees a physician; in fact, he has not been to one in several years. Because Han has two jobs, Grandfather must go alone, which means he will not have help translating what the physician says. He also wonders whether the physician understands him. Although Grandfather probably could receive government benefits of some kind, he always puts off seeking assistance. "They ask too many questions," he tells Han. Grandfather's pride and lack of language facility are more likely the reasons for his reluctance to apply for benefits.

Although Grandfather has lived in the United States since he was in his early 20s, his English is still poor. He never attended an American school, and the only English he knows is what he has picked up from talking with others and occasionally watching television. Moreover, living in the Japanese community has relieved him of undue pressure; everyone there speaks his language.

Although Grandfather is quite content, he does sense some erosion of traditional Japanese values. Of course, the family treats him with great respect, but the younger generations are somehow different now. It is difficult to pinpoint specific examples, but sometimes Han seems to want too much financial independence, and he does not seek out Grandfather's advice as much as he once did. Evidence of change is clearer in the neighborhood. Some of his elderly friends seem to be forgotten by their children, who seldom visit their elders.

Grandfather is closest to his grandchildren. He and Rieko speak Japanese at times, and although she is not fluent, she is making progress and Grandfather enjoys teaching her.

Strangely enough, it seems that Rieko is more interested in the traditional Japanese culture than her parents are.

What does the future hold for Grandfather? Right now, he is respected and needed by his family. It pleases him that the cultural assimilation of some Asian Americans is not affecting them to any significant degree. He is growing old, but his place in the family is secure.

Reflection Questions:

1. What challenges might Grandfather expect during the elderly developmental stage?
2. Grandfather senses "some erosion of traditional Japanese values." How might you respond should he bring this concern to a counseling session?

SUMMARY

Counselors of Asian American children, adolescents, adults, and elders face several challenges that require culturally appropriate knowledge, attitudes, and skills. Slight modifications in counseling intervention will not suffice. Counselors intervening with Asian Americans will need to recognize

- the rich diversity among the Asian cultures and that knowledge gained from working with Chinese American clients, for instance, may not be applicable to Samoan or Tongan clients;
- the communication problems facing many Asian Americans, such as limited English-language skills (comprehension and speaking);
- the incidence of poverty, which occurs in some Asian cultures more than in others;
- society's expectations that all Asians fit a stereotypical mold; and
- cultural differences that relate to the respective lifespan stage, such as possible differences between partially acculturated children and their grandparents.

Trying to fit an Asian American client into a mold or a model will only cause frustration for both client and counselor. Counselors who work effectively with Asian American clients will understand the need to learn about each client's specific culture and developmental stage and factors, such as differing cultural characteristics, language proficiency levels, educational attainments, and income levels, and the challenges associated with each developmental stage.

SUGGESTED READINGS

Chang, E., Chan, K. S. & Hae-Ra. (2015). Effect of acculturation on variations in having a usual source of care among Asian Americans and Non-Hispanic Whites in California. *American Journal of Public Health, 105* (2), 398–407. These authors examined associations with acculturation factors (English proficiency, length of residence, residence in a racially concordant neighborhood) and key enabling (employment, income, insurance) and predisposing (education) factors.

Dewell, J. A., & Owen, J. (2015). Addressing mental health disparities with Asian American clients: Examining the generalizability of the common factors model. *Journal of Counseling and Development, 93*(3), 80–87. Although mental health disparities for Asian Americans are known, reasons for the disparities are not well understood within the counseling process—this reading looks at empirically supported factors that might reduce the disparities.

Gnanadass, E. (2014). Learning to teach about race. *Adult Learning, 25*(3), 96–102. This article examines the intellectual and experiential journey of a South Asian American (SAA) feminist who teaches about race and antiracist praxis in the United States. It starts with her struggles trying to teach about race through the lens of White privilege and ends by sharing her current teaching practices, which foreground the concept of race as a learned identity.

Lund, T. J., Chan, P., & Liang, B. (2014). Depression and relational health in Asian American and European American college women. *Psychology in the Schools*, 51(5), 493–505. Research consistently demonstrates elevated rates of depression among college-aged women, yet evidence of racial differences in depression among this population are poorly understood.

Schachter, A. (2014). Finding common ground: Indian immigrants and Asian American panethnicity. *Social Forces*, 92(4), 1487–1512. The common political usage of the term Asian American includes Indians, but historical, religious, and phenotypical differences among Indians and East and Southeast Asians raise the question of how far the boundaries of Asian American identity extend.

10 Counseling Asian American Clients

QUESTIONS TO BE EXPLORED

- What unique challenges can counselors expect when intervening with Asian American children, adolescents, adults, and elders?
- How can counselors, especially counselors from other cultural backgrounds, effectively plan counseling intervention for Asian American clients, considering Asian Americans' unique cultural and individual differences?
- How have years of discrimination, prejudice, social injustices, and injustice affected Asian Americans and their worldviews?
- How can counselors address Asian Americans' tendency to seek mental health advice from sources other than counselors and psychotherapists?
- How can counselors conduct individual, group, and family therapy for Asian Americans?
- What concerns and problems related to development might Asian American child, adolescent, adult, and elder clients present to counselors?
- How can counselors of differing cultural backgrounds and lifespan stages intervene with Asian Americans of other backgrounds and lifespan stages?

OVERVIEW

Counselors need to understand Asian American people from historical, cultural, and lifespan perspectives. Many Asian Americans have experienced considerable hardships in the United States. Efforts to prohibit home ownership and to restrict educational, occupational, and political opportunities have taken a considerable toll on Asian Americans. Counselors also need to avoid making generalizations about this vastly diverse group of people. Given Asian Americans' diversity, it is essential that counselors consider languages, religions, and individual differences. As with all cultures, it is imperative that counselors learn about differences between younger-generation and older-generation Asian Americans. This chapter looks at how counselors can provide culturally appropriate individual, group, and family therapy to Asian American clients.

Since many Asian Americans have been successful in U.S. society, some people erroneously believe that discrimination is minimal or less severe and that Asian Americans do not need counseling intervention (Lee, 2003). Such an opinion often hides potential counseling problems resulting from acculturation, economic stress, family conflicts, or substance abuse. Lee (2003) also thought Asians might avoid situations and circumstances in which discrimination has already occurred.

ASIAN AMERICAN CHILDREN

Potential Problems Warranting Counseling Intervention

Problems Asian American children may experience include:

- failure to develop a strong Asian American cultural identity and a positive self-concept;
- the perception that they constitute a model minority; that is, they are all intellectually superior, hardworking, and academically successful, with superior mathematical skills;
- differing cultural characteristics;
- the inability to reconcile loyalties with conflicting Asian and majority cultures;
- pressures to excel in the majority-culture society yet maintain old-world Asian values;
- communication difficulties, which may hamper academic achievement and socialization;
- adverse effects of overt or covert racism, injustice, discrimination, and cultural history of oppression;
- an increasing tendency to move from a parent-centered world to a peer-centered world;
- family conflicts arising from children moving toward a peer-centered world and away from the parent-centered world;
- parents who are unwilling to accept contemporary Western viewpoints on child-family allegiances; and
- smaller physical size, which may create problems for children when small stature causes them to feel inadequate in other ways.

Counseling Considerations

Issues relative to Asian American children include (a) conflicts related to children's cultural background and the Western values advocated in school, (b) the significant influence of the patriarchal role of the father in nearly all aspects of children's lives, and (c) the European American cultural challenge to children's traditional place in the Asian family (valuing boys over girls, determining authority by sibling age, maintaining unquestioned obedience, or upholding the family's honor at all costs).

Recommendations for working effectively with Asian American children include the following:

- Determine individual strengths, experiences, and challenges.
- Determine the children's degree of acculturation to Western society.
- Understand Asian Americans' difficulty in being self-disclosing and open, especially with strangers, when discussing family matters.
- Understand that confrontational, emotionally intense approaches may cause additional problems and turmoil for Asian American clients.
- Learn about children as individuals and their respective cultural beliefs.

Asian American children experience many social, economic, and educational inequities that may warrant the intervention of elementary school counselors. These children may feel uncomfortable with or unable to deal with school situations. They may experience social and health problems or problems resulting from conflicting values and language differences. Asian American children often learn early in life to keep personal and family problems within the confines of the family so as to avoid shame and embarrassment. Therefore, children might be unfamiliar with counseling procedures and be reluctant to reveal inner feelings with a counselor with whom trust has not been established. Counselors who are aware of these cultural factors are in a better position to develop rapport that is conducive to the counseling process.

Individual and Group Therapy

What strategies are most appropriate for working with Asian American and Pacific Islander children? Counselors who understand the reserved demeanor of Asian American children and develop an enthusiasm for their Asian cultural heritage can enhance the client-counselor relationship. To promote cultural understanding, each child should be encouraged to share his or her background, values, needs, and problems.

Counselors should not misinterpret silence as apathy. During the session, Asian Americans may remain silent for quite some time, briefly verbalize a problem, and then wait for the counselor to offer directions.

Counselors should understand issues relating to four major areas: group orientation, concepts of time, communication and learning skills, and appropriate behavior. Counselors can understand the following issues:

- Individual competition should be minimized; children should not be recognized or punished in front of the group.
- Counseling activities should focus on the present time.
- Participation of parents and elders from the community should be sought whenever possible.
- The counselor should take the role of a mentor, because Asian American children and their parents might be reluctant to seek professional assistance.

In examining counseling techniques used with Asian Americans, counselors should be more formal and less confrontational than when working with European Americans. Also, although counseling decisions deserve individual consideration, group therapy sessions should be used less often with Asian American children; these children may be reluctant to disclose personal problems that could reflect negatively on the family. The child who might disclose problems and concerns in individual sessions may not wish to risk peers in a group session knowing personal or family problems.

Hanna and Green (2004) think school counselors should consider the spiritual backgrounds and traditions of Asian students. Such an understanding will improve counseling effectiveness and will also prove beneficial in establishing trust with Asian parents. When a counselor can demonstrate some depth of knowledge of an Asian parent's religious tradition, the degree of trust generated can be deeper and even more inspired than what results from a counselor's understanding of culture. Hanna and Green succinctly explain Hinduism, Buddhism, and Islam.

The key to establishing spiritual connections with Asian clients is through communicating empathic understanding. The concept of cultural empathy best explains the integration of cultural knowledge, counselor wisdom, and the awareness necessary for connecting with a student from a different spiritual background. It is not enough to simply understand a religion; it is also important to understand the religion in the cultural context of how it is practiced and who is practicing. It is also important to understand that a spiritual practice varies within the culture; that is, just as not all Christians are alike, not all Buddhists are alike.

Family Therapy

The Asian American family's sense of cohesiveness and their loyalty to the family welfare should not rule out family therapy altogether. Realistically, however, Asian American children may have to be encouraged to disclose significant information. Also, a child in a family therapy situation will probably be reluctant to speak, because the father is generally expected to speak for the family. Furthermore, the child's disclosure of a significant problem might reflect poorly on the father's ability to manage his home and family.

Elementary school counselors may want to involve parents and families in certain situations. Essential factors to consider include (a) reviewing the parents' backgrounds, (b) being aware of cultural differences, (c) developing a sense of trust, (d) respecting the "pride and shame" aspect, (e) recognizing the family's need to save face, and (f) learning how the parents feel about school.

Case Study 10.1 looks at a counselor's efforts with Mina, a ten-year-old Japanese American girl.

Case Study 10.1: Counseling Mina, an Asian American Child

Mina's teacher asked her on several occasions if she wanted to see the counselor, and although the teacher thought that Mina had several concerns, Mina was always hesitant. Finally, the teacher took the initiative to arrange an appointment.

During the first and second sessions, the counselor found that Mina was reluctant to reveal her problems. Mina trusted her teachers; they had shown a great deal of interest in her and her schoolwork. But as for the counselor—well, Mina couldn't imagine what to talk about.

Mina lived in a close-knit family in which her father reigned supreme. He made all the decisions, and Mina was afraid to ask him whether she could participate in the extracurricular activities her peers enjoyed. After completing her schoolwork and her piano practice, little time was left over; however, she did regard her peers with a sense of envy. Why couldn't she do some of the things they did? When would her father change? Couldn't he see that living in America required some change of ways? She worked very hard to live up to his high expectations for her, but her few friends did not have to meet such expectations. They enjoyed play a lot more than work. Mina thought that the exceptional demands of her family might be costing her friends.

Mina's other concern, which she was slow to admit, was her developing body. Was she developing too slowly, perhaps? Were all the changes normal? Luckily, her counselor was a woman; but even so, Mina did not admit her concerns until the eighth session. Now Mina feels fortunate that she has the counselor to answer her questions, because no one at home is willing to discuss such matters.

The counselor tried diligently to establish a trusting counseling relationship and proceeded slowly so as not to confront Mina "head-on." Finally, the counselor determined that Mina's problems could be attributed primarily to the pressure placed on her to excel in all endeavors, her perceived rejection by her peers, and her developing body. Because Mina probably would not disclose information in a group setting, the counselor scheduled several more individual sessions with her.

Counseling and Development 10.1: The Childhood Years

Feng, a nine-year-old Chinese American girl, was referred by her teacher to the counselor for several reasons: her reticent behavior, extreme quietness, reluctance to speak in class, and possibly too much concern with grades. The teacher says she believes the "model minority" notion because Feng's family members are high achievers. The teacher wanted Feng to be more like other class members, for example, taking a more active and social role. The counselor knew she had a professional responsibility to talk with the teacher about her stereotypical beliefs.

The counselor confided to herself. The counselor was definitely concerned about the teacher's belief in the "model minority," but she also knew Feng's developmental characteristics: changing self-esteem, developing cultural identity, and lack of social interaction; but there were still differing cultural perceptions of social interactions.

Counseling Strategies:

1. Explore the possibility of Feng being a second-language learner, especially if her parents spoke Chinese in the home.
2. Inquire about Feng's quietness—was it due to self-esteem issues? Or was it due to language difficulties?
3. Determine whether Feng's developing cultural identity was interfering with her overall development.

ASIAN AMERICAN ADOLESCENTS

Potential Problems Warranting Counseling Intervention

Problems Asian American adolescents may experience include

*   failure to develop positive adolescent and Asian American identities;
*   adverse effects of the model minority stereotype;
*   failure to meet cultural expectations for behavior (e.g., restraint of strong feelings, avoidance of outspokenness);
*   conflicts involving family cultural characteristics (e.g., rigidly defined roles);
*   problems with English-language proficiency and non-Asian Americans' inability to understand nonverbal communication;
*   conflicts between "individualism" and the Asian American commitment to family and the welfare of others;
*   conflicts arising from generational differences between adolescents and elders;
*   developmental differences (e.g., in height and weight);
*   problems associated with social interests expanding from family to the wider community and peers; and
*   adverse effects of racism, prejudice, and discrimination.

Counseling Considerations

Several challenges confront counselors working with Asian American adolescents. First, these adolescents often believe that they should seek out family members for advice and assistance rather than share concerns with an outsider. This situation may lead to the counselor having to explain the objectives, procedures, and confidentiality of the counseling process. Second, parent-adolescent conflicts stem from the traditional Asian commitment to the family, thus resulting in problems from acculturation, generational differences, and differing peer and family expectations (Lee, Su, & Yoshida, 2005). Third, nonverbal behaviors may be misinterpreted. Asian Americans' forward and backward leaning indicates specific feelings (a forward lean indicates politeness and concern; a backward lean indicates that the listener wants to withdraw from the conversation). Fourth, Asian Americans may choose to remain silent, perhaps due to their uncomfortableness with the counselor. Finally, Asian American college students may experience somatic discomforts, such as headaches, insomnia, palpitations, dizziness, and fatigue, for which they may seek counseling services (Lee et al., 2005).

Another barrier that interferes with the counseling of Asian Americans is a tendency to avoid disclosing personal problems. For example, Asian American students frequently have difficulty admitting emotional problems because of the shame it might bring to their families. These students may request help indirectly by referring to academic problems or somatic complaints. Asian Americans' difficulties with disclosure often require the counselor to emphasize the confidentiality of counseling relationships. Asian American clients often open up and express feelings quite directly once they develop trust in the counselor (Lippincott & Mierzwa, 1995; Yeh & Huang, 1996). Asian students tend to view counseling as a directive, paternalistic, and authoritarian process. Hence they are likely to expect the counselor to provide advice and a recommended course of action.

Perceptive counselors also consider Asian adolescents' adherence to both Asian and European American values, what some call bicultural competence. Helping students explore their own values as well as the extent to which they align with Asian and European American cultural norms may help them to be able to live comfortably with the values of both the dominant and indigenous cultural groups, a disposition that has been linked to positive facets of mental and cognitive functioning (Omizo, Kim, & Abel, 2008). Before setting counseling goals and directions with Asian American adolescents, it is important to examine how these goals and actions make sense in light of their cultural norms and values, as well as the extent to which these norms and values may affect their beliefs about their competence to follow through with counseling directions (Omizo et al., 2008).

Individual and Group Therapy

Several characteristics of group-oriented cultures—collectivism and primacy of group survival over individual survival—make them especially compatible with group career counseling techniques (Pope, 1999).

Although Asian Americans generally tend to underutilize formal mental health services, they tend to use or overuse career counseling. In Asian cultures, seeking assistance for career issues does not have the same stigma associated with seeking help for mental health issues (e.g., depression). Group career counselors must build self-credibility as well as credibility for the process of group career counseling. Specific group career counseling interventions include exploration groups, job interview skills, and culturally appropriate career decision-making skills.

Asian American adolescents may be reluctant to seek counseling, either for individual or group therapy. Ringel (2005) maintains that Asian Americans, specifically Chinese, Japanese, and Koreans, underutilize mental health services due to a variety of reasons, such as lack of access to counseling services, lack of familiarity with Western counseling models, and differences in values and worldviews. Dilemmas in cross-cultural practice often occur when counselors with Western cultural perspectives intervene with Asian American adolescents. Typical Western adolescent developmental themes such as individuation, identity consolidation, and peer relationships may be viewed very differently from an Asian immigrant family's point of view. This cultural difference has to be understood and appreciated by their non-Asian American clinicians. Also, Ringel (2005) found that some therapists advocated a Western point of view, encouraging their clients to become more independent of their families and more expressive of their feelings. Other therapists viewed their clients from the perspective of their Asian traditions, but perhaps missed some important aspects of their unique individuality. The culturally experienced therapists presented the most skillful ways of balancing their clients' individual struggles with their unique cultural traditions.

When deciding whether to use individual or group therapy with adolescents, counselors should recognize that Asian American adults might consider group counseling a threat because they want to protect and honor the family's name. For those who hold such an expectation, group therapy may be threatening. Adolescents may fear that friends and parents will learn of their counseling sessions; therefore, information that could jeopardize the adolescents' or families' status is not likely to be disclosed. Asian American adolescents frequently refuse to participate in group counseling; in a group setting, they may be quiet and withdrawn. Family sessions may be characterized by only the father speaking or by holding back information that casts doubt on his ability. Ethical dilemmas may arise when family members, who feel a sense of collectivism for the family and do not understand the confidentiality associated with the counseling profession, ask the counselor what another family member revealed during sessions.

Group therapy has the potential to be effective with Southeast Asian refugee adolescents: They have an opportunity to share troublesome experiences with others and to participate in the healing process. This sharing experience provided by group therapy decreases alienation and the belief that one's own experiences are unique. This is particularly relevant for counseling with adolescents in Vietnamese and Cambodian cultures, given the traditional nature of privacy and personal boundaries outside the family system. Groups could be structured to provide psychotherapy that addresses depression, isolation, loss, and post-traumatic stress (Bemak & Greenberg, 1994).

Generational differences between parents and adolescents in the United States reflect the ongoing acculturation process of Asian Americans. Some adolescent clients experience a dislike for their own culture, especially in their social life. Such a situation is illustrated in the following counseling interchange, wherein the Asian American adolescent girl discusses her parents' reluctance toward her dating European Americans:

COUNSELOR: You seem to prefer dating Caucasians. . . .

CLIENT: Well. . . . It's so stupid for my parents to think that they can keep all their customs and values. I really resent being Chinese and having to date all those Chinese guys. They're so passive, and I can make them do almost anything I want. Others [Chinese] are on a big ego trip and expect me to be passive and do whatever they say. Yes . . . I do prefer Caucasians.

COUNSELOR: Is that an alternative open to you?

CLIENT: Yes . . . but my parents would feel hurt . . . they'd probably disown me. They keep on telling me to go out with Chinese guys. A few months ago they got me to go out with this guy—I must have been the first girl he ever dated—I wasn't even polite to him.

COUNSELOR: I guess things were doubly bad. You didn't like the guy, and you didn't like your parents pushing him on you.

CLIENT: Well . . . actually I felt a little sorry for him. I don't like to hurt my parents or those [Chinese] guys, but things always work out that way.

The client's last statement reflects feelings of guilt over her rudeness toward her date. Although she was open and honest, she confused her desire to be independent with her need to reject her parents' attempts to influence her life. During a later session, she was able to express her conflict:

CLIENT: I used to think that I was being independent if I went out with guys that my parents disapproved of. But that isn't really being independent. I just did that to spite them. I guess I should feel guilty if I purposely hurt them, but not if I really want to do something for myself.[1]

Family Therapy

Asian American clients often do not understand family therapy; therefore, the first session should be planned so that the client and the family will want to return for future sessions. Often misunderstanding the role of a family therapist, clients sometimes perceive the therapist as a knowledgeable expert who will guide them through their problem. They expect the counselor to be more directive than passive. Being directive does not mean the counselor must tell family members how to live their lives, but it does involve guiding the family therapy process. In such cases, the family therapist must convey confidence and should not hesitate to disclose educational background and work experience. Asian Americans need to feel that the counselor has received proper training and has the ability to help them with their problems.

A basic consideration in implementing family therapy with Asian Americans is to plan counseling therapy in such a manner that all family members will feel free to speak. In family counseling situations, the father, acting as the head of the household, might assume the spokesperson role, with other family members for the most part remaining silent.

Case Study 10.2 looks at a counselor's efforts with Rieko, a 16-year-old Asian American girl.

Case Study 10.2: Counseling Rieko, an Asian American Adolescent

Rieko, age 16, was referred by her teacher for counseling. The teacher had advised Rieko to refer herself, but Rieko secretly thought that counseling was out of the question because she valued her family's wishes to keep problems within the family. Therefore, the teacher referred her, promising Rieko that her peers would not know and that her family's name and honor would not be shamed.

The 32-year-old European American counselor knew she would have to move cautiously with Rieko by ensuring confidentiality, building trust, explaining the counseling process and the client-counselor relationship, and allaying Rieko's fears about shaming the family. During the first session, Rieko was quiet and unwilling to disclose significant information. After the third session, the counselor decided that Rieko's two major problems were her lack of non-Asian American friends and her difficulties with English. Specifically, Rieko's loyalty to her family's wishes and her commitment to excel in all endeavors "turned off" some potential friends, and her problems with English resulted in an inability to communicate with ease. The counselor's goal was to help Rieko believe in herself as a worthwhile person, regardless of whether or not she had non-Asian American friends. Also, remedial assistance with the communication problems was long overdue, especially because Rieko's communication problems required her to study much harder than most of her peers.

The counselor decided that Rieko should enroll in a special English class and that she would continue in counseling on a regular basis to discuss making friends in multicultural situations and to explore ways for her to deal with students who seemed to turn their backs on her. The counselor quickly ruled out both group and family therapy because Rieko would be very unlikely to disclose information in either situation.

Counseling and Development 10.2: The Adolescent Years

Anh Dung, a 16-year-old Vietnamese American boy, has numerous socialization challenges with all cultures, not just his own. He has been referred to the counselor for anger management, his anger being directed at both his teachers and other students. There have been several minor altercations with others on school property, and he has one "discipline slip" for yelling at his teacher. The counselor wants to intervene before the situation grows more acute.

The counselor thought about Anh Dung's developmental period: growing need for social acceptance, changing self-esteem in a majority European American society, and failing to achieve developmental tasks, such as getting along with others and dealing with his anger.

Counseling Strategies:

1. Begin with individual therapy, and then, possibly, move on to small group counseling, because several other students had histories of violent outbursts.
2. Seek a "developmental" source of his anger (e.g., friendships, bravado, frustration with self-esteem or his Vietnamese identity).

3. Ask about more developmentally appropriate ways to deal with anger (e.g., trying to see others' perceptive and, generally speaking, less egocentric behaviors).

ASIAN AMERICAN ADULTS

Potential Problems Warranting Counseling Intervention

Problems Asian American adults may experience include

*   acceptance of the model minority stereotype and the belief that Asian Americans do not need counseling;
*   adverse effects of historical and contemporary discrimination;
*   low socioeconomic status of many Asian Americans;
*   the belief that discussing physical and mental problems actually causes these problems;
*   language and communication difficulties;
*   adverse effects of rigid and authoritarian family structures;
*   conflicts arising from acculturation, such as perceived discrimination, homesickness, stress due to culture shock, and refugees' guilt about leaving loved ones behind;
*   the belief that seeking counseling reflects negatively on the family;
*   problems associated with midlife (e.g., aging, successfully meeting adult tasks and crises); and
*   problems resulting from marriage and family situations (e.g., expecting to maintain traditional Asian American family roles in a majority culture that emphasizes equality).

Counseling Considerations

Traditional Western psychotherapeutic approaches based on individualism, independence, self-disclosure, verbal expression of feelings, and long-term insight therapy may be counter-productive for Asian Americans, who often value interdependence, self-control, repression of emotions, and short-term, results-oriented solutions. Kim, Ng, and Ahn (2005) maintain that Asian American adults underutilize and prematurely exit from counseling services, although their need is no less than that of other cultural groups. Some Asians, such as Korean Americans, are significantly more likely to cope with problems by engaging in religious activities, such as speaking with a religious leader. Asian American females are significantly more likely to have positive attitudes toward seeking professional counseling.

We think Derald Wing Sue and David Sue in their book *Counseling the Culturally Diverse: Theory and Practice*, sixth edition, offer the best suggestions for counseling Asian Americans. The following summarizes some of Sue and Sue's suggestions and implications for counseling Asian Americans.

Counseling Asian American Clients–Characteristics and Strengths

A word of caution: Counselors should never make assumptions based upon stereotypical beliefs—an objective assessment is essential to determine how individual Asian Americans clients think.

Collectivistic Orientation: Instead of promoting individual needs and personal identity, Asian American families tend to have family and group orientations.

Implications: Because of possible collectivistic orientation, counselors should consider the family and community. For traditionally oriented Asian Americans, a focus on individual client needs and wishes may run counter to the values of collectivistic orientations. Goals and treatment may need to include a family focus. Nevertheless, more acculturated clients might prefer a more individual orientation than the traditional collectivistic orientation.

Hierarchical Relationships: Traditional Asian Americans families tend to be hierarchical and patriarchal in structure, with males and older individuals occupying a higher status.

Implications: In family therapy, perceptive counselors determine the family and community pattern. Some modern families are moving toward an egalitarian structure; some continue to be hierarchical. Allowing children or adolescents to interpret language or communication styles might threaten the hierarchical or patriarchal structure. Also, if women have employment opportunities while the husband experiences unemployment, a sense of loss of male status might result in family conflict.

Parenting Styles: Asian Americans' parenting styles tend to be more authoritarian and directive than those of European American families.

Implications: Egalitarian or Western-style parent effectiveness may run counter to traditional child-rearing patterns. Some Asian American families might run counter to traditional child-rearing patterns. Traditional Asian American families exposed to Western techniques or styles may feel that their parenting skills are being criticized.

Source: Sue, D.W., & Sue, D. (2013). *Counseling the Culturally Diverse: Theory and Practice*, sixth edition. Hoboken, NJ: Wiley and Sons.

Kim and colleagues (2005) suggest that Asian Americans favor a logical, rational, and directive counseling style over a reflective, affective, and nondirective one, especially if the counselor is Asian American. Also, Asian Americans perceive culturally sensitive counselors as being more credible and culturally competent than less-sensitive counselors. Kim and colleagues (2005) concluded that

- clients with similar worldviews perceived stronger client-counselor alliance and counselor empathy than those in dissimilar conditions;
- client adherence to Asian cultural values was positively related to client-counselor working alliance;
- client adherence to European American values was positively associated with client-counselor working alliance and session depth; and
- clients with high expectations for counseling success and strong adherence to European American cultural values had increased perceptions of counselor empathy.

Some Asian cultures associate mental health problems with stigma and will deny mental illnesses or try to hide the presence of any disorder among family members. Counselors should understand the reasons why Asian Americans tend to underuse mental health services and should attempt to convince individuals that use of such services may be in their best interest. Although Asian Americans have emotional disturbances just like the rest of the population, their problems usually pertain to academics and careers. For Asian Americans, talking about problems of this nature is not as threatening as disclosing personal and emotional concerns. Counselors who understand the values and motivations of Asian Americans will use techniques that encourage these clients to be open about personal and family matters.

Once the counselor understands the Asian American culture and its tendency to underuse counseling services, what counseling strategies are appropriate? Specifically, what should the counselor do or not do? Counselors working with Chinese American clients should

- Exhibit considerable involvement by modulating voice tone and by asking questions at appropriate times concerning the clients' problems or feelings. Caution should be used, however, because clients may think they are being interrogated. It is important that questions be posed with tact and that they not be excessive.
- Demonstrate self-confidence, through voice control and sureness of presentation. Moderate pitch and volume suggest self-confidence; paraphrasing a client's comments often seems unnatural and suggests hesitancy or weakness on the part of the counselor.
- Present himself or herself as an expert, by projecting a solid, secure, and trustworthy image. Because too much movement may be perceived as nervousness or insecurity, the counselor should remain relatively still and not gesticulate excessively.
- Offer self-disclosing remarks to convey a sense of trustworthiness as well as a sense of caring.

Much of the literature on multicultural counseling suggests that traditional, nondirective counseling approaches may be in conflict with the values and life experiences of Asian American clients. Because of Asian American cultural orientations, nondirective approaches may even be counterproductive. Asian American clients also assign more credibility to counselors who employ a directive approach than to counselors who use a nondirective approach. It follows, then, that Chinese American clients expect to assume a passive role and expect the counselor to be more assertive. Exum and Lau (1988) suggest that counselors should use a directive counseling approach with Cantonese-speaking Chinese students, as in the following dialogue:

COUNSELOR: What would you like to share with me today?
CLIENT: (*sigh*) Well, I'm not sure if it's going to help to talk about it.
COUNSELOR: Since you're here, there must be something bothering you. I do believe that talking about it would help.
CLIENT: Maybe the more I talk about it, the worse I'll feel. Maybe I shouldn't talk as much and let time take care of itself.
COUNSELOR: Seems like you're feeling a great pain inside you. Can you tell me more about it? We'll see if we can find some ways to solve the problem.
CLIENT: Yeah, maybe I should do that; since you've seen so many difficult problems before, you might be able to give me some suggestions.
COUNSELOR: Well, since this is something bothering you so much, you might feel even worse if you keep it all inside. I think it's very courageous of you to come to seek counseling.

(p. 92)

Axelson (1999) used the following exchange between a career-training counselor and a Vietnamese American client to illustrate how the communication barrier poses a problem:

COUNSELOR: How are things going now that you and your family have settled into your new apartment?
CLIENT: Yes. (*Smiles and glances down*)
COUNSELOR: Sometimes moving into a strange neighborhood and new home brings problems.
CLIENT: Many things for Kien fix up, work hard . . . need stove, one [burner] only work, but cos' so much. Friends [sponsors] help get good price, and get TV.
COUNSELOR: A TV?
CLIENT: Yes, they get good education, get better life. Can no teach English Kim and Van, school help . . . (*pauses*) . . . worry abou' Lan. Change so much, go far from

Vietnamese way. She have American boyfriend. Want be like American. (*Smiles and becomes very quiet, looks at floor, seems embarrassed by what she has said*)

COUNSELOR: You seem sad.

CLIENT: (*Grins and laughs*) My father tell me take care of Lan. My brothers all made dead by soldiers . . . only me left to watch Lan . . . (*pauses*) . . . our boat ge' Thai pirates. Lan and me make face black, hide in boat . . . no see us! (*Laughs and begins to sob quietly*) Oh, excuse me.

COUNSELOR: That's okay. I know it's difficult to talk about those past days and the things that hurt you. And it's a big responsibility to look out for Lan. It's all right to show how you feel to me. I won't take it as being impolite to me and I'll try to help you in any way I can—including listening and caring for how you feel about something that hurts or makes you sad or angry. It's my job to help you with things that are difficult for you.

CLIENT: Oh (*faint smile*) so many problems wan' to please father; help Kien . . . .

COUNSELOR: Yes, that's all important to you. How is Kien's job training going for him?

CLIENT: Kien in Vietnam, big navy officer . . . now nothing feel bad, but training good . . . become computer-electronic man. That good for him, get job, more money, feel better.

COUNSELOR: Yes, that's a good thing for your family.

CLIENT: Thank you.

COUNSELOR: Let's talk now about the work that you want. You said before that you like to sew. That's a skill that you have that you can use right now to add to the family income.

CLIENT: Yes, make clothes for children, mend Kien's shirt.

COUNSELOR: I know. You showed me some of the good work you have done. There's a job that I'd like to see you try at the store. It will be to alter clothes that customers buy.

CLIENT: Oh . . . speak little English, so har' for me, makes others feel bad . . . no way go store . . . can't find . . . where bus?[2]

In working with some Asian American clients, counselors should realize that modesty, discretion, and self-deprecation should not be considered a negative opinion of oneself. Discussing family matters calls for considerable discretion; likewise, obtaining sexual information may prove difficult, due to modesty and feelings of privacy. When intervening with Vietnamese Americans, counselors may wish to remember several suggestions: Build trust and concern for the client and the client's family, understand Vietnamese concepts of rigidly defined gender roles, and address communication barriers (both verbal and nonverbal) and their effects.

Writing specifically of South Asian people (e.g., Indian Americans and Pakistani Americans), Ibrahim, Ohnishi, and Sandhu (1997) offer several implications for counseling. For example, for effective intervention with South Asian clients, the mental health counselor should do the following:

- Respect the client's cultural identity and worldview (South Asian clients want to feel that interventions are self-generated and that a mutually respectful relationship exists between them and the mental health professional).
- Understand the client's level of acculturation and identity status before planning counseling intervention.
- Clarify the client's spiritual identity before deciding on counseling goals and outcomes.
- Provide multidimensional interventions by using cognitive, behavioral, ecological, spiritual, and other relevant domains for these clients.
- Recognize the importance of the client's life stage and age.
- Be aware that the client may not understand the counselor's nonverbal attitudes.
- Recognize the role of humility in the client's cultural identity.
- Respect the client's integrity and individualism.

- Allow clients to educate the counselor regarding their identification level with their sub-cultures, religions, values and worldviews, and the mainstream society.
- Use a relational style that allows both counselor and client to explore value systems in conjunction with each other.

Individual and Group Therapy

Counselors need to realize several myths that often surround group therapy: (a) Discussion of racial or cultural differences will offend group members, (b) groups can be truly homogeneous, (c) group member differences do not affect the process and outcome of groups, and (d) group work theory is appropriate for all clients.

According to Yu and Gregg (1993), Asian Americans underuse counseling sessions in general and group counseling services in particular. These clients might be reluctant to share information and might be offended by, or react negatively to, other group members sharing their values and feelings and attempting to assimilate the minority member. They perceive requests for self-disclosure, comments on the group process, and requests for feedback as rude demands and attempts at domination. In fact, Asian American clients may be confused by traditional group counseling approaches that emphasize verbalization, confrontation, conflict resolution, individualism, and autonomy. The counselor who is unaware of or elects to ignore this confusion faces the possibility of a negative outcome, including premature termination of counseling.

Yu and Gregg (1993) also suggest for counselors the following:

- *Counselor self-exploration:* Counselors should recognize their biases and prejudices toward members of specific cultural groups.
- *Client orientation:* During the pregroup interview, counselors should take special care to explain to the Asian client the expectations of group membership, the purpose of the group, and the roles of the members and the leader.
- *Group composition:* Counselors should group Asian clients appropriately, such as in groups that are culturally homogeneous, that allow members to better understand others' communication styles and that allow Asian clients of a particular nationality or geographic locale to be together.
- *Rapport building:* Throughout the orientation session, counselors should develop rapport between all members and the leader.
- *Group orientation:* Counselors should begin professional intervention so that group members will be aware of cultural differences and eventually unite all group members.
- *Group facilitation:* Counselors need to recognize the special circumstances and values that Asian clients bring to the group.

Even when Asian Americans do engage in group therapy and psychotherapy, the likelihood of negative outcomes between the demands of the group therapy process and the cultural values of Asian Americans is high. This conflict includes verbal unassertiveness, reluctance to display strong emotion, and unwillingness to disclose problems to strangers. Conflicts may be exacerbated if the counselor is unaware of Asian American culture-based behavior. Such pressure may cause the client to withdraw from group counseling.

Professional interventions with the positive outcomes are those in which the groups are homogeneous in terms of gender, background, profession, and social class. Goal-oriented sessions are probably more productive than free-floating, process-oriented sessions.

Johnson, Torres, Coleman, and Smith (1995) offered the following suggestions for group leaders:

- Conduct an assessment of potential members' values, interests, abilities, personalities, and decision-making patterns.
- Challenge members to examine the basis for their assumptions, attitudes, and beliefs.

- Help members generate alternatives to their existing beliefs.
- Assist members in testing their assumptions by requesting that members verify information outside the group and bring that information back to share with the group.
- Help members receive feedback from other group members about the logic of their attitudes and beliefs.

Han and Vasquez (2000) reported that South Asian refugees showed greater approval of group therapy that had a bicultural focus, provided practical information, met concrete needs, and demonstrated flexibility.

Family Therapy

Family therapy usually focuses on one individual, protects the dignity of the individual, and preserves the honor of the family. Counselors often find the technique valuable with Asian Americans because it allows them to define and clarify family relationships by speaking directly to the therapist rather than, for example, by a husband or wife speaking with one another.

Discussions of feelings or psychological motives for a behavior are uncommon in most Asian American homes. Disturbed behavior is often attributed to lack of will, supernatural causes, or physical illness. Hard work, effort, and developing character are thought to be the most effective means to address the majority of problems.

Kung (2001) maintains that mental health professionals will continue to face challenges when working with Chinese American families, especially due to the cultural belief that families should be involved in clients' lives. Kung suggests educating the population, especially recent immigrants, about the prevention and treatment of mental disorders; ensuring the availability of accessible services provided by mental health professionals who speak their language or dialect; enhancing the sensitivity of clinicians to the needs and expectations of these clients in order to reduce the drop-out rate; and developing culturally sensitive information models to fit specific cultural needs.

Counselors may want to talk with the husband before the wife to show respect for Asian custom and tradition. They may also choose to place the husband and wife in different groups to prevent the wife's speaking from being considered an affront to the husband.

In family therapy, it is important for the therapist to take an active role in the therapeutic process, rather than the traditional passive and facilitory process favored by many Western-trained therapists. In particular, Vietnamese clients likely see the therapist in the role of teacher, adviser, and someone who is able to give guidance in time of trouble (Leung & Boehnlein, 1996). Case Study 10.3 looks at a counselor's efforts with Han, a Japanese American adult.

Kim, Lee, and Morningstar (2007) offered specific suggestions for Korean American parents' expectations and hopes for their adolescent child's future. While they focused attention on members of the Individualized Education Program (IEP), their strategies for promoting cultural competence included knowing one's own worldview, learning about families served, and respecting cultural differences.

Case Study 10.3: Counseling Han, an Asian American Adult

Han, age 36, was referred by his company's physician to a mental health counseling organization. The physician wrote to the counselor that Han was experiencing stress. "If it hadn't been for the physical examination, I wouldn't have to see that counselor, who will probably ask a lot of nosey questions," Han thought.

The 44-year-old African American male counselor immediately picked up several cues that did not bode well for the counseling relationship: (a) Han was reluctant to come to counseling, (b) he was quiet and withdrawn, and (c) he did not want to discuss personal problems with a stranger. The counselor explained the counseling process, its confidentiality, and its intent. Then the counselor cautiously encouraged Han to talk (taking care not to give the impression of interrogating or snooping). Although it was difficult at first for Han to reveal his problems, the counselor was able to reach several conclusions after several sessions: (a) Han was working two jobs and felt uncomfortable about being away from his family; (b) he was worried about his wife working a part-time job (Not only would this reflect badly on him, but who would take care of Grandfather?); and (c) he was also worried about his preadolescent daughter Mina (So far she had been an excellent daughter and student and had brought much honor to the family, but would she be swayed by her friends?).

The counselor decided to meet with Han individually for several more sessions. A group session would allow Han to see that other men shared similar problems, but Han would be unwilling to share personal information in such a setting. Also, Han's traditional ways of thinking would undermine the effectiveness of family sessions.

Counseling and Development 10.3: The Adult Years

Fudo, a 49-year-old Japanese American adult, lives with his wife and two teenage children. Fudo has worked diligently in the United States to "do the right thing," to treat his family well and to assimilate into the American culture. Now he faces problems: job concerns (the company he works for is cutting back on employees), his mortgage payments, and falling real estate values. His depression has resulted in his seeing a counselor.

The counselor considers Fudo's developmental stage: middle aged, turning 50; psychologically, he is questioning his future; and physically, he knows he might not be as strong as he once was. Since the counselor does not think Fudo will communicate in a group session, he decides on individual therapy.

Counseling Strategies:

1. Ask Fudo about "how he feels" physically at age 49—self-disclosure might be key here, depending on the counselor's age.
2. Inquire about the reasons Fudo thinks he suffers depression.
3. Ask (being extremely cautious) about his family—support, regrets, and challenges. Again, the counselor should be cautious because Fudo might think the familial challenges result from causes he created.

ASIAN AMERICAN ELDERLY

Potential Problems Warranting Counseling Intervention

Problems elderly Asian Americans may experience include

-   adverse effects of stereotypes;
-   being both Asian and elderly—the possibility of double or multiple jeopardy;
-   discrimination and injustices because of age and culture;

- cultural differences and characteristics;
- poor English-language skills;
- distrust of social and governmental agencies;
- lack of education, low income, unemployment, and poor housing;
- reluctance to disclose personal information;
- problems with developmental tasks and psychosocial crises;
- lack of systematically kept records with specific ethnic classifications;
- major health-related concerns, such as certain types of cancers, high blood pressure, and tuberculosis; and
- communication or cultural barriers that prevent them from receiving health benefits and services to which they are entitled.

Ageism has been well documented (Ryan, Jin, Anas, & Luh, 2004) in both the United States and Europe. Older adults are marginalized, given low status, and either ignored in the mass media or portrayed in roles reinforcing negative stereotypes. Unfavorable stereotypes characterize older people as forgetful, sick, unattractive, and useless. While strong traditional Confucian norms in the East have resulted in more positive images of old age, there are still images of declining vitality and negativity in the East (Ryan et al., 2004). In addition to prejudice, social injustices, and discrimination, Sue and Sue (2013) suggested the elderly face a multitude of problems: Physical and emotional health, mental deterioration, elder abuse and neglect, substance abuse, depression, and suicide. Also, counselors often consider "sexuality in older people" to be a controversial topic. Just because a woman or man is older, that does not negate their sexuality.

Focusing on the vulnerability of the older population, especially older women, Ofstedal, Reidy, and Knodel (2004) reported concern over Asians' economic support and well-being. Multiple economic factors were examined: sources of income, receipt of financial and material support, income levels, ownership of assets, and subjective well-being. Ofstedal and colleagues (2004) concluded:

- Whereas men tend to report higher levels of income than women, there is generally little gender difference in housing characteristics, in asset ownership, or in subjective reports of economic well-being.
- Unmarried women are economically advantaged as compared to unmarried men in some respects, in part because they are more likely to be embedded in multigenerational households and receive both direct and indirect forms of support from family members.

Counseling Considerations

Problems that elderly Asian American clients bring to counseling sessions often center on differing intergenerational expectations and the elderly's expectation that their kin and younger generations will care for them. When younger generations of the family attain middle-class or higher status, the elderly often experience conflict and strain: Will they continue to be cared for? Will they receive the same respect? It is imperative to understand the history of Asian family loyalty and allegiances and the concerns of the elderly as younger generations rapidly acculturate. Counselors may have to encourage elderly Asian Americans to utilize available services. They may need to provide a convincing argument that counseling professionals can be trusted, and they may need to overcome the reluctance of Asian Americans to reveal the family's personal problems and secrets.

Counselors are often at a loss to explain why Chinese Americans do not participate more actively in counseling sessions. Barriers might include external barriers such as language, culturally generated distrust of service providers, and lack of bilingual and bicultural staff or internal barriers such as individual negative attitudes, cultural beliefs toward services, and pre-ferred helping courses (Liu, 2003) as well as a simple "never thought of it" (Li, 2004, p. 253).

Counselors might interpret the undemonstrative demeanor of Asian Americans as the result of repressed emotional conflicts. Professionals should remember that behaving openly with strangers can be quite difficult for Asian Americans. To overcome this potential impediment to counseling progress, counselors should (a) show respect for elderly clients and their culture; (b) establish a trusting atmosphere and develop rapport; (c) understand that elderly Asian Americans may be hesitant to disclose personal problems; and (d) explain the counseling process to clients, including the concept of confidentiality. These strategies may encourage partici-pation and self-disclosure in Asian American clients (Liu, 2003).

Individual and Group Therapy

The decision whether to use individual or group therapy should take into consideration the individual Asian American client. Individual therapy might be the most effective technique, unless the client chooses to disclose personal information in a group session. Reluctance to reveal personal information may stem from the Asian American client's fear of shaming or degrading the family. Even in an individual counseling situation, Asian American men will be hesitant to reveal information that could reflect negatively on the family or on their perfor-mance in meeting responsibilities to the family.

Writing specifically about elderly Japanese American clients, Itai and McRae (1994) maintain that such individuals may be reluctant to engage in any counseling therapy. For example, the Japanese traditionally have not looked for causes of illnesses in the psychological realm. For this culture, "paying to talk" (Itai & McRae, 1994, p. 374) is a difficult concept to understand, and asking someone for help with one's emotional problems has been regarded with shame. Thus emotional difficulties have been converted to physical problems because physical symptoms have been more acceptable. The Japanese also have considerable respect for self-sufficiency and independence. All these factors can contribute to Asian Americans, and especially Japanese Americans, being reluctant to participate in counseling therapy.

Case Study 10.4 looks at a counselor's efforts with Grandfather Sukuzi, an Asian American elder.

Case Study 10.4: Counseling Grandfather Sukuzi, an Asian American Elder

Grandfather Sukuzi, age 85, finally decided to visit a physician because of his worsen-ing dizziness, fading hearing, and forgetfulness. His son Han took a half day off from work and drove Grandfather to the physician's office. The physician diagnosed the diz-ziness as the result of an ear infection, for which he prescribed an antibiotic. The mild hearing loss was nothing to worry about; it was common for people of Grandfather's age. The physician did refer Grandfather to a counselor, however, to discuss his fears that the family was becoming too Americanized.

The 43-year-old Hispanic counselor experienced considerable difficulty with Grandfa-ther Sukuzi. The client could hardly speak English, he was reluctant to talk about himself or his family, and he seemed to be waiting for the counselor to do something so that he could finally leave. Obviously, Grandfather was extremely uncomfortable. Little could be done, the counselor thought, during this first session except try to build trust. He would show Grandfather that he was interested in him and assure him that the counseling rela-tionship would remain confidential.

The counselor decided to schedule at least two or three more sessions with Grandfather to try to build rapport and to give Grandfather a chance to disclose significant personal information. Group therapy was out of the question, because Grandfather would not want to share his concerns in a group setting. Family therapy was impossible, too, because Grandfather would do all the talking for the family. In this case, the counselor thought, progress will be slow. Not only was there a communication barrier, but his client would not always have transportation, and the chance of Grandfather revealing personal information was remote.

Counseling and Development 10.4: The Elderly Years

Chang-Sun is an 85-year-old Korean American man living in a large city in the Northeast. He lives with his daughter, her European American husband, and their two children. His family shows him respect, both as a family member and as an elderly person. Still, he feels old and tired; he is suspicious of most European professions and wants to keep his problems within the family; and he views his life as about over.

The Hispanic American counselor looks at Chang-Sun's records and contemplates how best to address the challenges: developmental tasks, coming to grips with his age and impending death, and medical problems associated with some older men (e.g., blood pressure problems and prostate problems). The counselor sees individual therapy as the only viable means of helping Chang-Sun.

Counseling Strategies:

1. Ask about his family in such a manner that he sees the positive assets in his life.
2. Discuss his culture and death, helping him to come to grips with the elderly developmental period.
3. Seek information about his health problems to determine whether additional medical health can be provided.

Family Therapy

In the past 25 years, mental health professionals have given increased attention to the role of families in mental health treatment and rehabilitation processes. Part of this trend is due to an effort to move discharged patients into the community, thereby necessitating caregiving and assistance from their families.

It is important for counselors and elderly Asian American clients to understand their expectations of each other. For example, elderly Asian Americans may be reluctant to admit their need for counseling; also, they might have unrealistic or erroneous expectations of the counselor and counseling. The Asian American elder might view the counselor as a knowledgeable expert who will guide family behavior in the proper course. During the first session, the effective counselor will take an active role rather than waiting for the elderly client or a family member to initiate interaction. The counselor who adopts a passive approach to professional intervention might be considered lacking in knowledge or skill.

Counselors readily recognize the importance of communication in any counseling effort. Thus they may find communication with Asian Americans to be difficult and frustrating. The elderly Asian American's reluctance to speak could result from limited English proficiency or an unwillingness to disclose personal information. To address these barriers, counselors may choose to develop a trusting and comfortable alliance with the family, especially the elderly, to whom other family members will look for direction.

Another factor that must be considered during family therapy is the powerful Asian belief that the father is head of the household and the spokesperson for the family. This belief may cause other family members to remain silent. Certainly family members would be unlikely to disagree with the father under any circumstances. It is important for counselors to recognize this family dynamic in evaluating their clients' behavior.

SUMMARY

Several challenges await counselors of Asian American children, adolescents, adults, and elders: (a) understanding the Asian American culture and its tradition of individuals and families caring for those with mental health problems; (b) understanding Asian American cultural mannerisms (e.g., silence) and cherished cultural beliefs (e.g., filial duty); (c) understanding the adverse effects of racism, injustice, and discrimination among Asian Americans; and (d) understanding Asian Americans' unique problems, such as communication barriers, portrayal as a model minority, and the stress caused by younger generations acculturating toward individualistic perspectives and the older generations' expectation of being cared for.

NOTES

1   From *Counseling American Minorities* (pp. 100–101) by Donald R. Atkinson, George Morten, and Derald Wing Sue, 1983. Dubuque, IA: Brown. Reprinted with permission of McGraw-Hill Companies.
2   From *Counseling and Development in a Multicultural Society* (pp. 447–448) by J.A. Axelson, 1999. Monterey, CA: Used with permission.

SUGGESTED READINGS

Bowman, N.A., & Park, J. J. (2014). Interracial contact on college campuses: Comparing and contrasting predictors of cross-racial interaction and interracial friendship. *Journal of Higher Education*, 85(5), 660–690. Research on diversity in higher education has evolved to consider the nature of interracial contact and campus climate as well as the factors that may foster meaningful interactions.

Cokley, K., McClain, S., Enciso, A., & Martinez, M. (2013). An examination of the impact of minority status stress and impostor feelings on the mental health of diverse ethnic minority college students. *Journal of Multicultural Counseling & Development*, 41(2), 82–95. This study examined differences in minority status stress, impostor feelings (predictors of mental health status), and mental health of ethnic minority college students.

DuPree, W., Jared, B., Kruti A., Patel, P.S., & DuPree, D.G. (2013). Developing culturally competent marriage and family therapists: Guidelines for working with Asian Indian American couples. *American Journal of Family Therapy*, 41(4), 311–329. The growing Asian Indian population has prompted the need for counselors to consider multicultural factors when communicating with their clients—this study provides guidelines and recommendations for working with Asian Indian Americans.

Kim, B.S.K., & Park, Y.S. J. (2015). Communication styles, cultural values, and counseling effectiveness with Asian Americans. *Journal of Counseling and Development*, 93(3), 269–279. These authors examined counseling intervention designed for Asian Americans, using a congruent and incongruent communication styles.

Raque-Bogdan, T.L., Klingaman, E.A., Martin, H.M., & Lucas, M.S. (2013). Career-related parent support and career barriers: An investigation of contextual variables. *Career Development Quarterly*, 61(4), 339–353. The authors used social cognitive career theory as the basis for examining the person and contextual variables of gender, ethnicity, educational and career barriers, and career-related parent support for incoming first-year African American, Asian, Latino, and White college students.

Scott, K. D., & Scott, A. A. (2014). Adolescent inhalant use and executive cognitive functioning. *Health and Development*, *40*(1), 20–28. These authors examined adolescent inhalant and cognitive processing as well as cognitive speed—results revealed ploy-substance users had a direct influence on cognitive functioning.

11 Understanding European American Clients

QUESTIONS TO BE EXPLORED

- How many European Americans live in the United States today, and what are their origins?
- What societal, cultural, communication, familial, and socioeconomic characteristics most accurately describe contemporary European Americans? How have they benefited from White privilege and from living in a predominantly Caucasian society?
- What stereotypes should counselors of European Americans be aware of and work to avoid?
- What lifespan differences exist among European American children, adolescents, adults, and elders, and what are the counseling implications?
- What are the unique challenges faced by European American children, adolescents, adults, and elders, and how can counselors most effectively address these challenges?
- What challenges confront counselors intervening with European Americans?
- What suggested readings can be offered to counselors preparing to work with or currently working with European Americans along the lifespan continuum?

OVERVIEW

As with all other cultures in America, European Americans enrich and contribute to the nation's diversity with their varied traditions, customs, languages, and dialects. Counselors, regardless of their cultural background, need to understand this plethora of differences and how they affect counseling intervention. As with African, Asian, and Hispanic Americans, whose origins are quite diverse, European Americans originated from many locations, including England, France, Germany, Greece, Hungary, Ireland, Italy, Poland, and Portugal. This chapter focuses on European Americans in the four lifespan stages and their cultural, socioeconomic, family, and language diversity. To avoid overgeneralizing, specific cultural groups are discussed whenever possible.

EUROPEAN AMERICANS: DEMOGRAPHICS

Although they are generically referred to as Whites, there are 53 categories of European Americans living in the United States. The term *White ethnic* refers to all non-Hispanic White families of European American heritage. The term is quite ambiguous, because it originally referred to southern and eastern European immigrants rather than to Americans of British or German ancestry. More recently, it has been used to refer to a broader range of people. Projections of the White population numbered 378,857,056 in 2015.

European ancestry groups with the largest population numbers include German, Irish, English, Italian, French, Polish, Dutch, Scotch-Irish, Scottish, and Swedish. Europeans with smaller numbers include Czechs, Danes, Greeks, Hungarians, Norwegians, Russians, Slovaks, and Welsh (U.S. Census Bureau, 2015g, http://quickfacts.census.gov/qfd/states/00000. html).

At the time of the American Revolution, the American population was composed largely of English Protestants who had absorbed a substantial number of German and Scotch-Irish settlers and a smaller number of French, Dutch, Swedish, Polish, Swiss, Irish, and other immigrants. Over time, the White population crossed ethnic lines to create a conglomerate, but culturally homogeneous, society. People of different ethnic groups—English, Irish, German, Huguenot, Dutch, and Swedish—intermarried. The period from 1830 to 1930 was a time of mass immigration to the United States. In colonial days, most immigrants came from Great Britain and Ireland, with a few from Germany, France, the Netherlands, Belgium, and Luxembourg, later, they were followed by Norwegians and Swedes. Italians began arriving in 1890, and from 1900 until the start of World War I, about one-fourth of all immigrants to America were Italians. Many Germans arrived in the United States following World War II. Greek immigration began in the 1880s, when the Greek economy failed to show signs of improvement. Most Poles immigrated to the United States as a result of mass migration and World War II.

Significant numbers of Jews from the former Soviet Union migrated to Israel and to the United States. Although the majority of these Jewish immigrants chose Israel as their new home, 40,000 immigrated to the United States. However, this wave of Jewish immigrants was not the first to arrive in the United States; some emigrated from the Soviet Union following the Six Day War and the Leningrad Trial in the 1970s. The majority of the 90,000 Soviet Jews who chose the United States came from Russia, Byelorussia, and the Ukraine.

EUROPEAN AMERICAN CHILDREN

Social and Cultural Description

As with the many Asian and Hispanic cultures, the diversity of the many European American cultures makes accurate description difficult. A prerequisite to any discussion of such a diverse population is to recognize the tremendous societal, cultural and intracultural, socioeconomic, and individual diversity of these groups. Because children in all European cultures have not been studied, conclusions must be drawn from the most reliable available evidence. Acculturation also affects what children believe. Although first-generation children often hold on to native cultural beliefs, significant acculturation has occurred in subsequent generations.

Members of some European American cultures (e.g., Greeks) want their children to hold on to cherished traditional values and beliefs. Rapid acculturation often occurs as a result of U.S. schooling, which creates a strong pressure to adopt the predominant culture of the school.

Depending on their individual culture and degree of acculturation, it is likely that European American children feel a sense of bicultural allegiance. For example, European American children, especially first- or second-generation, may feel pulled between two cultures when they strive to accommodate majority-culture beliefs, values, and customs, as well as family expectations to maintain allegiance to old-world and time-honored traditions. Considerable stress and guilt can occur when other children of differing cultural backgrounds question a child's attire, foods, religious beliefs, or mannerisms.

One of the challenges facing European American children is actually due to another person's condition or lifestyle. Elden, Edwards, and Leonard (2004) examined the association between fathers' alcoholism and children's effortful control. Counselors of children (and, in fact, adults) should find several conclusions interesting: (1) Boys of alcoholic fathers exhibit lower overall levels of effortful control than boys of nonalcoholic fathers, (2) maternal warmth was a unique predictor of effortful control in boys, and (3) for girls, fathers' alcoholism was associated with lower paternal warmth, which was in turn a significant predictor of effortful control. Overall, the researchers found that sons of alcoholic fathers are at an increased risk of problems in self-regulation (or self-control) at young ages. Paternal warmth mediates the association between fathers' alcoholism and self-regulation for both boys and girls, although the nature of the mediation may vary with gender.

Communication

Some European American groups speak English sufficiently well that English has become the primary medium of communication and the language spoken at home. In all likelihood, many of these people encourage their children to speak English in order to assimilate into mainstream America. People who are less fluent in English may feel incapable of helping their children learn English and thus avoid situations requiring proficiency in English.

One significant problem usually associated with language-minority children is that they face two different sets of cultural perspectives and are forced to orient themselves to two different worlds, both socioculturally and psychologically. Such a communication dilemma often results in children thinking they have to choose between the cultural heritage of their parents and the culture of the school. The result is that some children try to develop both a school language and a home language, thereby taking on additional learning challenges. Others who adopt English as their primary language risk disappointing their elders, who may consider adherence to the native language to be an essential element of their cultural heritage.

Families

European American families differ, just as African American, Asian American, Hispanic American, and American Indian families differ. Differences may result from socioeconomic, cultural, intracultural, and other factors. Some European American families hold on to traditional beliefs, such as preference being shown to boys, expectations for girls to perform household duties, and expectations of both genders to show strong support and concern for the family. Likewise, the success or welfare of the family is more important than the welfare of the individual.

Children in some European American groups are taught traditional family values, such as maintenance of positive family relationships, nurturance of children, and obligations of the children toward the family. Depending on the cultural group, parents also instruct their children to respect and assist extended family members. Case Study 11.1 tells about 13-year-old Brea, who is growing up in a predominantly Irish American world.

Case Study 11.1: Brea, an Irish American Child

Brea is a 13-year-old Irish girl who attends an ethnically diverse middle school four blocks from her home. She lives with her mother, father, and brother in a large city in the Southeast. The grandfather lives in a small house behind the family house. Both the mother and the father work, and the family lives a modest middle-class life.

Although her grandfather has maintained his Irish accent, Brea has an accent only on a few words. Her parents wanted to be accepted (socially and economically) in the United States, so they tried to avoid any strong Irish accent. They did not feel comfortable with giving up the Irish accent but thought it was necessary for "survival" in the United States. Brea never realized the reasons why her parents gave up their accent, but she has noticed their vocal changes.

Brea and her grandfather are close—he tells her about his Irish past, how his grandfather described the potato famines, and the ill treatment many Irish received when they came to America. She thought the "No Irish Need Apply" signs must have been centuries ago. In her developmental period and with her worldview, she did not understand the relatively short distance in the past.

On St. Patrick's Day, attendance at schools in the large city was not taken so students could attend the large St. Patrick's Day parade. Her family members recognized their Irish history (e.g., the family's migratory status, religious beliefs, literature, folklore, and a sense of distinctiveness). Still, they did not demand that Brea adopt or adhere to all customs. Without using (and perhaps not even knowing) the term "melting pot," they felt success in America called for balancing "an appreciation for their cultural heritage" with middle-class expectations in a diverse society.

Reflection Questions:

1. Brea's parents are walking a fine line of balancing their Irish cultural expectations with middle-class expectations. How will this affect Brea's ethnic identity formation and self-esteem?
2. Will Brea feel "conflicted" between her Irish roots (as explained by her grandfather) and her parents' expectations to adhere to middle-class U.S. standards? What worldview will Brea adopt?
3. Remember, Brea is 13 and attends a middle school—what concerns might she bring to the school counselor?

Unique Challenges Confronting European American Children

Several challenges unique to European American children deserve the attention of counselors in multicultural settings (it is important to note, however, that counselors should avoid stereotypical conclusions about European American children, a problem faced by a specific child might be an entirely individual situation and have little or no cultural basis):

- Children, by the nature of their developmental period, may feel ignored or powerless to gain needed attention. Their mental health needs may go unrecognized until problems grow acute.
- Children may feel the need to become more bicultural to maintain social relationships. This need for biculturalism could result in guilt feelings as the children choose between majority-culture values and their parents' long-held cultural beliefs and traditions.
- Children learning English as a second language may have both social and academic problems in school and may feel overwhelmed and unable to deal with the demands of English-language schools.
- Children of some European American cultures may have difficulty with the usually greater freedom allowed for girls in the United States. They may be accustomed to seeing boys in more authoritarian roles and may be shocked at the gender equality in American schools.
- Children may experience academic problems because they lack understanding of the U.S. school system and of the roles of educators and counselors.
- Children may experience a decline in self-esteem because of being in a majority-culture school and because of their different cultural values, beliefs, and traditions.

Although these examples are representative of European American children's problems, other problems undoubtedly exist and will require the individual attention of the counselor to pinpoint them and to devise culturally appropriate intervention strategies.

EUROPEAN AMERICAN ADOLESCENTS

Social and Cultural Description

Estimated numbers of European American adolescents ages 15–19 are projected to be 6,143,000 in 2015. Although adolescents vary among cultures, they experience certain common developmental characteristics or tasks regardless of culture: making friendships, dealing with peer pressures, moving away from the immediate family to an expanding social world (this undoubtedly varies among cultures), and beginning the transition toward economic independence. These tasks may be more difficult for European American adolescents because they might be dealing with different cultural expectations for making and keeping friends, speaking a language other than English, and experiencing difficulty equating family and peer expectations.

Adolescents living in cultural enclaves (e.g., predominantly Italian, German, Hungarian, or Polish) might experience only minor difficulties. However, when forced to extend life activities outside the boundaries of the cultural enclave, adolescents might encounter problems with different world customs and expectations. For example, school activities may require adolescents to leave their cultural enclaves to participate in athletic events, academic competitions, school plays, and other activities requiring intraschool participation.

Although self-esteem (as well as a positive cultural identity) is important during all lifespan developmental periods, counselors need to recognize the importance of self-esteem during the adolescent years. Adolescents form self-esteem that might last a lifetime and that influences their attitudes toward self, significant others, and life's challenges. Yet self-esteem often declines, especially for females, during this developmental period. Living, socializing, and functioning in a majority-culture society may intensify problems with self-esteem. Adolescents' self-esteem can be damaged when they believe that significant others consider "cultural differences" wrong or in need of change, or when adolescents believe it is necessary to change long-held traditions and beliefs in order to gain acceptance in the majority-culture society. Although it is common for self-esteem to decline for both adolescent girls and boys, girls usually experience a more active decline. Cultural and societal expectations as well as students' self-esteem can either promote or limit career aspirations and decisions as to whether to seek employment in the United States or to return to one's native land.

Hazler and Mellin (2004) maintain that one of every four girls is likely to experience moderate to severe symptoms of depression during adolescence. Hazler and Mellin (2004) maintain that rates of female to male depression rapidly soar during adolescence to a 2:1 ratio despite fairly equal rates throughout childhood. The fact is that female adolescents face emotional, academic, and social problems more often and more extensively than male adolescents do at this critical age. With this clear problem, there has been a lack of research on the unique difficulties female adolescents face and the identification of techniques designed to meet their specific needs. Existing research suggests that throughout childhood and preadolescence, depression rates between the genders tend to be fairly equal, but at about the age of 14, female adolescents begin experiencing depressive disorders at twice the rate of male adolescents.

Communication

Communication plays a significant role in the socialization of adolescents, who increasingly widen their social worlds away from their immediate families to a widening circle of friends and peers. Although some European American cultures continue to have a high regard for and close allegiance to family members (immediate and extended), the demands of adolescence require increased socialization and communication. The ability to socialize with peers and others, as well as the ability to speak English to teachers and counselors, illustrates the importance of being able to communicate effectively.

It is difficult to draw conclusions. Just as with adolescents from Asian and Hispanic cultures, some European American parents speak English very well, whereas others do not. Counselors intervening with European American clients will find that an adolescent's ability to speak the language will greatly influence academic success and the ability to build satisfactory interpersonal relationships. Therefore, although an adolescent's native language should be a respected aspect of the cultural background, an increasing proficiency in English should be encouraged, especially if the adolescent's reasons for seeking or being referred for counseling stem from an inability to communicate in English.

European American adolescents who are confident in their English-language proficiency will be more likely to engage in the verbal interaction necessary for desirable socialization and social development. Conversely, adolescents who do not feel confident with their English-speaking abilities will probably avoid situations requiring English-language proficiency. Counselors working with students who have communication difficulties will readily recognize potential problems, such as academic, socialization, and employment difficulties. Taking care to avoid casting the adolescent's native language in a negative light, the counselor needs to help the adolescent client understand that at least a minimal degree of communication competency will be needed to cope in an English-speaking society.

Families

It is a commonly held belief that a primary source of problems for immigrant families is the differing values held by parents and adolescents. Even though adolescents and their families might disagree on issues and expectations, conflicts may not be as acute as some might expect. Such a lack of serious problems may result from adolescents being taught from an early age the importance of adhering to family expectations.

However, adolescent children of immigrants, unlike their parents, are often attracted to majority-culture values and behavior models in school and society. At the same time, their socialization is heavily influenced by their parents' ancestral cultures at home and in the community. Perceptive counselors recognize potential adolescent-family conflicts and that these problems will warrant serious consideration and attention.

Wang and Sheikh-Khalil (2014) maintained enhancing the academic achievement and mental health of students is an important educational goal. To achieve this, it is essential to identify the contextual factors that influence academic and emotional functioning and the pathways through which they operate. Parental involvement in education is an important way to facilitate positive youth development. In this study, Wang and Sheikh-Khalil (2014) conceptualized parental involvement in education as a multidimensional construct (i.e., school involvement, home involvement, and academic socialization) and examined the associations of each of these elements with adolescent achievement and depression in high school. This study contributes to the literature by identifying which types of parental involvement are most effective for high school students. They found that parental involvement in tenth grade improved not only academic but also emotional functioning among adolescents in eleventh grade.

Depending on the European culture, adolescents may perceive a conflict between the expectations and traditions of the majority culture and those of their own culture. Such a conflict may or may not cause a problem, depending on the adolescent's commitment to adhere to traditional family beliefs. For example, some aspects of adolescents' cultural backgrounds include (a) the father as the authority figure; (b) the mother as the nurturer; (c) more freedom and a more responsible place in the family for sons than for daughters; (d) the expectation that daughters stay closer to home, during both adolescence and adulthood, than sons; and (e) the high regard for the welfare of elderly family members. Acculturation often has dramatic effects on these expectations, second- or third-generation European American families might differ significantly from first-generation families. Case Study 11.2 tells about Art, an adolescent Irish American.

Case Study 11.2: Art, an Irish American Adolescent

Art is Brea's 16-year-old brother. Art and Brea are a lot alike, but Art tends to ignore his Irish cultural background. Art is somewhat quiet, but he is involved on the football team and a few other school activities. Different from Brea, he does not speed a lot of time with Grandfather, does not attend the annual St. Patrick's Day parade, and tries to suppress any Irish accent. Brea wonders sometimes whether Art is ashamed of his Irish heritage and whether he just wants to blend in with the majority culture. He obviously loves and respects his grandfather, but chooses not to spend as much time with him as Brea does.

Like many adolescents, he wants to feel accepted by his friends and peers. He does not engage in illegal activities, but he does engage in some behaviors at school that his parents would not approve of. His parents and grandfather want him to succeed in school so he will not be forced to work as they have had to. They view the United States as a place to succeed socially and economically, so they want Art to work diligently toward his education. Art sometimes feels a "pull" between his friends' expectations and his parents'.

Art thinks about his future—spending time with girls, participating on the football team, thinking about his increasing freedom, and concentrating on his appearance. While he thinks these are typical adolescent behaviors, he also wonders whether he "measures up to his friends" in physical appearance and social skills. His self-esteem appears to be positive in some areas and negative in other ways.

Art's teachers know him, but he is not particularly close to any of them. As far as he knows, the counselor does not even know his name. He has never had any one-on-one experiences with his counselor. She comes to his class about once a month to discuss appropriate topics, but the class is so large that she does not actually know him. Except for his participation on the football team, Art tends to "fade into the woodwork." One has to wonder whether Art is questioning his adolescent identity, denying his Irish heritage, or some combination of both.

Reflection Questions:

1. Suppose Art's teacher recommended him for counseling because he tends to "fade into the woodwork" and fails to participate in school activities except for the football team. Should a counselor ask about his Irish heritage, his adolescent years, or his family?
2. What approaches would you take to determine whether Art has a problem or just wants to be left alone?
3. Consider Art's relationship with his family—he acknowledges his sister, but does not want to spend time with his grandfather. Do you feel Art is ignoring his Irish culture or just that he is growing into independence?

Unique Challenges Confronting European American Adolescents

Tasks usually associated with adolescence, coupled with approaching adulthood in a majority-culture society, can have profound and intertwining effects on adolescents. Unique challenges that European American adolescents may face include

- problems resulting from trying to hold on to their family's traditional cultural beliefs while adopting the majority-culture beliefs necessary for social and economic survival;
- problems resulting from peer pressure to engage in popular social and school activities that their parents find objectionable;

- communication problems stemming from poor English-language proficiency or forced bilinguality;
- problems moving toward marriage or economic independence;
- inability to accept the responsibility that their parents expect children to accept (e.g., responsibility for helping the parents and elderly family members); and
- pregnancies in unwed adolescent mothers.

Adolescence is a period in which rapid and various changes occur. In this period, these changes affect adolescents' lives and relations with others. Teenagers are in dispute with their parents on topics such as clothing, choice of friends, getting permission, studying. Conflicts may vary according to parental attitudes. Examining the direct role of accepting and authoritarian parental attitude in life satisfaction and depression, the authors Acun-Kapikiran, Körükcüo, and Kapikiran (2014) maintained parental attitude was determined to be the positive predictor of life satisfaction. According to their findings, early adolescents whose decisions are respected, who are supported, and given autonomy by their parents have increased life satisfaction. Moreover, negative correlation between accepting parental attitude and depression was found. In other words, depression increases in adolescents when accepting parental behavior decreases. The findings showed that there is a negative correlation between authoritarian parental attitude and life satisfaction. Children whose parents pressure them into doing things, hinder their freedom, and make decisions for them have low life satisfaction and high depression levels (Acun-Kapikiran et al., 2014).

Adolescent violence is a problem facing many counselors—violent adolescents and the harm they inflict on others are not limited to any specific culture. Unfortunately, adolescents in all cultures are perpetrators and victims.

EUROPEAN AMERICAN ADULTS

Social and Cultural Description

Social and cultural characteristics vary among cultures, generational status, social class, gender, and age. Just as it is difficult to describe a typical Hispanic American because of the culture's many different origins and cultural backgrounds, it is equally difficult to describe a typical European American adult. Likewise, a southern European man will probably differ significantly from an eastern European woman. Therefore, the most valid cultural descriptions come from considering individual cultures (even then, one should use considerable caution because of intracultural and individual differences). Educational attainment varies with cultural groups. Some of this variation results from lack of opportunity or motivation to seek education. Nevertheless, one's education is indicative of one's potential to achieve economically and socially in U.S. society. Table 11.1 shows U.S. Census Bureau (2013) data on educational attainment of European Americans age 25 and older.

Table 11.1 Educational Attainments: European Americans (25 Years and Older), 2013 (in thousands)

Educational Attainment	Population
Some college or associate degree	13,332
Bachelor's degree or more	16,558
Master's degree	6,267
Doctorate degree	1,756

Source: U.S. Census Bureau. (2013). Educational attainment in the United States: 2013. Washington, DC: Author. Retrieved 2 December 2015 from http://www.census.gov/hhes/socdemo/education/data/cps/2013/tables.html.

Greek Americans may have difficulty cooperating with others, especially in business deals; they prefer a competitive atmosphere and usually are not willing to put aside their individual interests for the sake of the group. Greek Americans also (a) have clearly defined status and roles in work situations, (b) have patriarchal control and deeply binding extended kinship networks, (c) have a strong need to defend family honor, and (d) generally love *philotimo* or honor.

Italian Americans (a) have a strong allegiance to the family, (b) have a strong affection for living where they grew up, (c) believe that young people should be taught by their elders, (d) have an allegiance to a church (once the Catholic Church, but Italians are now seeking other religions), (e) are suspicious of strangers, and (f) expect filial obedience. Some of these tendencies (e.g., suspicion of strangers) decrease with education and advancing occupational position.

The religions of European Americans deserve careful consideration because a culture's religion often depends on its geographic origin and its members' degree of acculturation. Italian Americans remain heavily Catholic, in fact, in one survey, 90% of respondents had been raised as Catholics, and 80% considered themselves Catholic at the time of the interview. Because the Catholic Church has stood for tradition, family, and community, Italians continue to offer their support (Alba, 1985). Polish Americans also have a powerful allegiance to the Catholic Church. By 1923, about 140 Greek churches existed in the United States. Each community of Greeks formed a board of directors whose function was to build a Greek Orthodox Church. Attempts were made to consolidate the Greek Church with other Eastern churches into an American Orthodoxy, but this did not materialize; the church seemed inextricably intertwined with its role as transmitter of the Greek heritage.

Marriage

Most Jews newly arrived from the former Soviet Union view their primary motivation in leaving their homeland as fear of anti-Semitism rather than as the desire for religious freedom. Most Soviet Jews view themselves as culturally Jewish and are interested in the Jewish culture as expressed through history and literature. Broman (2005) maintains that high quality in marriage is important in its own right for a sense of well-being as well as being important for marital stability, yet the limited focus on the role of race on marital quality poses a barrier to our understanding of marriage.

Broman (2005) maintain that Blacks have lower levels of marital stability than do Whites. For example, collaborative styles have been found to be more important for Blacks than Whites. Blacks are more likely to participate in household chores, and conflictual styles do not seem to be as detrimental to Black marriages as they are for Whites. In his study of Black and White marriages, Broman concluded that Black spouses characterize their spouse's behavior as more negative than do Whites, thus resulting in lower levels of marital quality. Specifically, Broman concludes that Blacks feel less loved and feel their spouses waste money, hit or push (or exhibit more physical violence in general), and have affairs. He also raises the possibility of whether Blacks are just more honest and open to discussing their marriages and their spouses' behaviors than Whites; however, his research did not address this question. Although critical differences evidently exist between Black and White marriages, factors such as socioeconomic status and length of the marriage should be considered. Still, counselors intervening with both Black couples and White couples should understand that differences exist and deserve consideration during counseling.

Socioeconomics

Describing the socioeconomic status of the many European cultures is nearly impossible, because many variations exist among cultures. For example, there are both wealthy and poor

Italians. Many criteria affect family and individual socioeconomic status: Is the husband or father present? Does the wife work outside the home? How many children are in the family? Is the cost of living in the neighborhood high or low? How well do family members manage their money?

Communication

Most European Americans feel confident in their ability to speak English and probably place priority on speaking English in the home. In contrast with some Hispanic American cultures that continue to place high priority on speaking Spanish, some European American cultures, such as people from Germany, the United Kingdom, and Italy, value speaking English. European Americans with English-language proficiency probably cope better economically and socially than their counterparts with less proficient English-speaking skills. People who speak English fluently and who perceive English as their major medium of communication most likely live in mainstream society. Others feel forced to live and work in a native-language enclave with people speaking the same language or speaking English with a similar proficiency. Counselors may have clients with communication-related problems—problems resulting from the frustration of having limited English-speaking skills in a majority-English society. Potential problems include inability to interact socially, difficulty finding suitable employment, or difficulty conducting business transactions in a non-native language. It will be important for counselors to understand the dilemmas caused by communication problems. For example, English- or Spanish-speaking counselors need to realize the frustrations of their Greek- or Russian-speaking clients and vice versa.

As for people in all cultures, considerable variation exists in the English-language proficiency of European Americans. Cultural groups such as Italian Americans and German Americans may experience difficulty with the language. Due to tremendous individual differences, it is impossible to determine which cultures will or will not have language problems. Several factors influence an individual's ability to learn and speak English: (a) Parents and families may live in language enclaves where native people speak native languages, (b) parents may speak the native language in the home, (c) parents may try to learn to speak the language, and (d) schools may provide English as a second language (ESL) programs and show appreciation for native languages.

Families

Any discussion of family characteristics should be approached with considerable caution. Generally, adult European Americans grew up in families that taught men and women to be independent, strong, and self-sufficient. Exploration of the world was encouraged, self-control was highly valued, suffering was borne in silence, and conflicts were concealed, especially in public (McGoldrick, Giordano, & Garcia-Preto, 2005). Like all cultures, however, European Americans form a heterogeneous group. Family patterns differ according to the time of immigration, region of origin, economic class, and religious background. Many factors influence how a family lives, the roles of the husband and wife, how parents view their children, and the emphasis placed on extended family members. Although counselors need information about European families, providing a full description of these families risks stereotyping. To avoid stereotyping, an attempt is made here to use only the most objective information and the most widely accepted resources.

In the German American family, the husband/father is the head of the household and leader of the family. Traditionally, the father, although he is sometimes sentimental, has a stern side. He is usually self-controlled, reserved, unduly strict, and stubborn. The German American father is often somewhat distant and less emotionally available to the children than their mother is. The German American woman is regarded as hardworking, dutiful, and subservient. She adopts her husband's family and friends and gains his social status. Her contributions center primarily on household and family duties. In contemporary times, the wife's main tasks continue to be focused on the house and family; in fact, the appearance of her husband and children can be a source of pride (Winawer & Wetzel, 2005).

The Greek American family continues to maintain strict gender roles, with little overlap between these roles. Men provide economic necessities, while women cater to men's desires and wish to be considered good wives. Men are authoritarian fathers and husbands, who often seem emotionally distant, and they are parsimonious with praise and generous with criticism. They often tease their children (some say to toughen them), and the children learn that teasing is part of being loved. Typically, Greek men revere their mothers, value the family honor, and believe that a woman's place is in the home. Women expect to comply with tradition and view motherhood as fulfillment. Male children are still preferred over females, even in the urban areas of the United States, having a son is a wife's main source of prestige. Parents believe that some emotions, such as uncertainty, anxiety, and fear, are weaknesses and should be hidden from their children. Gay and lesbian couples or families are sometimes reluctant to seek counseling services because alternative lifestyles are usually stigmatized in the Greek community. In fact, gay and lesbian Greeks usually tend to seek services outside the culture (Killian & Agathangelou, 2005).

Irish American women have traditionally dominated family life, have primarily found their social life through the church, and have enjoyed more independence compared with women from other cultures. Unlike other cultures, the immigration rate of Irish women ranked higher than that of Irish men. Irish families often paid as much attention to the education of their daughters as to that of their sons. Traditionally, fathers have been shadowy or absent figures, and husbands dealt with wives primarily by avoidance. Discipline is still maintained by ridicule, belittling, and shaming. Children are generally raised to be polite, respectable, obedient, and well behaved. Parents rarely praise their children or make them the center of attention (McGoldrick, 2005).

A major characteristic of Polish American families is respect for family members. Although some acculturation has undoubtedly occurred, the father/husband is the leader of the household, whose wishes are to be respected and obeyed. Children are raised in a tradition of discipline and are expected to give their fathers unquestioning obedience. Second-generation children have become acculturated, but similar discipline expectations and practices continue to be practiced among many Polish families.

Italian Americans learn that the family is all-important and that sharing meals is a symbol of nurturing and family connectedness and a wonderful source of enjoyment. In Italian American homes, gender roles are distinct and defined, men always dominate and women nurture (Giordano, McGoldrick, & Klages, 2005).

The Dutch American family shares a strong sense of responsibility. The nuclear family maintains close ties with the family at large. Clear boundaries are maintained in the family consistent with the values of individualism and respect for privacy and personal freedom. Role definition and responsibilities are clear. Families expect the man to provide overall direction to the family, provide economic support, and set an example of uprightness in the community. The woman provides a rich home life for her husband, nurtures the children, and attends to and promotes social and cultural input for the family (De Master & Giordano, 2005).

Emotionality, romanticism, pessimism, isolation, and duality of identification between Eastern and Western values are common Hungarian characteristics. An old proverb says that Hungarians are the happiest when they are in tears. They want music at weddings and at funerals; the Hungarian culture has always appealed more to emotions than to logic. Although Hungarians are generally an emotional people, certain negative emotions are not always expressed openly. For example, conflicts, anger, and pain are not openly expressed, perhaps to preserve family loyalty (Laszloffy, 2005).

Case Study 11.3 describes Amon, an Irish American adult.

Case Study 11.3: Amon, an Irish American Adult

Amon is Brea and Art's father. A hardworking man, he does not have much formal education, but he is good with mathematics and works as a carpenter. He has steady work, even during bad economic times. He is skilled in carpentry and works conscientiously to please his customers. Amon learned a lot about carpentry from his father, Bartley, who was also a carpenter when he worked.

Amon and his family live in a modest house in a middle-class neighborhood. While bad economic times have not drastically affected him, he does wonder how he would support his wife, Brea, Art, and Bartley should something go wrong. Bartley draws a little social security, but it would not be sufficient to keep the household going for long.

Amon is turning 50 next month, and he does feel "challenged" by his situation. Brea is in middle school, Art is in high school, his wife takes care of the house and family, and his father, Bartley, is too old to work extensively. He knows he has established a reputation for being a skilled carpenter and a conscientious, trustworthy man, but what will happen if he is no longer able to work? He might be too old to learn another trade. Even if he could, it is unlikely he would have enough time to build another reputation such as the one he now holds. His reputation in the community as a good provider for his family and a skilled tradesman means a lot to Amon.

Amon is proud to be Irish, but wonders whether Brea and Art (especially Art) will "melt" into the middle-class, majority society. He knows his father holds on to cherished Irish beliefs more than he does, and he thinks Art might be less interested. Brea seems interested to a certain extent. He realizes his children must "remain" Irish, adopt middle-class majority values, or do some "balancing act" in between. If asked, he would probably not offer a suggestion for an option. Just as he has done, he realizes Brea and Art must find the right "combination" to get along in the majority culture.

Reflection Questions:

1. What challenges or tasks might Amon bring to a counseling session?
2. How might his concerns be developmentally different from those of Brea and Art?
3. How would you address the possibility of his father holding on to the Irish culture, Brea being at least interested, and Art leaning more toward the majority culture?

Unique Challenges Confronting European American Adults

European American adults face several challenges, including the four we will now describe. First, European groups, like all cultural groups, have been negatively stereotyped by other groups. Italians and Jews, in particular, have stood out because of the frightful stereotypes associated with them. Italians have been characterized as being "swarthy," bearing signs of physical degradation (e.g., low foreheads), having criminal tendencies, and being prone to passion and violence. Jews have been stereotyped as being "stingy," "shrewd," and "intellectual" (Atkinson, 2004). Poles have been subject to offensive and distasteful jokes and other ethnic slurs. The list continues, but this brief discussion serves to show the dangers of stereotyping.

Second, European Americans, especially first- and second-generation families, may have financial problems because of discrimination, unemployment or underemployment, poor English-language skills, and lack of education. Almost 16% of European Americans lived below the poverty level in 2014.

Third, European Americans, probably primarily first- and second-generation, may experience communication problems. People who choose to live (or are forced to live) in cultural enclaves where the majority of residents speak the same language will likely enhance their social interaction and economic survival; however, problems may arise when these people must venture out among predominantly English-speaking populations. Regardless of a counselor's native language, it may be advisable to encourage clients to improve their English-language skills as an excellent beginning point to solving communication problems caused by poor English proficiency.

Fourth, European Americans may experience confusion and frustration as family members increasingly move toward majority-culture family expectations. Traditional expectations of the father/husband being the breadwinner and decision maker and the mother/wife being the homemaker and nurturer may be affected by acculturation. For example, both men and women may experience psychological difficulties as women perceive the advantages associated with more egalitarian and liberated views. Older generations and men (and also women) who are accustomed to strict family traditions and customs sometimes experience problems with others' tendencies to forsake cherished cultural traditions in favor of a more acculturated lifestyle.

EUROPEAN AMERICAN ELDERLY

Social and Cultural Description

European American elderly, like clients in all cultures and developmental stages, must be considered as individuals because, for example, Romanian Americans differ from German Americans just as Mexican Americans differ from Cuban Americans. A number of factors—intracultural, socioeconomic, gender, and geographic—can affect the way European Americans think and live. Counselors in multicultural settings need to learn about individual European American elderly in an attempt to provide the most effective counseling intervention.

Some acculturation has undoubtedly occurred among second- and third-generation (and, to some extent, first-generation) European Americans. The degree of acculturation depends on educational level, initiative and ability to be a part of majority-culture activities, and residence in a cultural enclave.

European American elderly may be more likely than younger generations to retain valued cultural traditions and customs, such as the authority role of husbands or fathers. Elderly family members might look on with disbelief as younger women take assertive roles, men allow (and, in some cases, encourage) women to take crucial family roles, both men and women allow their children and adolescents greater freedom and independence, and younger family members place greater emphasis on proficiency in English. Another potentially threatening cultural belief is the nontraditional egalitarian value placed on both daughters and sons rather than giving sons privileged positions within the family.

Although cultures and generations vary, some European American cultures hold the elderly in high regard and believe that they deserve respect and care. Elderly European Americans may feel neglected because of changing familial status and changing cultural attitudes toward the elderly. They may think their children are more accepting of majority-culture values that favor personal concerns over traditional cultural beliefs toward the elderly.

Communication

As with the elderly in other cultures, considerable diversity exists among European Americans in their ability to speak English. The elderly in some European American cultures speak fluent

English, whereas others continue to hold on to their native languages, live in language enclaves to avoid the realities of a predominantly English-speaking society, or experience difficulty because they are confronted with a new language. Regrettably, there is no reliable information on the numbers of elderly who speak native languages to avoid English. First-generation elderly European Americans who may not have mastered English and elderly persons who have elected, or been forced, to live in language enclaves may experience the most serious communication problems.

Communication problems among some elderly persons indicate the need for intervention. Counselors working with elderly European Americans must understand the common problems of the elderly, as well as the special problems resulting from limited English-speaking skills. Language-minority persons, whether French, German, Romanian, Hungarian, or any other language, may have several problems—speaking with physicians and nurses, especially on the telephone; dealing with social services agencies designed to assist the elderly; getting groceries and medicines delivered to the home (even in places where businesses still provide such services); and other problems. Aging can potentially aggravate the existing problems seen in European Americans in other stages along the lifespan continuum. Perceptive counselors will recognize a possible double jeopardy—being elderly and a language minority—and plan counseling intervention that addresses the problems that are associated with aging.

Families

In most cases, the elderly hold on to cherished familial beliefs about family roles and treatment of the elderly. For example, elderly Italian Americans continue to see the family's role as providing family members with the training necessary to cope in a difficult world. The father has traditionally been the family's undisputed head—often authoritarian in his rule—who sets behavioral guidelines. He still usually takes seriously his responsibilities to provide for his family. As the ultimate authority on living, he offers advice on major issues. The mother provides the emotional sustenance. She yields authority to the father and traditionally assumes responsibility for the emotional aspects of the family. Her life centers on domestic duties, and she is expected to receive her primary pleasure from nurturing and serving her family. For children, there is marked differentiation between sons and daughters. Sons are given much more latitude. Daughters are expected to assume primary caregiving responsibility for an aging or sick parent. The extended family plays a central role in all aspects of Italian family life, including decision making (Giordano et al., 2005). Because many elderly European Americans continue to cling to such beliefs, seeing younger generations apparently adopt majority-culture values can pose difficult dilemmas for some elderly family members.

Case Study 11.4 looks at Bartley, an older Irish American.

Case Study 11.4: Bartley, an Irish American Elder

Bartley, Amon's father, realizes he is growing older. He is 72, in good mental and physical health, does not smoke, and drinks only occasionally. He lives a modest life, and he realizes his life is better now than during his younger days. Bartley does not remember actually seeing "No Irish Need Apply" signs—that was before his time. Still, he remembers what he considers discrimination due to his culture. Also, he has heard numerous comments (some subtle and some not so subtle) about his drinking habits. He was never a heavy drinker, but the stereotype followed him wherever he went.

Bartley sees changes that concern him. His son, Amon, is too busy to learn much about the Irish culture. He understands Amon's situation—he must make a living for this family. He appreciates Brea's visits and talking about what things used to be like. He is concerned that his grandson, Art, might be forsaking his Irish culture for majority-culture acceptance. Although he wants his family to remain "Irish," he understands the necessity of social acceptance and economic survival in the United States. He understands the dilemma, but he still has difficulty with the changes around him.

Bartley's age bothers him at times. He is experiencing the developmental decline related to growing older, not being able to contribute much financially, the necessity for his family to switch from traditional values to majority-culture values. Although his health is good now, he does question what health changes are coming and whether he will be able to take care of himself. He knows his family will help, just as he helped his family when he was younger, but still, he wants to be as independent as he can. Bartley remembers his wife, who died about ten years ago. He misses her, but he still appreciates having Amon and his family nearby.

Reflection Questions:

1. What familial concerns might Bartley bring to the counseling session?
2. Would you suggest individual or family counseling? (Remember, Bartley has individual problems related to his developmental period as well as family issues related to his grandchildren moving more toward majority-culture beliefs.)
3. Make a list of his developmental concerns (as related to the elderly developmental period) and suggest appropriate counseling strategies.

Unique Challenges Confronting Elderly European Americans

European American elders may face several challenges that are unique to their culture and developmental period. Challenges will, of course, depend on the client's generational status, overall health, economic status, and living arrangements (living alone or with relatives).

First, communication difficulties can pose a problem, especially for elderly European Americans who either have been unable to learn English or have lived in cultural enclaves where learning English seemed unnecessary. Coping with life's everyday demands and expectations can be hampered by lack of English-speaking ability. Communication problems between counselor and client can also limit the effectiveness of counseling intervention. In fact, some acute communication difficulties may result in the need for an interpreter.

Second, changing cultural expectations (e.g., perspectives toward family traditions, children living near and caring for the elderly, husband/father primarily assuming authoritarian roles) can result in frustration and confusion that counselors may need to address. Older European Americans may not have lived as long in the majority culture as their children and grandchildren and thus may be more reluctant to forsake cherished cultural customs and beliefs. The older generation's observations of younger generations acculturating toward majority-culture ways may create conflicts that require counseling intervention.

Third, elderly European Americans may experience financial problems. Difficulties arising from individuals being unable to work and possibly unable to benefit from some social services and monetary programs can necessitate a need for counseling. The Bureau of Labor Statistics reports that the elderly population is expected to increase by 16% by 2020. As the elderly populations have increased, so have their social and economic circumstances. Based on many socioeconomic measures, the many elderly people are as well off as, or perhaps better off than, the nonelderly (Finfgeld-Connett, 2005). This is not to imply that many elderly people do not continue to live in poverty. Actually, 9% live in poverty. Despite improved economic well-being of most elders generally, poverty remains prevalent among minorities, women, and rural residents. Clear links exist between poverty, lower educational attainment, residence in rural or nonmetropolitan areas, female gender, and living alone. People who did better financially during their working lives do better after they retire; that is, the advantages experienced during younger years will accumulate to enhance relative well-being during older ages.

Fourth, European American elderly, like their counterparts in other cultures, often experience declining health and increased medical expenses. The elderly often worry about health concerns ranging from impaired physical mobility to terminal diseases, living alone while ill, and paying for needed medical care. Thus the elderly may need counseling to help them cope with these problems.

Fifth, although not limited to one cultural group, alcohol abuse is considered to be one of the fastest growing health problems among aging adults in the United States. It is estimated that 2% of the 10% of community-based older adults have alcohol problems and 21% of aging hospitalized patients have a diagnosis of alcoholism.

Finfgeld-Connett (2005) discusses alcohol problems in aging adults and self-directed treatment models and their importance in helping aging adults resolve early and late onset of alcohol abuse problems. In general, early-onset alcohol abusers began abusing alcohol in their thirties and forties and may be well known to health-care and social service providers. Late-onset alcohol abusers develop problems in their fifties and sixties. These drinkers are often perceived as reactive drinkers because their problems stem from retirement or death of a spouse. Although distinct differences exist between the two types, they also share similarities. Both groups are likely to drink at home, alone, and in response to negative emotional states. Most consume alcohol on a daily basis, are widowed or divorced, are retired, and have minimal social support.

Suggestions for counselors and social workers (as well as others in the helping profession) include the following:

1. Employ age-specific, group treatment using a supportive versus a confrontational approach.
2. Concentrate on managing negative emotional states such as depression and loneliness.
3. Foster the expansion of social support networks.
4. Present treatment content at a pace that is appropriate for older clients.
5. Avoid using terms such as *group leader*, *therapist*, or *treatment program* (to preserve self-esteem)—instead, use terms such as *teacher*, *student*, and *class.*

SUMMARY

Counselors of European American children, adolescents, adults, and elders face several challenges that call for resolution prior to effective counseling intervention: differences and similarities in cultural backgrounds, language and communication problems, and selection of proper intervention strategies.

A counselor from a non-European American background may have difficulty understanding European American worldviews. Similarly, a young or middle-aged counselor may have difficulty understanding the developmental perspectives of children, adolescents, and elders. Counselors, regardless of their cultural backgrounds, need an understanding of European American perspectives on development, family, and languages, to name a few aspects. Likewise, because of the tremendous diversity within the greater European American culture, counselors may experience difficulty understanding some European American subcultures, for example, a French American counselor might experience difficulty intervening with a Romanian American client. Perceptive counselors in multicultural settings readily recognize that clients of European American cultural backgrounds differ, as do those of other diverse cultures, such as Asian or Hispanic. Professional responsibility demands, first, an understanding of the client in the individual European American culture and, second, the selection of culturally appropriate counseling strategies.

SUGGESTED READINGS

Andretta, J. R., Worrell, F. C., & Mello, Z. R. (2014). Predicting educational outcomes and psychological well-being in adolescents using time attitude profiles. *Psychology in the Schools, 51*(5), 434–451. The authors identified five time-attitude profiles based on positive and negative attitudes toward the past, present, and future. Adolescents with profiles characterized by higher positive attitudes than negative attitudes (i.e., Positive, Optimistic, and Balanced) reported more favorable educational and psychological outcomes than did adolescents with profiles marked by higher negative attitudes (i.e., Negative and Pessimistic).

Li, J., Fung, H., Bakeman, R., Rae, K., & Wei, W. (2014). How European American and Taiwanese mothers talk to their children about learning. *Child Development, 85*(3), 1206–1221. Little cross-cultural research exists on parental socialization of children's learning beliefs. This study compared European American and Taiwanese mothers and children regarding good and poor learning.

Lindsey, C. (2014). Trait anxiety in college students: The role of the approval seeking schema and separation individuation. *College Student Journal, 48*(3), 407–418. Mental disorders appear to be on the rise among college students and are having a significant effect on their attrition, with anxiety identified as one of the most common presenting issues. This study examined the relationship between separation individuation and the early maladaptive schema of approval seeking with trait anxiety to determine their predictive utility.

Wang, M. T., & Kenny, S. (2014). Longitudinal links between fathers' and mothers' harsh verbal discipline and adolescents' conduct problems and depressive symptoms. *Child Development, 85*(3), 908–923. This study examined relations between maternal and paternal harsh verbal discipline and adolescents' conduct problems and depressive symptoms.

Williams, L. R. (2014). Experiences with violence in Mexican American and European American high school dating relationships. *Children & Schools, 36*(2), 115–124. Violence in adolescent dating relationships has become increasingly normative in the United States, with the severity of the consequences increasing into adulthood. Minority youths are at an increased risk for experiencing moderate to severe forms of physical dating violence, yet they are less likely to seek professional services.

12 Counseling European American Clients

QUESTIONS TO BE EXPLORED

- What unique challenges can counselors expect when intervening with European American children, adolescents, adults, and elders?
- How can counselors, especially those from other cultural backgrounds, effectively plan counseling intervention for such a diverse group as European American clients? How can counselors avoid cultural stereotypes?
- How can counselors accommodate cultural differences in selecting individual, group, and family therapy?
- What concerns and problems related to development might child, adolescent, adult, and elderly clients present to counselors?
- How can counselors of differing cultural backgrounds and lifespan stages intervene with European Americans of other lifespan stages?
- How can counselors most effectively plan and implement counseling intervention for gay, lesbian, and bisexual European American clients?
- What sources provide information for professionals intervening with European American children, adolescents, adults, and elders?

OVERVIEW

European Americans and their diverse traditions, customs, languages, dialects, and communication styles will challenge counselors to plan counseling interventions that reflect both cultural backgrounds and lifespan stages. European Americans originate from diverse locations, including France, Germany, Greece, Hungary, Ireland, Italy, Poland, and Portugal. Perceptive counselors realize the need to consider European Americans' cultural differences, languages, family issues, and developmental concerns. This chapter examines European Americans in the four lifespan stages and how counselors can plan effective professional intervention. Also, gender differences and gay and lesbian perspectives have the potential to affect the outcome of counselor interventions and are examined whenever possible. Finally, this chapter includes a discussion of individual, group, and family therapies that may be appropriate for European American clients.

EUROPEAN AMERICAN CHILDREN

Potential Problems Warranting Counseling Intervention

Problems that European American children may experience include the following:

- Parents and families discourage children from seeking counseling at school; for example, children in some European cultures learn early that they alone understand their problems, the causes, and the possible solutions.

215

- Conflicts are caused by being raised in a culture that teaches children that the father is the primary decision maker and authority figure, even as the children attend more egalitarian-oriented schools.
- Old-world values taught at home may conflict with values of other cultures in the neighborhood and school (e.g., allegiance to the family, affection for the homeland, respect for elders, allegiance to a church).
- There may be peer pressure to engage in behaviors that would be considered "culturally inappropriate" by parents and families.
- Strangers are suspect.
- Communication difficulties may occur, especially when English is spoken at school and a different language is spoken in the home.
- Developmental and health concerns can include eating disorders and common childhood diseases and ailments.

Ingersoll, Bauer, and Burns (2004) report that estimates from 7.5 million to 14 million children in the United States experience significant mental health problems, many of which will be treated with psychotropic medications. The range is vague due to the ambiguity of psychiatric diagnoses and general problems with epidemiological research on diagnostic categories.

Niobe Way (2013) studied the importance for boys of being able to share their secrets with their close friends, the importance of close friendships for boys' mental health, and the loss of continued desire for close male friendships as boys transitioned from middle to late adolescence. Way concluded that if we take what boys tell us about their friendships seriously and if we take into account what we have learned over the past century regarding boys' and men's friendships, we should begin to reexamine our understanding of what it means to be male as well as what it means to be human. The previous emphasis on competition and aggression as defining attributes of humans is now widely challenged. We want to have close relationships, including friendships. Yet the conceptions of manhood and maturity in the United States and elsewhere rest on valuing emotional stoicism and autonomy exclusively. Those of us from the United States and in many other places typically tell our children, particularly as they reach late adolescence, that they must not only separate from their parents but also from their peers and move toward independence. We tell our children to think for themselves and not to worry about what others think or feel. In other words, we foster ways of being that are not natural and do not bring about psychological or physical health for boys or girls, men or women. American culture, in other words, appears to foster the crisis of connection that the boys in Way's study face in late adolescence and the crisis of connection that Americans are facing in the early twenty-first century (Way, 2013).

Counseling Considerations

Counseling European American children requires consideration of individual children and their respective cultures. Some children disclose freely, whereas others believe that talking about problems reflects negatively on their families as well as on their ability to deal with life tasks. Children, especially younger children, may not understand the purposes of counseling and may lack the cognitive structures and social skills to respond to counselors' efforts. Some children experience communication problems, while others may view counseling as the family's role. Counseling European American children will differ from counseling clients in other life-span stages and other cultural groups. A client's willingness to talk, to discuss family matters, and to trust counseling professionals varies significantly from culture to culture.

Ingersoll and colleagues (2004) maintained that the medical world in Western society, with its focus on alleviating symptoms using psychotropic medicines, continues to dominate in the treatment of emotional disorders. The convergence of increasing psychotropic medicines for children, the dominance of the medical model, and the economic power wielded by pharmaceutical companies are all issues that could be addressed through advocacy counseling. The primary issue is how counselors can best advocate for clients and their families regarding children and psychotropic medications. Even though treatment might involve some form of medication, advocacy counseling can help families explore treatment options, evaluate relevant literature, and become empowered to stand up against pharmaceutical companies.

Counselors intervening with children face several challenges. Children's limited concept of time may make it difficult for them to receive maximum benefit from the standard once-a-week session. Thus the counselor may wish to schedule shorter, twice-weekly (or more) sessions so that children can experience carryover between the sessions. Counseling effectiveness may also be hampered by communication difficulties resulting from differences in both communication and nonverbal behavior styles. Children are still in the process of developing a sense of self-esteem and a cultural identity. Thus both counselor and child may benefit greatly from activities that enable the child to explore the culture and immediate environment in a concrete fashion.

Counselors who work with children benefit from the realization that children, because of their developmental period, often feel that they are powerless and without a voice. In some situations, the counselor working with family issues might be perceived as a helpful force; in other ways, the counselor might be seen as further complicating the problem. For example, children may question whether to place allegiance with the counselor or with the family. Also, counselors will have to make individual decisions as to whether to select individual, group, or family counseling. One child might benefit from listening to other children talk about psychological discomfort resulting from family and peer allegiances, but for another child, hearing other children discuss problems might only solidify or intensify family concerns.

Individual and Group Therapy

Children can be confused in their thinking and may need the counselor to help them structure their ideas and feelings. In fact, many elementary-grade children simply do not understand counseling terms and the actual meaning of words. In such situations, the counselor's intuitive style and questioning skills become especially important. Other problems associated with thinking, language, and understanding counseling terminology might be even more acute with children from the vast number of European American subcultures. Several sessions may be necessary to establish rapport, an essential prerequisite when working with children, especially if the cultural backgrounds of the child and the counselor differ.

The model proposed by Ivey, D'Andrea, Ivey, and Simek-Morgan (2012) is as follows:

1. *Establishing rapport:* The counselor needs to tap personal and cultural strengths to establish rapport. Giving a smile, playing a game, or allowing children to do artwork or something else with their hands as they talk might open communication and build a sense of rapport or trust. Traditional therapy that begins with talk will probably be less effective with children.

2. *Gathering data that emphasize strengths:* Children often talk in short, random, and concrete segments. The counselor who works effectively with children often allows them to talk freely and in their own fashion while the counselor paraphrases, reflects feelings, and summarizes frequently. Children may need help organizing their thoughts as well as expressing themselves. With the less talkative child, it will be important to ask questions to encourage the child to talk, without leading the child in a specific direction. The counselor's questions and concepts should be concrete, rather than abstract. Data gathering also includes identifying children's strengths and assets. Children may sense if the counselor feels boredom, impatience, or frustration, which will negatively affect the intervention.

3. *Determining goals:* During this stage, the counselor can ask children what they want to happen. Such questioning gives children an opportunity to explore an ideal world and to

discover fantasies and desires. Some goals might be impossible (e.g., stopping their parents' divorce), but the counselor should try to get children to work toward concrete and realistic goals.

4. ***Generating alternative solutions and actions:*** Children respond well to brainstorming, which helps the counselor break down the problem into small, workable steps. Often, listing solution alternatives can be useful. This five-stage model is also useful in group work. For example, when three to five children who share similar problems are brought together in group therapy, they can often help one another or at least see that other children share similar problems. Simultaneously, imagining the future and the emotional consequences of alternatives can be especially helpful.

5. ***Generalizing:*** The counselor should try to give children a concrete goal for the next counseling session. Assignments work well when children know they need to work on specific things. Children should know that the counseling session had a specific purpose and that, afterward, they have a specific "assignment" to do prior to the next session.

Only the counselor can consider cultural and individual differences to determine the feasibility of individual and group therapy. As with other cultures and other lifespan stages, wide differences exist among European Americans. Also, both individual and group therapies have their advantages. Individual sessions allow children to tell and enact their own stories; such counseling interviews are conducted with an awareness of self in relation to others, family, and culture.

Family Therapy

Family therapy can be beneficial, especially if the counselor plans sessions to reflect the child's developmental stage and concerns. Several considerations are prerequisite to effective family therapy. The counselor needs to recognize the child's capabilities and potentialities and to plan the length of counseling sessions to reflect the child's shorter attention span and interest level.

During family counseling, the counselor needs to be sure that the child and family members understand the counseling process and the family's goals. The importance of communication should be paramount—the child should feel free to agree or disagree with family members, say what she or he really thinks, and bring disagreements out in the open. The child needs to feel that she or he will be treated with respect. The counselor should initiate professional intervention and open communication in several ways: (a) asking questions in a caring yet specific manner, (b) creating a counseling environment that allows children to look clearly and objectively at themselves and at their behaviors, and (c) asking questions the child will be able to handle.

Each child in the family should be spoken with individually. The counselor needs to convey sincerity in appreciating all the child's questions. The child should be asked about expectations of and reasons for seeking or referral to counseling. The counselor should repeat what the child says to make sure that the child's meaning is understood. In essence, the counselor (a) learns about communication within the family, (b) encourages the children to talk about themselves and their feelings in relation to the family, (c) helps the children to express frustration and anger, (d) encourages the children to question family members about troublesome issues, (e) uses confronting questions to provoke the children's thoughts, and (f) discusses the roles of family. After establishing rapport and a comfortable atmosphere, the counselor begins to bring out underlying feelings and confronts family members concerning the factors that are causing the family dysfunction.

It is important to look at family therapy from a cultural perspective. Counselors may experience more difficulty when intervening by using family therapy with some European American cultural groups. For example, some children are more reluctant to speak and voice concerns in family therapy because they have been taught to consider parents with great respect. In patriarchal families, children might think problems or disagreements reflect negatively on the father's ability to manage his household and family. Also, some families might perceive children in a subordinate role—children should be silent and avoid commenting on family matters. Next, on the one hand, communication problems might interfere with the effectiveness of a counseling session; some family members can communicate effectively, whereas others (perhaps older generations) may experience more difficulty with English. On the other hand, having family members present may be beneficial; those with greater facility in English can assist other members who have difficulty. Finally, some cultures might be reluctant to discuss family issues (particularly those of a personal nature) with a counselor of a different culture; for example, a Greek American family may feel uncomfortable with a female counselor or a non-Greek American counselor. Such a reluctance could, of course, occur in any counseling situation regardless of individual, group, or family.

Case Study 12.1 looks at Christina, a European American girl.

Case Study 12.1: Counseling Christina, a European American Girl

A teacher in Christina's school recommended her for counseling. Because Christina attended a school sponsored by the Greek Orthodox Church, no full-time school counselor was available. However, a guidance counselor who had been contracted to work among several Greek schools was available. Although Christina did not exhibit serious emotional problems, the teacher did think Christina had concerns of sufficient merit to warrant the counselor's attention. For example, Christina had demonstrated several stress-related ailments and had voiced a concern about venturing out from her Greek enclave and taking an active role in the broader majority-culture society.

After several meetings with Christina, the counselor found that Christina's basic problem centered on her lack of confidence in her ability to interact with potential friends in the majority-culture society. Her self-esteem allowed her to relate positively in her Greek American surroundings, yet she had considerable concerns, particularly when she visited other schools with her school teams.

Christina's counselor reached two conclusions: (a) Although Christina had the ability and motivation to deal interpersonally outside her immediate community, her perceived inadequacies deserved to be addressed, and (b) the counselor planned to initially provide individual counseling and then move to several small-group sessions. Specific plans included helping Christina realize that her ability to make friends and form interpersonal relationships within the Greek culture could transfer to the majority culture. Also, although Christina's self-esteem was not currently a problem, the counselor wanted to help Christina preserve her self-esteem and continue to respect the Greek culture. She had to convince Christina that it was not necessary to give up her Greek heritage to gain acceptance in a broader society.

Counseling and Development 12.1: The Childhood Years

Ansel, a 13-year-old French American boy (French mother and American father), was painfully quiet and shy. He had perhaps one or two friends, both males. He did not have any female friends, but it was difficult to determine whether that bothered him. His teacher decided that Ansel's problems might grow more severe once he attended a significantly larger secondary school. Ansel was referred for "excessive shyness," "lack of socialization," and possibly "lack of appropriate self-esteem for the developmental period."

The counselor considered Ansel and his developmental characteristics, for example socialization, lack of growing independence, and possible declining self-esteem. The counselor, a 38-year-old African American, decided on individual counseling due to Ansel's shyness.

Counseling Strategies:

1. Work to build a positive rapport with Ansel and to gain his trust and identify his strengths.
2. Ask Ansel who he valued as friends and get him to consider the traits he wanted in friends.
3. Determine whether having only a few friends "bothered" him or whether he was satisfied with the status quo.

The counselor decided to also talk with Ansel's teacher about cooperating learning or other small-group activities, so Ansel could have socialization opportunities.

EUROPEAN AMERICAN ADOLESCENTS

Potential Problems Warranting Counseling Intervention

Problems that European American adolescents may experience include

- conflicts between the quest for freedom and independence typically associated with adolescent conflict and the adolescent's traditional cultural expectations;
- challenges created by differing sexual orientations, whether gay, lesbian, transgendered, or questioning;
- frustration and stress caused by increased communication demands and limited English proficiency skills;
- a decreasing respect for oneself and one's cultural background as adolescents' social worlds broaden;
- increased stressors, such as arguments about getting chores done at home, pressure to get good grades or excel in school sports, and increased adolescent resistance to participating in family activities;
- acculturative stress resulting from being a first- or second-generation culture in a school and neighborhood where another culture is in the majority;
- peer pressure to experiment with illicit substances and to engage in other illegal activities;
- stereotypes often associated with certain European cultures; and
- typical concerns and stresses of the adolescent lifespan period, such as developing an identity, conflicts between independence and dependence, and being an adult in certain aspects and only an older child in others.

Although the general society, as a whole, in North America is becoming more tolerant of differing sexual orientations, substantial negative feelings toward the lesbian, gay, bisexual, and transgender/sexual (LGBT) still exist. Adolescents who are stigmatized as sexual minorities possess unique and complex needs that must be considered in the dynamics of counseling. This particular population includes LGBT adolescents who are questioning and struggling to accept their sexual identity. Lemoire and Chen (2005) describe the sexual identity development of LGBT adolescents and advocate Carl Rogers' person-centered approach for counseling intervention. They argue that this counseling approach seems to have potential to create the necessary conditions to counteract stigmatization. The person-centered approach has particular strengths, such as unconditional positive regard, congruence, and empathy; adoption of the client's perspective; the notion of self-concept; and growth process being client directed.

Counseling Considerations

Adolescents referred to the counselor by a teacher, parent, principal, or other authority figure often project onto the counselor the authority of those who "force" them to be in counseling. Whenever possible, adolescents should self-refer to avoid the feeling that another adult "made" them see a counselor. Even youths who have elected to seek counseling may find it difficult to share problems and concerns.

The counselor can take several directions to help the adolescent experiencing stress and frustration caused by inadequate communication skills. First, during intervention, the counselor may determine a need for a translator. There are drawbacks to having a translator present (e.g., the translator's choice of words and tone of voice), but if unaided, the client's problems with English (or the counselor's inability to speak the client's native language) may intensify the client's problems. Second, depending on the severity of the communication problem, the counselor may seek help from another professional (e.g., English as a second language (ESL) specialist) who can evaluate specific problems and provide an appropriate English-language program. Third, the counselor may decide to identify and arrange for intervention with a counselor whose native language is the same as the client's. This approach should be considered a short-term solution, however, because eventually the client will need to develop proficiency in English. Fourth, rather than take a comprehensive approach to intervention, the counselor may decide to focus intervention only on those areas related to the adolescent's development (e.g., communication for socialization or for dealing with a widening social world outside the immediate home and language enclave).

Maintaining prevention factors has become a major programmatic and investigative force in the child and adolescent mental health specialty. Counselors seeking to enhance the counselor-client relationship should work to be perceived as different from the adolescent's parents and teachers. Counselors should be perceived as being able to keep adolescents' disclosures confidential. They should be sensitive and sympathetic, yet honest, and work cooperatively with the client in providing feedback and openly seeking feedback from the client. Also, counselors should remember that developmental characteristics and cultural differences play a significant role in the counseling process and in the determination of counseling strategies.

Counselors intervening with adolescents will want to use as many resources as possible. These resources may include health departments, urban leagues, hospitals with comprehensive health programs, and other organizations geared toward helping adolescents. Counselors should maintain a current file of such organizations, especially service groups.

Individual and Group Therapy

Realistically speaking, counselors will have to limit their time with adolescents, due to their heavy workloads. Counselors might feel compelled to limit the number of sessions or plan for short-term interventions. Still, the counselor has a professional responsibility to provide effective counseling interventions. Such counseling interventions require the following:

1. *Professional relationships:* The counselor listens attentively, seeks an understanding of the student's worldview, and strives for mutual understanding. The counselor understands behavior from an adolescent developmental perspective and explores the problem in a positive and respectful climate.
2. *Student's strengths and resources:* The counselor assists the adolescent by believing in her or his capabilities, by fostering self-confidence, and by encouraging students to take responsibility to change behaviors or self-beliefs.
3. *Involvement:* The counselor demonstrates a sincere involvement or interest in the adolescent's welfare and overall well-being. During counseling intervention, the counselor uses role-playing and experiential activities to get the adolescent to understand behavior, its

causes, and different, more positive behaviors. The counselor carefully avoids being judgmental about behavior. The adolescent's worldviews (e.g., developmental, social class, and
cultural) about behaviors may differ significantly.

4. *Clear and specific goals:* The counselor and adolescent focus on current behaviors, future
plans, and expectations for change. The counselor also expresses hopes for change as well
as helps the adolescent to develop specific goals and plans for changing behaviors.

Counseling adolescents with differing cultural backgrounds can present several challenges.
The adolescent, especially in group sessions, might feel reluctant to share information due to
peer pressure or gang involvement. Others might be reluctant to share information about the
family—another cultural characteristic that deserves respect. When the counselor perceives this
cultural reluctance, she or he might choose individual counseling; however, developing professional relationships, recognizing and building on student's strengths and resources, maintaining involvement, and developing clear and specific goals remain valid.

Family Therapy

The extent to which families teach their adolescents to suspect professional counselors and
other cultures and to rely on family support networks, such as the extended family and the
church, will determine or significantly influence adolescents' tendencies toward, or rejection
of, family intervention.

Counseling interventions with culturally different families often require that counselors deal
with suspicion among groups, myths of sameness, treatment expectations, processes of acculturation, and communication barriers. Traditionally, family members have relied on informal
support networks such as the extended family and the church. Although more ethnic minorities are beginning to take advantage of family therapy, these issues and problems should be
addressed before trust can be developed.

Family therapy with adolescents who function in neither the child nor the adult developmental stage requires an understanding of developmental factors that have the potential to affect
counseling intervention. Adolescents may be reluctant to participate in any type of therapy if
their parents have taught them that mental health problems should be addressed only in the
family. Some beliefs (e.g., families should take care of their problems and problems can reflect
negatively on the father and his ability to manage the family) will contribute to adolescents'
reluctance to disclose information.

Counselors working with adolescents from European American cultures might choose to
meet with these clients several times prior to actual family counseling sessions to inform them
of expectations and techniques. Counselors may also need to encourage adolescents to disclose
information without making them feel guilty about disobeying their parents' wishes.

Case Study 12.2 looks at a counselor's efforts with Nikos, a European American adolescent.

Case Study 12.2: Counseling Nikos, a European American Adolescent

The school counselor, the same one who travels to various schools and works with
Nikos's sister Christina, was asked to meet with Nikos because of his low academic
achievement. Although Nikos was passing and did not exhibit significant behavior problems, he was not excelling, he felt guilty about his lack of academic achievement, he
wanted to make friends outside the Greek community, and he questioned how he would
equate family and peer expectations, especially when he started making friends of another

cultural background. What would his parents think if he dated non-Greek girls? With his academic achievement, how would he find a job or continue his education if he decided to do so? What would his parents think if they knew he was not working up to his potential? He confided these concerns to the counselor in an individual counseling session.

The counselor made several decisions regarding Nikos's problems. First, he had legitimate concerns, especially his feelings of guilt about letting his family down and concerns about equating family and peer expectations. As with Nikos's sister, the counselor decided on several individual counseling sessions with Nikos to be followed by several group sessions with other adolescents who had similar problems. Also, she decided to include two or three adolescents of other cultures with Nikos's group counseling sessions so that he could learn to appreciate his Greek culture yet simultaneously realize that he could relate to non-Greek peers. Next, she wanted to work on Nikos's feelings of guilt over schoolwork (his failure to meet his family's expectations). Finally, if Nikos did not disclose significant or confidential information during group counseling sessions, she would try to schedule more individual counseling sessions.

Counseling and Development 12.2: The Adolescent Years

Kirsten is a 16-year-old German American female. She is a stellar student in all aspects—dress, grades, and behavior. Still, Kirsten has a "hidden" problem—she appears calm and easygoing, but she feels she cannot handle the stress resulting from her high expectations. Kirsten thought, "Should I talk with the counselor about how I feel?" Would the counselor tell her teachers or worse yet, her parents? Then she decided she would mention her problem to the counselor. Kirsten finally decided to make the big move.

The counselor considered counseling strategies based on Kirsten's developmental characteristics: cognitive development and motivation, and psychosocial development (few friends and no one in whom she could confide).

Counseling Strategies:

1. Try to identify the source of Kirsten's stress—was the pressure hers, her parents', and/or her teachers'?
2. Ask Kirsten about her leisure activities (in addition to all her extracurricular activities), and ask whether she had considered joining some school clubs, where she would not feel compelled to "stand out."
3. Seek to determine whether Kirsten's self-esteem was dependent on her school success.

EUROPEAN AMERICAN ADULTS

Potential Problems Warranting Counseling Intervention

Problems that European American adults may experience include

- reluctance to seek mental health counseling because of confidence in their ability to determine and handle personal problems;
- the belief that if they seek counseling services, the counselor's role will be to tell them what to do rather than to help them resolve their own situation;

- suspicion of authority and actual distrust of strangers;
- stereotypical generalizations;
- conflicts caused by women seeking increased freedom, more equality in their marriages and families, more decision-making powers, more freedom to seek careers, and an overall egalitarian family life;
- problems associated with employment, such as discrimination, underemployment, unemployment, or decisions about career moves;
- challenges with children and adolescents who disobey parental expectations for behavior and family roles;
- age-related concerns such as midlife crises, the trials of caring for an elderly family member, and the difficulty of seeing one's children growing older and more independent;
- fear of illnesses and diseases;
- disruptions such as divorce, alcoholism, death of a loved one, relocation, loss of a job, and dual-career marriages; and
- racism (both individual and institutional), discrimination, prejudice, and stereotypes associated with differing European cultures.

Basically, social phobia can be defined as a persistent fear of social performance, one that has the potential for causing the person to experience embarrassment. Approximately 60% of the people who experience social phobia experience other troubling disorders such as depression and obsessive-compulsive disorder and are at greater risk of experiencing suicide ideation and suicide attempts.

Although people with social phobias report that the condition interferes with their lives, less than 20% seek professional help and only 6% say they have medications to treat the condition. Low treatment use results from the lack of information made available to people with social phobia about treatment options coupled with their fear of social interactions, including making contact with helping professionals. For people with social phobia, exposure to social situations can cause extreme anxiety and even panic. Symptoms include trembling, twitching, dizziness, rapid heart rate, feeling faint, difficulty speaking or swallowing, and sweating. Commonly feared situations include eating in public places, giving and receiving compliments, unexpectedly bumping into someone previously known, making eye contact, talking with unfamiliar people, and speaking to an audience (Curtis, Kimball, & Stroup, 2004).

Curtis and colleagues (2004) offer several implications for counseling intervention with clients experiencing social phobias. Counselors should

- make the general public more aware of social phobia, since most people with the condition never seek treatment;
- understand that anxiety can be a symptom of many medical conditions, such as diabetes, heart arrhythmia, thyroid conditions, and anemia;
- help clients change their irrational beliefs through cognitive restructuring and exposure to feared situations through role-play and then in-vivo exposure; and
- encourage clients to invite close family members and significant others to participate in therapy.

Counseling Considerations

Counselors who work with clients of differing cultures often contend with the negative consequences of racism and discrimination, as well as with the problems associated with clients' differing worldviews and structures of reasoning. To prepare for counseling European American adults, counselors should obtain a list of service and community organizations and agencies that assist with specific situations. Such organizations include crisis hotlines, family shelters, rape crisis networks, Sistercare for Abused Women, the Salvation Army, and the Urban League.

Counselors will also have to determine whether individual or family therapy will be most beneficial for European American adults.

Gender-related issues and needs should be addressed in counseling sessions. As counselors become increasingly sensitive to multicultural concerns, the culture of genders should be included for the male segment of the population to be better served. With traditional men being socialized to be independent, it is not surprising that they have sought the services of mental health professionals less often than women do. In treating men, specific factors need to be considered: counselors' flexibility and gender sensitivity as well as learning from male clients in the counseling process. Also, recognizing strengths that men bring to the counseling process can be integral.

The counselor should be cautious when intervening in family issues such as the following: (a) problems dealing with the defining of family roles; (b) frustrations of living in a patriarchal family in an egalitarian society; (c) frustrations of wanting to follow one's desires while feeling obligations to extended kinship networks; and (d) valuing and equating independence, rather than individualism, among people. These issues may be more or less acute, depending on the generational status of the family. For example, first-generation adults might experience more acculturation problems as their children adopt mainstream values, whereas second- or third-generation adults may have grown accustomed to these changes in values.

In 1988, the American Association for Marriage and Family Therapy (AAMFT) mandated that gender topics become a part of the curriculum of accredited programs. McCarthy and Holliday (2004) maintain that a traditional male gender role reflects an affirmation of masculine identity with such qualities as success and self-reliance. Males' perceived gender roles may affect their help-seeking attitudes and behaviors. In their excellent article, McCarthy and Holliday's (2004) suggestions include preparing clients to enter and undertake counseling, understanding stereotypes and how they may enter into counseling, considering positive and negative perceptions of cultural groups, and offering possible gender-specific strategies (understanding that no single intervention works for every client).

Individual and Group Therapy

The array of problems and issues that European American adults bring to counseling sessions will be as diverse as their individual cultures. Thus counselors cannot begin a session with a predetermined mind-set regarding a Hungarian American family's problems, for example. Once a problem has been determined, the counselor has the professional responsibility to decide whether individual or group therapy will be most effective. Only after an individual assessment will the counselor be able to determine whether to use individual or group therapy. To make this determination, the counselor may ask questions such as the following: Will the client disclose personal information in front of group members? How uncommon (e.g., individual or personal) are the individual's problems? Will the degree of cultural diversity of the counseling group contribute to or decrease the effectiveness of the counseling intervention?

Once the decision is made to use individual or group therapy, there are several guidelines that contribute to the effectiveness of counseling with European Americans.

Guidelines for individual therapy include (a) considering individual European American cultures rather than relying on stereotypical generalizations, (b) considering communication problems and making accommodations whenever possible, (c) considering individual problems rather than problems commonly associated with the cultural group, (d) considering problems and issues related to the adult lifespan period rather than overgeneralizing problems of other lifespan periods, and (e) basing decisions about whether to use individual therapy on specific and factual information.

Guidelines for group therapy include (a) knowing when group therapy is most effective—that is, if clients are willing to disclose personal information; (b) knowing "cultural backgrounds" sufficiently well to recognize how culture affects adult clients; (c) understanding issues such as sexual orientation, disabilities, and other differences; and (d) periodically reassessing group therapy to determine its continued effectiveness.

Family Therapy

Ethnicity is a filter through which families and individuals understand and interpret their symptoms, their beliefs about the causes of their illnesses, their attitudes toward helpers, and their preferred intervention methods. For example, Italian and Jewish family members may tend toward emotional expressiveness in sharing suffering, whereas Irish and British family members may tend to withdraw into themselves and not discuss their feelings with others. Attitudes toward mental health also vary. For example, Italians generally rely primarily on the family and seek professional help only as a last resort (Ivey et al., 2012).

In addition, the needs of lesbian and gay clients also deserve to be understood and addressed. (These topics are addressed in considerable detail in Chapters 15 and 16.) Laird (2000) explored lesbian relationships and offered several implications for marital and family therapists:

1. Lesbian couples seek therapy for many of the issues that trouble other couples—the loss of a partner or job, help in negotiating conflicts in parenting or work sharing, or relationships with their families of origin.
2. Models of marital and family therapy that have proved useful with heterosexual couples will likely prove helpful with lesbian couples (however, therapists should be knowledgeable about lesbian life; recognize the sexist, heterosexist, and homophobic biases in theories and models; and work to overcome their own sexism, heterosexism, racism, and classism).
3. "Matching" (Laird, 2000, p. 463) the gender and/or sexual orientation of therapist and client is not necessary—what is important is the therapeutic approach that follows.

Counselors employing family therapy with European American adults can maximize effectiveness by (a) preparing individual family members for family therapy (e.g., explaining the purposes of family therapy and the counselor's and family members' roles and responsibilities), (b) learning as much as possible about each family member's cultural background and developmental period, (c) understanding power structures and expectations within the family, and (d) formulating an intervention plan with clearly defined goals that reflect adults' cultural and developmental perspectives.

Rather than consider the European American family through the lens of the counselor (regardless of the counselor's cultural background), the counselor should use caution in developing an accurate cultural perspective of the family. Counseling based on middle-class, majority-culture perspectives (again, regardless of the counselor's cultural background) will not suffice, especially with European American adults who have a powerful allegiance to old-world customs and beliefs. In other words, family intervention needs to be based on and reflect the individual European American culture.

Franco-Americans have a history of self-help and of accepting advice from kinship networks or the local priest rather than from outsiders, who are viewed with suspicion and mistrust. Frequently clannish, most Franco-Americans are reluctant to acknowledge the need to seek help from mental health workers and resent any implication that they should. Personal problems, especially family issues, are considered too personal to share with a therapist. When therapy is sought as a last resort, Franco-Americans prefer a male who is the same age or older, Catholic, and also Franco-American. Because French is the primary language of most first-generation Franco-Americans, they will probably seek a parish priest or a sympathetic layperson who also speaks French. The counselor needs to avoid misunderstandings that result from cross-cultural and intrafamilial confusion (Langelier & Langelier, 2005).

Counseling German American families often violates a tacit rule: "Do it yourself" (Winawer & Wetzel, 2005, p. 565). German Americans who seek therapy think they have no other choice;

for example, a marriage is on the verge of collapse or some symptom impedes the family's functioning. During the initial interview, the therapist should move slowly and not be discouraged by a labored beginning. The German style of forming relationships is generally very structured and takes time. Once the therapist has been accepted in the family, German Americans usually take therapy seriously. Family therapists should understand that the German family is characterized by gender role complementarity (e.g., fathers provide for the family, and mothers take care of the household and the children) (Winawer & Wetzel, 2005).

With Greek American families, the first step is to ensure that each family member feels understood. During the first session, the therapist should display culturally sensitive behaviors to reassure family members that they are not involved with a complete outsider. The therapist should be respectful of relationship values and the traditional hierarchical family organization. If the therapist is unsure about the Greek culture, the session can begin by conducting an enthographic interview in which the family members are treated as experts. Inquiries can begin with cultural customs and lead to questions about the family's patterns. Because gender roles are rigidly defined in the Greek culture, the gender of the therapist will be a powerful determinant in the interactions among family members. Male and female counselors are perceived as having different kinds of power. It is likely that Greek parents will generally be more impressed with a formal, conservative manner (Killian & Agathangelou, 2005).

When Irish Americans attend family therapy, they probably view therapy sessions as being like a confession, during which they admit their sins and ask forgiveness. They may not understand their feelings and may experience considerable embarrassment during the process. As a general rule, structured therapy that is focused on a specific problem will be the most helpful to these clients. Brief, goal-oriented, and clearly stated therapy will likely have the greatest appeal. Value-centered, introspective, open-ended therapy may be considered very threatening. Therapy that is oriented toward uncovering hidden psychological problems probably increases clients' anxiety and their conviction that they are "bad" and deserve to suffer. Irish American clients may be helped more effectively by somewhat mysterious, paradoxical, and humorous techniques. For example, the counselor might use techniques that encourage clients to change without dwelling on their negative feelings and organize therapy around building on a positive connotation and a more hopeful vision of their lives (McGoldrick, 2005).

Italian Americans traditionally have turned to the family, rather than to mental health professionals, for help in solving problems. When they do seek outside help, the problem has probably reached a serious level, and they may feel ashamed that they are unable to solve it. The therapist needs to reassure these clients that they are not to blame and ensure that the family will be involved in counseling intervention. Gaining the family's trust is important because Italian Americans mistrust nearly everyone outside the family. Italian fathers, in particular, may feel threatened because seeking outside help implies their inability to remain in control of their families. In the beginning stages of therapy, the counselor can build trust by sharing common values, which makes the counselor seem warm and approachable (Giordano, McGoldrick, & Klages, 2005).

Therapists intervening with Scandinavian Americans should understand and respect several points. First, Scandinavians emphasize egalitarianism and, because of their suspicion of authority, will probably mistrust the therapist. Second, although most Scandinavians realize that depression negatively affects their lives, they do not admit depressive symptoms or seek professional help. Because Scandinavians are a pragmatic people, they prefer solution-focused approaches during which therapists need to be indirect. Therapy that emphasizes a total-reality approach may be considered shaming, thereby exposing them to humiliation for having called special attention to themselves. Perhaps the most effective way of intervening with Scandinavian Americans is to allow them to figure out as much for themselves as they can, with guidance. Such an approach allows them to maintain their dignity, independence, and sense of control of their lives (Erickson, 2005).

Case Study 12.3 looks at the counselor's efforts with Olympia, a European American adult.

Case Study 12.3: Counseling Olympia, a European American Adult

Olympia's Greek church provides a counselor one day per week to discuss problems experienced by members of the church. A friend suggested that Olympia visit the counselor, especially because the church provided the counseling services. Although Olympia did not think she had any serious problems, she agreed to see the counselor, mainly to satisfy her friend's request. Olympia revealed several potential problems, such as her belief that some Greek women were becoming more independent and assertive, whereas she was not; her holding Greek traditions in high regard even though she realized that both Christina and Nikos were experiencing considerable acculturation; the family's need of more money; and the grandfather's declining health. Again, she felt fortunate; her problems were not as serious as those of some of her friends, but she did have a better understanding of the problems that she and her family faced.

The counselor considered Olympia's problems to be somewhat typical of many women in the Greek culture who were torn between tradition—their own and their husbands' Greek traditions—and the acculturation of their children. They wanted a better life for their children and viewed the school (sponsored by the Greek Orthodox Church) as the means to achieve a better life. Also, like many other women, she felt obligated (although not resentful) to take care of older family members—in this case, Grandfather Costas. The counselor decided to include Olympia in a small-group counseling session at first. Then, if she could convince Olympia's husband to attend and participate, she might plan one or more family counseling sessions. The counselor realized that convincing Olympia's husband to attend might be difficult, especially because he probably did not understand Olympia's feelings. The counselor considered how many other Greek women might share similar feelings and concerns and wondered what special programs she might initiate at the church specifically to meet the needs of Greek women.

Counseling and Development 12.3: The Adult Years

Alisa, a 50-year-old Italian woman, lived with her husband for 25 years. Her three children were grown, married, and continued to live in the neighborhood. By no means wealthy, Alisa had a comfortable life and saw her grown children about once a week. Still, she knew changes were occurring: Her energy level was declining, depression sometimes bothered her, and she could sense body changes. She did not have her children to care for, but she did see her grandchildren once a week. Alisa attended a large Catholic church that offered the services of a counselor who was well versed in adult development.

The counselor considered Alisa's age, menopausal issues, feelings of not being needed, and occasional depression.

Counseling Strategies:

1. Ask Alisa about her overall health and whether she needs to consult a medical doctor for her depression. Will counseling work, or will medical treatment be necessary?
2. Understand that turning 50 is difficult for some people, did Alisa's depression result from age, menopausal issues, or something else? Ask Alisa what she thinks the root cause(s) are.
3. Ask Alisa about marital therapy. Will it be beneficial for her husband to attend counseling sessions? Will he attend if asked?

EUROPEAN AMERICAN ELDERLY

Potential Problems Warranting Counseling Intervention

Problems that European American elders may experience include

- varying degrees of acculturation, which affects their motivation and ability to deal with life;
- communication proficiency, which will depend on their generational status and whether they live in a native language enclave where learning English seems unnecessary;
- the belief that younger generations should give emotional and financial support, offer respect and loyalty, and in some cases live in proximity to them;
- health problems, physical and psychological, that limit mobility and their ability to deal with personal problems;
- lower standards of living and, in some cases, poverty and substandard housing;
- illness or death of a spouse or other loved ones;
- health problems and chronic illnesses and medical care;
- fear of living alone and lack of financial means to do so;
- communication problems that hamper the ability to deal with medical professionals and social service workers;
- changes resulting from acculturation and the younger generations' seeming lack of allegiance; and
- fear of counseling intervention that might appear intrusive or threatening.

One problem facing significant numbers of older adults (and many other age groups) is obesity, caused by heredity, poor eating habits, and lack of proper exercise. Reynolds, Saito, and Crimmins (2005) investigated the effect of obesity on life expectancy and concluded that obesity leads to higher mortality rates. Conflicting research holds that the relationship between obesity and life expectancy may differ by age; that is, some evidence suggests lower death rates among the obese at older ages. The effects of obesity may be more significant for younger rather than older adults. Reynolds and colleagues (2005) conclude that obesity has little effect on life expectancy in adults age 70 and older; however, the obese are more likely to become disabled. That means obese older adults live more years and a higher proportion of their remaining lives disabled. One significant implication is that health professionals and health-care providers should realize that obesity-related death is less of a concern than obesity-related disability in this age range. Given the steady increases in obesity among older Americans, more research is needed on the effects of obesity on life expectancy and disability.

Socioeconomically, the most elderly people today are as well off as, and perhaps better off, than the nonelderly. It is also important to point out that many elderly people are better off than children and adolescents. Undoubtedly, elderly people differ according to many factors, and counselors should avoid assumptions about the elderly clients' socioeconomic circumstances. Also, some elderly clients may not want to disclose their socioeconomic situation, especially if poverty conditions exist.

Counseling Considerations

Counselors will increasingly be called on to work with the elderly from various cultural backgrounds. However, without special training, counselors might feel unprepared to provide counseling intervention with elderly clients. Also, counselors must understand the need to redefine terminology that defines elderly people and perhaps be instrumental in the redefining process.

Decisions regarding counseling therapies with elderly European Americans should be grounded in both cultural and developmental perspectives. Problems of elderly European

Americans might result from their individual cultural diversity, limited communication skills, family problems, and concerns about growing older. No single intervention method can be suggested for a particular culture; such a decision must be reached on an individual counseling basis and must reflect the most effective approach for individual elderly persons. As with other cultures and developmental periods, the literature does not conclusively suggest a specific counseling approach.

Counselors may use several approaches with elderly European American clients who have communication problems, keeping in mind the value that these clients place on their languages. Counselors working with these clients may (a) arrange for a translator to assist with communication problems during counseling intervention, (b) arrange for English-language instruction from a person trained to work with the elderly, and (c) seek the help of bilingual social services specialists.

Individual and Group Therapy

Counselors employing individual therapy should (a) understand the perspectives of elderly European Americans and the challenges associated with the lifespan period; (b) build an effective counseling relationship (i.e., obtain the trust and confidence of the elderly client); (c) understand and address, whenever possible, problems resulting from limited English-language skills; and (d) determine the effectiveness of individual therapy.

Similarly, counselors intervening with group therapy can benefit from several guidelines, including the following: (a) An increased number of clients can be counseled simultaneously (although clients' individuality should never be forgotten); (b) comments and disclosures of other clients can contribute to the overall goals of counseling; (c) recognition of individual cultures and their members' propensity and reluctance to disclose personal information should guide intervention; and (d) disclosure should be encouraged, yet cultural perceptions of confidentiality should be respected.

Case Study 12.4: Counseling Costas, a European American Elder

Grandfather Costas was recommended for counseling when he visited his physician for arthritic-type pains. Costas visited a physician only rarely, and he thought it was even less likely that he would attend a counseling session. After being encouraged by the physician and his own family, however, he decided to attend "one or two" sessions. After extending considerable effort to get Costas to disclose personal information, the counselor listened attentively to Costas's concerns about his declining health, failing eyesight, and a slight loss of hearing. Other concerns included his dislike of Nikos and Christina increasingly adopting mainstream American values. "It is not like the old days," Costas once said with mixed emotions of concern and dismay.

The male counselor realized that Costas was experiencing concerns (aging, failing health, fear of losing traditions) similar to those of many elderly clients. In his determination of appropriate counseling interventions, he thought Costa might disclose more in individual sessions than in group or family sessions; however, family sessions might be most effective because other family members could learn how to help him. However, because Costas was the eldest male in the family and thought he had to be a "tower of strength," he probably would not disclose significant information or feelings in front of family members. Although one objective of counseling would be to address acculturation issues, the counselor might also be able to convince Costas to get visual and hearing tests to determine how he might be helped in those areas. The counselor decided that individual counseling would be most appropriate, and he would try to accomplish as much as possible in the first session because he was doubtful that Costas would attend many sessions before deciding to withdraw from counseling.

Counseling and Development 12.4: The Elderly Years

Anthony was an 86-year-old Italian male. He could speak Italian, but his English was limited. He had lived in an Italian enclave all his life, so learning English was unnecessary. He lived off his meager social security, and his modest house was paid for. His wife had died nine years previously, but his four grown children (especially his daughters) occasionally checked on him. Anthony had limited sight, an enlarged prostate, limited mobility, and weak English skills. He attended a state-supported "lunch gathering" five days a week. Nearly everyone there spoke Italian. The coordinator of the program recommended him for counseling because he appeared "lonely" and "depressed."

The Italian American counselor worked with elderly clients, so she thought she understood their developmental stage and worldviews. She considered his developmental characteristics: fading eyesight, prostate problems, limited physical mobility, and possible depression.

Counseling Strategies:

1. Ask Anthony about his "concerns" about physical and psychological health.
2. Determine whether Anthony wants to socialize more or whether he basically wants to be alone.
3. Learn Anthony's strengths (e.g., religious beliefs, children's support, and the ability to live alone at 86), and ask him to consider ways to improve his overall well-being.

Family Therapy

Family therapy with elderly European Americans requires that counselors (a) consider whether family members will respond to or disclose information, especially in cultures holding the elderly in high regard (family problems and issues might reflect negatively on the elderly or vice versa); (b) take advantage of family dynamics by establishing goals for all family members, not just the elderly client; (c) learn how elderly family members fit into the overall family structure; (d) understand language problems, especially if the family speaks a native language at home; and (e) recognize that generational differences might interfere with counseling effectiveness.

SUMMARY

Counselors of European American clients along the lifespan continuum may face several unique challenges. Counselors should avoid assuming that European Americans are a homogeneous group of people with similar problems and challenges; learn cultural and developmental characteristics and the complex relationship between the two; make valid decisions concerning when to use individual, group, and family therapies; provide for communication differences, both verbal and nonverbal, and recognize when to request the services of a translator; and realize the impossibility of learning about all European American groups and commit to learning about individual European cultural groups.

232   *Understanding and Counseling Clients*

SUGGESTED READINGS

Lockard, A. J., Hayes, J. A., Graceffo, J. M., & Locke, B. D. (2013). Effective counseling for racial/ ethnic minority clients: Examining changes using a practice research network. *Journal of College Counseling,16*(3), 243–257. Studies have shown that counseling decreases students' academic distress, primarily in European American students.

Meany-Walen, K., Bratton, S. C., & Kottman, T. (2014). Effects of Adlerian play therapy on reducing students' disruptive behaviors. *Journal of Counseling & Development, 92*(1), 47–56. This study examined the effectiveness of Adlerian play therapy with Latinos, European American, and African Americans exhibiting disruptive classroom behaviors.

Rigali-Oiler, M., & Kurpius, S. R. (2013). Promoting academic persistence among racial/ethnic minority and European American freshman and sophomore undergraduates: Implications for college counselors. *Journal of College Counseling, 16*(3), 98–212. This article discusses factors influencing persistence decisions; gender and racial/ethnic differences were found in centrality and public regard of racial/ethnic identity.

Scott, K. D., & Scott, A. A. (2014). Adolescent inhalant use and executive cognitive functioning. *Child Care, Health & Development, 40*(1), 20–28. This study investigates the association between inhalant use and executive cognitive functioning and processing.

13 Understanding Hispanic American Clients

QUESTIONS TO BE EXPLORED

- What are the childhood, adolescent, adult, and elderly years like in the Hispanic American culture?
- What social and cultural characteristics (e.g., *afecto*, *dignidad*, *machismo*, *respeto*, *spiritualism*) and familial traditions describe Hispanic Americans along the lifespan continuum?
- What unique challenges face Hispanic Americans during the various lifespan stages?
- What communication problems (and Hispanics' tendencies to hold on to the Spanish language) affect Hispanic Americans, and how do these problems and tendencies affect educational attainment, employment, and economic success?
- What unique challenges face counselors providing mental health services to Hispanic Americans in the four lifespan stages?
- What sources of information are available for counselors intervening with Hispanic American children, adolescents, adults, and elders?

OVERVIEW

Counselors undoubtedly will be called on to provide professional intervention for Hispanic Americans, the nation's fastest growing cultural group. Hispanic Americans will challenge counselors and psychotherapists, regardless of gender and cultural background, to understand Hispanic heritages, allegiances to the Spanish language, and cultural customs and practices. Also, Hispanic Americans experience problems on a daily basis that potentially can result in the need for professional counseling. Problems such as lack of English-language skills, low educational attainment, unemployment, poverty, discrimination, and acculturative stress can exact serious tolls on Hispanic Americans. This chapter looks at Hispanic Americans in the four lifespan stages and presents a portrait of Hispanic Americans and the lives they live.

HISPANIC AMERICANS: DEMOGRAPHICS

People who identify with the terms "Hispanic" or "Latino" are those who classify themselves in one of the specific Hispanic or Latino categories listed on the decennial census questionnaire and various Census Bureau survey questionnaires—"Mexican, Mexican Am., Chicano" or "Puerto Rican" or "Cuban"—as well as those who indicate that they are "another Hispanic, Latino, or Spanish origin." Origin can be viewed as the heritage, nationality group, lineage, or country of birth of the person or the person's ancestors before their arrival in the United States. People who identify their origin as Hispanic, Latino, or Spanish may be of any race (U.S. Census Bureau, n.d., https://www.census.gov/population/hispanic/).

Hispanic Americans may be identified as Mexican Americans, Central and South Americans, Chicanos, Spanish Americans, Latin Americans, Mexicans, Puerto Ricans, Cubans,

Guatemalans, and Salvadorans. Mexican-origin people live predominantly in the Southwest and Midwest, Puerto Ricans tend to live in the Northeast, and Cubans are mostly concentrated in the Southeast. The Hispanic population of the United States as of July 1, 2013, was 54 million, making people of Hispanic origin the nation's largest ethnic or racial minority. Hispanics constituted 17% of the nation's total population. The Hispanic population increased by 1.1 million between July 1, 2012, and July 1, 2013. This number is close to half of the approximately 2.3 million people added to the nation's population during this period. Hispanics increased 2% between 2012 and 2013. Projected Hispanic population numbers will be 128.8 million (or 31%) in the United States in 2060. Nearly 65% of the Hispanics in the United States were of Mexican background in 2012. Another 9.4% were of Puerto Rican background, 3.8% Salvadoran, 3.7% Cuban, 3.1% Dominican, and 2.3% Guatemalan. The remainder was of some other Central American, South American, or other Hispanic/Latino origin (U.S. Census Bureau, 2014a).

The term Hispanic or Latina/o American must be used carefully with considerable objectivity. Although these terms are widely used, many differences separate individual ethnic and cultural groups.

The Hispanics share many values and goals, yet they also differ in many respects. Still, in some ways, Hispanics constitute members of a single cultural group with a fairly common history and the sharing of language, values, and customs; in other ways, they are a significantly heterogeneous population that should be conceptualized as an aggregate of distinct subcultures. Tremendous cultural diversity exists among Hispanic Americans, such as the differences between Mexican Americans and Cuban Americans, among generations, and among Hispanics living in different geographic locations in the United States. Thus mental health professionals and social workers are encouraged to learn about individual clients and their respective cultural characteristics.

Like the arrival of European immigrants at the turn of the century, the tide of Hispanic immigrants and the fast growth of Hispanic American families have changed American's cities, including religion and politics. Hispanic Americans mainly choose the Catholic faith, although significant numbers are choosing other faiths. Hispanics are a powerful force in the nation's politics as politicians realize the strength of Hispanic numbers and seek to get their votes. The growing Hispanic vote cannot be taken for granted. Not only are there increasing numbers of voters, but the growing numbers of Spanish-language newspapers, radio stations, and television stations are better educating Hispanic voters about political issues. States with the largest Hispanic American populations include Arizona, California, Colorado, Connecticut, Florida, Idaho, Illinois, Iowa, Kansas, Massachusetts, Nebraska, Nevada, New Hampshire, New Jersey, New Mexico, New York, Oregon, Rhode Island, Texas, Utah, Washington, and Wyoming (U.S. Census Bureau, 2014a).

The median income of Hispanic households in 2012 was $39,005, with a poverty rate of 25.6%. Twenty-nine percent lacked health insurance in 2012, down from 30.1% in 2011 (U.S. Census Bureau, 2014a). While the most current numbers of Hispanics lacking health insurance is not available, we predict the number will be considerably lower due to the Affordable Care Act.

HISPANIC AMERICAN CHILDREN

Social and Cultural Description

A new collective majority of Hispanic children will soon present challenges in schools. A projected 50.3% of school-aged children will be driven largely by the dramatic growth of Hispanic children and the decline in the European American population. The United States has a responsibility to vastly improve the education outcomes for these diverse Hispanic students

(Maxwell, 2014). While Maxwell (2014) writes mainly of educational experiences, counselors will also experience challenges with this influx of students: language differences, different worldviews, a "different" school system with "different" expectations, and possibly misunderstanding the adult counselor as well as the goals of counseling.

A general cultural description of Hispanic Americans is difficult because of the marked diversity of the various subcultures. Diversity also exists in individual differences, generational differences, and socioeconomic levels within each Hispanic cultural group. In considering the social and cultural characteristics of Hispanic American children, counselors and psychotherapists must keep this intracultural diversity in mind to avoid the pitfalls of stereotyping. Considering the number of Hispanic adults of childbearing age, it is likely that the numbers of Hispanic children will continue to increase dramatically. One only has to look at the diversity of schools in the most populated Hispanic states to see the increasing numbers of Hispanic children.

Several cultural characteristics and values are instilled in children at an early age.

- *Children are taught about machismo.* This term may be translated as a strong sense of masculine pride and is used flatteringly among Hispanic Americans. Both Hispanic American boys and girls learn that machismo refers to manhood, the courage to fight, the masculine traits of honor and dignity, keeping one's word, and protecting one's name. More subtly, machismo also refers to dignity in personal conduct, respect for others, love for family, and affection for children. The term also implies a clear-cut distinction between the genders, whereby males enjoy rights and privileges that are denied to females, a fact that Hispanic children often learn early in life.

- *Children are taught to avoid competition and behaviors that would set them apart from their group.* To stand out among one's peers is to place oneself in great jeopardy and is to be avoided at all costs.

- *Children in some Hispanic groups,* such as Mexican Americans, *are often taught to regard European Americans with fear and hostility.* Children who are taught such attitudes have difficulty believing that a European American counselor has their best interests at heart.

Before discussing communication and families, it must be repeated that the tremendous cultural diversity among Hispanic Americans warrants consideration. For example, Mexican Americans and Cuban Americans may be very different with respect to culture-based values. In fact, each of the numerous Hispanic subgroups adheres to unique and distinguishing cultural and social practices. Acculturation rates, socioeconomic factors, educational levels, and region of residency deserve consideration.

As the number of single-parent families in the United States has continued to increase, so have concerns about the health and well-being of young children. Although exceptions certainly exist, as a whole, the majority of single parents are women, less educated, poorer, and more likely to experience racial discrimination than is the case for women in two-parent families

Unfavorable outcomes are often associated with single parenthood, particularly for children in late childhood, adolescence, and young adulthood. One must be careful with generalizations because many single parents are excellent caregivers—one cannot say or suggest single parents have more children with counseling needs. Also, a parent's social class, familial support, educational attainment, and economic well-being also play significant roles. Still, problems might include dropping out of high school, poor school achievement, problem behavior, increased health risk, and severe behavioral difficulties.

Communication

Spanish-speaking people represent the largest language-minority population in the nation. Often Hispanic American children feel encouraged to speak Spanish at home yet feel compelled to speak English at school. Which language should be considered the language of choice? Although children want their parents' approval for choice of language, they often hear in school that English contributes to academic success. Also, nonverbal language, as in other cultures, is important in the Hispanic American culture and should be understood by professionals of all cultures; for example, many Hispanic Americans tend to stand close while communicating and to touch one another; eye contact may be avoided.

Approximately 38 million U.S. residents five and older spoke Spanish at home in 2012. This is a 121% increase since 1990 when it was 17.3 million. Those who *hablan español en casa* constituted 13.0% of U.S. residents five and older. More than half (58%) of these Spanish speakers spoke English "very well" (U.S. Census Bureau, 2014a). While children should not feel obligated to forsake their native language, we do believe that some degree of proficiency in English is required for successful living in the United States. Implications for counselors are clear: The possibility of communication problems might interfere with counseling therapy, and, in some cases, an interpreter might be needed.

Also, many Hispanic American children are taught distinct communication customs, some of which professionals fail to understand. For example, children of Hispanic immigrants are taught to respect adult authority rather than express their own knowledge and opinions, yet teachers and counselors in the United States often value assertive speaking and typically equate Hispanic American children's silence as a negative attitude toward learning and professionals. Using a culturally valid communication style, the child listens politely and attentively but does not answer; then the counselor who misunderstands this communication custom thinks the child is being difficult or obstinate.

Families

Several interesting facts about Hispanic children and their families include:

> 11.9 million–The number of Hispanic family households in the United States in 2013.
>
> 62.4%–The percentage of Hispanic family households that were married-couple households in 2013. (For the total population in the United States, it was 73.2%.)
>
> 58.5%–The percentage of Hispanic married-couple households that had children younger than 18 present in 2013. (For the total population in the United States, it was 40.3%.)
>
> 65.1%–Percentage of Hispanic children living with two parents in 2013. (For the total population in the United States, it was 68.5%.)
>
> 43.1%–Percentage of Hispanic married couples with children under 18 where both spouses were employed in 2013. (For the total population in the United States, it was 58.0%; U.S. Census Bureau, 2014a).

Family lifestyles and activities in the Hispanic American culture play a large part in determining what the developing child will be like as an adult. Ethnic awareness in children is perpetuated by family gatherings for cultural holidays. Puerto Rican Americans have a deep sense of commitment to the immediate and extended family—kinship networks of Hispanic Americans are widely recognized.

Although acculturation undoubtedly is occurring, *traditionally*, the father in the Hispanic American family is clearly head of the household. Children learn early that their father's authority goes unchallenged, that he often makes decisions without consulting their mother, and that he expects to be obeyed when he gives commands. Male dominance extends to sons, who have more and earlier independence than daughters. Again, although these are traditional Hispanic values, counselors should carefully assess acculturation, social class, and economic status of both parents to avoid generalizations and stereotypes.

Professionals working with Hispanic American children and their families need to understand the traditionally defined gender roles. They should also be aware that changes are occurring: Hispanic American women are increasingly exerting their influence; indeed, in many cases, they are seeking equality with men. As women continue to redefine their roles in the Hispanic and White societies, children will also experience changes.

Unique Challenges Confronting Hispanic American Children

Hispanic American children face several challenges with regard to poverty, communication, and education. First, many Hispanic American children live in poverty. As previously suggested, the median income of Hispanic households in 2012 was $39,005, with a poverty rate of 25.6% (U.S. Census Bureau, 2014a). One can argue that significant numbers of Hispanic children live in poverty conditions and its effects on home conditions, nourishment, and educational attainment. Second, communication problems continue to plague Hispanic American children; their tendency to speak their native language at home and in the community but to speak English at school may prolong communication problems. In fact, significant numbers of Hispanic children speak a language other than English at home and have difficulty with everyday English usage. Although the use of the Spanish language is definitely increasing in the United States, many Spanish-speaking "pockets" still exist and probably continue to increase.

Hispanic American children face several educational challenges: (a) Generally speaking, Hispanic American children and adolescents begin school with less preschool experience; (b) gaps in Hispanic Americans' academic achievement appear at age 9 and persist through age 17; (c) the school drop-out rate for Hispanic American adolescents is declining but still remains high; (d) Hispanic American high school seniors experience more learning disruptions (e.g., fights, gang behaviors) than their European American counterparts; and (e) Hispanic Americans have lower educational aspirations. It is especially important to mention that Hispanic children should not be blamed for the challenges they face. Factors affecting their educational achievement include the fact that many attend segregated schools in urban areas, many are taught by teachers who do not understand Hispanic students and learning styles, and many face discrimination by both teachers and other students.

Case Study 13.1: Gonzalo, a Hispanic American Child

Gonzalo is a 12-year-old Hispanic American male child. He lives with his sister, his mother, and his maternal grandfather. The whereabouts of the father are unknown. The family lives off what Amelia makes in her cleaning ventures and the grandfather's social security. The family is not destitute, but its financial level is less than desirable. Medicaid provides the only health insurance, and the grandfather is on Medicare.

The family lives in an urban area in the Northeast. Gonzalo attends a large middle school with other Hispanic students and African American students. European American students represent the minority in his school and neighborhood. Although he does not realize that the educational concepts are actually relics of the junior high school era, he does know that the school is the old high school. The school is not a very "student-friendly" school—the administrators and teachers teach the basics from outdated textbooks and work to maintain discipline and order.

While Gonzalo puts forth some effort, his mother thinks he can do better. His grades are mediocre at best. His mother is not sure what Gonzalo's teacher thinks because there is little communication between the home and the school. His counselor knows little about him, other than he seems shy and withdrawn at times. He is awkward (which is a developmental characteristic of the age), has few friends, and tries to "hang out" with Hispanic male peers, although he is "noticing" girls lately. Some bullying occurs in this middle school, but so far, he has not been a victim more than once or twice. He has never missed school because of threats or fear of bullies.

Unlike some Hispanic families, Gonzalo is not close to his mother and grandfather. He and his sister discuss school matters, teachers, and other students. Gonzalo feels familial love for this mother and grandfather, but he does not seek their advice. Candidly speaking, Gonzalo thinks his mother is too busy working, and his grandfather is too old to understand his life events and worldviews.

Reflection Questions:

1. What problems might Gonzalo bring to a counseling session? Consider his world-views or life events, such as being awkward, having few friends, noticing girls, and lacking strong family relationships.
2. Consider the statement: *Gonzalo thinks his mother is too busy working, and his grand-father is too old to understand his life events and worldviews.* What are the possible repercussions of such thinking, especially his opinion that his "grandfather is too old to understand him"?

HISPANIC AMERICAN ADOLESCENTS

Social and Cultural Description

Hispanic American adolescents represent a sizable percentage of the Hispanic population. They represent a diverse group with varying levels of acculturation, socioeconomic class, proficiency in English, and region of residency within the United States.

Forces that influence the lives of Hispanic American adolescents include the social and psychological changes that accompany adolescence as well as the cultural customs and traditions considered sacred to the culture. These two forces, along with Hispanics' tendencies to speak only Spanish in the home or to live in predominantly bilingual areas, challenge both adolescents and their counselors.

Several Hispanic American cultural characteristics illustrate that European American standards are inappropriate when intervening with Hispanic Americans. First, European Americans often believe that equality within the family and self-advancement are consistent with the ideals of freedom, democracy, and progress. In contrast, Mexican Americans value placing one's family above self. Second, the adolescent male must adhere to cultural expectations or risk the loss of respect for himself and his manhood.

Too often, Hispanic American adolescents are negatively stereotyped. Emphasis has been placed on such issues as delinquency, gangs, drug and alcohol abuse, poor academic achievement, and dropping out of school rather than on the more average adolescent behavior in the culture. This is not to suggest that the negative aspects should be ignored, only that they should receive an objective and cautious interpretation.

A cultural description of Spanish-speaking people must include an understanding of certain attributes that play a significant role (in varying degrees, depending on the individual group) in the Hispanic American culture. These attributes include the following:

Spanish Term	Meaning
afecto	literally "affect"; refers to warmth and demonstrativeness
dignidad	dignity; one may oppose another person but should never take away his or her dignity
machismo	a strong sense of masculine pride; sometimes taken by non-Hispanics to imply an innate inferiority of women
respeto	respect for authority, family, and tradition
Espiritismo (or spiritualism)	the drawing out of spirit in one's life which is innate and unique to all people (there is no common definition of this term)

(Gold, 2010)

Reyes, Meininger, Liehr, Chan, and Mueller (2003) explain that the experience and expression of anger are common occurrences throughout the adolescent years. Feelings of unjust treatment or frustration often precipitate anger arousal. Although the experience and expression of anger are normal for everyone, emerging data suggest a relationship between how anger is experienced and expressed and risk factors for cardiovascular disease. Significant relationships have been found between anger control and a number of health conditions, for example, blood pressure and overall current health. The State-Trait Anger Expression Inventory (STAXI), a questionnaire, is designed to measure the experience and expression of anger. It is well established with African and European Americans, but Reyes and colleagues (2003) maintain that little is known about its use with Hispanic American adolescents. While their article is over a decade old, it continues to be relevant.

Poverty continues to plague the Hispanic American population and affects developing adolescents, just as previously discussed in the "Hispanic Children" section. Although some Puerto Ricans have experienced substantial improvement in socioeconomic status, poverty continues to be widespread in this population.

Determining appropriate programs and efforts has proved difficult because of the paucity of research on the mental health needs of some Hispanic adolescents (e.g., Mexican Americans). Despite the many risk factors for Hispanic American adolescents, research and scholarly literature on this population are almost nonexistent. Available research usually focuses on one of four categories: dropping out of school, substance abuse, delinquency, and teenage pregnancy. Although these topics are important, other areas of concern need attention so that counselors, social workers, and other mental health professionals will be able to plan appropriate intervention.

Communication

Spanish-speaking adolescents have much in common with other cultural groups. For example, communication poses a problem outside the immediate neighborhood. Many Hispanic Americans prefer to retain their native tongue rather than make the transition to English. Because they do not perceive a need to develop proficiency, some Spanish-speaking people continue to risk survival in a bilingual world. In the southwestern United States, many Hispanic Americans live in Spanish-speaking communities that are isolated from the English-speaking community.

A major concern in the education of Hispanic American adolescents is their language proficiency and literacy. Approximately one out of every six Mexican American high school students has not acquired academic English-language skills adequate for the levels of performance required to succeed in the various subject areas. Anyone trying to survive in a society speaking a language that is different from the dominant language can attest to the problems encountered. Communication problems during the adolescent years, however, have the potential to affect both individual self-concept and developing cultural identity negatively.

Counselors working with significant numbers of Hispanic American adolescents need to address their problems with English. Counselors, especially school counselors, might be called on to work with regular classroom teachers, bilingual specialists, and special educators. Addressing Hispanic Americans' communication challenges is a difficult task because of the tremendous cultural and language diversity. No one model or program meets all the needs of Hispanic American students.

Families

A counselor's understanding of the family's role in the Hispanic American culture is a prerequisite to understanding and counseling an adolescent client. A deep feeling for family, both immediate and extended, permeates the culture and often becomes the basis for individual and group decisions.

The Hispanic American family is like families of other cultures in some respects and different in others. First, as in Asian American and African American families, the extended kinship network plays a vital role; also, in the Hispanic American family the natural superiority of the male is a basic tenet. Grandparents and other family members may live in the same household or nearby in separate households and visit frequently. Second, with respect to the dominance of the male, in the Puerto Rican family the husband exercises the authority in the family and makes decisions without consulting his wife. It follows that he expects to be obeyed when he gives commands. Third, like American Indian and Asian American families, there is an emphasis on cooperation and placing the family's needs ahead of individual concerns. This does not imply that the family impedes individual achievement and advancement. One must be careful to distinguish between being cooperative and respectful and being docile and dependent. Any discussion of Hispanic American families must consider the effects of acculturation and recognize that second- and third-generation Hispanics have experienced change. Women are demanding more active and equal roles and increasingly are heading households.

Hispanic American adolescents living with a single parent often engage in risk-taking behaviors and have an earlier onset of sexual activity than adolescents living with both parents. On the other hand, the quality of the parenting relationship is more significant than the family's composition in predicting social deviance, substance use, and dropping out. Whether living with one or two parents, Hispanic adolescents face challenges that counselors will need to address.

Case Study 13.2: Jasele, a Hispanic American Adolescent

Jasele is a 16-year-old Hispanic American female who lives with her mother in a large urban area. She has one older brother, but he left home several years ago and only touches base occasionally. Her mother works at a restaurant and makes enough money for the two to survive financially. The house is clean and neat, but admittedly, the neighborhood is facing economic decline, resulting in criminal behaviors and drug sales.

Even with all the neighborhood and financial challenges, Jasele makes better than average grades. She wonders about her mother, her future, and the declining status of the neighborhood. She has a 19-year-old boyfriend who her mother appears to question. Drug use? Other criminal behaviors such as muggings and break-ins? Increasing unplanned pregnancies? Jasele knows her mother must be thinking of these situations, but at this point, her mother has only said things such as "Be careful who you choose as friends." Jasele thinks her mother might be wondering what will happen to her only daughter in a few years.

Jasele enjoys her high school experiences. As stated, she makes better than average grades and has mostly well-behaved Hispanic American friends. Jasele is developing through adolescence and into adulthood. She has the physical, psychosocial, and cognitive developmental characteristics of a young female her age. She is curious about drugs and sex. She does not want to disappoint her mother, but she has occasionally taken illegal drugs just to see what it would be like (and she thinks her mother does not know). She and her boyfriend have experimented sexually, but she has been careful to avoid pregnancy or a sexually transmitted disease. Still, she wonders how long she can avoid the consequences of sexual experimentation. Should she stop all sexual experimentation now and wait until marriage? Candidly speaking, will her boyfriend continue in such a relationship? What will she do after high school? What will happen to her mother?

Jasele appears to be a "problem-free" adolescent, but in reality, she is experiencing the conflicts of obeying her mother's expectations and the challenges associated with developing from an adolescent female to an adult woman.

Reflections Questions:

1. What *specific* challenges might Jasele bring to a counseling session? Do her concerns call for individual counseling or small-group counseling (because probably many other female adolescents experience similar challenges)?
2. What *developmentally appropriate* counseling strategies should be implemented?
3. To what extent should female counselors disclose similar concerns (hers rather than other students') during the adolescence developmental period?

Unique Challenges Confronting Hispanic American Adolescents

Counselors working with Hispanic American adolescents need to be aware of several challenges confronting this group. First, they are often stereotyped as gang members and involved with drugs. Second, these adolescents must try to reconcile the different family structures of the Hispanic American and European American cultures. Third, Spanish-speaking adolescents are faced with recognizing the need to speak the language of the majority culture; although the desire to maintain an allegiance to their native tongue is natural, learning English increases their chances of success in a predominantly English-speaking nation. Problems worsen when adolescents have some type of disabling condition (e.g., a learning disability). Fourth, Hispanic American females (ages 15–19) have the highest teen birth rate (83 per 1,000).

Many adolescent Hispanic American mothers have little chance of escaping the cycle of poverty. Poverty and financial stress can impede cognitive development and their ability to learn. It can contribute to behavioral, social and emotional problems, and poor health. The risks posed by economic hardship are greatest among those who experience poverty when they are young and among those who experience persistent and deep poverty. Adolescents experience similar consequences. With adolescents, the poverty situation might be worse because considerable numbers of Hispanic adolescents are not in school and are not working (Annie E. Casey Foundation, 2014, http://www.aecf.org/m/resourcedoc/aecf-2014kidscountdata book-2014.pdf).

HISPANIC AMERICAN ADULTS

Social and Cultural Description

Counselors should avoid labeling Hispanic Americans as a single cultural group based on their common language. Race and ethnicity figure largely in the diversity among Hispanic Americans, which is influenced by geographic origin (e.g., Mexico, Cuba, Puerto Rico, El Salvador, the Dominican Republic, Colombia, and Venezuela).

The median age (34.4) of Hispanics in Florida represents the highest Hispanic population in the United States. Such a median age (which includes continued childrearing ages) suggests their population will continue to increase. Ten million Hispanics reside in Texas. Fifty-five percent of all the Hispanic population lives in California, Florida, and Texas, compared with 47.3% of New Mexico's population being Hispanic in the most recent census count (U.S. Census Bureau, 2014a).

Some interesting facts about Hispanic Americans include the following: (a) Large numbers of Hispanic families are concentrated in just a few states, such as California, Texas, and New York; (b) Hispanic families are more highly urbanized than non-Hispanics; (c) the Hispanic population has a younger age distribution; (d) the Hispanic youth population is expected to increase substantially; and (e) compared with non-Hispanics, Hispanics have the largest family size. Hispanic Americans have experienced considerable difficulty achieving academic and economic success in the United States. Whether as a result of cultural discrimination, poor English-language skills, lack of employment skills, or problems coping in a predominantly European American society, the Hispanic American population generally has not made desired gains. Although the educational level of Hispanic Americans continues to rise, considerable diversity continues to exist among Hispanic groups. As previously mentioned, Hispanic Americans are reluctant to forsake their native language. While some acculturation undoubtedly has occurred, Hispanic Americans continue to emphasize *respeto, machismo, dignidad,* and *Espiritismo* in defining rigid family roles.

Educational attainments almost always predict socioeconomic success—money for food, shelter, and health care. Table 13.1 shows the educational attainments of Hispanic Americans 25 years old and older.

Meyer, Castro-Schilo, and Aguilar-Gaxiola (2014) investigated the underlying mechanisms of the influence of socioeconomic status and self-rated health. They concluded socioeconomic status plays an important role in self-rated health as well as mental health. Race/ethnicity and

Table 13.1 Educational Attainments of Hispanic Americans 25 Years Old and Older (in thousands)

Educational Attainment	Hispanic
Total	26,107
Less than 9th grade	6,142
9th to 12th grade, no diploma	4,069
High school graduate (or equivalency)	6,830
Some college; no degree	4,402
Associate's degree	1,377
Bachelor's degree	2,259
Graduate degree	1,030

Source: U.S. Census Bureau. (2015k). Selected characteristics of racial groups and Hispanic or Latino population. Washington, DC: Author. Retrieved from http://www.census.gov/comendia/statab/cats/population/elderly_racial_and_hispanic_origin_population_profiles.html.

gender also play a role. Counselors have long understood the effects of poverty, unemployment, and underemployment, but Meyer et al. (2014) provide conclusive evidence that interventions should be tailored to reflect clients' socioeconomic status.

Communication

Although discrimination cannot be discounted, the reluctance of the Hispanic American culture to speak English has also contributed to Hispanic Americans' employment problems; in all likelihood, their ability and reluctance to speak English has also hindered their acculturation. Some Hispanics do not feel confident in their English-speaking skills and, therefore, seek employment only in Spanish-speaking neighborhoods. Others seek jobs that require only minimal speaking. Some feel frustrated as employers refuse to employ Hispanics with limited English-speaking abilities. Those who are employed often feel that their limited ability to speak English reduces their chances of promotion and career advancement. Regardless of the reasons, lack of communication skills often results in Hispanics being unable to build the social and employment networks needed for economic and social success. Lack of English communication skills also affects many Hispanics' educational opportunities. Although they see the need for education and employment training, their communication skills prohibit them from filling out applications, seeking financial assistance, and actually attending classes.

The communication problem is not only a first-generation problem. Many second- and third-generation Hispanics continue to have difficulty with English. Even younger-generation Hispanic Americans tend to speak Spanish or "Hispanicized English" in the home. Their limited English-language skills have been debilitating and have contributed to increased discrimination and lack of opportunity.

Families

Describing the Hispanic is indeed difficult due to the tremendous diversity among Hispanic groups. Whenever possible, we will refer to specific ethnicities to avoid stereotypes and generalizations.

As for employment, 67% of Hispanics or Latinos 16 and older were in the civilian labor force in 2012; 19.5% of civilian employed Hispanics or Latinos 16 and older worked in management, business, science, and arts occupations in 2012. The percentage is in all likelihood higher now, due to increased educational opportunities, affirmative action, and more demand for native Spanish speakers.

Puerto Ricans

Although cultural differences exist between Puerto Ricans raised in Puerto Rico and those raised in the United States, both groups differ distinctly from the dominant European American culture, and both suffer disadvantages. In addition, one must proceed with caution when describing people's cultural characteristics.

The Puerto Rican family is viewed as the place where people are free to be themselves and where people come for affection and love. The family is also an institution that historically has oppressed women, although acculturation has occurred. Puerto Ricans place value on personalism, another cherished cultural characteristic. Puerto Ricans define their self-worth in terms of qualities that give them self-respect and earn them the respect of others. For example, a man can achieve respect by being able to protect and provide for his family and by being honorable and respectful in his behavior. Focusing on inner qualities allows people to experience self-worth, regardless of worldly success or failure. Respect plays a role in preserving the network of close personal relationships. Respect for authority is first learned in the home and then expands to the outside world. A deep appreciation of family life characterizes Puerto Rican families, regardless of socioeconomic status. Because the family unit is fundamental, individuals tend to evaluate themselves in relation to other members of the family. Another important characteristic is the notion of male superiority, with the male considered to be the unquestioned head of the household. Hispanic women have continued to redefine their roles, just as other cultures have changed gender roles and expectations.

Mexicans

As a group, Mexican Americans typically are proportionately more disadvantaged educationally and socioeconomically compared to their European counterparts; demographically speaking, these characteristics represent a real vulnerability for this group with regard to their mental health status and clearly suggest the need to ensure the presence of available, affordable, and effective health and mental health services for this population. Disadvantages can result from any number of factors, including discrimination, racism, and some Hispanics' ability to speak English. Also, unfortunately, some Mexicans are considered to be illegal immigrants, which in many cases is not true.

In a discussion of Mexican families, regional, generational, and socioeconomic variations make generalizations difficult. The following characteristics for the most part pertain to Mexican Americans of relatively poor and working-class backgrounds who migrated to the United States during the past three or four decades. First, the family includes grandparents, uncles, aunts, and cousins. Children who were orphaned or whose parents divorced may be cared for in the household of a relative. Second, a degree of interdependence characterizes this supportive network. Family functions such as caretaking, disciplining of the children, problem-solving, managing finances, and providing emotional support are shared. Third, the family protects the individual and demands loyalty. Family cohesiveness and respect for parental authority endure throughout an individual's lifetime. Autonomy and individual achievement are not particularly emphasized.

Cubans

The Cuban American population shares many characteristics with Mexican Americans. The family is the most important social unit in Cuban life and is characterized by a bond of loyalty. This bond unites family members as well as a network of friends, neighbors, and community members. As in other Hispanic cultures, the man is the leader and provider of the household. If the man is unable to find work, his self-esteem is damaged, and he may lose the respect of his wife and children. This loss of respect is likely to result in marital difficulties, especially if the wife assumes the role of economic provider. Because of improved relations between the Unites States and Cuba, travel might increase between the countries, which will contribute to the acculturation process.

Unique Challenges Confronting Hispanic American Adults

Regardless of the Hispanic group, professionals need to provide experiences that meet the needs of Hispanic immigrants. Hispanic American adults, who are no longer children or adolescents in developmental transition, have major responsibilities, such as being financial providers. Poverty continues to be a problem among some Hispanic people. Still, hope exists with increased educational opportunities as well as employment opportunities.

Health-care disparities exist for Hispanic Americans. Weinick, Jacobs, Stone, Ortega, and Burstin (2004) report that Hispanic Americans have poorer health status and higher incidences of illnesses such as diabetes, human immunodeficiency infection, and cervical cancer compared with non-Hispanic Whites. Despite this, Hispanics use fewer health-care services and are less likely to have entered the health-care system for any type of care than White non-Hispanic

Americans. Hispanic Americans are often treated as a monolithic ethnic group with a single pattern of health-care utilization. However, there are considerable differences within this population. This health-care disparity requires first understanding (and in fact, challenging) the myth that the Hispanic culture is a monolithic population. Weinick and colleagues (2004) report that Hispanics are less likely to be offered employer-sponsored health insurance, are recent immigrants to the United States, and lack familiarity with health care; they fear being deemed a public charge and face language barriers as a result of a lack of providers who speak their native language.

Case Study 13.3: Felicita, a Hispanic American Adult

Felicita is a 45-year-old Hispanic adult female living in a semirural area of a southeastern state. She works in a textile factory making minimum wage, with few opportunities for overtime. She lives with a Hispanic man who is about 52–53 years old. They are not married, and their arrangement is far more economic than sexual. They found it less financially expensive to live together in a small and cramped mobile home. The man does odd jobs—day laboring sometimes, doing odd jobs in the mobile home park, and cleaning stores and small restaurants. He does not have a serious alcohol problem, but he usually drinks on Friday and Saturday nights. By almost any standards, Felicita qualifies as poor, especially since she (like her live-in partner) does not have any medical insurance.

Felicita was married at one time, but her husband left and she has not seen him since. Stories of his disappearance abounded, but no one really knew what happened to him. In any event, Felicita was not receiving any financial support from him. Felicita had one child that she put up for adoption and another one that she decided to keep. She had not seen him in two to three years and actually did not know where he was living.

Felicita questioned her life and especially her future. What if her "live-in" decided to leave? What would happen if she lost her job? The textile factory was cutting back on some workers' hours. She had an expendable job, but to date, no one had mentioned her dismissal. The lack of medical insurance was another serious problem. Although she was only 45, she had never had a complete physical examination. What if there was a serious medical condition? How long would it be until she had to see a doctor? How would she pay the doctor? Would a doctor even see her without proof of insurance? The working conditions were poor—heat, humidity (to keep threads from breaking), and constant dust. Plus, she thought to herself, "I started smoking when I was 15—now working in bad breathing conditions might . . . , " and then she decided not to think about it right now.

Reflection Questions:

1. It is unlikely that anyone would actually refer Felicita to a counselor, but assume she came to you for counseling intervention. What counseling strategies would you use? How would you avoid stereotypical generalizations? How would you understand her worldviews?
2. Considering her developmental stage (adult and the challenges of the next developmental period), how would you provide developmentally appropriate counseling strategies?

HISPANIC AMERICAN ELDERLY

Social and Cultural Description

The elderly population will probably become even more racially and ethnically diverse in the future. Hispanic elderly will increase to 16% by the middle of 2050 (U.S. Census Bureau, 2014b). People are living longer due to advances in medical care as well as increased access to medical care. The Affordable Care Act will increase the likelihood of living longer as well as maintaining a better quality of life. Despite the growth of a large Hispanic American population, little systematic research has been conducted on elderly Hispanic Americans. Attempts to make generalizations about Cubans in Florida, Puerto Ricans in New York, and Mexicans in California are not likely to result in meaningful conclusions. Significant cultural differences, together with stereotypes about the elderly, frequently lead to misunderstandings; hence, counselors must identify specific subgroups and consider the individual client within this subgroup.

Although the Hispanic American population is concentrated largely in the southwestern states, such as California and Texas, clusters reside in other geographic regions. The various subgroups tend to remain distinct with respect to location. For example, most Hispanic Americans in California and Texas are of Mexican descent, whereas a majority of those living in New York and New Jersey are of Puerto Rican descent.

Lack of education, unemployment, and low income pose problems for a significant segment of the Hispanic American community. Of all the minority elderly populations, Hispanic elderly are the least educated. The proportion without formal schooling is ninefold greater than for elderly European Americans; most Hispanic Americans age 65 and older have little formal education. Not surprisingly, this lack of education has consequences that extend to employment and income. Income levels for elderly Hispanic Americans are dismal. Poverty rates are higher in nonmetropolitan areas than in metropolitan areas, and more Hispanic American women than men experience poverty.

Concern over potential health problems or declining health also characterizes Hispanic American elderly. They tend to have more activity limitations and spend more days per year in bed because of illness than other minority cultures. Common health problems include hypertension (high blood pressure), cancer, high cholesterol levels, diabetes, and arthritis. Shuster, Clough, Higgins, and Klein (2008) analyzed the relationship between health and health behaviors among elderly Hispanic American females. This population is expected to grow faster than any other segment of the population within the United States. Hispanics are at more increased risk for diabetes than non-Hispanic Whites, even with other variables (e.g., obesity, family history, smoking status, and hormone therapy) as well as increased risk of hypertension and related heart disease, alcoholism, and specific cancers. Still, cultural factors (e.g., language, acculturation, and fatalism) did not have a significant effect on disease prevention behaviors. Also, unfortunately, the diet of Hispanic women is higher in fat intake and lower in the daily intake of vitamins, fruits, and vegetables. Although adults age 65 or older make up only 4.6% of the Hispanic population today, their number is expected to grow faster than any other cultures and developmental periods (Shuster et al., 2008).

Hilton and Child (2014) researched spirituality and successful aging of older Hispanics, although they used the term Latinos. They maintained that the United States can expect major changes in the health-care system. The aging U.S. population is becoming far more ethnically diverse. Although ethnic minority groups currently account for one third of the nation's population, they will become the majority by 2042. Latinos are currently the largest and fastest growing ethnic minority group in the United States, and by mid-century they are expected to account for nearly 20% of the 65 and older population.

The aging process is associated with progressive losses that are often linked to depression. However, many older adults are able to maintain an optimistic outlook and a sense of well-being despite these losses. Most of the successful aging research to date has been conducted with Caucasians, at a time when the United States is becoming more racially and ethnically diverse. Latinos are currently the largest and fastest growing ethnic minority group in the United States and will constitute 30% of the population by mid-century.

All counselors, including marriage and family therapists, generally work from a strengths-based and systems perspective that addresses the multiple domains of the whole person. Many professionals also subscribe to the mission of the Association for Spiritual, Ethical, and Religious Values in Counseling (ASERVIC). The Association for Multicultural Counseling and Development offers additional competencies that can help professionals accurately evaluate the spiritual needs of their clients within a multicultural context. Spiritual assessments are an important part of practice, and they need to be tailored so that they are relevant for each minority group (Hilton & Child, 2014).

Faith-based communities can use the information from this study and the literature to help address the overlapping spiritual, religious, and financial needs of older Latinos. Pastoral counseling can help older Latinos find purpose and meaning in the cultural challenges that they face, which will promote their well-being (spiritual component). It is important to recognize that religious community and material support are particularly important to older Latinos compared with other groups (religious component). Catholic priests and nuns are often the most trusted advisers and source of support outside of the Latino family. They play an important role in connecting Latinos to community resources, including support for their physical and emotional health. Finally, it is important to assess and intervene with older Latinos' economic strain (financial component), which puts them at risk for depression. Faith-based organizations are trusted and may be the first line of support sought out by older Latinos. Therefore, partnerships need to be developed between faith-based organizations and other service providers that are less trusted by these older adults, including mental health. Keeping pastoral leaders informed about available services, giving them resource and educational materials in English and Spanish to distribute, and consulting with them about the specific needs of their parishioners would help move the trust that has been established within the church out into the community. The faith-based setting is both comfortable and convenient for older Latinos, who also may have transportation issues (Hilton & Child, 2014).

Perceptive counselors will avoid stereotypes and other erroneous beliefs about Hispanic Americans. First, sometimes, professionals and laypeople believe that the Hispanic elderly are surrounded by extended family members. In reality, although significant numbers of Hispanic Americans live with families, familial changes have resulted from increased acculturation rates, education, and upward mobility. Such factors result in Mexican American elderly feeling alone and abandoned. Second, we sometimes assume Hispanics hold a reverence for elderly people, so in old age they take on crucial roles in their family and community systems. Traditionally, the elderly have been given special status for their experience and wisdom. Yet family structures have changed as generations have acculturated; support and respect for the elderly have declined. Third, one should not assume Hispanics keep the elderly at home rather than using a nursing home. Acculturation and the need for more than one job often cause adult children to see the need to place elderly family members in nursing homes. The important point to remember is that elderly Hispanic clients need to be considered as individuals to avoid counseling intervention based on false premises.

Communication

The low academic attainment and low socioeconomic conditions of elderly Hispanic Americans are caused, at least in part, by communication difficulties. The elderly often speak little or no English. In fact, many older Hispanic Americans do not seek government benefits because of their inability to communicate in English. They feel frustrated and overwhelmed when they have to speak and write in English. Some take a bilingual person to help them with the application requirements.

To avoid communication problems, some elderly Hispanics tend to live in Spanish-speaking neighborhoods in which English is rarely spoken, which interferes with their acculturation. The convenience of being able to communicate in one's native language also undermines serious efforts toward learning to speak more fluent English. The growing numbers of newspapers and radio and television stations that are geared specifically toward Hispanic American audiences contribute to the problem.

Families

The importance of family kinship networks among Hispanic Americans can be seen in their effort to provide for the elderly in their own homes. Although we think most Hispanic elders would prefer to remain with the immediate or extended family, recent familial attitudes and acculturation have resulted in an increasing trend toward placing elderly family members in nursing homes. Respect for immediate and extended family members is an old tradition in the Hispanic culture. While some acculturation has occurred in younger Hispanic generations, many older Hispanics cherish the older worldviews and are more unwilling to change. Still, counselors of the Hispanic elderly will need to understand the individual client.

In short, Hispanic American customs and practices include a respect for the elderly and a concern for their welfare. Keeping the elderly in the home, or at least in the immediate community so that younger generations can provide care, appears to be the current norm. It may be safely assumed, however, that younger generations will continue to lean toward stronger immediate families, which may leave the elderly in an increasingly precarious situation. Although this trend is not yet firmly established, it is quite possible that Hispanic American clients will increasingly bring such familial problems to counseling sessions.

Case Study 13.4: Geo, a Hispanic American Male Elder

Geo is a 74-year-old Hispanic male who feels "old," as he describes himself to his friends and family. He lives alone in a modest one-bedroom house in a Southern city. His wife died eight years previously. He is a devout Catholic and maintains as much of his Hispanic culture as he can. Geo prays every day and attends church on a regular basis. He has been in the United States since the mid-1970s, so his English is good, but not excellent because he chose (or felt the need) to live predominantly in Spanish-speaking neighborhoods. He lives off social security, Medicare, and what little money he saved. A proud and independent Hispanic man, he does not feel good about taking money from social security and Medicare, but he does. His house is paid for, so he feels good about that, although it was a financial struggle for his wife and him.

During his working years, he was a master carpenter. Roofing was his specialty, but he could do almost all carpentry jobs except major construction. That would have been a possibility, but he did not have the "upfront money" to finance major construction jobs.

Geo meets with several friends almost every afternoon for cards and conversation. He is physically mobile and talks about the "old days" with his friends.

Geo appears to be a 74-year-old man without problems, but he has concerns: He misses his wife; he wonders what will happen if he runs out money; why are medical copayments increasing; and what if he can no longer live alone?

Geo has three children, but they do not live nearby. In any case, he would never ask to live with them or ask them for financial assistance. All three moved from the predominantly Spanish-speaking enclaves to better their economic and social status in life. Geo understood their motives, but that did not mean he missed them any less.

Reflection Questions:

1. Assume Geo was referred to you, and he confided, "I really miss my wife. We were married for nearly 50 years. What will happen if I can no longer live alone?" With your understanding of the developmental period and the Hispanic culture, what counseling strategies would you use?
2. What would you do to understand Geo's worldviews of being 74, living alone, his powerful religious beliefs, and his Hispanic culture?

Unique Challenges Confronting Hispanic American Elderly

Mental health providers, regardless of their cultural background, will be challenged to understand some Hispanics' attitudes toward the healing professions. Three widespread ethnomedical systems are found among Hispanics in the United States—*Espiritismo* (spiritualism), Santería, and *Curanderismo*. These beliefs and practices derived from separate neocolonial histories. *Espiritismo* (or spiritualism) is from a conjunction of European (French) and Afro-Caribbean traditions, and Santería is from a conjunction of folk Catholicism and West African traditions. *Curandero* literally means "healer." Stemming from the verb *curar* (to heal), *curanderos (as)* are recognized by Mexican Americans as having the special ability to heal. *Curanderismo* is a medical system, a view of healing with historical roots that combine Aztec, Spanish, spiritualistic, homeopathic, and scientific elements. Confusion often exists about the role of *curanderos (as)*, because these folk healers provide a wide range of services to their communities, and these services vary from region to region across the United States (Koss-Chioino, 2000).

Although Hispanic American elderly have undoubtedly experienced economic, personal, and social progress, considerable hurdles remain: illiteracy, unemployment, malnutrition, language, poverty, and discrimination. The following five specific areas need immediate attention:

1. Raising educational and income levels and decreasing the incidence of malnutrition.
2. Increasing understanding of the role of the elderly in the family.
3. Encouraging proficiency in English to allow the elderly to move out of Spanish-speaking enclaves.
4. Directing attention to problems of the elderly and ridding the elderly of their stereotypical image.
5. Improving the general health status of the elderly, which will contribute to their overall well-being.

The extent to which the Hispanic American elderly improve their lives will depend largely on the effort they put forth to raise their economic status and to improve their ability to speak English. Counselors working with elderly Hispanic Americans can contribute significantly to these efforts by understanding both the culture and the elderly period of the lifespan. Although challenges to both Hispanic Americans and counselors can be formidable, the future might reflect a genuine concern for the minority elderly and set the stage for long-overdue changes and accomplishments.

SUMMARY

The rapidly increasing Hispanic American population and their many problems (e.g., lack of English-language skills, low educational attainment, unemployment, poverty, discrimination) suggest that counselors, especially those living in states with significant Hispanic populations, will be called on to provide culturally and lifespan-appropriate counseling intervention. Successful counseling, although not easy, is attainable. Counselors will need to prepare themselves professionally and personally to understand the diverse Hispanic cultures and heritages and to provide intervention that reflects these differences. The rewards of understanding Hispanic cultures and being able to provide effective intervention will be worth the time and effort expended.

SUGGESTED READINGS

Gray, M.M. (2015). Your average American Catholic. *America, 212*(17), 16–19. The article discusses the demographics of U.S. Roman Catholics and explores topics such as the experiences of parish life by Catholics in relation to Mass attendance and church growth or decline, the religious identifications of former Catholics, and generational differences among U.S. Catholics.

Hill, G., & Downing, A. (2015). Effect of frequent peer-monitored testing and personal goal setting on Fitnessgram scores of Hispanic middle school students. *Physical Educator, 72*(2), 193–205. The purpose of this study was to determine the effects of frequent peer-monitored Fitnessgram testing, with student goal setting on push-up performance of 83.7% Hispanic middle school students.

Jacobson, L. (2015). The Hispanic dynamic. *State Legislatures, 41*(6), 16–20. This article discusses the growth of Latino population in the United States and their potential impact on politics and policy. Topics discussed include the top-ten fastest growing Hispanic states as of 2011, including Alabama, North Carolina, and Georgia; the gains made by Latinos in the nation's state legislatures in the November 2014 elections, including 73 serving in state senates and 229 in lower chambers; and issues of common concern for Latinos, including good schools and equal opportunity.

Méndez, L.I., Crais, E.R., Castro, D.C., & Kainz, K. (2015). A culturally and linguistically responsive vocabulary approach for young Latino dual language learners. *Journal of Speech, Language & Hearing Research, 58*(1), 93–106. This study examined the role of the language of vocabulary instruction in promoting English vocabulary in preschool Latino dual language learners (DLLs).

Parrinelio, C.M., Isasi, C.R. Xiaonan X., Bandiera, F.C., Jianwen C., Ji-Hyun L., David J., Navas-Nacher, E.L., Perreira, K.M., Salgado, H., & Kaplan, R.C. (2015). Risk of cigarette smoking initiation during adolescence among US-born and non-US-born Hispanics/Latinos: The Hispanic community health study of Latinos. *American Journal of Public Health, 105*(6), 1230–1236. These researchers assessed the risk of cigarette smoking among Hispanics/Latinos by gender and their age of migration to the United States.

Rhodes, S.D., Mann, L., Simán, F.M., Eunyoung S., Alonzo, J., Downs, M., Lawlor, E., Martinez, O., Sun, C.J., O'Brien, M.C., Reboussin, B.A., & Hall, M.A. (2015). The impact of local immigration enforcement policies on the health of immigrant Hispanics/Latinos in the United States. *American Journal of Public Health, 105*(2), 329–337. These authors sought to understand how local immigration enforcement policies affect the utilization of health services among immigrant Hispanics/Latinos and found fear of immigration enforcement policies and concluded interventions are needed to increase immigrant Hispanics/Latinos' understanding of their rights and eligibility to utilize health services.

Stambaugh, T., & Ford, D.Y. (2015). Microaggressions, multiculturalism, and gifted individuals who are Black, Hispanic, or low income. *Journal of Counseling and Development, 93*(2), 192–201. The authors hypothesize that gifted individuals are subject to microaggressions based on their unique characteristics (e.g., when gifted individuals are also Black, Hispanic, or low income). Research from the field of gifted education is combined with the counseling and psychology literature to explore the common assumptions that may lead to microaggressions.

14 Counseling Hispanic American Clients

QUESTIONS TO BE EXPLORED

- What unique challenges can counselors expect when intervening with Hispanic American children, adolescents, adults, and elders?
- How can non-Hispanic counselors effectively plan counseling intervention for Hispanic American clients, considering their diverse cultural and individual differences?
- How has a history of discrimination and injustice affected Hispanic Americans and their worldviews?
- How can counselors address Hispanic Americans' tendency to underuse counseling services?
- How can counselors conduct individual, group, and family therapy for Hispanic Americans?
- What concerns and problems related to development might Hispanic American child, adolescent, adult, and elderly clients present to counselors?
- How can counselors of differing cultural backgrounds and lifespan stages intervene with Hispanic Americans of other lifespan stages?
- What additional sources provide information for professionals intervening with Hispanic American children, adolescents, adults, and elders?

OVERVIEW

As discussed in Chapter 13, the rapidly increasing Hispanic economically disadvantaged status suggests that counselors will be called on to provide professional intervention with this group of people. Also, as emphasized in Chapter 13, counselors, social workers, and other professionals should use considerable caution when describing Hispanic Americans. This culture is composed of many diverse groups with historical, economic, social, individual, communication, generational status, rural/urban status, social class level, and sexual orientation differences. The likelihood of counselors intervening with Hispanic American children, adolescents, adults, and elders is increasing. Effective counseling will require an understanding of Hispanic American clients; their respective developmental period; and how cherished cultural beliefs such as *machismo, respeto, familismo, curerismo*, personalism, and *dignidad* will influence individual, group, and family therapy.

Counselors will need to understand cultural concepts such as *machismo, respeto*, and *familismo* from a Hispanic perspective and how these cherished concepts affect these clients' daily lives and counseling outcomes. As with other cultures, counselors, regardless of their cultural backgrounds, have a responsibility to understand and counsel from the Hispanic client's worldview. The Hispanic American community is diverse with respect to almost every conceivable domain, including education level, income, family structure, length of residence in the United States, maintenance of traditional gender roles and cultural values, and occupation. Stereotypes, however, have led to misconceptions about what it means to be Hispanic in terms of behaviors, attitudes, and position in society.

Another difference counselors will have to address is that many Hispanic Americans continue to show an allegiance to the Spanish language. Hispanic Americans may hold on to their native language because they expect to return to their native lands, live in Spanish-speaking enclaves, or lack the educational opportunities to learn English. Regardless of the reason, counselors likely will encounter clients with limited English-speaking abilities. More will be said about this reality in the counseling sections.

HISPANIC AMERICAN CHILDREN

Potential Problems Warranting Counseling Intervention

Problems that Hispanic American children may experience include

- failure to develop a strong cultural identity and a positive self-concept;
- adverse effects of stereotypes;
- distrust of and hostility toward European American professionals;
- conflicts between use of "home language" and "school language," as well as the child's belief that speaking English is disloyal to the "native tongue";
- inability to reconcile loyalties to conflicting values of Hispanic and European American cultures;
- different cultural expectations; for example, rigid gender roles—boys are "manly" and girls are "retiring and reserved";
- adverse effects of racism, injustice, and discrimination;
- physical, psychosocial, and intellectual differences;
- socialization to a peer-centered world;
- delayed psychosocial development if peers consider Hispanic American children inferior or troublemakers;
- lack of personal resources caused by widespread low socioeconomic status; and
- reconciling family loyalties with individual desires during a time of transition from a parent-centered world to a peer-centered world.

The last two decades have witnessed enormous growth in the Latino student population. The Hispanic school dropout rate is larger than that of White and twice as large as that of African American students. This is especially true of Mexican American students, who constitute the majority of the Hispanic student population. Several factors might contribute to the higher dropout rates: perceived or actual discrimination, language problems, and poverty, just to name a few. Students who perceived poor-quality school environments had lower grades and were most likely to be generally unsuccessful in school. Undoubtedly, as Maxwell (2014) stated, the U.S. school system must vastly improve the educational experiences of Hispanic learners—the same holds true for counselors. Counselors have a responsibility to understand the Hispanic ethnicity and culture as well as the challenges these students (certainly not all) face.

Brown and Chu (2012) examined ethnic identity and academic outcomes of Mexican immigrant children living in a predominantly European American community. The study also included schools' promotion of multiculturalism and teachers' attitudes about the value of diversity in predicting immigrant youths' attitudes and experiences. Although little research has examined perceptions of community discrimination, Brown and Chu believe Hispanic (Brown and Chu use the term Latino) adolescents perceive discrimination by teachers and peers; these experiences are often based on language or immigration status. For example, first and second-generation Latino immigrant students state that teachers have low expectations of them, often assuming their English is poor; report having hostile encounters with teachers who stereotype them as troublemakers; and report being treated as invisible by the teachers.

Brown and Chu (2012) found school and teacher characteristics were important in predicting children's perceptions of discrimination and ethnic identity. Children at schools with more Latino students perceived more peer, teacher, and community discrimination than children at schools with fewer Latino students. As the ethnic minority population approaches 50% and ethnic groups are evenly mixed, perceptions of discrimination have been shown to peak. Consistent with these findings, in the current sample, the children who perceived the most discrimination attended a school consisting of 59% Latino students. In addition, teachers who value diverse classrooms, and consider them an opportunity for enrichment rather than a burden, had immigrant students with more positive ethnic identities. In contrast to teachers who ignore cultural differences, teachers who value diversity create environments in which cultural backgrounds can be freely discussed. These teachers fostered students feeling positively about their ethnic group. These teachers had students who also perceived less peer discrimination, perhaps by setting a classroom norm in which teasing and exclusion on the basis of ethnicity was not acceptable. Further, among schools that valued multiculturalism and diversity, children perceived less community discrimination as their teachers more highly valued diversity (Brown & Chu, 2012).

Although Brown and Chu (2012) focused primary attention on teachers, the same conclusions hold true for counselors. Counselors who value multiculturalism, create diverse environments, and emphasize positive feelings about the individual culture are far more likely to provide successful intervention.

Counseling Considerations

Counseling Hispanic American children requires knowledge of individual Hispanic cultures whenever possible. Although Hispanic Americans are often considered a single cultural group because of their similarities in language, values, and traditions, the Hispanic American culture represents many heterogeneous subcultures, each possessing unique traits. Counselors of Hispanic American children should understand that these children have been taught to distrust European American professionals. This distrust can result in children being hesitant to disclose personal information.

When counseling Hispanic American children, counselors should understand

- their own cultural backgrounds, beliefs, values, and assumptions;
- Hispanic Americans' cultural backgrounds as well as their historical and contemporary contributions;
- problems that Hispanic American children face and how individual children may be helped;
- difficulties Spanish-speaking children may encounter in bilingual settings as well as their nonverbal mannerisms (e.g., preference for standing close);
- children's cognitive and psychosocial development;
- the importance of both immediate and extended families; and
- intricate relationships between culture and counseling and the role culture plays in counseling intervention.

Hojman (2014) maintains that language barriers limit the counselor's effectiveness and rapport.

Hojman explains that one out of five children younger than 18 are Hispanic. By 2051, the Hispanic children's population will be 25%. Hojman (2014) explains the impact of sociocultural factors, race, and ethnicity in health and clinical care. Effects of language barriers on Hispanic youth as a group are at a higher risk for depression, suicidal ideation, violence, academic underachievement, and dropping out of high school compared with the non-Hispanic. Hispanic children who require mental health services compose about 3% of the child population;

this could be approximately equal to half of all American children who suffer from ADHD. This group of children is at high risk and underserved.

Hojman (2014) also explains significant disparities among children in welfare as well as in the juvenile justice system. More than 50% of children and youth in the child welfare system are African American, Latino, and American Indian, and more than 65% of the children and youth in the juvenile justice system are African American and Latino. The lack of Spanish-language skills from a clinician can even prolong Latino children's social welfare and cause court system conundrums because of the lack of communication within their native language as well as the lack of Latino cultural knowledge. The current health-care system does not properly focus on the needs of a culturally diverse population and cultural competence, which would imperatively include the clinician's ability to communicate in the same language of the patients they see. This is often not the reality these days. When minorities seek treatment, they experience significant barriers toward maintaining a consistent level of outpatient care, such as financial needs, location of services and transportation, lack of adequate health insurance, and lack of linguistic support. These barriers generally lead to the premature interruption of services.

Individual and Group Therapy

What should counselors consider when planning intervention for Hispanic American children? Professionals will want to assist these children in coping with changing demands; feeling good about oneself (having a positive self-concept) is important for constructive life choices, helps prevent destructive behaviors, and may lead to higher academic achievement. For example, elementary school counselors are in unique positions to implement interventions that target students' self-concept. Counselors can implement activities as well as peer helper programs that include tutoring and remediation to improve self-concept in minority children as well as majority-culture students (Kenny & McEachern, 2009).

Counselors should consider four counseling priorities when intervening with Hispanic American children: (1) language, communication, and cognitive development; (2) expansion of career choice options; (3) personal respect and pride in the Hispanic culture; and (4) personal value exploration. Although all four factors are keys to the effectiveness of the counseling process, counselors who respect and convey an appreciation for a child's cultural heritage can have a positive impact on children and their developing identities and self-concepts.

Counselors can also take other steps to improve their effectiveness in counseling Hispanic American children. Counselors will find it beneficial to be able to speak both English and Spanish fluently. They should also have firsthand experiences with, and an understanding of, the Spanish culture. Counselors will also find it beneficial to refine their helping characteristics, such as empathy, warmth, positive regard, congruence, and authenticity.

Group therapy has the potential for helping Hispanic American children work toward solving school and home problems. School counselors often perceive group counseling as particularly effective for furthering Hispanic American children's skills in expressing their feelings in English, stimulating self-respect and pride in Hispanic culture, and clarifying personal values.

Family Therapy

Hispanic Americans' powerful allegiance to immediate and extended family suggests that effective family counseling requires including all the children in family therapy, not just the child with the problem. The complex relationships surrounding Hispanic American family members contribute to the effectiveness of family counseling. Unfortunately, it can lead to family counseling being ineffective. Perceptive counselors will understand effective family counseling as well as the nature of Hispanic American family relationships. The cultural concept of *familismo* is so important that Hispanic parents and families teach their children early to sacrifice self-interest to help other family members and the family unit as a whole.

To enhance the effectiveness of family counseling with Hispanic Americans, the counselor should (a) respect the family's hierarchical structure by interviewing the parents first and then the children and by communicating in Spanish with the parents and in English with the children to delineate blurred generational boundaries and (b) recognize that Hispanic Americans learned early to be cooperative in interpersonal relationships.

Case Study 14.1 looks at a counselor's efforts with Ramon, a Hispanic American child.

Case Study 14.1: Counseling Ramon, a Hispanic American Child

Eight-year-old Ramon's teacher referred him to the European American school counselor because of her concern for Ramon's academic achievement, communication problems, and self-concept. "I don't know what to do with Ramon," Mr. Perkins complained. "I encourage him, yet he just doesn't seem interested." After reading the referral sheet and speaking with Ramon, the counselor concluded that the child did have problems: low socioeconomic status, poor grades, weak self-concept, and communication difficulties. In addition, Ramon gave every indication of not trusting the counselor or the teacher.

The counselor, realizing he had to begin slowly, encouraged Ramon to speak with and trust him. In early sessions, the counselor chose to emphasize Ramon and his cultural background: his family, his language, and his life. Ramon hesitatingly began to trust and to speak—much to the counselor's surprise—in mixed English and Spanish. The counselor learned that Ramon came from a traditional Puerto Rican family and that Spanish was spoken in the home. The counselor also saw evidence of Ramon's reading difficulties and behavior problems.

The counselor decided that he had to work to improve Ramon's self-concept and arrange appropriate English instruction and remedial tutoring to help him catch up academically. The counselor recognized that he would have to proceed cautiously to convince Ramon he could still maintain his cultural identity and respect without getting into fights with other children. Finally, the counselor decided to arrange a conference with Ramon's parents, who might be able to help the boy if they knew exactly what to do. Although little could be done about Spanish being spoken in the home, the counselor would explain to the parents the conflict that Ramon experienced because of the dual language situation.

Counseling and Development 14.1: The Childhood Years

Angel, a ten-year-old Hispanic American girl, feels no one likes her in her new school. She and her parents recently relocated from a predominantly Hispanic neighborhood to a more predominantly European American area. At first, she was excited about the change. Angel appears lonely—low self-esteem, few friends, the boys make fun of her clumsy actions during physical education, and her grades had fallen slightly. Angel had not shared her perceived difficulties with her parents. When the teacher saw Angel alone and crying, she asked the guidance counselor (a 40-year-old African American) to meet with her.

The counselor was trained in counseling and children's development and quickly recognized several potential challenges: declining self-esteem, lack of friends, being laughed at during physical education, her maturing body, feelings of loneliness, and decline in academic achievement.

Counseling Strategies:

1. Focus on self-esteem issues by helping Angel realize her strengths, abilities, and her Hispanic culture.
2. Ask Angel what traits she valued in friends and who in the class might "fit that description."
3. Explain to Angel that her clumsy physical movements resulted from her maturing bones and muscles.
4. Focus on individual therapy and possibly small group, since Angel did not want her parents to know.

HISPANIC AMERICAN ADOLESCENTS

Potential Problems Warranting Counseling Intervention

Problems that Hispanic American adolescents may experience include

- failure to develop a positive Hispanic American identity and a healthy self-concept;
- commitment to such cultural values as *machismo, familismo, dignidad,* and *respeto,* which other cultures may misunderstand or reject;
- conflicts between other cultural expectations for "self-advancement" and the adolescent's commitment to family over self;
- failure to comply with traditional Hispanic family expectations: strict family roles, innate superiority of males, women assuming subordinate roles;
- academic problems;
- communication problems: reluctance to give up Spanish as the primary language, and to move out of a Spanish-speaking enclave;
- developmental differences (e.g., height, weight);
- adverse effects of racism and discrimination; and
- media stereotypes, such as being gang members and participating in gang-like behavior.

According to Zayas, Kaplan, Turner, Romano, and Gonzalez-Ramos (2000), mental health clinicians in inner-city mental health centers serving high concentrations of Hispanic American residents have observed that many of the adolescent Hispanic American females are referred after suicide attempts. While this article is 15–16 years old, it is still an important topic—counselors should be aware of any suicidal feelings Hispanic clients might harbor. The incidence of suicide attempts in adolescent Hispanic females is 21%, compared with 10.8% and 10.4% in African American and non-Hispanic adolescents, respectively. Also, adolescent Hispanic American girls are twice as likely as their African American and non-Hispanic American counterparts to have made suicide attempts requiring medical attention. On the bright side, the researchers report that the vast majority (80%) of adolescent Hispanic females do not attempt suicide. Zayas and colleagues propose an integrative counseling model that includes sociocultural, familial, psychological, and developmental domains. They discuss these domains in detail and explain how each appears to interact in the suicide attempts of Hispanic adolescent girls. One other point is worthy of mention. According to the authors, the research implies that adolescent Hispanic American girls who have attempted suicide may live in nuclear families that have less contact with extended families than do adolescents who do not attempt suicide. Having aunts, uncles, cousins, and others who can provide support, mentoring, and modeling to adolescent Hispanic girls may help prevent suicide attempts. Again, acculturation might have changed these findings, but suicide is sufficiently serious for counselors to reexamine the topic.

Agronick and colleagues (2004) reported the challenge of young Latino men being HIV positive or having AIDS. One factor that plays a role in sexual behaviors is the prevalence of bisexuality (a topic addressed in more detail in Chapter 15). Although correct estimates are difficult to determine, Agronick and colleagues (2004) believe that approximately 20% of men who have sex with men are bisexual. For bisexual and gay Latino men, the developmental passage may be complicated by strong sanctions against homosexuality that are supported by cultural norms stressing the importance of maintaining family and cultural connections. In fact, the strong value placed on family and religion might dictate a concealment of gay identity to protect the family from hurt or stigma.

Agronick and colleagues (2004) maintain that reaching bisexual men can be challenging. Some Latino men who have sex with men may not recognize themselves in HIV prevention programs primarily targeting gay-identified men and/or men of other cultural backgrounds. It will be important to develop media campaigns that specifically target the patterns of risky behaviors of bisexual men and crucial to increase public service announcements featuring Latino men who engage in homosexual behavior. Prevention campaigns have the potential to reduce the rate of HIV infections and transmission among Latino men and their partners, members of communities that currently carry a disproportionately large burden of the AIDS epidemic.

Stambaugh and Ford (2015) hypothesize that gifted individuals are subject to microaggressions based on their unique characteristics. They defined microaggressions as when gifted individuals are also Black, Hispanic, or low income. Ongoing exposure to microaggressions leads to negative emotional and physical stress responses, depression, physical and mental strain, higher dropout rates, and avoidance of more difficult course work or careers. Given these understandings, Stambaugh and Ford (2015) propose the following:

1. Gifted students are subject to microaggressions by the nature of their unique characteristics.
2. Students who are gifted and culturally different or poor are at even greater risk for encountering microaggressions and the consequences associated with these microaggressions compared with their White or affluent counterparts.
3. The more categories an individual subscribes to (e.g., gifted, Black, Hispanic, poor), the more difficult the therapeutic alliance if the counselor ignores or misunderstands any facet. Giftedness cannot be removed from the child any more than his or her race/ethnicity or background can be removed. All facets must be considered in a holistic way.
4. Counselors must be aware of their own assumptions and biases related to gifted students, including those who are culturally different or poor.
5. Counselors must be aware of cultural and learning differences of students who are gifted and culturally diverse so that they can incorporate effective strategies within the counseling relationship (Stambaugh, & Ford, 2015).

Counseling Considerations

Counselors need to understand the challenges facing adolescent Hispanic Americans. The Hispanic American male must eventually find gainful employment in a society where Hispanic American rates of unemployment and poverty run high and where limited educational attainment prevents them from competing in the job market. The Hispanic American female probably will witness such social changes as greater equality among the genders and more women in the workforce, perhaps at higher salaries than often poorly educated Hispanic American men.

The diversity in Hispanic American cultural characteristics complicates a discussion of generic counseling strategies. Thus counselors should seek knowledge of the specific population with which they expect to interact. When planning counseling intervention, counselors and psychotherapists need to remember that Hispanic American adolescents typically do not seek services themselves. Instead, they usually are referred by social service agencies. Also, parents who want counseling services for their adolescent might face considerable challenges: family embarrassment, communication problems, cultural differences, and the lack of health insurance.

Gloria and Rodriguez (2000), writing specifically about counseling Latino students in university counseling centers (UCCs), maintain that UCC service providers should assess university environment, ethnic identity, acculturation, social support, and other psychosocial issues when providing counseling services and promoting academic persistence with Latino students. Scales and surveys should be identified to measure perceptions of the cultural environment, ethnic loyalty and cultural awareness, ethnic identity, acculturation, acculturative stress, and social support. Beginning the counseling relationship with a paper-and-pencil test might not be the most productive approach and, in fact, might lessen trust with some students. This is particularly true with Latinos, because many value personalism (Gloria & Rodriguez, 2000).

According to Gloria and Rodriguez (2000), asking clients questions such as the following might provide the necessary information when attending to psychosocial issues:

- How do you identify yourself (e.g., Latino, Chicano, Mexican American)?
- What does being Latino (or other self-identifier) mean to you?
- How difficult has it been for you to maintain your cultural values, beliefs, and behaviors on campus?
- What is your primary language?
- Who do you hang out with on campus?
- What holidays and traditions do you and your family celebrate?
- As a Latino (or other identifier), what struggles and challenges have you encountered on campus?
- What expectations does your family have of you?
- Who have you sought help from on campus?
- Who do you seek help from in your home environment?
- If you were at home, how would you resolve these issues?

We also believe acculturated Mexican Americans are less likely than acculturated European Americans to receive mental health services. Less acculturated Mexican Americans tend to perceive psychiatric symptoms as physical problems rather than as emotional or mental problems. A wealth of factors can influence the decision to seek counseling intervention: immigration status, social class, health insurance, and the risk of embarrassment. When formulating counseling programs, effective counselors should understand several aspects of the Hispanic culture that influence counseling effectiveness. First, family structure and gender roles are important counseling considerations. For example, the extended family structure characteristically includes formalized kinship relations and loyalty to the family, which takes precedence over loyalty to others.

Perceptive counselors also see a possible discrepancy between client expectations and counselor expectations during the counseling process. Counselors can explore these expectations to determine client expectations. Generally speaking (and one must use extreme caution with these determinations), European American students expect counselors to be less directive and protective than did Chinese American, Iranian American, and African American students, who expect the counselor to be a more directive and nurturing authority figure. In addition, African Americans have lower expectations of personal commitment to the counseling process compared with their European American counterparts. Again, caution is urged—acculturation occurs, and individuals vary tremendously within cultures.

For the most effective counseling intervention, professionals working with Hispanic American adolescents should listen carefully and offer feedback to the clients, identify and label potential problems, raise the clients' expectations for change, and describe the attitudes and feelings of clients according to their cultural perceptions.

Individual and Group Therapy

The decision whether to use individual or group therapy must be reached with a solid understanding of the culture, the individual, and the advantages and disadvantages of each counseling modality. School counselors working with Hispanic American students sometimes find group counseling to be effective for developing students' skills in expressing their feelings in English, for stimulating self-respect and pride in the Hispanic culture, and for clarifying personal values.

The knowledge, attitudes, and skills of the group therapist have a significant effect on the outcome and effectiveness of group counseling. Effective group therapists intervening with adolescents demonstrate:

- understanding of the adolescent development period and the possibility of a sense of double jeopardy, being both adolescent and Hispanic;
- culturally appropriate expressions of nurturing, warmth, caring, acceptance, and openness;
- ability to engage clients in either English or Spanish, including appropriate self-disclosure when opportunities arise;
- genuine acceptance of cultural heritages expressed in language and communication, clothing, and knowledge of cultural events; and
- skills to develop and facilitate a sense of community within the group.

Other effective group therapy techniques include teaching listening skills, focusing on feelings, and reinforcing group members' interactions. Some group counselors begin with individual adolescents and then progress to group therapy after establishing rapport and trust.

Family Therapy

Family therapy offers particular promise with Hispanic Americans because of the high value placed on immediate and extended family relationships, unity, welfare, and honor. Many Hispanic Americans place major emphasis on the group rather than on the individual, which translates into a deep sense of family commitment, obligation, and responsibility. A family expectation holds that when a person experiences problems, others (often both immediate and extended family members) will offer assistance, advice, and consolation.

Issues brought to family therapy sessions might include conflicts caused by adolescents feeling torn between two worlds. Some adolescents, especially girls, might be caught between the worlds of peers and families; they have spent their childhood in the United States and have learned some cultural rules of other societies, but at home they continue to be expected to behave according to the cultural traditions of the family. Such situations, however, fluctuate with generational status, acculturation, and socioeconomic status.

Counselors provide information on group dynamics, and family members actually try to help one another solve their problems. The counselor then meets separately with each family member in an attempt to improve communication skills for use in the group sessions and in private life. The family can be included in therapy in several ways. Counselors may choose to work with the whole family directly or request specific family members to attend counseling sessions. Or the counselor may work with one family member, who in turn works with the family as a group.

Counselors should work with both the Hispanic American youth and the family in counseling. If such an arrangement is not possible, the counselor should at least meet with the family at some point. Because Hispanic Americans generally think the family can provide the greatest assistance, involving as many members as possible may result in a cooperative effort to help the client. By involving the family, the counselor also demonstrates awareness that the family can play a therapeutic role and that each person has something to offer.

When working with Puerto Rican adolescents, in particular, suggestions for counselors include

- using active, concrete, and specific counseling approaches;
- developing an awareness of the Puerto Rican culture and the adolescent developmental period;
- examining prejudices and attitudes toward Puerto Ricans;
- making home visits if possible and making reference to the family during sessions; and
- calling clients by their correct names.

Case Study 14.2 looks at a counselor's efforts with Carlos, a Hispanic American adolescent.

Case Study 14.2: Counseling Carlos, a Hispanic American Adolescent

Carlos, age 16, spoke in both English and Spanish as he told his 45-year-old European American counselor what had happened: Police had referred him to the counseling organization that worked with delinquent adolescents. Not having had any previous conflicts with the law, Carlos had been picked up with several other boys who had broken into a vacant store and done several hundred dollars' worth of damage. Carlos's parents had been notified, and his father and older married brother had come to the police station. Carlos further explained that he had been released because he had not actually taken part in the crime and because his father had agreed that Carlos would meet with the counselor.

During his first session, Carlos was cooperative. He discussed his academic problems, his poor self-concept, and his lack of European American friends. Although the counselor insisted that Carlos accept responsibility for his actions, he did believe that Carlos's friends were to blame for his encounter with the police.

In determining counseling priorities, the counselor decided to meet with Carlos on an individual basis for several sessions and then, if Carlos continued to disclose information, switch to group sessions with other Puerto Rican adolescents with similar problems. The counselor's first priorities were to help Carlos to better understand his culture, work to improve Carlos's self-concept, and help him understand his Hispanic identity. As secondary priorities, the counselor would attempt to convince Carlos to accept responsibility for his schoolwork and for selecting more appropriate friends.

Counseling and Development 14.2: The Adolescent Years

Julio, a 16-year-old Hispanic American boy, lives in a predominantly Spanish-speaking neighborhood. He attends a high school where he excels at academics. He is a "model student": He reads constantly, dresses well, and refuses all gang activities. He is well behaved and well spoken in English and Spanish. His problem: He lacks friends. Some students laugh at him (and bully him) for being a "good" student. Julio is proud of his accomplishments, but he would like to have some friends or someone he can call a best friend. The teacher knows Julio is being bullied and wrote a counseling referral.

The counselor could empathize with Julio's plight: being 16 years old without friends or social networks, being bullied, and having high expectations for himself when others did not. How long could he have a positive self-esteem under such conditions?

Counseling Strategies:

1. Work with the entire class about the effects of bullying (without mentioning Julio's name).
2. Form a small counseling group of excellent students to provide an outlet to share concerns and frustrations.
3. Mention to the teacher the possibility of small-group work where Julio can have someone with whom to communicate.

HISPANIC AMERICAN ADULTS

Potential Problems Warranting Counseling Intervention

Problems that Hispanic American adults may experience include

- conflicts caused by changing women's roles as women seek to change traditional roles to gain greater equality;
- negative effects of stereotypes that Hispanics are hot blooded, fighters, and drug dealers or gang members;
- the belief that all Hispanic adults, regardless of geographic origin, have the same cultural characteristics;
- commitment to long-held traditions of *respeto, familismo, machismo,* and *dignidad,* which may slow the acculturation process;
- language problems and communication barriers;
- differing cultural characteristics: allegiance to immediate and extended families, large families, patriarchal families, rigidly defined gender roles (in some cases), and belief in inherent male superiority (in some cases);
- conflicts caused by the changing role of women (e.g., increasing numbers of Hispanic American women working outside the home);
- low socioeconomic status;
- difficulties encountered in achieving equal educational and employment opportunities in European American society;
- problems associated with midlife: meeting tasks and crises, marriage and family problems;
- lack of positive cultural and individual identity and difficulty in successfully meeting psychosocial crises and developmental tasks;
- frustrations caused by maintaining allegiance and commitment to Hispanic traditions while living in a predominantly European American society; and
- stress caused by the realities of the aging process (e.g., loss of stamina, impaired sexual functioning).

Smith, Chesin, and Jeglic (2014) maintain the help-seeking behavior of racial and ethnic minorities should be considered when designing and implementing services for college students. Hispanic individuals, for example, have been found to underuse traditional treatment resources in the United States because of their belief that mental health problems should be addressed by the family or the faith community. Thus, to be effective, outreach efforts and service provisions must consider nontraditional means of engaging students, perhaps through religious and cultural organizations. Smith, Chesin, and Jeglic (2014) also maintain that adolescents were more likely to use mental health services when resources were available at school. Likewise, Spanish-speaking Hispanics were more likely to use community health services, especially when those health centers partnered with faith-based organizations. Meanwhile, to provide culturally competent treatment to racial and ethnic minority college students, college counselors and administrators could borrow and adapt treatments for diverse adolescents and college students. Including sessions on the acculturation process in family therapy for depressed and suicidal Latino teenagers is also recommended. College students may also benefit from such education that allows for a better understanding of their experience and recognition of their struggles within their diverging development. Immigrants and first-generation U.S. college students face unique challenges that might include a lack of guidance and familial support. Predictably, immigrants may be less likely to use mental health services than their U.S.-born peers (Smith et al., 2014).

Counseling Considerations

It is essential for professionals planning counseling intervention to understand that Hispanic Americans underuse counseling services. An ethnomedical system, *curanderismo*, is associated with Puerto Rican Americans, Cuban Americans, and Mexican Americans (Koss-Chioino, 2000). *Curanderos*, often called folk healers, are consulted for many maladies and are trusted the most for folk illnesses with psychological components, such as *susto* (fright), *empacho* (indigestion), and *envidia* (envy) (Falicov, 2005).

As we mentioned in Chapter 1, Graf, Blankenship, Sanchez, and Carlson (2007) wrote about Mexican Americans' attitudes toward disabilities and rehabilitation. Their article focuses on rehabilitation counselors who work with Hispanic American persons who have elected not to assimilate into the mainstream culture. Vocational rehabilitation counselors are likely to encounter adults who are entering the workforce for the first time because of having remained at home with their families. Counselors should be sensitive to the reluctance of family members of an adult entering the workforce. Family members should be invited to participate in initial assessments and planning discussions. In addition, social concerns about making a person with a disability feel bad or not knowing what to say may result in avoidance of the person with the disability. Employers and educators should learn more about disability etiquette as well as ways to interact with the disabled. By doing so, a Mexican American might consider vocational options in lieu of college plans (Graf et al., 2007).

Realistically speaking, many Hispanic American families are not likely to use community mental health services, resulting in unmet psychosocial needs. Problems with language, lack of knowledge of services, and low financial resources limit Hispanics' access to counseling intervention. Such a reluctance to seek mental health counseling might also result from illegal immigration status into the United States. An "illegal" person is unlikely to seek mental health services.

Withrow (2008) suggested implications for practice for early intervention with Latino families. Counselors and early interventionists increasingly serve Spanish-speaking families. Yet, often cultural accommodations merely imply use of interpreters or bilingual providers when professional tasks are much greater. Cultural competence requires self-awareness and understanding of the client's community and worldviews as well as the client's specific risk factors. Withrow (2008) suggested that counselors working with families typically visit families in their homes. Such a practice may feel intrusive to the families, who are often experiencing turbulence and transition during the time the intervention occurs. In these situations, immigrant families face many challenges: linguistic/communication issues, discrimination, and cultural misunderstandings (Smith et al., 2014). Two concerns for mental health counselors are awareness of one's own values and biases as well as understanding the client's worldview. Readers might recall in Chapter 1 that we described how Withrow (2008) believed some Spanish-speaking families thought a disability was an act of God or caused by something they had done wrong. Therefore, in addition to the counselor and family being culturally different, the early interventionist counselor has a professional responsibility to understand the clients' worldviews.

Garza and Watts (2010) suggest that filial therapy provides common ground for intervening with Hispanic families. Typically, family interventions focus on a problem; however, filial therapy focuses on positive behavioral or symptomatic changes that result from a changed parent-child relationship rather than specific problem-focused strategies. Filial therapy is both a therapeutic intervention and a preventive approach. One unique contribution of filial therapy is the recognition that parents typically have more emotional significance to children than does the therapist. Consequently, the objective of filial therapy is to place the parent in the therapeutic role by using the naturally existing bond between parent and child (Garza & Watts, 2010).

Similarly, Mexican Americans have a high rate of withdrawal from counseling. Reasons for withdrawal may include communication barriers, unfamiliarity with the mental health system, and counselor insensitivity. Several reasons might explain Hispanic Americans' underuse of counseling and their high withdrawal rates. First, there are too few counselors from Hispanic backgrounds (although the number is increasing). Second, counselors sometimes fail to offer culturally responsive professional intervention. Third, communication barriers, another reason to underuse or withdraw from therapy, have been effectively addressed by letting the children interpret for the adults. However, counselors should recognize that such an arrangement might put Puerto Rican parents in an inferior, powerless position. Whatever intervention the counselor decides to use, the effort should focus on empowering the client to effect change. Such an intervention focuses on skill building and moves away from "blaming the victim," which the counselor wants to avoid. Counselors, regardless of their cultural backgrounds, will need to examine their own assumptions and biases toward Puerto Ricans as well as other Hispanic groups.

While the Hispanic culture has tremendous diversity, counseling considerations that apply to most Hispanic American groups include the following:

- Because of the counselor's position of authority, family members might consider it impolite or inappropriate to disagree with her or him during the counseling session.
- To maintain a good working relationship with the Hispanic family, especially with the father, the counselor's communicative style should be businesslike and nonconfrontational.
- Hispanics consider the exertion of personal power to be threatening, disrespectful, and Western; hence, it is likely to alienate them.

Guidelines for mental health counselors with Hispanic American clients include:

- understand issues of immigration, acculturation, and bilingualism from Hispanic clients' worldviews;
- develop an understanding of Hispanics' developmental period as well as the complex relationship between development and culture;
- increase the availability of bilingual mental health services and staff, being sure that the mental health staff understands the Hispanic culture; and
- work to build multicultural counseling competencies to provide the most effective professional intervention for all clients.

The counseling relationship will be affected by differing opinions of what constitutes appropriate behavior and differing expectations for the counseling intervention. It is important, therefore, to recognize individual differences and to acknowledge the diversity among Hispanic cultures. We now turn attention to several specific Hispanic American populations and offer counseling suggestions for each.

Latino Americans

The counselor who understands the importance of *personalismo* to Latino American clients will want to greet them warmly, using the client's first name rather than a title. The counselor should employ small talk to build rapport and trust and should understand that because

Latinos perceive psychological problems as physical problems, sessions should be scheduled promptly.

Brazilian Americans

Most Brazilians come to treatment when an acute emotional crisis occurs and support is not available in their immediate network. Nonetheless, psychotherapy or counseling for emotional and family problems is not an alien concept for most middle-class Brazilians, especially younger generations. Compared with other ethnic groups, Brazilians in the United States seem more receptive to the idea of psychotherapy if a personal connection is made with a particular therapist, someone who can relate to them culturally and linguistically. Barriers do exist, however, such as communication barriers, time and financial constraints, and the scarcity of culturally sensitive counselors (Korin, 1996; although this reference might appear too old, it continues to be one of the best on Brazilian Americans).

Mexican Americans

Mexican Americans deserve individual consideration and counseling intervention based on their history and culture. With respect to expectations for counseling, Mexican American clients expect more openness from counselors and prefer more formality from professionals. Also, Mexican Americans favor counseling that deals with present, rather than past, events and psychoanalytic techniques. For effective counseling, counselors who work with Mexican Americans should (a) assume the role of family intermediary who can translate cultural behaviors, justify conduct, encourage compromise and negotiation, and ameliorate imbalances in hierarchies; (b) be flexible with language, allowing the alternation of Spanish and English (if needed); (c) use an emotive tone rather than a structured behavioral or contractual approach; (d) manifest genuine interest, rather than gaining data via referral sheets; and (e) encourage clients to express their reactions, both negative and positive (Falicov, 2005). The following counselor-client dialogue illustrates the client's frustrations in having to deal with several troublesome problems at once:

COUNSELOR: Juan, workers' employment compensation will pay for your lost time, but the health insurance will pay only for the authorized medical treatment that you received for the accident you had at work.

CLIENT: My eyes still don't work so I can see the assembly charts. I get so darn shaky whenever I think about all my money problems, bills, if I can't do the work, what's going to happen to my children. . . .

COUNSELOR: Yeah, I know, it seems like everything is hitting you all at once.

CLIENT: Ha! You know, maybe it sounds crazy or something, but there's this woman in my neighborhood who has some things that she gives me and advises me how to feel better. It really helps.

COUNSELOR: I can't really advise you on what type of treatment you should receive. If it helps and you feel better, why not use it? You're also getting the medical help for your visual problem. You're doing the most you can for yourself at this time.[1]

Another consideration for counselors is Mexican Americans' strong religious beliefs. The following case history attests to the powerful role of religious beliefs:

Jos, a young 35-year-old Spanish-speaking Mexican, came to the clinic complaining of trembling in his hands, sweating, and shortness of breath. He appeared to be a strong and straightforward individual. He stated that his work performance as an upholsterer had been deteriorating for several months. His major conflict focused on his wish to marry his girlfriend and the resulting need to decrease the amount of money he was sending to his parents and younger brothers and sisters in Mexico. He felt he would be committing a crime or a sin if he were to reduce his help to his family. He had sought advice in the mental health clinic because he thought he was going crazy. He had never experienced such sudden onsets of anxiety before. In addition to helping his patient express his feelings and his needs in short-term therapy, the therapist encouraged him to speak to a priest about his fears of committing a sin against his family. Jos did consult with a priest over several meetings and also completed eight sessions of short-term therapy. His anxiety diminished, his work improved, and he decided to propose marriage to his girlfriend when therapy ended.[2]

Sources of stress for Mexican American women include poverty, substandard housing, lower social status, and limited education. Many women struggle for increased equality and a greater range of personal and educational options. In seeking such goals, Mexican American women sometimes find themselves in a double bind: Not only are they treated as subordinate to men, they are considered inferior due to their ethnic group membership. Mexican American women are caught between two worlds—one that tells them to preserve and to abide by traditional customs and another that tells them to conform to the teachings and beliefs of the dominant culture.

Flores, Tschann, Marin, and Pantoja (2004) maintain that, despite the growing literature on Mexican American families and increased research on family relationships, few studies have examined the marital functioning between Mexican American husbands and wives. These researchers investigated the effects of acculturation on marital conflicts among Mexican Americans. They report that as individuals become more acculturated to European American cultural customs and take on more European American values, they may also develop fewer traditional gender role expectations within their marriages, which can be a source of marital conflict. Still, some Mexican American husbands and wives report that they have traditional gender role expectations of themselves and their spouses, even when the power balance is egalitarian. They found that

- more acculturated husbands and wives engaged in less avoidance of conflict and were more expressive of their feelings in an argument;
- husbands and wives who were more acculturated reported more conflict concerning sex and consideration of the other; and
- bicultural and more acculturated husbands reported that their wives were more verbally and physically aggressive, compared with mono-Mexican husbands.

Professionals should (a) identify mental health systems as appropriate sources of help by making personal appearances at meetings and by contacting doctors and clerics, (b) acquaint themselves with the most recent and effective innovations in counseling, and (c) ensure that bilingual informational materials explaining mental health services and how to use them are disseminated.

Puerto Rican Americans

The counseling literature provides several suggestions for planning intervention with Puerto Rican Americans. First, the vast differences between first- and second-generation Puerto Ricans deserve recognition in counseling strategies. Second, Puerto Ricans often have problems with American school systems. Parents initially surrender responsibility for their children to the school system because they think it is a benevolent institution; later, they become suspicious of the schools and are unwilling to cooperate. Third, counselors working with Puerto Rican American clients should understand the Spanish-speaking culture and its attitudes toward the family. Counselors should also be aware that the high incidence of depression in low-income Puerto Rican women has been attributed to cultural factors, such as women's subordinate status.

Individual and Group Therapy

The decision whether to use individual or group counseling may be difficult because of the tremendous diversity among Hispanic American groups. The choice of intervention approach should be based on which therapeutic mode is most beneficial for the individual client and culture. The selected approach should reflect the client's individual needs, socioeconomic status, place of birth, and language spoken.

Integrated groups composed of ethnic and nonethnic members often reflect attitudes and behaviors of the external world and may provide more information and mutual understandings, as well as skills in interacting with each other. In contrast, homogenous groups of ethnic minorities provide the opportunity for more immediate trust and cultural understandings, which can enhance and foster group cohesion. Hispanic Americans may be more comfortable in a homogeneous, Spanish-speaking group if they can speak both Spanish and English without fear of offending non-Spanish speakers.

Family Therapy

Bean, Perry, and Bedell (2001) encourage therapists to understand the diversity among Hispanic Americans—for example, national origin, level of acculturation, length of U.S. residency, social class, and other demographic factors. A definitive set of therapeutic guidelines cannot be applied to every family. Even after accepting this diversity, it is important to initiate a standard for defining and evaluating culturally competent therapy with Hispanic American families. Bean and colleagues (2001) offer the following guidelines for working with Hispanic American families:

- Use family therapy as the preferred treatment modality.
- Be prepared to collaborate with folk healers.
- Act as an advocate for the family with other helping agencies.
- Gather information on the immigration experience.
- Assess for level of acculturation.
- Be bilingual.
- Respect the father or father figure.
- Conduct separate interviews with family subsystems.
- Avoid forcing changes in family relationships.
- Provide the family with concrete suggestions that they can quickly implement.
- Engage the family during the first session with warmth and *personalismo*.

Counselors need to remember that because of the history of discrimination against Hispanic Americans, many clients distrust family therapists of the majority culture. Therapists should define their counseling roles carefully. They should show respect for the Hispanic culture by addressing the father first. Having an interpreter present might be necessary, because older family members may neither speak nor understand English. Counselors who are polite and willing to offer advice can develop rapport and trust and become a part of the family system.

It is important for family therapists to understand that the roles of family members in ethnic minority cultures may vary. For example, in African American families, the roles of husbands and wives tend to be relatively egalitarian, whereas in Hispanic American families, husbands often take a more dominant role. Counselors also need to be sensitive to family structure issues. Again, acculturation occurs and counselors have a professional responsibility to assess individuals in a specific ethnic or cultural group.

The Hispanic American family can be included in counseling in several ways: (a) Ask specific family members to join in the counseling process, (b) work directly with the entire family, or (c) counsel one member of the family as a consultant who then works with the client or other family members.

Most Puerto Rican males do not like to ask for help, because asking for help might threaten their *machismo* (although this Hispanic cultural trait has changed during the past two decades). If a wife wants the therapist to encourage her husband to join her in therapy, the therapist should assess the situation carefully before misinterpreting the request. Puerto Ricans who ask an outsider to intervene usually feel powerless and embarrassed, and they view authority figures as influential. Telling the woman to do the convincing herself may alienate her and result in her withdrawal from therapy. Every effort should be made to include the husband by appealing to his sense of responsibility to his family. Still, the counselor should avoid making the husband feel guilty for not attending counseling.

Studies of Cuban American family therapy suggest several guidelines for the engagement and treatment of Cubans. The counselor or psychotherapist should have family therapy skills, cultural competence, and sensitivity to cultural issues. More specifically, knowledge of the Spanish language is essential, because cultural issues are often best expressed in natural languages. Counselors also need to appreciate the phases of migration and the connectedness to the culture of origin and to evaluate the impact of the stress of migration, value conflicts, and developmental conflicts (Bernal & Shapiro, 2005).

Case Study 14.3 looks at a counselor's efforts with Carla, a Hispanic American adult.

Case Study 14.3: Counseling Carla, a Hispanic American Adult

Carla, age 35, referred herself to a neighborhood mental health organization. Lately she has been experiencing frustrations and stresses: her husband Oscar's job or the lack of one, the money the family has borrowed, Oscar's objection to her getting a job, problems with her son's progress in school, her inability to initiate change as other women can, her feelings of powerlessness, and her desire to put her husband's authority to the test. She has finally concluded that she should get a job and enroll in night school despite her husband's protests. "I want to improve my life," Carla says. "Oscar runs my life; I'm ready for a change."

The counselor, a 34-year-old European American woman, recognized that Carla needed immediate help and that she would be receptive to counseling. The counselor had some degree of multicultural expertise and understood some of the problems affecting contemporary Hispanic Americans. She told Carla that, although as a counselor she had a fairly good knowledge of the Hispanic culture, she still might make mistakes. She encouraged Carla to talk more about herself and what she wanted. She also advised Carla to consider the repercussions of her getting a job and attending school, as opposed to how she might feel if she failed to take action. The counselor decided that she would meet with Carla several times to counsel her as she moved against Oscar's authoritarian demands and that individual therapy would be best for the first few sessions. Afterward, group therapy might be appropriate, because the counselor knew other Hispanic American women in similar situations. Family therapy was not a possibility, because Oscar would stifle Carla's ambitions and monopolize the counseling session.

Counseling and Development 14.3: The Adult Years

Juan, a 49-year-old Hispanic male, works at a carpet mill in a Southern state. Juan has worked there for 31 years. Juan is worried about his family's future, turning 50, financial cutbacks in all manufacturing areas, his four children, and his aging father who lives with him.

Some workers have already been laid off; others, including Juan, have had hours reduced. "What will I do at age 50, if I lose my job?" He balked at the idea of a therapist, but the carpet mill offered counseling for people being laid off or having hours cut. He thought attending counseling might ensure his job.

The Hispanic counselor understood Juan's fears. The counselor considered developmental tasks beginning around 50, fear of the future (e.g., taking care of his family and father), and losing his job at 50. Juan was far from being elderly; he had skills, but he might have difficulty finding a job in a bad job market.

Counseling Strategies:

1. Individual therapy first, then ask whether Juan wants to join a group session with other employees—perhaps family therapy because the wife and father are probably also concerned.
2. Talk with Juan about his family—his concern for his wife, children, and father.
3. Talk with Juan about developmental tasks (or whatever selected term): middle-aged, relationships with families, and possibilities of not being the breadwinner.

HISPANIC AMERICAN ELDERLY

Potential Problems Warranting Counseling Intervention

Problems that Hispanic American elders may experience include

*   inability to overcome stereotypes about the Hispanic culture and about being elderly;
*   double jeopardy—being both Hispanic and elderly;
*   problems associated with urban life: poverty, crime, low socioeconomic status, lack of education, unemployment, low standard of living, or unmet basic needs;
*   illegal immigrant status;
*   health-related problems: chronic ailments, frequent bouts with illnesses, lack of transportation to obtain medical services;
*   developmental problems and psychosocial crises;
*   allegiance to Spanish, hampering improvement in English;
*   the patriarchal nature of the Hispanic American family and the inability to accommodate change; and
*   lack of transportation, financial difficulties, and communication problems that hamper access to health services.

Buki (2005), in a guest editorial for *Clinical Psychology News*, describes the condition of geriatric psychiatric Hispanic patients, aged 65 and older. Buki (2005) offers several descriptive comments:

*   Most know how to read and write in Spanish at a basic level.
*   Most have low rates of both alcohol and substance abuse, and many have stopped nicotine use.
*   Most describe their early years as difficult, largely because they began working at a young age.
*   Some report a history of verbal and physical abuse during years as political prisoners.
*   Most common psychiatric diagnoses include anxiety disorders, social anxiety disorders, depression, and age-related cognitive decline and dementias.

Many patients feel hopeless and have experienced suicidal ideations. Buki (2005) recommends psychological intervention that

- utilizes cognitive restructuring, medication, psychoeducation, support, and psychodynamic interventions;
- practices deep breathing and relaxation training; and
- takes about 25 minutes, because 45 minutes appears to be too long for patients' attention spans.

Counseling Considerations

Counselors confront several obstacles in planning professional intervention for elderly Hispanic American clients. First, the tremendous diversity among Hispanic Americans challenges counselors (especially non-Hispanic counselors) to understand Hispanics' unique cultural and social characteristics. The challenge grows more acute when one considers generational status, levels of acculturation, and socioeconomic differences. Second, questions surrounding the problems and crises of the elderly years further complicate the counseling process, for example, worldviews and economic hardships. Aging, grief from loss, and relationship problems are common and may lead to crises for elderly Hispanics, especially when racism and discrimination have taken a toll on their lives.

Counselors should make every effort to understand what it is like to face the double jeopardy of being both Hispanic American and elderly. Retirement and reduced income are two issues faced by elderly Hispanic Americans, who (a) probably cannot afford to retire and (b) do not have sufficient income to endure a reduction. Coping with these financial difficulties can result in a struggle to maintain one's integrity in times of despair, especially as one ages. Such problematic situations constitute an even greater challenge for the poor and uneducated Hispanic Americans confronted by racism and discrimination. The dismal picture of elderly Hispanic Americans also includes problems usually associated with the elderly lifespan period, such as loss of stamina, changes in physical appearance, and sometimes loss of sensory perceptions.

Professional intervention with Hispanic American elderly requires knowledge of elderly development, an ability to intervene with older clients, and culturally appropriate counseling skills to work with this cultural group. Two basic considerations crucial to the success of counseling elderly Hispanic Americans are (a) understanding what problems and issues might be raised during intervention and (b) understanding what techniques and strategies may enhance the counseling relationship. The following discussion centers on specific steps the counselor can take to increase the likelihood of gaining the client's confidence, building rapport, and getting the client to disclose information freely.

The counselor working with elderly Hispanic Americans must first let the clients know that he or she understands and accepts the traditional Hispanic familial structure. A client must be confident that the counselor does not harbor negative feelings about the culture or subscribe to damaging stereotypes. Second, the counselor must be aware of the client's commitment to speaking Spanish and understand why it has persisted as such an important cultural characteristic. Third, the counselor should appreciate the possible reluctance of the client to take a young counselor seriously, especially a female counselor. Fourth, the counselor must work to build trust and encourage disclosure of relevant personal information.

Language can also be a barrier to effective communication, especially for older Hispanic Americans. Planning appropriately for communication barriers will be all-important. If elderly family members cannot speak English, then conducting the interview in Spanish is essential to engaging them. Older Puerto Rican Americans are often hesitant and afraid to learn English; they may feel humiliated when they try to speak English and are not understood and are asked to repeat themselves. Even when Puerto Rican Americans do speak English, lack of fluency may lead to distorted information and vagueness.

If a counselor needs an interpreter, it is best to use a counselor or paraprofessional rather than a neighbor or friend. Finally, the Hispanic American client's need for respect, privacy, and dignity should not be overlooked.

As with other cultures and stages of the lifespan, counselors should consider the effects of being elderly, the effects of being a member of a particular culture, the complex relationship between age and culture, and the various intracultural and individual differences among elderly clients.

Individual and Group Therapy

As always, the counselor's decision whether to use individual or group therapy should be based on the individual, the specific culture, and the reasons for counseling. Several generalizations, however, may be noted in dealing with Hispanic Americans. Elderly Hispanic Americans, although generally not accustomed to disclosing significant information that may reflect poorly on the family, might be willing to discuss problems associated with aging in a group session. The elder's lack of experience with group counseling, however, would probably call for special effort on the part of the counselor to explain the group process, or the counselor may prefer to use individual therapy.

Family Therapy

What do research and scholarly opinion offer for counselors working with elderly Hispanic Americans? With respect to family therapy, counselors should (a) speak Spanish (if possible) if the elderly client has problems speaking English; (b) make the family comfortable by providing a warm and personal setting; (c) be active, personal, and respectful of the family's structure and boundaries; and (d) ask the family members when the problems began, what types of solutions they have tried, and what their expectations are for change. As with all cultures and ages along the lifespan, the most effective counselors understand the culture and the lifespan period, and the complex relationships between the two.

In all likelihood, the patriarchal nature of the Hispanic American family will dictate that only the father or husband will speak for the family. The possibility of the wife or children disagreeing with the head of the household is remote. Although some indications suggest that Hispanic American women are becoming more outspoken, they cannot be expected to disclose much personal information during the course of a family session.

Case Study 14.4 looks at a counselor's efforts with Papa Rafael, a Hispanic American elder.

Case Study 14.4: Counseling Papa Rafael, a Hispanic American Elder

Papa Rafael, age 75, referred himself to a community health organization for counseling. Although he was surprised that a 75-year-old man with difficulty speaking English had referred himself, the 48-year-old European American male counselor was eager to talk with Papa Rafael. Because he had come of his own volition, surely Rafael would be willing to discuss his problems and to disclose his feelings.

During the first session, the counselor explained the counseling process, assured confidentiality, and sought to establish trust and rapport. The client's problems became clear: his family's financial difficulties and his son's unemployment; his own meager government benefits; growing old poor; and concern that his family, like many others, might abandon traditional Hispanic beliefs. Rafael saw a solution to the family's financial woes, but it was not a satisfactory solution in his view: His daughter-in-law Carla could take a job to help make ends meet, but such a solution could also lead to "the downfall of the family." Women in his family had not worked outside the home; they had stayed home to care for the children. Who would cook, take care of the children, clean the house? The counselor understood how Rafael felt. Finances were a problem, and so was the threat of loss of traditional values. After assessing the situation, the counselor decided that he wanted to see Rafael again. Perhaps a group session would be appropriate because his other elderly clients were having similar difficulties. Because Rafael's problem involved the family, a family session might be in order. Meeting with Rafael, Oscar, and Carla to discuss their financial situation and possible solutions was an idea worth exploring.

Counseling and Development 14.4: The Elderly Years

Ernesto is a 75-year-old Hispanic male who ponders his future. He lives alone, but his three sons and one daughter live nearby. The family has always lived in the same Spanish-speaking neighborhood, which means that he speaks little English. Ernesto lives off his social security and Medicare. Before his health went bad, he worked as a bricklayer and part-time roofer. His daughter does more for him than the three sons combined, but Ernesto realizes his three sons have jobs. A professional social worker brings his lunch every day; the social worker recommended him to a counselor who works in her office.

Using both English and Spanish, the counselor spoke to Ernesto about his health and family. The counselor considered Ernesto and his development period: declining health and energy, increased medical problems (mainly heart, circulatory, and diabetes), and increasing dependence on his daughter. Ernesto was questioning his future and eventual death. Would he have enough money if he became ill? And what would happen if he could not continue to live alone?

Counseling Strategies:

1. Ask about his family and family relationships with his three sons and one daughter.
2. Discuss his concerns about growing older and his eventual death. Was he lonely, or did he just prefer to be alone?
3. Ask about the possibility of Ernesto joining some older "group" that had similar interests and concerns.

SUMMARY

Counselors of Hispanic Americans need to address numerous topics: cherished cultural concepts and beliefs, allegiance to Spanish and problems with limited English proficiency; problems associated with aging; low socioeconomic status; and racism and discrimination. The challenges will be to (a) understand clients, their individuality, and their respective Hispanic culture; (b) provide developmentally and culturally appropriate counseling intervention; and (c) understand Hispanics' reasons for underuse of, and early withdrawal from, counseling intervention. Professional training and firsthand contact with Hispanic American clients in the four lifespan stages are the most effective means of successfully meeting these challenges.

NOTES

1   Dialogue from *Counseling and Development in a Multicultural Society* (pp. 433–434) by J.A. Axelson, 1999, Monterey, CA: Brooks/Cole. Reprinted with permission.
2   From *Effective Psychotherapy for Low-Income and Minority Patients* (p. 47) by F.X. Acosta, J. Yamamoto, and L.A. Evans, 1982, New York: Plenum. Reprinted with permission.

SUGGESTED READINGS

Bidell, M.P. (2014). Are multicultural courses addressing disparities? Exploring multicultural and affirmative lesbian, gay, and bisexual competencies of counseling and psychology students. *Journal of Multicultural Counseling & Development*, 42(3), 132–146. Clinical training and counselor competency are essential for ethical practice when working with multiethnic, lesbian, gay, bisexual (LGB), and transgender clients. Multicultural courses significantly predicted students' multicultural but not LGB counselor competency.

Blount, A.J., & Young, M.E. (2015). Counseling multiple-heritage couples. *Journal of Multicultural Counseling & Development*, 43(2), 137–152. Multiple-heritage couples are one of the fastest growing client populations in the United States—they are challenged by societal perceptions, stereotypes, and other pressures associated with being in a multiple-heritage pairing.

Love, M.M., Smith, A.E., Lyall, S.E., Mullins, J.L., & Cohn, T.J. (2015). Exploring the relationship between gay affirmative practice and empathy among mental health professionals. *Journal of Multicultural Counseling & Development*, 43(2), 83–96. During the last several decades, psychologists have placed emphasis on multicultural competence as an essential aspect of training and practice; however, despite this emphasis, empirical data on the effects of multicultural training and practice are generally limited to variables such as race and ethnicity, with very little research on sexual minorities.

Magaldi-Dopman, D. (2014). An "Afterthought": Counseling trainees' multicultural competence within the spiritual/religious domain. *Journal of Multicultural Counseling & Development*, 42(4), 194–204. Although spiritual/religious identity development is included within multicultural training on the theoretical level, significant gaps exist in counseling trainees' practical preparation for spiritual/religious competence.

Soheilian, S.S., & Inman, A.G. (2015). Competent counseling for Middle Eastern American clients: Implications for trainees. *Journal of Multicultural Counseling & Development*, 43(3), 173–190. The authors used a factorial multivariate analysis of variance (MANOVA) to determine whether counselor trainees' group differences on measures of multicultural competence, empathy, and multicultural counseling self-efficacy (CSE) when working with Middle Eastern American (MEA) clients.

Tovar, E. (2015). The role of faculty, counselors, and support programs on Latino/a community college students' success and intent to persist. *Community College Review*, 43(1), 46–71. This study examines how interactions with institutional agents (faculty and academic counselors) and select student support programs influence success (i.e., grade point average) and intentions to persist to degree completion for Latino/a community college students.

Tufekcioglu, S., & Muran, J.C. (2015). Case formulation and the therapeutic relationship: The role of therapist self-reflection and self-revelation. *Journal of Clinical Psychology*, 71(5), 469–477. This article examines the role of the therapist's self-reflection and self-revelation in case formulation. Tufekcioglu and Muran believe that a collaboratively constructed case formulation must always be considered in the context of an evolving therapeutic relationship.

15 Understanding Lesbian, Gay, Bisexual, and Transgender Clients

QUESTIONS TO BE EXPLORED

- What terminology seems most appropriate when referring to lesbian, gay, bisexual, and transgender (LGBT) clients and to related terms, such as *homosexuality*, *sexual orientation*, and *queer*?
- What demographics and historical and cultural contexts do counselors of LGBT clients need to know?
- What do the terms *coming out* and *identity development* mean? How do definitions vary? What does the literature say about coming out and identity development in several cultures?
- What are the childhood, adolescent, adult, and elderly years like for LGBT clients in terms of social and cultural descriptions, coming out and identity development, and challenges unique to the developmental period?
- What challenges confront counselors of LGBT clients?
- How will the Supreme Court decision legalizing same-sex marriage affect counselors and counseling relationships?
- What resources are available to counselors who want to improve their counseling effectiveness with LGBT clients across the lifespan?

OVERVIEW

Previous chapters of this text have discussed clients of culturally different backgrounds and how counselors can address their various needs along the lifespan. A premise of this book is that lesbians, gay men, and bisexual men and women have a culture of their own, in addition to their other cultures. Such individuals have their own worldviews, perspectives on same- and different-sex orientations, and experiences with injustice and discrimination. As more lesbians, gay men, and bisexual persons come out and let their sexual orientations be known, counselors will be increasingly called on to provide professional intervention throughout the lifespan. This chapter focuses on understanding LGBT clients, their coming out and identity development, and the unique challenges they face in the lifespan continuum. As always, the emphasis will be on counselors understanding clients' cultures (mainly same-sex orientation in this chapter) and accepting the challenge to develop the attitudes, knowledge, and skills necessary to provide effective counseling intervention for LGBT clients.

LESBIANS, GAYS, BISEXUALS, AND TRANGENDERED

Terminology

Counselors working with LGBT clients readily understand the need for constructive rather than destructive terminology. Therefore, there needs to be at least some discussion of words and labels such as *queer, gay, lesbian, bisexual, transgender, sexual orientation*, and *lifestyle* as well as abbreviated labels such as *LGB* and *LGBT*.

In this book, *gays* refers to males with a same-sex orientation, whereas *lesbians* refers to females with a same-sex orientation. *Bisexuals* refers to individuals who have the sexual orientation to love and sexually desire both same- and other-gendered individuals. Transgender is an umbrella term for people who self-identify as other than their birth sex (male or female). *LGBT* is used as a convenient collective term to describe lesbians, gays, bisexuals, and transgender populations. Another term *GLBTQ* stands for gay, lesbian, bisexual, transgender, and queer/questioning. In this volume, the term *LGBT* will be used rather than *queer*, although *queer* is being reclaimed by the younger generation of LGBTs. Here, *queer* will not be used. *Homosexual* is not a preferred term for LGBTs, because many people consider it to be exclusionary. In this volume, *homosexual* is used as an adjective (e.g., the homosexual culture). *Sexual orientation* is used to denote one's sexual orientation; *lifestyle* is rarely used because it suggests that sexual orientation is a choice. Again, whatever terminology counselors and other readers choose to use, terms should denote positive perspectives and respect for LGBT clients, both as individuals and as a culture.

Demographics

Because LGBT clients are in all four lifespan stages and live in all parts of the United States, it is difficult to provide specific demographics. One might expect LGBT persons to live in larger urban areas, such as San Francisco, New York, and Chicago, but in reality, they also live in both suburban and rural areas. To avoid harassment, some LGBT persons, especially those in rural areas and small towns, might be less likely to let their sexual orientation be known. They must deal daily with the problem of whether to hide their sexual orientation or risk the condemnation of the community. In such situations, teachers, ministers, and medical doctors might risk their professional status and financial livelihood if their sexual orientation becomes public. Such tendencies to hide one's sexual orientation make it difficult to determine accurate numbers and geographical locations for this group.

Some LGBT persons might be reluctant to designate themselves as such. For example, some people have a same-sex orientation yet never engage in same-sex relationships. Others might have had only one same-sex encounter and, therefore, do not classify themselves as lesbian or gay. Counselors need to determine when (and if) the client accepted his or her sexual orientation. In other words, some clients might actually be LGBT and be unwilling to admit it to the counselor or to themselves.

Counselors might expect LGBT clients to be primarily in the younger lifespan stages, but significant numbers of older people accept and deal with their same-sex orientations and the attendant prejudices, humiliation, and hurtful remarks. It is safe to assume that regardless of their geographic location, counselors will be called upon to intervene with LGBT clients in all four lifespan stages. One key to effective professional intervention will be to consider homosexuality as a culture. LGBT persons have a number of cultures, as do heterosexual people; however, one subculture of the former is their sexual orientation and the accompanying perspectives and views.

Historical and Cultural Contexts

In some cultures, homosexuality and bisexuality have been assumed to be mental illnesses. One's sexuality is gaining more respect, especially in the United States. Many people (admittedly, certainly not all) have accepted the fact that one's sexual orientation is not a choice. Recent court decisions, and especially the Supreme Court decision legalizing same-sex marriage, demonstrate the acceptance of LGBT people and their right to marry. Regardless of the counselor's sexual orientation, professionals have a professional and ethic responsibility to provide responsive counseling environments and interventions.

Counselors and their clients benefit when they understand both historical and contemporary perspectives of same-sex orientation. Most people currently know little about the everyday experiences of LGBT persons in different historical periods. Also, much of what has been written focuses only on gay men. Attitudes appear to range from tolerance to oppression, with the norm in Western societies being hostility and condemnation. In fact, LGBT persons have largely been invisible in history, and most existing knowledge is derived from religious and legal sanctions against same-sex relationships.

After World War II, the increasing visibility of lesbians and gay men was accompanied by increased public hostility, including police raids of lesbian and gay bars and efforts to remove same-sex orientation people from government service. Many lesbians and gay men lived in fear that exposure could lead to loss of jobs, housing, violence or intimidation, or a place in the community. The last half of the twentieth century witnessed the gradual evolution of acceptance of LGBT people. Undoubtedly, challenges continue as some same-sex-oriented individuals face fear, prejudice, and discrimination.

In certain time periods and cultures, sexual orientation did not result in conflicts, whereas in others, considerable turmoil and violence surrounded the issue. For example, people with homosexual orientations have been honored among some American Indian tribes, tolerated in some countries such as Scandinavia, proscribed in ancient Greece among scholars, and condemned throughout much of the Anglo-Saxon world. Attitudes in the Far East have historically been benevolent. In Japan during the feudal period, male homosexual love was considered more manly than heterosexual love. In premodern China, where male brothels were common, parents often trained their sons to be prostitutes. Currently, among cultures in the United States, perhaps the greatest potential for cultural acceptance of diversity in sexual orientation lies in the traditional American Indian culture (Firestein, 1996). American Indians place value on two-spirited people (Reynolds & Hanjorgiris, 2000), that is, people possessing masculine and feminine qualities. Some American Indian cultures recognize the existence of people whose spirits are both feminine and masculine, not only accepting them as part of nature but also revering them as having particular spiritual qualities.

Lesbian, gay, and bisexual people of color may experience multiple layers of oppression, as they often not only contend with the negative societal reactions to their sexual orientation but also may experience racial prejudice, limited economic resources, and limited acceptance within their own cultural communities (Harper, Jernewall, & Zea, 2004).

Counselors who provide professional intervention for LGBT clients should recognize contemporary contexts and attitudes toward homosexuality. Although acceptance of homosexuality has increased as more LGBT persons have revealed their sexual orientations, many of these individuals continue to face discrimination and prejudice in schools, in the workplace, and in society. Many are afraid to let their sexual orientation be known. Professionals working with LGBT clients need to plan counseling intervention that recognizes the problems these clients face in a predominantly heterosexual society.

Some church leaders have explicitly spoken out against the physical violence and harassment experienced by sexual and gender minorities. Writing specifically of the Catholic Church, Perez (2014) wrote churches should condemn antigay violence. He specifically mentioned that in at least 76 countries, laws still criminalize particular expressions of sexuality and gender. These laws often make people vulnerable to prosecution by the state, as well as to attack and persecution by members of the public. Governments often use sexual and gender minority groups as convenient scapegoats for social, political and economic ills, thus increasing their vulnerability. The meaning and scope of unjust discrimination against homosexual persons is still subject to debate in Catholic circles. But church teaching suggests that, at a minimum, this includes a need to refrain from and condemn violence against people on account of their perceived or actual sexual orientation or gender expression. As Catholic leaders have noted, this includes the criminalization of consenting sexual behavior among adults. As church leaders continue to discuss the morality of same-sex unions and whether homosexuals are to be welcomed into the church, Perez (2014) thinks they would also do well to condemn clearly and categorically the violence that sexual and gender minorities face in communities around the world.

Coming Out and Identity Development

Coming Out Process: Forming a Definition and Understanding Challenges

Any legitimate discussion of coming out should include counselors' forming their definition of the term *coming out* and understanding the significant challenges associated with the process. Counselors often find that the term has multiple meanings, depending on individual clients and the extent to which these clients have accepted their sexual orientation and have chosen to come out.

The coming out process depends on gays', lesbians', or bisexuals' definition and the extent to which they want to "out." We think coming out means "the experience of acknowledging a lesbian, gay, bisexual orientation and identity to oneself and others." In some cases, coming out or accepting one's sexual orientation (rather than preference) has been seen as self-acceptance and the perception of positive acceptance of significant others. Sometimes gays', lesbians', and bisexuals' openness might be limited to family and close friends. Sometimes, coming out or accepting one's sexual orientation comes long after a same-sex sexual experience.

Regardless of the counselor's definition, it is essential to understand the difficulty of the coming out process. The process might be particularly detrimental to adolescents who feel emotionally and financially dependent on their family. About two-thirds of youth come out to their mother; about one-third come out to their father. Parents might also be affected as they question their parenting skills and practices, as well as the negative societal perceptions about sexual orientation (Sue & Sue, 2013).

A prerequisite to effective professional intervention with gays, lesbians, and bisexuals is to *avoid* thinking, "The client had a sexual choice and made the wrong one." Counselors working with clients of differing sexual orientations should readily understand the importance of coming out as well as how the process relates to and affects self-acceptance, self-esteem, and self-validation. Counselors also should recognize (and plan accordingly) that coming out is an individual experience. Although similarities exist in individuals' process of coming out, individual differences continue to exist based on self-acceptance and acceptance of family members and close friends. Some might come out rather quickly; others might never fully come out. Counselors should recognize that losses can accompany the coming out process; for example, the loss of a heterosexual lifestyle and loss of social acceptance of one's relationships.

Identity Models and Changes

Developing a gay or lesbian identity and its related developmental tasks, referred to as coming out, is generally considered a difficult process for LGBT persons, depending on gender, race, ethnicity, social class, age, religion, and geographic location. The coming out process includes confronting negative social attitudes as well as negative self-perceptions. LGBT individuals have few role models, inadequate support systems, lack of legal protection, added isolation, and potential loss of primary cultural identification and community.

While the next several models might appear somewhat dated, we continue to think they are the most informative and useful.

Van Wormer, Wells, and Boes (2000) maintain that, in the coming out process, the first stage is the initial or pre-coming out stage, during which an individual may not consciously recognize same-sex attraction but may experience uneasy feelings. During this stage, the person might defend himself or herself against any feelings associated with same-sex attractions and embrace heterosexuality. The second stage involves a beginning awareness of a same-sex romantic and sexual attraction. Individuals begin to examine heterosexist beliefs—that is, assuming everyone is heterosexual and that heterosexuality is preferred. During this stage, people choose to come out to someone about their feelings. In the third stage, people develop gay or lesbian friendships, perhaps a romantic-sexual partner relationship, and socialize with the gay and lesbian community. Through contacts in the LGBT community, individuals develop a social support network within the context of their emerging identity. The fourth stage includes self-acceptance of a gay or lesbian identity, which is then incorporated into other aspects of one's life (i.e., social, political, personal). People describe their sexual orientation as who they are and integrate other developmental tasks into their LGBT identity (van Wormer et al., 2000).

Several other models of lesbian and gay identity development have been proposed. Although it is not feasible to explore in detail all the models of lesbian and gay identity development, several models are listed and briefly described. Two models, those of Falco (1991) and Troiden (1989), are examined in more detail. Finally, McCarn and Fassinger's (1996) model is discussed. While these models might appear old, they continue to be valid in describing lesbian and gay identity development.

Falco Model

In her book *Psychotherapy with Lesbian Clients: Theory into Practice*, Falco (1991) proposes a generalized model for the sexual identity development of lesbians by combining and summarizing the models of other researchers. In the first stage, a person is aware of being different and begins to wonder why. In the second stage, she begins to acknowledge her lesbian feelings and may tell others. Sexual experimentation marks the third stage, as the person explores same-sex relationships while seeking a supportive community. She begins to learn to function in a same-sex relationship, establishing her place in the lesbian culture, while passing as heterosexual when necessary. In the final stage, she integrates her private and social identities.

Troiden Model

Troiden (1989) proposes a four-stage model of lesbian and gay identity formation that shows how lesbians and gay men see themselves as such and adopt corresponding lifestyles. The four stages are sensitization, identity confusion, identity assumption, and commitment. Each stage can be identified by its characteristics and personal behaviors.

Step 1   **Sensitization** During this stage, which occurs before puberty, most lesbians and gay men do not see homosexuality as personally relevant. They assume a sense of heterosexuality, if they think about their sexual status at all. Lesbians and gay men typically acquire social experiences during their childhood, however, that serve later as a basis for perceiving homosexuality in more relevant and personal terms. These experiences lend support to emerging perceptions of homosexuality.

Step 2   **Identity Confusion** Lesbians and gay men in this stage begin to perceive their sexual orientation during adolescence, when they reflect on the possibility that their feelings, behaviors, or both could be regarded as homosexual, which contradicts previously held self-images. The hallmark of this stage is identity confusion—inner turmoil and uncertainty surrounding ambiguous sexual status. Because their sexual identities are in limbo, these individuals can no longer accept their heterosexual identities as a given, yet they have not developed perceptions of themselves as homosexual.

During this stage, lesbians and gay men typically respond to identity confusion in several ways:

Denial: They deny the homosexual component of their feelings, fantasies, and activities.

Repair: They attempt to eradicate homosexual feelings and behaviors.

Avoidance: They recognize that their behaviors, thoughts, and fantasies are homosexual but see them as unacceptable and to be avoided.

Redefining: They reduce identity confusion by redefining behavior, feelings, and activities.

Acceptance: Women and men accept their behaviors; they accept that their feelings and fantasies may be homosexual and seek out additional sources of information to learn more about their sexual feelings.

Step 3   Identity Assumption Lesbians and gay men in this stage, during or after adolescence, develop a homosexual identity that becomes both a self-identity and a presented identity, at least to other lesbians and gay men. Defining oneself as lesbian or gay and presenting oneself as such to other lesbians or gay men are the first stages in a larger process of identity disclosure called "coming out" (Troiden, 1989, p. 59). The earmarks of this stage include self-definition as lesbian or gay, identity tolerance and acceptance, regular association with other lesbians or gay men, sexual experimentation, and exploration of the lesbian or gay subculture.

Step 4   Commitment Homosexuality is adopted as a way of life. The main characteristics of this stage include self-acceptance and comfort with the lesbian or gay identity and role. This commitment has both internal and external dimensions. It is indicated internally by (a) the fusion of sexuality and emotionality into a significant whole, (b) a shift in the meanings attached to homosexual identities, (c) a perception of the homosexual identity as a valid self-identity, (d) expressed satisfaction with the homosexual identity, and (e) increased happiness after self-defining as lesbian or gay. It is indicated externally by (a) same-sex love relationships, (b) disclosure of a homosexual identity to nonhomosexual audiences, and (c) a shift in the type of stigma management theories.

McCarn and Fassinger Model

After examining the previously mentioned models, McCarn and Fassinger (1996) proposed a model of lesbian identity:

Stage 1: Awareness	
Individual Sexual Identity	of feeling or being different
Group Membership Identity	of existence of varying sexual orientations
Stage 2: Exploration	
Individual Sexual Identity	of strong/erotic feelings for women
Group Membership Identity	of one's position regarding lesbians as a group
Stage 3: Deepening/Commitment	
Individual Sexual Identity	to self-knowledge, self-fulfillment, and crystallization of choices about sexuality
Group Membership Identity	to commitment with reference group and with awareness of oppression and consequences of choices
Stage 4: Internalization/Synthesis	
Individual Sexual Identity	of love for women and sexual choices into overall identity
Group Membership Identity	of identity as a member of a minority group, across context

Bisexual Model

Although many theories have attempted to explain the development of positive gay and lesbian identities, less scholarly activity has focused on bisexual identity development. Bilodeau and Renn (2005) analyzed LGBT identity development and suggest that bisexuals experience identity processes differently from the way gays and lesbians do. Some individuals may accept a bisexual identity after self-labeling as lesbian or gay. Others may identify bisexual feelings from childhood onward. Still others may not become aware of bisexual feelings until after experiencing heterosexual relationships or marriages. Stage models do not always account for Eurocentric notions of culture, sexual orientation, gender identity, and spiritualism.

Malebranche, Arriola, Jenkins, Dauria, and Patel (2010) report on same-sex behavior among Black bisexual men. While the African American population is about 13% of the U.S. population, Black men accounted for 49% of the estimated 56,300 incidents of HIV infection in 2006. Their research focused on factors influencing sexual behavior, disclosure of same-sex behavior, and condom use practices among bisexual Black men. Their discussion included disclosing that same-sex or bisexual behavior entailed weighing the pros and cons, considering the gains and costs to self and others, and considering the approval or disapproval from others that may result from disclosure.

LESBIAN, GAY, BISEXUAL, AND TRANSGENDER CHILDREN

Unfortunately, little literature exists on LGBT children, perhaps because it is not until the adolescent developmental period that most boys and girls begin to realize their sexuality, and in this case, their same-sex sexual orientation. However, some children as young as five or six years of age realize their attraction and interest in the same sex. Most research on LGBT children focuses on topics such as living in a predominantly heterosexual society (and the accompanying harassment experienced by many LGBT children), feeling different, and dealing with gender-role conformity.

Research by Murray and McClintock (2005) examined whether a parent's nondisclosure of his or her homosexual or bisexual orientation within the family unit negatively affects self-esteem and anxiety in children. Murray and McClintock concluded that the children of lesbian mothers did not show a significant difference in trait anxiety when compared to children of heterosexual mothers. Also, self-esteem was not affected. Children of gay fathers, however, often experienced a negative effect. This effect may have resulted from the length of the family secret or the fact that cultural attitudes toward gay men tend to be more negative than attitudes toward lesbians.

Social and Cultural Description

Researchers do not know how many LGBT children exist, and, in fact, many children might not realize their attraction toward the same sex. Still, some children have erotic or sexual fantasies that associate with sexual desire. In fact, the mean age of same-sex attraction has been reported to be 9.7 years for both boys and girls (Giorgis, Higgins, & McNab, 2000). Undoubtedly, LGBT children do exist and might bring their unique challenges to counseling sessions. Therefore, counselors need to recognize the challenges that these children face and be prepared to offer professional intervention that reflects children's sexual orientation and cultural backgrounds.

Some LGBT children often know at a young age that something is different about them—the way they think, the way they feel, and what they like and do not like. Just because a child feels different does not mean that the child is necessarily lesbian, gay, or bisexual; however, emotional problems can result when children feel they are not like others. Van Wormer et al. (2000) tell of a five-year-old boy who felt an attraction for other boys. Although LGBT children might be too young to understand their feelings, they undoubtedly feel different and question themselves about why they are not like others. Then they hear words such as *fag, homo,* or other derogatory terms. Although they might not understand the meaning of the words, they know the words are directed at them. Also, a child who is culturally different from the majority culture (regardless of the respective majority culture) might feel a double sense of oppression; that is, a child might also feel different because he or she is African American, Hispanic American, Arab American, or Asian American. The sad reality is that a child might feel different in more than one way. The child might be of a cultural minority that is noticeably obvious and also harbor feelings of being attracted to the same sex.

Coming Out and Identity Development

Identity formation refers to the development of a personal identity as core individual characteristics and social identity or as one's relation to others. Children face the developmental task of understanding and coming to terms with their sexual identity in an environment that denies and devalues their sexuality. Many children feel pressure to adopt expected gender roles; that is, they are taught that boys and girls are expected to behave in specific ways. Still, all children who refuse to adhere to specific gender roles do not develop same-sex identities and orientations.

When LGBT children go through the process of understanding their sexual identity, they might experience considerable inner conflict. They do not understand their feelings and their differences, especially when they perceive that society promotes opposite-sex attractions. As previously suggested, the problem of identity development grows more acute when the child comes from a culturally different background. Being a child in such an environment can result in problems such as confused sexual identity, guilt, and lower self-esteem, all of which counselors might be called on to address.

Perceptive counselors realize they cannot use generalizations or stereotypes (e.g., appearance, personality, or behaviors) to determine who is lesbian, gay, or bisexual. Although many young children might realize they differ in some way, they might not be old enough to realize their same-sex sexual orientation. Also, due to harassment and ridicule, most children will not engage in a coming out process. Coming out and being out are crucial to self-perceptions of being stable—those positive self-images that would normally be considered crucial to the sense of self in children. Depending on the culture, sexual play might have been encouraged; in other cultures the practice might have been taboo. Years later, these children may wonder why the same-sex urges continued to exist. Still, as children, coming out (if they had even known the meaning of the term and process) would have been difficult or impossible due to parental punishments and peer harassment.

Case Study 15.1 looks at Manuel, a ten-year-old Hispanic American boy who showed possible indicators of being gay.

Case Study 15.1: Ten-Year-Old Manuel

Ten-year-old Manuel was a Hispanic American boy in the fifth grade who seemed different from other boys his age. He liked to read and to be alone, and he did not participate in physical activities at recess.

Manuel was required to take an active role in the physical education class. However, it was evident that he did not enjoy the physical activities; other boys did not want him on their teams, so he was always the last one chosen. One boy said, "We don't want the gay fag on our team." The coach heard the comment, but he chose not to take action. On several occasions, Manuel made up excuses (e.g., having a hurt leg) so that the coach would not make him play.

Manuel was referred to the counselor, an Asian American man. During the third meeting with the counselor, Manuel confided that he felt different. "I like to read; they don't. They like to play ball; I don't. I think I am more like the girls, but I don't think they like me either." He never mentioned the possibility that he might have a different sexual orientation, and the counselor avoided seeking information in that area, especially during the early stages of counseling.

The teachers felt Manuel was different and knew he was the recipient of considerable taunting and verbal abuse, but they did not take any deliberate action to help him. One teacher thought Manuel might be gay and concluded that if he were, he should keep quiet about it. "He gets enough ridicule now," the teacher thought. Another teacher knew a problem existed but did not know what action to take. "Telling the others to stop picking on him might make the situation worse," the teacher said. In the meantime, Manuel managed to make it through the day, although some days were far from pleasant. He stayed quiet most of the time, read more and more, and strove to avoid social contact.

Reflection Questions:

1. The coach heard the "gay fag" remark but chose to ignore it. Was the coach right or wrong? What would you have done had you been the coach?
2. Preferring reading over physical activity is not an indicator of sexual orientation. Do you think Manuel was gay or just questioning (or neither)?
3. At what point should the counselor mention sexual orientation? Soon? Never? Should he wait for Manuel to broach the subject?

Unique Challenges Confronting Lesbian, Gay, Bisexual, and Transgender Children

Selected challenges facing LGBT children and their counselors include the following:

1. School and societal messages emphasize (subtly or not so subtly) heterosexual attraction over homosexual attraction. Peers might harass and call suspected LGBT children names (e.g., "sissy," "fag," or "dyke"), provoking fear, humiliation, and self-hatred, which can have long-lasting negative effects on personal identity and self-esteem.
2. LGBT children might assume that the majority of other children are heterosexual, recognize their own differences, and thus assume they are wrong. Differences can take many forms; sometimes differences indicate sexual orientation and at other times they do not. Some people erroneously suggest that effeminacy in boys and masculinity in girls indicate signs of the homosexuality that will continue in adolescence and adulthood. Counselors need to avoid predicting future sexual orientations based on children's feminine or masculine behaviors.
3. LGBT children may sometimes fear for their safety. Just because they are different, other children might pick fights or beat them up. In some particularly unfortunate situations, adults do not take appropriate action when they know a child is being harassed because of sexual differences.
4. In addition to their sexual orientation, children might also be of a culture different from the majority culture or perhaps disabled in some way. Forming a positive sexual and cultural identity can be even more difficult when children have to deal with several differences, especially in schools and communities that place major emphasis on heterosexualism and majority culture values.

LESBIAN, GAY, BISEXUAL, AND TRANSGENDER ADOLESCENTS

It is important to remember that homosexuality and bisexuality are normal variations in both sexual identity and sexual behavior; adolescent homosexuality and bisexuality are not phases that lead to heterosexuality; sexual orientation is established in early childhood, and attempts to change it are unscientific and unethical (White, Oswalt, Wyatt, & Peterson, 2010).

White and colleagues (2010) maintain that lesbian, gay, and bisexual youth may be at higher risk for depression, suicide, and negative risk taking. Speaking mainly about physical education and recreational opportunities for lesbian, gay, and bisexual youth, the authors report youth hearing "that's so gay" or "you're so gay." Also troubling, only 16.5% of students reported that faculty or staff intervened to address negative remarks.

LGBT adolescents often face a multitude of life stressors due to their minority status, including discrimination and an increased risk of harassment, violence, and sexual abuse. Bebes, Samarova, Shilo, and Diamond (2015) examined the associations between perceived parental acceptance, perceived parental psychological control, and self-reported psychological symptoms among a sample of 234 lesbian, gay, bisexual, and transgendered (LGBT) Israeli adolescents aged 14–21. Two parenting behaviors that have received special attention are acceptance and psychological control. Parental acceptance is typically defined as warmth, affection, approval, support, and positive involvement. Adolescents who feel accepted have greater self-esteem, function more effectively in the world, and are generally more protected against psychological distress. Conversely, lack of parental acceptance appears to increase the risk for both externalizing and internalizing symptoms, including depressive symptoms and suicidal ideation (Bebes et al., 2015).

Bebes et al. (2015) maintained parental acceptance and psychological control may be particularly important for lesbian, gay, bisexual, and transgendered (LGBT) adolescents for a number of reasons. First, LGBT youth are at added risk for parental rejection due to their same-sex orientation, gender identity, and/or gender atypical behavior. Bebes et al. (2015) also maintain that over half of parents initially react to their LGBT adolescents' disclosure with some degree of negativity. Although most parents become more accepting, or at least more tolerant, over time, a substantial minority remain persistently intolerant or even rejecting. For example, in prior research on Israeli adolescents and young adults, 9% of mothers and 12% of fathers remained fully or almost fully rejecting a year and half after disclosure. Second, and relatedly, LGBT adolescents are at greater risk for a wide variety of psychological symptoms. This heightened risk may be, at least in part, due to parental rejection and psychological control (Bebes et al., 2015).

Transgender students have unique stressors in their lives. Because transgender identity can involve the presentation of one's body as a gender that is different from one's physiology, a transgender student may face body shame, ridicule, harassment, or violence. Changing names or pronouns, clothing, appearance, or pursing medical services to physically transition can be a difficult process. Such transitions can be affirming when pursued with the support and empathy of adult advocates, such as school professionals, mentors, and family members (Ludeke, 2009).

Goodenow, Szalacha, Robin, and Westheimer (2008) conducted research on adolescent females, sexual orientation, and HIV-related risks. During adolescence, sexuality and sexual issues assume a high degree of importance for most adolescents; the majority become sexually active at some point during this period. These researchers maintained that few studies have focused on HIV/AIDS risk among adolescent girls, although patterns of risk behavior often begin during adolescence. Conventional wisdom suggests that lesbians and women who have sex with women are at low risk for HIV/AIDS. Nevertheless, some evidence indicates that sexual-minority females—those who self-identify as lesbian or bisexual or those who engage in same-sex activity—may have a risk of HIV infection as high as or higher than women who identify themselves as heterosexual and who have sexual activity exclusively with males.

Fields et al. (2015) explored gender-role strain arising from conflict between homosexuality and cultural conceptions of masculinity among young Black men who have sex with men (MSM). Black men who have sex with men aged 13 to 24 years have a higher HIV incidence rate than other racial subgroups, a rate that increased by 49% between 2007 and 2010. Understanding the culturally relevant factors influencing sexual behavior among Black MSM may help identify processes that increase their HIV risk. Fields et al. (2015) explored family, peer, community, and racial expectations of masculinity described by young Black MSM, the gender-role strain associated with these expectations. Participants perceived rigid manhood expectations from important others, demanding that they avoid femininity and maintain an appearance of hypermasculinity. Although gender and sexual orientation are distinct social constructs, our results suggest that participants' important others equated homosexuality with femininity, such that the masculine expectations experienced by participants were both antihomosexual and antifeminine. Participants described being ridiculed and reprimanded as children by important others if they fell short of these expectations. Thus many experienced gender-role strain as part of their childhood masculine socialization. This type of strain is thought to be particularly prominent for gay men.

Adolescents with disabilities deserve equal opportunities during the promotion of positive sexual development. Harader, Fullwood, and Hawthorne (2009), writing about adolescents with disabilities and sexual development, suggested concrete guidelines for modifying discussions, materials, and activities for adolescents with moderate disabilities. Those related to sexual development include increasing supervision when sexual development occurs and remaining calm when sexual activity occurs.

Social and Cultural Description

Adolescence is the developmental period many boys and girls sense and act upon their LGBT orientations. According to Giorgis, Higgins, and McNab (2000), the age of first homosexual activity is reported to be 13.1 years for boys and 15 years for girls. However, there have been some relatively small differences in these ages reported by other researchers. Dubé and Savin-Williams (2000) reported that youths, regardless of ethnicity, labeled their same-sex attractions at age 15 to 17 years. Most bisexual people usually engage in such sexual activity in early to middle adolescence and young adulthood. It is possible for young people to develop passionate attachments to persons of the same gender during adolescence. In some cases, these emotional attachments may lead to physical sexual activity.

Minority culture adolescents often face double challenges owing to their same-sex orientations and their differing cultural backgrounds. They might face problems due to the majority culture's emphasis on personal independence compared to the minority culture's tendency toward group allegiance. Adherence to religious beliefs and family expectations for heterosexual unions and offspring affect African Americans, where close ties exist between church and community. Mexican Americans, Cuban Americans, and Puerto Rican Americans, as well as other cultures from primarily Catholic nations, would also be affected by adolescents' LGBT orientations. Likewise, many Asian Americans (e.g., Chinese, Japanese, Koreans, Vietnamese, Thais, Cambodians, Filipinos) emphasize family tradition and adherence to community expectations. In addition, minority LGBT persons are less likely than majority-culture Americans to have family support when they come out (van Wormer et al., 2000).

Whereas European American cultures think adolescents should gain individuation from the family, Greeks think adolescence is a time when individuation occurs within the family. Adolescents learn to emulate their parents, take on more gender role–appropriate responsibilities, and develop their sense of increased maturity. Greek adolescents rarely discuss thoughts, feelings, or changing life values with their parents. Family traditions make coming out difficult for adolescent daughters. Adolescent males would also have difficulty sharing same-sex sexual orientations, especially considering the Greek culture's expectation for adolescents to accept gender role–appropriate responsibilities and behaviors.

Coming Out and Identity Development

Many LGBT adolescents report feeling different since earliest childhood; however, contemporary studies (Hershberger & D'Augelli, 2000) have suggested that most adults who self-identify as lesbian or gay realize that their attraction to others of the same sex began during early adolescence. A developmental approach to sexual orientation must take into account the individual's developmental status. This means that same-sex eroticism will be experienced, thought about, and expressed not only in different ways at different ages but also in ways that reflect the individual's physical, cognitive, emotional, and social development at a particular point of personal development (Hershberger & D'Augelli, 2000). Until quite recently, adolescent homosexuality was thought to be a passing phase on the road to heterosexuality. These feelings take on sexual meaning during puberty as homosexual attractions occur. After a period of confusion, the individual typically adopts a gay or lesbian label but still may need years to reach a final stage of acceptance.

Sexual identification is not embraced immediately upon self-recognition; instead, it is a gradual coming out to oneself. Most individuals pass from awareness to positive self-identity between the ages of 13 and 20, with the process of establishing a positive lesbian, gay, or bisexual identity occurring earlier today than in the past. Few middle school students self-identify as lesbian, gay, or bisexual, compared with as high as 6% to 7% of high school students who describe themselves as primarily lesbian, gay, or bisexual. Still, even in middle school, evidence suggests lesbian, gay, and bisexual students feel different (Schneider & Owens, 2000). If they come out, many lesbian, gay, and bisexual adolescents do not believe that they can rely on traditional sources of support, such as their families, friends, peers, teachers, neighbors, clergy, and physicians.

Even under the threat of condemnation and harassment, some LGBT persons come out during the adolescence stage. They have or are in the process of developing an LGBT identity and are prepared to let their same-sex sexual orientation be known. Some have had heterosexual contacts, either experimentally or perhaps just to prove their heterosexuality to others; however, they become so certain of their same-sex sexual orientation that they decide to come out. The process may be more difficult for disabled adolescents or adolescents from culturally different backgrounds, who might already feel isolated and oppressed due to their culture and ethnicity and, therefore, may believe that coming out will only worsen their plight.

Case Study 15.2 tells about Suzie, an Asian American adolescent who was not ready to come out and, in fact, tried to deny her same-sex sexual orientation even to herself

---

Case Study 15.2: Suzie, a Lesbian Asian American Adolescent

Suzie, a 16-year-old, third-generation Asian American girl in the tenth grade, refused to let her same-sex sexual orientation be known. In fact, she denied her feelings even to herself. Suzie came from a typical and "normal" middle-class home. The family attended church, they had big family gatherings, and they visited friends during vacation time each year. Both of Suzie's parents were heterosexual, and, as far as she knew, no one in her family was homosexual. Suzie had several friends who were girls, and, as far as she knew, none of them even suspected that she was feeling different. She had not even confided to her best friend that she might be a lesbian. She had dated several boys, tried to enjoy their company, and had even tried having sexual relations on two occasions. However, having sex with the boys was more for experimentation than for feelings of closeness with them. Her parents did not have any idea that she had had sexual relations with the boys, and it was clear that she did not want them to learn of her experiences. She had never had any physical contact with any of the girls she knew. She denied her feelings and thought (as she said several years later), "I have too much to lose. My parents want me to go to college, and I know I need to—I will just have to face life somehow without people knowing I am a lesbian. Who knows? I might not be a lesbian anyway. As soon as I meet the right guy, I will be close to him, sex will be good, and I will forget these feelings. I have been feeling this way since I was nine years old, and if I have been hiding my feelings all this time, I know I can keep hiding them."

In addition, as she confided several years later, another reason she would never let her feelings be known was because of the school. "I had heard all those names lesbians (although they might not actually have been lesbian, other students thought they were) were called. I would have been so embarrassed, especially if my parents had ever heard I was being called those names."

Suzie was in a bind. She had same-sex feelings that she continued to hide and deny to others and herself. She had no intention of ever letting anyone know. As she said later, "I was so embarrassed. No one could ever know about me."

Reflection Questions:

1. In fact, she (Suzie) denied her feelings even to herself. Was Suzie a lesbian, or was she only questioning her sexuality? If she was a lesbian, why did she have sexual relations with boys on several occasions?
2. Suzie said to herself, "I have no intention of ever letting anyone know." What are the implications for counseling intervention of leading such a life of secrecy?
3. Assume the unlikely event Suzie discloses her sexual feelings to you, what counseling approaches would you recommend?

Unique Challenges Confronting Lesbian, Gay, Bisexual, and Transgender Adolescents

Selected challenges facing LGBT adolescents include

- school and societal messages that heterosexuality is the norm and that homosexuality should be ignored;
- prejudice and discrimination in schools and society whereby LGBT adolescents receive intentional or unintentional ill treatment;
- harassment, name-calling, and humiliation that some students (and teachers) inflict on LGBT students and heterosexual students who are perceived as lesbian, gay, or bisexual;
- safety and health risks such as suicide, drug and alcohol abuse, and risky sexual behaviors resulting in sexually transmitted diseases; and
- parents and family members who condemn LGBT adolescents for their homosexuality.

LESBIAN, GAY, BISEXUAL, AND TRANSGENDER ADULTS

These adults face a number of challenges, primarily due to society's rejection of homosexuality on moral and religious grounds or lack of knowledge of differing sexual orientations. Coming out also poses problems, either because LGBT adults are reluctant to reveal their sexual orientations or because they fear loss of employment and social status as well as harassment and physical harm. Also, as previously suggested, counselors need to understand the unique situation facing minority LGBT adults, because being a cultural minority plus being LGBT can lead to multifaceted oppression and discrimination.

Social and Cultural Description

Although it is impossible to pinpoint specific numbers of minority LGBT adults and their geographical location, they probably compose about 10% of the population. LGBT adults may be found in all cultures and all social classes.

The American Indian culture used the term *berdache* to describe a man or woman who departs from a socially constructed gender role and acquires traits and obligations of the opposite sex. Rather than crossing gender lines, the *berdache* actually blurs them, thus constituting a third sex. In traditional cultures, *berdaches* have married individuals of the same sex, and these marriages were recognized by Indian law (Potgieter, 1997). Therefore, at least in the past, American Indian adults have tolerated same-sex sexual orientations. American Indian adults might be as reluctant as those of other cultures to reveal their homosexuality.

In the Asian American culture, open disclosure that one is lesbian or gay (or even the possibility of transgender) poses a threat to the continuation of the family line as well as a rejection of one's culturally accepted social roles. Also, LGBT Asians might fear that their parents will think their sexuality is a deviant behavior, a "disappointment," or a reflection on their parenting skills. However, the persistent invisibility of Asian American lesbians and gay men is slowly changing with the development of lesbian and gay support groups within Asian communities.

Western concepts of minority sexual orientations are influencing other countries. Discovering that one has an affectionate, an erotic, or a sexual attraction to others of one's own sex has profoundly different meanings in China, Korea, and Japan. During the nineteenth and twentieth centuries, this tolerant attitude was largely replaced by Western ideas that same-sex attraction was abnormal. Research by Kimmel and Yi (2004) reviewed past and contemporary thinking about gays, lesbians, and bisexual people, especially those of Asian descent. Some opinions were affected by Western thought, the work of Christian missionaries, and Asian allegiance to family expectations and honor. Kimmel and Yi (2004) focus their attention on four aspects: differences between life in Asia and in the United States, differences between immigrants and nonimmigrants in the United States, differences of lifestyle variations, and age differences. Kimmel and Yi offer four conclusions:

1. A gay, lesbian, and bisexual community is clearly emerging in Asia.
2. Gay men and lesbians in the United States are freer than in Asia to be open and to live their lives as sexual minorities.
3. Gender differences parallel those found in studies of lesbians and gay men in Western countries.
4. Nationality, culture, and ethnic background do make an important difference when studying Asian lesbians, bisexuals, and gay men.

As previously stated, Hispanic American cultures differ widely and represent a wide range of persons with different languages and different cultural norms. Consideration should be given to individual Hispanic cultures as well as to individuals within each culture. Generally speaking, in Hispanic cultures, women are expected to be submissive, virtuous, respectful of elders, and willing to defer to men; men are expected to provide for, protect, and defend the family. Still, perceptive counselors realize the importance of considering individual cultures as well as clients' socioeconomic status, spiritualism, generational status, and geographic location.

Coming Out and Identity Development

Many adults have lived their entire lives without ever acknowledging their same-sex sexual orientation. These adults may consider coming out to be more risky and psychologically damaging than hiding their sexual orientation. In their research, Parks, Hughes, and Matthews (2004) report findings from a sample of African American, Hispanic American, and White American lesbians. In their discussion, Parks and colleagues maintain that lesbians of color were less likely than their White counterparts to disclose their sexual identity to nonfamily groups, regardless of age. However, they found an interesting pattern of age-related differences in disclosure to family. Older women of color were more likely than younger women of color to be out to their families, whereas the opposite was true for White women: Older White women were substantially less likely than their younger counterparts to be out to their family members. Also, lesbians of color had to simultaneously confront and manage the triple oppressions of sexism, heterosexism, and racism that exist both within the dominant culture and within their own racial or ethnic groups. According to Parks and colleagues

- challenges of these triple oppressions can be stressful and daunting tasks; and
- stress and isolation place individuals at risk of negative health consequences, yet health-care providers cannot assume that lesbians will disclose information about their sexual orientation.

Simonsen, Blazina, and Watkins (2000) suggest that counselors should be sensitive to the importance of emotional and affection expression issues to the well-being of gay men and, where appropriate, incorporate those issues into counseling. They also note that gay men experience unique issues related to their sexual orientation; however, some concerns (e.g., emotionality, work, and family conflicts) are similar to those experienced by heterosexual men. Therefore, although counselors should identify differences between gay men and heterosexual men, Simonsen and colleagues suggest that it is equally important to recognize the fundamental similarities between the two groups.

The coming out process can be an emotional experience for LGBT adults and largely depends on expected consequences. For example, some LGBT adults may confide in trusted friends in order to gain needed emotional support but choose not to tell coworkers in order to protect job security. Particularly for cultural minority LGBT adults such as Asian Americans, Hispanic Americans, and African Americans, coming out tests family acceptance and relationships. Some families, especially those that place emphasis on continuing the family line, may totally reject the coming out of a family member. Also, even if a family agrees to conceal a family member's same-sex sexual orientation, the family's allegiance to the church might still be a reason to reject the LGBT family member. Again, although coming out is difficult for LGBT persons in all developmental stages, it can also be an emotional and traumatic event for adults, especially considering the potential loss of family, social status, and financial livelihood. Other considerations regarding the decision to come out may include a desire to protect other family members. LGBT adults might want to avoid problems with the extended family, especially among the older generation, who might experience difficulty with a family member coming out.

Case Study 15.3 looks at Alisa, a bisexual Hispanic American adult.

Case Study 15.3: Alisa, a Bisexual Hispanic American Adult

Alisa, a 45-year-old wife, had been hiding her bisexuality for decades. She had been married for 23 years and had three grown children who, to the best of her knowledge, were heterosexual. She and her husband had a good marriage, and he did not have any idea about her bisexuality (or at least he never gave any indication that he knew). They had enjoyed a good sex life together, but still Alisa knew she had feelings for two other females. In fact, she did not know whether she preferred her husband or other females—both were pleasing and satisfying in their unique ways.

Because she did not have a profession and was a stay-at-home wife, she knew she could not come out as a lesbian or bisexual. She was unwilling to risk her marriage and her grown children's opinion of her. Alisa did not have a large number of lesbian partners; she had only two women who she met with on a fairly regular basis—once or twice a month. She believed her two lesbian lovers were selective about their lovers, so she was not concerned about contracting a disease. Between these sexual encounters with the women, she and her husband enjoyed their sex life.

Alisa felt she should feel a "sense of guilt," but she continued her lesbian encounters. Her husband was a good man, a good provider, and a good father—how could she live her lifestyle? Alisa knew (as well as anyone can know) that her husband was heterosexual and had never had sex with another man. Perhaps she was the only woman he had had sex with. Although he knew Alisa's friends, he never suspected a lesbian relationship among the three women. Alisa felt that he would be greatly concerned about her encounters with other women, so the subject never came up. In the meantime, she thought she would just continue her bisexual behaviors.

Reflection Questions:

1. How is Alisa handling her bisexuality? She enjoys sex with both her husband and her lesbian friends. What will be the effects of her "sense of guilt"?
2. If Alisa told you (the counselor) of her lesbian encounters, how would you respond? How would you respond if you were a marriage and family therapist? Would the type of counselor even matter?
3. What might be the possible long-term effects for consequences for Alisa actually living two "lives"?

Unique Challenges Confronting Lesbian, Gay, Bisexual, and Transgender Adults

Although some of these challenges (e.g., prejudice, discrimination) apply to all LGBT adults regardless of their developmental stage, others apply primarily to LGBT adults. For example, LGBT adults might experience

- problems with career needs and barriers due to their sexuality, especially those who come out in the workplace;
- prejudice, discrimination, and harassment in all aspects of society;
- problems that arise when lesbians, gay men, and bisexuals are in heterosexual marriages as well as problems in adoption and parenting issues;
- challenges dealing with depression, especially in lesbians; and
- dangers resulting from risky behaviors: suicide, substance abuse, and HIV/AIDS.

Merrill and Wolfe (2000) maintain that battered gay and bisexual men suffer patterns, forms, and frequencies of physical, emotional, and sexual abuse similar to what has been documented by research on battered heterosexual and lesbian women. Domestic violence appears to be as common and as serious a problem in same-gender relationships as in heterosexual ones. Likewise, the most commonly reported reasons for staying—namely, hope for change and love for partner—appear to be universal to the experience of being battered, regardless of sexual orientation. Merrill and Wolfe offer several conclusions:

1. All people associated with and working with gay and bisexual battered men (and women) should avoid "recognition failure" (p. 24), whereby people fail to recognize behaviors that constitute domestic violence.
2. Most professionals should receive training in assessing and responding to same-gender battering; for example, some helping professionals, when they arrive at a domestic violence scene, fail to realize that two women or two men can share a romantic relationship and that one can still be a victim of domestic violence.
3. Workers at battered women's shelters tend to admit women without completely assessing whether they are the victim or batterer who is seeking shelter as a ploy.
4. Workers tend to assume that "women are not as violent to one another" and "men can protect themselves" (p. 25), and, therefore, the man must be the perpetrator and the woman must be the victim.

LESBIAN, GAY, BISEXUAL, AND TRANSGENDER ELDERLY

Contrary to commonly accepted myths, many elderly people (both homosexual and heterosexual) remain sexually active and are generally satisfied with their sex lives. With better health treatment and drugs for erectile dysfunctional, many elderly people enjoy sexually satisfying lives. Some people might think the elderly do not have same-sex urges. Not only might counselors neglect addressing their elderly clients' sexuality, but they might also assume that all elderly people are heterosexual. Elderly LGBT persons who have not come out might never let their sexual orientation be known.

Social and Cultural Description

Elderly LGBTs face multiple challenges owing to their age, possible minority status, and same-sex sexual orientation. Older lesbians are thought to be nonexistent by both society and the lesbian community. Thus elderly lesbians are in triple jeopardy because of age, gender, and sexual orientation. Gay men place more emphasis on youth, yet there is speculation that older gay men often learn to deal with their stigmatized status and, therefore, are better prepared to deal with aging than heterosexual men are. Another commonly held belief is that young gay men find older gay men unattractive because of the reminder that they will also be old someday (van Wormer et al., 2000).

The popular belief that older lesbians and gay men live their lives alone is a myth. The vast majority of older lesbians and gay men live with a partner, a roommate, friends, or family members. Sharing an apartment or a home with another LGBT person provides a haven from the hostile outside world. Some older LGBT persons have meaningful relationships throughout their lives. Perhaps the most important consideration for gay men is that their living situation can solve a range of political and social problems. Sharing a home with another person provides companionship and lightens the financial burden of housing. This companionship is important to gay men who might have few friends or to those who live in rural areas distant from an accessible gay community. The plight facing minority LGBT elderly can be multiply oppressive. The presence of any of these three conditions—minority status, elderly status, and same-sex sexual orientation—alone can create difficulties, but the presence of all three at once can make oppression more acute. Counselors need to understand the challenges associated with the elderly developmental period as well as those associated with being a minority and lesbian, gay, or bisexual.

Coming Out and Identity Development

In one of the few studies of older gay men coming out, Berger's (1996) seminal study concluded that some men in this study thought coming out meant their first sexual encounter with a man; others thought the term meant being honest with others about their sexual orientation; and others thought it meant self-recognition and self-acceptance. Regardless of their definition, they all considered coming out to be one of their most significant life experiences. It could also be a very difficult and frightening step that was taken only after years of soul-searching. With one exception, all the men had had their first same-sex sexual experience during early puberty or adolescence. Even though they recognized their same-sex sexual interests, some of the men had married and raised children before returning to same-sex interests in their forties and fifties. Some of the men had their first experience with peers, usually friends from school or in the neighborhood. Only a small number had had sexual experiences with an older man.

Case Study 15.4 looks at Adamos, an elderly Greek American "questioning." Case Study 15.4 raises an important point: *Elderly clients and sexuality. There is a myth that older people are not interested in sexual activities.*

Case Study 15.4: Adamos, an Elderly Greek American "Questioning"

Adamos is 69 years old and is questioning his sexuality. While he knows that 69 is no longer youthful, he does not feel elderly. In fact, he does not like to be called elderly. He still has sexual desires for women, but he is questioning how he feels about men. His wife died about ten years ago, and he has been lonely. His four or five male friends (all heterosexual as far as he knows) come to his house almost every late afternoon during the week. They have a drink or two and discuss world and neighborhood events.

At 69, Adamos is in reasonably good health and is capable of sexual activity. He has never been "with a man," but he is considering what it would be like to be "with a man." "I am too old for these thoughts," he said to himself, but the thoughts continue. He has known one of the male visitors for about 18 years and wonders whether the man (although married) has sexual feelings for him. Still, Adamos wonders what his friend's reactions might be. What if his friend was shocked? Would he continue the long friendship? Also, Adamos asked himself, "Do I really want to do this?" There were women in the neighborhood—maybe he should just spend more time with them, he thought.

Adamos met with a counselor twice a month at a community clinic where lunch was served, but he knew he would never disclose his feelings to a counselor. No one knew his thoughts, and they would have to remain his secret.

Reflection Questions:

1. Adamos will not disclose his feelings about another man to the counselor. If a counselor suspected Adamos' feelings or possible desires to be sexually active with a man, how might he or she assist him to explore (with the counselor taking an objective stance)?
2. Should Adamos "forget" his feelings and spend more time with the women in the neighborhood? Why or why not? Is Adamos facing an "either-or situation," or could he explore both possibilities?
3. Why do you think Adamos is exploring these feelings at 69? Has he always had such feelings and just would not consider his feelings a viable possibility?

Interestingly, the majority of gay men reported shame over their sexual feelings at some point in their lives. Most gay men overcame their initial feelings of shame and guilt as they reached adulthood. In fact, older gay men are less anxious about their same-sex sexual relations than are their younger counterparts. As gay men age, they no longer have to conform to the mental image of the sexually active gay man in his twenties and thirties (van Wormer et al., 2000).

Unique Challenges Confronting Lesbian, Gay, Bisexual, and Transgender Elderly

As for LGBTs in the other developmental periods, it is important for counselors to consider challenges unique to LGBT elderly, including:

- deciding whether to come out during the elderly years (assuming the elderly person has not already come out);
- prejudice and discrimination in housing, retirement benefits, and medical attention;
- difficulties in obtaining assisted living facilities, nursing home care, and long-term health care stemming from their sexual orientation;
- challenges associated with increased health problems and the possibility of these problems being aggravated by HIV/AIDS and lack of proper medical attention; and
- problems stemming from being elderly in a society that ignores LGBT sexuality of the elderly and thus does not work to address their needs.

SUMMARY

Counseling LGBT clients in the various developmental stages will challenge counseling professionals, especially counselors who do not understand the effects of cultural diversity and same-sex sexual orientations. In order to provide effective counseling intervention, counselors must have the professional training, experience with minority LGBT persons in the various lifespan stages, and a genuine professional motivation to effectively counsel LGBT persons in the four lifespan periods. Specific challenges include:

- understanding that LGBT persons have a culture of their own, in addition to their own ethnicity;
- developing the counseling competencies (e.g., attitudes, knowledge, skills) necessary to counsel LGBT persons in the various cultures and lifespan stages;
- providing counseling intervention (e.g., individual, group, and family) that reflects LGBT persons' worldviews and same-sex sexual orientation;
- understanding and accepting one's own sexuality (homosexuality, bisexuality, or heterosexuality) and making a commitment to avoid letting one's sexuality interfere with counseling clients who have different sexual orientations.

SUGGESTED READINGS

Enke, F. (2015). Understanding and teaching U.S. lesbian, gay, bisexual, and transgender history. *History Teacher, 48*(3), 588–590. Enke explains the importance of lesbian, gay, bisexual, and transgendered students and also offers suggestions for teaching about sexual orientation.

Fatemi, A., Khodayari, L., & Stewart, A. (2015). Counseling in Iran: History, current status, and future trends. *Journal of Counseling & Development, 93*(1), 105–113. The counseling profession in Iran currently faces challenges in addressing the needs of women; ethnic minorities; and lesbian, gay, bisexual, transgender, and queer individuals. In this article, the authors focus on the historical background, current trends, and future challenges of the counseling profession in Iran.

Hansen, L. E. (2015). Encouraging pre-service teachers to address issues of sexual orientation in their classrooms. *Multicultural Education, 22*(2), 51–55. In the article, the author discusses the ways in which teacher educators can encourage future teachers to tackle lesbian, gay, bisexual and transgender (LGBT) issues in their classrooms.

Hipolito-Delgado, C. P. (2015). Beyond cultural competence. *Counseling Today, 56*(10), 50–55. The article discusses a study led by researcher Judith Hermosillo, which highlighted the concept of "ally" in the lesbian, gay, bisexual, transgender, queer, intersex, and questioning

(LGBTQIQ) community. It mentions the multicultural counseling competencies that were adopted by the U.S. Association for Multicultural Counseling & Development and the American Counseling Association (ACA) in 1992.

McGill, C.M., & Collins, J.C. (2015). Creating fugitive knowledge through disorienting dilemmas: The issue of bottom identity development. *New Horizons in Adult Education & Human Resource Development*, *27*(1), 29–40. Rather than examining only lesbian, gay, bisexual, and transgender (LGBT) people, professionals need conversations about sexuality that focus on sub-identity groups, such as gay men who identify as bottoms (generally prefer receptive roles during anal and/or oral intercourse).

Zirkel, P.A. (2015). LGBT students. *Principal*, *94*(4), 50–51. The article considers legal issues relating to lesbian, gay, bisexual, and transgender (LGBT) students in the United States. Selected topics include the Supreme Court's decision wherein a transgender student in Maine challenged a school district's exclusion of the student from the use of the girls' bathroom, the application of the court's decision to transgender students in other states, and the civil rights of LGBT students.

16 Counseling Lesbian, Gay, Bisexual, and Transgender Clients

QUESTIONS TO BE EXPLORED

- How does counseling intervention differ for lesbian, gay, bisexual, and transgender (LGBT) clients and for heterosexual clients?
- What are the American Psychological Association (APA) guidelines for counseling LGBT clients?
- What counseling concerns and issues are particularly relevant to LGBT clients in each of the specific developmental stages?
- How can counselors help LGBT clients deal with harassment, prejudice, discrimination, and other types of physical and psychological abuse?
- How can counselors provide effective individual, group, and family counseling for LGBT clients in the four lifespan stages?
- What factors should counselors consider when planning professional intervention for LGBT clients who are also minority and/or disabled?
- How can counselors provide professional intervention for LGBT clients who have HIV/AIDS or who are experiencing bereavement because LGBT friends and relatives have died?
- How can counselors most effectively intervene with clients who are suicidal or engaged in substance abuse?
- What special challenges might confront counselors of LGBT clients who might not be experienced in working with homosexual clients?

OVERVIEW

Throughout history, lesbian, gay, bisexual, and transgender persons have experienced prejudice, harassment, discrimination, and violence, all of which resulted in adverse psychological, health, and job-related outcomes. Many same-sex orientation people never "came-out" or let their sexual orientation be known. Living a life of secrecy had adverse effects, but being honest with another person about one's sexual orientation could result in violence and even death. Fortunately, some people have evolved to more positive attitudes and views, but certainly not all people. Counselors are in a unique position to demonstrate understanding and acceptance; plus, counselors, regardless of sexual orientation, have an ethical responsibility to the counseling profession.

Most counseling professionals agree that people have more than one culture, and lesbians, gay men, and bisexuals have a "same-sex sexual orientation" culture, just as heterosexual people share a culture of heterosexualism. However, counselors of LGBT clients will want to improve their knowledge, attitudes, and skills because there are indications that LGBT clients will increasingly make their sexual preferences known during counseling sessions. Counselors also have a responsibility to be aware of their own values in helping others. Standard A.4.b of the *ACA Code of Ethics* (American Counseling Association, 2014) includes a statement about the ethical responsibility of counselors to be aware of their own values and how these may influence the counseling process. Likewise, counselors should never impose their own values on the client during the counseling process. This chapter looks at the differences in counseling LGBT clients; some special concerns and issues LGBT clients might experience; and the use of individual, group, and family counseling for LGBT clients in the four lifespan periods. Also, whenever possible, attention will be given to LGBT clients who are minority and/or disabled.

DIFFERENCES IN COUNSELING LESBIAN, GAY, BISEXUAL, AND TRANSGENDER CLIENTS

Counselors who intervene with LGBT clients encounter different challenges, concerns, and issues than those encountered while counseling heterosexual clients. One cannot assume that the only difference will be the client's sexual orientation. Table 16.1 shows difficult issues LGBT clients might encounter.

Other differences undoubtedly will surface as counselors intervene with LGBT clients. The brief list that follows provides only representative examples; counselors will need to consider individual LGBT clients to determine the extent to which their sexual orientation affects counseling. The important point for counselors to remember is that a client's sexual orientation will affect the client's perceptions of problems, concerns, and issues. Just as Hispanic American counselors need to understand African American and other cultures' worldviews and culturally related issues, the heterosexual counselor needs to understand the differences in intervening with LGBT clients and vice versa. In addition to understanding the differences in counseling LGBT clients, it will be necessary to gain the knowledge, develop the attitudes, and refine the skills needed to intervene with these clients, just as this book has repeatedly recommended for counselors working with differing cultural groups.

Table 16.1 Differences in Counseling LGBT Clients

---

1. LGBT clients face challenges resulting from their different worldviews.

    Example: Their sexual orientation will affect their individual experiences (and perceptions of those experiences) as well as their social, moral, religious, educational, economic, and political views.

2. LGBT clients experience different types of discrimination and injustice.

    Example: They experience discrimination because of their sexual orientation and their minority or disabled status, resulting in multiple types of jeopardy or discrimination.

3. LGBT clients experience career problems caused by their coming out.

    Example: They might feel their careers will be jeopardized (or employment might actually be terminated) if they formally come out.

4. LGBT clients experience family problems caused by coming out or perceived sexual orientation.

    Example: Their family members object to their sexual orientation on moral, religious, or other grounds, resulting in loss of family support and family cohesiveness.

Kirk and Belovics (2008) provide a list of guidelines for providing equitable treatment in the workplace. We selected several guidelines that we think are appropriate for counselors in all situations, whether it be employees, counseling programs and clinics, or community counseling centers.

Specific policies that prohibit discrimination based on sexual orientation or identity include

- creation of safe environments that are free of heterosexist, homophobic, and AIDS-phobic behaviors;

- organization-wide policies and education about LGBT individuals and about AIDS;
- an equitable benefit program that recognizes domestic partners of gay, lesbian, and bisexuals; and
- support groups for LGBT individuals.

What approach should the counselor take when the client does not know whether or not to come out? Should the counselor encourage the client to come out or to conceal his or her sexual orientation? These are difficult questions, and the answer often depends on the individual client. The overriding counseling principle should be the welfare of the client. The counselor should try to establish a safe, comfortable climate so that the client can come out if she or he wishes. The decision to come out should be strictly the client's decision. If the client is considering coming out, the counselor can help by discussing possible plans and their consequences; however, the final decision needs to be made by the client.

GUIDELINES FOR PSYCHOTHERAPY WITH LESBIAN, GAY, BISEXUAL, AND TRANSGENDER CLIENTS

It is useful for counseling professionals to be aware of the nature and availability of community resources for LGBT clients and their families. Particularly useful are those organizations that provide support to the parents, young and adult children, and friends of LGBT clients; programs that provide assistance to victims of hate crimes; programs for LGBT youth; and groups that focus on parenting issues, relationships, and coming out. There are also professional organizations for LGBT persons of color, groups for HIV/AIDS issues, groups for socializing and networking in business, and groups that provide spiritual assistance. Psychologists who are unfamiliar with available resources for LGBT persons may obtain consultations or referrals from local agencies and state psychological associations. The list that follows provides guidelines for psychotherapy with LGBT clients.

Guidelines for Psychotherapy With LGBT Clients

Attitudes Toward Homosexuality and Bisexuality

Guideline 1: Psychologists understand that homosexuality and bisexuality are not indicative of mental illness.

Guideline 2: Psychologists are encouraged to recognize how their attitudes and knowledge about LGBT issues may be relevant to assessment and treatment and seek consultation or make appropriate referrals when indicated.

Guideline 3: Psychologists strive to understand the ways in which social stigmatization (i.e., prejudice, discrimination) pose risk factors for the mental health and well-being of LGBT clients.

Guideline 4: Psychologists strive to understand how inaccurate or prejudicial views of homosexuality or bisexuality may affect the client's presentation in treatment and the therapeutic process.

Relationships and Families

Guideline 5: Psychologists strive to be knowledgeable about and respect the importance of LGBT relationships.

Guideline 6: Psychologists strive to understand the particular circumstances and challenges faced by parents who are lesbian, gay, or bisexual.

Guideline 7: Psychologists recognize that the families of LGBT persons may include people who are not legally or biologically related.

Guideline 8: Psychologists strive to understand how a person's sexual orientation may have an impact on his or her family of origin and the relationship to that family.

(*Continued*)

Issues of Diversity

Guideline 9: Psychologists are encouraged to recognize the particular life issues or challenges that are related to multiple and often conflicting cultural norms, values, and beliefs that LGBT persons of racial and ethnic minorities face.

Guideline 10: Psychologists are encouraged to recognize the particular challenges that bisexual individuals experience.

Guideline 11: Psychologists strive to understand the special problems that exist for LGBT youth.

Guideline 12: Psychologists consider generational differences within LGBT populations and the particular challenges that LGBT older adults may experience.

Source: Developed from "Guidelines for Psychotherapy with Lesbian, Gay, and Bisexual Clients," by American Psychological Association, 2000, *American Psychologist*, 5(2), 1440–1451.

COUNSELING LESBIAN, GAY, BISEXUAL, AND TRANSGENDER CHILDREN

Counselors providing professional intervention with LGBT children need to recognize the unique challenges of the childhood developmental period. For example, children may realize they are different in some way, but they may not understand how they differ or what the feelings of being different mean. Effective counselors of LGBT or questioning children usually try to understand children's worldviews and perceptions of their home, school, and community. Also, it will be imperative that counselors understand children's perceptions of the problems. Being called derogatory names on a daily basis can take a significant toll on a child. Telling a child to "just ignore those who call you names or laugh at you" will probably be ineffective. The counselor's challenge is to recognize that few children will have formally come out, so the counselor might not actually know whether the child has a same-sex sexual orientation.

Counseling Concerns and Issues

The LGBT child (or a child whom others suspect as such) experiences concerns and issues that other children might not experience. Disabled children might be laughed at and taunted, but LGBT children experience their own particular forms of fear, harassment, and prejudice.

LGBT children often face a hostile school and societal environment. In many schools, the needs of LGBT children largely go unnoticed and unmet. Their identity as a minority group is ignored, even though in many schools they are often the most hated group. LGBT children are fair game for adults and other students to harass, demean, and threaten. Although parents and community members often consider schools to be safe places where teachers prohibit harassment, such is not always the case. Children are physically and psychologically abused on buses, playgrounds, hallways, and even in classrooms, while teachers either are unaware of it or choose to ignore it. LGBT children are left to fend for themselves, although they often fear for their physical and psychological safety. They dread going to school because they know they will be taunted by other students. Most school districts have policies against name-calling and harassment due to sexual orientation (or perceived sexual orientation), but all too often students who harass and cause physical or psychological damage go unpunished. Counselors can play significant roles in this area—they can encourage other students not to harass and taunt, and they can also encourage teachers and administrators to take strong and decisive action to stop harassment of LGBT children.

Although Robert McGarry (2013) was writing only about curriculum, he explained that for schools to accommodate LGBT students, educators must do more than just add LGBT to the curriculum. (Note while we use LGBT in this book, McGarry presented the findings from a study conducted by GLSEN—The Gay, Lesbian, Straight Education Network.) McGarry suggested schools with LGBT-inclusive practices provide less hostile learning and educational experiences for LGBT students and increased feelings of connectedness to the school community. When students do not feel connected, they are more likely to miss classes and even full days from school. Not only does this affect their learning, but it also denies them the identity development benefits that result from the activities and in-person interactions that occur in schools. McGarry maintains that schools too often ignore the existence of LGBT students; demonize LGBT students as being wrong; stigmatize these students as unacceptable; and exclude transgendered students (e.g., discussing only gays, lesbians, and bisexuals and ignoring transgendered students).

LGBT children often misunderstand the "differences" they feel. Although they might not realize that their feelings indicate a different sexual orientation, many feel a need to share their feelings with someone. These children have not formally engaged in a coming out process, so the counselor should not automatically make assumptions about their sexual orientation. They may have same-sex orientation feelings, but the feelings might never be acted upon. However, the counselor can still attempt to help LGBT children understand their perceptions of feeling different.

Another counseling concern or issue is when LGBT children are from a culture different from the majority culture of the school (regardless of what the school's majority culture is). To be lesbian, gay, or bisexual or to be perceived as such and to be of a minority culture as well can result in multiple jeopardy for harassment. The presence of a disability is yet another reason for being harassed. Counselors who are effective with LGBT children (or those children who are harassed because others suspect they are LGBT) are sufficiently perceptive of other reasons for harassment. Counselors should make a commitment to take planned action to stop all harassment, whether owing to culture, disability, or perceived sexual orientation.

Counseling Considerations

Counselors of LGBT children often must deal with several special considerations. Are the child's perceptions of feeling different a result of sexual orientation? Should sexual orientation even be mentioned during counseling sessions? Should all therapy be individual to avoid the possibility of harassment resulting from group therapy? How realistic is family therapy? These are difficult questions to answer, and a decision can be reached only through consideration of each individual case.

Individual and Group Therapy

As discussed in Chapter 15, counselors and all professionals, as well as the general population, should refrain from assuming that a person is lesbian, gay, or bisexual based on that person's appearance or actions. Just because a boy is effeminate and prefers books over football does not mean he is gay or ever will be gay. The same is true with girls who prefer more rugged clothes to dresses or soccer over cooking; they may or may not be lesbians, but counselors cannot make assumptions based solely on preferences.

It is another matter if the child shares with the counselor that his or her "feelings of difference" include a same-sex sexual orientation. Some people have told us that they knew they had a same-sex sexual orientation as early as age eight or nine. If, during individual therapy, the child openly confides to the counselor a same-sex sexual orientation, then the counselor has the professional responsibility to avoid judgmental statements, to help the child to accept the feelings, to help the child to understand the meaning of same-sex orientation, and to agree to provide support and acceptance. The counselor should not engage in any attempts to change the child's sexual orientation. Likewise, the counselor should maintain strict confidentiality about the child's disclosure.

Schneider and Owens (2000) offer recommendations for schools fostering a supportive community at three levels:

1. *Institutional:* School leaders need to communicate to all educators and counselors that value is placed on safe, nurturing environments.
2. *Classroom:* Educators and counselors can discuss the fact that people differ and that these differences have the potential to enhance our understanding of the world and one another.
3. *One-on-one:* Educators and counselors need to create a safe environment in which to learn and safe places where LGBT students feel supported.

Unless the school has a sufficient number of LGBT students who have formally come out, group therapy is probably not an effective means of intervention. Few, if any, elementary schools have group therapy solely for LGBT students; the number of group therapy instances might be higher in middle schools and high schools. Most children who think their perceptions of feeling different resulted from same-sex sexual orientations would be reluctant to share this information in a group therapy session owing to possible harassment and taunting.

Counselors can and should use group or class opportunities to discuss children's differences, the need to accept differences, and the need to avoid harassing others. In these group or class presentations, the counselor makes an individual decision about whether to refer to issues about people with same-sex sexual orientations—such a decision should be based on children's ages and developmental levels. For example, referring to same-sex sexual orientation might be risky for first graders but more realistic for sixth graders. The counselor might have to consider how broadly to consider the term *group therapy.* If the term *group therapy* is sufficiently flexible to include class discussions, then diversity of all types should be discussed, with an emphasis on acceptance and positive treatment of others.

Family Therapy

Some children may confide their perceptions of feeling different to their parents; however, in all likelihood, most children will not, especially if they know their feelings relate to (and if they understand the meaning of) their sexual orientation. Theoretically, children can disclose their same-sex sexual orientation during family therapy sessions, but from a practical perspective this is unlikely. First, they may not know these feelings relate to sexual orientation. Second, they may be reluctant to share these feelings, especially if they come from a culture that believes children's behaviors reflect on the mother's and father's parenting ability. In such cultures, the embarrassment they experience and the accompanying feelings of shame they bring to their families will be too great for most children to admit they feel different.

Assuming that a counselor does decide on family therapy, and assuming the child does share feelings of same-sex sexual orientation, the counselor should strive to understand the parents' feelings (especially if they are both heterosexual) as well as their acceptance levels regarding the child's disclosure. The counselor should also help parents to understand the child's need for continued love and acceptance. The counselor should work to keep family therapy from becoming negative; for example, the counselor should prevent parents from assigning blame for their child's sexual orientation or prevent parents from reprimanding the child for being different. The session should not end with despair over the child's disclosure, disappointment with the child, or anger toward any person in the family therapy session.

Case Study 16.1 focuses on a counselor's challenges with Troy, an African American boy who felt "different."

Case Study 16.1: Counseling Troy, an African American Child

The counselor, an Asian American, knew that Troy, a sixth-grade African American boy, faced a number of problems. One of Troy's teachers had recommended him for counseling. After one visit, the counselor concluded the boy faced a number of problems. He avoided participation in physical activities, he felt he was "different" ("I am not like them," he once told the counselor), he avoided social contact, and he received considerable ridicule and verbal abuse from fellow students. The counselor concluded that Troy had sufficient problems to warrant special counseling. He decided against group therapy because Troy would be uncomfortable admitting his feelings and accompanying problems, and he decided against family therapy because Troy had indicated that his parents did not know the problems he faced.

The counselor considered his intervention plan. He decided not to mention sexual orientation because Troy had never said that his "different" feelings were sexually related. He would discuss Troy's feeling different and the origins of these feelings, his lack of participation in voluntary school activities, the ridicule and psychological abuse (and its negative effects), and his avoidance of social contact. He would also work on self-acceptance and self-esteem as well as his treatment of others—that is, giving others the impression that he was ignoring or avoiding them. He and Troy would also discuss Troy's apparent giving up on this year—as he said, "It [his different feelings and being called derogatory names] really doesn't matter—I am going to middle school next year anyway."

The counselor thought that Troy would receive as much or more psychological abuse at the middle school as he had received in the elementary school. Although he did not tell Troy that, he still wanted to work on Troy's self-esteem and the other negative effects of ridicule and taunting. Also, although he did not plan to ask Troy about his sexual orientation, he still planned his response should Troy disclose any same-sex feelings. "I don't want to look shocked, dismayed, or disappointed," the counselor thought. "It is imperative that Troy have someone to accept him, especially if he discloses information regarding his sexuality."

The counselor decided on two primary approaches. First, he planned to determine Troy's reasons for feeling different, and second, he planned to work on Troy's self-acceptance and self-esteem. He thought, "There might be a time when Troy will want to involve his parents, but this is probably not the time."

Counseling and Development 16.1: The Childhood Years

Trey, an 11-year-old boy, seemed too attached to two boys in his class. His teacher noticed that he seemed overly interested in male anatomy from books he read, drawings, and overheard conversations. She realized that one characteristic of the developmental period was an interest in sexual curiosity. She talked with the counselor, who agreed that Trey's interest was a bit intense, but as long as he was not being abused, there was little that she could do.

The counselor met with Trey. Nothing was mentioned about sexual orientation or sexual abuse, mainly because Trey was standoffish and it was their first session. Still, the counselor decided on several strategies.

Counseling Strategies:

1. Discuss with him the teacher's observations to hear what he has to say; such a discussion may or may not lead to the topic of sexual orientation.

2. Continue individual therapy with a focus on confidentiality, friendships, and physical development.

3. Guide the discussion to friendship development and self-esteem issues.

COUNSELING LESBIAN, GAY, BISEXUAL, AND TRANSGENDER ADOLESCENTS

Mayer, Garofalo, and Makadon (2014) examined ways to promote the successful development of sexual and gender minority youths. Because of societal discomfort with atypical expressions of sexual orientation and gender identity, lesbian, gay, bisexual, and transgender (LGBT) youths have experienced enhanced developmental challenges compared with their heterosexual peers.

Mayer et al. (2014) maintained that despite major advances in the extension of civil liberties for sexual and gender minority populations, bias and stigma remain a concern for young people, who often live in social environments that expose them to rejection and isolation, discrimination, and abuse. Such issues can lead to loss of self-esteem, depression, and other emotional distress.

According to Mayer et al. (2014), sexual attraction begins with onset of puberty, if not sooner. The usual processes of developing sexual and gender identities is particularly stressful for sexual minority youths, because they are likely to experience identity confusion and lack of support for their emerging identities, resulting in high levels of stress as they realize they have a stigmatized identity. They may feel shame, guilt, or denial. Likewise, possibilities exist that heterosexuals, as well as sexual and gender minority youths, are recognizing their sexual identities at earlier ages than in previous decades, and for LGBT youths, they confront social challenges when they may be less intellectually and socially mature and may have fewer social supports than older adolescents and young adults.

Adolescent health education in schools is often primarily focused on pregnancy prevention rather than assessing risks for HIV and sexually transmitted infections, while having satisfying sex lives. At least some clients desire to discuss sexual orientation and gender identity with clinicians. With respect to speaking openly to LGBT youths, bias among clinicians toward sexual and gender minorities has been identified as a cause of health disparities. Clinical training needs to be improved by providing new knowledge and addressing clinician attitudes toward sexual and gender minority youths and to enhance open and nonjudgmental discussions in clinical settings to facilitate clients' health and resilience. A primary issue for clinicians is to recognize the importance of, and become comfortable with, talking openly with their patients and clients about their sexual orientation and gender identity (Mayer et al., 2014).

Counselors intervening with clients in the adolescent developmental stage need to remember that adolescents differ from both children and adults. All too often, people mistakenly view adolescents as older children or younger adults. However, adolescence is a distinct developmental period with its own unique challenges and developmental tasks. As previously mentioned, many children might not understand why they feel "different" and few will have engaged in a formal coming out process. Many adolescents have engaged in at least some form of sexual experimentation, either different-sex, same-sex, or both. Most LGBT adolescents fully understand their same-sex sexual orientation, and many will have engaged in some type of same-sex sexual activity.

Counselors working with adolescents need to remember that this developmental period requires the achievement of specific developmental tasks, such as building wholesome attitudes toward self, sexual identity, and cultural identities; learning to get along with peers of all cultures and both genders; developing positive attitudes and behaviors toward social groups; and achieving socially responsible and acceptable behavior. Perceptive counselors will bear in mind that because some developmental tasks vary with culture, such tasks may also vary with sexual orientation.

LGBT adolescents face many of the same problems as their heterosexual counterparts, with the added burden of attempting to incorporate a stigmatized sexual identity. Schools often do little to provide support for LGBT adolescents as they develop a sexual identity. Teachers usually avoid the subject of same-sex sexual orientations. Nor do LGBT adolescents view the counselor as a person with whom they can share problems. Studies have found that two-thirds of counselors surveyed expressed negative attitudes toward same-sex sexual orientations.

General recommendations for counseling gay men, lesbians, and bisexuals include adapting paperwork to allow clients to indicate their sexual orientation (as well as the nature of the intimate relationships); offering educational activities, groups, and outreach programs; providing books and other literature specific for LGBT individuals in waiting rooms; and demonstrating tolerance and actual affirmation for LGBT people. Finally, the presence of openly gay, lesbian, and bisexual people in the counseling centers can serve as positive role models for clients seeking help.

It is important that counselors understand the unique difficulties and risks that LGBT adolescents face. Prominent concerns of LGBT youth include social vulnerability and isolation and verbal and physical abuse, all of which have been associated with academic problems, running away, prostitution, substance abuse, and suicide. LGBT youth may experience estrangement from their parents when they reveal their sexual orientation. Parental rejection places LGBT adolescents at increased risk for homelessness, prostitution, HIV/AIDS infection (caused by risky sexual behavior or other factors), and stress. Youth are also at increased risk for being victims of violence, even within their families; substance abuse; and attempting suicide.

Counseling Concerns and Issues

As with other stages along the lifespan, LGBT adolescents experience prejudice, discrimination, harassment, and name-calling in school and society. Some LGBT adolescents actually fear for their physical and psychological safety. When this violence occurs at school, dropping out seems to be the only solution to many victims. Speaking primarily of institutional practices and lesbians, educational institutions often refuse to deal with prejudice, discrimination, and abuse against lesbians in the same way they protect other oppressed groups. Schools can help lesbian adolescents by establishing homosexually affirmative school environments that provide external support for students with same-sex sexual orientation.

Although coming out can produce psychological well-being, it can also be dangerous. Coming out prematurely presents the possibility of rejection as well as verbal and physical abuse. Coming out should be postponed until the adolescent gains a reasonable degree of self-worth and a support network. The lesbian adolescent needs to be secure in her identity before coming out, because her self-doubt or hesitancy may heighten the confusion of others, thus making her acceptance more difficult. Counselors should advise adolescents to weigh the pros and cons of coming out, while also examining their reasons for coming out.

Several developmental tasks occur during the coming out period. The first involves the development of interpersonal skills to meet and socialize with others with similar sexual orientations. Second, adolescents need to develop a sense of personal attractiveness and sexual competence. Third, it is helpful for the adolescent to realize that self-esteem is not based on sexual conquests, to help prevent seeing oneself in only a sexual manner.

LGBT adolescents often have difficulty dealing with parents and family members who condemn same-sex sexual orientations. They often experience alienation from family members; they face mistreatment and disapproval or rejection from parents who react with shame, anger, and guilt. LGBT adolescents also deal with developmental and health concerns as well as HIV/AIDS. They deal with the typical developmental concerns (e.g., physical size, developmental tasks, socialization, cognitive abilities) that many heterosexual adolescents deal with daily, but LGBT adolescents have another set of concerns related to their sexual orientation. Such concerns as whether to come out and its effects on sexual identities and self-esteem take a serious toll. Although the adolescent developmental period is a relatively healthy time of life, LGBT adolescents know they are at increased risk for HIV/AIDS, especially when they have sexual relations with adolescents whom they do not know well. Counselors of LGBT adolescents can play significant roles as they focus professional intervention toward health concerns, such as HIV/AIDS prevention; the need to have some information about partners' sexual history; and the need to choose an appropriate time (and appropriate reasons) for coming out.

Finally, some LGBT adolescents deal with being lesbian, gay, or bisexual, being from a different culture and perhaps being disabled. As previously mentioned, being LGBT and from a nonmajority culture can result in double jeopardy. Although there is not sufficient research on specific cultures to draw major conclusions, counselors know enough to conclude that minority LGBT adolescents can experience difficult situations.

While we hope perceptions of Asian American lesbian and gay adolescents have changed, Chung and Katamaya (1998) explain how same-sex sexual orientation is at serious odds with the Asian American culture. Having a same-sex sexual orientation in Asian cultures conflicts with traditional gender roles for men (e.g., continuation of the family) and women (e.g., taking care of husband and children). Because traditional gender roles and the family system are central to most Asian cultures, violation of gender roles and threats to the family system are unacceptable. Therefore, same-sex sexual orientations are often condemned. Other reasons exist for same-sex sexual orientations being unaccepted in Asian cultures. Many modern Asian countries developed out of agricultural societies that relied primarily on human labor. Larger families meant more human power and economic potential. Therefore, men and women traditionally have been expected to get married and have many children so that they can secure greater economic status. Same-sex sexual orientations work against this economic tradition and, therefore, are condemned in most Asian cultures (Chung & Katamaya, 1998).

In conclusion, American society deals with issues related to same-sex sexual orientations primarily at the adult level and at the expense of adolescents. Even within the lesbian and gay communities, adolescents are not given adequate attention. Counselors who understand the concerns of LGBT adolescents realize that those who do not work out their concerns may direct their fears and hostility inward, resulting in low self-esteem and self-defeating behaviors.

Counseling Considerations

LGBT adolescents will be more likely than children to seek counseling intervention. Unlike children, who often do not understand why they feel "different," LGBT adolescents will likely understand their same-sex sexual orientations. Counselors might be called on to provide individual therapy for adolescents. Likewise, depending on the number of LGBT adolescents and the level of school affirmation LGBT students receive, counselors might be expected to have group therapy solely for LGBT adolescents. Keeping in mind researchers who maintain that families often object vehemently to their adolescents' same-sex sexual orientation, counselors might need to plan family therapy to discuss adolescent and family concerns.

Individual and Group Therapy

Counselors planning individual counseling therapy for LGBT adolescents should base professional intervention on several beliefs. First, the adolescent who is disclosing a same-sex sexual orientation is overcoming considerable peer and cultural pressure to remain hidden. Therefore, a thorough history is needed to ascertain the adolescent's developmental level, values, and social mores. Questions about sexual activity should be asked in a nonjudgmental manner. The lack of same-sex activity or heterosexual activity may not indicate a lack of interest; instead, the lack might result from guilt, fear, insecurity, religious beliefs, parental injunctions, and lack of opportunity. Second, counselors should consider their attitudes, both cognitive and emotional, toward homosexuality. Counselors demonstrating positive attitudes can help alleviate the stigmatization felt by many LGBT adolescents. Third, some counselors tend to minimize the adolescent's same-sex sexual orientations, which can be intimidating and overwhelming and may actually increase anxiety. Counselors who genuinely want to help LGBT adolescents show understanding and concern so that these clients know their sexual orientation is neither being ignored nor condemned.

A group counseling experience for LGBT adolescents can be a powerful and positive vehicle for acquiring the social identification and self-pride that enables successful life adjustment. Exposure to other LGBT adolescents provides models for a variety of experiences, insights, and alternative behaviors in solving problems and developing healthy coping styles. This exposure will include information on how to resolve problems of identity disclosure, obtain support, manage a career, and build relationships.

Group counseling with LGBT students has several advantages. First, a group allows a safe, secure atmosphere in which to establish trusting relationships that can encourage members to risk more authentic relationships outside the group. Second, choosing goals, planning action, and modifying ideals and personal values tend to be accelerated in the group process. Third, the group experience tends to minimize the disadvantages of individual counseling for those LGBT students who might be threatened by the intimacy inherent in client-counselor relationships. A peer-oriented, self-help approach to group counseling defines LGBT persons as members of an oppressed minority group, as opposed to a group that is considered psychologically impaired. The group helps break the social isolation and can focus on personal adjustment rather than a shift in sexual orientation. Support groups seem to be the most valuable resources for lesbian and gay adolescents because they provide an opportunity for developing social skills, discussing the meaning of sexual identity and sexuality, finding support and understanding from peers, sharing information, and socializing.

Giorgis, Higgins, and McNab (2000) maintain that lesbian and gay students face discrimination manifested in acts of isolation, physical abuse, and denial of basic rights of speech, assembly, and association. Counselors should

* keep strict confidence when a student comes out;
* ask "Are you seeing anyone?" rather than "Do you have a boyfriend/girlfriend?";
* encourage library media specialists to purchase lesbian- and gay-friendly books;
* provide counseling services designed specifically for lesbian and gay students and their parents and families; and
* promote established policies to protect lesbian and gay students from harassment, violence, and discrimination.

The following list looks at counseling issues and the counselor's roles in group counseling for sexual minority youths.

Group Counseling: Counseling Issues and Counselor's Roles

Counseling Issue: *Development of Social Identity*

Counselor's Roles
1. Avoid assuming all clients are heterosexual.
2. Understand the developmental stages and challenges of both heterosexual and homosexual youth.

(Continued)

3. Gain knowledge of same-sex sexual orientation in order to be able to dispel myths and negative stereotypes.

4. Provide intervention focused on developing positive self-esteem and self-acceptance.

5. Become aware of one's own sexual prejudices.

Counseling Issue: *Isolation*

Counselor's Roles

1. Let LGBT clients know they are not alone in the world—they have people who care about them.

2. Convince LGBT clients that they have someone with whom they can confide their sexual orientation and their concerns and challenges.

3. Be willing to engage in dialogue with clients and support clients in clarifying their feelings about sexual orientation.

Counseling Issue: *Educational Issues*

Counselor's Roles

1. Move toward destigmatizing homosexuality through professional development, support staff and services, addressing sexuality in the health curriculum, library services, and general curriculum changes.

2. Commit to individuality of and fairness for all students, both heterosexual and homosexual.

3. Provide training for other educators in ways to promote individuality and equality.

4. Provide educative experiences in all discussions of sex education (both heterosexual and homosexual), including dating and relationships, parenting, sexually transmitted diseases, and available services.

5. Work to eliminate administrative discrimination in the hiring of lesbian and gay staff members.

Counseling Issue: *Family Issues*

Counselor's Roles

1. Help LGBT adolescents and their family members in dealing with family issues.

2. Help adolescents and their families explore the possible consequences (both positive and negative) of coming out.

3. Seek help in dealing with anger, guilt, and concerns about religious issues, and the parents' own sexual prejudices.

4. Help family members deal with the stigmatization of having an LGBT family member.

5. Convince parents and family members that familial background appears to have nothing to do with the development of a same-sex sexual orientation.

6. Help parents and family members identify community resources.

Counseling Issue: *Health Risks*

Counselor's Roles

1. Address the health issues and possess the communication skills necessary to deal with sensitive health topics.

2. Ensure that LGBT adolescents have sufficient information to protect themselves from HIV/AIDS.

3. Help LGBT adolescents feel secure and comfortable discussing issues such as fear of HIV exposure, the need for HIV testing, test results, safe-sex practices, sexual orientation concerns, alcohol and drug use, and suicidal thoughts.

4. Increase LGBT adolescents' awareness of evidence and indicators of victimization, suicidal tendencies, and substance abuse in clients, especially for LGBT adolescents who are uncomfortable with their sexual orientation.

Source: Adapted from "Gay and Lesbian Adolescents: Presenting Problems and the Counselor's Roles," by J. J. Cooley, 1998, *Professional School Counseling, 1*(3), 30–34.

Family Therapy

Counselors who choose family therapy as a means of intervention are usually aware that LGBT adolescents might not admit their sexual orientation to their families, or when "coming out" during family therapy, serious problems might arise. The counselor should be knowledgeable and comfortable with adolescents (and other family members) with same-sex sexual orientations, be prepared to deal with fears of being stigmatized for working with LGBT clients, and be able to genuinely communicate acceptance and understanding of the family. Being familiar with LGBT community organizations and resources will also help the family.

Topics that counselors might choose to address during family therapy sessions include clarifying myths and stereotypes regarding what it is like to be lesbian, gay, or bisexual; encouraging LGBT adolescents to socialize with people who can help them the most (e.g., other LGBT persons and relevant support groups); and helping LGBT adolescents and their family members realize that sexual orientation is only one facet of a person's life.

Case Study 16.2 describes a counselor's intervention with Suzie, a lesbian Asian American adolescent.

Case Study 16.2: Counseling Suzie, a Lesbian Asian American Adolescent

Suzie met with her counselor in the twelfth grade. One of her teachers who thought she seemed unhappy and stress recommended her for counseling. The counselor, a 45-year-old heterosexual man, agreed to meet with Suzie several times, mostly to satisfy the teacher.

After several meetings, the counselor saw no reason to continue. Suzie disclosed little about her personal life and nothing about her sexual orientation or her previous sexual relations with boys. Although the counselor made his confidentiality clear, Suzie was still unwilling to disclose personal information that the counselor might "tell" or that she would not want her parents to know. The counselor learned that Suzie had a close family, and he perceived that something was bothering Suzie, but whatever the problem was, Suzie would not disclose it. Because there was no indication that Suzie was a lesbian or was disturbed by same-sex feelings, the counselor did not pursue the topic.

The closest any discussion came to sexual matters was when Suzie told him about the boys she had dated. However, she did not disclose that she had engaged in sexual relations. The counselor wondered why Suzie had not dated more boys, but he assumed that Suzie's parents did not approve of her dating, especially non-Asian boys.

The counseling sessions were unproductive because Suzie refused to disclose information. Several years later, Suzie wished she had told the counselor about her feelings for other girls. She said, "I was embarrassed—I could not possibly let my counselor know I was one of those lesbians. What if my parents had found out? No, I just could not tell anyone."

Counseling and Development 16.2: The Adolescent Years

Rhonda was a developmentally mature 16-year-old, interracial adolescent. A teacher saw Rhonda and another girl kissing beside the school. She told the two girls, "You girls shouldn't be doing that," and walked away. Then she began to think that maybe she should have ignored the embrace. Were her sexual values interfering with her ability to consider the situation objectively? She mentioned her concern to the counselor for several reasons—her own inability to accept two girls kissing, whether the counselor should speak with Rhonda, and whether the two girls were lesbians.

The counselor decided to speak with Rhonda about the kiss. Whether Rhonda was a lesbian really did not matter, but the school had a rule about romantic relationships at school. The counselor knew her professional responsibilities required objectivity and acceptance of others' sexuality.

Counseling Strategies:

1. Develop Rhonda's confidence in the counseling process—let her know her comments will be confidential, as long as the ACA (2005) *Code of Ethics* is followed.
2. Mention (objectively and matter-of-factly) the incident that the teacher observed to gauge Rhonda's perception of the embrace and kiss.
3. Do not mention possible lesbianism—let Rhonda disclose what she feels comfortable sharing.

The following list shows strategies for involving and educating parents and families of lesbian students.

Strategies for Helping Families of Lesbian Students

---

1. Be sincere, because these students might have been on guard most of their lives trying to determine who can and cannot be trusted.
2. Use the same-sex terminology the students use and remember that students might appear confused about their sexual orientation.
3. Respect confidentiality of students' sexual orientation and personal concerns.
4. Deal with feelings first—most young lesbians feel alone, guilty, ashamed, and angry.
5. Anticipate some confusion—understand that sexual orientation is a biological fact and counselors cannot talk students out of their sexual orientation.
6. Be aware of the potential for depression, especially as lesbians let go of their heterosexual identity.
7. Provide accurate information on depression as well as how sexually transmitted diseases, including HIV/AIDS, can be passed among women.

COUNSELING LESBIAN, GAY, BISEXUAL, AND TRANSGENDER ADULTS

Counseling LGBT adults is both similar to and different from counseling children and adolescents. Some similar issues include coming out, prejudice, and harassment, which affect LGBT adults in much the same way as they affect LGBT children and adolescents. Some differences during the adult development period include career barriers; issues surrounding adoption, parenting, and same-sex marriages; and bereavement issues. There may also be added health concerns that usually occur during the adult developmental period. Therefore, counselors of LGBT adults need to plan for those challenges that cross developmental stages and also plan for challenges specific to the adult developmental period.

Counseling Concerns and Issues

MacGillivray and Kozik-Rosabal (2000) provide an excellent discussion of terminology in which they define GLBTQ as gay, lesbian, bisexual, transgender, and queer/questioning.

They describe the terms they prefer and provide rationales. In their article, they look at sexual orientation as "simply a state of being" (p. 289). Other topics explored include gender identity, the roles schools play in the creation and perpetuation of discrimination directed toward GLBTQ students, the difficulty of determining demographics of GLBTQ students, and the fact that being GLBTQ is not just an urban issue.

Interesting aspects of MacGillivray and Kozik-Rosabal's work include the following:

1. The term itself, GLBTQ, seems to support the inclusion the authors want: No client is being excluded due to his or her sexual orientation.
2. The assertion is that GLBTQ is not just an urban issue—such students also attend schools in rural and suburban schools.
3. In addition to meeting the needs of GLBTQ students, schools need to prepare heterosexual students for democratic citizenship in communities with significant populations of politically active and out GLBTQ people.

MacGillivray and Kozik-Rosabal suggest that educators have an enormous task before them as they make schools safe for GLBTQ students. Undoubtedly, counselors also will play significant roles, both helping GLBTQ students as well as helping heterosexual students accept diversity among all people.

Counselors of LGBT adults will be called on to provide professional intervention for a number of concerns and challenges. One key to effective intervention for LGBT adults is to remember that counseling efforts should reflect perspectives unique to the adult developmental period. First, many LGBT clients face social stigmatization, violence, and discrimination. Belonging to a sexual minority can cause increased stress related to long-term daily hassles ranging from hearing antigay jokes to more serious problems, such as loss of employment, home, and custody of children or actual violence. Also, LGBT adults sometimes fear for their physical and psychological safety, which results in a reluctance to come out and in their decision to limit their activities to predominantly homosexual communities.

Second, LGBT adults face challenges associated with coming out. Will they be rejected by their social and business peers? Will their jobs be threatened? What is the right time (assuming there is a right time) for coming out? Will family members support the adult's same-sex sexual orientation and the decision to come out publicly? Because heterosexism is so intense in Asian cultures, an openly homosexual lifestyle often is not an option; the consequences of disclosing one's sexual orientation are just too threatening. Most lesbians and gay men in Asian American societies suppress their sexual orientation and outwardly follow the expectations of a heterosexual lifestyle, although there might be some discreet homosexual activities. Counseling implications include the following:

1. Encourage clients to realize that it might be necessary to resolve additional losses of friends and partners.
2. Know of and encourage clients to take advantage of the potential sources of support in the gay community.
3. Examine personal beliefs about gay men, HIV/AIDS, and AIDS-related deaths to determine actual misinformation and stereotypes.
4. Help clients facilitate the acknowledgment of anger and feelings.
5. Help HIV-positive gay men explore feelings of guilt or shame over the possibility that they have infected their lovers.
6. Plan for the fact that the loss of a partner is often not marked by the same societal rituals designed to aid the resolution of grief (e.g., memorial services, time off from work, support from family and friends).
7. Understand that families might not be a source of support during times of bereavement, particularly families who have rejected clients due to their sexual orientation.

8.   Understand and plan appropriately for self-destructive behaviors, such as bitterness, alcohol and drug use, and aggressive behaviors that might result from multiple losses.

Career counselors working with LGBT clients need to be sensitive to the fact that lesbian clients are a special group and need special assistance with self-exploration and job search strategies. Pope et al. (2004) recommend specific interventions directed at counselors, at individual counseling activities, at career counseling programs within institutions, and at advocacy and community action. Program-focused interventions for career counseling include

- supporting gay and lesbian professionals as role models for students;
- providing information on national gay and lesbian networks of professionals and community people such as the Association for Gay, Lesbian, and Bisexual Issues in Counseling;
- sharing information on existing local gay and lesbian resources;
- offering special programming, such as talks by lesbian and gay professionals;
- arranging career shadowing opportunities with other lesbian and gay professionals;
- facilitating internships or cooperative education placements in gay- and lesbian-owned or operated businesses; and
- establishing mentoring programs.

The gay community has been disproportionately affected by HIV/AIDS. Counselors who plan professional intervention for infected LGBT persons include topics such as risk-reduction education, knowledge of the diseases, safe-sex practices, and assistance with grieving the loss of loved ones. Other topics include potential pain, possibility of death, feelings of being dirty and damaged, social rejection, and job loss. Anger might be targeted at former lovers or sexual partners, at oneself for being careless, and at the medical establishment. In addition to providing emotional support during periods of anxiety, counselors can help patients with education, relaxation, and assistance in using existing coping methods that have been successfully used in the past. Counselors can also help patients who are near death to resolve unfinished business and personal issues. Making out wills and implementing a power of attorney for health care are among the last preparations for death.

LGBT couples experience problems that are both similar to and different from those of heterosexual couples. Problems can include communication difficulties, sexual problems, dual-career issues, and commitment issues. Problems that may be presented in therapy that are specific to LGBT couples include the couple's disclosure of sexual orientation to their families, work colleagues, health professionals, and caregivers; differences between partners in the disclosure process; issues derived from the effects of gender socialization in same-sex couples; and HIV/AIDS status. External issues such as pressure from families of origin or current or former heterosexual partners may also arise (APA, 2000).

There appear to be no significant differences in the capabilities of LGBT parents compared with heterosexual parents. However, LGBT parents face challenges not encountered by most heterosexual parents because of the stigma associated with homosexuality and bisexuality. Prejudice has led to institutional discrimination by the legal, educational, and social welfare systems. In a number of cases, LGBT parents have lost custody of their children, have been restricted from visiting their children, have been prohibited from living with their domestic partners, or have been prevented from adopting or being foster parents based on their sexual orientation (APA, 2000). LGBT parents face the same problems and issues as those faced by heterosexual parents, such as how to maintain age-appropriate discipline or how to nurture children's self-esteem.

Some LGBT persons face additional problems when they are from a different culture and/ or have a disability. Counselors have greater challenges when working with clients who have more than one difference. It will be necessary to understand the multifaceted discrimination these clients might face due to their same-sex sexual orientation, minority status, and disabling condition.

In offering professional intervention to racially and ethnically diverse LGBT populations, it is not sufficient that psychologists simply recognize the racial and ethnic backgrounds of their clients. A multiple minority status may complicate and exacerbate the difficulties these clients experience. For example, clients may be affected by the ways in which their cultures view homosexuality and bisexuality. LGBT persons with disabilities may not have access to information, support, and services that are available to their nondisabled counterparts. Lack of social recognition for LGBT persons in relationships affect those with ongoing medical concerns, such as medical coverage for domestic partners, family medical leave policies, hospital visitation, medical decision making by partners, and survivorship issues.

Counseling Considerations

The assessment and treatment of LGBT clients can be adversely affected by therapists' explicit or implicit negative attitudes. For example, when heterosexual norms for identity, behavior, and relationships are applied to LGBT clients, their thoughts, feelings, and behaviors may be misinterpreted as abnormal, deviant, and undesirable. Psychologists should avoid making assumptions that a client is heterosexual, even in the presence of apparent markers of heterosexuality, for example, marital status.

Counselors need to assess both the heterosexist and sexist context in which their lesbian clients live and ask about their lesbian clients' experiences of prejudice, harassment, discrimination, and violence that are related both to their sexual orientation and to their gender. Counselors can also help clients understand how living in a society that is both heterosexist and sexist might be influencing their mental health. Counselors might also become actively involved in social change efforts aimed at eradicating heterosexism and sexism in order to improve the lives of lesbians.

Feminist therapy theorists have made significant contributions to enhancing counselors' understanding of how social, economic, political, and institutional factors affect women's lives and the particular problems that women bring to counseling. LGBT adults need individual, group, and family therapy that reflect the needs of the adult developmental period. Although some issues (e.g., prejudice, discrimination) affect LGBT persons in all lifespan periods, counselors need to focus on specific issues faced by adults. Another challenge will be for the counselor to decide whether individual therapy, group therapy, or family therapy will be the most effective approach. Key issues for practice include an understanding of human sexuality; the coming out process and how variables such as age, gender, ethnicity, race, disability, and religion may influence the process; same-sex relationship dynamics; family-of-origin relationships; struggles with spirituality and religious group membership; career issues and workplace discrimination; and coping strategies for successful functioning (APA, 2000).

Faith and spirituality play a major role in many peoples' lives. A challenge is how to provide counseling intervention with different religious beliefs, such as Jewish, Christian, and Muslim perspectives. Balkin, Watts, and Ali (2014) examined recent challenges to counselor education and the *ACA Code of Ethics* (American Counseling Association, 2005) and focus on how the three major Western religions address counseling and counselor training with diverse clients. They examine Jewish, Christian, and Muslim perspectives as related to counseling and training issues across faith, sexual orientation, and gender issues. Recent legal challenges center on the practice of counseling referrals that are made on the basis of a values conflict between a counselor and the client (i.e., *Walden v. Centers for Disease Control*) or counselor educators' actions in removing students from counseling programs for behaviors that are in conflict with the *ACA Code of Ethics* (American Counseling Association, 2005). These challenges provided the stimulus for our exploration of the intersection of faith and sexual orientation as it affects the counseling profession and counselor education. Each of the aforementioned court cases centers on the principle of how a counselor with strong religious values can practice counseling in an increasingly diverse world where there is a possibility of providing services to a client whose values or behaviors are in direct conflict with the counselor's religious value system. Of special note is the fact that, in each of the cases, issues affecting lesbian, gay, bisexual, transgender, and questioning (LGBTQ) individuals were the focus of the values conflicts and corresponding legal disputes. Sometimes, counselors offer referrals to other mental health providers when a values conflict occurs. However, this practice can be construed to be discriminatory, especially when the professional does not first seek consultation, supervision, or further education (Balkin, Watts, & Ali, 2014).

Individual and Group Therapy

LGBT clients may be in individual counseling for any number of reasons, such as convenience, the counselor's decision, or because they have not formally come out and do not wish to share their sexual orientation with a group. One essential consideration in deciding whether to use individual or group therapy is whether the LGBT client has come out and to whom. Although group therapy has a number of advantages, individual therapy is usually used until the client has formally engaged in a coming out process. Once the client has shared his or her sexual orientation and is comfortable with his or her sexuality, then often group counseling is recommended so clients can know others' perspectives. Any of the previously discussed issues (e.g., prejudice and harassment, feeling unsafe, coming out, health concerns, and disabilities) would be appropriate topics.

   Counselors will increasingly be challenged to provide group therapy with same-sex couples. Jacobson, Pappalardo, and Super (2009) suggest the need for psychoeducational group therapy for same-sex couples exists to teach couples how to develop successful and healthy relationships by using PAIRS (Practical Applications of Intimate Relationship Skills) to introduce tools and techniques for healthy communication. The authors justify the group in that same-sex couples lack role models or social norms desirable for learning necessary positive relational skills essential to navigate establishing a healthy and loving relationship. Same-sex couples contain more egalitarian qualities and do not need to overcome traditional heterosexual gender roles to develop supporting relationships. After an analysis of how same-sex couples could benefit from a group teaching relational skills, how the group will be formed and structured, the selection of participants, the rules of the group, and a functional explanation, the authors hope to garner support for the proposed group.

   The PAIRS curriculum specifically develops ground rules for facilitators when running a group. These ground rules help keep the group feeling safe and comfortable sharing. The rules, referred to as "The Basics" include: (a) we must respect each other's privacy; anything discussed in this group is confidential; confidential means not sharing or discussing any information learned about others in the group with anyone other than your partner; (b) sharing with others in the group is voluntary; when doing activities you can choose to say and express whatever feelings you have, you can also choose to remain silent; your silence will be respected; (c) speak only for yourself, not your partner; one way to remember this is to make "I" statements rather than "we" statements; (d) when sharing about your couples relationship, check it out with your partner first; checking it out with your partner before sharing something personal about your relationship demonstrates respect for your partner, just in case they feel uncomfortable about having the information shared in the group; (e) a goal of the group is to feel safe, to learn, and to have fun; this group experience is unique and is designed so that each individual experiences with their partner a sense of community that will be shared with others in the group; through this experience of community relationships strengthen; and (f) be respectful and considerate of others; please turn off cell phones during the group; at times of need it may be necessary that you be reached via your cell phone, please, at these times, put the cell phone on vibrate and kindly take the call outside the room. Ethical considerations important to remember when facilitating a group are the ethical considerations that the group requires to run both smoothly and effectively. Along with ground rules, ethical considerations are guidelines the group adheres to, ensuring both the safety of its members and allowing the facilitators to evaluate the overall effectiveness. (Jacobson et al., 2009). For additional information on PAIRS program, we suggest the American Counseling Association (http://www.counseling.org/docs/vistas/vistas_2009_jacobson-pappalardo-super.pdf?sfvrs).

Family Therapy

Flores and Carey (2000), who specialize in family therapy for Hispanic Americans, presented several questions family therapists might ask:

1. Can therapists describe and define the intersection between being Hispanic and being a man without resorting to stereotypical and all-encompassing descriptions?
2. How do we challenge internalized conceptions about the role, position, and power of family members?
3. Are we reconstructing a definition of men that reproduces heterosexist, patriarchal biases, addressing masculinity in universal terms while neglecting racial and cultural variations?
4. How do we integrate an affirmative practice in the treatment of Hispanic men?

Undoubtedly, counselors working with LGBT Hispanic Americans and their families (as well as LGBT persons and families from other cultures) can think of other questions that deserve to be answered in order to provide effective intervention for LGBT family members.

Case Study 16.3 focuses on counseling Carlos, a bisexual Hispanic American adult.

Case Study 16.3: Counseling Carlos, a Bisexual Hispanic American Adult

Carlos finally had to admit to his bisexual life, which he had long kept secret from his wife and employer. However, it still was not to them that he confided. He had to see a doctor. On one of his business trips to a large city, he had a sexual encounter with a man he met at a bar. Although this was not his first encounter, he said this was the first time he did not use protection. Afterward, his concerns about sexually transmitted diseases grew daily, and he made up excuses to avoid having sexual relations with his wife so that he would not pass any possible infection to her. Finally, he went to a family practitioner (not his family doctor) to be tested for sexually transmitted diseases. The medical tests were negative, but the doctor strongly recommended counseling. Carlos agreed mainly because if his wife and employer discovered his bisexualism, he could at least say he had entered counseling.

The counselor, a 40-year-old heterosexual Hispanic American man, met with Carlos and listened to his concerns: Carlos feared being found out by his wife and employer. As he said, "My wife and family would never understand this—I don't even understand it." The counselor knew group therapy was not practical in this case. He also concluded that family therapy was an impossibility, because Carlos was so intent on concealing his bisexualism from his wife and employer. Therefore, the counselor chose individual therapy but later admitted that he really did not know what Carlos hoped to accomplish. It was clear that Carlos had no intention of coming out; also, he had no intention of trying to negate his bisexuality (even if that were possible).

The counselor planned several topics to discuss with Carlos: coming out (which already appeared to be impossible for Carlos), how to deal with the challenges brought on by his bisexuality, how his family and employer might react, how he could have safer sex in future bisexual encounters, and, generally speaking, topics that Carlos considered important. Overall, the counselor felt that because Carlos never planned to come out, the goal should be to help Carlos accept his bisexuality and, as previously suggested, help him to use greater caution to engage in safe-sex practices, which, after his recent scare, Carlos had probably already realized.

Counseling and Development 16.3: The Adult Years

Alex was a 45-year-old married man. He and his wife had been married for 15 years. She suspected he was a bisexual. Her suspicions were confirmed when she saw him and another man exiting a motel together. She confronted him and demanded that he stop. He showed reluctance. She threatened to leave if he either did not stop or seek counseling at a local center.

Having little choice, he agreed to meet with the counselor, a male in his late 40s. Alex explained to the counselor that he had been a bisexual before he was married, and his wife caught him with another man. He expected the counselor to tell him to stop his bisexuality. Quite the contrary, the counselor adopted an objective manner.

Counseling Strategies:

1. Let Alex know that a counselor has an ethical responsibility to be objective and avoid passing judgment on others' sex lives.
2. Let Alex know his sex life (either same-sex, different-sex, or both) is his choice and responsibility.
3. Ask Alex to consider whether he and his wife would attend a marriage/family therapy session—not immediately, but sometimes in the future.

With sexual attitudes such as those described by Flores and Carey (2000), we question the effectiveness of family therapy for LGBT Hispanic Americans. Same-sex sexual orientation is at serious odds with the Asian American culture, and we also question the effectiveness of family therapy for LGBT Asian Americans. In these cultures, men are expected to be "manly," providers, and patriarchal; women are expected to be nurturing and able to take care of their husbands and families. Although times have changed, owing to acculturation and changing mores, there are still gender and family role expectations that do not include being LGBT.

However, counselors should consider family therapy if they think family members will be supportive of the LGBT clients. Questions to be considered when deciding whether to use family therapy include the following:

1. Will LGBT clients openly disclose and discuss their sexual orientation and its effects on their lives (and their family members' lives)?
2. Will they risk losing family support?
3. Will family members be supportive or condemning?
4. Will the close ties of some families be more powerful than their condemnation of same-sex sexual orientations?

Other questions will undoubtedly be raised as counselors consider individual LGBT clients and their families.

COUNSELING LESBIAN, GAY, BISEXUAL, AND TRANSGENDER ELDERLY

Two problems confront authors who write about the LGBT elderly. First, there is a common misconception that the elderly do not have sex, are not interested in sex, or both. Second, there is a paucity of literature on counseling LGBT elderly. There is a growing body of literature on the elderly and on LGBT persons; however, literature on the two subjects combined—counseling the LGBT elderly—is, unfortunately, somewhat more difficult to find. Also, as with previous discussions, it is imperative that this section will focus as much as possible on LGBT persons in the elderly developmental period. Although prejudice and discrimination challenge LGBT persons in all developmental periods, it is necessary to look at the special challenges experienced by those in the elderly developmental period.

As marginalized populations, lesbians and gay males are frequently overwhelmed by a sense of powerlessness. For example, powerlessness manifests itself in various forms of oppression, such as language, curtailment of civil rights, and criminalization of same-sex sexual contact.

Counseling Concerns and Issues

LGBT persons in the elderly lifespan period experience the problems and challenges experienced by people in the other three lifespan periods, including dealing with a hostile social environment, fearing for physical and psychological safety, dealing with coming out issues, and dealing with suicide and substance abuse. Because all LGBTs deal with these challenges, this section will focus on specific problems faced by the LGBT elderly.

First, American society ignores elderly sexuality, especially in the LGBT elderly population. Although stereotypes follow people in all developmental periods, two stereotypes about the elderly are that they either cannot function sexually or that they have no interest in sex. Both stereotypes are wrong—many elderly people are interested in sex and continue to have the capacity to engage in sexual relations. The LGBT elderly, like their heterosexual counterparts, continue their sexual interest. Another challenge for researchers and writers is that additional studies of the LGBT elderly are needed so that recommendations can be made for mental health services and counseling professionals. A challenge for counselors is to recognize that sexual activity is not just for young and middle-aged people. Counselors who assume that the elderly have neither a sex life nor an interest in sexual activities make a serious mistake and should examine their personal stereotypes and assumptions.

Second, although all LGBT persons experience prejudice and discrimination, the elderly also deal with problems in housing, assisted living facilities, nursing homes, retirement benefits, medical attention, and long-term health care. Some elderly LGBT people experience discrimination as they attempt to find housing. Although they probably will not be told that their sexual orientation is the reason for being unable to find a place to live, realistically speaking, some landlords will not rent to LGBT persons. Sometimes LGBT persons are told that the place has already been rented, or they will be quoted an exorbitant rental fee that far exceeds the value of the dwelling or comparable places in the neighborhood. Assisted living facilities and nursing homes often take deliberate action to deny access to elderly LGBT people, perhaps because of outright prejudice or fear of HIV/AIDS and other diseases. Elderly LGBT people face the typical problems that most elderly people experience, but they also experience problems associated with being lesbian, gay, or bisexual. Lack of legal rights and protection in medical emergencies and a lack of acknowledgment of couples' relationships, particularly following the loss of a partner, have been associated with feelings of helplessness, depression, and disruption of normative grief processes in LGBT elderly (APA, 2000).

Third, some elderly LGBT people deal with issues arising from their sexual orientation, minority status, and, perhaps, having a disability. Although all elderly people probably experience discrimination at some time, the situation undoubtedly grows more acute when the elderly person has one or more of these risk factors for discrimination.

Fourth, some elderly deal with developmental and health concerns as well as HIV/AIDS. Most elderly people experience some health problems as they grow older. However, LGBT elderly might also be concerned about their sexual orientation and related health problems, such as HIV/AIDS. Unless they live with others (e.g., a roommate) of similar sexual orientation or in an LGBT community, they might lack a support system to discuss developmental and health concerns. In order to receive the medical attention they need, elderly LGBT people often feel required to share their sexual orientation, which may result in additional discrimination.

Counseling Considerations

Some counselors erroneously think sexual issues, particularly those surrounding same-sex sexual orientation, will not surface when counseling the elderly. Some counselors think the elderly will be more concerned with how long they will live, with whom they will live, and whether their health will decline. Although these are all legitimate concerns, LGBT elderly may also be concerned with coming out issues, HIV/AIDS, and other sexual orientation issues. As with LGBT clients in other lifespan periods, the counselor will be challenged to decide whether to intervene with individual, group, or family therapy.

Individual and Group Therapy

Counselors working with elderly LGBT people will want to consider their clients' personal circumstances in the decision to use individual or group therapy. Are there other elderly LGBT people who are willing to meet as a group? Are they willing to disclose their sexual orientation and the related problems (if their problems relate to their sexual orientation)? Has the client in question engaged in a formal coming out process? Will individual or group therapy be most effective for the individual in question?

Once the counselor makes the decision to use individual or group therapy, approaches might include topics such as coming out, health problems related to both sexual orientation and aging, discrimination and prejudice, problems with family (immediate and extended) acknowledging the elderly person's same-sex sexual orientation, financial concerns, housing problems, retirement benefits, medical attention and long-term health care, and any other problems that individual elderly LGBT clients want to discuss. In addition, counselors will need to consider whether cultural diversity and disabling conditions result in multiple forms of jeopardy and contribute to the elderly LGBT client's problems.

In both individual and group therapy, counselors should also consider the community in which the elderly LGBT person resides. Does the elderly LGBT client perceive the community as supportive or condemning? What community resources are available to assist the elderly LGBT client? The acceptance of the community will be significant in elderly LGBT clients' decisions to disclose their sexual orientation and the extent to which they feel the community will help them in their time of need.

Family Therapy

As when counseling clients in the other lifespan periods, counselors need to consider whether family members will support or condemn elderly LGBT clients. In some cases, family members think the elderly family member's sex life is nonexistent anyway, so trying to address the client's sexual orientation is a moot point. As with other developmental periods, some family members will be supportive, others will not. The counselor should carefully consider whether including family members will contribute to or harm the elderly LGBT client's situation. In some ways, if the family is supportive, family therapy can be helpful because the client then will see the support and assistance the family offers. Once the decision is reached to engage in family therapy, any of the aforementioned topics will be appropriate. Again, the perceptive counselor will consider the individual LGBT client to determine problems to be discussed and how family members can contribute to the counseling effort.

Case Study 16.4 looks at a counselor's efforts with Calliope, an elderly Greek American lesbian.

Case Study 16.4: Counseling Calliope, an Elderly Greek American Lesbian

Calliope, a 74-year-old Greek American lesbian, had attended the senior lunch center for several years. Things in her life were about the same: She was lonely, she still had to share apartment costs, and she still had sexual feelings for women. The counselor, a 43-year-old heterosexual Greek American who worked at the lunch center, continued to discuss group concerns, but these sessions could not legitimately be called group counseling. The participants had general discussions concerning growing old, being somewhat poor, and having health problems. Because the lunch center group was relatively small, the counselor decided to have 20-minute individual "screening" sessions with participants. Then she could decide which people needed individual counseling. She was not sure she could take on such a task, but she knew Calliope and several others seemed to want to discuss topics they were reluctant to disclose in the group.

During the first session, Calliope did not feel comfortable disclosing her lesbianism, yet the counselor felt she should see her another time or two. During the fourth session, Calliope disclosed that she had been a lesbian all her life. She had come out with a few close friends and had lived with two or three lesbian lovers, but she had never publicly come out, and she did not plan to do so, although the counselor assured her that she could still come to the lunch center. They discussed reasons for Calliope's not coming out earlier in life (e.g., her family expecting her to accept traditional Greek roles as wife and mother), why some LGBT people tried to hide their same-sex sexual orientation all their life, and her fears of prejudice and discrimination, especially at her doctor's office. In addition, as Calliope said more than once, "If my landlord knew about the real me, I would probably have to move."

The counselor concluded that Calliope had no intention of ever coming out. She had concealed her sexual orientation all her life, and she would not come out now. Still, the counselor thought discussing Calliope's feelings about herself and her sexual orientation might prove helpful. The counselor thought, "Calliope disclosed her lesbianism to me, so I need to take her concerns seriously. I will talk with her several more times."

Counseling and Development 16.4: The Elderly Years

Maxine was 73-year-old life-long lesbian, although she had been married. Her children did not think she could live alone, so she lived in a nursing home. Some of the other women living in the facility complained to the manager that Maxine was being more sexually explicit than they felt comfortable with. The manager asked the part-time counselor to speak with Maxine about her unwanted advances.

The counselor had been trained in a variety of settings, one being with elderly clients and one being with sexually different clients. She felt comfortable with both. Maxine freely admitted she had been a lesbian since elementary school.

Counseling Strategies:

1. Get Maxine to realize there was nothing "wrong" with her developmental period or her lesbianism.
2. Remember friendships are important for healthy development (in all developmental stages), yet she will probably need to seek another approach. Such a suggestion must be made with objectivity and no value setting on the part of the counselor.
3. Determine whether there are enough lesbians to begin a group on sexuality.

SUMMARY

Sometimes, counselors feel uncomfortable intervening with LGBT clients, possibly due to lack of professional training in working with this population. We recommend the following guidelines for counselors working with LGBT clients:

1. Know the interrelatedness of clients' developmental period, culture, sexual orientation, and disabling conditions—major premises of this book.
2. Consider sexual orientation to be a biological fact, rather than a matter of choice or preference.
3. Work toward eliminating any personal vestiges of prejudicial feelings about LGBT persons.
4. Know development in the four lifespan stages sufficiently well to know developmental issues and problems LGBT clients in each lifespan period might experience.
5. Take deliberate and planned action to gain knowledge, refine attitudes, and develop the skills needed to provide effective professional intervention with LGBT clients.
6. Refine individual, group, and family counseling skills; for example, know when to use each type of therapy and how to make a particular therapy work to achieve desired results in individual situations.

As LGBT clients increasingly disclose their same-sex sexual orientation during counseling sessions, counselors need to feel comfortable discussing such orientations, knowing the unique challenges LGBT clients face, and the effects of culture and disabling conditions on those with same-sex sexual orientations.

SUGGESTED READINGS

Laska, M. N., Van Kim, N. A., Erickson, D. J., Lust, K., Eisenberg, M. E., & Rosser, B. R. S. (2015). Disparities in weight and weight behaviors by sexual orientation in college students. *American Journal of Public Health, 105*(1), 111–121. The authors assessed disparities in weight and weight-related behaviors among college students by sexual orientation and gender and found disparities in weight, diet, and physical activity—related factors across sexual orientation among college youths.

Lindley, L. L., & Waisemann, K. M. (2015). Sexual orientation and risk of pregnancy among New York City high school students. *American Journal of Public Health, 105*(7), 1379–1386.

Lindley and Waisemann examined associations between sexual orientation and pregnancy risk among sexually experienced New York City high school students.

Love, M. M., Smith, A. E., Lyall, S. E., Mullins, J. L., & Cohn, T. J. (2015). Exploring the relationship between gay affirmative practice and empathy among mental health professions. *Journal of Multicultural Counseling and Development, 43* 83–96. These authors maintain multicultural competence has been emphasized, but more research is needed on sexual minorities.

Mueller, A. S. James, W., Abrutyn, S., & Levin, M. L. (2015). Suicide ideation and bullying among US adolescents: Examining the intersections of sexual orientation, gender, and race/ethnicity. *American Journal of Public Health, 105*(5), 980–985. These authors examined how race/ethnicity, gender, and sexual orientation shape adolescents' likelihood of being bullied and vulnerability to suicide ideation.

Muratori, M. C., & Smith, C. K. (2015). Guiding the talent and career development of the gifted individual. *Journal of Counseling & Development, 93*(2), 173–182. The authors highlight challenges that gifted individuals may encounter in their career development and propose a theory-informed career counseling framework, with special attention to socioeconomic status, race, gender, and sexual orientation included.

Olive, J. L. (2015). The impact of friendship on the leadership identity development of lesbian, gay, bisexual, and queer students. *Journal of Leadership Education, 14*(1), 142–159. This qualitative study explores the past experiences of six post-secondary students who self-identified as lesbian, gay, bisexual, and/or queer (LGBQ) and held leadership roles in student organizations at one large public institution.

Troutman, O., & Packer-Williams, C. (2014). Moving beyond CACREP standards: Training counselors to work competently with LGBT clients. *The Journal for Counselor Preparation and Supervision, 6*(1), 1–17. As the title suggests, Troutman and Packer-Williams maintain moving beyond CACREP standards in an effort to improve counseling intervention with LGBT clients.

Part III

Professional Issues in Multicultural Counseling

17 Issues in Multicultural Counseling

QUESTIONS TO BE EXPLORED

- What issues will confront counselors as American society grows increasingly diverse?
- How inclusive should a definition of multicultural counseling be (e.g., should sexual orientation, gender, spirituality, and disability be included in the definition)?
- What ethical and legal standards should be considered when counseling clients of differing backgrounds?
- How can counselors most effectively assess clients of differing cultural backgrounds, and how can spirituality be understood and assessed?
- What is distance or online counseling, can it replace face-to-face counseling, and how can it be most successful?
- What research issues remain to be resolved?

OVERVIEW

Counselors will increasingly intervene with clients of differing races, ethnic groups, cultural backgrounds, lifespan periods, genders, sexual orientations, and degrees of disability. Clients also have differing definitions of spirituality as well as differing levels of commitment to their spiritual beliefs.

Some clients' problems will be specific to their particular culture, whereas other problems and frustrations will cross cultural lines. This chapter examines selected issues: (a) how inclusive a definition of multicultural counseling should be, (b) how clients' diversity can be addressed, (c) how ethical and legal standards affect intervention, (d) how assessment can be effective in multicultural settings, (e) how online or distance counseling can play a role in the counseling process, and (f) how counselors can address research concerns in the twenty-first century. This chapter also shows how these issues affect the counseling process and the counseling profession.

ISSUE 1: HOW INCLUSIVE SHOULD A DEFINITION OF MULTICULTURAL COUNSELING BE?

Defining the Issue

We discussed whether we need to include a section on "inclusivity" in this edition. Then we decided inclusivity was sufficiently important to include—we have always encouraged inclusive approaches, but new perspectives have appeared recently that deserve support: cisgender, transsexual, queer, intersex and invisible minority. (For information on these topics, we refer the reader to the Irving (2014) interview.)

Some counselors think the definition should be restricted to interactions between counselors and clients of varying ethnic backgrounds, mainly because racism, injustice, and discrimination might be given short shrift if a more inclusive definition is adopted. Instead of broadening the definition, those who are opposed to an inclusive definition would prefer to use the phrase "counseling multicultural populations" when dealing with differences related to men and women, gays, lesbians, elderly people, people with disabilities, and various levels of spirituality. Other counselors maintain that unequal treatment and discrimination have widespread effects in the United States and are not limited to racial and ethnic differences.

Individuals who differ from others have two important characteristics in common. First, clients usually cannot change their status, and they may experience discrimination because of differences. Second, equal respect for people from all cultures is a primary explicit value of multicultural counseling. At the same time, however, multiculturalism has been criticized as being too negative toward European cultures. Focusing multicultural counseling only on certain racial and ethnic minorities at the exclusion of others contradicts the concept of inclusiveness.

Our Position on Inclusiveness

We advocate an inclusive definition of multicultural counseling—one that includes lesbians, gay, bisexuals, transgender, cisgender, transsexual, queer, intersex, and invisible minority people. We think lesbians, gay men, bisexuals, and people with disabilities have a culture of their own, in addition to their overall culture. In this text, we have included chapters on lesbians, gays, bisexuals, and transgender persons as well as European Americans. To the extent the research allowed, we included gender, spirituality, disabilities, and rehabilitation perspectives. Our rationale for inclusiveness is as follows:

* LGBT persons share specific cultural characteristics, experience injustice and discrimination similar to racial and ethnic minorities, and deserve counselors capable of providing effective professional intervention.
* The definition of multicultural counseling should include European Americans. European American clients, although extremely diverse, deserve to have their cultural worldviews recognized during counseling intervention. Just as we have advocated European American counselors understanding clients' differing cultural backgrounds, we advocate counselors of differing cultural backgrounds respecting and addressing European Americans' cultural backgrounds.
* People with disabilities have a culture of their own and often experience injustices. Because of their "culture of disability" and the threat of injustice, people with disabilities should be part of an inclusive definition of multicultural counseling.
* People's spirituality deserves consideration during counseling intervention. Some cultures place significant value on spiritualism. The spiritualism does not have to be the same, and some clients have more or less reliance on it. Still, counselors have an obligation to consider a client's spirituality during the counseling process.

ISSUE 2: HOW CAN COUNSELORS PERCEIVE CLIENTS' DIVERSITY?

Counselor perceptions of clients' backgrounds undoubtedly affect intervention strategies. As previously suggested, the events experienced during multicultural intervention may take a variety of forms, each having the potential for promoting or hindering the effectiveness of counseling. The stresses and strains of multicultural interaction may result in conflict that actually may increase or intensify clients' problems. Other counseling outcomes may result in improved relationships among people of varying cultural backgrounds. In any event, how the counselor and the client perceive their multicultural relationship and their perceptions of the actual outcome of the intervention warrants consideration. Considering our nation's growing diversity, counselors will continue to focus attention on several models of cultural deficiency/ difference, conflicting opinions regarding counseling approaches, and the effects of verbal and nonverbal communication between counselor and clients.

Models of Cultural Deficiency and Difference

The study of differences in intelligence as a function of race has sometimes been flawed with inaccurate scientific data or faulty analysis. This situation has resulted in some researchers contributing, knowingly or unknowingly, to racism and stereotyping. The issue has far greater implications, however, than whether clients are categorized according to the genetic deficiency model, the cultural deficit model, or the cultural difference model. For example, counselors who believe that low intelligence and strong athletic ability characterize African Americans or that Asian Americans are by nature mathematically oriented will have a biased perception of the client.

The Genetic Deficiency Model

The genetic deficiency model holds that culturally different people are genetically inferior. Scholarly opinion that was offered around the turn of the twentieth century argued for the genetic intellectual superiority of Whites and the genetic inferiority of the "lower races." Some people considered minority cultures to be lacking in desirable attributes and to be uneducable. Such mind-sets undoubtedly resulted in discrimination and other forms of ill treatment. People forming friendships, college administrators making admissions decisions, and employers making employment decisions obviously considered some people to be genetically deficient and either consciously or unconsciously discriminated against them. Rather than considering a person's record of achievement or motivation for self-improvement, many people used the genetic deficiency model as the basis for making such decisions. Although the genetic deficiency model is not as powerful as it once was, some people continue to subscribe to the theory that genetic inheritance plays a significant role in the determination of intelligence, motivation, and ability to achieve, academically and otherwise.

The Cultural Deficit Model

In the cultural deficit model, social scientists described culturally different people as "deprived" or "disadvantaged" because they demonstrated behavior at variance with middle-class values, language systems, and customs. From a class perspective, middle-class people assumed that other cultures did not seek to advance themselves because of a cultural deficit. Thus, rather than attribute undesirable differences to genetics, social scientists shifted the blame to cultural lifestyles or values.

Both the genetic deficiency and the cultural deficit models failed to address the implicit cultural biases that shaped these negative perceptions of people. The cultural difference model has refuted and largely superseded both models.

The Cultural Difference Model

The cultural difference model holds that people with culturally diverse backgrounds have unique strengths, values, customs, and traditions that can serve as a basis for enriching the overall counseling process. Researchers have begun to establish an information base documenting that cultural differences are not deficiencies and that the differences can be built on as counseling progresses. In order for counselors to provide the most effective professional intervention, they must make deliberate attempts to capitalize on differences as resources, rather than disregard them or view them as deficits to be eliminated.

Proponents of the cultural difference model believe that people of all backgrounds, regardless of lifespan period, still need to be aware of mainstream cultural values and knowledge. A degree of cultural compatibility is attained as counselors and clients increasingly develop an awareness of each other's cultural differences. In any event, people should not be condemned for their language, culture, age, sexual orientation, or other differences.

Etic-Emic Approaches

Two basic approaches to multicultural study and related research are the etic and the emic. Kurasaki, Sue, Chun, and Gee (2000) define etic as culture-general concepts or theories and emic as culture-specific phenomena. They offer the example of the psychotherapist using catharsis, or the expression of pent-up emotions, to relieve tension or depression directly. For a principle to be etic in nature, it should be applicable to different cultural groups. If it is not applicable to different cultural groups, the principle is emic, perhaps applicable only to a particular client or a particular cultural group.

Regardless of the etic or emic approach, counselors should be cautious of theories and studies that fail to take into account individual differences among clients. The psychotherapist who assumes that nondirective techniques are effective with all clients may be confusing etics and emics to the extent that an individual client's needs are not met. In clinical practice, some researchers and clinicians believe that current psychotherapies based on Western modes of thought and treatment may be culturally inappropriate with certain members of ethnic minority groups; they advocate more culturally relevant forms of treatment. It is essential to have professional intervention consistent with clients' cultural lifestyles (Kurasaki et al., 2000).

It is probably impossible to conduct counseling purely on the basis of etic or emic approaches. Counseling that ignores multicultural differences demonstrates cultural insensitivity; yet counselors should not focus exclusively on such differences. Realistically speaking, neither the etic nor emic approach can be used exclusively, because the emic approach accentuates the differences among groups and complicates the multicultural counseling process, and the etic approach tends to overlook important cultural differences and may fail because of cultural insensitivity. The most effective counselors blend the two approaches.

Autoplastic and Alloplastic Approaches

People of all cultures adapt to their environmental situations by changing themselves in an autoplastic approach, by changing the environment in an alloplastic approach, or by combining the two approaches. The question has been raised concerning the extent to which multicultural psychotherapy and counseling lean toward changing the individual as opposed to helping the client change the environment. Traditionally, counseling has been directed at those who are socially and culturally deviant, with the goal of changing client behavior to be more conforming with the norms of the dominant majority group. The situation becomes more complex when the counselor considers multicultural situations. Does the counselor prepare the client to change external reality or help the client accommodate to that reality? Our increasingly pluralistic society expands the client's options as to the nature of personal relationships, reference groups, and ethnic and cultural identities. However, this issue continues to be crucial to counselors who must decide whether to foster assimilation or to encourage self-development. The autoplastic-alloplastic distinction has the potential to create controversy. How much should the client be helped to accept or change a situation? One must consider the role of culture in this regard. Whereas Hispanic Americans traditionally are socialized to accept and endure life gracefully, European Americans are taught to confront obstacles and, if possible, remove them.

Existentialist Approaches

Although counseling usually draws on psychological theories, the existentialist approach to counseling emphasizes philosophical concepts. Existential philosophy and multicultural counseling both respect and recognize cultural differences as they organize human experiences in ways that reflect universal concerns of humankind. For counseling to be effective, counselors have a responsibility to explore their own and their clients' differences resulting from race, ethnicity, culture, gender, and sexual orientation.

Ivey, D'Andrea, Ivey, and Simek-Morgan (2012) maintain that the existentialist point of view is an attitude toward the counseling interview and toward the meaning of life. These authors offer several main points concerning existentialist approaches to counseling:

- Our task is to understand what existence in the world means; these meanings vary from culture to culture.
- We know ourselves through our relationship with the world and, in particular, through our relationships with other people.
- Anxiety can result from a lack of relationship with ourselves, others, or the world at large or from a failure to act or choose.
- We are responsible for our own construction of the world. Even though we know the world only from a personal interaction, it is we who decide what the world means and who must provide organization for that world.
- The counselor's task is to understand the client's world as fully as possible and ultimately to encourage the client to be responsible for making decisions. However, existentialist counselors will also share themselves and their worldviews with clients when appropriate.
- Some people might not view the world as meaningful and, therefore, develop a negative and hopeless view of what they observe to be absurdity and cruelty of life.
- If a person sees the many possibilities in the world as difficulties, then that person has a problem. If a person sees problems as opportunities, then that person will choose to act.

Communication: Verbal and Nonverbal Language

The outcome of any psychological intervention ultimately depends on the degree to which counselors and clients understand each other. Simply understanding a client's spoken language may not be enough, however. Other variables enter the picture. First, communication styles (both verbal and nonverbal) must be understood. We have already mentioned the Native American tendency to avoid eye contact, the tendency of some African Americans to "play it cool" and act "together," the Asian American confusion over whether to speak loudly or softly because of contrasting cultural expectations, and the Hispanic American tendency to maintain allegiance to the mother tongue. Second, the communication issue is further complicated when counselors consider the lifespan periods and generations of their clients. The language that children learn in American schools is quite different from the language used by a teenage dropout dealing drugs on the street. Moreover, the language used by children and adolescents might differ from that of adult and elderly clients. Older clients are more likely to feel a sense of obligation to remain faithful to their native tongue.

Although all aspects of communication style are in play during a counseling session, some are likely to be more salient than others, depending on the individual and the culture. It may be very important with some clients to consider appropriateness of topics, tone of voice, or taking turns in conversation.

The complex issue of maintaining effective communication between counselor and client does not allow for broad generalizations. For example, the decision of whether to seek an interpreter, to speak the client's native language (if the counselor is fluent in it), or to use a respected third party to assist with communication depends on the individual client, the nature of the client's problems, the extent of the language barrier, and how the client perceives the communication problem.

Lifespan Differences

The fairly recent attention to lifespan development and the recognition of characteristics associated with each stage have resulted in more appropriate assessment and intervention. Counselors have long recognized that children differ from adults, but only recently have serious attempts been made to provide developmentally appropriate counseling and psychotherapy for adolescents and the elderly. The need for additional scholarly research on counseling and on the lifespan continuum becomes clear in the light of critical differences between lifespan stages and the myriad changes occurring during each stage. Complications arise from the fact that various cultures differ in their perception of lifespan stages.

Intracultural, Generational, Sexual Orientation, Spirituality, Disability, Geographical, and Socioeconomic Differences

As mentioned in previous chapters, the tremendous diversity among clients makes generalizations difficult. Any number of examples can be offered as evidence that a "single" culture or ethnicity should not be the sole determining factor in reaching professional decisions. For example, considerable differences are found between relatively uneducated, lower-class African Americans living in the inner cities and highly educated, middle-class African Americans residing in the suburbs. Similarly, differences between first-generation Asian Americans and subsequent generations may be substantial. Differences may also occur as a function of geographic region of residency; for example, Hispanic Americans residing in Texas may exhibit characteristics different from those living in New York or Florida. Counseling professionals should have the knowledge and skill to intervene with individuals within a given culture, recognizing intracultural and individual differences as significant variables in planning appropriate intervention.

ISSUE 3: WHAT ETHICAL AND LEGAL STANDARDS SHOULD GUIDE COUNSELORS?

Counselors have an obligation to abide by the ethical standards subscribed to them by the American Association for Counseling and Development (AACD), the American Counseling Association (ACA), and the American Psychological Association (APA) and to respect other ethical standards. Other standards exist, but space will not allow an explication of more than one.

Ethics Associated With Multicultural Counseling

The *ACA Code of Ethics* states that counselors should embrace a cross-cultural approach; specific standards related to nondiscrimination and multicultural competence permeate the code. The *2014 ACA Code of Ethics* provides guidelines for sound multicultural professional practices. (We strongly suggest counselors and counselors in training read ACA's code of ethics.)
   Ethical multicultural practice involves three primary goals:

1.   Self-attitudes–becoming more aware of one's own values, biases, assumptions, and beliefs.
2.   Knowledge of cultural values, biases, and assumptions of diversity among clients.
3.   Commitment to developing culturally appropriate intervention strategies.

The counselor's ethical responsibility, however, is not only to understand the differing cultural orientations and values of clients but also to examine cultural biases and stereotypes that affect clients. By gaining knowledge about clients' cultural differences and by assessing personal feelings, the counselor reaches a level of awareness that values are culture-specific, rather than right or wrong; that is, it is not for the counselor to judge the correctness of values esteemed by clients of other cultures.

Although psychotherapists often avoid them, ethical concerns and issues often arise. Ethical standards of professional counseling associations require members to treat each client as a unique individual and to provide services uniquely tailored to meet individual needs. Should school counselors make their services available to all students at the risk of practicing beyond their scope of competence? Or should they limit their scope of practice to areas in which they feel confident and therefore withhold services from clients of diverse backgrounds about which they have not received training. Such questions help explain the ethical aspects of psychotherapy, contexts that can prove destructive or constructive.

Ethics and ethical decision making are critical elements of counseling practice, and a component of competent training in ethical decision making should be a component of professional training programs. Cottone and Claus (2000) question whether ethical decision-making models really work. They maintain that there is much work to be done in ethics; surprisingly little research has been done on ethical decision making or models of decision making in counseling. Although there are many models available, it is difficult to determine whether one model is better than another. In fact, the criteria for what makes a better model are not clearly defined. The authors conclude that additional dialogue on these matters is needed. Over a decade and a half has passed, we hope the issue of ethics is more defined.

Many counselors in nonschool settings work with children during their practice, which emphasizes our belief that counselors understand the legal and ethical issues relevant to working with children and adolescents. Attention should be given to several critical ethical issues: counselor ability and motivation to work with children, the child's or adolescent's right to confidentiality (e.g., sexual orientation, if the child or adolescent chooses to disclose or not disclose), and the counselor's responsibilities with child neglect or mistreatment. Counselors need to protect themselves by being cautious and judicious. The authors suggest the following guidelines:

- Inform families of the limits of your abilities as defined by education, training, and supervised practice.
- Maintain familiarity with state statutes regarding privilege.
- Clarify policies concerning confidentiality with both the child and the parents at the first therapy session.
- If you choose to work with a minor without the parents' informed consent, ask the minor to provide informed consent in writing.
- Keep accurate and objective records of all interactions and counseling sessions.
- Maintain adequate professional liability coverage.
- When in need of help or advice, confer with colleagues and have professional legal help available.

Clearly, the many ethical and legal dilemmas surrounding the counseling profession are too complex to summarize here. It is apparent, however, that additional research is warranted to determine the effect of the differing perceptions of ethical matters when the cultural backgrounds of counselors and clients differ. Ethical decisions in counseling relationships become more complex when one works with clients who have differing worldviews and unique cultural perspectives of their lives.

ISSUE 4: HOW CAN COUNSELORS MOST EFFECTIVELY ASSESS CLIENTS OF DIFFERING CULTURAL BACKGROUNDS?

Assessment in counseling and psychotherapy includes interviewing, observing, testing, and analyzing data from cultural perspectives. Counselors should determine the extent to which diversity affects assessment as well as provide an adequate response to several questions or concerns, such as culturally appropriate testing and assessment. Counselors must carefully avoid ethnocentrism and considering clients only from the counselor's worldviews.

The Extent to Which Cultural Diversity Affects Assessment

One basic issue concerns the extent to which cultural diversity affects assessment: Will a characteristic representative of a specific culture be mistakenly perceived and assessed by using European American middle-class standards? Will a counselor of a Hispanic or Asian cultural background mistakenly assess a European American or an African American client? Counselors need to make sure that their cultural assumptions and worldviews have a minimal effect on clients of differing cultural backgrounds.

Five questions come to mind as counselors plan assessment in multicultural settings:

1. What needs to be assessed, and are those needs culturally based?
2. What types of assessment instruments reflect cultural perspectives and most effectively assess those needs?
3. What evidence do assessment instruments provide that indicates they are culturally responsive?
4. What precautions should counselors heed when interpreting assessment results?
5. What ethical and legal responsibilities are associated with multicultural assessment?

Also, counselors need to be fairly certain that assessment instruments are culturally appropriate. Without appropriate assessment strategies, counseling professionals are unable to diagnose problems, develop appropriate goals, and assess the outcomes of intervention. Initial client assessment, clinical judgments, selection of assessment instruments, and the outcomes of counseling evaluation are assessment factors that warrant attention.

Spirituality or religious beliefs should also be considered. Some clients might hold very conservative or liberal views, which may differ from the counselor's or other members of the group therapy. Spirituality is critical for sound mental health and effective growth and development.

To be candid, counselors do experience problems with cross-cultural assessment. For example, counselors and clients may experience difficulty establishing equivalence across cultures, lack of appropriate cultural norms may exist, and composition of test items might be culturally inappropriate. Cultural influences on testing can be minimized only through increased awareness, training, and instrument development, but they cannot be totally eliminated.

Until assessments and psychological evaluations are as fair as possible and common to all cultures, testing practitioners have a responsibility to continue to scrutinize the content of tests. Practitioners can contribute to test fairness by being aware of the difficulties involved in the comparison of test performance across cultures. Practitioners also need to share, in the literature and at professional meetings, their observations regarding cross-cultural testing.

ISSUE 5: WHAT IS ONLINE OR DISTANCE COUNSELING? DOES IT PLAY A ROLE IN THE MULTICULTURAL COUNSELING PROCESS?

In "Considerations for the use of Distance Learning," Stolsmark (2015) maintains that the lack of accessible mental health services limits those with mental health issues. Therefore, counselors have a responsibility to be knowledgeable about the available resources for distance counseling. Counselors should also understand all ethical and legal requirements (Stolsmark, 2015).

The *2014 ACA Code of Ethics* outlines this topic in Section H, which focuses on distance counseling, technology, and social media. Specifically, counselors should adhere to Standards H.1.a., H.1.b., H.2.a., H.2.b., H.2.c., H.2.d., H.3., H.4.a., H.4.b., H.4.c., H.4.d., H.4.e., and H.4.f. In addition, per Standard I.1.b., the first step in making an ethical decision is to use an ethical decision-making model (Stolsmark, 2015).

According to these standards, counselors have the freedom to choose whether to use technology and distance counseling in their practice. Counselors should first make sure they are practicing within their legal rights and limitations with regard to distance counseling. If a client is asking to receive distance counseling in another state, it would be important to research the licensing rules and requirements for that state. The American Counseling Association recommends that counselors be licensed in the client's state. Those who decide to use distance counseling should take into consideration their own knowledge and competencies. Specific certifications or additional course work may be required to provide such services.

As always, keys to resolving any ethical dilemma include consulting with other counselors, referring to ACA standards and documenting the decision-making process and rationale in order to provide an explanation if the decision is called into question (Stolsmark, 2015).

ISSUE 6: WHAT RESEARCH CONCERNS WILL BE RELEVANT IN THE FUTURE?

It goes without saying that counselors should stay abreast of research developments in the field; furthermore, they should conduct research of their own. In reality, however, the majority of counseling practitioners do not actively participate in research endeavors, nor do they always keep up with the latest developments reported in the literature. This section examines some research issues that are likely to confront counselors during the next decade.

The Multicultural Counseling Process

What research issues are particularly relevant to the multicultural counseling process? What areas must be considered to provide a more enlightened perspective on counseling clients in multicultural settings? Although research goals and methodologies in the various areas of counseling may be similar, a prerequisite to all research endeavors in a multicultural context is the understanding and acceptance that client diversity significantly affects outcomes. Also, it must be understood that ethical standards and legal aspects relevant to the counseling profession also apply to research endeavors in multicultural situations.

Research Techniques and Outcomes

Whether counselors employ comparative group research designs, field studies, single-subject studies, or case studies, differences should be taken into account. An important cultural consideration that may have a bearing on gathering research data is the possibility of a communication problem (verbal or nonverbal) between researcher and subject. For example, the researcher may construe the Native American tendency to gaze into space as indicative of boredom, or the researcher may not understand an Asian American's shyness or tendency not to disclose personal information, or the Hispanic American's valuing of family over self may be misinterpreted in a variety of ways. Although these represent only selected examples, the point is clear that researchers of one culture may make erroneous judgments with respect to the behavior of subjects of other cultures.

Multicultural Counseling and the Lifespan Continuum

Research undoubtedly needs to be directed toward the relationships between multicultural counseling interactions and the client's lifespan stage. These intricate relationships can be understood only by directing research toward (a) the multicultural aspects of the counseling relationship, (b) the actual counselor-client interactions, and (c) the counselor's perception of the client's lifespan stage. Specifically, attention needs to be focused on the actual effects of culture and the client's developmental period in the multicultural counseling endeavor.

Research Directions, Tasks, and Challenges

In reviewing what we know, West-Olatunji (2014) maintained there are six areas representing the next frontier for multicultural counselors: 1) transnationalism, 2) moving from knowing that cultural differences exist to accessing culture-centered interventions, 3) the impact of oppression and marginalization on cultural identity, 4) understanding multiple identities (or the intersectionality of identity), 5) diverse White identities, and 6) exploring the silenced voices of faculty of color as insider researchers.

The ultimate determination of counseling effectiveness depends largely on a credible research base. In order for this base to accrue, studies must seek to synthesize knowledge of clients' cultures with that of lifespan differences. Selected research directions that will lead to greater multicultural awareness include the following:

- Evaluate the impact of multicultural counseling training.
- Determine which assessment instruments most effectively assess the needs of clients of differing cultural backgrounds.
- Determine client preference for counselor race or ethnicity (both intergroup and intra-group differences).
- Study identity development within the context of majority and minority status.
- Determine the effect of race and ethnicity on diagnosis, treatment, and counseling outcomes.
- Examine the relationship between therapist prejudice and differential diagnosis, process, treatment, and outcome.
- Examine multiple oppressions (e.g., the effects of being minority, gay or lesbian, and elderly, or being a Hispanic American with a disability).
- Ascertain approaches to culture and counseling beyond the current theoretical basis.
- Identify variables that explain past and present occurrences, as well as those that predict future events with respect to people, ideas, and cultures.
- Inform counselors of means of providing services based on new counseling theories and new training so that counseling and psychotherapy services can be more equitably distributed among the multicultural society.

It is important to note that the resolution of research issues will depend on collaborative efforts of researchers and counseling professionals. Practical solutions to counseling dilemmas can emerge only through such collaboration.

SUMMARY

Counselors, now and in the future, will need to (a) determine the inclusiveness of the definition of multicultural counseling, (b) deal with the challenges of all clients' diversities, (c) consider lifespan issues, (d) assess the effects of diversity on counseling intervention, (e) recognize the ethical and legal dimensions of counseling, and (f) conduct research on diversity and its effects on counseling intervention. The enthusiasm with which counselors and researchers tackle these tasks will greatly influence counseling efforts in multicultural situations.

SUGGESTED READINGS

Burton, S., & Furr, S. (2014). Conflict in multicultural education classes: Approaches to resolving difficult dialogues. *Counselor Education & Supervision, 53*, 97–110. These authors discuss how to handle conflicts within multicultural education classes and explained that conflicts were often directed at the instructor.

Schnall, E., Kalkstein, S., Gottesman, A., Feinberg, K., Schaeffer, C. B., & Feinberg, S. S. (2014). Barriers to mental health care: A 25 year follow-up study of the Orthodox Jewish community. *Journal of Multicultural Counseling and Development, 42*, 161–172. Orthodox Jewish communities have been overlooked—their results revealed increased acceptance of mental illness and its treatment.

Stolsmark, E. (2015, March). Considerations for the use of distance counseling. *Ct.counseling.org*, 16. As the title implies, Stolsmark focuses on the possibilities of distance counseling and clients who live afar and cannot visit the counselor face-to-face.

West-Olatunji, C. (2014, March). Multicultural counseling: The next frontier. *Counseling Today, 56*(9), 5–6. West-Olatunji discusses several areas such as 1) transnationalism, 2) moving from knowing that cultural differences exist to accessing culture-centered interventions, 3) the impact of oppression and marginalization on cultural identity, 4) understanding multiple identities (or the intersectionality of identity), 5) diverse White identities, and 6) exploring the silenced voices of faculty of color as insider researchers.

Zeren, Ş. G. (2014). Information and communication technology in education of psychological counselors in training. *International Online Journal of Educational Sciences, 6*(2), 494–509. Using information and communication technology in the psychological counseling and guidance field is a current field of psychological counseling.

Epilogue

Increased knowledge of cultural diversity and lifespan development and improved understanding of how they are interrelated contribute to better relationships between clients and counselors and to more favorable outcomes. The goal of this epilogue is to tie together some recurrent themes of the preceding chapters. Considered here are the current status of multicultural counseling and the effects of cultural, intracultural, lifespan, sexual orientation, gender, and disability differences among clients, as well as rehabilitation counseling, the continuing challenges associated with racism and discrimination, and the dangers of basing counseling decisions on erroneous generalizations.

MULTICULTURAL COUNSELING AND PSYCHOTHERAPY

Its Beginning

Multicultural counseling as a legitimate area of counseling specialization has evolved rather quickly during the past several decades. The growing interest in multicultural counseling is evidenced in the increasing numbers of multicultural studies and in the acceptance of this subspecialty in professional circles. As the United States continues to become increasingly culturally diverse, counselors in public agencies, schools, and private practice will no doubt be challenged to provide effective counseling intervention for clients of many different cultures.

A Rationale

The rationale for multicultural counseling is clear: Rather than expect clients of various cultural backgrounds to adapt to the counselor's cultural expectations and intervention strategies, multicultural counseling proposes that the counselor base intervention on each client's individual, intracultural, gender, socioeconomic, geographic, generational, sexual orientation, disability, and lifespan differences. Without doubt, this text has proposed and demonstrated that all clients, regardless of cultural background, need individual consideration that takes into account the client's cultural as well as many other differences.

Growing Acceptance: Present and Future

Considerable evidence suggests that multicultural counseling has gained professional respect and points toward an overall acceptance and a bright future: (a) the growth of the Association of Multicultural Counseling and Development (AMCD), (b) the *Journal of Multicultural Counseling and Development*, (c) the growing number of multicultural counseling textbooks, (d) the various conferences and seminars addressing multicultural concerns and issues, (e) the appearance of new college courses designed to enhance the counselor's knowledge and skills, and (f) the possibility of distance or online counseling.

People and Their Diversity

To say that American society is growing more diverse is an understatement. Not only is the size of the minority population continuing to increase, but we are also seeing an increasing variety of cultures at all stages of the lifespan. From a historical viewpoint, culturally different people have been the recipients of cruel and inhumane treatment. Much has been written about the enormous problems that immigrants face upon entering the United States. Consider, too, the unjust treatment directed toward American Indians; it is difficult to even guess at how many were enslaved or killed. Racism continues to exist, impeding the progress of all groups victimized by it.

Despite the grimness of the historical record, the twenty-first century can be a time for recognition and acceptance of others' diversity. Factors that may contribute to such recognition include (a) the efforts directed at children and adolescents (e.g., multicultural counseling in elementary and secondary schools), (b) the multicultural emphasis of the National Council for Accreditation of Teacher Education and the Council for Accreditation of Counseling and Related Educational Programs, (c) the increasing evidence that the nation actually benefits from cultural diversity, and (d) the American Counseling Association's work on counseling the culturally diverse.

Realities: Racism, Injustice, Discrimination, White Privilege, and Social Injustices

As previously mentioned, racism, injustice, discrimination, White privilege, and social injustices continue to affect people in the United States. Although overt acts of violence and hatred, such as those of the skinheads and the Ku Klux Klan, may not be as overt as they have been in the past, the more covert forms of racism are widespread and continue to undermine people's progress and well-being. One only has to search the Internet for racism against all people and hate groups from all ethnic and cultural groups. Acts of violence toward ethnic and cultural minorities are evidenced in the media. Such racism and hatred cannot be attributed to one group—still, regardless of the ethnic or cultural group, counselors need to maintain objectivity and strive to promote racial harmony. Still, we maintain these are realities of the times, and we hope counselors can and will do their part to improve relations among all ethnicities and cultures.

Counselors of all cultures will have to deal with problems resulting from these realities; they will also have to sort through personal biases and long-held misconceptions with respect to race and ethnicity.

An Increasing Knowledge Base: Cultural Diversity and Lifespan Recognition of Cultural Diversity

The professional literature of the past several decades will increase counselors' knowledge of cultural diversity. More than ever before, counselors have access to objective information describing African American, American Indian, Asian American, European American, and Hispanic American cultural groups. No longer should counseling intervention be based on inaccurate generalizations about cultural differences. Through personal interaction with people of differing cultural backgrounds and through careful review of pertinent journals, books, and other resources, counselors can gain valuable insights into the unique problems of all clients. The American Indian concept of sharing, the African American unique dialect and concept of extended family, the Asian American concept of generational and family relationships, the European American respect for individualism, and the Hispanic American *machismo* and commitment to speaking Spanish can provide an accurate basis for counseling intervention. Equally important is the understanding that individuals may vary according to generation, socioeconomic status, gender, sexual orientation, disability, geographic location, and other variables.

KNOWLEDGE OF HUMAN GROWTH AND DEVELOPMENT

Counselors can benefit from the increasing knowledge of lifespan development. No longer should a counselor plan assessment and intervention without first considering the client's lifespan period and its unique characteristics, crises, and tasks; for example, the adolescent's view of the role of the family may be quite different from the elderly person's view or the child's view. The intricate relationship between culture and development can be seen in the generational differences between some younger and older Asian Americans. Although the work of some developmentalists (e.g., Erikson, Havighurst, Piaget) may be culturally specific and based on European American and middle-class norms, the growing body of developmental literature is providing a sound foundation for counseling across cultures and developmental periods.

Using the Knowledge Base to Enhance Counseling Effectiveness

There are numerous benefits of counseling intervention based on lifespan development. Counselors are better able to plan appropriate strategies if they understand, for example, (a) the child's problems growing up in a society that often discriminates against culture and age; (b) the adolescent's need to reconcile peer pressure and family expectations; (c) the adult's frustrations in coping with economic, educational, and employment discrimination; and (d) the daily reality of multiple jeopardy often faced by people who are elderly, LGBT, disabled, or some combination thereof.

Responding to Individual and Cultural Diversity Differences

Classifying a client by culture or ethnicity may describe very little about the person. Each client should be considered on an individual basis, with the recognition that many differences affect the counseling process. It may be accurate to describe someone as an African American, but that description does not provide sufficient information with which to plan assessment and intervention. The problems of an unemployed African American man who never finished high school are very different from those of a college-educated African American man working in middle management. Along the same lines, the diverse Hispanic culture requires that counselors consider individual populations and individual clients. A Puerto Rican American living in New York is probably quite different from a Mexican American residing in southern Texas.

Avoiding Stereotypes and Generalizations

Stereotypes and generalizations have the potential to severely damage counseling relationships and intervention outcomes. It should be obvious that all minorities are not underachievers, that all adolescents are not sexually promiscuous, and that all elderly are not helpless. Stereotypical thinking continues to persist, however, even in people who are well educated and who pride themselves on their sound logic and reason.

Stereotypes and generalizations apply not only to culture but also to the various lifespan periods. To characterize all children as carefree, all adolescents as troublemakers, all adults as prone to midlife crises, or all elderly as helpless and senile is an affront to individuals all along the lifespan continuum. The expectation that a client will demonstrate certain adverse behaviors because of age may even foster those behaviors.

What steps should be taken to reduce the presence of stereotyping and generalizations with respect to age groups? First, counselors should learn more about lifespan development and the unique problems of each stage. Then the necessity of basing counseling decisions on accurate and objective information is likely to become clear. Second, counselors should seek firsthand experiences with people along the lifespan continuum. Third, counselors should strive to recognize the severe consequences of age-related stereotypical thinking for their clients.

SEEKING HELP IN A MULTICULTURAL SOCIETY

Tendencies to Not Seek Professional Help

Counselors intervening in multicultural situations should recognize that, in some cultures, people tend to seek assistance from the immediate and extended family rather than from professionals. Although logical reasons underlie this tendency, counselors are still faced with the need to explain the counseling process and its confidentiality to clients and to gear the first session to increase the likelihood of clients returning for additional sessions. Some cultural groups may avoid professional help because of a reliance on folk rituals. Others may be reluctant to disclose confidential matters to outsiders. Language and communication difficulties and transportation problems may also be factors. Although it is important for the counselor to be aware of a client's reluctance to seek counseling help, it is even more important to understand the cultural basis for the reluctance. With this understanding, the counselor is better able to foster receptivity to the counseling process and willingness to disclose significant personal information.

SOURCES OF MENTAL HEALTH SERVICES

Counselors may encounter clients in various settings, such as community mental health agencies, hospitals, schools, or private practice. Clients may seek counseling because of problems and frustrations associated with acculturation, racism and discrimination, or family relationships. Regardless of the problem or the counseling setting, counselors who understand multicultural groups will be more likely to address their clients' needs objectively and accurately.

THE FUTURE: A TIME FOR RESPONSIVE ACTION

Multicultural counseling, lifespan development, and an understanding of the relationship between culture and development have progressed to a point where counseling professionals can take positive action to help clients from differing cultural backgrounds. To encourage such action, efforts should be directed toward training culturally effective counselors and promoting recognition of the relationship between cultural diversity and lifespan development.

Training Culturally Effective Counselors

The increasing likelihood that counselors will intervene in multicultural situations underscores the need for counselors to (a) understand their own cultural identities, (b) understand clients' cultural backgrounds, and (c) employ strategies that reflect cultural characteristics and expectations. Responsive counselor education programs will take into account the increasing cultural diversity in the United States by providing training and experiences designed to impart the knowledge and skills necessary for effective counseling in multicultural settings.

Recognizing the Relationship Between Cultural Diversity and Lifespan Development

Responsive action calls for counselor education programs that assist counselors in recognizing the relationship between cultural diversity and lifespan development. As previously stated, the Asian American elder has unique problems that the African American child or adolescent has not encountered and may never encounter. Intervention should be based on accurate knowledge of the client's culture and lifespan period and, of course, the client's many individual differences.

SUMMARY

Multicultural counseling is beginning to come into its own. Increasing numbers of profession-als are recognizing the need to consider a client's cultural background and valued cultural tra-ditions and expectations. Continued advances in the area of lifespan growth and development are enhancing counselors' understanding of clients' developmental periods. In the twenty-first century, professionals will be better able to provide counseling services that are culturally and developmentally appropriate. It is hoped in the years ahead that the needs and problems that clients bring to counseling sessions will increasingly receive the kind of attention they deserve.

Appendix

Suggested Multicultural Experiential Activities

The following activities can be used as a part of the multicultural counseling course. Feel free to modify them to reflect the needs and diversity of your class. If you use additional experiential activities, please send a description to either author for inclusion in future editions of this text.

1. Establish the tone for multiculturalism and its acceptance at the beginning of each class with an exercise in multiculturalism. Exercises may include a poem that relates to the topic or a short story or music selection reflecting cultural diversity.

2. Use an ethnobiography to help the class get acquainted with the various backgrounds and differences of each class member. Such a biography will aid in building respect for differences in people and for clients in the future. Suggestions include students' names, why their parents gave them these names, what growing up was like, educational backgrounds, greatest successes, biggest failures, and ways in which students feel different.

3. Show *The Color of Fear*, an excellent video, to facilitate discussion of topics of racial differences, social class, and gender issues. This powerful and thought-provoking video tells about a group of men from various backgrounds who discuss their feelings on these issues. Students can then react to the video and discuss their feelings about the issues.

4. Show *A Class Divided*, another excellent video, which tells about the "blue eye" experiment and brings attention to the unfair nature of discrimination. Then students can discuss their feelings and reactions to the video and to discrimination in general.

5. Replicate the "blue eye" experiment. Place all the students with blue eyes into one group and those with nonblue eyes into another group. Ask the blue-eyed students to wait in the hall. Explain to the nonblue-eyed students to treat the blue-eyed students in a discriminatory fashion. Invite the blue-eyed students back into the class with the "normal class." Toward the end of the class, each group can discuss how the discrimination felt.

6. Administer a cultural attitudes inventory to the class to determine attitudes demonstrated in books, television, and movies about cultures. Thinking about images portrayed in the media can help explain some of the stereotypes that people have about cultures.

7. Arrange for a panel discussion of members of different cultures in an attempt to eliminate stereotypes by learning objective and factual information. Students in the class can ask questions about particular cultures to distinguish between fact and stereotype.

8. Ask students to do a cultural anthropology project by investigating people in their area and neighborhood. Selected and interesting topics might include what type of people live in the vicinity, how they arrived there, their reasons for selecting the area, and what they do there now. Such an exercise can be extended into the past several generations.

9. Arrange for a multicultural "adventure" by trying a culturally different type of food. Students in the class may cook the food, or they may go to an ethnic restaurant they have never visited.

10. Have students think of at least one saying from five famous people from different cultural backgrounds. Then analyze each saying in regard to cultural values.

11.   Encourage class members to identify their family motto from their family of origin. What cultural values are implied by the motto?

12.   Ask each class member to select an American Indian name and to explain its origin and significance.

13.   Have students prepare a coat of arms in the shape of a shield that depicts various aspects of their cultural background and explain its meaning to the class.

14.   Arrange for class members to visit with the elderly, because some people harbor stereotypes about older people and generally feel uncomfortable around them. Visiting a nursing home or senior center can be helpful in overcoming anxiety about counseling elderly clients. Students can tell or write about what they learned, such as stereotypes they had before visiting and how those stereotypes have changed.

15.   Have the entire class set aside a time outside of or during class to visit a homeless shelter. The class can help clean and prepare meals for the people who live there. Students will benefit from helping the homeless and from learning about the reasons for homelessness and the problems faced by homeless people.

16.   Arrange for class members to visit with people with disabilities to help dispel stereotypes about such people. Students can share in class what they learned and how their newfound knowledge can be reflected during counseling intervention.

17.   Ask class members to share experiences during which they felt discrimination. These experiences can be from racial and cultural discrimination or from any type of discrimination (e.g., disability, height, weight, religious affiliation, social class). How did they feel, and how might such discrimination be lessened?

18.   Ask students to share experiences when they were the only one of their cultural group in a large group of people. Did they feel accepted by others or uncomfortable being the only one of their cultural group? What might they or others have done to lessen the feelings of anxiety (if anxiety existed) and promote mutual acceptance within the group?

19.   Ask students to visit the homes of people from another cultural background. How did the homes differ? What differences were seen in cultural backgrounds and expectations? Have students suggest how knowledge of home environments might contribute to the effectiveness of counseling, especially with children and adolescent clients.

20.   Have individual students or small groups interview a gay man or lesbian or read about the problems (as well as the joys and satisfactions) faced by people with differing sexual orientations. What forms of discrimination or harassment do they experience? What do they think counselors need to know? How can the information the students gained contribute to their effectiveness when counseling gay and lesbian clients? The individual students or small groups can report to the class and create guidelines for improving the effectiveness of counseling intervention for gay and lesbian clients.

References

Acosta, F. X., Yamamoto, J., & Evans, L. A. (1982). *Effective psychotherapy for low-income and minority patients* (p. 47). New York: Plenum.

Acun-Kapikiran, N., Körükcüo, Ö., &, Kapikiran, S. (2014). The relation of parental attitudes to life satisfaction and depression in early adolescents: The mediating role of self-esteem. *Educational Sciences: Theory & Practice, 14*(4), 1246–1252.

Adkison-Johnson, C. (2015). Child discipline and African American parents with adolescent children: A psychoeducational approach to clinical mental health counseling. *Journal of Mental Health Counseling, 37*(3), 221–233.

Agoratus, L. (2014). Alternatives to out-of-home placement for families. *Exceptional Parent, 44*(12), 48–49.

Agronick, G., O'Donnell, L., Stueve, A., Doval, A. S. Duran, R., & Vargo, S. (2004). Sexual behaviors and risks among bisexually and gay-identified young Latino men. *AIDS and Behavior, 8*(2), 185–197.

Aguilera, D., & LeCompte, M. D. (2007). Resiliency in native languages: The tale of three indigenous communities' experiences with language immersion. *Journal of American Indian Education, 46,* 11–36.

Akos, P., & Ellis, C. M. (2008). Racial identity development in middle school: A case for school counselor individual and systemic intervention. *Journal of Counseling and Development, 86*(1), 26–33.

Alba, R. D. (1985). *Italian Americans into the twilight of ethnicity.* Upper Saddle River, NJ: Prentice Hall.

Altman, A. N., Inman, A. G., Fine, S. G. Ritter, H. A., & Howard, E. (2010). Exploration of Jewish identity. *Journal of Counseling and Development, 88,* 163–173.

American Counseling Association. (2005). ACA Code of Ethics. Alexandria, VA: Author.

American Counseling Association (2014). *2014 ACA Code of Ethics.* Author: American Counseling Association, ct@counseling.org

American Psychological Association. (2000). Guidelines for psychotherapy with lesbian, gay, and bisexual clients. *American Psychologist, 55*(2), 1440–1451.

Amola, O., & Grimmett, M. A. (2015). Sexual identity, mental health, HIV risk factors, and internalized homophobia among Black men who have sex with men. *Journal of Counseling & Development, 93,* 236–245.

Andretta, J. R., Worrell, F. C., & Mello, Z. R. (2014). Predicting educational outcomes and psychological well-being in adolescents using time attitude profiles. *Psychology in the Schools, 51*(5), 434–451.

Annie E. Casey Foundation. (2014). *Kids count data book 2014.* Baltimore, MD: Author.

Appiah, K. A. (2015). Race in the modern world: The problem of the color line. *Foreign Policy, 94*(2), 3–8.

Arredondo, P., Toporek, R., Brown, S. P., Jones, J., Locke, D.C., Sanchez, J., & Stadler, H. (1996). Operationalization of the multicultural counseling competencies. *Journal of Multicultural Counseling and Development, 24*(1), 42–78.

Arthur, N., & Achenbach, K. (2002). Developing multicultural counseling competencies through experiential learning. *Counselor Education and Supervision, 42*(1), 2–14.

Atkinson, D. R. (2004). *Counseling American minorities: A cross-cultural perspective* (6th ed.). New York: McGraw-Hill.

Awe, T., Portman, A., & Garrett, M. T. (2005). Beloved women: Nurturing the sacred of leadership from an American Indian perspective. *Journal of Counseling and Development, 83*(3), 284–292.

Axelson, J. A. (1999). *Counseling and development in a multicultural* society (3rd ed.). Pacific Grove, CA: Brooks/Cole.

Bailey, D. F., & Paisley, P. O. (2004). Developing and nurturing excellence in African American males. *Journal of Counseling and Development, 82*, 10–17.

Balkin, R. S., Watts, R. E., & Ali, S. R. (2014). A conversation about the intersection of faith, sexual orientation, and gender: Jewish, Christian, and Muslim perspectives. *Journal of Counseling and Development, 92*, 187–193.

Ballard, E. D., Musci, R. J., Tingey, L., Goklish, N., Larzelere-Hinton, F., Barlow, A., & Cwik, M. (2015). Latent class analysis of substance use behavior in reservation-based American Indian youth who attempted suicide. *American Indian & Alaska Native Mental Health Research: The Journal of the National Center, 22*(1), 77–94.

Baskin, T. W., Russell, J. L., Sorenson, C. L., & Ward, E. C. (2015). A model for school counselors supporting African American youth with forgiveness. *Journal of School Counseling, 13*(7), 1–17.

Bean, R. A., Perry, B. J., & Bedell, T. M. (2001). Developing culturally competent marriage and family therapists: Guidelines for working with Hispanic families. *Journal of Marital and Family Therapy, 27*(1), 43–54.

Bebes, A., Samarova, V., Shilo, G., & Diamond, G. M. (2015). Parental acceptance, parental psychological control and psychological symptoms among sexual minority adolescents. *Journal of Child and Family Studies, 24*, 882–890.

Bell, K. E. (2007). Gender and gangs: A quantitative comparison. *Crime & Delinquency, 2009, 55*(3), 363–387.

Bemak, F., Chung, R. C., Siroskey-Sabdo, L. A. (2005). Empowerment groups for academic success: An innovative approach to prevent high school failure for at-risk, urban African Americans. *Professional School Counseling, 8*, 377–389.

Bemak, F., & Greenberg, B. (1994). Southeast Asian refugee adolescents: Implications for counseling. *Journal of Multicultural Counseling and Development, 22*, 115–124.

Berger, R. M. (1996). *Gay and gray: The older homosexual man* (2nd ed.). Binghamton, NY: Haworth.

Berk, L. E. (2008). *Development through the lifespan* (6th ed.). Boston: Allyn & Bacon.

Berman, M. (2014). Suicide among young Alaska Native men: Community risk factors and alcohol control. *American Journal of Health, 104*(S3), S329-S335.

Bernal, G., & Shapiro, E. (2005). Cuban families. In M. McGoldrick, J. Giordano, & N. Garcia-Presto (Eds.), *Ethnicity and family therapy* (3rd ed., pp. 202–215). New York: Guilford.

Bidell, M. P. (2014). Are multicultural courses addressing disparities? Exploring multicultural and affirmative lesbian, gay, and bisexual competencies of counseling and psychology students. *Journal of Multicultural Counseling & Development, 42*(3), 132–146.

Bilodeau, B. L., & Renn, K. A. (2005). Analysis of LBGT identity development models and implications for practice. *New Directions for Student Services, 111*, 25–39.

Blanks, A. B., & Smith, J. D. (2009). Multiculturalism, religion, and disability: Implications for special education practitioners. *Education and Training in Developmental Disabilities, 44*(3), 295–303.

Blount, A. J., & Young, M. E. (2015). Counseling multiple-heritage couples. *Journal of Multicultural Counseling & Development, 43*(2), 137–152.

Bowman, N. A., & Park, J. J. (2014). Interracial contact on college campuses: Comparing and contrasting predictors of cross-racial interaction and interracial friendship. *Journal of Higher Education, 85*(5), 660–690.

Bradley, C., Johnson, P., Rawls, G., & Dodson-Sims, A. (2005). School counselors collaborating with African American parents. *Professional School Counseling, 8*(5), 424–427.

Brandon, R. R. (2007). African American parents: Improving connections with their child's educational environment. *Intervention in School and Clinic, 43*(2), 118–120.

Broman, C. L. (2005). Marital quality in Black and White marriages. *Journal of Family Issues, 26*(4), 431–441.

Brown, C. S., & Chu, H. (2012). Discrimination, ethnic identity, and academic outcomes of Mexican immigrant children: The importance of school context. *Child Development, 83*(5), 1477–1485.

Brydolf, C. (2009). Getting real about the "model minority." *The Education Digest*, 74(5), 37–44.

Buki, V. M. V. (2005). Treating the Hispanic elderly. *Clinical Psychology News*, 33(4), 8–9.

Burton, S., & Furr, S. (2014). Conflict in multicultural education classes: Approaches to resolving difficult dialogues. *Counselor Education & Supervision*, 53, 97–110.

Caire, K. (2009). Educating African American boys. *Education Next*, 9(4), 88.

Carrola, P., & Corbin-Burdick, M. F. (2015). Counseling military veterans: Advocating for culturally competent and holistic interventions. *Journal of Mental Health Counseling* 37(1), 1–14.

Case, K. A. (2012). Discovering the privilege of whiteness: White women's reflections on anti-racist identity and ally behavior. *Journal of Social Issues*, 68(1), 78–96.

Centers for Disease Control. (2013). *HIV among African Americans*. Atlanta, GA: Author.

Chang, E., Chan, K. S. & Hae-Ra. (2015). Effect of acculturation on variations in having a usual source of care among Asian Americans and Non-Hispanic Whites in California. *American Journal of Public Health*, 105 (2), 398–407.

Chung, R. C., & Bemak, F. (2013). Use of enthographic fiction in social justice graduate counselor training. *Counselor Education and Supervision*, 52, 56–69.

Chung, R. C., Bemak, F., & Wong, S. (2000). Vietnamese refugees' level of distress, social support, and acculturation: Implications for mental health counseling. *Journal of Mental Health Counseling*, 22, 150–161.

Chung, Y. B., & Katamaya, M. (1998). Ethnic and sexual identity development of Asian-American lesbian and gay adolescents. *Professional School Counseling*, 1(3), 21–25.

Clauss-Ehlers, C. S., & Parham, D. (2014). Landscape of diversity in higher Education: Linking demographic shifts to contemporary university and college counseling center practices. *Journal of Multicultural Counseling & Development*, 42(2), 69–76.

Cohen, C. I., Goh, K. H., & Yaffee, R. A. (2009). Depression outcome among a biracial sample of depressed urban elders. *American Journal of Geriatric Psychiatry*, 17, 943–952.

Cokley, K., Cody, B., Smith, L., Beasley, S., Miller, I.S.K., Hurst, A., Awosogba, O., Stone, S., & Jackson, S. (2014/2015). Bridge over troubled waters: Meeting the mental health needs of black students. *Kappan*, 96(4), 40–45.

Cokley, K., McClain, S., Enciso, A., & Martinez, M. (2013). An examination of the impact of minority status stress and impostor feelings on the mental health of diverse ethnic minority college students. *Journal of Multicultural Counseling & Development*, 41(2), 82–95.

Comas-Diaz, L. (2001). Hispanics, Latinos, or Americanos: The evolution of identity. *Cultural Diversity and Ethnic Minority Psychology*, 7(2), 115–120.

Cooley, J. J. (1998). Gay and lesbian adolescents: Presenting problems and the counselor's role. *Professional School Counseling*, 1(3), 30–34.

Cottone, R. R., & Claus, R. E. (2000). Ethical decision-making models: A review of the literature. *Journal of Counseling and Development*, 78, 275–283.

Cross, T L. (2014). The Indian Child Welfare Act: We must still fight for our children. *Reclaiming Children and Youth*, 23(2), 23–24.

Curtis, R., Kimball, A., & Stroup, E. L. (2004). Understanding and treating social phobia. *Journal of Counseling and Development*, 82, 3–8.

David, R. J., & Collins, J. W. (2014). Layers of inequality: Power, policy, and health. *American Journal of Public Health*, 104, S8–S10.

Davis, P., Davis, M. P, & Mobley, J. A. (2013). The school counselor's role in addressing the advanced placement equity and excellence gap for African American students. *Professional School Counseling*, 17(1), 32–39.

Day-Vines, N. L., & Day-Hairston, B. O. (2005). Culturally congruent strategies for addressing the behavioral needs of urban, African American male adolescents. *Professional School Counseling*, 8, 236–243.

De Master, C., & Girodano, M. D. (2005). Dutch families. In M. McGoldrick, J. Giordano, & N. Garcia-Preto (Eds.), *Ethnicity and family therapy* (3rd ed., pp. 334–344). New York: Guilford.

de Ravello, L., Jones, S. E., Tulloch, S., Taylor, M., & Doshi, S. (2014). Substance abuse and sexual risk behaviors among American Indian and Alaska Native high school students. *Journal of School Health*, 84(1), 25–32.

Degges-White, S., & Stoltz, K (2015). Archetypal identity development, meaning in life, and life satisfaction: Differences among clinical mental health counselors, school counselors, and counselor educators. *Adultspan Journal, 14*(1), 49–61.

Denevi, E. (2004). White on White: Exploring White racial identity, privilege, and racism. *Independent School, 63*(4), 84–87.

DePaul, J., Walsh, E., & Dam, U. C. (2009). The role of school counselors in addressing sexual orientation in schools. *Professional School Counseling, 12*(4), 300–308.

Desselle, D. D., & Proctor, T. K. (2000). Advocating for the elderly hard-of-hearing population: The deaf people we ignore. *Social Work, 45*(3), 277–281.

Deutsch, F. M. (2007). Undoing gender. *Gender & Society, 21*(1), 106–127.

Dewell, J. A., & Owen, J. (2015). Addressing mental health disparities with Asian American clients: Examining the generalizability of the common factors model. *Journal of Counseling and Development, 93*(3), 80–87.

Dinkes, R., Kemp, J., Baum, K., & Snyder, T. D. (2009, December). *Indicators of school and safety: 2009.* Washington: U.S. Department of Education, U.S. Department of Justice Office of Justice Programs.

Downing, N. E., & Roush, K. L. (1985). From passive acceptance to active commitment: A model of feminist identity for women. *Counseling Psychologist, 13*(4), 695–709.

Dubé, E. M., & Savin-Williams, R. C. (2000). Sexual identity development among ethnic sexual-minority male youths. *Developmental Psychology, 35*(6), 1389–1398.

DuPree, W., Jared, B., Kruti A., Patel, P. S., & DuPree, D. G. (2013). Developing culturally competent marriage and family therapists: Guidelines for working with Asian Indian American couples. *American Journal of Family Therapy, 41*(4), 311–329.

Dykes, F., & Thomas, S. (2015). Meeting needs of the hidden minority: Transition planning tips for LGBT youth. *Preventing School Failure, 59*(3), 179–185.

Elden, R. N., Edwards, E. P., & Leonard, K. E. (2004). Predictors of effortful control among alcoholic and nonalcoholic fathers. *Journal of Studies on Alcohols, 65*(3), 309–320.

Enke, F. (2015). Understanding and teaching U.S. lesbian, gay, bisexual, and transgender history. *History Teacher, 48*(3), 588–590.

Erickson, B. (2005). Scandinavian families: Plain and simple. In M. McGoldrick, J. Giordano, & N. Garcia-Preto (Eds.), *Ethnicity and family therapy* (3rd ed., pp. 641–653). New York: Guilford.

Erikson, E. (1963). *Childhood and society.* New York: Norton.

Erikson, E. (1968). *Identity: Youth and crisis.* New York: Norton.

Estrada, A. U., Durlak, J. A., & Juarez, S. C. (2002). Developing multicultural counseling competencies in undergraduate students. *Journal of Multicultural Counseling and Development, 30*(2), 110–123.

Exceptional Parent Magazine. (2008). www.eparent.com.

Exum, H. A., & Lau, E. Y. (1988). Counseling style preference of Chinese college students. *Journal of Multicultural Counseling and Development, 16,* 84–92.

Falco, K. (1991). *Psychotherapy with lesbian clients: Theory into practice.* New York: Brunner/Mazel.

Falicov, C. J. (2005). Mexican families. In M. McGoldrick, J. Giordano, & N. Garcia-Preto (Eds.), *Ethnicity and family therapy* (3rd ed., pp. 229–241). New York: Guilford.

Fatemi, A., Khodayari, L., & Stewart, A. (2015). Counseling in Iran: History, current status, and future trends. *Journal of Counseling & Development, 93*(1), 105–113.

Ferdman, B. M., & Gallegos, P. I. (2001). *Racial identity development and Latinos in the United States.* In C. Wijeyesinghe & B. Jackson (Eds.), New perspectives on racial identity development: A theoretical and practical anthology (pp. 32–66). New York: New York University Press.

Ferguson, T. M., Leach, M. M., Levy, J. J., Nicholson, B.C., & Johnson, J. D. (2009). Influences on counselor race preferences: Distinguishing Black racial attitudes from Black racial identity. *Journal of Multicultural Counseling and Development, 36,* 66–76.

Fields, E. L., Bogart, L. M., Smith, K. C., Malebranche, D. J., Ellen, J., & Schuster, M. A. (2015). "I always felt I had to prove my manhood": Homosexuality, masculinity, gender role strain, and HIV risk among young Black men who have sex with men. *American Journal of Public Health, 105*(1), 122–131.

Finfgeld-Connett, D. L. (2005). Self management of alcohol problems among aging adults. *Journal of Gerontological Nursing, 31*(5), 51–58.

Firestein, B. A. (1996). *Bisexuality: The psychology and politics of an invisible minority*. Thousand Oaks, CA: Sage.

Flores, M. T., & Carey, G. (2000). *Family therapy with Hispanics: Toward appreciating diversity*. Boston: Allyn & Bacon.

Flores, R., Tschann, J. M., Marin, B., & Pantoja, P. (2004). Marital conflict and acculturation among Mexican American husbands and wives. *Cultural Diversity and Ethnic Minority Psychology*, *10*(1), 39–52.

Fuertes, J. N. (2004). Supervision in bilingual counseling: Service delivery, training, and research considerations. *Journal of Multicultural Counseling and Development, 32*(2), 84–94.

Gallardo, M. E., & McNeill, B. W. (2009). *Intersections of multiple identities*. New York: Routledge.

Garrett, M. T., & Carroll, J. J. (2000). Mending the broken circle: Treatment of substance dependence among Native Americans. *Journal of Counseling and Development, 78*(4), 379–388.

Garrett, M. T., & Wilbur, M. P. (1999). Does the worm live in the ground? Reflections on Native American spirituality. *Journal of Multicultural Counseling and Development, 27*(4), 193–206.

Garza, Y., & Watts, R. E. (2010). Filial therapy and Hispanic values: Common ground for culturally sensitive helping. *Journal of Counseling and Development, 88*, 108–113.

Giordano, J., McGoldrick, M., & Klages, J. G. (2005). Italian families. In M. McGoldrick, J. Giordano, & N. Garcia-Preto (Eds.), *Ethnicity and family therapy* (3rd ed., pp. 616–628). New York: Guilford.

Giorgis, C., Higgins, K., & McNab, W. L. (2000). Health issues of gay and lesbian youth: Implications for schools. *Journal of Health Education, 31*(1), 28–36.

Gloria, A.M., & Rodriguez, E. R. (2000). Counseling Latino university students: Psychosocial issues for consideration. *Journal of Counseling and Development, 78*, 145–154.

Glover-Graf, N. M., Marini, I., Baker, J., & Buck, T. (2007). The perceived impact of religious and spiritual beliefs for persons with chronic pain. *Rehabilitation Counseling Bulletin, 51*(1), 21–33.

Gnanadass, E. (2014). Learning to teach about race. *Adult Learning, 25*(3), 96–102.

Gold, J. M. (2010). *Counseling and spirituality: Integrating spiritual and clinical orientations*. Columbus, OH: Merrill Prentice-Hall.

Goldsmith, J. S., & Kurpius, S. E. Robinson. (2015). Older adults and integrated health settings: Opportunities and challenges for mental health counselors. *Journal of Mental Health Counseling, 37*(2), 124–137.

Goodenow, C., Szalacha, L. A., Robin, L. E., & Westheimer, K. (2008). Dimensions of sexual orientation and HIV-related risk among adolescent females: Evidence from a statewide survey. *American Journal of Public Health, 98*(6), 1051–1058.

Graf, N. M., Blankenship, C. J., Sanchez, G., & Carlson, R. (2007). Living on the line: Mexican and Mexican American attitudes toward disabilities. *Rehabilitation Counseling Bulletin, 50*(3), 153–165.

Gray, M. M. (2015). Your average American Catholic. *America, 212*(17), 16–19.

Han, A. Y., & Vasquez, M. J. T. (2000). Group intervention and treatment of ethnic minorities. In J. F. Aponte & J. Wohl (Eds.), *Psychological intervention and cultural diversity. Education and Supervision* (2nd ed., pp. 110–130). Boston: Allyn & Bacon.

Hanna, F. J., & Green, A. (2004). Asian shades of spirituality: Implications for school counseling. *Professional School Counseling, 7*(5), 326–333.

Hansen, L. E. (2015). Encouraging pre-service teachers to address issues of sexual orientation in their classrooms. *Multicultural Education, 22*(2), 51–55

Harader, D. L., Fullwood, H., & Hawthorne, M. (2009). Sexuality among adolescents with moderate disabilities: Promoting positive sexual development. *The Prevention Researcher, 16*(4), 17–20.

Harper, G. W., Jernewall, N., & Zea, M. C. (2004). Giving voice to emerging science and theory for lesbian, gay, and bisexual people of color. *Cultural Diversity and Ethnic Minority Psychology, 10*(3), 187–199.

Hart, J. E. (2009). Strategies for culturally and linguistically diverse students with special needs. *Preventing School Failure, 53*(3), 197–206.

Havighurst, R. J. (1972). *Developmental tasks and education* (3rd ed.). New York: McKay.

Hayden, L., Cook, A., Scherer, A., Greenspan, S. Silva, M. R., Cadet, M., & Maki, E. (2014). Integrating physical activity, coach collaboration, and life skill development in youth: School counselors' perceptions. *Journal of School Counseling, 12*(3), 1–38.

Hays, D. G., Chang, C. Y., & Dean, J. K. (2004). White counselors' conceptualization of privilege and oppression: Implications for counselor training. *Counselor Education & Supervision, 43,* 242–257.

Hazler, R. J., & Mellin, E. A. (2004). The developmental origins and treatment needs of female adolescents with depression. *Journal of Counselor & Development, 82,* 18–24.

Healey, A. C., & Hays, D. G. (2012). A discriminant analysis of gender and counselor professional identity development. *Journal of Counseling and Development, 90,* 55–62.

Hebard, S. P., & Hebard, A. J. (2015, March). Beyond LGB. ct.counseling.org

Helms, J. E. (1984). Toward a theoretical explanation of the effects of race on counseling: Black and White model. *Counseling Psychologist, 12*(4), 163–165.

Helms, J. E. (1990). *Black and White racial identity: Theory, research, and practice.* Westport, CT: Greenwood.

Helms, J. E. (1994). Racial identity in the school environment. In P. Pedersen & J. C. Carey (Eds.), Multicultural counseling in schools (pp. 19–37). Boston: Allyn & Bacon.

Henderson, D., Carjuzaa, J., & Ruff, W. G. (2015). Reconciling leadership paradigms: Authenticity as practiced by American Indian school leaders. *International Journal of Multicultural Education, 17*(1), 211–231.

Henfield. M. S., Washington, A. R., & Byrd, J. A. (2014). Addressing academic and opportunity gaps impacting gifted Black males. *Gifted Child Today, 37*(3), 147–154.

Hermann, M. A., & Herlihy, R. (2006). Legal and ethical implications of refusing to counsel homosexual clients. *Journal of Counseling and Development, 84*(4), 414–418.

Hershberger, S. L., & D'Augelli, A. R. (2000). Issues in counseling lesbian, gay, and bisexual adolescents. In R. M. Perez, K. A. DeBord, & K. J. Bieschke (Eds.), *Handbook of counseling and psychotherapy with lesbian, gay, and bisexual clients* (pp. 225–247). Washington, DC: American Psychological Association.

Hill, G., & Downing, A. (2015). Effect of frequent peer-monitored testing and personal goal setting on Fitnessgram scores of Hispanic middle school students. *Physical Educator, 72*(2), 193–205.

Hilton, J. M., & Child, S. L. (2014). Spirituality and the successful aging of older Latinos. *Counseling and Values, 59,* 17–34.

Hines, P.M., & Boyd-Franklin, N. (2005). African American families. In M. McGoldrick, J. Giordano, & N. Garcia-Preto (Eds.), *Ethnicity and family therapy* (3rd ed., pp. 87–100). New York: Guilford.

Hipolito-Delgado, C. P. (2015). Beyond cultural competence. *Counseling Today. 56*(10), 50–55.

Ho, M. K. (1987). *Family therapy with ethnic minorities.* Newbury Park, CA: Sage.

Hojman, H. (2014). Spanish is coming to a child psychiatry practice near you. *The Brown University Child and Adolescent Behavior Letter, 30*(1), 1–3.

Hooper, L. M. (2014). Mental health services in primary care: Implications for clinical mental health counselors and other mental health providers. *Journal of Mental Health Counseling, 36*(2), 95–98.

Horwitz, A, (2014, February 9). New law offers protection to abused Native American women. The *Washington Post,* National Security Section, 1–14.

Hwang, W., Chun, C., Takeuchi, D. T., Myers, H. F., & Siddarth, P. (2005). Age of first onset of major depression in Chinese Americans. *Cultural Diversity and Ethnic Minority Psychology. 11*(1), 16–27.

Ibrahim, F. A., Ohnishi, H., & Sandhu, D. S. (1997). Asian American identity development: A culture-specific model for South Asian Americans. *Journal of Multicultural Counseling and Development, 25*(1), 34–50.

Ingersoll, R. E., Bauer, A., & Burns, L. (2004). Children and psychotropic medication: What role should advocacy counseling play? *Journal of Counseling and Development, 82,* 337–343.

Irving, D. (2014, September). Counselor career stories—An ally's perspective in LGBTQIA issues and training, ct.counseling.org, 26–27.

Itai, G. I., & McRae, C. (1994). Counseling older Japanese American clients: An overview and observations. *Journal of Counseling and Development, 72,* 373–377.

Ivey, A. E., D'Andrea, M., Ivey, M. B., & Simek-Morgan, L. (2012). *Theories of counseling and psychotherapy: A multicultural perspective* (7th ed.). Boston: Pearson Allyn & Bacon.

Jacobson, L. (2015). The Hispanic dynamic. *State Legislatures, 41*(6), 16–20.

Jacobson, L., Pappalardo, K., & Super, J. (2009). Group therapy to build strong relationships for same-sex couples. Paper based a program presented at the American Counseling Association Annual Conference and Exposition, Charlotte, NC. Accessed 11 November 2014 from http:/// www.counseling.org/docs/vistas/vistas_2009_jacobson-pappalardo-super.pdf?sfvrsn=3.

Johnson, I. H., Torres, J. S., Coleman, V. D., & Smith, M. C. (1995). Issues and strategies in leading culturally diverse counseling groups. *Journal for Specialists in Group Work, 20*, 143–150.

Johnson, S. K., & Johnson, C. D. (2005). Group counseling: Beyond the traditional. *Professional School Counseling, 8*(5), 399–400.

Kaslow, N. J., Price, A. W., Wyckoff, S., Grall, M. B., Sherry, A., Young, S., Scholl, L., Millington, U.V., Rashid, A., Jackson, E. B., & Bethea, K. (2004). Person factors associated with suicidal behavior among African American women and men. *Cultural Diversity and Ethnic Minority Psychology, 10*(1), 5–22.

Keats, D. M. (2000). Cross-cultural studies in child development in Asian cultures. *Cross-Cultural Research, 34*(3), 339–350.

Kenny, M. C., & McEachern, A. (2009). Children's self-concept: A multicultural comparison. *Professional School Counseling, 12*(3), 207–212.

Kerr, B. A., & Multon, K. D. (2015). The development of gender identity, gender roles, and gender relations in gifted students. *Journal of Counseling & Development, 93*(2), 183–191.

Killian, K. D., & Agathangelou, A. M. (2005). Greek families. In M. McGoldrick, J. Giordano, & N. Garcia-Preto (Eds.), *Ethnicity and family therapy* (3rd ed., pp. 532–551). New York: Guilford.

Kim, B. S., & Lyons, H. Z. (2003). Experiential activities and multicultural counseling competence training. *Journal of Counseling and Development, 81*(4), 400–408.

Kim, B. S., Ng, G. F., & Ahn, A. J. (2005). Effects of client expectation for counseling success, client–counselor worldview match, and client adherence to Asian and European American cultural values on counseling process with Asian Americans. *Journal of Counseling Psychology, 52*(1), 67–76.

Kim, B. S. K., & Park, Y. S. J. (2015). Communication styles, cultural values, and counseling effectiveness with Asian Americans. *Journal of Counseling & Development, 93*(3), 269–279.

Kim, K., Lee, Y., & Morningstar, M. E. (2007). An unheard voice: Korean American parents' expectations, hopes, and experiences concerning adolescent child's future. *Research and Practice for Persons with Severe Disabilities, 32*, 253–264.

Kimmel, D.C., & Yi, H. (2004). Characteristics of gay, lesbian, Asian, Asian Americans, and immigrants from Asia to the USA. *Journal of Homosexuality, 47*(2), 143–171.

Kirk, J., & Belovics, R. (2008). Understanding and counseling transgender clients. *Journal of Employment Counseling, 45*(1), 29–43.

Konstam, V., Cook, A. L., Tomek, S., Mahdavi, E., Gracia, R., & Bayne, A. H. (2015). What factors sustain professional growth among school counselors? *Journal of School Counseling, 13*(3), 1–40.

Korin, E. C. (1996). Brazilian families. In M. McGoldrick, J. Giordano, & J. K. Pearce (Eds.), *Ethnicity and family therapy* (2nd ed., pp. 200–213). New York: Guilford.

Koss-Chioino, J. D. (2000). Traditional and folk approaches among ethnic minorities. In J. F. Aponte & J. Wohl (Eds.), *Psychological intervention and cultural diversity* (2nd ed., pp. 149–166). Boston: Allyn & Bacon.

Kottler, J. (2013). Reenvisioning a new counselor identity. *Counseling Today, 52*, 10–12.

Krause, N. (2004). Lifetime trauma, emotional support, and life satisfaction among older adults. *The Gerontologist, 44*(5), 615–623.

Krogstad, J. M. (2014). *One-in four Native Americans and Alaskan Natives are living in poverty.* Pew Research Center. Accessed 15 March 2015 from http://www.pewresearchorg/author,jkrogstad.

Kung, W. W. (2001). Consideration of cultural factors in working with Chinese American families with a mentally ill patient. *Families in Society: The Journal of Contemporary Human Services, 82*(1), 97–107.

Kurasaki, K. S., Sue, S., Chun, C., & Gee, K. (2000). Ethnic minority intervention and treatment research. In J. F. Aponte & J. Wohl (Eds.), *Psychological intervention and cultural diversity* (2nd ed., pp. 234–249). Boston: Allyn & Bacon.

Laird, J. (2000). Gender in lesbian relationships: Cultural, feminist, and constructionist reflections. *Journal of Marital and Family Therapy, 26*(4), 455–467.

Langelier, R., & Langelier, P. (2005). French Canadian families. In M. McGoldrick, J. Giordano, & N. Garcia-Preto (Eds.), *Ethnicity and family therapy* (3rd ed., pp. 545–554). New York: Guilford.

Laska, M. N., VanKim, N. A., Erickson, D. J., Lust, K., Eisenberg, M. E., & Rosser, B. R. S. (2015). Disparities in weight and weight behaviors by sexual orientation in college students. *American Journal of Public Health, 105*(1), 111–121.

Laszloffy, T. A. (2005). Hungarian families. In M. McGoldrick, J. Giordano, & N. Garcia-Preto (Eds.), *Ethnicity and family therapy* (3rd ed., pp. 586–595). New York: Guilford.

Lee, R. M. (2003). Do ethnic identity and other-group orientation protect against discrimination for Asian Americans? *Journal of Counseling Psychology, 50*(2), 133–141.

Lee, R. M., Su, J., & Yoshida, E. (2005). Coping with intergenerational family conflict among Asian American college students. *Journal of Counseling Psychology, 52*(3), 389–399.

Lee, S., & Rotherham-Borus, M. J. (2009). Beyond the "model minority" stereotype: Trends in Health risk behaviors among Asian/Pacific Islander high school students. *Journal of School Health, 79*(8), 347–354.

Lemoire, S. J., & Chen, C. P. (2005). Applying person-centered counseling to sexual minority adolescents. *Journal of Counseling and Development, 83*, 148–154.

Leung, P. K., & Boehnlein, J. (1996). Vietnamese families. In M. McGoldrick, J. Giordano, & J. K. Pearce (Eds.), *Ethnicity and family therapy* (2nd ed., pp. 295–306). New York: Guilford.

Li, H. (2004). Barriers and unmet needs for supportive services: Experiences of Asian American caregivers. *Journal of Cross-Cultural Gerontology, 19*, 241–260.

Li, J., Fung, H., Bakeman, R., Rae, K., & Wei, W. (2014). How European American and Taiwanese mothers talk to their children about learning. *Child Development, 85*(3), 1206–1221.

Limb, G. E., White, C., & Holgate, M. (2014). American Indian couples' relationship quality to improve parenting. *Journal of Human Behavior in the Social Environment, 24*(2), 92–104.

Lindley, L. L., & Waisemann, K. M. (2015). Sexual orientation and risk of pregnancy among New York City high-school students. *American Journal of Public Health, 105*(7), 1379–1386.

Lindsey, C. (2014). Trait anxiety in college students: The role of the approval seeking schema and separation individuation. *College Student Journal, 48*(3), 407–418.

Lippincott, J. A., & Mierzwa, J. A. (1995). Propensity for seeking counseling services: A comparison of Asian and American undergraduates. *Journal of American College Health, 43*, 201–204.

Littlebear, R. E. (2003). Chief Dull Knife community is strengthening the Northern Cheyenne in language and culture. *Journal of American Indian Education, 42*, 75–84.

Liu, Y. (2003). Aging service and use among Chinese American seniors. *Journal of Cross-Cultural Gerontology, 18*, 273–301.

Lo, L. (2008). Expectations of Chinese families of children with disabilities towards American schools. *The School Community Journal, 18*(2), 73–90.

Lockard, A. J., Hayes, J. A., Graceffo, J. M., & Locke, B. D. (2013). Effective counseling for racial/ethnic minority clients: Examining changes using a practice research network. *Journal of College Counseling, 16*(3), 243–257.

Lokken, J. M., & Twohey, D. (2004). American Indian perspectives of Euro-American counseling behavior. *Journal of Multicultural Counseling and Development, 32*, 320–331.

Lonborg, S. D., & Bowen, N. (2004). Counselors, communities, and spirituality: Ethical and multicultural considerations. *Professional School Counseling, 7*(5), 318–325.

Loos, J, Manirankunda, L., Hendrickx, K. Remmen, R., & Nöstlinger, C. (2014). HIV Testing in primary care: Feasibility and acceptability of provider initiated HIV Testing and counseling for Sub-Saharan African migrants. *AIDS Education & Prevention, 26*(1), 81–93.

Love, M. M., Smith, A. E., Lyall, S. E., Mullins, J. L., & Cohn, T. J. (2015). Exploring the relationship between gay affirmative practice and empathy among mental health professionals. *Journal of Multicultural Counseling & Development, 43*(2), 83–96.

Lovejoy, M. (2001). Disturbances in the social body: Differences in body image and eating problems among African and White women. *Gender & Society, 15*(2), 239–261.

Ludeke, M. (2009). Transgender youth. *Principal Leadership, 19*(3), 12–16.

Lund, T. J., Chan, P., & Liang, B. (2014). Depression and relational health in Asian American and European American college women. *Psychology in the Schools, 51*(5), 493–50.

Ly, P. (2008). Caught between two cultures. *Diverse Issues in Higher Education, 25*(14), 24–25.

MacGillivray, I. K., & Kozik-Rosabal, G. (2000). Introduction. *Education and Urban Society*, *32*(3), 287–302.

MacLeod, B. P. (2014). Addressing clients' prejudices in counseling. *Counseling Today, 56*(8), 50–55.

Magaldi-Dopman, D. (2014). An "Afterthought": Counseling trainees' multicultural competence within the spiritual/religious domain. *Journal of Multicultural Counseling & Development, 42*(4), 194–204.

Malebranche, D. J., Arriola, K. J., Jenkins, T. R., Dauria, E., & Patel, S. N. (2010). Exploring the "bisexual bridge": A qualitative study of risk behavior and disclosure of same-sex behavior among Black bisexual men. *American Journal of Public Health, 100*(1), 159–164.

Malott, K.M., Paone, T. R., Schaefle, S., Cates, J., & Haizlip, B. (2015). Expanding White racial identity theory: A qualitative investigation of Whites engaged in antiracist action. *Journal of Counseling & Development, 93*, 333–343.

Malott, K. M., & Schaefle, S. (2015). Addressing clients' experiences of racism: A model for clinical practice, *Journal of Counseling and Development, 93*, 361–369.

Marbley, A. F., Bonner, F. A, McKisick, S., Henfield, M. S., & Watts, L. (2007). Interfacing culture specific pedagogy with counseling: A proposed diversity training model for preparing preservice teachers for diverse learners. *Multicultural Education, 14*, 8–16.

Maslim, A. A., & Bjorck, J. P. (2009). Reasons for conversion to Islam among women in the United States. *Psychology of Religion and Spirituality, 1*(2), 97–111.

Maxwell, L. A. (2014, December). U.S. school enrollment hits majority-minority milestone. *Education Week*, www.eddigest.com.

Mayer, K. H., Garofalo, R., & Makadon, H. J. (2014). Promoting the successful development of sexual and gender minority youths. *American Journal of Public Health, 104*(6), 976–981.

McCabe, P. C., & Rubinson, F. (2008). Committing to social justice: The behavioral intention on school psychology and education trainees to advocate for lesbian, gay, bisexual, and transgendered youth. *School Psychology Review, 37*(4), 469–486.

McCarn, S. R., & Fassinger, R. E. (1996). Revisioning sexual minority identity formation: A new model of lesbian identity and its implications for counseling and research. *Counseling Psychologist, 24*(3), 508–534.

McCarthy, J., & Holliday, E. L. (2004). Help-seeking and counseling within a traditional male gender role: An examination from a multicultural perspective. *Journal of Counseling and Development, 82*, 25–30.

McGarry, R. (2013). Build a curriculum that includes everyone. *Phi Delta Kappan, 94*(5), 27–31.

McGill, C.M., & Collins, J. C. (2015). Creating fugitive knowledge through disorienting dilemmas: The issue of bottom identity development. *New Horizons in Adult Education & Human Resource Development, 27*(1), 29–40.

McGoldrick, M. (2005). Irish families. In M. McGoldrick, J. Giordano, & N. Garcia-Preto (Eds.), *Ethnicity and family therapy* (3rd ed., pp. 395–615). New York: Guilford.

McGoldrick, M., Giordano, J., & Garcia-Preto, N. (Eds.). (2005). *Ethnicity and family therapy* (3rd ed.). New York: Guilford.

McMahon, T. R., Kenyon, D. B., & Carter, J. S. (2013). "My culture. my family, my school, me": Identifying strengths and challenges in the lives and communities of American Indian youth. *Journal of Child & Family Studies, 22*, 694–706.

Meany-Walen, K., Bratton, S. C., & Kottman, T. (2014). Effects of Adlerian play therapy on reducing students' disruptive behaviors. *Journal of Counseling & Development, 92*(1), 47–56.

Méndez, L. I., Crais, E. R., Castro, D.C., & Kainz, K. (2015). A culturally and linguistically responsive vocabulary approach for young Latino dual language learners. *Journal of Speech, Language & Hearing Research, 58*(1), 93–106.

Merrill, G. S., & Wolfe, V. A. (2000). Battered gay men: An exploration of abuse, help-seeking, and why they stay. *Journal of Homosexuality, 39*(2), 1–30.

Meyer, O. L., Castro-Schilo, L., & Aguilar-Gaxiola, S. (2014). Determinants of mental health and self-rated health: A model of socioeconomic status, neighborhood safety, and physical activity. *American Journal of Public Health, 104*(9), 1734–1741.

Meza, N. (2015). Indian education: Maintaining tribal sovereignty through culture and language preservation. *Brigham Young University Education & Law Journal*, Issue 1, 353–366.

Milan, S., & Keiley, M. K. (2000). Biracial youth and families in therapy: Issues and interventions. *Journal of Marital and Family Therapy, 26*(3), 305–315.

Moghaddam, J. F., Momper, S. L., & Fong, T. (2013). Discrimination and participation in traditional healing for American Indians and Alaska Natives. *Journal of Community Health, 38,* 1115–1123.

Molock, S. D., & Barksdale, C. L. (2013). Relationship between religiosity and conduct problems among African American and Caucasian adolescents. *Journal of Child and Family Students, 22,* 4–14.

Moore, D. L., (2005). Expanding the view: The lives of women with severe work disabilities in context. *Journal of Counseling and Development, 83,* 343–348.

Moore-Thomas, C., & Day-Vines, N. L. (2008). Culturally competent counseling for religious and spiritual African American adolescents. *Professional School Counseling, 11,* 159–165.

Morgan, H. (2010). Teaching Native American students: What every student should know. *Education Digest, 75*(6), 44–47.

Moss, J. M., Gibson, D. M., & Dollarhide, C. T. (2014). Professional identity development: A grounded theory of transformational tasks of counselors. *Journal of Counseling and Development, 92,* 3–12.

Mueller, A. S. James, W., Abrutyn, S., & Levin, M. L. (2015). Suicide ideation and bullying among US adolescents: Examining the intersections of sexual orientation, gender, and race/ethnicity. *American Journal of Public Health. 105*(5), 980–985.

Muller, L. E. (2000). A 12-session, European American led counseling group for African American females. *Professional School Counseling, 3*(4), 264–269.

Muratori, M. C., & Smith, C. K. (2015). Guiding the talent and career development of the gifted individual. *Journal of Counseling & Development, 93*(2), 173–182.

Murray, P. D., & McClintock, K. (2005). Children of the closet: A measurement of the anxiety and self-esteem of children raised by a non-disclosed homosexual or bisexual parent. *Journal of Homosexuality, 49*(1), 77–95.

Nadal, K. L., (2004). Pilipino American identity development model. *Journal of Multicultural Counseling and Development, 32*(1), 45–62.

National Education Association. (2008). *Native American 101: Basic facts about American Indian, Alaska Natives, and Native Hawaiian education.* Washington, DC: Author.

Newman, D. L. (2005). Ego development and ethnic identity formation in rural American Indian adolescents. *Child Development, 76*(3), 734–747.

Ofstedal, M. B., Reidy, E., & Knodel, J. (2004). Gender differences in economic support and well-being of older Asians. *Journal of Cross-Cultural Gerontology, 19,* 165–201.

Oguntoyinbo, L. (2015, May 7). Behind the mask. *Issues in Higher Education, 32*(7), 14–15.

Olive, J. L. (2015). The impact of friendship on the leadership identity development of Lesbian, Gay, Bisexual, and Queer students. *Journal of Leadership Education. 14*(1), 142–159.

Omizo, M. M., Kim, S. K., & Abel, N. R. (2008). Asian and European American cultural values, bicultural competence, and attitudes toward seeking professional psychological help among Asian American adolescents. *Journal of Multicultural Counseling and Development, 36*(1), 15–28.

Orel, N. A. (2004). Gay, lesbian, and bisexual elders: Expressed needs and concerns across focus groups. *Journal of Gerontological Social Work, 43*(2/3), 57–77.

Pan, L., May, A. L., Wethington, H., Dalenius, K., & Grummer-Strawn, L. M. (2013). Incidence of obesity among US children living in low-income families, 2008–2011. *Pediatrics, 132*(6), 2013–2045.

Papalia, D. E., Olds, S. W., & Feldman, R. D. (2009). *Human development* (11th ed.). Boston; McGraw-Hill.

Papalia, D. E., Feldman, R., & Martorell, G. (2014). *Experience Human development* (13th ed.). Boston: McGraw-Hill.

Parks, C. A., Hughes, T. L., & Matthews, A. K. (2004). Race/ethnicity and sexual orientation: Intersecting identities. *Cultural Diversity and Ethnic Minority Psychology, 10*(3), 241–254.

Parrinelio, C. M., Isasi, C. R. Xiaonan X., Bandiera, F. C., Jianwen C., Ji-Hyun L., David J., Navas-Nacher, E. L., Perreira, K. M., Salgado, H., & Kaplan, R. C. (2015). Risk of cigarette smoking initiation during adolescence among US-born and non-US-born Hispanics/Latinos: The Hispanic community health study of Latinos. *American Journal of Public Health, 105*(6), 1230–1236.

Pearson, B. Z., Conner, T., & Jackson, J. E. (2013). Removing obstacles for African American English-speaking children through greater understanding of language difference. *Developmental Psychology, 49*(1), 31–44.

Pennachio, D. L. (2004). Caring for your Filipino, Southeastern Asian, and Indian patients: More than half of Asian Americans say their doctors don't understand their cultures: Sensitivity to diversity is essential for good patient care. *Medical Economics, 81*(2), 36–42.

Perez, C. (2014, December 8–15). Zero tolerance: Why Catholics must condemn anti-gay violence. *America,* 16–19.

Pew Research Center (2009). A religious portrait of African Americans. Washington, DC: Author.

Phan, L. T., Rivera, E. T., & Roberts-Wilbur, J. (2005). Understanding Vietnamese refugee women's identity development from a sociopolitical and historical perspective. *Journal of Counseling and Development, 83,* 305–312.

Phillips, I. (2003). Infusing spirituality into geriatric health care: Practical applications from the literature. *Topics in Geriatric Rehabilitation, 19*(4), 249–256.

Pica-Smith, C., & Poynton, T. A. (2014). Supporting interethnic and interracial friendships among youth to reduce prejudice and racism in schools: The role of the school counselor. *Professional School Counseling, 18*(1), 82–89.

Pinguart, M., & Sorensen, S. (2005). Ethnic differences in stressors, resources, and psychological outcomes of family giving: A meta-analysis. *The Gerontologist, 45,* 90–106.

Ponterotto, J. G., Utsey, S. O., & Pedersen, P. B. (2006). *Preventing prejudice: A guide for counselors, educators, and parents* (2nd ed.). Thousand Oaks, CA: Sage.

Pope, A. (1999). Applications of group career counseling techniques in Asian cultures. *Journal of Multicultural Counseling and Development, 27*(1), 18–30.

Pope, M., Barret, B., Szymanski, D. M. Chung, Y. B., Singaravelu, H., McLean, R, & Sanabria, S. (2004). Culturally appropriate career counseling with gay and lesbian clients. *The Career Development Quarterly, 53*(2), 158–177.

Pope, R. L. (2000). The relationship between psychosocial development and racial identity of college students of color. *Journal of College Student Development, 41*(3), 302–311.

Poston, W. S. C. (1990). The biracial identity development model: A needed addition. *Journal of Counseling and Development, 69,* 152–155.

Potgieter, C. (1997). From apartheid to Mandel's constitution: Black South African lesbians in the nineties. In B. Greene (Ed.), Psychological perspectives on lesbian and gay issues, Vol. 3: *Ethnic and cultural diversity among lesbians and gay men* (pp. 88–116). Thousand Oaks, CA: Sage.

Prosek, E. A., & Hurt, K. M. (2014). Measuring professional identity development among counselor trainees. *Counselor Education & Supervision, 53*(4), 284–293.

Qasqas, M. J., & Jerry, P. (2014). Counselling Muslims: A culture-infused antidiscriminatory approach. *Canadian Journal of Counselling & Psychotherapy, 48*(1), 57–76.

Raque-Bogdan, T. L., Klingaman, E. A., Martin, H. M., & Lucas, M. S. (2013). Career-related Parent support and career barriers: An investigation of contextual variables. *Career Development Quarterly, 61*(4), 339–353.

Reyes, L. R., Meininger, J. C., Liehr, P., Chan, W., & Mueller, W. H. (2003). *Nursing Research, 52*(1), 2–11.

Reynolds, A. L., & Hanjorgiris, W. F. (2000). Coming out: Lesbian, gay, and bisexual development. In R. M. Perez, K. A. DeBord, & K. J. Bieschke (Eds.), *Handbook of counseling and psychotherapy with lesbian, gay, and bisexual clients* (pp. 35–55). Washington, DC: American Psychological Association.

Reynolds, S. L., Saito, Y., & Crimmins, E. M. (2005). The impact of obesity on active life expectancy in older American men and women. *The Gerontologist, 45*(4), 438–444.

Rhodes, S. D., Mann, L., Simán, F. M., Eunyoung S., Alonzo, J., Downs, M., Lawlor, E., Martinez, O., Sun, C. J., O'Brien, M. C., Reboussin, & B. A., Hall, M. A. (2015). The impact of local immigration enforcement policies on the health of immigrant Hispanics/Latinos in the United States. *American Journal of Public Health, 105*(2), 329–337.

Rigali-Oiler, M., & Kurpius, S. R. (2013). Promoting academic persistence among racial/ethnic minority and European American freshman and sophomore undergraduates: Implications for college counselors. *Journal of College Counseling, 16*(3), 98–212.

Ringel, S. (2005). Therapeutic dilemmas in cross-cultural practice with Asian American adolescents. *Child and Adolescent Social Work Journal, 22,* 57–66.

Rivas-Drake, D., Syed, M., Umana-Taylor, A., Marstrom, C., French, S., Schwartz, S. J., & Lee, R. (2014). Feeling good, happy, and proud: A meta-analysis of positive ethnic-racial affect and adjustment. *Child Development*, 85(1), 77–102.

Robinson, T. L. (2005). *The convergence of race, ethnicity, and gender: Multiple identities in counseling* (2nd ed.). Columbus, OH: Merrill/Prentice-Hall.

Robinson-Wood, T. L. (2009). *The convergence of race, ethnicity, and gender: Multiple identities in counseling* (4th ed.). Columbus, OH: Merrill Prentice Hall.

Rodenborg, N. A., & Boisen, L. A. (2013). Aversive racism and intergroup contact theories: Cultural comparisons in a segregated world. *Journal of Social Work*, 49(4), 564–679.

Roscoe, J. L. (2015). Advising African American and Latino students. *Research & Teaching in Developmental Education*, 31(2), 48–60.

Rothman, T., Malott, K. M., & Paone, T. R. (2012). Experiences of a course on the culture of Whiteness in counselor education. *Journal of Multicultural Counseling and Development*, 40, 37–40.

Rowe, W, Bennett, S. K., & Atkinson, D. R. (1994). White racial identity: A critique and alternative proposal. Counseling Psychologist, 22(1), 129–146.

Rowles, J. C., & Duan, C. (2012). Perceived racism and encouragement among African American adults. *Journal of Multicultural Counseling and Development*, 40, 11–23.

Ryan, B. (2013). You are not alone. *Education Today*, 2, 2–4.

Ryan, E. B., Jin Y., Anas, A. P., & Luh, J. J. (2004). Communication beliefs about youth and old age in Asia and Canada. *Journal of Cross-Cultural Gerontology*, 19, 343–360.

Saucier, M. G. (2004). Midlife and beyond: Issues for aging women. *Journal of Counseling and Development*, 82, 420–425.

Schachter, A. (2014). Finding common ground: Indian immigrants and Asian American panethnicity, *Social Forces*, 92(4), 1487–1512.

Schnall, E., Kalkstein, S., Gottesman, A., Feinberg, K., Schaeffer, C. B., & Feinberg, S. S. (2014). Barriers to mental health care: A 25 year follow-up study of the Orthodox Jewish community. *Journal of Multicultural Counseling and Development*, 42, 161–172.

Schneider, M. E., & Owens, R. E. (2000). Concern for lesbian, gay, and bisexual kids: The benefits for all children. *Education and Urban Society*, 32(3), 349–367.

Scott, K. D., & Scott, A. A. (2014). Adolescent inhalant use and executive cognitive functioning. *Health and Development*, 40(1), 20–28.

Sharma, M. (2004). Substance abuse and Asian Americans: Need for more research. *Journal of Alcohol Drug Education*, 47(3), 1–3.

Shuster, G. F., Clough, D. H., Higgins, P. G., & Klein, B. J. (2008). Health and health behaviors among elderly Hispanic women. *Geriatric Nursing*, 30(1), 18–27.

Simonsen, G., Blazina, C., & Watkins, C. E. (2000). Gender role conflict and psychological well-being among gay men. *Journal of Counseling Psychology*, 47(1), 85–89.

Skogrand, L., Mueller, M. L., Arrington, R., LeBranc, H., Davina, S. E., Dayzie, I., & Rosenbrand, R. (2008). Strong Navajo marriages. *American Indian and Alaska Native Mental Health Research: The Journal of the National Center*, 15, 25–41.

Smart, J. F., & Smart, D. W. (2006). Models of disability: Implications for the counseling profession. *Journal of Counseling and Development*, 84(1), 29–40.

Smedley, B. D. (2012). The lived consequences of race and its health consequences. *American Journal of Public Health*, 102(5), 933–935.

Smith, A., & Koltz, R. L. (2015). Supervision of school counseling students: A focus on personal growth, wellness, and development. *Journal of School Counseling*, 13(2), 1–34.

Smith, K. M., Chesin, M. S., & Jeglic, E. L. (2014). Minority college student mental health: Does majority status matter? Implications for college counseling services. *Journal of Multicultural Counseling and Development*, 42, 77–92.

Smith, L., Foley, P. F., & Chaney, M. P. (2008). Addressing classism, ableism, and heterosexualism in counselor education. *Journal of Counseling and Development*, 86(3), 303–309.

Soheilian, S. S., & Inman, A. G. (2015). Competent counseling for Middle Eastern American clients: Implications for trainees. *Journal of Multicultural Counseling & Development*, 43(3), 173–190.

Stambaugh, T., & Ford, D. Y. (2015). Microaggressions, multicultural, and gifted individuals who are Black, Hispanic, or low income. *Journal of Counseling & Development*, 93, 192–201.

Steen, S., Bauman, S., & Smith (2007). Professional school counselors and the practice of group work. *Professional School Counseling, 11*, 72–83.

St. Lawrence, J. S., Kelly, J. A., Dickson-Gomez, J., Owczarzak, J., Amirkhanian, Y. A, & Sitzler, C. (2015). Attitudes toward HIV voluntary counseling and testing (VCT) among African American men who have sex with men: Concerns underlying reluctance to test. *AIDS Education & Prevention, 27*(3), 195–211.

Stolsmark, E. (2015, March). Considerations for the use of distance counseling. *Ct.counseling. org*, 16.

Sue, D. W., & Sue, D. (2013). *Counseling the culturally diverse: Theory and practice* (6th ed.). New York: Wiley.

Sutton, C., & Broken Nose, M. A. (2005). American Indian families. In M. McGoldrick, J. Giordano, & N. Garcia-Preto (Eds.), *Ethnicity and family therapy* (3rd ed., pp. 43–54). New York: Guilford Press.

Thomas, A., Hacker, J., & Hoxha, S. (2011). Gendered racial identity of Black young women. *Sex Roles*, 64(7/8), 530–542.

Thomason, T. C. (2000). Issues in the treatment of Native Americans with alcohol problems. *Journal of Multicultural Counseling and Development, 28*(4), 243–252.

The Washington Post. (2014, November 29). From broken home to broken system. Accessed 2 December 2014 from http://www.washingtonpost.com/sf/national/2014/11/28/from-broken-homes-to-a-broken-system/.

Tovar, E. (2015). The role of faculty, counselors, and support programs on Latino/a community college students' success and intent to persist. *Community College Review*, 43(1), 46–71.

Townes, D. L., Chavez-Korell, S., & Cunningham, N. J. (2009). Reexamining the relationship between racial identity, cultural mistrust, help-seeking attitudes, and preference for a Black counselor. *Journal of Counseling Psychology, 56*, 330–336.

Townsend, S. S. M., Fryberg, S. A., Wilkins, C. L., & Markus, H. R. (2012). Being mixed: Who claims a biracial identity? *Cultural Diversity and Ethnic Minority Psychology, 18*(1), 91–96.

Trahan, D. P., & Lemberger, M. E (2014). Critical race theory as a decisional framework for the ethical counseling of African American clients. *Counseling & Values, 59*(1), 112–124.

Troiden, R. R. (1989). The formation of homosexual identities. *Journal of Homosexuality, 17*, 43–73.

Troutman, O., & Packer-Williams, C. (2014). Moving beyond CACREP standards: Training counselors to work competently with LGBT clients. *The Journal for Counselor Preparation and Supervision, 6*(1), 1–17.

Tufekcioglu, S., & Muran, J. C. (2015). Case formulation and the therapeutic relationship: The role of therapist self-reflection and self-revelation. *Journal of Clinical Psychology, 71*(5), 469–477.

U.S. Census Bureau. (n.d.). Hispanic origin. Washington, DC: Author. Retrieved 12 October 2015 from https://www.census.gov/population/hispanic/.

U.S. Census Bureau. (2009). *Statistical abstracts of the United States 2009* (128th ed.). Washington, DC: Author.

U.S. Census Bureau. (2010). Marital status. *American fact finder*, S1201. Washington, DC: Author. Retrieved 3 January, 2010, from http://factfinder.census.gov.

U.S. Census Bureau. (2013). Educational attainment in the United States: 2013. Washington, DC: Author. Retrieved 2 December 2015 from http://www.census.gov/hhes/socdemo/education/data/cps/2013/tables.html.

U.S. Census Bureau. (2014a). *Facts-for-features—Hispanic Heritage Month.* Washington, DC: Author.

U. S. Census Bureau. (2014b). Population projections of the United States, by age, sex, race, and Hispanic origin. Washington, DC: Author. Retrieved 14 November 2014 from http://www.census.gov/population/pop-profile/adobe/24_ps.pdf.

U.S. Census Bureau. (2015a). *U.S. Census Bureau projections show a slower growing, older, more diverse nation a half century from now.* Washington, DC: Author.

U.S. Census Bureau. (2015b). *Sex by age (Black or African American alone, 2009–2013 American Community Survey 5 year estimates).* Washington, DC: Author.

U.S. Census Bureau. (2015c). *America's families and living arrangements: 2012.* Washington, DC: Author.

U.S. Census Bureau. (2015d). *Race, population estimates program.* Washington, DC: Author.

U.S. Census Bureau. (2015e). American Indians by the numbers. Washington, DC: Author. Retrieved 3 June 2015 from http://www.infoplease.com/spot/aihmcensus1.html.

U.S. Census Bureau. (2015f). *Asian Americans: Income, poverty and health insurance.* Washington, DC: Author.

U.S. Census Bureau. (2015g). *Quick census facts.* Washington, DC: Author:

U.S Census Bureau. (2015h). *Census Bureau reports 64 percent increase in number of children living with a grandparent over the last two decades.* Washington, DC: Author.

U.S. Census Bureau. (2015i). *One-in-four Native Americans and Alaskan Natives are living in poverty.* Washington, DC: Author.

U.S. Census Bureau. (2015j). Facts-for-features. Washington, DC: Author. Retrieved 2 December 2015 from http://www.census.gov/newsroom/facts-for-features/2015/cb15-ff 07.html.

U.S. Census Bureau. (2015k). Selected characteristics of racial groups and Hispanic or Latino population. Washington, DC: Author. Retrieved from http://www.census.gov/comendia/statab/cats/population/elderly_racial_and_hispanic_origin_population_profiles.html.

van Wormer, K., Wells, J., & Boes, M. (2000). *Social work with lesbians, gays, and bisexuals: A strengths perspective.* Boston: Allyn & Bacon.

Vander Zanden, J., Crandell, T., & Crandell, C. (2006). *Human development* (7th ed.). New York: McGraw-Hill.

Wainryb, C. (2004). The study of diversity in human development: Culture, urgencies, and perils. *Human Development, 47,* 131–137.

Wang, M., & Kenny, S. (2014). Longitudinal links between fathers' and mothers' harsh verbal discipline and adolescents' conduct problems and depressive symptoms. *Child Development, 85*(3), 908–923.

Wang, M., & Sheikh-Khalil, S. (2014). Does parental involvement matter for student achievement and mental health in high school? *Child Development, 85(2),* 610–625.

Watari, K., & Gatz, M. (2004). Pathways to caring for Alzheimer's disease among Korean Americans. *Cultural Diversity and Ethnic Minority Psychology, 10*(1), 23–28.

Way, N. (2013). Boys' friendships during adolescence: Intimacy, desire, and loss. *Journal of Research on Adolescence, 23*(2), 201–213.

Weinick, R. M., Jacobs, E. A., Stone, L. C., Ortega, A. N., & Burstin, H. (2004). Hispanic health-care disparities: Challenging the myth of a monolithic Hispanic population. *Medical Care, 42*(4), 313–320.

West-Olatunji, C. (2014, March). Multicultural counseling: The next frontier. *Counseling Today,* 5–6.

Wexler, L., Chandler, M. Gone, J. P., Cwik, M., Kirmayer, L. J., LaFromboise, T., Brockie, T., O'Keefe, V., Walkup, J. & Allen, J. Framing health matters: Advancing suicide prevention research with rural American Indian and Alaska Native populations. *American Journal of Public Health. 105*(5), 891–899.

White, C. S., Oswalt, S. B., Wyatt, T. J., & Peterson, F. L. (2010). Out on the playing field: Providing physical education and recreational opportunities for lesbian, gay, and bisexual youth. *The Physical Educator, 67*(1), 46–56.

Who is a Jew? (2014). *The Economist, 410*(8869), 51–52.

Williams, J. M., Greenleaf, A. T., Albert, T., & Barnes, E. F. (2014). Promoting educational resilience among African American students at risk of school failure: The role of school counselors. *Journal of School Counseling, 12*(9), 1–34.

Williams, L. R. (2014). Experiences with violence in Mexican American and European American high school dating relationships. *Children & Schools. 36*(2), 115–124.

Winawer, H., & Wetzel, N. A. (2005). German families. In M. McGoldrick, J. Giordano, & N. Garcia-Preto (Eds.), *Ethnicity and family therapy* (3rd ed., pp. 555–572). New York: Guilford.

Withrow, R. L. (2008). Early intervention with Latino families: Implications for practice. *Journal of Multicultural Counseling and Development, 36,* 245–256.

Wolff, K. E., & Munley, P. H. (2012). Exploring the relationships between white racial identity consciousness, feminist identity development and family environment for white undergraduate women. *College Student Journal, 46*(2), 91–96.

Yager, T. J., & Rotheram-Borus, M. J. (2000). Social expectations among African American, Hispanic, and European American adolescents. *Cross-Cultural Research, 34*(3), 283–305.

Yakushko, O., & Chronister, K. M. (2005). Immigrant women and counseling: The invisible others. *Journal of Counseling and Development, 83*, 292–298.

Yeh, C. (2003). Age, acculturation, cultural adjustment, and mental health symptoms of Chinese, Korean, and Japanese immigrant Youth. *Cultural Diversity and Ethnic Minority Psychology, 9*(1), 34–48.

Yeh, C., & Huang, K. (1996). The collectivistic nature of ethnic identity development among Asian American college students. *Adolescence, 31*, 645–661.

Yeh, C. J., Okubo, Y., Winnie Ma, P., Shea, M., Ou, D., & Pituc, S. T. (2008). Chinese immigrant high school students' cultural interactions, acculturation, family obligations, language use, and social support. *Adolescence, 43*(172), 775–787.

Yu, A., & Gregg, C. H. (1993). Asians in groups: More than just a matter of cultural awareness. *Journal for Specialists in Group Work, 18*, 86–93.

Zayas, L. H., Kaplan, C., Turner, S., Romano, K., & Gonzalez-Ramos, G. (2000). Understanding suicide attempts by adolescent Hispanic females. *Social Work, 45*(1), 53–63.

Zeren, Ş. G. (2014). Information and communication technology in education of psychological counselors in training. *International Online Journal of Educational Sciences, 6*(2), 494–509.

Zirkel, P. A. (2015). LGBT students. *Principal, 94*(4), 50–51.

Index

Tables are identified with an italicized page number.

Multicultural Pluralistic Assessment (MPA) 102
multicultural society: clients 4–5; counseling and
    psychotherapy 14–21; seeking help in 336
multiple dimensions of identity 42

National Council for Accreditation of Teacher
    Education (NCATE) 14
noninterference, American Indian adolescents
    128–9

online counseling 328–9

PAIRS (Practical Applications of Intimate
    Relationship Skills) 310–11
patience, American Indian adolescents 128
personalismo 263, 266
personally mediated racism 19–20
Pilipino American identity development model
    37–8
pluralistic society, diversity among clients 5–14
Polish Americans 206, 208
post-traumatic stress disorder 184
poverty: Asian Americans 160; definitions 8–9
power 20
prejudice, identity 28–9
prenatal: crucial periods 64, 67;
    developmental characteristics 65;
    multicultural differences 67
psychological processes 31–2
psychotherapy: guidelines for LGBT clients
    295–6; multicultural counseling 333–4;
    multicultural society 14–21
Puerto Rican Americans 5, 47, 81, 87, 233–4,
    243–4, 262, 265, 267, 269, 283

queer 273, 274

race 6
Racial/Cultural Identity (R/CID)
    development model 32–4
racial discrimination, African American adults
    113–14
racial identity, adults 77
racial identity development 26; definition 35
racism 19–20; identity 28–9
Rehabilitation Act (1973) 22
rehabilitation counseling 22–3
religion 9–10; Black church 93–4; European
    Americans 206; Islam and African American
    families 86–7, 94
research, multicultural counseling 329–30
resources, multicultural counseling 17
respeto 233, *239*, 242, 251, 256, 261
risk taking 130, 165, 240, 282
Rogers, Carl 220

Scandinavian Americans 227
self-awareness 30–2; counselors 49–55
self-concept: adolescents 72–3; children 70
self-esteem, adults 77
sexually transmitted diseases (STDs),
    adolescents at risk 73

sexual orientation 11–12, 273, 274, 326
social identity 26; LGBT adolescents 303–4
social injustice, identity 28–9
social justice 20–1
social phobia 224
socioeconomics, European American adults
    206–7
socioeconomic status (SES) 7–8, 73, 77, 334;
    African Americans 84–5, 91, 95, 102, 106,
    112, 114, 116–18; American Indians 136,
    140, 147, 154; Asian Americans 161–2,
    164, 169, 186; European Americans 206–7;
    Hispanic Americans 239, 242–4, 252, 255,
    259, 261, 266, 268; lesbian, gay, bisexual
    and transgender (LGBT) 286
soft-spokenness 133, 145
Southeast Asians, Asian American elderly 172
spiritualism. *See Espiritismo*
spirituality 9–10, 326
Standard English 85, 94, 116
State-Trait Anger Expression Inventory
    (STAXI) 239
stereotyping 19; avoiding 335; clients 47
stress, adults 76–7
subculture 6
substance abuse 12, 23; adolescent identity
    71; adolescents at risk 73; African American
    adolescents 106; African American adults
    95; American Indian adolescents 130, 143;
    American Indian adults 149
Sue, David 186–7
Sue, Derald Wing 186–7
susto 262

targeted prevention 12
Themes Concerning Black (TCB) 102
Themes of Black Awareness (TOBA) 102
training and preparation, counselors 58–60
transgender 274
Troiden model 277–8

United States (n.) 7–8, 11, 15; African
    Americans 88, 92–3, 97, 113; American
    Indians 123–5, 131–3; Asian Americans
    159–62, 168, 170, 172, 174–5, 178,
    184, 192–3; biracial identity development
    model 34; cultural diversity 45–6, 57, 59;
    depression 73, 106; elderly stereotypes 78;
    European Americans 198–213, 216; health-
    care disparities 18; Hispanic Americans
    233–49, 251, 259, 261–4; individualism
    29; infant mortality 64, 67; Islam and
    African American families 86; lesbians, gays,
    bisexuals, and transgender (LGBT) 274–5,
    286; lifespan difference 18; multicultural
    differences 68, 322, 333–4, 336; racial
    discrimination 113; racism 19–20; self-
    awareness 30–1
university counseling centers (UCCs) 258

Vietnamese Americans 168, 184–5, 188–9,
    191, 283